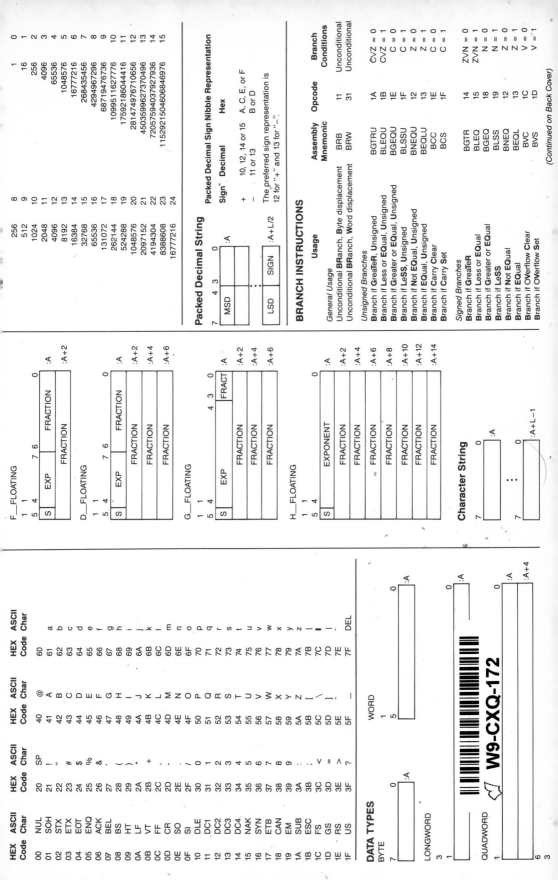

ASCII Character Set

HEX Code	ASCII Char	HEX Code	ASCII Char	HEX Code	ASCII Char	HEX Code	ASCII Char
00	NUL	20	SP	40	@	60	`
01	SOH	21	!	41	A	61	a
02	STX	22	"	42	B	62	b
03	ETX	23	#	43	C	63	c
04	EOT	24	$	44	D	64	d
05	ENQ	25	%	45	E	65	e
06	ACK	26	&	46	F	66	f
07	BEL	27	'	47	G	67	g
08	BS	28	(	48	H	68	h
09	HT	29	)	49	I	69	i
0A	LF	2A	*	4A	J	6A	j
0B	VT	2B	+	4B	K	6B	k
0C	FF	2C	,	4C	L	6C	l
0D	CR	2D	-	4D	M	6D	m
0E	SO	2E	.	4E	N	6E	n
0F	SI	2F	/	4F	O	6F	o
10	DLE	30	0	50	P	70	p
11	DC1	31	1	51	Q	71	q
12	DC2	32	2	52	R	72	r
13	DC3	33	3	53	S	73	s
14	DC4	34	4	54	T	74	t
15	NAK	35	5	55	U	75	u
16	SYN	36	6	56	V	76	v
17	ETB	37	7	57	W	77	w
18	CAN	38	8	58	X	78	x
19	EM	39	9	59	Y	79	y
1A	SUB	3A	:	5A	Z	7A	z
1B	ESC	3B	;	5B	[	7B	{
1C	FS	3C	<	5C	\	7C		
1D	GS	3D	=	5D	]	7D	}
1E	RS	3E	>	5E	^	7E	~
1F	US	3F	?	5F	_	7F	DEL

Powers Tables

Powers of 2:

Value	n	Value	n
1	0	4096	12
2	1	8192	13
4	2	16384	14
8	3	32768	15
16	4	65536	16
32	5	131072	17
64	6	262144	18
128	7	524288	19
256	8	1048576	20
512	9	2097152	21
1024	10	4194304	22
2048	11	8388608	23
		16777216	24

Powers of 16:

Value	n
1	0
16	1
256	2
4096	3
65536	4
1048576	5
16777216	6
268435456	7
4294967296	8
68719476736	9
1099511627776	10
17592186044416	11
281474976710656	12
4503599627370496	13
72057594037927936	14
1152921504606846976	15

Packed Decimal Sign Nibble Representation

Sign	Decimal	Hex
+	10, 12, 14 or 15	A, C, E, or F
−	11 or 13	B or D

The preferred sign representation is 12 for "+" and 13 for "−".

Packed Decimal String

```
7    4 3    0
 MSD  | ... |     :A
 ...              :A+L/2
 LSD  | SIGN |
```

BRANCH INSTRUCTIONS

Usage	Assembly Mnemonic	Opcode	Branch Conditions
General Usage			
Unconditional BRanch, Byte displacement	BRB	11	Unconditional
Unconditional BRanch, Word displacement	BRW	31	Unconditional
Unsigned Branches			
Branch if GreaTeR, Unsigned	BGTRU	1A	$C \lor Z = 0$
Branch if Less or EQual, Unsigned	BLEQU	1B	$C \lor Z = 1$
Branch if Greater or EQual, Unsigned	BGEQU	1E	$C = 0$
Branch if LeSS, Unsigned	BLSSU	1F	$C = 1$
Branch if Not EQual, Unsigned	BNEQU	12	$Z = 0$
Branch if EQual, Unsigned	BEQLU	13	$Z = 1$
Branch if Carry Clear	BCC	1E	$C = 0$
Branch if Carry Set	BCS	1F	$C = 1$
Signed Branches			
Branch if GreaTeR	BGTR	14	$Z \lor N = 0$
Branch if Less or EQual	BLEQ	15	$Z \lor N = 1$
Branch if Greater or EQual	BGEQ	18	$N = 0$
Branch if LeSS	BLSS	19	$N = 1$
Branch if Not EQual	BNEQ	12	$Z = 0$
Branch if EQual	BEQL	13	$Z = 1$
Branch if OVerflow Clear	BVC	1C	$V = 0$
Branch if OVerflow Set	BVS	1D	$V = 1$

(Continued on Back Cover)

Floating Point Data Types

F_FLOATING
```
15 14      7 6          0
 S | EXP | FRACTION      :A
      FRACTION           :A+2
```

D_FLOATING
```
15 14      7 6          0
 S | EXP | FRACTION      :A
      FRACTION           :A+2
      FRACTION           :A+4
      FRACTION           :A+6
```

G_FLOATING
```
15 14       4 3         0
 S |  EXP  | FRACT       :A
      FRACTION           :A+2
      FRACTION           :A+4
      FRACTION           :A+6
```

H_FLOATING
```
15 14       4 3         0
 S |  EXPONENT           :A
      FRACTION           :A+2
      FRACTION           :A+4
      FRACTION           :A+6
      FRACTION           :A+8
      FRACTION           :A+10
      FRACTION           :A+12
      FRACTION           :A+14
```

Character String
```
7          0
           :A
 ...
           :A+L−1
```

DATA TYPES

BYTE
```
7   0
    :A
```

WORD
```
15      0
        :A
```

LONGWORD
```
31          0
            :A
```

QUADWORD
```
31          0
            :A
            :A+4
```

Programming
in
Assembly
Language
VAX-11

Programming in Assembly Language
VAX-11

Edward F. Sowell
CALIFORNIA STATE UNIVERSITY, FULLERTON

Addison-Wesley Publishing Company
Reading, Massachusetts   Menlo Park, California   Don Mills, Ontario
Wokingham, England   Amsterdam   Madrid   San Juan
Bogotá   Sydney   Santiago   Singapore   Tokyo

Library of Congress Cataloging-in-Publication Data

Sowell, Edward F.
  Programming in assembly language, VAX-11.

  Includes index.
  1. VAX-11 (Computer)—Programming.   2. Assembler
language (Computer program language)   I. Title.
QA76.8.V37S68   1987   005.2'45   86-26577
ISBN 0-201-10886-0

DEFGHIJ-DO-89

Preface

Background

The study of assembly language remains an essential element of the computer science curriculum in spite of the increasing use of high-level languages. The justifications for this study are twofold. First, there are still programming tasks that are best done in assembly for reasons of efficiency and access to machine capabilities not available in high-level languages. Indeed, the number of programmers using assembly language has *increased* in recent years because of the need for high performance software for microcomputers. The versatile computer scientist or programmer must therefore be able to code in assembly language when the need arises. The second reason is more fundamental: Assembly is really just a way of expressing the actual native language of the computer; namely, machine code. The study of assembly is therefore, in a sense, a study of the machine and its architecture. Important issues that come up naturally in this study include fundamental instructions that a computer is capable of carrying out; the concept of hardware memory cells as the basic units of storage; the way that the machine stores and accesses data and instructions; the instruction fetch-execution cycle which constitutes the most fundamental characteristic of a digital computer; the fundamental aspects of computer input and output; data structures such as stacks, queues, lists, and pointers; and the use of stacks in recursion. Thus the study of assembly language can serve as a bridge between the skills learned in an introductory programming course and many advanced topics that the student will study in greater depth in later courses.

Aim of This Book

This book is divided into two parts. Part I, Chapters 1–10, is intended for a one-semester introductory course in assembly language programming and computer architecture. Part II, Chapters 11–17, is intended as supplementary material for the introductory course, and for a second course in advanced assembly.

Part I is written for students who have had only one prior course in introductory programming (in any high-level language), and no prior exposure to assembly language,

v

number theory, logic, or computer architecture. The dependence on the programming course is actually minimal. For example, it is not assumed that the student is thoroughly familiar with any particular programming language. All concepts are developed from the beginning. Part II assumes that the student has completed an introductory course covering the material in Part I, or otherwise has mastered assembly language programming for some computer.

This book is also written for the instructor. In particular, it will be appreciated by instructors who are teaching assembly or VAX MACRO for the first time. To this end, the organization of Part I of the book is in the order of classroom presentation, so that a course outline for the core material will closely follow the contents in Chapters 1–10. Additionally, sufficient exercises are presented so that different assignments can be given in alternate semesters. Because of the inclusion of material on operating system interaction, and on the use of editors and debugging tools, it should not be necessary to develop supplementary handouts for most installations. The appendixes provide complete details on these matters, in addition to examples within the text.

Because of the detailed explanations and examples, the book will also be useful for self-study. Those already familiar with an assembly language may find the discussion too detailed and the pace too slow, especially in Part I. Nonetheless, such readers will appreciate that nearly every VAX-11 instruction is discussed and most are presented with examples. Other things that should aid the student in using this book are the frequent examples explained in detail, end-of-chapter summaries, and answers to selected exercises.

Approach

The pedagogic approach taken in this text reflects its principal aim, namely, guiding first- and second-year students in the study of assembly and machine language programming. To this end, the order of presentation, especially in Part I, is designed to keep the motivation level high, and the new-concept load low. Rather than presenting all related instructions at once, as would be done in a manual, a small group of instructions and a single addressing mode are presented first, followed by examples using only this subset of the language. These instructions and addressing modes were selected as those easiest for students to understand, as well as to provide a repertoire sufficient to work a small class of programming problems. Assembler directives (pseudo-ops) are introduced in the same manner. This knowledge of VAX MACRO is then gradually expanded, enlarging the class of workable problems and programming competence in a metered way. Machine code translation and execution on the machine are emphasized throughout this process. The purpose of this is to integrate the study of architecture with the programming. Initial use of the simplest addressing modes and instructions makes the translation easy to learn.

As a rule, young computer science students like to use the computer more than they like to deal with abstract information. Capitalizing on this, the book moves into programming as quickly as possible. In Chapter 1, examples and exercises get the student onto the machine. Number theory is initially covered only in sufficient depth to provide necessary skills in binary, hexadecimal, and octal arithmetic using integers. By deferring the remainder of number theory to later chapters, motivation is kept high. Naturally, the initial subset of the language has been carefully selected to require only integers.

Input and output (I/O) can be major stumbling blocks in learning (and teaching!) assembly. The primary approach taken in this book is to sidestep the issue until the student's level of programming skill is high enough to properly handle I/O. In the meantime, we use the Symbolic Debugger to load input directly into registers and memory, and to examine contents after program execution. This approach has an important side benefit. It maintains an emphasis on architecture by requiring the student to think in terms of data and instructions as they actually exist in memory, rather than allowing the assembly mnemonics to be viewed as the end product of the exercise. Also there is no better way to develop skills in the hexadecimal base than to examine memory using the Symbolic Debugger. Recognizing that some instructors will want to use terminal I/O rather than the Symbolic Debugger approach, preprogrammed hexadecimal I/O routines are presented in Appendix E. Both terminal and file routines are provided. Programmed I/O using the device registers with polling, and interrupt-driven I/O are covered in later chapters.

Another central idea in the pedagogical approach of this book is that most students learn best in going from the specific to the general, rather than the reverse. It is for this reason that instructions are demonstrated by simple examples as well as being given in the general form. This theory of learning also supports the basic approach of using a specific assembly language and computer instead of working in terms of an idealized, imaginary computer and contrived assembly language. With the approach taken here, students "learn by doing" in a real computing environment. Although machine and assembly code are highly machine-specific, the basic *concepts* remain the same for practically any modern computer. This means that students who learn MACRO on the VAX-11 will be able to transfer much of this knowledge to learning another machine and assembly language on their own.

The Computing Environment

The VAX-11 family of computers and the VAX MACRO assembler are the vehicles for the presentation. Maximum benefit will be derived if students have access to such equipment and software, either through a central facility (e.g., VAX-11/780 with VMS operating system) or stand-alone machines such as the MICRO VAX. However, in situations in which this is not possible, there are sufficient examples of actual machine interaction so that much could be learned without a machine.

he decision to include actual machine interaction examples in the text required the selection of a particular operating system. The widely used Digital Equipment Corporation (DEC) multi-user operating system called VMS was selected for this purpose. All necessary reference materials for VMS and its user-support software have been summarized in the appendixes, so additional books, manuals, or software should not be required.

Preprogrammed terminal and file I/O macros and subroutines are presented in Appendix E. These can be entered manually from the listings given, or can be obtained from Addison-Wesley on magnetic diskettes. *The instructor should have these macros and subroutines installed before instruction begins if they are not presently on the system to be used.* Once these are installed, all examples in the text will operate exactly as shown.

How to Use This Book

Part I of *Programming in Assembly Language: VAX-11* is intended for a one-semester (three hours per week) or one quarter (four hours per week) course in assembly language and computer architecture. Such a course will fulfill the CS-3 requirement, *Introduction to Computer Systems*, in Curriculum 78 recommended by the Association for Computing Machinery, and typically enrolls students with one prior programming course. Accelerated courses for exceptionally well-prepared students can also interject selected advanced topics from Part II. The pace will depend upon student preparation and ability. Normally, the first one-third of the course would be devoted to Chapters 1–5, while Chapters 6–8 comprise the second third of the course. The final one-third of the course should be devoted to the material in Chapters 9 and 10, and any advanced topics to be covered from Part II.

Chapters 1, 2, and 3 provide an introduction to the course. Chapter 1 shows by example what is meant by machine and assembly programming, and explains the process of creating a program with an editor, as well as assembling, linking, and running it on the machine. Chapter 2 is intended to give the student essential skills in base conversion and nondecimal arithmetic with integers, including the two's complement system. Chapter 3 deals with computer architecture and organization. In the first part of the chapter, the von Neumann machine is used to convey general concepts. Subsequently, the architecture of the VAX-11 itself is focused upon, with the aim of preparing students to deal with more specific aspects of this machine needed later in the book. Virtual memory and microprogramming features of the VAX are covered in sufficient depth to allow these terms to be properly used when needed. These chapters can be covered easily in the first six, one-hour lectures, with the majority of time devoted to Chapters 2 and 3.

Chapter 4 begins the process of introducing instructions, addressing modes, and directives. The subset introduced here will allow only "straight-line" programs, manipulating longword integers in registers. Manual translation, assembler listing, and the use of the Symbolic Debugger and simplified I/O routines are also introduced here. Two or three lectures will be required to cover this chapter.

The purpose of Chapter 5 is to sufficiently enlarge the student's repertoire to allow programming with branches and loops, and to use data organized in arrays. (The full treatment of data structures is presented in Chapter 14.) Unsigned branching instructions are described without specific reference to condition codes. The student is given several standard "templates" for programming decision structures and loops. Immediate, short literal, relative, register deferred, and autoincrement and autodecrement addressing modes are introduced. Three to four lectures should be allocated for this chapter.

Chapter 6, "Computer Arithmetic," is a treatment of integer arithmetic within the constraints imposed by digital computers. The differences between signed and unsigned integers are thoroughly discussed. The chapter also introduces the condition codes, and then the signed branch instructions. Other arithmetic concepts discussed here include shift and rotate operations, double-precision arithmetic, and the multiply and divide operations, both in hardware and software forms. Four lectures will be adequate for this chapter, although an extra lecture will be required for thorough coverage of the software multiply and divide algorithms.

The purpose of Chapter 7 is to introduce the character (byte) data handling capability of the machine. This includes coverage of the ASCII code, byte instructions, character string instructions, and byte and character storage directives. Logical bit instructions are also discussed here. A comprehensive example deals with a simple word processing problem. Depending on the students' prior experience with string manipulation, three or four lectures will be required to cover this material.

Input and output are finally discussed in Chapter 8. By this point, the student has a sufficient grasp of assembly language and architecture to deal with the intricate steps involved in I/O. Character I/O using supplied macros (as shown in Appendix E) is discussed first. This is intended to expose the student to I/O at the "system macro" level, such as is available in most assembly language environments. The concept of a string buffer is thereby introduced. Programmed I/O at the device register level is discussed in an optional section. The PDP-11 is used here to avoid intricate explanations of the VAX multi-user environment. This is followed by a detailed explanation of hexadecimal and decimal numerical I/O routines. At least four lectures will be required for this chapter.

Chapter 9 presents the concepts of subroutines and stacks. Basic ideas of subroutines, including elementary usage in MACRO, are presented first, followed by an introduction to stacks. This leads into a discussion of linkage and argument transmission. The latter is thoroughly treated, including call-by-value and call-by-reference methods with several implementations of each method. After gaining an understanding of these fundamental subroutine concepts, the student should be prepared for the treatment of VAX procedures which follows. Examples include procedures that can be called from Pascal and FORTRAN. Five lectures will suffice for this chapter if the instructor is selective in classroom coverage of the several argument transmission methods presented in the chapter.

Chapter 10 covers the macro definition facility of MACRO, as well as assembly expressions, symbols, direct assignment, repeat directives, and conditional assembly. The assembly process is also outlined. By selecting among the topics, the chapter can be covered in four lectures.

If the above guidelines are followed, and six hours are reserved for review and examinations, there will be five to eight hours left for coverage of advanced topics selected from Part II. The chapters in Part II are independent of one another, so that the instructor can choose such topics freely.

When using the book for a second course in assembly language programming, it is assumed that the students have mastered the concepts in Part I. The starting point is Chapter 11 which is devoted to programming considerations that are not often covered in an introductory course, but are important in larger projects. These topics include modular programming, programming style and standards, linkage and memory maps, position-independent code, and the creation and use of libraries.

Chapter 12 contains a complete discussion of the VAX-11 addressing modes, followed by a treatment of data structures in the assembly language context. For the reader who has completed Part I, this will fill gaps and unify the VAX-11 addressing mode picture developed earlier. For those who learned assembly on another computer, this material will provide all needed information on VAX-11 addressing. In either case, this chapter prepares the student for the second topic of Chapter 12—data structures. Multidimensional arrays, strings, tables, stacks, queues, and linked lists are covered in detail, with examples.

Chapter 13 presents the fundamental ideas of recursion, then shows implementation of recursive algorithms with MACRO subroutines. The coverage assumes no prior experience with recursive programming. Examples include the traditional factorial function and the Quicksort algorithm operating on a character string.

Chapters 14 and 15 deal with floating-point and decimal representation, respectively. In the floating-point chapter, the discussion includes VAX-11 storage formats, arithmetic operations, and errors, as well as the VAX-11 instructions and MACRO directives for programming with this data type. The decimal chapter shows VAX-11 storage conventions for decimal strings, decimal arithmetic, and the VAX-11 decimal instructions. There is also a discussion on why decimal programming is sometimes desirable.

Chapter 16 is a treatment of exceptions and interrupts. The concepts are first discussed at a fundamental level, including vectoring and priorities. This is followed by a treatment of exception and interrupt programming using the facilities provided under VAX/VMS. Examples include arithmetic exception handlers, a simple interrupt-driven input process running in parallel with a sorting process, software traps, and timing events with the interval timer.

Chapter 17 concludes Part II and the book with an overview of input/output using the VAX/VMS Record Management Services (RMS). While the treatment is not exhaustive, it shows how this important part of VMS can be used to read and write files. It also provides sufficient orientation for the reader to seek more detailed information in the RMS manual.

The appendixes should be examined by the reader early in the course. Found there will be much useful information in summary form. Appendix A gives the complete VAX-11 instruction set and the VAX MACRO assembler syntax. Appendixes B, C, and D deal respectively with the EDT editor, the Symbolic Debugger, and the VMS operating system. Appendix E has the source code, installation instructions, and usage instructions for the simplified I/O routines referred to in the text. Appendix F contains a complete, modular program that exemplifies the assembly programming style discussed in the text. Appendix G is an abbreviated list of error reports that might be generated by VMS software, including the assembler, the linker, and the Symbolic Debugger. With these appendixes it should be possible to use this book effectively without any other books or manuals.

Acknowledgments

I wish to acknowledge the many people who have contributed either directly or indirectly to the development of this book. Direct contributions were made by the reviewers, including David W. Burry (Perkin-Elmer Corporation), Thomas W. Lynch and John E. Rager III (Northwestern University), Dennis J. Volper (University of California, Irvine), Kenneth M. Long (The Computer School), Lawrence Naylor (Drake University), and William F. Decker (University of Iowa). It was with the assistance of my editor James DeWolf that I was able to integrate many of their suggestions into the final product. I am also grateful for the insights offered by my colleagues at CSUF, including Mahadeva Venkatesan, David Falconer, and Martin Katz. They, too, have helped me improve the text. Further credit must be given to Vaclav Rajlich (Wayne State University) for his influence on my earlier PDP-11 book, much of which carries over to the present work. I could not have brought all of this together without the assistance of Phyllis M. Mercer who did the word processing and provided me with constant support throughout the project. The usefulness of the book as a university text has been enhanced by my students, including Donald Purpura who developed the solutions for the exercises, Thiem Gian who proofread the entire manuscript for technical accuracy, and the many students who helped in the refinement process by using early versions in the classroom. There were others who helped me in less direct but equally important ways. In this category I especially want to mention my family for their support and encouragement, and Dean A. James Diefenderfer, (C.S.U.F.) who originally encouraged me to enter the field of computer science.

Fullerton, California   E. F. S.

Contents

3

Computer Organization and Architecture 39

4

Introduction to
Assembly Language Programming 65

5

Programs with Branches and Simple Data Structures 91

6

Computer Arithmetic 127

7

Character Data and Byte Operations 157

8

Input and Output 184

9

Subroutines and Stacks 209

PART II   ADVANCED TOPICS

12

Addressing and Data Structures 317

13 | Recursive Programming 357

14 | Floating-Point Representation 370

15 | Decimal Representation 395

APPENDIXES

D

VMS Operating System **508**

E

Simplified I/O Macros and Subroutines **522**

PART I

Fundamentals

1

Preliminaries

1.1 | Programming Concepts

A digital computer is a machine that is capable of accepting a prepared sequence of instructions and carrying them out. For example, the VAX-11 series of computers discussed in this book has over 300 different instructions, called its **instruction set,** and can be configured with sufficient memory space to retain a sequence of many thousands of these instructions. Preparation of a sequence of these instructions to accomplish some desired purpose is called **programming** of the computer. The sequence of instructions, or some set of statements from which they can be derived, is called a **program.**

There are many different ways in which a program can be expressed. We begin our discussion by considering the most fundamental way, that is, when it is expressed in terms of numerical instruction codes recognizable directly by the machine. An example of this is:

```
01010100    01010001    11010000
01010100    01010010    11000000
01010100    01010011    11000000
                        00000000
```

Although difficult to recognize, this is a segment of a program in the "machine language" or "machine code" of the VAX-11 computer; it causes the VAX-11 to add three numbers. As you can see here, the instructions in this native language of the VAX-11, like those for other digital computers, are strings of 1's and 0's called bit (*binary digit*) strings. Each particular pattern has a very precise meaning to the machine; these meanings were imparted to the machine by its builders.

Earlier computers, including Digital Equipment Corporation's PDP-11 (the predecessor to the VAX-11), allowed programming directly in terms of these bit patterns. These machines had a set of switches across the front (see Figure 1.1) so that an operator could set up a particular bit pattern using switch up to represent a 1, or down to represent a 0. Depressing another, momentary-contact switch "deposited" the instruction code

3

FIGURE 1.1/Front panel of PDP-11 computer

FIGURE 1.2/Front panel of VAX-11 computer

set on the switches into memory. The process would be repeated until an entire (small) program had been entered. After entry, the program could be executed.

It is easy to see that machine language programming in this manner is tedious and time-consuming. Another disadvantage is that programs expressed in machine code are very difficult for *human beings* to read. This is important because sooner or later most programs have to be modified to meet a new need, requiring a programmer to review them long after they were originally written. The only advantage of machine code is that it is the easiest form of a program for the machine to understand. At the same time, it is the most difficult for human beings to understand.

Because of these disadvantages, programming computers directly in machine code is rarely done today. Modern computers such as the VAX-11, shown in Figure 1.2, do not even have the front panel switches necessary for such programming.

Even though we no longer program in machine code, it is still important to be able to recognize and interpret the machine language. As we saw above, actual machine code is represented in binary in the computer. However, machine code programs are often expressed in a slightly different form that makes them easier (although still not easy!) for us to read. To convert to this alternate form, we begin at the right in each instruction and replace each group of four binary digits according to the rule:

$$
\begin{array}{ll}
0000 = 0 & 1000 = 8 \\
0001 = 1 & 1001 = 9 \\
0010 = 2 & 1010 = A \\
0011 = 3 & 1011 = B \\
0100 = 4 & 1100 = C \\
0101 = 5 & 1101 = D \\
0110 = 6 & 1110 = E \\
0111 = 7 & 1111 = F
\end{array}
$$

The preceding example then becomes:

$$
\begin{array}{lll}
54 & 51 & D0 \\
54 & 52 & C0 \\
54 & 53 & C0 \\
   & 00 &
\end{array}
$$

This is said to be "hexadecimal" (base 16) representation, whereas the original version is expressed in binary (base 2). This is merely a convenience for people, because the machine actually works in terms of binary instructions. When it becomes necessary for a programmer to write out a machine language instruction, he or she most often will do so in hexadecimal, often called "shorthand binary." Fortunately, it is not often necessary to write programs in machine language.

The inconvenience of machine language programming is overcome to a large extent by the use of **assembly language programming.** The fundamental idea of assembly language is that each machine language instruction has a short, meaningful symbol that is more easily recognized by human programmers than are the binary or hexadecimal representations. Such symbols are called **mnemonics,** because they are selected by the language designer to have the quality of being easily remembered. For example, ADDL is the mnemonic for the addition instruction. Later, we will see that the "L" at the end of the mnemonic part of the instruction tells the computer the size of the numbers to be added.

Rewriting the above program segment in terms of the VAX-11 assembly language (called MACRO) produces:

```
MOVL    R1,R4
ADDL    R2,R4
ADDL    R3,R4
HALT
```

It is much easier to see how the program works when expressed this way. The program assumes that originally there are three numbers, each stored in one of the **registers** R1, R2, and R3, which may be viewed as "number boxes." In the first instruction, the contents* of R1 is moved into a fourth box R4, destroying whatever was there before. Next, the contents of R2 is added to the contents of R4, producing a partial sum of the contents of R1 and R2, with the result being placed back in R4. Likewise the contents of R3 is added to R4, producing the final result of R1 + R2 + R3, leaving it in R4. The last instruction, HALT, stops the computer.

To see the relationship between the machine code and the assembly, you must know the equivalent numeric code for each element of the assembly language, and vice versa. For example, on the VAX-11 we have:

Mnemonic	Code
MOVL	D0
ADDL	C0
Rn	5n
HALT	00

With this information, you can read the machine code in much the same way as you read the assembly. It is necessary to note only that the machine code is usually written right-to-left rather than the normal left-to-right. In this book we will emphasize the relationship between assembly and machine code in order to develop a better understanding of the way the machine works.

This example demonstrates the correspondence between machine and assembly language programming. It should be understood, however, that ultimately every program, however it was expressed originally, must be reduced to machine code prior to execution, since the computer "understands" only its own native language. Thus when one writes a program in assembly language, it is with the expectation that it will be **translated** into machine code. Now very little would be gained from programming in assembly language if this translation had to be done by the programmer, i.e., by hand. Fortunately,

---

* In this text, the word "contents" will be construed as a singular noun meaning "that which is contained in the storage cell."

this problem has a solution—namely *another* program (written earlier by someone else!) that can read the assembly language and generate automatically the patterns of 1's and 0's representing the corresponding machine code. Such a program is called an **assembler,** and most likely already exists on the computer system which you will be using. The process is shown in Figure 1.3. The programmer creates the program in assembly language and passes it through the assembler, producing machine code.

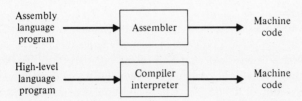

FIGURE 1.3/Translation of assembly or high-level language to machine code

Programming in assembly language is easier than programming in machine code, but not as easy as using a "high-level" language such as BASIC or Pascal. Contrast, for example, the single Pascal statement:

```
W := X + Y + Z;
```

with the assembly language program above that accomplishes essentially the same thing; i.e., it adds three numbers together. A single Pascal statement expresses what it took three *instructions* to express in MACRO. Moreover, the meaning, at least to those familiar with conventional notation of algebra, is much clearer. This is true in general: a high-level language program is easier for people to read and is more compact in its original (source) form than the equivalent assembly language program. However, we must not forget that, as with assembly language programs, high-level language programs have to be translated to machine code prior to execution. The pre-existing program that does this job for high-level languages is called a **compiler** or, in some cases, an **interpreter.** This process is also shown in Figure 1.3.

1.2 | Why Assembly Language?

Because it is usually easier to program in high-level languages, one might ask, "Why use assembly language?" The answer to this question depends heavily on the particular problem being addressed. One thing that usually indicates the desirability of assembly language is the requirement of extremely fast execution of the final program. As a rule, compilers and interpreters generate machine code that uses more machine instructions than a well-designed assembly language program uses. Fewer instructions often mean faster execution. The actual size of the machine language program is sometimes critical as well. Computers aboard spacecraft may have limited memory, so that shorter programs created by talented assembly language programmers may be an important advantage or even a necessity. Another reason may be that a compiler or interpreter is *not available* for the host computer, or those available may be limited in some way, precluding the use of some useful feature of the machine. This happens very frequently in the task known as "systems programming." As a result most computer installations have at least one programmer who works with assembly language.

Programmers must examine their task in view of these factors when making the decision. If the problem does not need extremely efficient, compact, code, and if a suitable high-level language translator is available, one most likely should not use assembly language.

There are valid reasons for studying assembly language programming even if you are never called upon to write a program in assembly language. First, a study of assembly language develops a deeper understanding of the computer itself, which will improve one's programming skills in any language. Secondly, the computer science curriculum properly includes study of the design and organization of computers. Many of the issues encountered in computer design cannot be fully understood without a knowledge of machine and assembly language programming. These considerations are enough cause for one to learn assembly language.

1.3 | Support Programs

Solving a problem on a computer always involves more than just the program, regardless of the language selected. For example, one must somehow "enter" the program into the computer before it can be executed. As already observed, if it is not in the native language of the machine, it must be assembled, compiled, or interpreted, and, as we shall see later, "linked" to put it into a form suitable for execution. Finally, one must instruct the computer to run the program, and enter any necessary input data. In most cases, the programmer is assisted in these tasks by the **operating system,** and a number of supporting **system programs** available on the computer being used. Here we briefly introduce these concepts, using the VAX-11 VMS operating system as an example. A more complete treatment of the use of these support systems is presented in Appendices B, C, and D.

The creation of an assembly language program is aided by a system program called an **editor.** Several editors are usually available on VAX-11 computers. The one selected for use here is EDT (called the DEC Editor in Digital Equipment Corporation literature). This, or any other editor, allows the programmer to create and save programs as files on the "mass storage device"* serving the computer. Commands to the editor also allow the correction of typographical errors, or later modification of the program. One task facing the beginning assembly language programmer is the mastery of EDT or some other available editor program so that programs can be easily created and modified.

We will now do a complete example of a simple program to demonstrate the procedure. You should carry out the example yourself as your first experience in assembly language programming. Before proceeding, however, you should check with your instructor or computer center staff to see if the support programs needed by many examples in this

---

* Unfamiliar terms may be looked up in the Glossary.

book, namely MACLIB and SUBLIB, have been installed on your computer as shown in Appendix E.

First, you have to "log on" to the computer, using a terminal. This begins by establishing a connection to the computer, following directions available from your instructor or your computer center staff. Once the connection is established, pressing the carriage return key <CR> causes the VMS operating system to issue the "log on prompts," as shown below by underlining. You respond to these prompts with your "user name" and "password," as assigned by your computer center or instructor.

```
Username: Smith
Password: secret
$ ▒
```

Here the $ is the VAX-11 VMS command prompt, meaning that VMS is ready to respond to your commands. All of the VMS commands you need to know are presented in Appendix D. For now, we will learn how to use only those commands needed to create, assemble, link, and execute a MACRO program.

As we continue with this example and others, we will indicate computer-issued prompts by *underlining*. Although not shown, your response must always be followed by a carriage return.

After signing onto the computer, enter:

```
EDIT MYPROG.MAR
```

This causes entry into the EDT editor. The system responds with an asterisk (*) which should be answered with I, standing for input:

```
* I
  ▒
```

Your assembly language program can now be entered. A simple one that can actually be executed is:

```
        .TITLE    FIRST TRY
        .ENTRY    START, 0
        .PUTSTR   MSG1
        $EXIT_S
MSG1:   .ASCIZ    /HI THERE!/
        .END      START
```

Simultaneously pushing the "control" and "Z" keys (called control-Z and written ^Z or CTRL Z) will cause the system to respond with another asterisk, to which you respond with EX, standing for EXIT from the EDT program. This also saves the results. The complete sequence, which should be tried, is:

```
EDIT MYPROG.MAR
*I
        .TITLE    FIRST TRY
        .ENTRY    START, 0
        .PUTSTR   MSG1
        $EXIT_S
MSG1:   .ASCIZ    /HI THERE!/
        .END      START
  ^Z
*EX
$ ▒
```

This creates a "file" or permanent copy of these entered lines on your disk space. If typing errors are made, they can be corrected using other features of EDT as explained in Appendix B.

To assemble this program the MACRO assembler can be invoked with the following sequence:

```
$ MACRO/LIST  MYPROG+MACLIB/LIB
```

The assembler responds with a report of any programming errors. After printing the errors, VMS provides another $ prompt. (If any errors are reported after you have carefully checked each step, check the installation of the support programs described in Appendix E.)

Now, your assembled program must be prepared for loading and execution. This process is called linking, and is done by a system program called LINK. To execute LINK, enter:

```
$ LINK/MAP  MYPROG+SUBLIB/LIB
```

To execute your program, enter:

```
$ RUN  MYPROG
```

whereupon it will print:

```
HI THERE!
$ ▒
```

(*Note:* If it doesn't, it is probably because SUBLIB or MACLIB has not been installed. See Section E.2.)

The process described above is shown diagrammatically in Figure 1.4. Each of the first three steps—editing, assembling, and linking—requires the use of a system program, invoked by entering their names. Each system program receives your program in one form and from it creates a different version. For example, the command EDIT invokes the EDT editor, receives keyboard entries of MACRO statements, and creates a source file, conventionally identified as *name*.MAR, where *name* is selected by the programmer. The file is automatically saved on mass storage. The assembler, MACRO, accepts *name*-.MAR as input, and produces two files as output—*name*.LIS and *name*.OBJ. Both are also saved. The LIS file is a "listing" which can be printed or displayed on your terminal; it gives the assembled program (as hexadecimal addresses and instructions) as well as the assembly language itself. Any errors encountered by the assembler will also be included in LIS. To see the LIS file, enter:

```
$ SET TERMINAL/WIDTH = 132
$ TYPE  MYPROG.LIS
```

You can omit the SET TERMINAL command if your terminal only displays 80 characters per line. The interpretation of the LIS file is given in Section 4.9. The OBJ file produced by the assembler is "machine code," sometimes called the **object** version of your program, and cannot be listed at your terminal. It is in the binary form needed by the LINK program.

The OBJ version becomes input to the LINK program, which also creates two files. The first of these, *name*.MAP, can be printed or displayed and has information

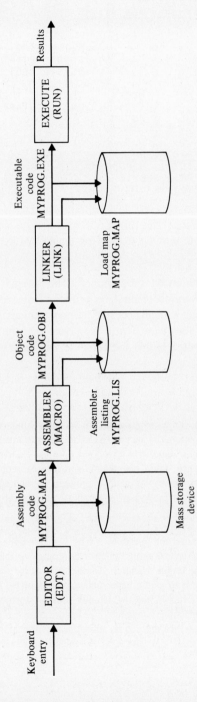

FIGURE 1.4/Procedure for creating and running a MACRO program

```
$ EDIT MYPROG.MAR
Input file does not exist
[EOB]
*I
                                    .TITLE FIRST TRY
                                    .ENTRY START,0
                                    .PUTSTR MSG1
                                    $EXIT_S
                        MSG1:       .ASCIZ/HI THERE!/
                                    .END    START
                    ^Z
[EOB]
*EX
DSA1:[50,004]MYPROG.MAR;1 7 lines
$ MACRO/LIST    MYPROG+MACLIB/LIB
$ LINK MYPROG,SUBLIB
$ RUN MYPROG
HI THERE!
$ ▒
```

FIGURE 1.5/Complete terminal activity for simple MACRO exercise

which is useful to an experienced programmer. The second, *name*.EXE, is, like *name*.OBJ, in binary and therefore cannot be printed. However, it is the complete, ready-to-execute program along with all necessary system routines. The complete terminal activity for this example is shown in Figure 1.5. Note that the system responses are underlined. The $ prompt indicates that the computer is ready for the next command.

1.4 | Summary

We have seen that a computer program, in its most fundamental form, is a set of **instructions** represented as bit patterns in successive locations in the computer's memory. These bit patterns are recognizable *by the hardware of the machine itself* and are therefore referred to as **machine code.** For convenience, these bit patterns can also be represented in hexadecimal. Assembly language is a way of expressing such a program in "human readable" form, and there is a system-provided program (called an assembler) that converts assembly language to machine code.

Briefly mentioned was the relation between assembly language and still more convenient higher-level languages, which raised the question, "Why use assembly language?" The answer to this may be greater execution speed, more compact programs, or the mere absence of high-level language translators for the target machine. Another reason for the study of machine and assembly language programming is to gain a better understanding of the machine itself.

We also covered, at least briefly, how to actually create, assemble, link, and execute a simple MACRO program. If a machine is available the reader should repeat the given examples and work the provided exercises, since there is no substitute for practice.

1.5 | Exercises

In the exercises below, you should obtain paper copy of your terminal activity for assignments to be turned in.

1.1 Go to your computer center and determine which text editor you should use. If your editor is different from EDIT/EDT then find out how to do the examples in this chapter with your editor.

1.2 Create the program given in Section 1.3 using your system text editor. Assemble, link, and run this program.

1.3 Revise the program given in Section 1.3 to print out your name, street address, city, state, and zip code in three separate lines.

1.4 Using Appendix D, the reference manuals available in the computer center, or materials from your instructor, determine how to do the following things on your computer system:

(a) Obtain a directory listing of your permanent files.

(b) Erase a file.

(c) Rename a file.

(d) Merge two files.

▶ **1.5** Describe in your own words the differences between machine, assembly, and high-level language programs.

2

Binary, Hexadecimal, and Decimal Number Systems

2.1 | Numbers for Machines and People

As we have already noted, digital computers work internally in terms of binary codes. This is almost universally true since it is easy to devise electronic hardware that can represent two different states, e.g., on and off, and binary codes require only two different symbols, 0 and 1. Thus there is a natural match between electronic machines and binary codes. On the other hand, human beings are adapted to working principally with the decimal representation of numbers using the Arabic digit symbols 0, 1, 2, . . ., 9. In order to bridge this gap, we digress from our discussion of programming to review the fundamental notions of number representation, conversion of bases, and arithmetic operations in the machine-preferred systems. We focus on binary, hexadecimal (shorthand binary), and the familiar decimal system.

The term **representation** is used in this discussion to distinguish the manner in which we choose to *write or store* a number from the number itself. For example, 16 people or 16 pounds of corn can be represented with Arabic numerals in decimal as we have done here, Roman numerals, tally marks, or any one of many other numeric representation systems. Regardless of representation, the abstract concept of the number is the same. This is an important distinction to keep in mind as we proceed.

We begin our discussion with a review of the positional number system using various bases. We then develop basic arithmetic skills, such as addition and subtraction, in these different bases, and learn how to convert between bases. All of this is done initially with positive integers only. After developing this foundation, we then learn how negative numbers can be represented using what is called the **two's complement system,** and see that all of our skills with positive numbers extend directly into this system.

14

2.2 | Positional Notation and Bases

As we learned in junior high school, a number such as 428 in the Arabic decimal system can be viewed as a sum of products:

$$4 \times 10^2 + 2 \times 10^1 + 8 \times 10^0 = 428$$

Here we are acknowledging that each digit position has a certain **place value**, i.e., from right-to-left 1, 10, 100, 1000, etc., which multiplies the digit value. These are obviously the successive powers of ten, 10^0, 10^1, 10^2, 10^3, and so forth, so that the place value of a decimal digit is 10 raised to the power of its position, counting from 0 at the least significant digit. Here 10 is said to be the **base** of the decimal number system. Where there is any possibility for ambiguity, we note the base of the representation used by a subscript, e.g., 428_{10}.

In general, a positional notation number in any base can be expressed as:

$$N = \sum_{i=0}^{m-1} D_i b^i \tag{2.1}$$

where the D_i are the m individual digits and b is the base.

Binary (base 2) and hexadecimal (base 16) numbers employ the same kind of positional notation. For example, the binary number 101_2 can be viewed as:

$$1 \times 2^2 + 0 \times 2^1 + 1 \times 2^0$$

If we express the place values, e.g., 2^2, 2^1, and 2^0, as *decimal* numbers, we achieve the decimal equivalent of this number:

$$1 \times 4 + 0 \times 2 + 1 \times 1 = 5_{10}$$

Similarly, the binary number 11111 is:

$$1 \times 2^4 + 1 \times 2^3 + 1 \times 2^2 + 1 \times 2^1 + 1 \times 2^0 = 31_{10}$$

This last example demonstrates that when we limit ourselves to a particular number of digits, the size of the number that can be represented is also limited. The largest possible value of a number composed of a specified number of digits occurs when each digit has the largest value allowed by the base. Thus in the above example, 31_{10} is the largest value representable with five bits. In general, if the base is b and there are m allowed digits, the decimal representation of the largest allowed number is:

$$b^m - 1$$

In the preceding example, this is $2^5 - 1 = 31_{10}$. This observation is very important when a binary number is stored in the computer, because the largest number that can be represented in binary positional representation is determined by the number of bits allowed in the storage cell. We shall see in the next chapter that the VAX-11 has several different sizes of storage cells, each having its own maximum size of binary number. The most important of these cells are bytes, words, and longwords, with capacities shown in Table 2.1.

TABLE 2.1

Cell	Size (bits)	Largest Positive Integer
Byte	8	255_{10}
Word	16	$65,535_{10}$
Longword	32	$4,294,967,295_{10}$

As we learned in Chapter 1, hexadecimal numbers are used primarily as a more convenient way for human beings to write binary codes (see Section 1.1). However, it is also true that hexadecimal numbers are the positional representation in base 16. Thus we can also view them as sums of place value times digit products. For example, applying Equation (2.1), 165_{16} is:

$$1 \times 16^2 + 6 \times 16^1 + 5 \times 16^0 = 375_{10}$$

We have seen that the significance of the base of a number system is that it determines the *place values* in a positional notation. In going from right to left, each successive place value is the base times the previous place value. It is also important to note that the base determines the number of unique symbols required in a positional number system. For example, in the binary system, base 2, we need two symbols (0 and 1), while in the decimal system we need ten symbols (0, 1, 2, . . ., 9). The reason for this is simply that there must be enough symbols to "span" the distances between place values. Consider the simple process of numbering mileposts along a highway using the decimal system and beginning at 0. The post at the end of the ninth mile is marked 9, and the next post must mark the end of the tenth mile. We observe that because we have chosen the decimal system, the second digit place value is 10, and therefore we have no need for another symbol. We can mark the post with two of the already used symbols, i.e., a 1 and a 0. Indeed, if there *had* been an eleventh symbol, it would have been possible to mark the post in two different ways, which would be a redundant and confusing system. On the other hand, had there been only nine symbols, 0 through 8, we would not have had any symbol with which to mark the ninth mile! Thus the selection of base in a positional notation determines the required number of symbols.

The hexadecimal system, base 16, is used in expressing machine code for many modern computers, including the VAX-11. Observe, however, that with hexadecimal we need 16 symbols to span the ranges between place values of successive digits. Thus the customary ten arabic digits are insufficient. This problem is solved by using the *alphabetic* characters A, B, C, D, E, and F to augment the digits 0, 1, 2, . . ., 9, as shown in Table 2.2. Thus the number E4A, for example, is:

$$14 \times 16^2 + 4 \times 16^1 + 10 \times 16^0 = 3658_{10}$$

where we have made use of Equation (2.1) and the fact that E has the decimal value of 14 and A has the decimal value of 10.

TABLE 2.2/Digit Symbols for Various Bases

Base	Name	Digit Symbols
2	Binary	0 1
8	Octal	0 1 2 3 4 5 6 7
10	Decimal	0 1 2 3 4 5 6 7 8 9
16	Hexadecimal	0 1 2 3 4 5 6 7 8 9 A B C D E F
Value of Digital Symbol (All bases)		0 1 2 3 4 5 6 7 8 9 10 11 12 13 14 15

Table 2.2 also refers to octal or base 8 representation. This is the base used to express machine code on many computers, including the Digital Equipment Corporation PDP-11 family. Octal and hexadecimal are similar in that they allow convenient conversion to and from binary and are therefore used as "shorthand" for binary numbers. For reasons that are discussed in Chapter 3, the hexadecimal system has now largely displaced octal in machine code expressions. We mention octal here primarily because some machines continue to use this system.

2.3 | Arithmetic Operations in Binary and Hexadecimal

From time to time it will be necessary for the assembly language programmer to perform simple addition and subtraction in binary, octal, and hexadecimal. The rules learned in elementary school for performing these operations in decimal have to be modified slightly to account for the different bases. We will show these operations by example, and encourage the reader to practice using the exercises at the end of the chapter.

2.3.1. Addition

Addition is performed one digit at a time, working from the right. When the sum of digits exceeds the value of the highest symbol available in the base, one must "carry" the excess into the next position. In binary the highest symbol value is 1, so 1 plus 1 generates a zero and a carry as shown in the following simple examples:

$$
\begin{array}{cccc}
1 & 1 & 11 & 101 \\
+1 & +0 & +01 & +100 \\
\hline
10 & 1 & 100 & 1001 \\
\end{array}
$$

A slightly more difficult case occurs when more than two numbers have to be added. Consider, for example, the following:

$$
\begin{array}{r}
1 \\
1 \\
+1 \\
\hline
11 \\
\end{array}
$$

In performing this addition we add the first two 1's getting a carry to the second-digit position. The 0 added to the remaining 1 yields 1 in the first digit. Since there are no second-place 1's in the summands, the final result is just the carry generated by the first addition. A more interesting case occurs when adding four 1's:

$$
\begin{array}{r}
1 \\
1 \\
1 \\
+1 \\
\hline
100
\end{array}
$$

Adding the first two 1's yields 0 with 1 carried to position two. Adding the third summand to the first-position 0 yields 1. Adding this first-position 1 to the fourth summand yields 0 and *another* carry to the second position. One must then *add the two carries,* yielding a 0 as the final second-position value, and a carry into the third position.

As a final example of binary addition consider:

$$
\begin{array}{r}
1\ 1\ 1 \\
+1\ 1\ 1 \\
\hline
1\ 1\ 1\ 0
\end{array}
$$

Here we added a number to itself, so that we should expect the result to be twice the number. Our answer of 1110 is indeed twice 111, and demonstrates an important principle: Multiplying a binary number by 2 shifts the bit pattern left by one bit, with a 0 filling in the first position. This can be stated another way: Multiplying by 2 adds a 0 at the right. This operation is commonly called an **arithmetic shift left.** The reader will recognize that this is similar to what happens when we multiply a decimal number by 10. Indeed, when any number is multiplied by its base, a 0 digit is added to the right.

Addition of hexadecimal numbers follows similar rules. In this case, however, the highest available digit, F, has the value 15 so that any partial sum greater than 15 necessitates a carry. Some examples will demonstrate the hexadecimal techniques.

We refer to Table 2.2 for the place values of each digit.

(a)		(b)		(c)		(d)		(e)		(f)		(g)	
	1		A		E		A		B		E		FF
+3		+1		+2		+C		+D		+F		+1	
	4		B		10		16		18		1D		100

Examples (a) and (b) yield sums which are 15 or less and therefore involve no carries. In (c) 2 added to E yields a value of 16_{10}, but there is no single symbol in hexadecimal for representing 16_{10}. We therefore write the amount by which the partial sum exceeds the base, in this case 0, and carry a 1, giving the answer 10_{16}. Similar reasoning applies to (d), (e), and (f). In (f) note that the partial sum is 29_{10}, which exceeds the base by 13_{10}. Table 2.2 shows that the symbol D has the decimal value 13, so we write D for the first digit of the answer and carry a 1 into the second place. Example (g) demonstrates a carry which also generates a carry. Also, note that FF is another representation of an 8-bit binary number in which all bits are 1's. It is therefore the largest 8-bit binary number, and the largest 2-digit hexadecimal number. It is not surprising then that adding 1 gives a 3-digit hexadecimal number. This is analogous to adding 1 to 99_{10} and getting 100_{10}.

When there are more than two hexadecimal summands, there may be more than one carry to be added into the adjacent position. For example, consider:

$$
\begin{array}{r}
F \\
F \\
+F \\
\hline
2D
\end{array}
$$

Addition of the first two F's yields E with a carry of 1 to the second-position digit. The first-position E added to the third F yields a D with *another* carry to the second-position digit. Finally, the two carries are added to yield 2 in the second position.

The reader may wish to test his or her skills by verifying the following examples of hexadecimal addition:

$$
\begin{array}{llllll}
\text{(a)} & \text{1A3} & \text{(b)} & \text{C999} & \text{(c)} & \text{1ABC} \\
& \text{F1C} & & \text{A888} & & \text{ABC1} \\
& +\text{EAD} & & +\text{B777} & & +\text{1A2B} \\
\hline
& \text{1F6C} & & \text{22998} & & \text{E0A8}
\end{array}
$$

2.3.2 Subtraction

Subtraction is only slightly more difficult than addition. Rather than carrying, we may have to "borrow" from the digit to the left, in a manner completely analogous to decimal subtraction. We will demonstrate first with binary, then hexadecimal. We defer the consideration of negative numbers until Section 2.5. Therefore, in this section we do not consider problems that have negative operands, or that lead to negative results.

When no borrowing is required, the subtraction process is completely straightforward, e.g.:

$$
\begin{array}{ccc}
1 & 11 & 111 \\
-1 & -10 & -101 \\
\hline
0 & 01 & 010
\end{array}
$$

Now consider the case when there is a 1 to be subtracted from a 0, e.g.:

$$
\begin{array}{r}
10 \\
-1 \\
\hline
1
\end{array}
$$

Here it is necessary to borrow from the second position before subtracting the 1. The following scratch work shows the process and compares it to the analogous situation in decimal subtraction:

Binary	Decimal
0 2	8 10
$\not{1}\,\not{0}$	$\not{9}\,\not{0}$
−1	−1
1	8 9

Note that borrowing a 1 from the next binary digit reduces that digit by 1, and converts the 0 to a 2. The 1 can then be subtracted from this 2, yielding the answer. If the position to be borrowed from is itself a 0, it is necessary to borrow also from the *next higher* digit. Note the following example:

$$
\begin{array}{r}
1 \\
0 \; \cancel{2} \; 2 \\
\cancel{1} \; \cancel{0} \; \cancel{0} \\
-1 \\
\hline
1 \; 1
\end{array}
$$

Here we borrowed from the third position giving the second position a value of 2. This allowed borrowing from the second position, leaving it as a 1 and making the first-position value 2. The subtrahend can then be subtracted from the first-position 2, giving a 1. Finally, the second-position value is brought down, giving the correct answer.

Note in the above examples that in the borrowing process we choose to express the sum of the borrow and the minuend digit in *decimal* form rather than binary. That is, we could either write (and think!) in binary or in decimal, as shown in the following:

$$
\begin{array}{r}
10 \\
\cancel{1} \; \cancel{0} \\
-1 \\
\hline
1
\end{array}
\qquad \text{Binary}
$$

$$
\begin{array}{r}
2 \\
\cancel{1} \; \cancel{0} \\
-1 \\
\hline
1
\end{array}
\qquad \text{Decimal}
$$

We chose decimal, since that enabled us to use the subtraction facts which we learned for decimal arithmetic, rather than learning their counterparts in binary, hexadecimal, or whatever base we happened to need.

The following examples further demonstrate the process of binary subtraction, and should be verified by the reader:

$$
\begin{array}{llll}
\text{(a)} & \begin{array}{r} 1110 \\ -1101 \\ \hline 0001 \end{array}
& \text{(b)} & \begin{array}{r} 1000 \\ -111 \\ \hline 0001 \end{array}
& \text{(c)} & \begin{array}{r} 1010 \\ -0101 \\ \hline 0101 \end{array}
\end{array}
$$

Subtraction of hexadecimal numbers parallels the process in decimal or binary. That is, we proceed digit-by-digit from right to left, subtracting the subtrahend from the minuend. For example,

$$
\begin{array}{r}
774 \\
-153 \\
\hline
621
\end{array}
$$

In this case it is impossible to tell that hexadecimal subtraction is being done, because every digit of the subtrahend is smaller than the corresponding digit in the minuend. When this is not the case, one must increase the minuend digit by borrowing from the digit to the left. This is the same as in decimal, with the exception that in hexadecimal the borrow contributes 16_{10} rather than 10_{10}. Observe this in the following example, where we again choose to "borrow in decimal":

$$
\begin{array}{r}
25 \\
0 \ \cancel{A} \ 30 \\
\cancel{1} \ \cancel{A} \ E \\
- \quad C \ F \\
\hline
D \ F
\end{array}
$$

Let's go through this a digit at a time. To subtract F from E we need to borrow. The borrow adds the base value 16_{10} to the E, yielding 30_{10}. Subtracting the decimal equivalent of F (15_{10}) from the 30_{10} yields 15_{10}, which we write down as F for the first hexadecimal digit of the answer. The borrow, however, has reduced the second digit to 9_{10}, so we need to borrow from the third digit before subtracting the C. When we do, we get $9_{10} + 16_{10} = 25_{10}$. We can then subtract the C (12_{10}) from 25 and get $13_{10} = D_{16}$.

Hexadecimal subtraction is an especially important skill when working with VAX-11 machine code. The following detailed examples will help you master the process.

$$
\begin{array}{lll}
\text{(a)} \quad
\begin{array}{r}
16 \\
A \ \cancel{B} \ 29 \\
F \ \cancel{B} \ \cancel{1} \ \cancel{B} \\
- \ A \ 2 \ E \\
\hline
F \ 0 \ E \ F
\end{array}
&
\text{(b)} \quad
\begin{array}{r}
25 \ 18 \\
\cancel{A} \ \cancel{A} \ 27 \\
1 \ \cancel{A} \ \cancel{A} \ \cancel{B} \\
- \ C \ 9 \ F \\
\hline
D \ 9 \ C
\end{array}
&
\text{(c)} \quad
\begin{array}{r}
26 \\
9 \ \cancel{A} \ 18 \\
1 \ F \ \cancel{A} \ \cancel{B} \ \cancel{A} \\
- \ F \ C \ D \ 9 \\
\hline
F \ D \ D \ 9
\end{array}
\end{array}
$$

2.4 | Conversion of Bases

We have already observed that the same number can be represented in many different bases. The conversion from one base to another is something that every assembly language programmer has to do regularly, so some proficiency in this is necessary. Here we will show selected conversion techniques for:

binary	to	hexadecimal
hexadecimal	to	binary
hexadecimal	to	decimal
binary	to	decimal
decimal	to	hexadecimal
decimal	to	binary

2.4.1 Binary/Hexadecimal

The conversions from binary to hexadecimal and hexadecimal to binary are particularly easy, as we have already seen in Chapter 1. There is a one-to-one correspondence between hexadecimal digits and groups of four bits (called nibbles), as shown in the following table.

Hexadecimal	Binary	Hexadecimal	Binary
0	0000	8	1000
1	0001	9	1001
2	0010	A	1010
3	0011	B	1011
4	0100	C	1100
5	0101	D	1101
6	0110	E	1110
7	0111	F	1111

This table can be constructed easily by counting in binary from 0 to 16_{10}. With frequent usage it is quickly memorized. Then a binary number is simply partitioned into groups of four bits, starting at the right, and the corresponding hexadecimal digit is substituted for each group. Examples follow.

EXAMPLE 2.1 Convert 11011100111010101 to hexadecimal.

Binary: 0001 1011 1001 1101 0101
Hexadecimal: 1   B   9   D   5

Note that we grouped the bits by four, starting at the right. If the number of bits is not evenly divisible by four, we simply add leading zeros to complete the leftmost hexadecimal digit.

EXAMPLE 2.2 Convert E94A to binary.

Hexadecimal: E   9   4   A
Binary: 1110   1001   0100   1010

The great ease with which we do these conversions is the reason why we use hexadecimal as shorthand for binary. In fact, binary numbers are seldom written out, and some programmers will refer to hexadecimal as "binary" because they tend to visualize the implied bit pattern instead of the hexadecimal digits.

2.4.2 Binary and Hexadecimal to Decimal

We have also already seen conversion from binary and hexadecimal to decimal. This can be done by using Equation (2.1), repeated here:

$$N = \sum_{i=0}^{m-1} D_i b^i \tag{2.1}$$

where

D_i = value of the ith digit *represented in decimal*, and
b^i = base raised to the ith power *and represented in decimal*.

In binary-to-decimal conversion the b^i's are the powers of two. Because the D_i's are just 0 or 1, this conversion amounts to a simple addition of the powers of two for the bits that are 1. The powers of two are tabulated inside the front cover of this text. Several examples of this are given in Section 2.1.

There are other methods for conversion to decimal. One binary-to-decimal conversion that can be done without the aid of powers-of-two tables is called the **double dabble** method. The steps are:

1. Double the leftmost bit.
2. Add the next bit (this is the "dabble").
3. Double the result.
4. Repeat from Step 2 until there are no more bits.

Although this method can, with practice, be done without writing anything down, we show a step-by-step example below for clarity.

EXAMPLE 2.3   Convert 1011110 to decimal using double dabble.

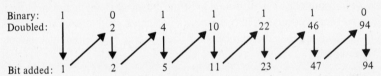

Here ↗ shows the doubling operation, and ↓ shows the "dabbling" operation.

See also Exercise 2.9.

2.4.3 Decimal to Binary

Conversion from decimal to hexadecimal or binary is significantly more difficult than the reverse. Theoretically, the formula in Equation (2.1) could be used, but this is not a practical method for hand calculations. To see why, consider conversion of 42_{10} to binary by using Equation (2.1):

$$4 \times 10^1 + 2 \times 10^0$$

In order for conversion to take place, each of these numbers must be expressed in the target base, binary, and the arithmetic must be carried out in binary. Let's do this just once:

$$100 \times 1010 + 10 \times 1 = 101010$$

The reader can prove this to be correct by converting back to decimal. Note, however, that to do it this way we had to know the binary representation of 4, 2, 10, and 1, and had to know how to perform multiplication in binary. These are not particularly difficult concepts, but on the other hand, most of us have far better skills in *decimal* arithmetic. Most programmers, therefore, apply different methods for the reverse conversions.

Decimal-to-binary conversion can be done quite easily with the **subtractive** method, since the coefficients on the place values are always 0 or 1. The method goes rapidly with a calculator and a powers-of-two table. One simply attempts to subtract the largest possible power of 2, and records a 1 for the corresponding bit when successful, or a 0 otherwise. The following example demonstrates this method.

EXAMPLE 2.4 (Subtractive method)   Convert 42_{10} to binary.

$$42 - 32 = 10 \qquad D_5 = 1 \qquad (2^5 \text{ subtracted})$$
$$D_4 = 0$$
$$10 - 8 = 2 \qquad D_3 = 1 \qquad (2^3 \text{ subtracted})$$
$$D_2 = 0$$
$$2 - 2 = 0 \qquad D_1 = 1 \qquad (2^1 \text{ subtracted})$$
$$D_0 = 0$$

Therefore, $42_{10} = 101010$.

An alternate approach is known as the division or **remainder** method. With this method, the number is divided by the base, and the quotient and remainder are written separately. The quotient is then divided by the base, and again the resulting quotient and remainder are recorded. This process is repeated until the quotient is zero. The succession of remainders is the number in the new base. The following example demonstrates this method.

EXAMPLE 2.5 (Remainder method)   Convert 94_{10} to binary.

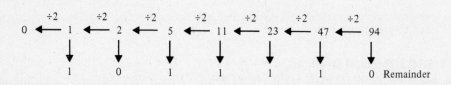

Therefore, $94_{10} = 1011110_2$. Note that this method is the inverse of the double dabble method. This is evidenced by the similarity in intermediate results. (See example 2.3.)

2.4.4 Decimal to Hexadecimal

Decimal-to-hexadecimal conversion can be done in several different ways. Some prefer to convert first to binary using the subtractive method, and then perform the easy binary-to-hexadecimal conversion. Direct decimal-to-hexadecimal conversion by the subtractive method is complicated by the fact that the hexadecimal digits act as multipliers on the place value. This means that the powers must be subtracted repeatedly, in contrast to the decimal-to-binary conversion which requires only a single subtraction per power. One must first determine the largest power of 16 that can be subtracted. The first hexadecimal digit is then the number of times that this power can be subtracted. Repetition of the process gives the rest of the digits, as shown in the following example.

EXAMPLE 2.6 (Subtractive method)   Convert 4640_{10} to hexadecimal.

$$
\begin{array}{rl}
4640 & \\
\underline{-\ 4096} & \quad (16^3 \text{ subtracted once; } D_3 = 1) \\
544 & \\
\underline{-\ 256} & \\
288 & \\
\underline{-\ 256} & \quad (16^2 \text{ subtracted twice; } D_2 = 2) \\
32 & \\
\underline{-16} & \\
16 & \\
\underline{-\ 16} & \quad (16^1 \text{ subtracted twice; } D_1 = 2) \\
0 & \quad (16^0 \text{ subtracted 0 times; } D_0 = 0)
\end{array}
$$

Therefore, $4640_{10} = 1220_{16}$.

An alternate method for decimal-to-hexadecimal conversion is called the remainder method. Here one divides the number by 16 repeatedly; on each division the next digit is given by the *remainder*.

EXAMPLE 2.7 (Remainder method)   Convert 4640_{10} to hexadecimal.

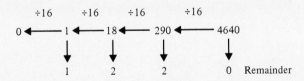

Therefore, $4640_{10} = 1220_{16}$. It is observed that the procedure is the same as that used in decimal-to-binary conversion by the remainder method; only the base is different.

2.5 | Negative Numbers

2.5.1 The Two's Complement Number System

In Section 2.2 it was shown that the number of bits available, i.e., the cell length, limits the size of numbers that can be stored using binary positional notation. We saw, for example, that a 4-bit binary number can represent only sixteen different numerical values. We used these bit patterns to represent the sixteen hexadecimal digits, that is:

Binary	Hexadecimal	Binary	Hexadecimal
0000	0	1000	8
0001	1	1001	9
0010	2	1010	A
0011	3	1011	B
0100	4	1100	C
0101	5	1101	D
0110	6	1110	E
0111	7	1111	F

Similarly, with 32-bit cells such as we have in the VAX-11, there are $2^{32} = 4,294,967,$ 296 different bit patterns that can be used to represent zero and the positive integers up to 4,294,967,295. We now note that if we used *all* of these available bit patterns for *positive* numbers, we would have none to represent negative numbers. If the programmer wishes to use negative numbers, it will be necessary to assign some of the bit patterns for their representation.

There are many ways that this could be done. For example, using a 4-bit cell length for convenience of demonstration, we could make the following assignments:

Bit Pattern	Value
1111	−7
1110	−6
1101	−5
1100	−4
1011	−3
1010	−2
1001	−1
1000	−0
0000	+0
0001	+1
0010	+2
0011	+3
0100	+4
0101	+5
0110	+6
0111	+7

This would give us a way to represent the integers from −7 to +7, and as a bonus we would have a −0 as well as a +0 (for whatever value that might be!). This system could be used, but poses some slight inconveniences. For example, one might expect that 2+(−1) would be +1. In this system, however, 2+(−1)= −3, as shown here:

$$
\begin{array}{rl}
0010 & (\ 2) \\
+1001 & (-1) \\
\hline
1011 & (-3)
\end{array}
$$

This difficulty could, of course, be overcome by devising new rules for subtraction. Indeed, some computers do use this system, which is called the **sign-magnitude** system. However, there is another system which was viewed as a better one by the designers of the VAX-11 computers. This is called the **two's complement** system and is used on many other digital computers as well as the VAX-11.

The two's complement system offers an attractive way to divide the available bit patterns for a cell of given length into positive and negative integers. To demonstrate this system we will again use a 4-bit cell for convenience. The positive integers are represented by the positional binary numbers:

Decimal System	Two's Complement System (4-bit)
0	0000
1	0001
2	0010
3	0011
4	0100
5	0101
6	0110
7	0111

The negative numbers are represented by defining 1111 to be -1 and then counting *downward* in binary as the numbers become more negative, as shown here:

Decimal System	Two's Complement System (4-bit)
0	0000
-1	1111
-2	1110
-3	1101
-4	1100
-5	1011
-6	1010
-7	1001
-8	1000

With this system we observe that the integers between -8 and $+7$ can be represented, including a single 0. However, if we attempt to go beyond $+7$ we get 1000, which is the same as the pattern assigned to -8. Similarly, attempting to achieve a value more negative than -8 yields 0111, which is really a $+7$. It is therefore very important to recognize the range limits with this (or any other) digital representation of numbers.

The two's complement property of generating the most negative number by exceeding the positive range by 1 (and vice versa) invites a circular representation of the real line, as shown in Figure 2.1. You may also observe the similarity between this system and an automotive odometer which goes back to 0 after reaching 99999.

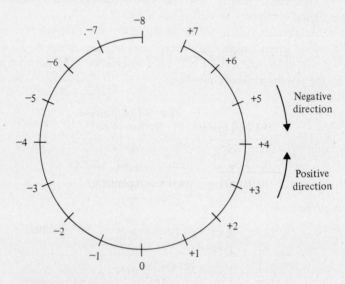

FIGURE 2.1/Circular representation of the real line for the 4-bit two's complement system

The two's complement system has many interesting and convenient properties. For example, subtraction obeys familiar rules.

$$
\begin{array}{cc}
0010 & (\ 2) \\
+1111 & +(-1) \\
\hline
1 \leftarrow \quad 0001 & (+1)
\end{array}
$$

Here we have shown that $(+2)+(-1)$ produces $+1$, using the conventional rules for binary addition and ignoring the carry from the most significant bit (MSB). Also, the negative of a number is produced by subtracting it from 0 (assuming a borrow into the MSB).

$$
\begin{array}{cc}
1 \rightarrow \quad 0000 & (\ 0) \\
-0011 & -(+3) \\
\hline
1101 & (-3)
\end{array}
$$

This property, in fact, gives the two's complement system its name. The term "complement" in mathematics means the amount that will make a value "complete." The complement of an acute angle is the value one must add to obtain 90 degrees. The two's complement of an n-bit binary number is the value which must be added to yield 2^n which, in a sense, is complete. Thus we can determine the two's complement of an n-bit binary number by subtracting it from 2^n. This is what we did, in effect, when we subtracted 0011 from 0000 with a carry into the MSB in the preceding example.

Many people find it easier to find the two's complement of a number by taking the one's complement and adding 1. This can be shown to be mathematically equivalent to subtracting it from 2^n. The operation is easy since the one's complement is found simply by "flipping the bits," i.e., changing 1's to 0's and 0's to 1's. Addition of the 1 usually requires only a few carries, and the entire process is often quicker than the subtraction process implied in the definition. The following examples show both methods.

EXAMPLE 2.8 (a) Find the two's complement of 01010111. By the definition:

$$
\begin{array}{ll}
100000000 & (2^n) \\
-01010111 & \text{(minus original number)} \\
\hline
10101001 & \text{(two's complement)}
\end{array}
$$

By one's complement plus 1:

$$
\begin{array}{ll}
10101000 & \text{(one's complement of original number)} \\
+1 & \text{(plus 1)} \\
\hline
10101001 & \text{(two's complement)}
\end{array}
$$

(b) Find the two's complement of 111. By the definition:

$$
\begin{array}{r}
1000 \\
-111 \\
\hline
001
\end{array}
$$

By one's complement plus 1:

$$
\begin{array}{r}
000 \\
+1 \\
\hline
001
\end{array}
$$

(c) Find the two's complement of 0100111011000101. By the definition:

$$
\begin{array}{r}
10000000000000000 \\
+0100111011000101 \\
\hline
1011000100111011
\end{array}
$$

By one's complement plus 1:

$$
\begin{array}{r}
1011000100111010 \\
+1 \\
\hline
1011000100111011
\end{array}
$$

(d) Show that the two's complement *of the two's complement* of a number, say 0110, yields the original number. By one's complement plus 1:

$$
\begin{array}{ll}
1001 & \text{(one's complement)} \\
\underline{+\quad 1} & \\
1010 & \text{(two's complement)} \\
\\
0101 & \text{(one's complement)} \\
\underline{+\quad 1} & \\
0110 & \text{(original number)}
\end{array}
$$

This example demonstrates the important property $-(-N) = N$ in the two's complement system.

There is the possibility of confusion due to several usages of the term "two's complement." This term is used as the name of the number system, as an adjective describing a number in this system, and as an arithmetic operation. When we say, "Find the two's complement of" or "Take the two's complement of" we refer to an arithmetic operation otherwise known as **negation.** When we say, "A two's complement number," i.e., use the term as an adjective, we are identifying the representation system employed. Note in particular that "two's complement" used as an adjective is not synonymous with *negative*. Indeed, in the preceding examples we found that by two's complementing 111 (a negative number) we achieved 001 (a positive number). Both 111 and 001 can be viewed as two's complement numbers. We have already noted that either could also be viewed simply as positive integers in a positional binary system. Saying that they are two's complement numbers is a necessary clarification, and says nothing about their sign. In general, an integer on a computer that employs this system will either be viewed as a two's complement representation, in which case we say it is **signed,** or as a positive integer representation, in which case we call it **unsigned.** The latter is used when the quantity being represented cannot be negative, and a larger range of positive values is needed.

2.5.2 The 32-bit and 8-bit Two's Complement Systems

The VAX computer provides several cell sizes for storing integers, as we shall see in Chapter 3. In this book we shall use primarily a cell which provides 32 bits (called a longword), and sometimes a byte cell which provides 8 bits (called a byte). The longword allows 2^{32} different bit patterns. As already noted, these can be used exclusively to represent unsigned integers, in which case the allowable range is 0 to $4{,}294{,}967{,}295_{10}$. By use of the 32-bit two's complement system, however, this same cell can be used to represent the range $-2{,}147{,}483{,}648_{10}$ to $+2{,}147{,}483{,}647_{10}$. The two's complement scheme of representation is shown in Table 2.3. Note that as with the 4-bit two's complement system, the largest positive value is a 0 in the MSB with the rest set to 1, and the largest negative value is a 1 in the MSB with the rest set to 0. Noting that *all* negative numbers have the MSB equal to 1, we see why the MSB is often called the

sign bit. Table 2.3 also lists the *hexadecimal translation* of the bit patterns, which we call 32-bit two's complement hexadecimal. In Figure 2.2 (a) we show the 32-bit two's complement system on a circular "real" line to emphasize that exceeding the allowed range, positive or negative, produces an erroneous result.

It is sometimes convenient or necessary to work in terms of 8-bit two's complement numbers rather than 32-bit longwords. Table 2.4 shows this system, with the circular diagram appearing in Figure 2.2(b). The similarities to the 4-bit and 32-bit systems are quite apparent in the table.

Tables 2.3 and 2.4 should be studied until negative and positive numbers can be readily recognized in both 8- and 32-bit systems, whether written in hexadecimal or binary. Observe that a two's complement hexadecimal number is positive if the most significant digit is 0,1,2, . . . , 7, but is negative if this digit is 8,9,A, . . . , F. In the binary form, a 1 in the MSB indicates negative. Comparison of the negative 8-bit numbers in binary representation with the negative 32-bit numbers similarly represented reveals an important fact: The representations are the same except for more leading 1's in the 32-bit representation. Similarly, the 8-bit and 32-bit positive numbers differ only by more leading 0's. Thus one could convert from 8-bit to 32-bit representation by *extending the sign bit to the left*. This is an important property, called **sign extension,** used when we take up bit and byte manipulations in later chapters.

TABLE 2.3/32-bit Two's Complement System

Decimal	Two's Complement (binary)	Two's Complement (hexadecimal)
−2,147,483,648	1000 0000 0000 0000 0000 0000 0000	80000000
−2,147,483,647	1000 0000 0000 0000 0000 0000 0001	80000001
−2,147,483,646	1000 0000 0000 0000 0000 0000 0010	80000002
.	.	.
.	.	.
.	.	.
−2	1111 1111 1111 1111 1111 1111 1110	FFFFFFFE
−1	1111 1111 1111 1111 1111 1111 1111	FFFFFFFF
0	0000 0000 0000 0000 0000 0000 0000	00000000
1	0000 0000 0000 0000 0000 0000 0001	00000001
2	0000 0000 0000 0000 0000 0000 0010	00000002
.	.	.
.	.	.
.	.	.
2,147,483,645	0111 1111 1111 1111 1111 1111 1101	7FFFFFFD
2,147,483,646	0111 1111 1111 1111 1111 1111 1110	7FFFFFFE
2,147,483,647	0111 1111 1111 1111 1111 1111 1111	7FFFFFFF

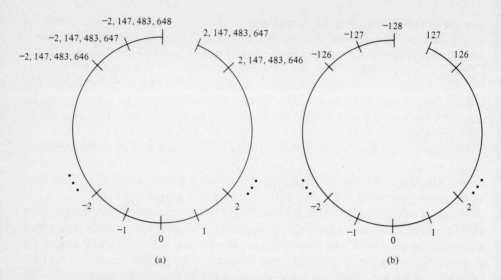

FIGURE 2.2/ Circular representation of the real line for (a) 32-bit and (b) 8-bit two's complement systems (numbers shown in base 10)

TABLE 2.4/8-bit Two's Complement System

Decimal	Two's Complement (binary)	Two's Complement (hexadecimal)
−128	1000 0000	80
−127	1000 0001	81
−126	1000 0010	82
.	.	.
.	.	.
.	.	.
−2	1111 1110	FE
−1	1111 1111	FF
0	0000 0000	00
1	0000 0001	00
2	0000 0010	02
.	.	.
.	.	.
.	.	.
125	0111 1101	7D
126	0111 1110	7E
127	0111 1111	7F

2.5.3 Two's Complement Arithmetic

Facility in two's complement arithmetic is important to the assembly language programmer. Here we demonstrate the most common operations—addition, subtraction, and negation—using longwords. In this discussion, recall that the MSB is called the 31st bit, and the adjacent one, the 30th.

Addition of two positive two's complement numbers is no different than adding positional binary numbers, provided the allowable range is not exceeded. When it is exceeded, the result is not valid. For example, adding 3 to $2,147,483,646_{10}$ produces:

$$
\begin{array}{r}
0111\ 1111\ 1111\ 1111\ 1111\ 1111\ 1111\ 1110 \\
+0000\ 0000\ 0000\ 0000\ 0000\ 0000\ 0000\ 0011 \\
\hline
1000\ 0000\ 0000\ 0000\ 0000\ 0000\ 0000\ 0001 \quad \text{(Overflow)}
\end{array}
$$

which is $-2,147,483,647_{10}$. Here an **overflow** is said to have occurred. Note that this condition is always marked by a carry from the 30th to the 31st bit. Because the 31st bit is reserved for the sign, the carry invalidates the result.

However, if there is *also* a carry out of the MSB there is no overflow. This is demonstrated by the following example, where we add a negative number and a positive number:

$$
\begin{array}{r}
1100\ 0000\ 0000\ 0000\ 0000\ 0000\ 0000\ 0000 \\
+0100\ 0000\ 0000\ 0000\ 0000\ 0000\ 0000\ 0000 \\
\hline
1 \leftarrow 0000\ 0000\ 0000\ 0000\ 0000\ 0000\ 0000\ 0000 \quad \text{(Correct Result)}
\end{array}
$$

Here, because we get a carry from bit 30 to bit 31, as well as the carry out of bit 31, the result is correct.

Subtraction can be carried out either by following the normal rules of binary subtraction, or by negating the subtrahend and adding. If the minuend is larger than the subtrahend and both are positive, normal subtraction is no different than that discussed in Section 2.3.2. Let us consider then the more interesting case of subtracting a larger positive number from a smaller one, for example, $2 - 3$. We use the 4-bit two's complement system for convenience.

$$
\begin{array}{rll}
1\rightarrow\ 0010 & (2) & \text{(minuend)} \\
-0011 & -(3) & \text{(subtrahend)} \\
\hline
1111 & (-1) &
\end{array}
$$

Note that by simply borrowing from an imaginary bit to the left of the MSB we arrived at the correct result. This same result can be obtained by forming the two's complement of the subtrahend (i.e., negating it) and adding:

$$
\begin{array}{rl}
0010 & (\ 2) \\
+1101 & +(-3) \\
\hline
1111 & (-1)
\end{array}
$$

Some will find this a more convenient method because addition may be easier than subtraction.

The preceding operations can also be carried out entirely in the *hexadecimal* representation of two's complement numbers. In fact, most assembly language programmers learn to think and work entirely in hexadecimal (or octal, depending upon the computer). We have already considered hexadecimal addition in Section 2.3.1; this remains unchanged for the two's complement system if the sum is within the allowed range. Even if one or both of the addends are negative the rules do not change. For example, the following 32-bit two's complement hexadecimal numbers are both negative:

$$
\begin{array}{ll}
 8\,0\,0\,0\,0\,0\,0\,2 & (-2{,}147{,}483{,}646_{10}) \\
+\text{F F F F F F F E} & +(\phantom{-2{,}147{,}483{,}64}-2_{10}) \\
\hline
1\leftarrow\ \ 8\,0\,0\,0\,0\,0\,0\,0 & (-2{,}147{,}483{,}648_{10})
\end{array}
$$

As usual, the carry out of the most significant digit is ignored.

The **negation** operation, i.e., two's complementing, can also be carried out entirely in hexadecimal. It is only necessary to observe the *maximum value* that each digit can take on as you follow the rules previously established. Let us consider the negation of the 8-bit two's complement hexadecimal number 62. First find its one's complement by subtracting each digit from its maximum possible value.

$$
\begin{array}{ll}
\text{FF} & \text{(maximum value of each digit)} \\
-62 & \\
\hline
9\text{D} & \text{(one's complement of 62)} \\
+\ 1 & \\
\hline
9\text{E} & \text{(two's complement of 62)}
\end{array}
$$

Observe that this is a negative number by virtue of the leading 9 (see Table 2.4).

A common problem is to convert a negative two's complement hexadecimal number to its decimal equivalent. The easy way to do this is to *negate* the number, i.e., form its two's complement, then convert the result to decimal and append the customary minus sign. For example, suppose we are given E6 and told that it is in an 8-bit two's complement hexadecimal representation (we could *not* tell this just by looking at it). Since its leading digit is E, it is negative. Its two's complement is

$$
\begin{array}{l}
\text{FF} \\
-\text{E6} \\
\hline
19 \\
+\ 1 \\
\hline
1\text{A}_{16} = 26_{10}
\end{array}
$$

Therefore, two's complement E6 $= -26_{10}$.

Two's complement hexadecimal subtraction is facilitated by negation. That is, rather than perform subtraction, we can two's complement the subtrahend and add. In the following example we find the difference FFFFFF7B $-$ 73, in which both operands are 32-bit two's complement hexadecimal representations. Observe that we are subtracting a positive number from a negative number, so we expect a negative result.

$$
\begin{array}{rl}
\text{FFFFFFFF} & \text{(maximum digit values)} \\
-\phantom{\text{FFFFFF}}73 & \text{(subtrahend)} \\
\hline
\text{FFFFFF8C} & \text{(one's complement)} \\
\phantom{\text{FFFFFFF}}1 & \\
\hline
\text{FFFFFF8D} & \text{(two's complement)} \\
+\text{FFFFFF7B} & \text{(minuend)} \\
\hline
\text{FFFFFF08} &
\end{array}
$$

It is left as an exercise for the reader to show that this is correct by converting the original numbers to decimal and carrying out the subtraction. The result is -248_{10}.

2.6 | Summary

Assembly language programming is complicated by the fact that the machine works with binary numbers, while people are more familiar with decimal numbers. Some effort is necessary to bridge this gap.

We first distinguished between the abstract concept of a number and the way we choose to *represent* it. For example, 13_{10} is a **representation** of a baker's dozen, but so is 1101_2. It was seen that **positional notation** is used in binary (base 2) and hexadecimal (base 16) number systems as well as in the familiar decimal system. For any positional number system the **place values** and the number of required **digit symbols** are determined by the base. The place values are found by raising the base to the position index, counting from 0 at the rightmost digit. Thus it was necessary to augment the ten Arabic numerals with the characters A, B, C, D, E, and F in order to have enough symbols in the hexadecimal system. We also saw that with the positional formula, if the digits and place values are expressed in a *different base*, the number is *converted* to that base.

We also discussed the mechanics of simple arithmetic in the binary and hexadecimal systems. Addition was seen to be much the same as decimal addition. However, it was found necessary to recognize the impact of the base on the **carry** operation. For example, we saw that in hexadecimal $15+1 = 10$ because there is no symbol for 16 in hexadecimal and 16 is the place value of the second digit. Similarly, in subtraction the borrow operation provides an additional 16 in hexadecimal or 2 in binary, analogous to 10 in decimal. However, we found that we could make use of our decimal addition and subtraction "facts" learned in elementary school by representing borrows in decimal.

The chapter also included a discussion of algorithms for converting from one base to another. We found that binary to hexadecimal, or the reverse, was a simple substitution process. This ease of conversion is in fact the justification for use of hexadecimal; it is a "shorthand" for binary. Slightly more difficult are the conversions from binary or hexadecimal to decimal. The positional notation, **sum-of-products formula,** is the most straightforward method for converting to decimal from either binary or hexadecimal, but not necessarily the easiest method. The alternate **"double dabble"** method is applicable for binary-to-decimal conversion. The more difficult conversions are *from decimal* to binary or hexadecimal. The sum-of-products formula would work, but not many of us have sufficient facility in base 16 or base 2 arithmetic to make this attractive. Instead, we demonstrated the use of the **subtraction-of-powers** method and the **remainder** method for conversion to either binary or hexadecimal. Most will find one or the other of these most suitable to their needs. Do not overlook the fact that you can convert first to binary, and then convert the binary to hexadecimal by substitution.

Finally, we introduced the **two's complement system** to represent negative numbers. It has several interesting properties, such as a subtraction mechanism which negates the subtrahend and adds. It was shown that the real line in a two's complement system is "circular," in the sense that exceeding the allowed range of positive numbers produces negative values, and vice versa. Since one bit is used for the sign, the allowable range for two's complement numbers is less than the range for unsigned integers in the same cell length.

2.7 | Exercises

2.1 Convert the following binary numbers to decimal using either Equation (2.1) or the double dabble technique.
- (a) 11110111
- (b) 1010
- (c) 10011100010000
- (d) 10000001
- (e) 10101001
- (f) 10101101
- (g) 1100100
- (h) 10000000
- (i) 11111111
- (j) 1010011100101110
- (k) 1111101000
- (l) 11000011010100000

2.2 Perform the indicated binary arithmetic.

- (a) 101010 + 10101 =
- (b) 10000000 − 1 =
- (c) 1111 + 111 =
- (d) 1111 − 111 =
- (e) 10000000 − 1010101 =
- (f) 1100100 − 101111 =
- (g) 110110110 + 111111111 =
- (h) 100110011001 + 110000111001 =
- (i) 1 + 11 + 111 + 1111 =
- (j) 11 + 1001 + 11011 + 1010001 =
- (k) 1 + 111 − 110 + 111110100 − 11100001 =
- (l) 1111101000 − 1100100 − 1010 − 1=

2.3 Convert the following binary numbers to hexadecimal and decimal.
- (a) 1010
- (b) 1111101000
- (c) 10101101
- (d) 10111111
- (e) 10000001
- (f) 1010011100101110

2.4 Convert the following decimal numbers to hexadecimal and binary.
- (a) 15
- (b) 1000
- (c) 384
- (d) 255
- (e) 169
- (f) 65535

Try both the subtraction of powers and the remainder methods.

2.5 Convert the following hexadecimal numbers to decimal and binary.
- (a) CC
- (b) E9DD
- (c) FFFF
- (d) 67
- (e) ABCD
- (f) 123456

2.6 Convert the following octal numbers to decimal and binary.
- (a) 314
- (b) 147
- (c) 164735
- (d) 377
- (e) 177777
- (f) 123456

2.7 Perform the indicated arithmetic. All values are in hexadecimal.

(a)   E12A   -(b)   1 2EF   (c)   FF 92
   +0E5B   +ABCD   −EA89

(d)   AC79   -(e)   1234   (f)   FF
   −79AC   +9876   −19

2.8 Perform the indicated arithmetic. All values are in octal.

(a)   432   (b)   063257   (c)   063254
   +371   +025653   −025667

(d)   375   (e)   145   (f)   563
   −177   654   351
           +717   +666

2.9 In this chapter we learned a method of converting binary numbers to decimal using the double dabble technique. This technique can be generalized readily to create a fast method for converting hexadecimal numbers to decimal. In fact double dabble and its generalization are simply an efficient way to evaluate the positional polynominal representation of the number to be converted. Can you generalize double dabble for hexadecimal-to-decimal conversion? Explain why your generalization works.

Hint: Convert hexadecimal 1ABC to decimal.

$$((1 \times 16 + 10) \times 16 + 11) \times 16 + 12 = 6844.$$

What was done? Try your generalization with the following hexadecimal numbers.

(a) F1AB   (b) 1E20   (c) FF2   (d) 123456

2.10 Develop a program in BASIC or Pascal (or other high-level languages with which you are familiar) that will convert a decimal number to binary, octal, or hexadecimal, depending upon the user's request. Your program should accept the number and the desired base and print the representation in the specified base.

2.11 Convert each of the following decimal numbers to its 32-bit two's complement hexadecimal representation.

-(a) 14   -(b) −14   (c) 6954 -(d) 1048575
(e) 30000 (f) −28481 (g) −195 .(h) −1048575

2.12 Convert the following 32-bit two's complement hexadecimal numbers to decimal.

(a) 00006DB6 (b) 80006DB6 -(c) FFFFFFF1
(d) 00000041 (e) EAAAAAAA (f) 70000000
-(g) 80000000 -(h) 1FFFFFFF

2.13 Perform the following arithmetic. All numbers are 32-bit two's complements, expressed in hexadecimal. Indicate if overflow has occurred, and whether the result is positive or negative.

-(a)   01ABCDEF - (b)   FFFFFFFF -(c)   7FFFFFF7 - (d)   000001A3
   +01FEDCBA   +00000001   +000000F   +8FFFFFF 8

_ (e)   8000000F -(f)   7000000F(g)   000001A3 − (h)   000001A3
   −1000000F   −1000000F   −8FFFFFF 8   −7FFFFFF 7

2.14 The one's complement system is an alternative numbering system that allows negative numbers. In this system, the negatives are the positives with each bit reversed. Explore this system for a 4-bit length system. (a) Show the decimal equivalent of each bit pattern. (b) Show what happens when the positive and negative ranges are exceeded. (c) What happens when a positive is added to a negative of equal magnitude using normal rules of binary addition?

— **2.15** Explain the term "sign extension" with regard to the two's complement number system. Demonstrate by showing -25_{10} and $+25_{10}$ represented in 8-bit, 16-bit and 32-bit two's complement binary and hexadecimal forms.

3

Computer Organization and Architecture

3.1 | Overview

One of the reasons for studying machine and assembly language programming is to become familiar with the way that digital computers actually work. Conversely, one can become proficient in machine and assembly language only by developing an understanding of the machine operation and characteristics. We therefore now take up these matters, referring to them as **computer organization** and **architecture.**

The terms organization and architecture are used to broadly describe the machine from a *functional* point of view. **Organization** refers to a description of the machine in terms of its major components. In particular, we are referring to the function of these components, i.e., what each component does, and how they are interconnected, i.e., how data and control information are communicated between components. **Architecture** refers to a description of the machine in terms of its programming elements and operations that are available to the assembly language programmer. Thus the machine's architecture includes aspects such as its instruction set, how data and instructions are stored in its memory, what kinds of registers are available, and how data items are referred to or "addressed" in memory.

Our primary intent in this chapter is to introduce these topics and discuss them in sufficient depth to allow development of machine and assembly programming concepts. Secondarily, we will be laying the groundwork for a broader understanding of the way digital computers work, to be further developed in later courses. To this end, we will explore certain important topics beyond what would be needed just to perform programming on the VAX-11.

In order to avoid unnecessary complications in our early discussions, we will first use a somewhat simplified, general model of the digital computer. Afterwards, we will examine the VAX-11 itself, focusing on a particular member of the family called the VAX-11/730. Even then, however, we will purposely omit many details in order to keep the discussion at an appropriate level. This approach will meet the needs of most readers. Those wanting further details of the VAX-11 architecture and organization may consult the Digital Equipment Corporation Publications, *VAX-11 Architecture Hand-*

book and *VAX-11 Hardware Handbook*. First, however, we must discuss exactly how information is stored in a digital computer, since this is fundamental to all elements of the machine.

3.2 | Stored Digital Information

A digital computer must have the capability to store information, including instructions and data. Conventionally, this is done by using electronic circuits that can store strings of binary digits called **bit patterns.** The binary numbers of Chapter 2 are examples of bit patterns. For the moment we shall refer to the basic unit of storage for these bit patterns as a **storage cell.** Storage cells can be implemented in various ways, but the implementation is not as important to us here as the concept itself. An 8-bit cell containing a bit pattern is shown in Figure 3.1.

7	6	5	4	3	2	1	0
0	1	0	0	1	1	0	0

FIGURE 3.1/The 8-bit cell (a byte) containing a bit pattern

Each "box" in the cell can hold either a 1 or a 0. Thus in such a cell we can store any information that can be represented by a binary code. For example, it is possible to represent an integer number in binary code. As a specific case, let's work with the decimal number 76, which is 01001100 in binary. The binary representation of this number can be stored in the cell as shown in Figure 3.1.

However, the information to be stored need not be a binary representation of numbers. Observe, for example, that the program shown in Section 1.1, when represented as *binary* machine code, can be stored in ten such cells. Furthermore, we shall later see that by assigning binary codes to alphabetic or other characters, e.g., "A", "B", "#", and "?", they too can be stored in these 8-bit cells. Indeed, *any* information can be represented by some kind of binary code and therefore can be stored in a cell. Conversely, a bit pattern in a cell can have many different meanings; the particular meaning depends on *how it is used*.

Different kinds of information have certain characteristics that are important when they are to be stored. The length of a binary representation is an important characteristic, since it determines the size of the cell needed to store it. For example, the decimal number 76 used in the preceding example has a binary representation that is seven bits long and therefore can be stored in the 8-bit cell as shown in Figure 3.1.

Other kinds of information can have characteristics other than just the binary code length. The term **data type** provides a general way for us to refer to a class of information items with common characteristics. For example, we can refer to "8-bit integers" as a data type, "16-bit integers" as a different data type, and so on. Modern computers and programming languages provide appropriate storage cells for all commonly encountered data types.

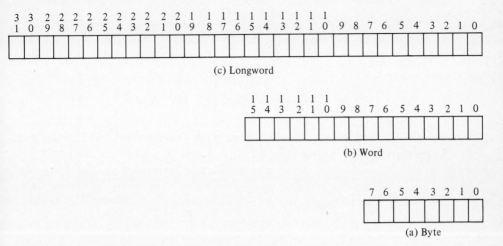

FIGURE 3.2/Information storage and storage cell types

Figure 3.2 shows cells of appropriate length for 8-, 16-, and 32-bit integer data types. Storage cells for various data types are assigned names by the computer manufacturer. For example, Digital Equipment Corporation refers to the 8-bit cell as a **byte,** the 16-bit cell as a **word,** and the 32-bit cell as a **longword.** Unfortunately, these names are not standardized, so other manufacturers may use the same name to refer to cells of different lengths.

3.3 | Basic Elements of Digital Computers

As we discussed in Chapter 1, digital computers are based on the idea of a stored "program" of binary instruction codes that are automatically executed, one after the other. We now examine how this is accomplished. A simplified model of a typical digital computer allows us to study the concepts involved before we consider the VAX-11 itself. This model is basically that proposed by John von Neumann in 1946, although newer concepts are also discussed.

3.3.1 Overall Organization

Figure 3.3 is a diagram of a typical digital computer. The three major elements are the Central Processor Unit (CPU), the Main Memory Unit (MMU), and the Input/Output system. These are interconnected so as to allow transfer of information between the units.

Instructions and data are stored in the MMU. As we will see later, there is no real difference between instructions and data in the sense that both are binary coded information. It is the *usage* of the information that gives it particular meaning.

Let us now examine the major elements of digital computers, one at a time, and investigate their functions and methods of operation.

Central Processor Unit (CPU)

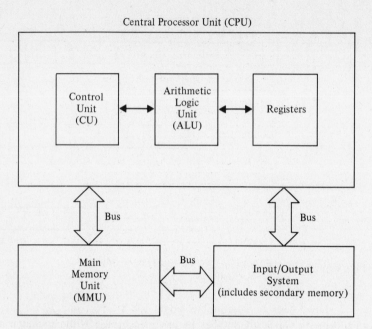

FIGURE 3.3/Organization of a typical digital computer

3.3.2 The Main Memory Unit and Cell Addresses

The computer has a large number of storage cells, as described above, comprising the **main memory unit.** This is often shown diagrammatically as in Figure 3.4. The total number of cells is referred to as the **physical memory size.** This size can be stated in terms of various memory cell units, such as bytes, words, or longwords. Most often, the size is stated in terms of bytes. The physical memory size can vary from a few thousand to several million bytes, depending on the particular machine and installation.

Each cell in physical memory has a unique number called an **address** assigned at the time the machine is designed. These are shown at the right of each cell in Figure 3.4. It is customary to state addresses in a nondecimal base such as octal or hexadecimal. Many modern computers, including the VAX-11, use hexadecimal for this purpose.

In machine and assembly language programming it is often necessary to refer to addresses in the program. The range of numbers between the lowest and highest allowable address which can be used in machine and assembly language programming is referred to as the **address space.** Furthermore, addresses themselves often need to be stored in main memory storage cells, or CPU registers, and hence the addresses are limited to a definite number of allowed bits. The number of bits provided by the hardware for an address is called the **address length.** The address length determines the address space because, as we saw in Chapter 2, the number of different bit patterns that can be represented by a binary string of length n is 2^n. For example, the PDP-11 computer has an address length of sixteen bits and therefore an address space of 0 to $2^{16}-1$

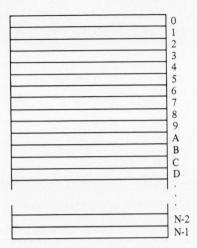

FIGURE 3.4/Main memory unit comprising N bytes

($65,536_{10}$ addresses). The VAX-11, on the other hand, has 32-bit addresses, giving it an address space of 0 to $2^{32}-1$ ($4,294,967,295_{10}$ addresses).

At first thought, it would seem that the physical memory size and the address space should be the same. Should there not be an address for every cell and a cell for every address? In fact, this is not necessarily the case in modern computers. With the concept of **virtual memory,** it is possible for the address space to be larger than the physical memory. Virtual memory is part of a larger concept called **memory management,** and is covered more fully in later courses. Here we briefly describe the concept so that you can understand how VAX-11 machine language programs can refer to addresses that are larger than the physical memory of the machine. Although not discussed here, it should also be noted that there are other methods of memory management that allow use of physical memory larger than the normal address space of the processor.

With the virtual memory concept, the addresses referred to in machine and assembly language programs are logical or **virtual addresses** that are automatically translated by special hardware and the operating system to get physical addresses. This concept is shown diagrammatically in Figure 3.5. When a virtual address in an instruction refers to a cell not currently assigned to physical main memory, the memory management system automatically moves the needed cells from secondary memory, e.g., magnetic disk storage units. The action of bringing in new information from secondary memory in this manner is called **paging,** because memory is subdivided into units called pages (usually 512 bytes) which is the amount of information loaded each time. Many modern computers, including the VAX-11, use the virtual memory concept. These are called **virtual memory machines.**

Fortunately, all of this is carried out automatically, so that it is of little concern to the beginning assembly language programmer. Throughout this book we will work entirely with the VAX-11 virtual addresses and not be concerned with where these cells are stored in the physical memory.

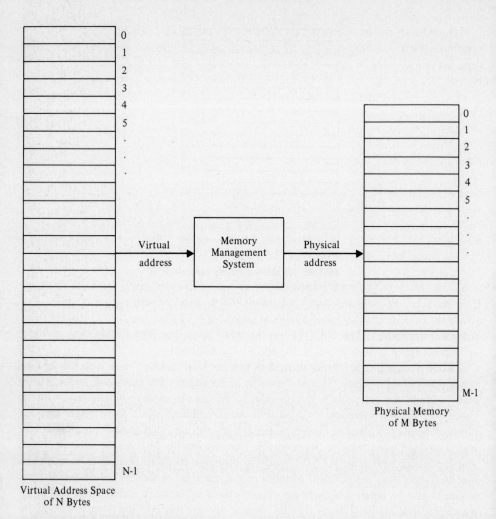

FIGURE 3.5/Virtual memory concept

3.3.3 The Central Processor Unit

The Central Processor Unit (CPU), in broad terms, is the device that automatically executes instructions. In Figure 3.3 we see that it is composed of the **Control Unit** (CU), the **Arithmetic Logic Unit** (ALU), and a group of internal **"registers."**

The **CU** has three tasks: It gets an instruction from the program stored in main memory (called a **fetch**); it decodes this instruction to determine what tasks the ALU has to perform; and it issues control and timing signals to all parts of the system to initiate and terminate the various actions needed to complete the instruction. It is the CU which carries out the Instruction Fetch Execute Cycle described below. In Figure 3.3 we do not show all control and data paths within the CU, but if we did we would see that the CU communicates with the main memory and the ALU.

The **ALU** is the device that does the actual computation work. That is, it performs operations such as addition, subtraction, complementing, shifting bits right or left in a cell, and so on. The actual operations performed are determined by the CU, which periodically sends decoded instructions and data to be operated on (called **operands**) to the ALU. The power of a CPU is determined to a large extent by the capabilities built into the ALU. Simple computers have ALU's that can perform a very small number of basic operations as mentioned above. More complex operations such as multiplication and division must then be done by the program using the basic operations. More sophisticated machines have a more extensive set of instructions built into the ALU, enhancing speed of program execution. Many modern computers, such as the VAX-11, actually have the *instructions* to be recognized by the ALU *stored as programs,* so that the ALU can have an almost unlimited variety of instructions. Such machines are said to be "microprogrammed." However, even microprogrammed computers normally have a standard instruction set so that they are no different from fixed instruction computers to the assembly language programmer.

The **registers** shown as part of the CPU in Figure 3.3 may be thought of as a small, high-speed memory for the CPU. They are physically and functionally different from cells in the main memory, but conceptually they are still digital storage cells. When we take up the VAX-11 computer later in this chapter we will discuss the role of registers in more detail.

3.3.4 Input/Output System and Secondary Storage

The final block in Figure 3.3 can be called the Input/Output (I/O) system. Actually, this is a collection of devices that includes terminals, printers, magnetic disk and tape units, and many other devices that must communicate with the computer. Sometimes these devices are referred to collectively as the **peripheral devices.** Units such as magnetic disk and tape units are often called **secondary memory** or **mass storage** devices. Their function is to provide long-term storage and storage for amounts of information too large to fit in main memory.

The information paths that connect the units of the computer are groups of wires called **buses.** A group of wires is needed since the transmitted information items are binary codes often having 8, 16, or 32 bits, all of which are transmitted in parallel. Additionally, control information must be transmitted. An important consideration regarding the bus system is that it often connects many different devices rather than just two. This is made to work by using a "time-sharing" concept, whereby each device that needs to transmit or receive data gets to use the bus for only a short period of time, and then must relinquish it to other devices. Synchronization of this process is carried out by various attachments to the CPU.

3.3.5 Instruction Fetch Execute Cycle

One of the most fundamental characteristics of a digital computer is its ability to automatically execute, one after another, a series of stored instructions. The procedure whereby this is carried out is referred to as the **Instruction Fetch Execute Cycle.**

The CU and the ALU within the CPU are the devices that actually carry out this cycle. To facilitate this, the CU uses a special register within the CPU, called the **program counter** (PC) register. Initially, the main memory cell address of the first program instruction is placed into the PC. The CU is designed to automatically fetch the contents of the memory location whose address is in the PC. The CU then decodes this instruction and sends control signals telling the ALU to execute it. Before execution, however, the CU *increments* the PC. This is a key step, since then the next time through the cycle the PC will contain the address of the *next* program instruction. After execution of the instruction, the cycle is repeated. Once started, this results in automatic execution of the entire program. Naturally, the process has to stop sometime. A special instruction, called HALT, serves to tell the CU when to stop the instruction execution cycle.

The preceding description of the Instruction Fetch Execute Cycle omitted some steps in order to allow you to see the most important concepts. One additional complexity that should be mentioned, however, is obtaining the data to be operated on, called the **operands.**

Most instructions have one or more operands that must be found from the registers or main memory. For most computers, the information needed to find the operands is either embedded within the instruction, or stored in the main memory in cells following the principal part of the instruction. Part of the Instruction Fetch Execute Cycle is decoding this ''addressing'' information and fetching the operands from main memory if required. Note that when the addressing information or the operand itself is stored in memory following the operation code, there is the additional problem of advancing the PC past this data so that the next instruction is available on the next cycle. This is, of course, handled automatically.

The Instruction Fetch Execute Cycle can be summarized as follows:

1. On start-up, the address of the first instruction of the program is put into the PC.

2. Fetch the contents of the main memory cell whose address is in the PC. Save a copy of this instruction in a special register within the CPU.

3. Increment the PC so that it refers to the next cell beyond the instruction.

4. Decode the instruction and locate and obtain any required operands.

5. Increment the PC beyond the operand addressing information so that it contains the address of the next instruction.

6. Execute the instruction and, if necessary, store the results. If it was HALT, stop the instruction execution cycle.

7. Repeat from Step **2**.

It must be recognized that the Instruction Fetch Execute Cycle is built into the machine itself. After being initiated, this cycle is repeated continuously until a HALT instruction is encountered. Further, we describe it here as it would function if the computer were serving a single user without an operating system. When the computer is under the overall control of an operating system, it executes continuously and should never encounter a HALT in your program. Rather, upon reaching the end of your program it should return to the operating system while the Instruction Fetch Execute Cycle continues. Indeed, the HALT is not a valid instruction for an unprivileged VAX-11 program.

Although we use HALTs in most of the early machine code examples of this book, as a rule programs should end with a special instruction to return to the operating system instead. This is discussed further in Section 4.2.5.

3.3.6 Instruction Format

One of the principal features of a computer's architecture is the way instructions are stored in the memory cells. The issue here is that an instruction must carry with it several pieces of information, and the way it is encoded affects the way instructions are stored and used by the CPU. First, it has to contain a code indicating the nature of the instruction, i.e., what it is supposed to do. This is called the **operation code** or **opcode.** Secondly, it has to contain information on the data to be operated on, called the **operands.** Here, operand information can imply either the data item itself embedded in the instruction, or information on where to find the data, such as in main memory. Depending on the kind of instruction, there might be from zero to several operands. All of this information must somehow be codified in the instruction. The exact way in which this is done is called the **instruction format.**

As a simple example, we can examine the instruction format of the PDP-11 family of computers. These machines have instructions with zero, one, or two operands. The formats used to store the opcode and operand information for these three types of instructions are shown in Figure 3.6. The design is such that the opcode plus the operand information, called "address codes," fit into the 16-bit storage cell used by the

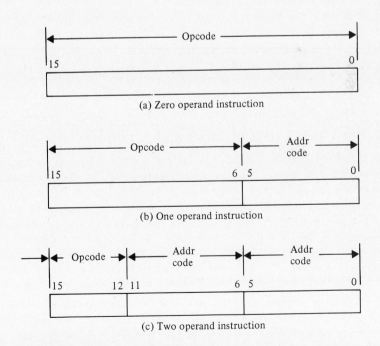

(a) Zero operand instruction

(b) One operand instruction

(c) Two operand instruction

FIGURE 3.6/PDP-11 instruction formats

PDP-11. Note that the address codes are six bits in length, so that two operands is the maximum possible, and furthermore, a two-operand instruction has only four bits left available for the opcode. This places a clear limitation on the architecture in that there can be only $2^4 = 16$ different two-operand instructions, and instructions with more than two operands cannot be implemented.

There are a number of ways that a computer designer can avoid the limitations on the number of operands and opcodes noted above. One way is to relax the requirement that the available length for the instruction (opcode plus address code) be exactly two bytes (one word). Later in this chapter we will see that the VAX-11 exploits this idea, allowing instructions to be of various legnths depending upon the number and type of operands needed by the instruction. Naturally, the instruction execution cycle has to account for this, ensuring that the program counter is properly advanced beyond the end of the instruction regardless of its length.

Another technique is to have the opcode *imply* the location of the operand. Some computers, for example, have many instructions that carry out the indicated operation with the result always going into the same destination cell, called the **accumulator.** Thus an addition instruction only needs to embed the address code for a single addend in the instruction format.

Other computers are based on the idea of always operating on the data in the topmost position of a data storage area, called a stack. The details of how such a machine might work must be deferred until we study the stack data structures in Chapter 9. Here we simply point out that computers based on this principal need at most one operand, and none at all for many instructions.

Thus it is seen that there is a wide variety of instruction formats for computer designers to choose from. Furthermore, the rest of the computer's architecture, such as its instruction set, the instruction execution cycle, and the requirements placed on the ALU, is strongly affected by the choice.

3.4 | The VAX-11 Organization and Architecture

The description of digital computers given in the preceding section is general in nature, rather than specific to a particular machine. We now turn our attention to the organization and architecture of the VAX-11 itself, since it is this machine that we will be concerned with in the remainder of this book. Our aim will be to learn enough about the VAX-11 organization and architecture to support later programming discussion and examples.

3.4.1 Overview of the VAX-11 Computer Family

The VAX-11 is actually a family of computers which includes several models. These machines have a common architecture, meaning that they have identical instruction sets, instruction formats, data storage elements, addressing methods, and addressing space, and in general, are the same with respect to all issues that affect the programmer. They differ, however, in the way in which the architecture is implemented.

Some of the architectural features common to all models include:

- Virtual memory with address space of 4.3×10^9 bytes (4.3 gigabytes)
- 32-bit data path width
- Sixteen 32-bit general purpose registers
- Microprogrammed CPU with a standard set of over 300 instructions
- Nine addressing methods for accessing instruction operands
- Fourteen data types that can be used as instruction operands
- A variable-length instruction format that allows zero to six operands
- A Program Status Longword (PSL) that maintains a record of the current state of the machine

We will examine each of these features in the following sections.

Currently, the VAX-11 architecture is implemented in several machine configurations. These are all called VAX-11 computers, but are designated with different model numbers. One of these models is the VAX-11/730, which is shown in Figure 1.2. Physically it is a small machine and properly called a "mini" computer. A more powerful model is the VAX-11/782, which is really two computers operating in parallel, and is in a class sometimes called "super-mini" computers. Recent additions to the VAX-11 family include an even larger model, called the VAX-11/8600, and a micro version called the Micro-VAX, implemented with large-scale, integrated circuits. It is to be expected that Digital Equipment Corporation will continue to release newer VAX-11 models to meet particular computing needs in the future.

The VAX-11 models differ considerably in physical characteristics, organization, and computing capacity. Figure 3.7 shows the block diagrams that the manufacturer uses to describe the models. We see that they have certain elements in common, such as the CPU, the console subsystem, the main memory, and the I/O adaptor. However, even though these elements serve the same basic functions, they differ in the way they are designed and constructed. For example, the VAX-11/750 and 780 have special "cache" memories internal to the CPU that act as temporary storage for frequently needed data, while the 730 does not. Also, it is seen that the larger machines can have more physical memory, and more I/O devices. These differences are what give the higher-numbered VAX-11 models greater processing speed and power than the smaller machines.

The variety of machines in the VAX-11 family is important from the standpoint of selecting a particular machine to match computing needs. However, because of similarities in architecture already noted, these differences will not be of major concern to us in our study of machine and assembly language programming. Most of our discussion in subsequent chapters will be independent of the VAX-11 model. When we do need to be specific, we will refer to the VAX-11/730. It must be realized, however, that even specific models can be equipped quite differently. For example, the amount of main memory installed and the peripherals which are present can vary from one machine to another.

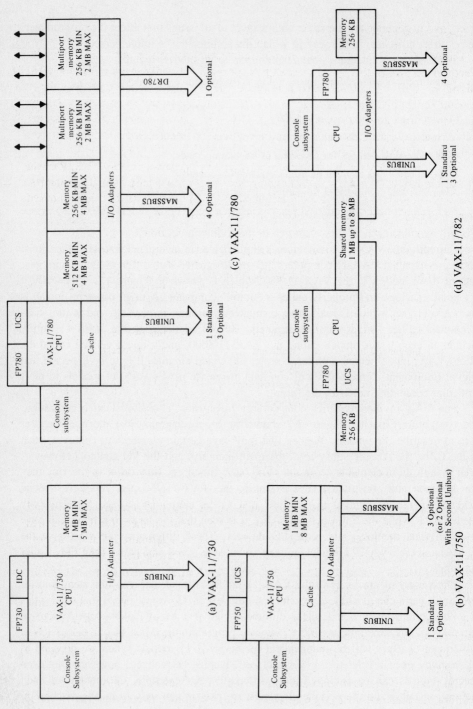

FIGURE 3.7/Block diagrams of VAX-11 models (Copyright © 1982, Digital Equipment Corporation. All rights reserved. Reprinted with permission.)

3.4.2 VAX-11 Data Types

The VAX-11 recognizes fourteen different data types, each with an appropriate storage cell length. In this book we shall be concerned with only seven of the fourteen, as listed in Table 3.1. As indicated here, each cell type has a name, e.g., *byte* for 8-bit, *word* for 16-bit, and *longword* for 32-bit. These names were assigned by Digital Equipment Corporation and reflect the VAX-11 heritage in the earlier PDP-11 computer family. Note that these designations are not universal. Other computer manufacturers use the term "word" for cells of other lengths.

Initially we will not need all of the storage cell types shown in Table 3.1. We will find that the longword is a convenient storage cell for our first programming examples, so we will use it exclusively in early chapters. The other cell types will be introduced when we consider programming concepts that need them.

TABLE 3.1/VAX-11 Data Types and Storage Cells (abbreviated list)

Data Type	Storage Cell Name	Storage Cell Size
Integer (8-bit)	Byte	8 bits (1 byte)
Integer (16-bit)	Word	16 bits (2 bytes)
Integer (32-bit)	Longword	32 bits (4 bytes)
Integer (64-bit)	Quadword	64 bits (8 bytes)
Character	Byte	8 bits (1 byte)
Character string	Byte string	0–65535 bytes
F-floating point	Longword	32 bits (4 bytes)
Decimal	Packed decimal string	0–16 bytes
Decimal	Leading separate numeric string	0–32 bytes

For convenience of discussion, it is sometimes necessary to refer to particular bits within the cell. For this purpose it is conventional (at least on the VAX-11) to assign position numbers beginning with 0 at the right, so that the leftmost bit in a longword is numbered 31. Additionally, one sometimes refers to the rightmost bit as the least significant bit (LSB), and the one at the left end as the most significant bit (MSB). This terminology refers to the numeric interpretation of the cell *contents*. As we saw in Chapter 1, the MSB contributes 2^{n-1} to the value of the contained number, while the LSB contributes only 2^0. Bits can also be referred to in groups using their position numbers separated by a colon. For example, (15:13) refers to the three leftmost (i.e., most significant) bits in a word, while (31:24) refers to the leftmost byte of a longword (see Figure 3.2).

The longer storage cell types are also conventionally viewed as collections of bytes. When this is done, the first group of eight bits is called byte 0, the next one is called byte 1, and so on. Also, the first and last bytes in a storage cell are sometimes called the low and high bytes, respectively.

3.4.3 VAX-11 Main Memory

The VAX-11 is a virtual memory machine, so we must distinguish between virtual memory and the physical memory. As noted in Section 3.3.2, the virtual addresses are those that are employed by the assembly language programmer. Also the virtual address space is the same for all VAX-11 models. Physical memory size, on the other hand, varies considerably among the VAX-11 models, but is seldom of concern to the assembly language programmer. Physical addresses are normally of concern only to the designers of the hardware and software that perform address translation. Thus in the following section, and in the remainder of this book, we shall refer only to virtual addresses.

VAX-11 virtual memory may be thought of as a collection of bytes organized linearly, as shown in Figure 3.8. Each byte has a unique number assigned to it, called its **virtual address.** Since the virtual addresses are represented by 32 bits, the virtual addresses range from 0 to $2^{32}-1$. The addresses are usually stated in hexadecimal, so that we have the lowest address of $0000\ 0000_{16}$ and the highest address of $FFFF\ FFFF_{16}$. Conceptually, our programs could refer to addresses anywhere within this range. However, the upper half of this address space is reserved for operating system programs and is therefore not accessible to most programmers. Also, addresses 0 to $0000\ 01FF_{16}$ are reserved for other uses. Thus your programs will use virtual addresses in the range of

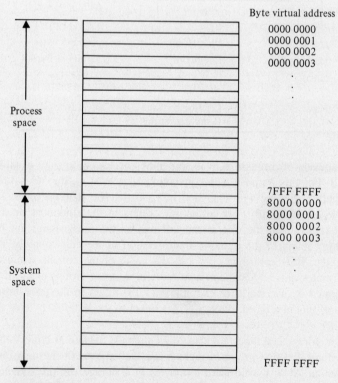

Byte virtual address

0000 0000
0000 0001
0000 0002
0000 0003

7FFF FFFF
8000 0000
8000 0001
8000 0002
8000 0003

FFFF FFFF

Process space

System space

FIGURE 3.8/VAX-11 virtual memory space

0000 0200$_{16}$ to 7FFF FFFF$_{16}$. Digital Equipment Corporation refers to the lower half of the virtual address space as **process space,** meaning the address space for user processes such as your program. The upper half of the virtual address space, i.e., from 8000 0000$_{16}$ to FFFF FFFF$_{16}$, is called **system space.** Operating systems programmers use addresses in this range.

As we saw in the previous section, there are a number of different data types that can be manipulated with VAX-11 instructions and which need to be stored in main memory. The VAX-11 assignment of an address to each byte in virtual memory lends itself nicely to storage and retrieval of these various data types. Regardless of length, it is necessary only to refer to the address of where the first byte is placed in memory, with the understanding that the rest of the data item occupies the successive bytes. For example, a longword containing the hexadecimal number B3F4 D157 might be stored beginning at the byte with address 0000 1A39. The memory diagram for this would then be:

								Byte addresses	Longword address
									0000 1A39
0	1	0	1	0	1	1	1	0000 1A39	
1	1	0	1	0	0	0	1	0000 1A3A	
1	1	1	1	0	1	0	0	0000 1A3B	
1	0	1	1	0	0	1	1	0000 1A3C	

Longword cell

If we needed to refer to this number, we need only identify the longword address 0000 1A39, since the number of successive bytes is inferred from the fact that we said it was a longword. We shall later see that all VAX-11 instructions imply the operand data types, and hence the number of bytes.

The preceding diagram shows the byte contents as binary to emphasize that the cells are eight bits in length, and that the data is in fact stored in binary code. As a convenience, however, we shall most often show such diagrams with all addresses and data in hexadecimal. Also, we showed the address as eight hexadecimal digits, since VAX-11 virtual addresses are indeed 32 bits in length. However, we will most often omit the leading zeros in such diagrams. Thus the same information is conveyed by the simpler diagram:

57	1A39
D1	1A3A
F4	1A3B
B3	1A3C

The contents of successive, related memory cells can also be displayed horizontally. With this method, the preceding diagram becomes:

Contents				Address
B3	F4	D1	57	1A39

Note that when thus displayed, the given address is that of the first byte, and the bytes with successively higher addresses are arranged from right to left. This is the way that machine code is printed in VAX-11 assembly program listings, so it is important that you learn to read memory contents displayed in this manner. (What is the address of the byte containing B3?)

Also note the storage *order* of the hexadecimal digits relative to the main memory addresses in the preceding example. On the VAX-11, multi-byte integers are always stored with the least significant digit at lower addresses and the more significant digits at higher addresses. (Some computers employ the reverse of this order.)

3.4.4 VAX-11 Registers

Section 3.3.3 referred to special memory cells within the CPU called **registers**. All VAX-11 computers have sixteen such registers, as shown in Figure 3.9. Each is 32 bits in length. These are called **general registers** since they play multiple roles in the VAX-11 architecture. For example, they can be used to hold instruction operand data, addresses of operand data, indexes to be added to operand addresses, or pointers in special data structures such as stacks. In contrast, other computers often have special registers for each of these functions.

The general registers are of paramount importance in programming the VAX-11 and therefore should be thoroughly understood. Our early programming examples in Chapter 4 will use these registers to hold operand data as we learn the basic elements of assembly language programming. In later chapters we will use them to address operand data in the main memory.

Although they are all called general registers, some are used by the computer in special ways that make their use for other purposes hazardous. In particular, the register

R0
R1
R2
R3
R4
R5
R6
R7
R8
R9
R10
R11
AP
FP
SP
PC

FIGURE 3.9/VAX-11 general registers

designated PC is used as the Program Counter and thus should never be used otherwise. Anything that causes the PC to change has the effect of changing the order of instruction execution. The Argument Pointer (AP), Frame Pointer (FP), and Stack Pointer (SP) also have special uses that we shall discuss at appropriate points in later chapters. Usage of these registers should be avoided until you understand their normal functions. The other registers, i.e., R0, R1, . . . , R11, can be used freely in your programs. Normal programming conventions, however, suggest that registers R0 through R5 be used for information that has only local, temporary significance. This is because these registers are often used to supply data to, or return results from, character handling instructions, and certain system routines, such as those for input and output. Nonetheless, we shall use these registers in many examples in this book, and alert you whenever their usage may pose difficulties.

As we learn more about programming in assembly, you will see that you often have a choice as to whether to use a register to hold a data item, or to store it in the main memory. In making this choice, probably the most important criterion is how frequently the data item will be used over its lifetime. Things that are accessed infrequently should be stored in the main memory. On the other hand, items that are used frequently, for example, loop control variables, are best stored in registers, because storing them in main memory would require unnecessary memory fetches and degrade program efficiency. Keep in mind that registers are implemented with much faster circuits than is main memory, and are also in closer communication with the ALU. In general, an item to be used repeatedly in some part of the program should probably be temporarily placed in a register even if its primary storage is to be in main memory.

In addition to the general registers, the VAX-11 architecture provides us with a special register called the **processor status longword (PSL).** This register is used by the CPU to keep track of its status. A diagram of the PSL is shown in Figure 3.10.

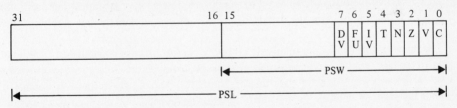

FIGURE 3.10/Processor status longword (PSL) and processor status word (PSW)

Most often, normal assembly language programming uses only bits (15:0) of the PSL, referred to as the processor status word (PSW). In this book, we will only be concerned with the rightmost eight bits of the PSW.

Bits (3:0), labeled N, Z, V, and C, are called the **condition codes.** The VAX-11 uses these codes to indicate the outcome of the previous operation. For example, an operation resulting in zero sets the Z bit to 1. Bits (7:4) can be used by the programmer to "trap" certain errors that may have occurred on the previous instruction. We will go into the use of these bits in the PSW as need arises in our programming.

3.4.5 VAX-11/730 Organization

As discussed in Section 3.4.1 the VAX-11 architecture is implemented quite differently in different members of the family. However, our purposes here will be served if we choose a single member of the family to study the CPU and overall organization of the machine in greater detail. The VAX-11/730 is a good choice since it has all elements needed for our discussion and is one of the least complicated members of the family.

The VAX-11/730 organizational diagram is shown in Figure 3.11. This diagram is like Figures 3.3. and 3.7, but shows more of the internal details of the machine. As before, the principal element is the CPU. Auxiliary units include the main memory unit, the buses, the peripheral devices, and the console subsystem.

Main Memory Unit

The VAX-11/730 main memory unit consists of one to five memory modules connected to the CPU through an array bus and memory controller. Each memory module contains 1,048,576 bytes (1 megabyte or MB), so the VAX-11/730 can have up to 5MB of physical memory. The memory controller performs a number of functions, including the translation of virtual addresses in our programs to physical addresses in the memory unit.

VAX-11/730 Bus System

As shown in Figure 3.11, the VAX-11/730 communicates with user terminals, printers, disk storage units, and other peripheral devices through UNIBUS, which is a trademark used by Digital Equipment Corporation for their particular implementation of the bus concept. Basically, a bus is just a group of wires that carries data and control information as electrical signals. All devices are connected to it in parallel, and circuitry coordinates access by each device. At any one time, only two devices can be communicating with one another over the bus. In one mode of operation, a device is granted access to the bus and can use it for one cycle, lasting approximately one-millionth of a second. During this time the data transfer takes place and then the bus is relinquished to another device.

Because of this sharing, a relatively complex control process is needed to coordinate usage of the bus. That is, devices must request usage, await permission, await acknowledgment of the receiver, transfer data and/or addresses, and finally relinquish control of the bus to another device. This control function is carried out physically by circuits within the memory controller. Some devices connected to UNIBUS have the capability to use it in the direct memory access (DMA) mode of operation. In this mode, data is transferred directly to/from main memory without going through the CPU. This process is initiated by the CPU, but proceeds under the control of the memory control unit.

VAX-11/730 Console Subsystem

The console subsystem allows operator control of the VAX-11. It is actually another computer that is dedicated to communicating with the VAX-11 CPU. In a sense, it is a much enhanced replacement for the switches found on the front of earlier computers such as the PDP-11, described in Chapter 1.

Among other devices, the console subsystem has a terminal, a cartridge-type magnetic

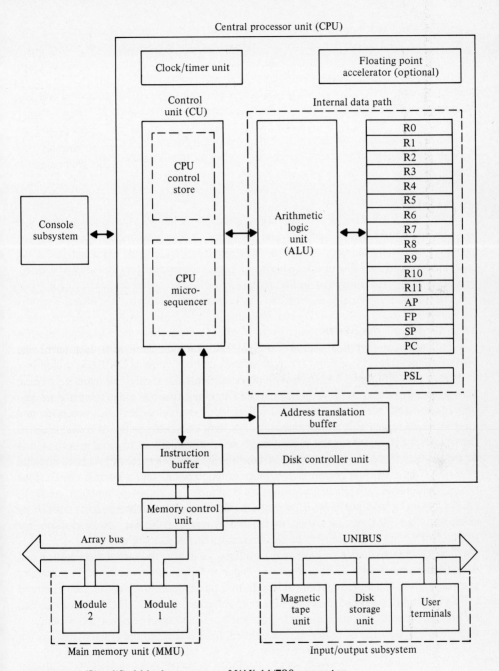

FIGURE 3.11/Simplified block structure of VAX-11/730 computer

tape drive unit, and control switches that establish its own mode of operation as well as that of the VAX-11. When the console subsystem is in the **console** mode, the operator can issue special, privileged commands to the VAX-11 CPU that cannot be issued by a normal user. Another important function of the console mode is to perform the initial start-up of the VAX-11, called "bootstrapping" or booting. This process reads the microcode representing the VAX-11 instruction set from the cartridge tape drive and places it in the control store unit, as well as other important initialization operations. When in its other mode of operation, called the **program** mode, the terminal connected through the console subsystem acts just like other terminals connected through the bus system.

VAX-11/730 CPU

Since the VAX-11/730 is a microprogrammable computer, the general functional breakdown of subsystems such as used in Figure 3.3 is not strictly applicable. For example, the control unit of the 730 is composed of the separate elements called the **control store** and the **CPU micro sequencer.** Together they function as a normal controller, so we group them together in Figure 3.11.

The functions normally ascribed to the arithmetic logic unit (ALU) and registers are performed by a unit that Digital Equipment Corporation calls the **internal data path.** To preserve functional similarity to Figure 3.3, we show the ALU and registers within the internal data path, although the 730 does not have distinct hardware elements for these functions.

The CPU in Figure 3.11 has several other elements not shown in Figure 3.3. These are enhancements that improve performance. The **clock/timer** is a device that generates time-of-year and interval timing signals. Both can be accessed by user programs and used for timekeeping and timing purposes. The **disk controller** is the hardware element that interfaces the CPU to the disk storage unit, allowing you to save programs and data other than in the main memory. The **floating point accelerator** (FPA) is an optional element of the CPU that performs certain arithmetic operations faster than can be done by the internal data path alone. Operations affected include addition, subtraction, multiplication, division, and polynomial evaluation. The design is such that the presence or absence of the FPA is transparent to the programmer. If absent, the operations are simply carried out (more slowly) by the standard internal data path.

The CPU is also seen to have two "buffers," namely, the **instruction buffer** and the **address translation buffer.** The term *buffer* is frequently encountered in computer science, and its use here is typical, referring to a place where information can be stored temporarily until it is needed. The instruction buffer on the VAX-11/730 is a longword register that always contains the next instruction. The control logic of the machine is such that the instruction buffer is being filled from main memory while the current instruction is being executed. This overlapping of the fetch and execute functions significantly increases processing speed and is employed in one form or another by nearly all modern computers.

The address translation buffer is related to the address translation process that accompanies the virtual memory concept. Recall that virtual memory addresses must be translated to physical memory addresses each time information is fetched from or stored in main memory. This is done by the memory management hardware, and although it can be done very quickly, it nonetheless is slower than if the machine worked in terms of physical addresses. The address translation buffer acts to alleviate this problem by retaining the translated values of frequently needed virtual addresses within the CPU. Thus when the CPU refers to a virtual address, the address translation buffer is checked first. If it is there, the translation does not have to be performed, freeing the CPU for other tasks. The VAX-11/730 can save up to 128 translated addresses in this buffer.

3.4.6 VAX-11 Instruction Format

In Section 3.3.6 we discussed the way that computer instructions are stored in memory cells. We saw there that an important issue is how to arrange the needed information, such as operation codes and operand information, in a simple but flexible way. We called the result of the designer's decisions on these matters the **instruction format.**

The instruction format for the VAX-11 computer allows any given instruction to have an opcode, and anywhere between zero and six operands. The opcode occupies the first position in the instruction format. For most instructions the opcode is one byte in length. However, there are a number of instructions, all beginning with the hexadecimal codes FC through FF, that are two bytes long. In either case, information needed to find each operand, called the **operand specifiers,** is stored in successive bytes in memory following the opcode. The general form is shown in Figure 3.12.

opcode
operand specifier 1
operand specifier 2
operand specifier 3
operand specifier 4
operand specifier 5
operand specifier 6

FIGURE 3.12/VAX-11 instruction format

It is thus apparent that VAX-11 instructions can be as short as one byte, which is the case when there are no operands. The length for instructions with operands depends on the number of operands and the complexity of the operand specifier. The simpler addressing methods, for example register addressing to be used in Chapter 4, have operand specifiers that are one byte in length. In such cases the instruction length is just the opcode length plus the number of operands. However, the operand specifiers depend on the addressing method being used and can be between one and five bytes in length. We will explain these more complex operand specifiers as we discuss the individual addressing methods in later chapters.

3.4.7 Instruction Fetch Execute Cycle

The Instruction Fetch Execute Cycle for the VAX-11 differs somewhat from that given in Section 3.3.5 due to the variable length of VAX-11 instructions. Fortunately, the basic ideas are the same. That is, at the beginning of the cycle the program counter (PC) contains the address of the next instruction to be fetched, and is updated to point to the next instruction during the cycle. Because the operand specifiers can be of any length and number, the PC cannot be advanced a fixed amount as is possible with the fixed length instruction formats. The VAX-11 deals with this problem by fetching the instruction a piece at a time, and using information encoded in the currently available part to determine how much more needs to be fetched. With this basic idea, the VAX-11 Instruction Fetch Execute Cycle can be described as follows:

1.   Fetch the first byte of instruction whose address is in PC, i.e., "pointed at" by the PC.
2.   Advance the PC by 1 byte.
3.   Examine the first byte of the instruction. If it is in the range FC–FF it is a 2-byte opcode, so fetch the next byte and advance PC by 1.
4.   Examine the instruction and determine the number, type, and access method of the operand. If it is HALT, stop the cycle.
5.   For each operand:
    (a) Fetch the first byte of the operand specifier and advance PC by 1 byte.
    (b) Examine the first byte of the operand specifier and determine the length of the rest of the operand specifier.
    (c) Fetch the rest of the operand specifiers and advance PC accordingly.
    (d) Locate the operand and fetch it if it is in main memory.
6.   Execute the instruction.
7.   Repeat from Step 1.

The cycle can be difficult to follow if the instruction has several operands and complicated operand specifiers. We will defer these complicated cases for now, and look at a simple example.

EXAMPLE 3.1   Trace the Instruction Fetch Execute Cycle for MOVL R1,R4.

The VAX-11 instruction MOVL R1,R4 moves the contents of register R1 to register R4. The instruction opcode for MOVL is D0, which implies that a longword (four bytes) is to be moved. Also implied by this code is the fact that there are to be two operands. The notation used for the operands, i.e., R1 and R4, implies what is called **register addressing,** which has an operand specifier format one byte in length and is coded as follows:

```
 7  6  5  4  3  2  1  0
┌──────────┬────────────┐
│ 0  1  0  1│     n      │
└──────────┴────────────┘
```

Here the $0101_2 = 5_{16}$ means register addressing, and the n is a hexadecimal integer representing the register number. Thus from Figure 3.12 we see that the entire instruction gets stored in main memory in three consecutive bytes. Let us assume that it is stored beginning at location A000, so that we have:

opcode	D0	A000
operand specifier	51	A001
operand specifier	54	A002
		A003

The Instruction Fetch Execute Cycle can now be traced taking the initial address in PC to be A000. The opcode D0 is fetched and the PC advanced to A001. Since D0 is not between FC and FF, the VAX-11 knows that it is a one-byte opcode and therefore does not fetch the next byte as part of the opcode. Rather, it examines the D0 and determines that it requires two operand specifiers for longwords. It therefore fetches the next byte and treats it as the first byte of the first operand specifier, incrementing PC to A002 in the process. From the 51 it is able to determine that it is a single-byte operand specifier, and that the operand itself is in R1 so that no fetch is required for the operand. Because the opcode indicated two operands, the operand specifier fetching process is repeated, this time detecting R4 as the destination operand, and advancing PC to A003. Finally the MOVL is executed, transferring the contents of R1 to R4. When the cycle repeats, it will begin with the PC pointing at A003, which presumably contains the next instruction. This would continue until a HALT was encountered.

The Instruction Fetch Execute Cycle bears close study because it is closely tied to proper understanding of the VAX-11 instructions and methods of addressing. In particular, observe that PC is incremented *before* the decoding of the instruction. This will be of great importance when we later observe that the contents of PC may be used to help locate operands for the instruction. The reader will also observe that at the beginning of each cycle the CPU, rather blindly, accepts whatever it finds in the memory location pointed at by the PC and attempts to interpret it as an instruction. If the programmer inadvertently places a *data* item in a cell whose address is reached by the PC, the CPU will treat this data as an instruction. This often will result in an error message. However, if the data item by chance has a valid interpretation as an instruction, the results are unpredictable but almost certainly wrong.

3.5 | Summary

In this chapter we introduced the main ideas of computer **organization** and **architecture.** We began by discussing these topics in the context of a simplified model of the digital computer, then built on these ideas to describe the more complex VAX-11 family of computers, and in particular the VAX-11/730.

Organization and architecture are two different levels of description of a digital computer. The **architecture** of a computer is a description in terms of what facilities it provides to the programmer, how it is programmed, and how it behaves as viewed by the machine and assembly language programmer. Thus it refers to the basic units of storage available, the logical organization of these storage cells in main memory, the instructions available, the format of instructions in memory, registers that are available to the programmer, the Instruction Fetch Execute Cycle, and other characteristics needed to program at the machine language level. A given architecture can be implemented many different ways, as evidenced by the widely different VAX-11 models having a common architecture. On the other hand, **organization** is a functional description of the machine in terms of its major hardware elements. This term refers to the way that the principal elements, namely the CPU, main memory unit, and input/output system, are designed and interconnected to implement a specified architecture.

In our discussion of organization, the CPU was further broken down into subunits called the **arithmetic logic unit** (ALU), the **control unit** (CU), and the **registers.** The ALU carries out arithmetic and logical operations necessary to execute the instructions, while the CU initiates and controls these and other actions. One of the principal activities of the CU is the continuous process known as the **Instruction Fetch Execute Cycle,** whereby the program instructions stored in main memory are sequentially fetched and executed. The **registers** are special, high-speed data storage cells used by the CU and ALU to carry out their tasks.

The **main memory unit** was seen to comprise a large number of individual storage cells that actually hold binary coded data and instructions. We introduced two memory concepts, **physical memory** and **virtual memory.** Physical memory refers to the actual memory as implemented in electronic circuits. The virtual memory concept, however, allows the programmer to work in terms of virtual addresses that are automatically translated by the hardware and system software into physical memory addresses. This concept is used on the VAX-11 and allows a much larger range of addresses, called the **virtual address space,** and therefore larger programs, for a given size of physical memory. Also, virtual addressing allows the address space to be independent of the physical machine, so that programs are the same for any member of the VAX-11 family.

In our discussion of storing digital information, we found it helpful to use the term **data type,** referring to the descriptive attributes of a piece of information. At this point in our development we have only talked about binary integer data types, with the number of bits being the only attribute. Commonly encountered data types in this category include 8-bit, 16-bit, and 32-bit integers. Paralleling the concept of data types is the concept of different units of digital storage, which we called **data cells.** We found, for example, that the VAX-11 computer allows fourteen different data types and provides data cells of appropriate length for each. VAX-11 data cells introduced in this chapter are called **bytes** (8-bit), **words** (16-bit), and **longwords** (32-bit). Each of these is a multiple of the byte, which allows the virtual addressing of the data cell to be the same as that of its first byte. To support this idea, the VAX-11 virtual addresses are byte addresses, which means that each byte in the virtual address space has its own address. Conventionally, these addresses are stated in hexadecimal representation.

The VAX-11 architecture, and to a lesser extent its organization, will be of importance in later chapters. We learned that it is a virtual address machine with an address space of over four gigabytes. However, half of this is accessible only to system programs, so that most assembly programs will use addresses in the range of 0 to 7FFF $FFFF_{16}$. Also, we have available sixteen 32-bit **general purpose registers.** Among these are R0 through R11, which can be used with few restrictions, and AP, FP, SP, and PC, which have special uses and therefore should not be used for normal data storage. An additional register called the **program status longword** (PSL) is used to store codes that reflect the outcome of the previous instruction. The VAX-11 **instruction format** was seen to be of variable length, consisting of an **operation code** followed by any **operand specifiers** required for the operation. For elementary addressing methods that we will use first, the operand specifiers are one byte in length, and are simple codes indicating the addressing method and the register employed. The Instruction Fetch Execute Cycle is designed to fetch the instruction one part at a time from main memory. By examining the portion currently available, the control unit can then determine if there are remaining parts of the instruction to be fetched. The most important aspect of the Instruction Fetch Execute Cycle is that it advances the PC to the next instruction. This results in sequential execution of a list of instructions in main memory, i.e., a program, which is the fundamental characteristic of all digital computers.

3.6 | Exercises

–3.1 For each of the following decimal numbers, show its internal representation as it would exist in a VAX-11 longword. Give the binary and hexadecimal representations.

⁓(a) 29652   (b) 43957   ⁓(c) 465   (d) 268435456
(e) 19754   •(f) 05693   (g) 65535   ⁓(h) 131071

–3.2 Assume the hexadecimal contents of main memory as shown below:

57	F00E
63	F00F
A1	F010
00	F011
FF	F012
1A	F013
09	F014

Give the hexadecimal and decimal values for each of the following data items:

(a) byte at F00E   (b) word beginning at F013
(c) longword beginning   (d) longword beginning at F00E
    at F011
(e) word beginning F010   (f) byte at F010

⁓3.3 If the longword with address 101A contains the hexadecimal number BB1F 6342, what is the decimal representation of the word with address 101C?

⌐3.4 Assume that you are working with a computer that has an architecture similar to the VAX-11, but allows sixteen bits for storing addresses and has an address for each byte.
(a) What is the address space?
(b) What is the address of the highest memory location?
(c) What is the address of the highest *word?*

– 3.5 Explain in your own words the terms "physical memory" and "virtual memory." State the advantages and disadvantages of the virtual memory concept.

3.6 What are the functions of:

    (a) the CPU   (b) the ALU
    (c) the CU   (d) the MMU
    (e) the I/O system   (f) the bus

3.7 How many general registers does the VAX-11 provide? Which of these are available for general programming usage? What is the special function of the PC register?

3.8 Assume that the following program is stored in the VAX-11 main memory:

Contents	Address
D0	0100
5 1	0101
5 4	0102
C0	0103
5 2	0104
5 4	0105
C0	0106
5 3	0107
5 4	0108
0 0	0109

The codes D0 and C0 are opcodes for MOVL and ADDL, respectively, and each expects two operands. The 51, 52, 53, and 54 are operand specifiers.

(a) What is the content of PC after the first opcode has been fetched?
(b) What is the content of PC after the entire first instruction has been fetched, but before it has been executed?
(c) What is the content of PC when execution terminates?
(d) What does this program do?

3.9 How many one-operand instructions can the PDP-11 computer have?

3.10 How many instructions with one-byte opcodes can the VAX-11 computer have? How does it in fact provide us with over 300 instructions?

3.11 Discuss the implications of the instruction MOVL R1,PC. What effect might this have? Does it appear to be good programming practice? Does the MACRO assembler accept it?

3.12 We saw that the VAX-11/730 can have up to five megabytes ($5,242,815_{10}$) of physical memory. Assuming that all bits of the physical addresses are transmitted at the same time, how many bits in width does the address bus data path have to be?

3.13 Explain the fact that the VAX-11 architecture has an address space of 4.3 gigabytes, but the VAX-11/730 can have at most five megabytes of physical memory.

3.14 How does the VAX-11/730 ALU differ from a conventional ALU?

3.15 Discuss the difference between the VAX-11 instruction format and that of the PDP-11 computer.

4

Introduction to Assembly Language Programming

4.1 | Overview

In Chapter 1 we saw that assembly language programs consist of a sequence of simple instructions, each of which causes a certain action to be taken by the computer. The VAX-11 has a large set of these instructions, some of which cause operations to be carried out on data (operand instructions) and others that affect the execution sequence in the program (control instructions). In this chapter we discuss five of these instructions (MOVL, ADDL, CLRL, INCL, and HALT). The first four of these are operand instructions that exemplify single- and double-operand formats. The last, HALT, is a simple control instruction.

These five instructions allow us to develop the fundamental concept of assembly language programming with simple programs and without unnecessary complications. These instructions will also serve as models for more advanced instructions introduced in later chapters. Because branching instructions are not covered, the programs that can be considered in this chapter are restricted to those with straight-line logic, i.e., strictly sequential execution of the instructions.

The five instructions of this chapter also provide us with an opportunity for further discussion of **addressing,** mentioned in Chapter 3. This term refers to the manner in which the data to be operated on by the instruction, i.e., the **operands,** are identified. We restrict our discussion to a single addressing mode (register addressing), postponing exploration of the full VAX-11 addressing capabilities until later chapters. In this way we allow the concept of addressing to be firmly established in the context of simple, straight-line programs. This restriction does limit the programs we can write to those operating only on the registers. Data which is stored in main memory will remain out of our reach temporarily.

The restricted set of instructions and addressing modes also allows us to begin developing skill in **translation** to machine code. Translation is important because the best understanding of assembly language programming comes by trying to visualize the resulting machine code instead of thinking solely in terms of the assembly language mnemonics. The idea here is simply that every assembly language instruction translates

65

into 8-bit binary patterns in one or more sequential bytes. For convenience, however, we will write these as their hexadecimal equivalents.

This chapter also introduces the idea of **assembler directives.** These are lines embedded in an assembly language program that are *not* VAX-11 instructions; rather, they are instructions to the assembler. Directives are sometimes called **pseudo-ops** because they look like other operation codes recognized by the assembler, but do not result in machine instructions. In keeping with the theme of this chapter, we again restrict our discussion to a small initial subset of the available directives, in particular, .TITLE, .ENTRY, and .END.

The chapter also includes three sections dealing with program execution and debugging. The first, Section 4.9, deals with how to read a MACRO listing. You will recall that the listing is produced by the assembler and shows the results of the translation in human-readable form. Section 4.10 is an introduction to the VAX-11 Symbolic Debugger. This is a system program that allows the programmer to interact with and examine the results of the program as it executes. This provides an extremely powerful learning mechanism, as well as affording a means for finding programming errors. Also, we shall use the Symbolic Debugger as a means of providing input data and examining the results of our early programs.

As an alternative to using the Symbolic Debugger for input and output, we will learn how to use special, preprogrammed routines for this purpose in Section 4.11.

4.2 | Five Instructions: MOVL, ADDL, CLRL, INCL, and HALT

4.2.1 MOVL

When you are programming in assembly language you will often find it necessary to move a piece of data from one place to another. For example, a value may be stored in main memory and the program may require it in a register, or you may wish to transfer the result of an operation from one register to another or to main memory. In fact, in large programs this is often one of the most frequent operations. To facilitate this, MACRO has the MOVL instruction. For example,

```
MOVL   R1,R2
```

causes the contents of register R1 to be moved into register R2. More precisely, the bit pattern in register R1 is *copied* into R2, leaving R1 unchanged. For example, if R1 and R2 initially contain:

R1:   6F 5B CA 0D
R2:   F6 CA 05 DB

then after MOVL, R1, R2 is executed they will contain:

R1:   6F 5B CA 0D
R2:   6F 5B CA 0D

Note that the previous contents of R2 has been overwritten in the process.

We show the above example with the register contents represented in hexadecimal. However, we should not forget that binary is the actual form of storage in the register. As we learned in Chapter 3, the registers are 32 bits in length, so each bit pattern in the example has 32 bits, hence eight hexadecimal digits.

Using the terms introduced in Section 3.2, we refer to these bit patterns as **longword** data types. Thus the MOVL instruction moves a longword from the first operand to the second, as indicated by the L suffix. In later chapters we will see that the MOVL instruction, as well as other VAX-11 instructions, has counterparts with different suffixes that operate on various data types. In this chapter, however, we restrict ourselves to longword operations.

4.2.2 ADDL

Another widely used instruction is ADDL. As might be expected, the purpose of this instruction is to add one number to another. For example, if we have:

R1:   00 00 00 02
R2:   00 00 00 4A

and the instruction:

```
ADDL   R1,R2
```

is executed the registers will then contain:

R1:   00 00 00 02
R2:   00 00 00 4C

Note that the contents of R1 remains unchanged, while the sum is placed in R2. Also observe that the original contents of R2 is overwritten with the result of the addition.

The MOVL and ADDL instructions are what we call double-operand instructions. That is, it is necessary to indicate the **source** and **destination** registers for the MOVL operation, or in the case of ADDL, the registers containing the two numbers to be added. There is a convention in MACRO that the first operand is called the source, and the second operand is called the destination in most double-operand instructions. That is,

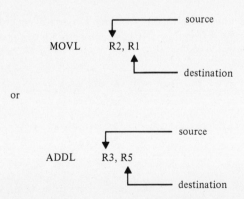

Actually, the second operand of the ADDL instruction is at once the source of the second summand, as well as the destination for the sum. Nonetheless, we refer to it as the destination operand, emphasizing that the result always goes to the second operand.

The ADDL instruction can also be written as ADDL2, where the suffix 2 means "two operands." Thus we could have written:

```
ADDL2   R1,R2
```

with exactly the same meaning as the above example. The VAX-11 also has instructions with three or more operands. The suffix notation provides a convenient means for indicating the number of operands while preserving the mnemonic quality of the MACRO name for the instruction. Because we will not often use the instructions with more than two operands, we will usually omit the suffix on two operand instructions.

4.2.3 CLRL

Very often a procedure within a program will begin by initializing registers or main memory locations to 0. This is called **clearing,** and the MACRO instruction to do it is the CLRL instruction. Unlike the MOVL and ADDL instructions, there is only a *single operand* for CLRL, namely the register to be cleared. For example, if we have in register R4:

R4:   1E 01 DF AB

and the instruction:

```
CLRL   R4
```

is executed, R4 will then be:

R4:   00 00 00 00

In later chapters we will see how other forms of the clear instruction can also be used to clear words, bytes, and other data cell types in memory in addition to registers.

4.2.4 INCL

The need to add unity to a quantity occurs frequently in programming. MACRO provides a single-operand instruction, INCL, specifically for this purpose. To demonstrate its use, assume that R2 initially contains 2858_{10} or:

R2:   00 00 0B 2A

If

```
INCL R2
```

is executed we will have:

R2:   00 00 0B 2B

which you can confirm to be 2859_{10}.

The INCL instruction can be used in conjunction with the CLRL instruction to initialize a register to 1. That is,

```
CLRL R2
INCL R2
```

will result in R2 being set to unity.

4.2.5 HALT

The MOVL, ADDL, CLRL, and INCL instructions are similar in that they operate on data, i.e., they each have one or two operands. The next instruction we will examine, HALT, has no operands. Its role is simply to stop the Instruction Fetch Execute Cycle (see Section 3.4.7). It is placed at the *logical end* of the program, i.e., after the last instruction to be executed. Often this will be different from the *physical end* of the program because nonexecutable lines, e.g., data storage, are sometimes placed after the last executable instruction. In Section 4.5 we will see how to mark the physical end of the program.

We use the HALT instruction in early examples in this book. As a practical matter, however, the HALT instruction has very little use in most modern assembly language programming. This is because most assembly language programs run under the control of an operating system, e.g., VAX/VMS, and in such an environment it is not appropriate for the Instruction Fetch Execute Cycle to be stopped at the conclusion of a normal program. Instead, control of the computer should simply revert back to the operating system. It is for this reason that when the CPU encounters a HALT in a normal user program an error message is displayed, followed by return to the operating system. This error report is purely informative and can be ignored. If desired, the system "macro instruction" $EXIT_S can be used instead of HALT, as shown in the example in Section 1.3.1. The use of $EXIT_S will, however, introduce machine code that cannot be explained in terms of the material covered thus far. For this reason HALT is used in our early examples.

4.3 | Register Addressing Mode

It should be apparent that if the machine uses an item of data it is necessary to identify where the data is stored. Specifying the locations of data items to be used in an operation is referred to as **addressing.** The VAX-11 has a variety of different ways of doing this, called **addressing modes.** However, in this chapter, only the direct **register addressing mode** is considered.

When the operand of any instruction is one of the general registers, register addressing mode is implied. This means that the *contents* of the named register is itself the operand.

As discussed in Section 3.4.4, the VAX-11 has sixteen general registers. For MACRO assembly language these registers are identified by the special symbols shown below:

General Usage		Special Usage
R0	R6	AP or R12
R1	R7	FP
R2	R8	SP
R3	R9	PC
R4	R10	
R5	R11	

When one of these symbols appears by itself as an operand, the MACRO assembler recognizes it and infers register addressing.

As discussed in Section 3.4.4, R0 through R11 can be used for general purposes in your programs. However, registers 12 through 15 have special usage and should not be used otherwise. Actually, the MACRO assembler does not even allow you to refer to registers 13, 14, or 15 with the Rn notation. Instead, they are recognized only by the names FP, SP, and PC to emphasize their special usage. Register 12 can be referred to either as R12 or AP.

Certain routines and instructions, such as those for input and output and character string instructions (Section 7.9), use R0 through R5 for their own purposes and therefore will destroy the previous contents of these registers. One should therefore not depend on a value in these registers after the use of input/output routines or the character string instructions. The problem of saving and restoring registers is discussed in Chapter 9.

4.4 | Translation to Machine Code

In Chapter 1 we learned that every assembly language instruction can be translated into an equivalent machine language instruction. This idea was expanded upon in Section 3.4.6 where we discussed the format of the machine instruction as it is stored in successive bytes in main memory. With this background we are now able to show the machine code form of each new instruction and addressing method as they are introduced. By doing this, we will be developing a better understanding of how the machine works, as well as learning to program in assembly language. We shall now see how this is done for the no-operand HALT instruction and for the MOVL, ADDL, CLRL, and INCL instructions using the direct register addressing mode.

4.4.1 No-Operand Instructions

Certain instructions do not operate on data and therefore require no operands. The HALT instruction is an example. It causes the computer to cease repetition of the Instruction Fetch Execute Cycle. On the VAX-11 the HALT instruction is represented by a one-byte opcode of zero. Thus we have the translation:

Assembly Instruction	Opcode
HALT	00

When the MACRO assembler encounters the mnemonic HALT, it generates a 00 as the next byte of machine code.

When the program is then linked and executed, this opcode will exist somewhere in main memory, which we represent as follows:

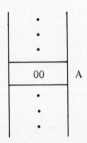

The address of the byte in which the opcode is stored, represented here as A, is determined by the assembly and linkage processes. The MACRO assembler places the first instruction byte of the program in location 0, the second in location 1, and so on, thus establishing addresses of each instruction relative to the beginning of the program. The linkage process then adjusts these addresses as it prepares the program for loading into a specific place in main memory, thus determining the run-time virtual addresses. Most often, however, we will not need to know the run-time addresses. It will be sufficient to work in terms of the addresses as measured from the beginning of the program, called **offsets.** Moreover, we will often just refer to these addresses symbolically, as we did above.

4.4.2 Single-Operand Instructions, Register Addressing

Let us now consider the translation of instructions that have a single operand. The CLRL and INCL instructions are examples. When the operands are register names, as in the examples in Section 4.2, the addressing mode is register addressing. These facts cause the MACRO assembler to generate a two-byte machine code instruction of the form:

operation code	opcode	A
destination operand specifier	5n	A + 1

By convention, the single operand is referred to as the destination operand. The main memory location address where the instruction begins is represented here by A, and the address of the second byte is A+1. We see that the second byte is the operand specifier, which is 5n for register addressing. Here n represents the register number.

The CLRL and INCL instructions have one-byte opcodes. They are:

Assembly Mnemonic	Opcode
CLRL	D4
INCL	D6

Thus the translation of the instruction CLRL R5 is:

D4	A
55	A + 1

As discussed in Section 3.4.3, the machine code instructions are often shown horizontally with the first byte at the right. Thus the above translation can be shown as:

$$55 \qquad D4$$

Note that when written this way the hexadecimal codes appear in reverse order when compared to the assembly mnemonics.

The following examples illustrate translations of several single-operand instructions using the horizontal format.

Machine Code		Assembly	
51	D4	CLRL	R1
54	D6	INCL	R4
50	D4	CLRL	R0
55	D6	INCL	R5
5A	D6	INCL	R10

4.4.3 Double-Operand Instructions, Register Addressing

The MOVL and ADDL instructions are examples of double-operand VAX-11 instructions. As with single-operand instructions, the use of a general register name for either or both operand(s) implies register addressing. Double-operand instructions, when both operands use register addressing, have the format:

operation code	opcode	A
source operand specifier	5n	A + 1
destination operand specifier	5n	A + 2

Thus we see that such instructions are three bytes in length. For the MOVL and ADDL instructions, the opcodes are:

Assembly Mnemonics	Opcode
MOVL	D0
ADDL	C0

Therefore, if we have the instruction MOVL R1,R2 the translation is:

D0	A
51	A + 1
52	A + 2

Similarly, ADDL R7,R11 translates to:

C0	A
57	A + 1
5B	A + 2

In horizontal format these are written:

Machine Code			Assembly
52	51	D0	MOVL R1,R2
5B	57	C0	ADDL R7,R11

4.5 | Labels

A label is an identifier placed at the beginning of a line in an assembly language program and followed by a colon. For example, in the instruction:

```
BEGIN:   CLRL R0
         INCL R0
```

BEGIN is a label. Although you can attach a label to any line, customarily labels are attached only to those lines that need to be referred to elsewhere in the program.

Labels can be any combination of characters beginning with a letter. They can be of any length up to 31 characters, but must be unique. In addition to numbers and alphabetical characters, you can use the underscore (_), dollar sign ($), and period (.) in labels. However, the dollar sign and period are used by system programs, so you should not normally use these in your labels.

Normally, labels begin in the first column of a line. However, a label can actually begin in any column as long as nothing precedes it. Also, a label can appear on a line by itself, in which case it acts as a label for the following line. For example,

```
BEGIN:
        CLRL R0
        INCL R0
```

has the same effect as the preceding example.

In the above discussion labels were viewed in relation to the assembly language program. In that context they appear as identifiers for convenient reference to various lines in the program. It is important, however, to also understand their relation to the machine code. That is, labels are in fact symbolic representations of *addresses* in main memory. Thus in the examples above the label BEGIN is in fact synonymous with the virtual memory address where the first byte of the CLRL R0 instruction is stored. It is the MACRO assembler that creates this relationship. When a label is encountered during an assembly, it is assigned the value that represents the address of the next location to be used to store the translated instruction or data. Thus we say that a label has a *value* which is an address, and referring to a label anywhere in the program is like referring to the corresponding address.

4.6 | Comments

Whether written in high-level or assembly language, comments in programs improve readability, both for you and for others who may have to read your work. In MACRO, anything following ";" is treated as commentary and therefore does not result in generation of machine instructions. The ";" can appear to the right of the instruction to say what is being done. For example,

```
CLRL   R4  ;INITIALIZE COUNTER
```

Comments that simply repeat that which is obvious from the mnemonics, e.g., ";CLEAR R4", are not useful. Instead, you should try to convey the *significance* of the instruction in the algorithm.

4.7 | Assembly Language Directives

An assembly directive is an instruction to the assembler which tells it something about *how* the program is to be assembled. Unlike assembler mnemonics for instructions (e.g., MOVL), directives do not generate VAX-11 machine instructions. Instead, they control certain aspects of the translation process. Directives are sometimes called **pseudo-ops.** We shall restrict the discussion here to three directives that are necessary or helpful in simple programs. These are:

```
.TITLE name
.ENTRY label,0
.END   label
```

The directive **.TITLE NAME** simply assigns a programmer-selected name to the program. It is used as the first line of the program. The effect of this will be that the operating system will print out this name whenever the program is executed or listed. It is merely a convenience and is not required. The name assigned by .TITLE has no role in the logic of your program. Nonetheless, its use is encouraged.

The **.ENTRY** directive serves to mark the logical beginning of your program, and to give it a logical name. It should precede the first instruction to be executed when the program begins. The label that is part of the .ENTRY directive can be thought of as the *logical name* of your program, in that the operating system uses it to call your program into execution. Also, you can refer to it elsewhere in your program like any other label.

The zero following the label in the .ENTRY directive is called a **register mask.** We will discuss this further when we take up subroutines in Chapter 9. This directive introduces two bytes (i.e., a word) into the machine code and sets them to zero. For example,

```
.ENTRY START,0
CLRL    R5
```

will be translated as:

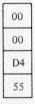

```
┌────┐
│ 00 │
├────┤
│ 00 │
├────┤
│ D4 │
├────┤
│ 55 │
└────┘
```

The **.END label** directive is required and does two things. First, it represents the *physical* end of the program. That is, the assembler will process line after line until it reaches an .END directive. Thus any lines after the .END will not be assembled. The second function of the .END directive is to indicate the entry point of the program. That is, if one writes:

```
.END A
```

where A is a label in the preceding program, the program counter will be initialized to the address assigned to A before execution begins. In many examples in this text, we use:

```
.END START
```

because we customarily use START as the label for the .ENTRY directive preceding the first executable instruction in the program.

There are many other directives in the MACRO assembly language. They all begin with a period. We will introduce other directives as the need arises.

4.8 | Example Programs

With the instructions and the addressing mode discussed thus far, a limited range of simple programs can be written. The following examples are designed to exercise these tools on problems of minimal complexity.

EXAMPLE 4.1 Let us consider first a program to compute the sum of the contents of R1, R2, and R3 and place the result in R0. The contents of R1, R2, and R3 are not to be changed in the process. The algorithm we shall use is as follows:

1. Copy contents of R1 into R0.
2. Add contents of R2 to R0.
3. Add contents of R3 to R0.
4. Stop.

The corresponding MACRO program is shown in Figure 4.1, and the translation into machine code is shown in Figure 4.2. In the translation it is seen that there are five lines. We show the translation as the MACRO assembler would, listing the opcodes and operand specifiers at the left of the addresses and in right-to-left order. Also as the assembler would, we show addresses as offsets relative to the first byte. Observe that .TITLE and .END START do not result in any machine code because they are assembly directives. The .ENTRY directive causes a one-word (four hexadecimal digits) zero to be generated at location 0000, so that the first actual machine instruction begins at location 0002. You should be able to confirm the remainder of this translation from the examples earlier in this chapter.

```
          .TITLE  ADDITION
    ;
    ;     ADDS R1,  R2,  AND R3 INTO R0
    ;
          .ENTRY  START,0
          MOVL    R1,R0          ;ADD THREE
          ADDL    R2,R0          ;  NUMBERS
          ADDL    R3,R0          ;   INTO R0
          HALT
          .END    START
```

FIGURE 4.1/MACRO program to add contents of R1, R2, and R3 into R0

Machine Code			Address
(hexadecimal)			**(hexadecimal)**
		0000	0000
50	51	D0	0002
50	52	C0	0005
50	53	C0	0008
		00	000B

FIGURE 4.2/Translation of program ADDITION

Note that the assembler treats anything to the right of a semicolon as comment, so that lines 2, 3, and 4 in the assembly code result in no machine code.

In Example 4.1 we also demonstrated some elements of programming style. In particular, note that:

1. The program has a title block indicating what it does and what registers are used. This is placed immediately after the .TITLE directive.
2. Instructions and directives begin in Column 9.
3. Operands begin in Column 17.
4. Comments begin in Column 33.

The column numbers correspond to the normal settings of the TAB key when using the EDIT/EDT editor. While these rules of style are not mandatory, they do tend to make programs more readable, and therefore we should try to adhere to them.

It will also be observed that the example program accepts no input data and generates no output. Those familiar with programming in high-level languages will find this curious, and may ask, "Why not read in R1, R2, and R3 and print out R0?" The answer to this is that input and output (I/0) are considerably more difficult in assembly language, and we choose therefore to postpone considering them until more programming skills have been developed. In order to circumvent this problem, we will learn in Section 4.10 how to set and examine memory locations and registers using the Symbolic Debugger.

EXAMPLE 4.2 Suppose that it is necessary to *interchange* the contents of two registers. For example, suppose we have:

> R4:   00000002
> R5:   00000004

and we wish to have:

> R4:   00000004
> R5:   00000002

One way of accomplishing this is with the algorithm:

1. Copy contents of R4 into R0.
2. Copy contents of R5 into R4.
3. Copy contents of R0 into R5.
4. Stop.

The program and translation are shown in Figures 4.3 and 4.4. You should be able to easily confirm that the program works and that the translation is correct.

EXAMPLE 4.3 Consider the calculation of the sixth Fibonacci number. Fibonacci numbers are the sequence of integers that obey the rule that each number in the sequence is the sum of the previous two. That is,

$$F(n) = F(n-1) + F(n-2)$$

starting with:

$$F(1) = F(2) = 1$$

```
              .TITLE SWITCH
       ;
       ;      INTERCHANGE R4 AND R5
       ;
              .ENTRY  START,0
              MOVL    R4,R0           ;SAVE R4
              MOVL    R5,R4           ;PUT R5 INTO R4
              MOVL    R0,R5           ;PUT R4 INTO R5
              HALT
              .END    START
```

FIGURE 4.3/MACRO program to interchange R4 and R5

Machine Code			Address
(hexadecimal)			**(hexadecimal)**
		0000	0000
50	54	D0	0002
54	55	D0	0005
55	50	D0	0008
		00	000B

FIGURE 4.4/Translation of interchange program

Here is a list of the first six Fibonacci numbers:

n	F(n)
1	1
2	1
3	2
4	3
5	5
6	8

An algorithm to calculate F(6) is as follows:

0. Initialize R1 and R2 to 1.
1. Copy R2 in R0.
2. Add R1 to R2.
3. Copy R0 into R1.
4. Repeat steps 1, 2, and 3 three more times.

The strategy behind this algorithm is that R1 and R2 always contain the previous and current Fibonacci numbers, respectively. The next Fibonacci number is therefore the sum of R1 and R2, as indicated by Step 2. However, because the sum is to be placed in R2, a copy of the current value (i.e., the current Fibonacci number) must be set aside for safekeeping; this is the justification for Step 1. After execution of Step 2, R2 has the new current Fibonacci number, R0 has the previous one, and R1 has the no-longer-needed value from the still earlier stage. Step 3 therefore moves R0 into R1,

```
        .TITLE FIBONACCI
;
;       CALCULATES 6TH FIBONACCI NUMBER AND
;       PLACES IT IN R2
;
        .ENTRY  START,0
        CLRL    R1              ;INITIALIZE
        CLRL    R2              ; R1 AND R2
        INCL    R1              ;  TO 1
        INCL    R2              ;
        MOVL    R2,R0           ;CALCULATE
        ADDL    R1,R2           ;  F(3)
        MOVL    R0,R1           ;
        MOVL    R2,R0           ;CALCULATE
        ADDL    R1,R2           ;  F(4)
        MOVL    R0,R1           ;
        MOVL    R2,R0           ;CALCULATE
        ADDL    R1,R2           ;  F(5)
        MOVL    R0,R1           ;
        MOVL    R2,R0           ;CALCULATE
        ADDL    R1,R2           ;  F(6)
        MOVL    R0,R1           ;
        HALT
        .END    START
```

FIGURE 4.5/MACRO program to calculate sixth Fibonacci number

re-establishing the pattern. After Steps 1, 2, and 3 are done the first time, R2 will have F(3). After Steps 1, 2, and 3 are completed for the fourth time, R2 will have the desired result, F(6).

The MACRO implementation of the Fibonacci algorithm is shown in Figure 4.5 with the corresponding translation to machine code in Figure 4.6. It is seen that after

Machine code			Address
(hexadecimal)			(hexadecimal)
		0000	0000
	51	D4	0002
	52	D4	0004
	51	D6	0006
	52	D6	0008
50	52	D0	000A
52	51	C0	000D
51	50	D0	0010
50	52	D0	0013
52	51	C0	0016
51	50	D0	0019
50	52	D0	001C
52	51	C0	001F
51	50	D0	0022
50	52	D0	0025
52	51	C0	0028
51	50	D0	002B
		00	002E

FIGURE 4.6/Translation of FIBONACCI

initialization, the MOVL, ADDL, MOVL instruction sequence is simply inserted four times. (The last MOVL R0,R1 is unnecessary, but is included to retain the similarity in each stage.)

In this problem you will probably find the opportunity to save programming effort and program size by looping back to reuse the same code rather than repeating it. In the next chapter we will develop this capability and will revisit this problem at that time.

4.9 | Interpretation of Assembly Listings

When a MACRO program file is submitted to the assembler (see Section 1.3), two output files are generated: the object file and the listing. The object file is intended only for machine interpretation, but the listing file is for the programmer to read. The listing file contains much useful information, including errors uncovered by the assembler. Examination of the listing is especially helpful when you are just beginning to understand the translation process performed by the assembler, because it shows the machine code and the mnemonics side by side. It is also a source of enlightenment if the program is not working as anticipated. Errors are often due to misunderstanding the meaning of the mnemonic codes, and it is therefore very helpful to see exactly how the assembler translates them.

In this section we use the assembler listing for Example 4.3 to explain its contents and format. Figure 4.7 shows this listing

```
FIBONACCI  9-FEB-1985  18:05:32   VAX-11 Macro V03-00           Page   1
           9-FEB-1985  18:05:08   QSA1:[50,004]F4P5.MAR;2              (1)
Machine code    Addr   Ln           Assembly source code
                0000    1              .TITLE FIBONACCI
                0000    2  ;
                0000    3  ;  CALCULATES 6TH FIBONACCI NUMBER AND
                0000    4  ;      PLACES IT IN R2
                0000    5  ;
          0000  0000    6             .ENTRY    START,0
       51   D4  0002    7             CLRL      R1          ;INITIALIZE
       52   D4  0004    8             CLRL      R2          ; R1 AND R2
       51   D6  0006    9             INCL      R1          ;  TO 1
       52   D6  0008   10             INCL      R2          ;
   50  52   D0  000A   11             MOVL      R2,R0       ;CALCULATE
   52  51   C0  000D   12             ADDL      R1,R2       ;  F(3)
   51  50   D0  0010   13             MOVL      R0,R1       ;
   50  52   D0  0013   14             MOVL      R2,R0       ;CALCULATE
   52  51   C0  0016   15             ADDL      R1,R2       ;  F(4)
   51  50   D0  0019   16             MOVL      R0,R1       ;
   50  52   D0  001C   17             MOVL      R2,R0       ;CALCULATE
   52  51   C0  001F   18             ADDL      R1,R2       ;  F(5)
   51  50   D0  0022   19             MOVL      R0,R1       ;
   50  52   D0  0025   20             MOVL      R2,R0       ;CALCULATE
   52  51   C0  0028   21             ADDL      R1,R2       ;  F(6)
   51  50   D0  002B   22             MOVL      R0,R1       ;
           00   002E   23             HALT
                002F   24             .END      START
```

FIGURE 4.7/Assembler listing for FIBONACCI

The top line of the listing shows the name of the program as given in the .TITLE directive, along with the date and time of the assembly. The version of the assembler, which changes from time to time as DEC modifies it, is also shown on this line. The second line gives the date, time, and name of the *source file* which was assembled.

The program is then printed. In order to help you interpret this listing the headings "Machine code", "Addr", "Ln", and "Assembly source code" have been added to this figure; they are not part of the MACRO listing. The Machine code columns contain the translated program. We see that the first translated code appears in line 6. This is because the .TITLE directive and comments do not generate machine code. The Addr column contains the offset address assigned to the first byte of the translated instruction. We say offset address here because it is relative to the first instruction in the program. Later we will see that the entire program is loaded for execution in an entirely different position in memory, but this need not concern us for the moment. The Ln column contains the line numbers of the source assembly language program. These are for reference purposes only. They are not part of the source or translated programs. Obviously, the assembly source code columns show the original MACRO program as it was created.

Earlier we pointed out that assembly directives are not MACRO instructions. In the listing, this is quite clear because .TITLE and .END do not have corresponding machine code instructions. The 0000 in line 6 is the zero word created by the .ENTRY directive, but technically it is not an instruction.

Certain parts of the listing have been omitted from Figure 4.7 in order to conserve space. The second page of the actual MACRO listing contains the symbol table which gives the offset address values assigned to labels, plus other information. We will discuss these items as the need arises in later chapters.

Some kinds of programming errors are detectable by the assembler. When such errors are found, you are alerted by a message at your terminal after the MACRO command has been executed. You can then look at the listing to see the source of the error because the lines in which the errors occur are identified there. Also the total number of errors, warnings, or other messages are printed at the bottom of the listing file. Table G.1 presents a list of assembler code messages and their most likely causes.

4.10 | Use of the Symbolic Debugger

MACRO programs that are not working properly are sometimes difficult to debug because errors are often caused by misunderstanding the opcodes and/or addressing modes. A powerful method of debugging such a program is a software tool that allows execution of the program to some preselected stopping point, called a **breakpoint,** and then allows the examination of the contents of each register and main memory location. The Symbolic Debugger, provided with the VAX-11/VMS operating system, is such a software tool. Many commands are provided by the Symbolic Debugger, including setting breakpoints, running the program, examining locations, modifying locations, and single-step execution.

This section shows how to use the Symbolic Debugger, which may be helpful in debugging your MACRO programs. It will also be a useful tool for program input and output before we develop better methods. Here we develop the concept of such a tool and show simple examples of its use. More details for using the Symbolic Debugger with VAX/VMS are provided in Appendix C.

To use the Symbolic Debugger, you give the DEBUG option in both the assembly and linkage commands. Then when you issue a RUN command for your program, the Symbolic Debugger takes over. From that point you issue the Symbolic Debugger commands, such as setting breakpoints, running the program, and examining contents. To use the Symbolic Debugger effectively, you will need to look at your MACRO listing as described in the previous section. Note that we continue the practice of showing the machine response with an underline.

It is assumed that you have a MACRO source file such as PROG1.MAR (see Section 1.3). To assemble and link for debugging enter the sequence:

```
$ MACRO/DEBUG/LIST PROG1
$ LINK/DEBUG PROG1
$ ▨
```

At this point you have an executable file named PROG1.EXE that consists of your program linked with the Symbolic Debugger. To execute, enter:

```
$ RUN   PROG1
```

The response will be:

```
VAX-11 DEBUG Version 4.1
% DEBUG-I-INITIAL,language is MACRO, module set to 'PROG1'
DBG> ▨
```

The Symbolic Debugger now awaits commands. Normally, you would next want to set breakpoints at the addresses of instructions where you want it to stop. Execution will stop *prior* to execution of the breakpoint instruction. The usual sequence of commands is then:

1. Set breakpoints at locations where you want the program to stop. See your MACRO listing to decide where to place them.
2. Run the program using the GO command.
3. Examine register and memory locations.

When referring to addresses with the Symbolic Debugger it is most convenient to work relative to some label in your program. For example, we customarily use START as the entry point label, so we refer to the first program location as START, the next as START+1, the next as START+2, and so on. With this technique the number added to START is just the offset address as shown in the listing. You can also use numerical addresses with the Symbolic Debugger. However, because LINK normally assigns addresses to your program beginning with 200_{16}, you must add 200_{16} to the offset addresses shown in your assembler listing in order to arrive at the numerical addresses. For example, to look at address 20 in your assembler listing, type 220 as the Symbolic Debugger address.

The most important Symbolic Debugger commands are shown below, with acceptable abbreviations underlined:

Setting a breakpoint:	SET BREAK addr
Removing a breakpoint:	CANEL BREAK addr
	(or BREAK/ALL without addr)
Show all breakpoints:	SHOW BREAK
Examine a memory location:	EXAMINE addr
Modify a memory location:	DEPOSIT addr = value
Examine contents of R1:	EXAMINE R1
Modify contents of R2:	DEPOSIT addr = value
Examine Proc. Status Word:	EXAMINE PSL
Start program execution:	GO addr (addr defaults to ENTRY addr at startup)
Continue execution after HALTing at a breakpoint:	GO
Single instruction:	STEP
Run program for next n instructions:	STEP n
Stop (return to VAX/VMS):	EXIT

Note that after you type GO, execution continues until a HALT, breakpoint, error, or $EXIT_S is encountered.

A complete terminal session using the Symbolic Debugger to check the working of the Example 4.3 program is shown in Figure 4.8. The first two lines assemble and link with the Symbolic Debugger. The RUN command then results in an entry message and the command prompt DBG>. Our first command is to set a breakpoint at the HALT, which is seen to be $2E_{16}$ bytes beyond START in the listing (Figure 4.7). The GO START command then causes execution to begin at START+2, since it automatically skips the .ENTRY word.* When it halts at the breakpoint, we EXAMINE the contents of R1 and R2, and see there the fifth and sixth Fibonacci numbers. This confirms that the program works. To further our understanding of the machine code, we EXAMINE the main memory contents where the program is stored. Note that a range of addresses can be examined by using a colon between the beginning and ending addresses after the EXAMINE command. The results are shown as hexadecimal longwords, with the convention that values beginning with an alphabetical digit are prefixed with a zero. (This is how the Symbolic Debugger differentiates between a number and a symbol.) Finally, the EXIT command returns us to the operating system.

Another important command available in the Symbolic Debugger is the DEPOSIT command for setting registers or memory locations to particular values. To demonstrate this, let us execute the program of Example 4.2 under control of the Symbolic Debugger. Figure 4.9 shows the listing, and the sample terminal session with the Symbolic Debugger

---

* The automatic skipping of two bytes when starting at a routine entry point is called a "routine start."

```
$ MACRO/DEBUG F4P5                 {Assemble with Debug turned on}
$ LINK/DEBUG F4P5                  {Link with Debug turned on}
$ RUN F4P5                         {Run}
                    VAX-11 DEBUG Version 4.1
%DEBUG-I-INITIAL, language is MACRO, module set to 'FIBONACCI'
DBG>SET BREAK START+2E             {Set break point at the HALT}
DBG>GO START                       {Execute the program}
routine start at FIBONACCI\START
break at FIBONACCI\START+2E
DBG>EXAMINE R1                     {Look at contents of R1}
R1:  00000005                      {This is F(5)}
DBG>EXAMINE R2                     {Look at contents of R2}
R2:  00000008                      {This is F(6)}
DBG>EXAMINE START+2:START+2E       {Look at the program machine code}
FIBONACCI\START+02:    52D451D4  ⎫
FIBONACCI\START+06:    52D651D6  ⎪
FIBONACCI\START+0A:    0C05052D0 ⎪
FIBONACCI\START+0E:    50D05251  ⎪
FIBONACCI\START+12:    5052D051  ⎪   {These are the program opcodes
FIBONACCI\START+16:    0D05251C0 ⎬    and operand specifiers represented
FIBONACCI\START+1A:    52D05150  ⎪    as hexadecimal longwords. Compare
FIBONACCI\START+1E:    5251C050  ⎪    to listing in Fig.4.7}
FIBONACCI\START+22:    0D05150D0 ⎪
FIBONACCI\START+26:    51C05052  ⎪
FIBONACCI\START+2A:    5150D052  ⎪
FIBONACCI\START+2E:    00000000  ⎭
DBG>EXIT                           {Leave the debugger}
$ ▒
```

FIGURE 4.8/Symbolic debugger execution of FIBONACCI

is shown in Figure 4.10. In Figure 4.10 the first two Symbolic Debugger commands set registers 4 and 5 to 19_{16} and 40_{16}. In the third and fourth commands we assure ourselves that R4 and R5 have the assigned values. We then set the breakpoint to START+0B (the HALT) and execute the program from START. When it reaches the breakpoint, we re-examine R4 and R5. It is evident that the program does work as planned. As a final exercise, we examine the entire program, confirming that the translation developed in Figure 4.4 was correct. In this case we use an option of the EXAMINE command which allows the contents to be viewed as individual bytes. The more extensive

```
    SWITCH      9-FEB-1985 18:46:03  VAX-11 Macro V03-00        Page  1
                9-FEB-1985 17:41:05  QSA1:[50,004]F4P3.MAR;1        (1)
Machine code    Addr   Ln        Assembly source code
                0000   1         .TITLE SWITCH
                0000   2  ;
                0000   3  ;  INTERCHANGE R4 AND R5
                0000   4  ;
          0000  0000   5         .ENTRY  START,0
50  54  D0      0002   6         MOVL    R4,R0        ;SAVE R4
54  55  D0      0005   7         MOVL    R5,R4        ;PUT R5 INTO R4
55  50  D0      0008   8         MOVL    R0,R5        ;PUT R4 INTO R5
        00      000B   9         HALT
                000C   10        .END    START
```

FIGURE 4.9/Assembler listing of SWITCH program

```
$ MACRO/DEBUG F4P3                    {Assemble with Debug turned on}
$ LINK/DEBUG F4P3                     {Link with Debug turned on}
$ RUN F4P3                            {Run}
                   VAX-11 DEBUG Version 4.1
%DEBUG-I-INITIAL, language is MACRO, module set to 'SWITCH'
DBG>DEPOSIT R4=19                     {Put hexadecimal 19 into R4}
DBG>DEPOSIT R5=40                     {Put hexadecimal 40 into R5}
DBG>EXAMINE R4                        {Check R4}
R4:  00000019
DBG>EXAMINE R5                        {Check R5}
R5:  00000040
DBG>SET BREAK START+0B                {Set break point at the HALT}
DBG>GO START
routine start at SWITCH\START
break at SWITCH\START+0B
DBG>EXAMINE R4                        {Look at R4}
R4:  00000040                         {Previous R5 contents}
DBG>EXAMINE R5                        {Look at R5}
R5:  00000019                         {Previous R4 contents}
DBG>EXAMINE/BYTE START+2:START+0B {Look at the program machine code as bytes}
SWITCH\START+02:   0D0
SWITCH\START+03:   54
SWITCH\START+04:   50
SWITCH\START+05:   0D0
SWITCH\START+06:   55       {These are the program opcodes
SWITCH\START+07:   54        and operand specifiers represented
SWITCH\START+08:   0D0       as hexadecimal bytes. Compare
SWITCH\START+09:   50        to listing in Fig.4.9}
SWITCH\START+0A:   55
SWITCH\START+0B:   00
DBG>EXIT                              {Leave the debugger}
$ ▓
```

FIGURE 4.10/Symbolic Debugger execution of SWITCH program

treatment of the Symbolic Debugger in Appendix C shows that other options allow you to view the contents in many other ways.

The preceding two examples show how we enter data into our programs and read the results until we develop the necessary skills for true I/O. While this method is not suitable for practical programs, it is adequate for our immediate needs. Moreover, it is very instructive to see the exact form that our programs take in the memory of the machine.

4.11 | Simplified Input and Output (Optional)

Normally, a computer program is written so as to allow its user to easily change the values that it operates on. For example, the program in Example 4.1 would be much more useful if a user who did not necessarily understand MACRO programming could cause it to add *any* three numbers. That is, we would like to allow the user to **input** the three summands, perhaps from a terminal keyboard. Additionally, for a user unfamiliar with machine code and the Symbolic Debugger, we should have a means of displaying the results. This would be called **output**.

Input and output (I/O) are surprisingly complicated tasks when considered at their most fundamental levels. These complexities arise for several reasons, including differences between the representation of data internal to and external from the computer. Also, external devices such as keyboards and printers tend to be much slower than the CPU, and the program must compensate for this difference in speed. Finally, the facilities for input and output available to the programmer vary considerably from one computer installation to another. This complexity of I/O presents a dilemma for those just beginning the study of assembly language programming (and for those who teach it!). Naturally, we would like to be able to conveniently allow program input and to display program results *early* in our studies, but the programming skills necessary to handle the complexities of I/O cannot be developed until we are well into the subject. One approach to this dilemma is to sidestep it through the use of the Symbolic Debugger. We showed this approach in the preceding example, where we wrote programs without I/O and used the Symbolic Debugger to set input data registers and to examine the contents of registers where results were placed. The disadvantages of this approach are obvious. Another approach is to use **preprogrammed routines** that perform the required operations for input or output. This approach is described below. The principal disadvantage is that it introduces into the program concepts that cannot be fully understood by the beginning programmer. Many will be willing to accept this disadvantage in order to be able to do I/O earlier in the study of assembly language programming.

The preprogrammed I/O routines to be used here are called .GETHEX and .PUTHEX. The first, .GETHEX, gets a hexadecimal integer from the keyboard and leaves it in R0. The second, .PUTHEX, prints the number found in R0 on the user's terminal display in hexadecimal representation. These routines can be made available in your MACRO program in any one of several ways, as described in Appendix E. In the examples below, we assume that they have been installed and that they exist in the library files called MACLIB.MLB and SUBLIB.OLB in the VAX/VMS directory of the user.

Usage of .GETHEX and .PUTHEX is not difficult. The instruction:

```
.GETHEX
```

anywhere in the program causes an asterisk (*) to be printed or displayed on the screen, and a pause to allow input of a *hexadecimal* number (00000000 to FFFFFFFF). The value typed in will be stored as a binary number in R0. Similarly, the instruction:

```
.PUTHEX
```

will result in the binary number stored in R0 being printed or displayed on the screen in *hexadecimal*. We shall defer explanation of the full meaning of these instructions until later chapters. For now, it is sufficient to say that they will cause jumps to subroutines which do the operations. The resulting machine code is not shown in your listing file. Note, however, that these instructions *do* cause machine code to be generated, so there will be a gap in the offset addresses whenever they are used.

As an example of the use of .GETHEX and .PUTHEX, we revise Example 4.1 to allow input of the three numbers to be added and the printing of their sum. The necessary

```
        .TITLE .GET/.PUTHEX DEMONSTRATION
;
;       READS AND ADDS THREE NUMBERS FROM THE KEYBOARD
;
        .ENTRY  START,0
        .GETHEX                     ;INPUT 1ST NUMBER TO R0
        MOVL    R0,R1               ;SAVE 1ST NUMBER IN R1
        .GETHEX                     ;INPUT 2ND NUMBER TO R0
        MOVL    R0,R2               ;SAVE 2ND NUMBER IN R2
        .GETHEX                     ;INPUT 3RD NUMBER TO R0
        ADDL    R1,R0               ;ADD 1ST NUMBER TO SUM
        ADDL    R2,R0               ;ADD 2ND NUMBER TO SUM
        .PUTHEX                     ;PRINT THE SUM
        $EXIT_S                     ;RETURN TO VAX/VMS
        .END    START
```

FIGURE 4.11/Using .GETHEX and .PUTHEX to add three numbers

revisions are shown in the listing in Figure 4.11. Observe that for input of each number we use a .GETHEX followed by a MOVL R0,Ri where Ri is the register where the input value is to be placed. To print the result, we simply use .PUTHEX because the result already resides in R0; otherwise it would have been necessary to move the result to R0 before the .PUTHEX.

Figure 4.12 shows a complete terminal session using the .GETHEX and .PUTHEX routines. Notes that the MACRO command line now contains "+MACLIB/LIB" after the program name. Also, the LINK step is revised to include "+SUBLIB/LIB" after the file name. As explained previously, these routines are assumed to exist as libraries saved in your VMS directory. If this is not the case, see Appendix E. Execution is as before, except now the program prints * and awaits keyboard entry; it does this three times. After the third number has been entered, it prints the results on your terminal display in hexadecimal.

```
$ MACRO F4P11+MACLIB/LIB          {Assemble with macro library}
$ LINK F4P11+SUBLIB/LIB           {Link with object library}
$ RUN F4P11                       {Run}
*11111                            {Values
*22222                                 to be
*88888                                    added}
000BBBBB                          {Result}
$ RUN F4P11                       {Run again}
*34                               {First value}
*3J                               {Demonstrate error handling}
ERROR--- SOME CHARACTER WAS NOT HEX.    START OVER.
*37                               {Reenter second value}
*33                               {Third value}
0000009E                          {Sum in hexadecimal}
$ ▓
```

FIGURE 4.12/Terminal session using .GETHEX and .PUTHEX

4.12 | Summary

This chapter introduced five fundamental instructions and one addressing mode. The instructions were:

MOVL	Rn,Rn	; double operand.
ADDL	Rn,Rn	; double operand.
CLRL	Rn	; single operand.
INCL	Rn	; single operand.
HALT		; no operand.

The addressing mode introduced here was the **direct register mode,** which enables us to work only with data in the general registers. Use of memory for our data must await introduction of other addressing modes in later chapters. By considering this single addressing mode and small set of instructions, we were able to focus better on the underlying concepts of assembly language programming.

The process of **translation** from assembly language mnemonics to machine code was examined in detail for each of these instructions and register addressing. We saw that for each instruction there is a unique **opcode** in the form of a binary number (but most often *represented* in hexadecimal). Additionally, there is a binary code for the operand specifier, also represented most often in hexadecimal. The opcode and the operand specifier comprise the machine code translation of the assembly language instruction. You should be able to carry out such translations with ease once the ideas are firmly understood.

Among the new concepts introduced in the chapter were **labels** and **comments.** Labels are placed at the beginning of lines in the assembly language program, giving the line a symbolic address that can be referred to anywhere in the program. The MACRO assembler assigns a numerical value to each label, which is the offset address of the first byte of the translated line relative to the beginning of the program. Comments are brief explanations inserted at appropriate places in the program. Everything to the right of a semicolon is treated as commentary and does not affect the program logic.

This chapter also introduced the idea of **assembly directives,** using .TITLE, .ENTRY, and .END as examples. Directives are instructions *to the assembler* telling it *how* to assemble the program. They do not result in any machine code in the actual assembled program. More directives will be introduced in later chapters as the need arises.

This chapter included several examples that demonstrated the instructions and addressing modes introduced. From these examples you can see the elements and structure of a MACRO program. They also provided us with practice in translating from assembly to machine code.

Also presented were two important aids for the assembly language programmer: the **listing file** generated by the MACRO assembler, and the **Symbolic Debugger.** The listing shows us exactly how the assembler translated our program and where it stored each instruction relative to the program beginning. The Symbolic Debugger is a system-provided program that allows us to interact with our own program as it executes. We demonstrated the use of the Symbolic Debugger as a mechanism for entering data into our program and examining results produced by the program. The Symbolic Debugger will serve as our principal I/O mechanism until we develop better I/O facilities in later chapters. However, those who wish to use interactive I/O earlier can use the preprogrammed routines **.GETHEX** and **.PUTHEX** introduced in Section 4.11.

4.13 | Exercises

4.1   Translate the following MACRO instructions into hexadecimal machine code:

(a) MOVL R5,R3   (b) ADDL R0,R0   (c) CLRL R4
(d) INCL R1   (e) ADDL R1,R10 (f) HALT
(g) ADDL SP,AP   (h) MOVL R12,R3 (i) ADDL2 R11,R4
(j) INCL R12

4.2   Translate the following VAX-11 hexadecimal machine code to MACRO. This is called "disassembly." (*Note:* Instruction codes are shown right-to-left as they would be shown in a MACRO listing.)

(a) 50 50 C0   (b)   5B D4
(c)   00   (d)   51 D4
(e) 5A 52 C0   (f) 57 53 D0
(g) 5C 54 D0   (h)   5A D6
(i) 5B 56 C0   (j) 55 58 D0

4.3   The VAX-11 instruction opcode is divided into two fields as follows:

```
7          4 3          0
 ┌─────────┬───────────┐
 │  mode   │ register  │
 └─────────┴───────────┘
```

Here, *Mode* represents the addressing mode, and *Register* is the general purpose register used. Any of the general purpose registers can be used in an opcode. How many addressing modes can the VAX-11 support?

4.4   The following is a VAX-11 program given in hexadecimal. What are the contents of the affected registers when it halts?

```
      50 D4
      50 D6
   51 50 D0
      50 D6
   50 51 C0
      00
```

4.5   Discuss the differences between instructions and directives.

4.6   Assemble the following MACRO program by hand beginning in location 0000.

```
      .TITLE EXAMPLE
      .ENTRY START,0
      CLRL   R0
      INCL   R0
      ADDL   R0,R0
      ADDL   R0,R0
      ADDL   R0,R0
  A:  HALT
      .END START
```

(a) What value will the label A have?

(b) What value will the label START have?

(c) What is the contents of the memory location that A labels?

(d) What is the contents of the memory location that START labels?

(e) What is the contents of R0 when the program halts?

4.7 Create the program to calculate the tenth Fibonacci number and assemble and link it with debug as shown in Figure 4.8. Set breakpoints at appropriate places so as to be able to examine R2 and see F(3), F(4), . . . , F(10) as they are calculated. Submit to your instructor a hard copy of your listing file, and the Symbolic Debugger activity while generating and examining the Fibonacci numbers.

4.8 Write MACRO programs to carry out each of the calculations shown below. If requested by your instructor, run them with the Symbolic Debugger to verify their correctness. For test cases use the following hexadecimal values:

$$X = 25, Y = 10, Z = 5$$

(*Hint:* Use registers to hold the values of each variable. Use only those instructions covered in this chapter.)

(a) X + Y   (b) Z + Y

(c) 2 (X + Y)   (d) 2 (X + Y) + 3 (Z + Y)

4.9 Write a MACRO program to reverse the order of the contents of R1, R2, R3, and R4. Run the program, using the Symbolic Debugger to load 10_{16}, 20_{16}, 30_{16}, and 40_{16} into R1, R2, R3, and R4, and to show that they have been reversed after execution. Submit listing and execution results.

4.10 Repeat Exercise 4.8 but use the input/output routines discussed in Section 4.11 to read in X, Y, and Z, and to print out the final results. Ask your instructor how to access .GETHEX and .PUTHEX, or see Appendix E.

4.11 Repeat Exercise 4.9 but use the input/output routines discussed in Sec 4.11 to read in the initial values for R1, R2, R3, and R4, and to print out the final contents.

5

Programs with Branches and Simple Data Structures

5.1 | Overview

In the previous chapter we introduced a limited set of instructions and a single addressing mode that allowed us to undertake simple programming problems in MACRO assembly language. This restricted MACRO subset allowed us to maintain a focus on the concepts of instructions, addressing, and translation. It is not a practical subset, however, because it does not allow branching, repetitive calculations, or even the use of main memory. In this chapter we will expand our programming capability by introducing several new instructions and addressing modes. In particular, we will introduce **branching** instructions and their supporting comparison instructions. With the branches introduced, it will be possible to build **loops** for repetitive calculations. The discussion is limited, however, to those branches and comparisons which deal with **unsigned** integers, i.e., the MACRO unsigned branches. Signed branches are deferred until after further discussion of the two's complement system in Chapter 6.

In order to allow use of main memory for our data, we introduce several new addressing modes in this chapter, some of which are useful in working with linear data structures such as arrays. These include the **immediate, relative, register-deferred, autoincrement,** and **autodecrement** modes.

In this chapter it will become evident that when addressing modes that refer to memory are used, the program must set aside storage space for the data in the main memory. New assembler directives, namely, **.BLKL** and **.LONG**, will be introduced for this purpose.

It is shown that memory reference addressing modes can generate instructions with formats different from those using register addressing. The translation technique in these cases is discussed, as are the effects on the appearance of the listing file.

5.2 | MACRO Branching

Recall that machine language instructions are stored sequentially in the main memory, and that the execution cycle normally fetches them sequentially for execution.

91

The need often arises to alter the sequence of instructions depending on conditions that arise in the calculations. One example would be when one or more instructions are to be performed or skipped, depending upon the outcome of a previous calculation. Another is when a sequence of instructions is to be repeated a number of times. Any alteration of the normal fetching of instructions from sequential memory locations is called a **branch.**

There are a number of VAX-11 instructions that can be used to cause branching. They work by *resetting* the PC to the destination address, whereupon the normal sequential fetching and execution resumes. The branching instructions include two unconditional branches and several groups of related conditional branches. We shall first discuss the **unsigned conditional branches,** followed by the **unconditional branch** instructions.

The conditional branches require a two-step process—the setting of a "condition," followed by a branch that depends on the condition. For now, we may think of the condition as simply the outcome of a comparison, subtraction, or test. To set the condition, we may use either the compare instruction, CMPL, the subtract instruction, SUBL, or the test instruction, TSTL. This is then followed by the appropriate branch instruction. An example of this is:

```
CMPL   R1,R2
BGTRU PLACE
```

Here the contents of R1 will be compared to the contents of R2. The following BGTRU instruction will then cause a branch to a label PLACE if the contents of R1 is greater than that of R2. If, on the other hand, R1 is less than or the same as R2, the branch will not take place. Instead, the instruction immediately following the BGTRU instruction will be executed.

There are other branch instructions that can be used in the same way. Those considered in this chapter include:

BGTRU	Branch if **G**rea**T**e**R** than **U**nsigned
BLSSU	Branch if **L**e**SS** than **U**nsigned
BEQLU	Branch if **EQ**ua**L** **U**nsigned
BGEQU	Branch if **G**reater than or **EQ**ual **U**nsigned
BLEQU	Branch if **L**ess than or **EQ**ual **U**nsigned
BNEQU	Branch if **N**ot **EQ**ual **U**nsigned

The workings of these instructions are shown in the following examples. In these examples, A and B are labels of instructions somewhere in the program.

EXAMPLE 5.1   R1 is set to 100_{16} and R2 to 50_{16}.

```
CMPL    R1,R2
BGTRU   A
```

Control will be transferred to A.

EXAMPLE 5.2   R1 is set to 100_{16} and R2 to 50_{16}.

```
CMPL    R1,R2
BLSSU   A
```

Control will *fall through* the BLSSU instruction to the code that follows in sequence.

EXAMPLE 5.3 R1 is set to 25_{16}, R2 to 50_{16}.

```
CMPL    R1,R2
BLSSU   A
```

Control will transfer to A.

EXAMPLE 5.4 R1 is set to 25_{16}, R2 to 25_{16}.

```
CMPL    R1,R2
BLSSU   A
BGTRU   B
```

Control will fall through both branches.

EXAMPLE 5.5 R1 is set to 25_{16}, R2 to 25_{16}.

```
CMPL    R1,R2
BGEQU   A
```

Control will transfer to A.

EXAMPLE 5.6 R1 is set to 50_{16}, R2 to 25_{16}.

```
CMPL    R1,R2
BGTRU   A
```

Control will transfer to A.

EXAMPLE 5.7 R1 is set to 50_{16}, R2 to 50_{16}.

```
CMPL    R1,R2
BLEQU   A
```

Control will transfer to A.

EXAMPLE 5.8 R1 is set to 50_{16} and R2 to 100_{16}.

```
CMPL    R1,R2
BLEQU   A
```

Control will transfer to A.

EXAMPLE 5.9 R1 is set to 100_{16} and R2 to 50_{16}.

```
CMPL    R1,R2
BEQLU   A
BNEQU   B
```

Control will transfer to B. Note that any unlabeled instruction following this BNEQU B cannot be reached.

In these examples, we have used only the CMPL instruction to set the condition in each case. This instruction, in effect, performs a subtraction, forming the result of the first argument minus the second argument (in the examples, R1 minus R2) in the ALU. It is important to note, however, that CMPL *has no effect on either operand*. It merely establishes a condition to determine if subsequent branching should be done.

There are other instructions that can be used to set branching conditions. For example, the SUBL instruction performs subtraction, placing the result of the *second operand minus the first into the second operand*. At the same time, conditions are set for subsequent branch instructions. Note that the roles of the operands are reversed from those of the CMPL instruction. An example will clarify this.

EXAMPLE 5.10 R1 is set to 50_{16} and R2 to 100_{16}.

```
SUBL    R1,R2
BGTRU   A
```

Now the first operand is subtracted from the second and the result ($B0_{16}$) is greater than zero. Since branches, in effect, examine the previous result relative to *zero*, the branch to A will take place.

The choice between CMPL and SUBL as a means of setting a branch condition depends upon whether the difference will be needed later. The SUBL instruction makes this difference available, whereas the CMPL does not. Normally you would not use SUBL unless you needed the difference. In Chapter 6 we will see that there is a more important reason for using CMPL when signed numbers are considered (Section 6.5).

There is often a need to branch depending on the *existing* state of a register or memory location, i.e., without comparing or subtracting. This can be done using the TSTL instruction. The two instructions:

```
TSTL    R1
BGTRU   A
```

will cause a branch to A if the contents of R1 is greater than zero. The contents of R1 remains unchanged.

It should also be recognized that *many* other instructions will act to set branching conditions. If there is any doubt that the conditions are properly set, a TSTL or CMPL should be done immediately preceding the branch. This is discussed further when we take up condition codes in Chapter 6.

The simplest branching statements have been left until last. These are the **unconditional branches,** BRB and BRW. Each has a single operand, namely, the label to which control is to be transferred. For example,

```
BRB    A
```

will branch to A regardless of what precedes or follows it. The only difference between BRB and BRW is the distance of the branch destination from the branch instruction. The BRB stands for **BR**anch with **B**yte displacement, and can transfer only to points relatively close to the branch instruction. The BRW, on the other hand, stands for **BR**anch with **W**ord displacement, and can transfer to more distant points. This is explained more fully below. The usefulness of these instructions will become apparent in later examples. An instruction without a label immediately following an unconditional branch indicates a good possibility of error. This is because under normal circumstances an instruction after an unconditional branch can be reached only by another branch instruction. Therefore, one would normally label this instruction to be used as a branch target.

5.3 | **Translation of Branches**

The translation process for branching instructions is similar to other instructions. Each branch instruction has an opcode that can be represented as a 1-byte hexadecimal number. For example, the opcode for BGTRU is $1A_{16}$. Table 5.1 shows the opcodes for the branches discussed so far.

The machine code translation of most branch instructions is two bytes in length, with the following format:

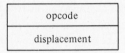

The **displacement** is the number of bytes that the PC must be advanced in order to position it at the destination address. The MACRO assembler determines the necessary displacement during the translation process so that the assembly language programmer seldom has to be concerned with it. Nonetheless, we shall examine exactly how the displacement is determined during assembly, and used during execution.

The displacement is best understood by first looking at how the branch instruction works during program execution. As described in Section 3.4.7, the first byte of the instruction is first fetched and decoded. The PC is advanced to the byte beyond the opcode in this step. When it is determined that the opcode is a branch instruction, the next byte (the one containing the displacement) is fetched, and the PC is again advanced. The condition established by the previous instruction is then checked, and if the condition is correct for the branch to occur, the displacement is added to the PC. Otherwise, nothing is added to the PC.

Two things should be clear from the above description. First, in order for the resulting PC contents to be the branch destination address, the quantity that we have called the displacement must be the distance between the byte *following* the last byte

TABLE 5.1/Unsigned Branches

Instruction	Opcode
BGTRU	1A
BLSSU	1F
BLEQU	1B
BGEQU	1E
BEQLU	13
BNEQU	12
BRB	11
BRW	31

of the branch instruction and the destination. Thus if we label the branch instruction itself α and the destination β, the displacement is

$$\text{displacement} = \beta - (\alpha + 2)$$

If it is a *backwards* branch, the displacement is negative.

The preceding displacement formula assumes branch instructions with a 1-byte displacement. The displacement for such branches is limited to the size of integer that can be represented in eight bits, so that we can use these instructions to branch at most 127_{10} bytes forward or 128_{10} bytes backwards, relative to the byte *following* the branch instruction. The origin of these numbers can be seen in Table 2.4.

We should observe that there are instructions for branching to more distant points in the program. One of these is the unconditional branch instruction, BRW, which is just like the BRB instruction but has two bytes (one word) reserved for the displacement. The modification of the displacement formula for the BRW instruction is left as an exercise.

Some examples will clarify branch instruction translation.

EXAMPLE 5.11 Show the translation of the following program segment.

Translation	Address		Instruction
52 51 D1	0000		CMPL R1,R2
09 1A	0003		BGTRU A
53 52 D0	0005		MOVL R2,R3
52 51 D0	0008		MOVL R1,R2
51 53 D0	000B		MOVL R3,R1
00	000E	A:	HALT

The Translation and Address columns are determined using techniques explained in Chapter 4, but the second byte of the BGTRU instruction translation is temporarily left blank. We can then use the branch displacement formula with:

$$\alpha = 3 \qquad \beta = E$$

to get:

$$\text{displacement} = E - (3 + 2)$$
$$= 09$$

Thus 09 is the second byte of the BGTRU instruction.

EXAMPLE 5.12 Show the translation for the following program segment with forward and backward branches. Register R0 is assumed to be initialized prior to its execution.

Translation	Address		Instruction
51 D4	0000		CLRL R1
52 D4	0002		CLRL R2
50 51 D1	0004	A:	CMPL R1,R0
07 13	0007	B:	BEQLU OUT
52 51 C0	0009		ADDL R1,R2
51 D6	000C		INCL R1
F4 11	000E	C:	BRB A
00	0010	OUT:	HALT

For the forward branch, BEQLU OUT:

$$\text{displacement} = 10 - (7 + 2)$$
$$= 07$$

For the backwards branch, the BRB A:

$$\text{displacement} = 4 \quad - (E + 2)$$
$$= F4$$

5.4 | Implementing Decision and Loop Structures

Certain cases of conditional branching arise frequently in programming. It is worthwhile to develop standard implementations for these cases. Three of the most common cases are the **single-alternative decision** structure, the **double-alternative decision** structure, and a **loop** structure. Collectively, these are called **control** structures. Logical flow charts for these control structures are shown in Figure 5.1. Those familiar

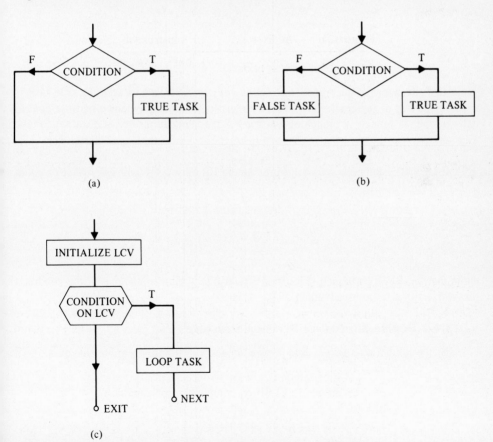

(a)

(b)

(c)

FIGURE 5.1/Control structures: (a) single-alternative decision structure; (b) double-alternative decision structure; (c) loop structure (leading decisions)

with modern high-level languages will recognize these as the IF-THEN, IF-THEN-ELSE, and WHILE structures.

While there are many different ways that these structures can be implemented in MACRO, there is some value to adopting a standard implementation for each. This will speed up the programming effort by reducing the number of choices facing the programmer, and will also make the program easier for others to understand. To this end, we present a single implementation for each structure in Figure 5.1. In later sections, as other instructions are introduced, we will offer other more efficient implementations for some of these.

5.4.1 Single-Alternative Decision Structures

The suggested MACRO implementation of the single-alternative decision structure is:

> Set condition
> Branch to END on complement of condition
>
> _____
> _____ (true task)
> _____
>
> END:
> (program continues)

Note that the appropriate branch instruction must be selected to skip the true task if the *complement* of the condition is true. The test logic is complemented because control falls through a branch if branching *does not* occur, and the preferred location for the true task is immediately after the branch instruction. An example will clarify this.

EXAMPLE 5.13   Suppose we wish to increment R0 only if R1 is *greater than or equal to* R2. We then write:

```
        CMPL    R1,R2    ;   CONDITION IS SET
        BLSSU   END      ;   BR OUT IF NOT TRUE
        INCL    R0       ;   TRUE TASK
END:
        (program continues)
```

Note that the BLSSU (branch if R1 is *less* than R2) is the *complement* of the condition for which R0 is to be incremented.

5.4.2 Double-Alternative Decision Structures

For the double-alternative structure we suggest the following implementation:

> Set condition
> Branch to ELSE on complement of condition
> THEN: _____
>   _____ (true task)
>   _____
>
> BRB END

```
ELSE:        _____
             _____ (false task)
             _____
             _____
END:
```
            (program continues)

Observe that we again branch around the true task if the condition *complement* is true. In this structure, however, the branch is to the false task, commonly labeled ELSE. Attention is also called to the BRB END instruction, which is necessary to prevent execution of the false task after completion of the true task.

Let us now consider the following example of the double-alternative decision structure.

EXAMPLE 5.14   Suppose R1 is to be incremented by one if it is less than R0, or by two if it is greater than or equal to R0. The instructions to accomplish this using the standard structure are:

```
        CMPL    R1,R0       ; CONDITION IS SET
        BGEQU   ELSE1       ; BRANCH TO ELSE1 IF R1 > =R0
THEN1:  INCL    R1          ; TRUE
        BRB     END1        ;   TASK
ELSE1:  INCL    R1          ; FALSE
        INCL    R1          ;   TASK
END1:
```
            (continuation of program)

As a matter of programming style, it is possible to indent the instructions in the true and false tasks. This helps to improve program readability. However, this is not customarily done in assembly language programming. Note that use of the labels THEN1, ELSE1, and END1 is optional and strictly a matter of style. In particular, the THEN1 label is unnecessary because control will automatically fall through the BGEQU if R1 is smaller than R0. Many programmers choose to omit THEN labels because each added symbol in the program adds to the amount of memory required in the assembly process. On very large programs, this can be a problem. On the other hand, these labels do improve readability, especially for those who are not thoroughly familiar with the MACRO instructions. Note that because each label in a program must occur only once, we append an integer, 1 in this case, to the labels. If other structures occur in the same program, we would use THEN2, ELSE2, END2, etc.

5.4.3 Loop Structures

Loop structures are often helpful and may be essential whenever the same set of instructions needs to be executed repeatedly. An example of this was shown in Figure 4.5 where we saw that the instructions:

```
MOVL    R2,R0
ADDL    R1,R2
MOVL    R0,R1
```

occur four times. If a loop structure had been used, this program would be significantly shorter. Moreover, if the instructions had to be done many times, it would be impractical to write the program any other way.

There are many different ways to implement loop structures in assembly language. Here we will show a versatile implementation of a WHILE loop, which is not greatly different from the WHILE loops familiar to high-level language programmers. The general structure is:

> Initialize LCV
> WHILE: Set condition using LCV
> Branch to END on complement of condition
>
> ——————
> —————— (loop task)
> ——————
>
> Update LCV
> BRB WHILE
> END:
> (continuation of program)

Here LCV stands for loop control variable, which is the quantity examined when the loop condition is set. It must be initialized prior to the first execution of the instruction that sets the condition, and updated prior to looping back after each execution of the loop task. The looping will continue while the tested condition remains true, and control will branch to the loop END the first time this condition is false. The following example shows how to multiply two unsigned integers using this structure.

EXAMPLE 5.15 Suppose that the two numbers to be multiplied are in R1 and R2. We will perform the multiplication by adding R2 to R0 exactly R1 times. Register 3 will serve as our LCV. The necessary instructions are:

```
         CLRL   R0        ; INITIALIZE RESULT
         MOVL   R1,R3     ; INITIALIZE LCV AND CONDITION
WHILE1:  TSTL   R3        ; SET CONDITION
         BLEQU  END1      ; CHECK COMPLEMENT
         ADDL   R2,R0     ; LOOP TASK
         DECL   R3        ; UPDATE LCV
         BRB    WHILE1
END1:
         (continuation of program)
```

Let us now go through this program segment line by line and understand how it works. R0 is cleared because it will be the destination register for holding the running sum. The LCV, R3, is initialized by moving the first multiplicand, R1, into it. The TSTL instruction compares R3 with zero, setting the condition for the subsequent BLEQU instruction. Note that BLEQU is the complement condition in that we wish to execute the loop task only if R3 is *greater than zero*, whereas BLEQU will branch if R3 is *less than or the same as zero*. The loop task is a single instruction in this example, and adds the second multiplicand, R2, to R0. This is followed by *decrementing* the LCV, R3, and an unconditional branch back to the instruction at WHILE1.

The decrement instruction, DECL, subtracts unity from the single operand. It is a single-operand instruction with a translation format exactly the same as the INCL instruction discussed in Section 4.4.2. Its operation code is D7.

The reader will find it helpful to select small integers for R1 and R2 and follow through the entire sequence, verifying that the algorithm works. Also, check to see that it performs correctly for either operand being 1 or 0.

The method used in the preceding example is not an efficient way to multiply. In fact, the VAX-11 has a multiply instruction that is preferable. On machines that do not support the multiply instruction there are much more efficient algorithms (see Section 6.13.1).

The loop implementation developed above is quite versatile. Note that it can be used as an indexed loop similar to the BASIC or Pascal FOR loop or the FORTRAN DO loop. In this case, the LCV is an index that is incremented beginning with an assigned initial value and until the assigned limit value is reached. This is coded in the following way if we identify R3 and the LCV, R2 as the initial value, R4 as the limit value, and R5 as the step or increment value.

```
          MOVL    R2,R3      ; INITIALIZE INDEX
WHILE1:   CMPL    R3,R4      ; SET CONDITION
          BGTRU   END1       ; CHECK COMPLEMENT
          _____            ; LOOP TASK

          _____

          _____
          ADDL    R5,R3      ; INCREMENT INDEX
          BRB     WHILE1
END1:
          (continuation of program)
```

Note that the loop will be done only when the index is less than or equal to the limit value, R4. In particular, it will not be done at all if the initial value exceeds the limit value. This is similar to the way that the DO and FOR loops are implemented in modern, high-level languages. In the following section we consider other loop implementations that offer certain efficiencies.

5.5 | Efficient Loop Structures

The loop control structure described in Section 5.4 has the advantage of looking like the WHILE structure in modern high-level languages. However, there are penalties for this appearance, namely, program length and execution time. Very often programs are written in assembly language specifically for compactness and speed advantages over high-level languages. Therefore, one looks for the most efficient assembly language structures.

As an alternate, more efficient loop structure, consider the following:

```
              Initialize LCV
      REPEAT:
              _____
              _____ (loop task)
              _____

              _____
              Update LCV
              Set condition for loop
              Branch to REPEAT if condition is true
```

Note that in this structure there is a single branch, whereas in the structure given in Section 5.4 two were required. There is, therefore, a saving in program length. More importantly, one instruction execution time interval is saved on each pass through the loop. In programs with many loops to be repeated thousands of times the savings can be substantial.

This loop structure has another important difference when compared to the earlier one. Note that the loop task is performed *at least once,* even if the loop condition is not met. This is because it uses the **method of trailing decisions,** instead of leading decisions. With this structure it is therefore necessary to use greater care in initializing the loop control variable, and to branch around the entire structure under conditions for which the task is not to be done at all. With leading decisions, i.e., the WHILE structure, the loop exit without task execution when the conditions are not met upon entry is a built-in feature.

It is possible to construct a loop in MACRO that is efficient as well as possessing the advantages of leading decisions. The structure having both features is:

```
                    Initialize LCV
                    BRB WHILE
          LOOP: _____
                    _____ (loop task)
                    _____
                    Update LCV
          WHILE: Set condition for loop
                    Branch to LOOP if condition is true
```

Observe that although the loop task appears before the decision physically, it occurs after the decision logically. This is, therefore, the logical equivalent of the WHILE structure presented in Section 5.4. It is more efficient, however, because the unconditional branch to WHILE is executed only once. Its only disadvantage is that the physical location of the loop task before the condition test will appear out of place to those more familiar with structured languages.

The frequently encountered need to loop a specified number of times has an even more efficient implementation. This is with the use of the SOBGTR instruction (**S**ubtact **O**ne and **B**ranch on **G**rea**T**e**R**). This instruction performs an automatic decrement of the specified register *and* branches if the result is greater than zero. Suppose that the number of times the loop is to be executed is stored in R1. The following implementation will accomplish this:

```
          LOOP: _____
                    _____
                    _____ (loop task)
                    _____
                    SOBGTR R1,LOOP
```

This is similar to:

LOOP: _____
            _____ (loop task)
            _____

            DECL   R1
            BGTRU LOOP

Thus the use of the SOBGTR instruction results in saving one instruction execution cycle per loop pass. This will be a preferred structure for highly efficient code when the loop is to be performed a known number of times upon entry to the loop. Another advantage of the SOBGTR instruction is that it does not alter the condition set by earlier instructions. It loses its advantages if exit from the loop is dependent upon more complicated conditions.

The method of leading decisions can also be used with the SOBGTR instruction. This is done by placing a branch instruction just above LOOP, which transfers control directly to the SOBGTR instruction at the end of the loop. The loop control register must be initialized with exactly the number of times that the loop is to be executed.

The SOBGTR instruction translates as a 3-byte machine instruction of the following format:

$$
\begin{array}{|c|}
\hline
F5 \\
\hline
n \\
\hline
\text{displacement} \\
\hline
\end{array}
$$

where F5 is the opcode, n is the register number employed, and *displacement* is as described for branch instructions. However, the displacement formula must be modified to account for the fact that it is a 3-byte instruction. An example is provided below.

EXAMPLE 5.16   Translate the following loop structure.

Translation	Address	Instruction	
52 D6	0000	A:	INCL	R2
FB 51 F5	0002		SOBGTR	R1,A
00	0005		HALT	

$$\text{displacement} = 0 - (2 + 3)$$
$$= FB$$

5.6 | **Immediate and Relative Addressing**

Up to this point we have dealt with only one addressing mode, register addressing. This limits our programming capability considerably, because it does not allow access to data in the main memory. We now wish to introduce two addressing methods that allow the use of main memory for program data, namely **immediate** and **relative** addressing. One important advantage of these methods is that they give us other ways to initialize program variables.

We avoid calling the immediate and relative addressing methods "addressing modes." The term addressing mode is used to refer to a specific set of addressing techniques used by the VAX-11 hardware. Immediate and relative methods are actually just special cases of more general VAX-11 addressing modes, even though they have special assembler mnemonics. More will be said on addressing modes in Chapter 11.

5.6.1 Immediate Addressing

Immediate addressing is exemplified by:

```
MOVL I^#25,R4
```

and

```
MOVL I^#A,R5
```

The presence of the I^# indicates immediate addressing. The meaning of the operand I^#25 is *the immediate number 25*. Therefore, in the first example above, at run time we are moving 25_{10} into R4. This is a frequent use of immediate addressing, i.e., putting a numerical value into a register or memory location. Also, symbols I^# tell the assembler where to store the number until it is needed. Note that the MACRO assembler assumes that any numbers appearing in the source code are in *decimal* representation. Thus the 25 is taken as decimal rather than hexadecimal.

The meaning of the operand I^#A requires careful thought, and we call attention to the fact that it is often misunderstood. To develop the correct understanding of this operand, note that the assembler *assigns a value* to every *symbol* that it finds in the program. Most often, the symbol will be a *label* in the program. In this case the assembler assigns to the label A the value of the memory location address where it placed the translated code for the attached instruction. In Example 5.11, A is a label on the HALT instruction, and the assembler has placed this instruction into location 000E. Thus it has assigned to A the value 000E. Therefore, if the instruction MOVL I^#A,R5 occurred anywhere in that program, it would, *upon execution*, place 000E into register five. (This is a simplification. Actually, the hexadecimal value placed in R5 will be 000E plus the loading point address determined when the program is LINKed. See Section 16.4 for a detailed discussion of execution-time addresses.) Note that I^#A does *not* mean the contents of A, although it is often mistakenly thought to mean that.

The preceding discussion relates to the assembly language syntax for immediate addressing, and when it is used. We now discuss its translation into machine code, which will reveal why it is called **immediate** addressing. Whenever the assembler encounters the form "I^#symbol" (e.g., I^#A or I^#25) in the program, it determines the numerical value of "symbol" and stores it in the memory location *immediately following* that in which the operand specifier is placed. It also assigns the code 8F to the operand specifier field of the instruction format. For example, the instruction:

```
MOVL I^#25,R3
```

translates to:

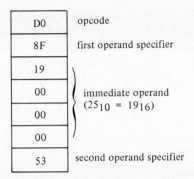

The reason for calling this immediate addressing is now apparent: the value to be used is placed *immediately* after the operand specifier. This is in contrast to other addressing methods, to be developed later, which place the operand elsewhere in memory.

The fact that this is a 7-byte instruction raises the question of proper positioning of the program counter for the next instruction. That is, how does the PC get properly positioned to the next instruction after fetching and carrying out this instruction? The answer lies in careful study of the Instruction Fetch Execute Cycle (Section 3.4.7). The D0 is fetched and PC is advanced to the operand specifier, 8F. Upon decoding the D0, the CPU knows that there will be two operand specifiers, and that the operands are longwords (four bytes). Upon fetching the first operand specifier (8F), PC advances to the first byte of the immediate operand. From the 8F the CPU knows that the operand begins in the byte whose address currently resides in the PC, and from the opcode it knows that it is four bytes long. This causes the CPU to fetch the next four bytes, advancing PC after each fetch and leaving it pointing at the second operand specifier, 53. Remembering that it needed two operand specifiers, the CPU fetches the 53 and advances the PC again. Thus after completion the PC is properly positioned at the next instruction.

Before leaving immediate addressing, let us briefly discuss two possible usage errors. One is when the programmer writes:

```
MOVL I^#A,R4
```

thinking that this moves the *contents* of a memory location labeled A into R4. Actually it moves the *address* of A into R4, because the assembler replaces A with its value, which is an address. The same erroneous thinking could lead a programmer to the statement:

```
MOVL R4,I^#A
```

but the result is different. Here, we are causing the *assembler* to place the address of A into the memory location following the first operand specifier. When it is executed, the contents of R4 is moved into the same location, overwriting what was there before! This leads us to say that if there is an immediate mode indication for the *destination operand* for any instruction that *changes* the destination, this is probably an error. However, note that an instruction:

```
CMPL R5,I^#CR
```

is correct and is often used. There is nothing wrong here because the CMPL instruction does not affect the destination address.

The VAX-11 has another addressing method that is closely related to immediate addressing. This is called **short literal mode,** which has the syntax:

```
MOVL S^#25,R4
```

From an assembly language viewpoint, there is no real difference here. At execution time, the number 25_{10} is moved into R4. The difference, however, is in how it is translated. The above instruction translates to:

D0	opcode
19	first operand specifier and operand value
54	second operand specifier

Here it is seen that the operand value ($19_{16} = 25_{10}$) is stored in the place where the operand specifier is placed for immediate mode, saving considerably memory. The disadvantage, however, is that you cannot use values larger than 63_{10} as the operand value with this mode. The reason for this limit is that the CPU has to be able to determine the addressing method by looking at the byte following the opcode. The rule that it follows is that if the two highest-order bits, (i.e., bits (7:6)) are 0, then literal mode is assumed and it uses the byte as an operand instead of an operand specifier. Thus the format of the byte is:

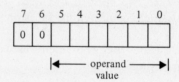

As we learned in Chapter 2, the largest number that can be stored in the 6-bit operand field is 63_{10}.

Conceptually, the immediate and short literal modes are the same. That is, they both provide a means of conveniently using a constant as an operand, and they both result in the operand being stored as part of the instruction. The choice between the two is made based on the size of the operand. For this reason, the MACRO assembler has been designed to make the choice automatically if the I^ and S^ are omitted. For example, if you write:

```
MOVL #25,R4
```

the assembler will choose the short literal form, giving the same translation as if we had used S^#. On the other hand,

```
      MOVL  #1274,R4
```

will be assembled as immediate mode.

5.6.2 Relative Addressing

Relative addressing allows us to store, retrieve, and otherwise operate on data *any-where* in main memory, rather than just immediately after the instruction. Relative addressing is indicated to the assembler by a symbol or expression* *without prefix* in an operand field. For example, in the instruction:

```
      MOVL  A,R4
```

the first operand is in the relative mode. This says, in effect, to take the *contents* of a memory location labeled A and move it into register 4. Here the symbol A plays a role identical to variables in high-level languages. The instruction:

```
      MOVL  A,X
```

is equivalent to the FORTRAN statement:

```
      X = A
```

in that they both say, "Copy the contents of A into the location identified by X." Note that here, for the first time, we are doing operations directly on memory.

The assembly language programmer must take specific steps to allocate memory locations for symbols to be used in relative addressing. This is done by use of assembler directives such as **.BLKL** and **.LONG**. To demonstrate their use, consider the problem of interchanging the contents of two registers using a memory location for intermediate storage. The program segment to do this might be:

```
             .
             .
             .
      MOVL    R1,SAVE
      MOVL    R2,R1
      MOVL    SAVE,R2
             .
             .
             .
      HALT
SAVE: .BLKL  1
             .
             .
             .
```

Here we assume that meaningful values have been placed into the registers R1 and R2. The .BLKL 1 is a directive that causes the assembler to reserve one longword immediately after the HALT instruction. In this example the address of this word would be assigned to the symbol SAVE. The first MOVL instruction then copies the contents of R1 into this location, and the third one copies it into R2.

The .LONG directive allows the assignment of an initial value into a reserved

---

* We will restrict ourselves to symbols only until expressions are discussed in Chapter 10.

memory location one longword in length. To demonstrate this, consider the following program segment that adds 1,10 and 100 (all decimal), leaving the result in R0:

```
        MOVL    A,RO
        ADDL    B,RO
        ADDL    C,RO
        HALT
A:      .LONG   1
B:      .LONG   10
C:      .LONG   100
```

Here one longword each has been allocated for A, B, and C, and they have been initialized *by the assembler* to be 1, 10, and 100, respectively, all interpreted as decimal. We emphasize that this takes place at assembly time rather than execution time, because the distinction is important. In particular, note that instructions can alter the contents of a memory location initialized by .LONG. Consider the following example:

```
        .
        .
        .
X:      .LONG   4
START:  CLRL    X
        .
        .
        .
```

This sequence is clearly not useful code, because the CLRL instruction cancels the effect of the .LONG directive. Another common error is:

```
        .
        .
        .
        CLRL    X
        .
        .
        .
X:      .LONG   4
        .
        .
        .
```

where the programmer perhaps thinks that the .LONG directive will cause X to be reset to 4 during execution. It will not. Moreover, there is another trap in this example: the implication that .LONG 4 generates an instruction. It does not. In fact, the appearance of .LONG or .BLKL anywhere after the first instruction should be preceded by a HALT, $EXIT_S, or an unconditional branch. Otherwise, the current contents will be interpreted as an instruction, even though the programmer probably intended it as data.

Let us now consider the machine code translation of relative addressing. It will then become apparent why it is so named. As with immediate addressing, relative addressing employs the locations immediately following the first byte of the operand specifier. In this case, however, the information stored there by the assembler and linker *helps to find the operand,* rather than actually being the operand as it is for immediate addressing. Specifically, the distance between the current PC and the operand is stored there. This distance is called the **PC-relative address,** or relative address for short.

The translation of relative-addressed operands is somewhat involved. It is partially done by the assembler, and finished by the linker. The part of the translation done by the assembler is carried out in two passes. During the first pass through the source code, it translates those instructions, directives, and operand specifiers that it can fully determine.* When it comes to a relative operand, however, it cannot always determine the relative address. This is the case when the operand is a label occurring *after* the place where it is used, which is called **forward referencing.** The assembler deals with this by leaving one longword of space for the relative address immediately after the first byte of the operand specifier, which will be EF. When a relative operand whose storage location is already known is encountered, the relative address can be determined at that time. In this case the assembler determines whether to allocate a byte, word, or longword for the relative address, depending on the size of the relative address. There is a different operand specifier code for each relative address length. The complete operand specifier for relative addressing can therefore be any of the following forms:

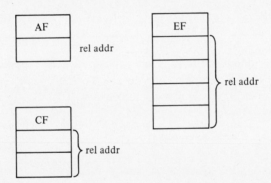

At the end of the first pass the assembler knows the locations of all operands measured from the location of the first byte of the program. These are called **offsets.** During the second pass, it goes through the entire program and places the offsets of the relative operands into the locations reserved for any undetermined relative addresses.

The final part of the translation is performed by the linker. Its task is to step through the translated code, calculate the actual relative addresses for those left in offset form by the assembler, and replace the offsets with the correct relative addresses.

In all cases, whether done by the assembler or the linker, relative addresses are calculated by the formula:

$$\text{rel address} = \alpha - \beta$$

---

* Actually, only the *lengths* of instructions and data are determined in pass 1, and the object code is developed in pass 2. The explanation given here is conceptually correct and shows the relative address calculation more clearly.

where:

$$\alpha = \text{address of byte } \textit{following} \text{ the locations}$$
$$\text{where rel address is to be stored}$$

$$\beta = \text{address of the operand}$$

We will now demonstrate the translation process for relative addressing with an example.

EXAMPLE 5.17 Figure 5.2 shows a short program that clears two memory longwords, labeled A and B, using relative addressing. The CLRL B instruction is a case where the relative operand is stored *after* the instruction, i.e., forward referencing, while CLRL A exemplifies the case where the relative operand is stored *before* the instruction. Both locations are initialized to 100_{10} (64_{16}) with the .LONG directive during assembly.

Part (a) of Figure 5.2 shows the situation after the first pass of the assembler. Note that in line 4 the first byte of the operand specifier has been determined as EF, and one longword has been reserved for the relative address of B. This is shown by the underlining to the left of the EF code. In line 5, a 1-byte relative address is sufficient,

Machine code	Offset addr	Ln	Assembly source code
	0000	1	.TITLE RELATIVE
00000064	0000	2 A:	.LONG 100
0000	0004	3	.ENTRY START,0
EF D4	0006	4	CLRL B
F1 AF D4	000C	5	CLRL A
00	000F	6	HALT
00000064	0010	7 B:	.LONG 100
	0014	8	.END START

(a) After assembler pass 1.

Machine code	Offset addr	Ln	Assembly source code
	0000	1	.TITLE RELATIVE
00000064	0000	2 A:	.LONG 100
0000	0004	3	.ENTRY START,0
00000010'EF D4	0006	4	CLRL B
F1 AF D4	000C	5	CLRL A
00	000F	6	HALT
00000064	0010	7 B:	.LONG 100
	0014	8	.END START

(b) After assembler pass 2.

Machine code	Virtual addr	Ln	Assembly source code
		1	.TITLE RELATIVE
00000064	0200	2 A:	.LONG 100
0000	0204	3	.ENTRY START,0
00000004 EF D4	0206	4	CLRL B
F1 AF D4	020C	5	CLRL A
00	020F	6	HALT
00000064	0210	7 B:	.LONG 100
		8	.END START

(c) After linker processing.

FIGURE 5.2/Relative addressing translations

so the first byte of the operand specifier is set to AF. The relative address of A is found from:

$$\text{relative address A} = 0000 - 000F$$
$$= F1$$

This relative address is coded as F1, as shown in Figure 5.2(a).

Figure 5.2 (b) shows the translation after the second assembler pass. The only difference is that the locations reserved for the relative address of B have been filled in with the offset address of B which is seen in line 7 to be 0010. The apostrophe at the right of the offset address in line 4 indicates that this number will be modified by the linker.

Figure 5.2 (c) shows the final translation as adjusted by the linker. Now the offset of B has been replaced by the relative address, calculated as:

$$\text{relative address B} = 0010 - 000C$$
$$= 04$$

We have also replaced the numbers in the address column by run-time virtual addresses. These are determined by the linker by adding 0200_{16} to the offset addresses assigned by the assembler.

Careful study of the above example will show that there can be considerable reduction of program length if data is stored *before* the first place where it is used when relative addressing is employed. Because this addressing method is used so often, most MACRO programmers take advantage of this by placing all data storage before the .ENTRY directive.

5.7 | Deferred, Autoincrement, and Autodecrement Addressing

In the preceding section we found that data in main memory could be individually referenced by the use of relative addressing. It will be observed, however, that with relative addressing a separate symbol is needed to label each individual data item used. For example, if three values are to be added, it is necessary to write:

```
        MOVL    A,R1
        ADDL    B,R1
        ADDL    C,R1
          .
          .
          .
        HALT
A:      .LONG   5
B:      .LONG   3
C:      .LONG   12
```

Clearly, this method of addressing is practical only for a few data items to be referenced. If the task is to add or otherwise manipulate a large collection of data, i.e., an **array,** a more convenient addressing method is called for. Because of the frequent need to work with arrays of data, usually stored in sequential main memory locations, MACRO provides several addressing modes especially designed for this purpose. In this section we describe the autoincrement and autodecrement modes, both of which are useful in dealing with arrays. Both are based on the concept of **indirect** or **deferred** addressing, which we will discuss first.

5.7.1 Register Deferred (Indirect) Addressing

When we write:

```
MOVL   R1,R2
```

we tell the processor to move the value found *in* register 1 *into* register 2. Thus the register addressing mode gives the processor the necessary information to find the values to be operated on (the operands) in a very *direct* way. We shall now contrast this with an alternative way of finding the operands, called *indirect* or *deferred* addressing.

Using what is called **register deferred** addressing, we might write the MACRO instruction:

```
MOVL   (R1),R2
```

Here we are telling the processor that the main memory *address* of the operand is to be found in R1. This is often called deferred or indirect addressing because the processor first gets the address of the operand, then uses that address to find the operand itself.

An analogy may be helpful in understanding deferred addressing. Books in a library are organized on the shelves according to topic. If you know the *author* of a particular book, however, the librarian will likely direct you to the card catalog. In the card catalog you will find the *location* (address) of the book, not the book itself. Thus the librarian who refers you to the card catalog is telling you the book's address *indirectly*. This is the same concept as a register having in it the *address* of an operand, rather than the operand itself.

Register deferred addressing is indicated as a register symbol enclosed in parentheses. For example, in the instruction:

```
SUBL   (R4),A
```

we are employing register deferred addressing for the first operand. This will cause the value found in the memory location whose address is contained in R4 to be subtracted from the current value in the location whose address is A.

Because indirect addressing requires an address to be in a register, an instruction using this mode is usually preceded by an instruction placing an address into the register. A typical sequence is therefore:

```
MOVL   #X,R5
ADDL   B,(R5)
```

Where X is a label somewhere in the program, i.e., an address.

While it is not necessary that the address be placed in a register *immediately* before its use in register deferred addressing, it is necessary to do so somewhere prior to its use. Programs are more easily understood if this is done close to where it is used.

It will be observed that the instruction:

```
ADDL   B,X
```

Has the same effect as the preceding example. Both add the contents of B to the contents of X. Nevertheless, there is an important advantage to the deferred addressing method, in that with it the operand address can be easily *changed* by subsequent operations on the register. For example, if we write:

```
MOVL      #X,R5
ADDL      B,(R5)
ADDL      #4,R5
ADDL      B,(R5)
```

we are adding the contents of B to X, and to the contents of the *succeeding* memory longword as well, without the need for another label. This advantage becomes very important when working with arrays of memory locations, as demonstrated in the following example.

EXAMPLE 5.18   Suppose we wish to clear 100_{10} successive memory longwords, beginning at location RESULT. Using the loop structure suggested earlier, we can write the following program segment:

```
            MOVL    #RESULT,R2   ; INITIALIZE RESULT ADDR.
            MOVL    #100,R3      ; INITIALIZE LCV
WHILE:      TSTL    R3
            BLEQU   END
            CLRL    (R2)         ; CLEAR RESULT ARRAY
            ADDL    #4,R2        ; UPDATE POINTER TO NEXT
                                 ; ARRAY LONGWORD ELEMENT.
            DECL    R3
            BRB     WHILE
END:
            HALT
RESULT:  .BLKL    100
```

The first instruction places the *address* of the first longword in the block of 100_{10} longwords reserved for RESULT into R2. The loop control variable, R3, is then initialized to 100_{10}. Because the loop structure works exactly as described earlier (see Section 5.4.3), we will not repeat the details, but will go directly to the loop task. On the first pass the instruction CLRL (R2) clears the first longword of the array stored at the address RESULT. Then R2 is incremented by 4, so that now R2 contains the address of the *second* longword in the block of 100_{10} longwords. The next time through the loop, the CLRL (R2) will therefore clear the second longword, and the ADDL instruction will increment R2 to the third longword. This continues until all 100_{10} longwords are cleared. Note that this could not have been done easily using relative addressing.

We will return to this example and improve the program somewhat when we take up autoincrement addressing.

When using register deferred addressing to reference successive elements in an array of data, the register can be viewed as a **pointer** into the array. That is, the register always contains the address of the next element, and is said to *point* at it. This terminology allows discussion of deferred addressing in more concise terms. For example, we can simply say, ''R2 points at,'' rather than saying, ''R2 contains the address of.''

Register deferred addressing has the operand specifier 6n where n is the register number employed. Thus the instruction:

```
SUBL  (R3),(R10)
```

translates as:

C2	opcode for SUBL
63	operand specifier for (R3)
6A	operand specifier for (R10)

We have noted that register deferred addressing requires an address to be placed in the employed register. Other VAX-11 deferred addressing modes have this same requirement. This can always be accomplished with immediate addressing of a label as exemplified in:

```
MOVL  #RESULT,R2
```

There is, however, a special VAX-11 instruction for moving addresses. The assembly mnemonic for this instruction is MOVAL, standing for ''move address of longword.'' Thus instead of the above we could accomplish the same thing by:

```
MOVAL  RESULT,R2
```

While the effect of these two forms is the same, the translated code and the steps that the CPU goes through during execution are quite different. We have already seen the translation used with the immediate addressing version. When MOVAL is used, the opcode is DE, and the first operand specifier is as for relative addressing. During execution of the immediate version, the virtual address is fetched from its position within the operand specifier and placed into the register. With the MOVAL form, the PC relative address is fetched from the operand specifier and the effective address is *calculated* by adding PC to the fetched value. The choice between the two methods is left to the programmer. One advantage of the MOVAL is that the mnemonic is more suggestive of the programmer's intentions. Another is that the resulting machine code is **position independent,** meaning that it is independent of the virtual address where the instruction is located. The importance of position independence is discussed in Section 11.5.

5.7.2 Autoincrement and Autodecrement Addressing

The need to increment the pointer register by 4 as in the preceding example occurs so often that it is provided automatically in the autoincrement addressing mode. To show how this works, we replace the two instructions (CLRL and ADDL) in the loop task in Example 5.18 by:

```
CLRL  (R2)+
```

which accomplishes exactly the same result. The "+" sign following the closing parenthesis indicates to the assembler that we are using **autoincrement** addressing. As with register deferred addressing, the operand is found in the memory location whose address is contained in R2. Now, however, the *register contents is incremented by 4 after the operand is fetched*. Thus the ADDL #4,R2 instruction is not needed. This has the advantage of greater execution speed, and the number of instructions required is reduced as well.

Autodecrement addressing is a companion to autoincrement addressing. It has the effect of *decrementing* the employed register by 4, and it does this *before* the operand is fetched. An example is:

```
MOVL -(R5),R1
```

which first decrements R5 by 4, then uses the result as an address. Whatever it finds at that address it copies into R1. If R5 was originally 0214, for example, this instruction would move the contents of memory location 0210 into R1, and would leave R5 set at 0210. In contrast, the instruction:

```
MOVL (R5)+,R1
```

would move the contents of 0214 into R1, leaving R5 set at 0218. Note that the assembly mnemonics has the "+" *following* the operand symbols (autoincrement), while the "−" *precedes* the operand symbols (autodecrement). This is suggestive of the way in which the addressing modes work.

If both operands in a double operand instruction use autoincrement and/or autodecrement addressing, careful thought must be given to the addresses actually referenced. The rule is that the operands are fetched and the registers are incremented or decremented *one at a time* beginning with the first operand. Consider the instruction:

```
ADDL (R1)+,(R1)+
```

where R1 initially contains 0200. The first operand is fetched from 0200, and R1 is incremented to 0204. The contents of 0200 is therefore added to the contents of location 0204, and R1 is *subsequently* incremented to 0208.

Let us now consider two frequent errors in autoincrement/autodecrement addressing. The instruction:

```
CMPL (R1)+,-(R1)
```

may not have the expected result, because R1 is both incremented and decremented after fetching the first operand. This means that the first operand and the second operand are precisely the same memory longword! This instruction leaves both R1 and main memory unchanged. The only effect is that the conditions have been set so that a branch on equal (BEQLU) instruction will branch. As another example of this type of situation consider the instruction:

```
CMPL (R3),(R3)+
```

Both operands are addressed before R3 is incremented; therefore, we again have the case where both operands are the same memory word. However, in this case there is a difference: after the instruction is finished R3 has been incremented by 4. This instruction has the effect that we have set up the conditions so that a branch on equal (BEQLU) instruction will branch, and that R3 gets incremented. This is an unusual, but sometimes useful, operation. A more normal instruction is:

```
CMPL  (R3)+,(R3)
```

The value that R3 initially points to is compared to the value in the next sequential memory longword. In the process R3 gets incremented so that the instruction finishes with R3 pointing at the second longword.

The autoincrement and autodecrement addressing modes are sometimes used with the TSTL instruction purely as a means of incrementing or decrementing a register by 4. For example,

```
TSTL  (R1)+
```

will increment R1 by 4, while:

```
TSTL  -(R5)
```

will decrement R5 by 4. This requires fewer memory locations and executes faster than two INCL (DECL) instructions or an ADDL #4,R1 (SUBL #4,R1) instruction, which accounts for the frequent usage. Usually, whenever TSTL (Rn)+ or TSTL −(Rn) appears without being followed immediately by a branch this usage is indicated. Note, however, that the register must contain a valid address or an access violation error will occur.

The operand specifiers for the autoincrement and autodecrement modes are:

$$8n \qquad \text{(autoincrement)}$$
$$7n \qquad \text{(autodecrement)}$$

where n is the number of the register employed. For example, the translation of:

```
ADDL  -(R3),(R2)+
```

is

C0	opcode for ADDL
73	operand specifier for −(R3)
82	operand specifier for (R2) +

5.8 | Example Programs

EXAMPLE 5.19 The decimal integers from one to ten are to be placed in a block of ten longwords. The program is to add the tenth to the first, leaving the result in the first longword; add the ninth to the second, leaving the result in the second longword; and so on for the rest of the block. Thus, upon halting, the first five longwords of the block should contain 11_{10}.

The listing file for an assembled MACRO program to do this is shown in Figure 5.3. In this program R2 is used as a pointer that is initialized to the top of the array beginning at A. This is done by the MOVL #A,R2 instruction. Similarly, R3 is a

Machine code			Addr	Ln		Assembly source code	
			0000	1		.TITLE	EXAMPLE 5.19
		0000	0000	2		.ENTRY	START,0
52	0000001B'8F	D0	0002	3		MOVL	#A,R2
53	00000043'8F	D0	0009	4		MOVL	#EOA,R3
	52 53	D1	0010	5	WHILE:	CMPL	R3,R2
	05	1B	0013	6		BLEQU	END
	82 73	C0	0015	7		ADDL	-(R3),(R2)+
	F6	11	0018	8		BRB	WHILE
		00	001A	9	END:	HALT	
00000004 00000003 00000002	00000001		001B	10	A:	.LONG	1,2,3,4,5
	00000005		002B				
00000009 00000008 00000007	00000006		002F	11		.LONG	6,7,8,9,10
	0000000A		003F				
	00000047		0043	12	EOA:	.BLKL	1
			0047	13		.END	START

FIGURE 5.3/Assembler listing for Example 5.19

pointer initialized at one longword beyond the end of the array, which is labeled EOA (end of A). A loop then begins, with the single instruction task of adding the value pointed at by R3 to that pointed at by R2. Autoincrement addressing is used on R2, and autodecrement is used on R3, so that each time through the loop a new sum is generated. Registers R2 and R3 are also used as loop control variables; so long as R3 is greater than R2 (after each has been incremented/decremented) the loop will continue. When the two pointers meet in the middle, the loop is terminated. Observe that R3 is initialized to the address one longword *beyond* the end of A. This ensures that the correct longword is addressed when it is decremented *prior* to fetching of the operand in the ADDL instruction.

Figure 5.3 also shows how some of our new addressing modes are displayed in the MACRO listing file. The two MOVL instructions use immediate addressing for their first operands. The addresses of these operands are shown on the same lines as the translated instructions. Note that the assembler has selected the immediate mode rather than the short literal form (coded 8F) because A and EOA occur *after* they are referenced. Also, it has placed an apostrophe after the addresses, meaning that the linker will modify these to reflect the effective addresses of A and EOA at run-time.

In line 10 of the listing we see the beginning of the block of longwords reserved for the A array. The values given in the .LONG directives are displayed four longwords per line beginning at offset address 001B. The single longword reserved with the label EOA by the .BLKL directive is stored at 0043. Note that the assembler does *not* give this longword a value. The 00000047 shown in the listing is really just the next available address and is later removed by the linker.

Figure 5.4 shows how the program is assembled, linked, and run with the Symbolic Debugger. In part (a) of the figure we look at the memory contents where the instructions are stored, that is, between START+2 and the END label.* By carefully comparing

---

* Note that the Symbolic Debugger displays hexadecimal longwords unless other representation is requested. Also, hexadecimal values that have an alphabetic symbol as the leftmost digit are given a leading zero in order to distinguish them from symbols.

```
$ MACRO/LIST/DEBUG E5P19
$ LINK/DEBUG E5P19
$ RUN E5P19
                    VAX-11 DEBUG Version 4.1
%DEBUG-I-INITIAL, language is MACRO, module set to 'EXAMPLE'
DBG>EXAMINE START+2:END                    DBG>SET   BREAK END
EXAMPLE\START+02:   021B8FD0               DBG>GO
EXAMPLE\START+06:   0D0520000              routine start at EXAMPLE\START
EXAMPLE\START+0A:   0002438F               break at EXAMPLE\END
EXAMPLE\START+0E:   53D15300
EXAMPLE\START+12:   0C0051B52              DBG>EXAMINE/DECIMAL A:E0A-1
EXAMPLE\START+16:   0F6118273              EXAMPLE\A:   11
EXAMPLE\START+1A:   00000100               EXAMPLE\A+4:   11
DBG>EVALUATE START                         EXAMPLE\A+8:   11
00000200                                   EXAMPLE\A+12:   11
DBG>EXAMINE/DECIMAL A:E0A-1                 EXAMPLE\A+16:   11
EXAMPLE\A:   1                             EXAMPLE\A+20:   6
EXAMPLE\A+4:   2                           EXAMPLE\A+24:   7
EXAMPLE\A+8:   3                           EXAMPLE\A+28:   8
EXAMPLE\A+12:   4                          EXAMPLE\A+32:   9
EXAMPLE\A+16:   5                          EXAMPLE\A+36:   10
EXAMPLE\A+20:   6                          DBG>EXIT
EXAMPLE\A+24:   7                          $ ▓
EXAMPLE\A+28:   8
EXAMPLE\A+32:   9
EXAMPLE\A+36:   10

        (a)                                        (b)
```

FIGURE 5.4/Symbolic Debugger execution of Example 5.19

this machine code with that in Figure 5.3 you can see how the linker has modified the immediate operands by adding 0200 to each. This is because the linker prepares the program for loading beginning at virtual address 0200. We verify this by using the EVALUATE command on the START label, seeing that it has been assigned a value of 0200. The EXAMINE command with the DECIMAL option specified is used to display the contents of array A. Then in part (b), a breakpoint is set at the HALT statement, and the program is executed. The EXAMINE command is again used to display the array after execution, showing the desired contents.

EXAMPLE 5.20   An array of data comprising n values is to be stored beginning at a main memory location labeled DATA. The program is to sort the data into ascending order.

We choose to perform the task using a straightforward bubble sort technique. In this method, n passes are made through an array of n values. On each pass, each successive value is compared with its successor, and if it is found to be larger than the successor the two are interchanged. We forego easy improvements to this algorithm in the interest of simplicity. The MACRO listing is shown in Figure 5.5. In this program R1 is the loop control variable for the outer loop, and R2 for the inner loop. Register R3 serves as a pointer into the DATA array, and as such is initialized to the first address in the DATA block before each entry to the inner loop. The inner loop performs

Machine code			Addr	Ln	Assembly source code	
			0000	1		.TITLE EXAMPLE 5.20
		0000	0000	2		.ENTRY START,0
00000050'EF	0000004C'EF	D0	0002	3		MOVL N,NM1
00000050'EF	01	C2	000D	4		SUBL #1,NM1
51	0000004C'EF	D0	0014	5		MOVL N,R1
	51	D5	001B	6	WHILE1:	TSTL R1
	2C	1B	001D	7		BLEQU END1
53	00000054'8F	D0	001F	8		MOVL #DATA,R3
52	00000050'EF	D0	0026	9		MOVL NM1,R2
			002D	10	WHILE2:	
	52	D5	002D	11		TSTL R2
	16	1B	002F	12		BLEQU END2
	63 83	D1	0031	13		CMPL (R3)+,(R3)
	0D	1B	0034	14		BLEQU END3
	54 73	D0	0036	15		MOVL -(R3),R4
	83	D5	0039	16		TSTL (R3)+
	73 63	D0	003B	17		MOVL (R3),-(R3)
	83	D5	003E	18		TSTL (R3)+
	63 54	D0	0040	19		MOVL R4,(R3)
			0043	20	END3:	
	52	D7	0043	21		DECL R2
	E6	11	0045	22		BRB WHILE2
			0047	23	END2:	
	51	D7	0047	24		DECL R1
	D0	11	0049	25		BRB WHILE1
			004B	26	END1:	
		00	004B	27		HALT
	00000004		004C	28	N:	.LONG 4
	00000054		0050	29	NM1:	.BLKL 1
00000001 00000002 00000003	00000004		0054	30	DATA:	.LONG 4,3,2,1
			0064	31		.END START

FIGURE 5.5/Assembler listing for Example 5.20

a pass through the array, comparing adjacent values and doing an interchange on any pair that is out of order. Note that a single pass requires advancing the pointer n-1 times, where n is the length of the array. It is known that n such passes will ensure a completely ordered array.

To further explain the operation of this algorithm we shall use the term "current" to represent the memory location pointed at by R3, or its contents, when the CMPL instruction is encountered. The term "next" is used to represent the next higher longword or its contents. Note that in the compare instruction, the first operand employs autoincrement addressing and represents the current array element, while the second operand represents the next array element by register deferred addressing. The exchange process is then *skipped* if the current value is less than or equal to the next value. The exchange process employes autoincrement, autodecrement, and register deferred addressing. The strategy employed is:

1. Place the current value into R4 for safekeeping.
2. Place the next value into the current location.
3. Retrieve the current value and place it into the next location.

The exchange begins by autodecrementing the pointer in the first MOVL so that the current value is copied into R4. The following TSTL then advances the pointer so that the second MOVL picks up the next value as its first operand. Autodecrement of the destination operand of this instruction causes the next value to be copied into the current location, leaving the pointer at this location. The second TSTL again advances the pointer to the next location so that it is properly positioned for the destination operand of the third MOVL. Observe that there are equal numbers of increments and decrements, so that R3 is left pointing at the next location, as it was when the interchange began.

It is worthwhile noting that there are other ways to accomplish the interchange which could be more efficient. However, addressing modes and/or instructions not yet discussed would be required. The method we have shown provides an interesting exercise in the use of autoincrement, autodecrement, and register deferred addressing. The reader who follows this example carefully will have no further difficulty with these modes.

Figure 5.6 shows the execution of Example 5.20 with the Symbolic Debugger. Figure 5.6(a) shows the memory contents before execution. Figure 5.6(b) shows that the contents of the DATA array have indeed been sorted after execution.

```
$ MACRO/LIST/DEBUG E5P20
$ LINK/DEBUG E5P20
$ RUN E5P20
                    VAX-11 DEBUG Version 4.1
%DEBUG-I-INITIAL, language is MACRO, module set to 'EXAMPLE'
DBG> EXAMINE START+2:END1          DBG>SET BREAK END1
EXAMPLE\START+02:   0044EFD0       DBG>GO
EXAMPLE\START+06:   43EF0000       routine start at EXAMPLE\START
EXAMPLE\START+0A:   0C2000000      break at EXAMPLE\END1
EXAMPLE\START+0E:   003CEF01       DBG>EXAMINE/DECIMAL N:N+20
EXAMPLE\START+12:   0EFD00000      EXAMPLE\N:     4
EXAMPLE\START+16:   00000032       EXAMPLE\N+4:    3
EXAMPLE\START+1A:   1B51D551       EXAMPLE\N+8:    1
EXAMPLE\START+1E:   548FD02C       EXAMPLE\N+12:   2
EXAMPLE\START+22:   53000002       EXAMPLE\N+16:   3
EXAMPLE\START+26:   0024EFD0       EXAMPLE\N+20:   4
EXAMPLE\START+2A:   0D5520000      DBG>EXIT
EXAMPLE\START+2E:   0D1161B52      $ ▓
EXAMPLE\START+32:   0D1B6383
EXAMPLE\START+36:   0D55473D0
EXAMPLE\START+3A:   7363D083
EXAMPLE\START+3E:   54D083D5
EXAMPLE\START+42:   1152D763
EXAMPLE\START+46:   1151D7E6
EXAMPLE\START+4A:   000400D0

DBG>EXAMINE/DECIMAL N:N+20
EXAMPLE\N:     4
EXAMPLE\N+4:    0
EXAMPLE\N+8:    4
EXAMPLE\N+12:   3
EXAMPLE\N+16:   2
EXAMPLE\N+20:   1
```

           (a)   (b)

FIGURE 5.6/Symbolic Debugger execution of Example 5.20

EXAMPLE 5.21   Assume the following initializations of the registers and memory locations prior to execution of *each* of the sample instructions given. The effects on registers and main memory are shown.

Register	Contents	Longword Address	Contents
R0	514	0500	1
R1	508	0504	2
R2	50C	0508	3
R3	504	050C	4
		0510	5
		0514	6

Instruction	Register Effects		Main Memory Effects	
	Register	New Value	Address	New Value
(a) `CLRL (R0)`	None	—	514	0
(b) `CLRL (R0)+`	R0	518	514	0
(c) `CLRL -(R1)`	R1	504	504	0
(d) `MOVL (R2),-(R2)`	R2	508	508	4
(e) `MOVL #514,R0`	R0	514	none	—
`ADDL (R0),-(R3)`	R3	500	500	7
(f) `SUBL (R1),(R1)+`	R1	50C	508	0
(g) `SUBL (R1)+,(R1)`	R1	50C	50C	1
(h) `MOVL (R0)+,-(R0)`	None	—	none	—

5.9 | Successive Refinements of Loops (Optional)

There are many important points to remember in the process of efficient loop construction. A very important point is to remain flexible in your thinking. Rigid structures make templates to guide one's development of first-cut programs, but the next step is refinement. To illustrate this point, consider the following simple program:

```
        MOVL   #ADR1,R1     ; POINT TO FIRST ARRAY.
        MOVL   #ADR2,R2     ; POINT TO SECOND ARRAY.
        MOVL   COUNT,R3     ; NUMBER OF ARRAY LONGWORDS.
WHILE:  TSTL   R3           ; TEST THE LOOP COUNTER.
        BEQLU  END          ; HAVE COMPLETED THE LOOP TASK.
        ADDL   (R1)+,(R2)+  ; ADDL LONGWORD FROM 1ST ARRAY TO 2ND.
        DECL   R3           ; DECREMENT THE LOOP COUNTER.
        BRB    WHILE        ; GO AROUND THE LOOP AGAIN.
END:
```

This program adds the longwords of the array at ADR1 to the corresponding longwords of the array at ADR2. COUNT is the number of additions to be done. As a simple refinement we observe that both the MOVL COUNT,R3 and the DECL R3 instructions test R3. This means that the TSTL instruction is redundant. Removing it leads us to:

```
            MOVL    #ADR1,R1        ; POINT TO FIRST ARRAY.
            MOVL    #ADR2,R2        ; POINT TO SECOND ARRAY.
            MOVL    COUNT,R3        ; NUMBER OF ARRAY LONGWORDS.
    WHILE:  BEQLU   END             ; HAVE COMPLETED THE LOOP TASK.
            ADDL    (R1)+,(R2)+     ; ADD LONGWORD FROM 1ST ARRAY TO 2ND.
            DECL    R3              ; DECREMENT THE LOOP COUNTER.
            BRB     WHILE           ; GO AROUND THE LOOP AGAIN.
    END:
```

This refinement may not seem significant, but the point to remember is that one good refinement may open pathways to other refinements. The BRB WHILE instruction can be replaced by a BNEQU instruction so that we have a speed gain for large values of COUNT without sacrificing any loss of efficiency (even in the zero loop case).

```
            MOVL    #ADR1,R1        ; POINT TO FIRST ARRAY.
            MOVL    #ADR2,R2        ; POINT TO SECOND ARRAY.
            MOVL    COUNT,R3        ; NUMBER OF ARRAY LONGWORDS.
            BEQLU   END             ; HAVE COMPLETED THE LOOP TASK.
    WHILE:  ADDL    (R1)+,(R2)+     ; ADD LONGWORD FROM 1ST ARRAY TO 2ND.
            DECL    R3              ; DECREMENT THE LOOP COUNTER.
            BNEQU   WHILE           ; GO AROUND THE LOOP AGAIN.
    END:
```

Now it is clear that DECL R3 and BNEQU WHILE can be replaced by a simple SOBGTR R3,WHILE instruction:

```
            MOVL    #ADR1,R1        ; POINT TO FIRST ARRAY.
            MOVL    #ADR2,R2        ; POINT TO SECOND ARRAY.
            MOVL    COUNT,R3        ; NUMBER OF ARRAY LONGWORDS.
            BEQLU   END             ; HAVE COMPLETED THE LOOP TASK.
    WHILE:  ADDL    (R1)+,(R2)+     ; ADD LONGWORD FROM 1ST ARRAY TO 2ND.
            SOBGTR  R3,WHILE        ; DECREMENT AND LOOP IF NOT ZERO.
    END:
```

We have created a simple-to-understand program that is now more efficient in both memory space and execution time. Something else was gained which was so subtle that you may not have even noticed; that is, this program is also globally more flexible than the original one. The SOBGTR instruction does its operation without altering the conditions set by any previous test. This allows for more testing conditions to occur and to be used easily while going around the loop. This is a subtle point that may eventually become clear as you gain more experience with larger programs.

5.10 | Summary

This chapter introduced a number of new instructions and addressing methods which greatly increase our programming capability in MACRO assembly language. Three new instructions used to establish branching conditions are **CMPL**, **SUBL**, and **TSTL**. Eight branching instructions, **BGTRU**, **BLSSU**, **BEQLU**, **BNEQU**, **BGEQU**, **BLEQU**, **BRB**, **BRW**, were introduced. Recall that CMPL and SUBL both do a subtraction. However, SUBL subtracts the first operand from the second and places the result in the second, while CMPL subtracts the second from the first and does not permanently place the result. Thus CMPL only establishes branching conditions. TSTL is also used to set branching conditions, but examines only a single operand, comparing it with zero. All conditional branching instructions decide whether or not to branch based on conditions set by preceding instructions such as SUBL, CMPL, or TSTL. The conditional branches discussed in this chapter are intended for use with unsigned numbers. Conditional branching that involves negative numbers is discussed in Chapter 6. We also encountered the **DECL** instruction, which is a counterpart of INCL; it decrements its single operand by one.

It was seen that **branch instructions** have a **translation** process similar to the other instructions. However, the operand specifier of a branch instruction is a **displacement** which is the **PC-relative address.** The actual address for the branch destination is automatically generated (when needed at execution time) by adding the current PC value to the relative address. It was seen that the branch instructions can be used to build three important classes of control structures: **single-alternative decision structures**, **double-alternative decision structures**, and **loops**. Standard implementations of these were presented and demonstrated in examples. Rigid adherence to the use of these standard forms is not necessary. However, the forms can be used to simplify the programming task and make programs more readable.

New addressing methods introduced included **immediate**, **relative**, **register deferred**, **auto-increment**, and **autodecrement methods**. All of these allow us to reference data in the main memory. **Immediate** is indicated by "I^#symbol" where "symbol" can be any numeric value or label. The numerical value is stored *immediately* after the operand specifier. We saw that there is also a **short literal** form of relative addressing with mnemonics of "S^#symbol" that can be used for small numbers. When the # symbol is not prefixed with I^ or S^, the assembler automatically selects the most appropriate form for translation. **Relative addressing** is indicated by a symbol alone as an operand. The symbol is assumed to be a label, and the assembler determines its address *relative* to the PC and stores this address in the locations following the first byte of the operand specifier. In later chapters we will see that the symbols for both of these modes can be replaced by expressions or can be defined other than as labels.

The **autoincrement** and **autodecrement** addressing modes allow reference to contiguous blocks of main memory using a single register. This makes them suitable for working with arrays. Both of these methods use the concept of **deferred** or **indirect** addressing, which is also exemplified in the **register deferred** method. In deferred addressing, the *address* of the operand is in the register, rather than the operand value itself. This is convenient because registers can be incremented or decremented, causing the same instruction to reference sequential memory locations as it is encountered repeatedly in a loop. Register deferred operands are indicated by registers enclosed in parentheses, e.g., (R5). Here we say that R5 points to the operand in memory. Such usage must, of course, be preceded by an instruction that places a valid address into the register employed, e.g., MOVL #A,R5 or MOVAL A,R5. **Autoincrement** addressing is indicated by a + sign *following* a register enclosed in parentheses, e.g., (R2)+. As suggested by this notation, R2 is incremented *after* the operand is fetched from the main memory location pointed at by R2. In **autodecrement**, the operand is written −(R4), which causes the register to be *decremented before* the operand value is fetched.

We found that use of main memory to store data obligates the programmer to allocate room. This is done by the use of the assembler directives **.BLKL** n that sets aside n longwords, or **.LONG** $n_1, n_2, \ldots, n_k$ that sets aside k longwords and initializes them to the given values: $n_1, n_2, \ldots, n_k$.

5.11 | Exercises

5.1 On a separate sheet, set up a table with BGTRU, BLSSU, BLEQU, BGEQU, BEQLU, BNEQU, and BRB across the top, and a,b, . . . , h down the left side. Indicate by X which branches will occur after CMPL R1,R2 with the following values of R1 and R2:

	R1	R2		R1	R2
(a)	1F6A	1F6A	(b)	01C5	0186
(c)	88C9	08C8	(d)	0000	0000
(e)	FF82	007E	(f)	0001	8999
(g)	020E	586A	(h)	FFFF	FFFF

5.2 Translate the following branch instructions, assuming that the branch operand label A is at the given address.

Addr of Branch Instruction		Branch Instruction		A
(a)	0202	BGTRU	A	020A
(b)	0208	BLSSU	A	0214
(c)	0124	BLEQU	A	0134
(d)	10A6	BGEQU	A	10A0
(e)	11A2	BEQLU	A	119E
(f)	22F4	BNEQU	A	22EA
(g)	251C	BRB	A	2512

5.3 We want to set R2 to 3 if R0 is greater than R1, or to set R2 to 4 if R0 is less than or equal to R1. Implement this in MACRO using first the standard control structure, then the most compact and efficient way you can devise using the instructions introduced so far. How many memory bytes and instruction executions did you save with the more efficient method?

5.4 Write a MACRO program to sort the contents of R1 through R10 into ascending order using register addressing only. Use the decision structures and loop implementations presented in this chapter. Translate *manually,* then assemble and run using the Symbolic Debugger or .GETHEX/.PUTHEX for I/O.

5.5 Revise the FIBONACCI program in Figure 4.5 to compute $F(n)$ where n is a value stored in R5. Demonstrate this program using the Symbolic Debugger or .GETHEX/.PUTHEX. How large can n be while still producing a valid result?

5.6 Translate the following into machine code:

```
ADDL  #62,R4
MOVL  #100,R1
```

5.7 Translate the following into assembly:

```
50 00000036 8F DO
         50 D5
```

5.8 Derive the formula for branch displacement for the BRW instruction.

5.9 Manually translate the following into machine code:

```
L1:
        DECL    A
        BEQLU   L1
        BRB     L2
        .BLKL   5
L2:     MOVL    #A,R1
        MOVL    A,R2
        HALT
A:      .LONG   10
```

(a) Assuming that this segment of code is loaded beginning at 0200_{16}, what value does the assembly and linkage process assign to A?

(b) To what value does the assembler initialize the *contents* of A?

(c) What value is stored in the location labeled A at HALT?

(d) What is the value in R2 at HALT?

(e) What is the value in R1 at HALT?

5.10 Identify the branch instructions and displacements implied by the following machine-code branches. Also state how many *bytes* forward or backward they will branch, measured from the branch instruction. Give answers in both hexadecimal and decimal.

(a) 36   1A   (b) 7F   1B   (c) 16   1E

(d) F6   11   (e) 7FFF 31   (f) 04   11

(g) FB   1F   (h) 81   12

5.11 Before *each* instruction below assume that memory and registers are set as follows:

Memory		Registers	
0220:	00000000	R0:	00000000
0224:	00000701	R3:	00000228
0228:	00000456	R4:	00000238
022C:	00000537		
0230:	00000174		
0234:	00000304		
0238:	00000663		

Indicate the effects of each instruction on the register and memory locations.

(a) CLRL   R3   (b) MOVL   (R3),R0

(c) CLRL   (R3)   (d) MOVL   (R3)+,R0

(e) CLRL   (R3)+   (f) MOVL   -(R3),R0

(g) CLRL   -(R3)   (h) MOVL   -(R3),-(R3)

(i) MOVL   R3,R0   (j) MOVL   -(R4),(R4)+

(k) ADDL   (R3)+,-(R4)   (l) DECL   (R4)+

5.12 Manually translate the following program into machine code. Also indicate the final contents of all registers and memory locations affected by the program as they would be after execution.

```
          .ENTRY   START,0
          MOVL     N,R1
          MOVL     #A,R2
          MOVL     #B,R3
  LOOP:   TSTL     R1
          BEQLU    OUT
          CMPL     (R2)+,(R3)+
          BGTRU    L1
          CLRL     -(R2)
          TSTL     (R2)+
  L1:     DECL     R1
          BRB      LOOP
  OUT:    HALT
  N:      .LONG    4
  A:      .LONG    1,2,3,4
  B:      .LONG    4,3,2,1
          .END     START
```

5.13 Write a program that reverses the contents of an array of length N beginning at A. That is, if A is initially 1,2,3,4, it should be 4,3,2,1 after execution. Your program should work with arrays of any size up to 1000 decimal without changing any instructions. Use either the Symbolic Debugger or .GETHEX/.PUTHEX to initialize N and A and demonstrate your program.

5.14 Write a MACRO program in which .LONG directives initialize an array A to the integers 0,1,2,3,4 and an array B to 4,3,2,1,0. A third array C is reserved with a .BLKL directive, uninitialized. After execution, each element of the array C must contain the larger of the corresponding elements in A and B. That is, $C_i = \max (A_i, B_i)$. Use the Symbolic Debugger to show that the program works.

5.15 Write a MACRO program that finds the largest value in an array and places it in R0. Demonstrate your program by using either .PUTHEX or the Symbolic Debugger to examine R0.

5.16 Manually translate the following MACRO instructions into machine code. Show the contents of R0 and memory after execution of each instruction. Describe what happens.

```
       MOVL   #A,R0
       ADDL   I^#7,R0
  A:   MOVL   I^#-5871,(R0)
       INCL   R0
       HALT
```

Hint: -5871_{10} will be stored as $FFFFE911_{16}$. Recall that the low bytes are stored before the high bytes. After manual translation, go through the machine code step by step, as the machine would, and note all changes in register and memory contents after each step.

6

Computer Arithmetic

6.1 | Overview

Up to this point our focus has been on elements of programming. In order to maintain this focus, we discussed numbers and arithmetic operations in a somewhat superficial way. In this chapter we change this focus to numbers and calculations with numbers, which we call **computer arithmetic.**

Arithmetic operations impose certain requirements on the computer and language not dealt with up to this point. In particular, a complete arithmetic capability requires operations on negative numbers, whereas up to this point we have dealt with instructions operating on positive integers almost exclusively. In this chapter we introduce examples using the **two's complement system,** so that negative numbers are allowed. Numbers in this system are called **signed numbers.** We will see that such numbers make use of a special class of VAX-11 instructions. This class includes, in particular, the **signed branch** instructions.

In order to understand signed numbers and these new instructions we must consider an element of the computer hardware called the **Processor Status Word,** which was introduced in Section 3.4.4. This special register monitors developments during calculations and allows us to guard against erroneous results.

Other new instructions which are introduced in this chapter, because of their particular importance in arithmetic operations, include the **shift** and **rotate** instructions, which allow us to deal with cell contents on a bit-by-bit basis. We also take up **multiply** and **divide** instructions that are available on VAX-11 computers.

When dealing with arithmetic it is possible to encounter numbers too large to be stored in a single memory cell in the positional binary representation. Although this is seldom encountered with a VAX-11 when using longwords, it can be a problem when working on computers with smaller cells. In order to deal with this we introduce the concept of **multiple-precision** representation of integers, which allows us to use two or more cells to store a single number. This requires the introduction of new VAX-11 instructions for **add with carry** and **subtract with carry** operations, and new directives for 64-bit cells called **quadwords.**

6.2 | Two's Complement Numbers and the VAX-11

The VAX-11 computer is designed to make use of the two's complement system described in Section 2.5. We do not wish to infer, however, that *all* numbers *must* be so represented on this machine. In fact, the computer stores *bit patterns,* on which the programmer can place whatever interpretations he or she wishes. Sometimes it is most convenient to place in a longword, or view its contents as, a 32-bit, unsigned, positional notation binary number. At other times we may wish to use the same longwords to store 32-bit, signed, two's complement numbers (positive or negative). Although seldom done on the VAX-11, it would also be possible to devise some other system of representing both positive and negative numbers with the same 32-bit longwords.

The reason one might say that the VAX-11 "uses" the two's complement system is that all instructions that are affected by algebraic sign or require negative numbers *assume* the two's complement representation. For example, as we saw in Chapter 5, a backwards branch of four bytes has a displacement of FC, which is the 8-bit two's complement representation of -4. Also, any negative result will be automatically represented in the two's complement system. For example, the DECL instruction decrements the longword operand by unity. Thus when the instructions:

```
CLRL R1
DECL R1
```

are executed, we would expect to find in R1 the hexadecimal number FFFFFFFF, which is -1. There are many other examples of this. Consider the immediate addressing example below:

```
MOVL I^#−14,R3
```

After execution of this we would find FFFFFFF2 in R3, which is -14_{10} in 32-bit two's complement representation.

The VAX-11 has a special instruction for creating the two's complement of a number. This instruction has the mnemonic MNEGL. For example,

```
MNEGL #14,R1
```

will place FFFFFFF2 in R1. A more typical usage would be the negation of the contents of some register or main memory location. For example,

```
MNEGL   R0,R1    ; Place negated contents of R0 into R1
MNEGL   R0,R0    ; Negate contents of R0
MNEGL   X,X      ; Negate contents of longword cell
                 ; Labeled X
```

The opcode for MNEGL is CE. Any addressing mode can be employed.

When we take up the subject of signed branch instructions in a later section of this chapter, we will see another important implication of the two's complement system on the VAX-11. That is, a set of branching instructions is included especially for two's complement numbers.

6.3 | **Condition Codes and the Processor Status Word**

In our earlier discussion of branching instructions, we used the loosely defined concept of "setting a condition" for a branch (see Section 5.2). We shall now refine this understanding by examining the mechanism whereby the machine establishes and retains these conditions.

The outcome of an instruction execution can be described in terms of four "condition codes," designated N, Z, V, and C. These codes are stored in four bits in a special register called the **Processor Status Word** or PSW (see Section 3.4.4). The approximate meanings of these codes, clarified in the following discussion, are:

N: Negative condition code, which is set to 1 if the previous result was less than 0.

Z: Zero condition code, which is set to 1 if the previous result was 0.

V: OVerflow condition code, which is set to 1 if the previous result exceeded the valid range of two's complement numbers that can fit in the destination cell.

C: Carry condition code, which indicates whether or not the previous operation caused a carry out of or a borrow into the MSB. Set to 1 if a previous operation *caused* a carry or a borrow.

It is important to remember that *many* instructions cause the condition codes to be set or cleared. We will develop the more important situations below. Refer to Table A.1 to see exactly how a particular instruction will affect these codes.

The importance of the condition codes lies in the fact that they allow the programmer to take appropriate action when a particular condition arises. Although we did not discuss the exact mechanism, we have already seen this with the unsigned conditional branch instructions, which are affected by the outcome of previous instructions, e.g., SUBL, CMPL, or TSTL. Here we merely point out that information about the outcome of previous operations is represented in terms of the four condition codes. We shall see that the condition codes have many other important uses, including guarding against invalid results.

Because the condition codes are *set* or *cleared* during execution of one instruction and must be *examined* during execution of subsequent instructions, their values must be temporarily stored. This is done in the PSW. As we saw in Section 3.4.4, the PSW is really the low-order sixteen bits, i.e., (15:0), of the Processor Status Longword, which is a 32-bit register in the CPU. Here we are concerned with only the four least significant bits that contain the current values of N, Z, V, and C. This is shown in Figure 6.1.

The condition codes can be examined when using the Symbolic Debugger. To see how the condition codes are set after an instruction, set a breakpoint *after* the instruction, execute the program, and when it stops at the breakpoint, issue the command:

```
DBG> EXAMINE PSL
```

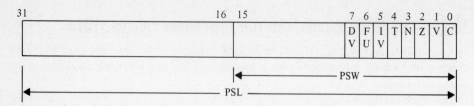

FIGURE 6.1/Processor status longword (PSL) and processor status word (PSW)

The sections which follow show several important usages of the information represented by the condition codes in the PSW.

6.4 | Using the C Condition Code to Detect Unsigned Overflow

In Section 2.5 we learned that if we use the entire 32-bit longword length to represent only positive (i.e., unsigned) numbers, the maximum possible value is $2^{32} - 1$. It was also mentioned that it is entirely possible to perform an arithmetic operation which would produce a larger result, in which case the machine-produced result is in error. Unless the program is written to detect this error and take appropriate action, however, the computer will simply proceed, using the incorrect value. The C condition code provides a means of detecting this error.

To see how the carry condition code (sometimes called the carry bit) can help us, consider the following four examples, each of which operates on 32-bit *unsigned* integers. We emphasize that these numbers should be viewed as unsigned integers because whether or not the result is "correct" depends on how we view the numbers.

Addition

1111 1111 1111 1111 1111 1111 1111 1111	(4,294,967,295)
+0000 0000 0000 0000 0000 0000 0000 0001	(1)
1 ← 0000 0000 0000 0000 0000 0000 0000 0000 (error)	(0)

This result is wrong because we added two positive integers and got a smaller result.

Subtraction (by two's complement add)

0000 0000 0000 0000 0000 0000 0000 0010	(2)
+1111 1111 1111 1111 1111 1111 1111 1100	+(−4)
1111 1111 1111 1111 1111 1111 1111 1110 (error)	(4,294,967,294)

This result is wrong because we subtracted one positive integer from another and got a result larger than the minuend.

Addition

1111 1111 1111 1111 1111 1111 1111 1110	(4,294,967,294)
+0000 0000 0000 0000 0000 0000 0000 0001	+(+1)
1111 1111 1111 1111 1111 1111 1111 1111 (correct)	(4,294,267,295)

This result is correct because we added two positive integers and got a result larger than either addend.

Subtraction (by two's complement and add)

0000 0000 0000 0000 0000 0000 0000 0100	(4)
1111 1111 1111 1111 1111 1111 1111 1110	+(−2)
1 ← 0000 0000 0000 0000 0000 0000 0000 0010 (correct)	(2)

This result is correct because the minuend was greater than the subtrahend, and we got a smaller result.

A study of these examples reveals that erroneous results are produced whenever the maximum values are exceeded. In the addition problems, we see that an error is accompanied by a carry out of the MSB; a correct result does not generate such a carry. In subtraction, on the other hand, a correct result of a two's complement addition generates a carry from the MSB; an error does not generate such a carry.

The VAX-11 is designed to take advantage of these properties. It does so by the way the C condition code is set by addition and subtraction operations. Specifically, we have:

After ADDL or INCL instructions:

$C = 0$ if there was not a carry from the MSB

$C = 1$ if there was a carry from the MSB

After SUBL, DECL, or CMPL instructions:

$C = 1$ if there was *not* a carry from the MSB

$C = 0$ if there was a carry from the MSB

Thus we see that for 32-bit unsigned numbers, $C = 0$ indicates a valid result, while $C = 1$ indicates an invalid result. (Later we shall see that this conclusion is not warranted for two's complement numbers.)

The programmer can use this property and the **B**ranch on **C**arry **S**et (BCS) instruction to take corrective action as shown below:

```
ADDL    X,Y
BCS     ERROR
```

Here ERROR is the label of an instruction which initiates the appropriate corrective action. For example, one may wish to simply halt execution at ERROR. The BCS instruction examines the C condition code and branches if it is *set,* i.e., it is 1. The same instruction would detect an unsigned overflow error after any instruction that affects the C condition code. The BCS is translated as any other branch instruction. It has an opcode of 1F.

Again we caution that the C condition code, used as shown here, is a valid test only for unsigned numbers. Error checking for signed numbers is discussed in the next section.

6.5 | Using the V Condition Code to Detect Signed Overflow

If the results of arithmetic operations are to be viewed as two's complement numbers, the C condition code is not a valid test for an overflow. This is because bit 31 (i.e., the MSB) is, in a sense, reserved for the sign in the two's complement system, and any carrys that change it create errors. The C condition code would not reflect this. The V condition code is therefore provided to allow checking for this kind of overflow.

The V condition code is based on the fact that a carry from bit 30 to bit 31 (without a compensating carry out of bit 31) produces a result with an obviously incorrect sign bit. For example, addition of two positive numbers should yield a positive result. Yet, it we add 1 to the largest allowable 32-bit two's complement number we get:

```
  0111 1111 1111 1111 1111 1111 1111 1111          (2,147,483,647)
 +0000 0000 0000 0000 0000 0000 0000 0001        +(          +1)
  1000 0000 0000 0000 0000 0000 0000 0000 (error) (−2,147,483,648)
```

Because both operands were positive, the sign bit of 1 is a clear indication of an erroneous result due to overflow. Similarly, adding two negative numbers should give a negative result. However, when we add -1 to $-2,147,483,468_{10}$ we get:

```
     1000 0000 0000 0000 0000 0000 0000 0000          (−2,147,483,648)
    +1111 1111 1111 1111 1111 1111 1111 1111        +(          −1)
 1←  0111 1111 1111 1111 1111 1111 1111 1111 (error) (−2,147,483,649)
```

The positive result is obviously in error. Moreover, if there is a carry out of the MSB without a compensating carry into it the result is in error.

In addition to the observations above, it should also be apparent that if the operands are of opposite signs, no overflow error can occur as a result of addition. You should be able to demonstrate this to yourself.

The V condition code is designed to allow you to detect any of the above errors, which are called **two's complement overflow.** *

---

* Digital Equipment Corporation uses the term *overflow* exclusively to refer to two's complement overflow. Unsigned integer overflow is just called a *carry*.

Because the V condition code is designed to reflect two's complement overflow, it is set or cleared after *addition* (i.e., ADDL or INCL) according to the following rule:

V = 1   if both operands are of the same sign and the result is of the opposite sign

V = 0   otherwise, i.e., operands of opposite signs, or both have the same sign as the result

Thus we see that the V = 1 is a reliable indicator of two's complement overflow in addition.

The rules whereby the VAX-11 determines if two's complement overflow has occurred in *subtraction* (SUBL or DECL) are slightly more complex. Once again, these rules are based on what sign the result has in relation to the operands. To explain these rules, we shall use the notation S to represent the subtrahend and M to represent the minuend. Note that with the SUBL instruction, the first operand is S and the second is M. With DECL the single operand is viewed as the minuend, and the subtrahend is unity.

There are only four possibilities for the signs of the operands:

1.   Subtrahend and minuend positive, designated here (S^+, M^+).

2.   Subtrahend and minuend negative (S^-, M^-).

3.   Subtrahend negative and minuend positive (S^-, M^+).

4.   Subtrahend positive and minuend negative (S^+, M^-).

In cases 1 and 2, no error is possible, since the result *must* be smaller than either operand. In case 3, the result should be positive; if the result is negative (i.e., same sign as S) it is in error. In case 4, the result should be negative; if the result is positive (i.e., same sign as S) it is in error. Observe from the preceding analysis that an error is indicated whenever S and M are of *opposite* signs and the result is the *same sign as* S. In all other situations the result is correct. Thus the VAX-11 applies the following rules in determining V when SUBL or DECL is executed:

V = 1   if subtrahend and minuend are of opposite sign *and* and the result is of the same sign as the subtrahend

V = 0   otherwise

Note that, as with addition, V = 1 is therefore an indication of a two's complement overflow during subtraction.

When the addition and subtraction effects on V are compared it is found that for *either* operation V = 1 is a reliable indicator of overflow in two's complement arithmetic. Thus the instruction:

```
BVS   ERROR
```

will "trap" a two's complement overflow after any instruction. Here ERROR is the label for the first statement in an error-handling sequence of instructions. The instruction BVS means **B**ranch on **OV**erflow **S**et, and has an opcode of 1D. It branches to ERROR only if V is 1.

The CMPL instruction differs from subtraction in two important ways on the VAX-11. First, with CMPL the subtrahend is the *second* operand rather than the first, as discussed in Section 5.2. The other difference is that the subtraction is carried out with a sufficient number of bits to *prevent signed overflow*. This means that after a CMPL the V condition code will always be *clear,* and the N condition code will be set if the first operand was less than the second in a two's complement sense. This reinforces the rule mentioned in Section 5.2, namely, use CMPL instead of SUBL for making branch decisions, especially if you are working with signed numbers. If the actual difference is needed, use SUBL, but then check for overflow before depending on the condition code if there is any possibility of the result being out of range.

6.6 Using the Z Condition Code to Detect Zero

Of the four condition codes, Z is the easiest to understand and use. The Z condition code is set to 1 by any operation which produces a zero result, and cleared by any nonzero result. The machine will examine all bits of the result, and if they are all zero, it will set Z to 1.

There are two VAX-11 branch instructions which use only the Z condition code:

BEQL/BEQLU   Branches if Z = 1

BNEQ/BNEQU   Branches if Z = 0

Observe that there are two different assembler mnemonics for each of these instructions, even though there is a single opcode for each. That is, both BEQL and BEQLU have the same opcode, and therefore the two mnemonics are equivalent. We are provided with different mnemonics so that, as a matter of programming style and clarity, we can use unsigned mnemonics (the U form) when we are working with unsigned integers, and signed mnemonics (without U) when working with two's complement numbers. We do not need different forms of the actual machine code because zero is represented the same way regardless of the integer type. Typical usage would be:

```
TSTL   (R1)
BEQLU  L1
```

where a branch to label L1 will take place if the location pointed at by the address in R1 is zero, causing Z to be set.

6.7 Signed Conditional Branch Instructions

With the preceding understandings of the two's complement number system and the condition codes, we are in a position now to deal with the signed branch instructions. These are **BGEQ, BLSS, BGTR,** and **BLEQ.** Simply stated, these branch instructions are intended to be used only with two's complement numbers, whereas the unsigned branch instructions BGEQU, BLSSU, BGTRU, and BLEQU (discussed in Chapter 5) should be used only with unsigned positive integers.

The need for different branch instructions for two's complement numbers can best be seen in terms of diagrams of the real line. Figure 6.2(a) shows the real line for the unsigned integers that can be represented with 32-bit, positional binary notation, and Figure 6.2(b) shows the real line for the 32-bit two's complement system. Let us choose the two numbers:

$$M = FFFFFFFE_{16} \quad \text{and} \quad S = 7FFFFFFF_{16}$$

and show them on both of these diagrams. When M and S are viewed as positive integers, M is greater than S, whereas the opposite is true if they are viewed as two's complement numbers.

If the programmer wishes to view the values of M and S as unsigned integers, the instructions:

```
CMPL   M,S
BGTRU  OUT
```

can be relied upon to branch to OUT if and only if M lies to the right of S in Figure 6.2(a). However, if M and S are to be viewed as two's complement numbers, these instructions *do not* guarantee a branch to OUT when M is algebraically greater than S. Indeed, the example in Figure 6.2(b) clearly shows that M = FFFFFFFF is *less than* S = 7FFFFFFF, yet the above instructions will cause the branch to occur. If M and S are to be viewed as two's complement numbers and we wish a branch to OUT if and only if M > S, we should write instead:

```
CMPL   M,S
BGTR   OUT
```

The CMPL instruction performs exactly the same operation, regardless of the programmer's view of the representation of the operands. However, the BGTR instruction will properly assess the two's complement comparison and branch to OUT if M is *algebraically* larger than S. In the following discussion we shall see that BGTR and the other signed branch instructions do this by examining the N and Z condition codes in the PSW. From a programming perspective, it is often sufficient to note that in the absence of signed overflow the preceding branch occurs whenever M lies to the right of S in Figure 6.2(b).

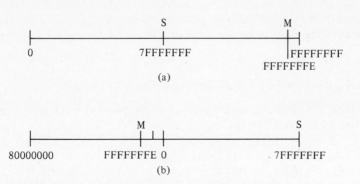

FIGURE 6.2/The real lines for (a) 32-bit unsigned integers and (b) 32-bit two's complement numbers

To see how the signed branch instructions use the information in the PSW, let us begin with the BLSS instruction. In Figure 6.3 we show the ten possible relationships between two nonzero operands of a subtraction-type instruction (SUBL or DECL). Let us temporarily set aside cases (h) and (j) because they represent overflow situations, i.e., situations where the difference would be too large to fit in a longword. Of the remaining cases, (c), (d) and (g) should branch upon execution of:

```
SUBL S,M
BLSS L1
```

The condition codes that would result from subtracting S from M in each case are shown in Table 6.1. (The determination of these condition codes using rules established in Sections 6.4, 6.5, and 6.6 is left as an exercise.) It will be observed that of the four cases in which M<S, three (c, d, and g) have the N bit set. Moreover, of the six

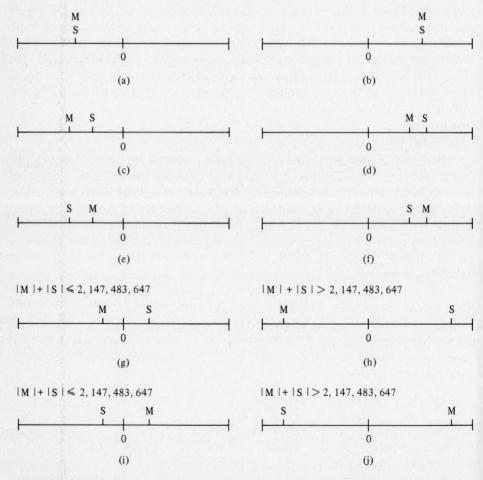

FIGURE 6.3/Eight cases of subtraction of two's complement numbers (M = minuend, S = subtrahend)

TABLE 6.1/Condition Codes after SUBL or DECL (cases defined in Figure 6.3)

Case	Condition Codes			
	NZVC	N∀V	Z∀N	ZV(N∀V)
(a)	0100	0	1	1
(b)	0100	0	1	1
(c)	1001	1	1	1
(d)	1001	1	1	1
(e)	0000	0	0	0
(f)	0000	0	0	0
(g)	1000	1	1	1
(h)	0010	1	0	1
(i)	0001	0	0	0
(j)	1011	0	1	0

cases in which M≥S, five (a, b, e, f, and i) have the N bit cleared. Thus the only cases for which the N bit does not reliably determine whether or not M<S are (h) and (j). These cases are the ones in which a signed overflow occurs during the subtraction process. This overflow causes the sign bit to be corrupted, so that the N condition code, which *always* reflects the final outcome of the operation, gives an incorrect assessment of the relation between M and S.

We conclude that in the absence of overflow the N condition code is a reliable indication of M<S. Thus the VAX-11 is designed such that the BLSS instruction examines the N condition code when deciding whether or not to branch. Because BGEQ is the logical complement of BLSS, it will branch if N = 0. Thus we have:

$$\text{BLSS} \quad \text{branches if} \quad N = 1$$
$$\text{BGEQ} \quad \text{branches if} \quad N = 0$$

Let us now consider the cases where overflow occurs, i.e., cases (h) and (j). Examination of Table 6.1 shows that V is set in both cases, and clear in all other cases. This suggests that V could somehow be used to branch correctly, even if the difference were too large to be stored. When we look at the N and V condition codes for each and every case, we observe that if either N or V is set, *but not both,* a branch should take place. This logical combination is called "Exclusive or," represented by N∀V. Table 6.1 shows the exclusive or of N and V for each case.

Some computers, such as the PDP-11, have branch instructions equivalent to BLSS and BGEQ, but which base the branching decision on N∀V, instead of N alone. This allows correct assessment of the algebraic relationship even when the result is out of range. On the VAX-11, however, the assumption is that the programmer would use a larger data cell if needed, or trap the overflow with a BVS instruction. Alternately, using CMPL instead of SUBL will cause a correct branch.

As noted in the previous section, the CMPL instruction carries out subtraction with sufficient precision to avoid overflow. This means that:

```
CMPL   M,S
BLSS   L1
```

will correctly handle cases (h) and (j) because the N condition code will always reflect the true difference.

The BLEQ conditional branch instruction is analogous to BLSS, except that it must also branch if the result of the subtraction is 0. Thus the condition to be checked is whether N is 1 *or* Z is 1. The logical expression of this condition is $Z \lor N = 1$ where $\lor$ is read "OR".

Examination of Figure 6.2 and Table 6.1 reveals that BLEQ will branch for cases (a) and (b) as well as for all those cases for which BLSS will branch. The logical complement of BLEQ is BGTR. Therefore, BGTR will branch only under those conditions for which BLEQ will not; that is, BGTR branches when $Z \lor N = 0$. Like the BLSS instruction, BLEQ and BGTR following a SUBL or DECL will not detect the overflow cases.

6.8 | Condition Codes and the Unsigned Conditional Branch Instructions

In Section 5.2 we discussed a number of branching instructions intended for usage with unsigned integers. There we described the operation of these instructions from a strictly algebraic point of view. We now wish to show that these branch instructions in fact rely upon the condition codes Z and C for their operation.

Let us examine first the BLSSU instruction that is supposed to branch when the minuend is less than the subtrahend, with both treated as unsigned integers. Figure 6.4

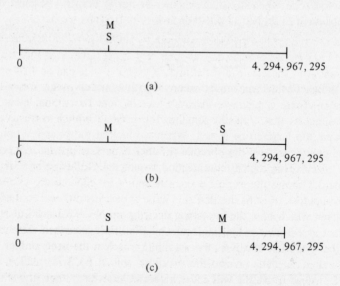

FIGURE 6.4/Three cases of subtraction of unsigned integers

TABLE 6.2/Evaluation of Unsigned
Branch Instructions in Terms of
Condition Codes

Case	Z	C	C$\lor$Z
(a)	1	0	1
(b)	0	1	1
(c)	0	0	0

shows all possible relationships between two unsigned integers. It is apparent from the figure that only in case (b) should BLSSU branch after CMPL M, S. Table 6.2 shows the corresponding Z and C condition codes, where it will be observed that case (b) is the only case where C = 1. It is for this reason that C = 1 is the condition that the VAX-11 checks for the BLSSU instruction. In fact, the machine code translation for the BLSSU instruction is exactly the same as for the BCS instruction.

Because M $\geq$ S is the logical complement of M < S, the BGEQU instruction also examines C and branches if C = 0. It has the same machine code as BCC.

The instruction BLEQU will branch if the minuend is less than or equal to the subtrahend. Thus the check is based on C $\lor$ Z = 1. As may be seen in Table 6.2, this occurs for cases (a) and (b). Note that BLEQU is the unsigned equivalent of BLEQ.

The instruction BGTRU is the logical complement of BLEQU. Therefore, this instruction causes a branch if C $\lor$ Z = 0.

6.9 | Summary of the Branch Instructions

We have discussed a number of branch instructions and their intended usage. All of these branch instructions are summarized in Table 6.3, grouped according to their most common usage. Those listed under General Usage can be safely used in any situation. All other branch instructions have recommended usage for either positive integers (unsigned) or two's complement integers (signed). Although an experienced programmer may find other valid usages, the novice should adhere to these recommendations.

Table 6.3 also provides the opcodes for each branch instruction. As explained in Section 5.3, the translation of any branch is the opcode followed by a displacement. The displacement is the number of bytes that must be added to the current PC (i.e., after the displacement has been fetched) in order to reset PC to the destination. All conditional branches have a single byte allowed for the displacement, and therefore can branch at most 80_{16} (-128_{10}) backward or $7F_{16}$ (127_{10}) forward. The unconditional branch has two forms: BRB, which allows a single byte displacement, and BRW, allowing a 2-byte displacement. Thus with BRW you can branch 8000_{16} (-32768_{10}) backward or $7FFF_{16}$ (32767_{10}) forward. This instruction can be used to conditionally branch to distant points by combining it with a conditional branch in which the logic has been

TABLE 6.3/Condition Codes for Branch Instructions

Instruction and Usage	Assembly Mnemonic	Opcode	Branch Conditions
General Usage			
Unconditional **BR**anch, **B**yte displacement	BRB	11	Unconditional
Unconditional **BR**anch, **W**ord displacement	BRW	31	Unconditional
Unsigned Branches			
Branch if **G**rea**T**e**R**, **U**nsigned	BGTRU	1A	$C \lor Z = 0$
Branch if **L**ess or **EQ**ual, **U**nsigned	BLEQU	1B	$C \lor Z = 1$
Branch if **G**reater or **EQ**ual, **U**nsigned	BGEQU	1E	$C = 0$
Branch if **L**e**SS**, **U**nsigned	BLSSU	1F	$C = 1$
Branch if **N**ot **EQ**ual, **U**nsigned	BNEQU	12	$Z = 0$
Branch if **EQ**ua**L**, **U**nsigned	BEQLU	13	$Z = 1$
Branch if **C**arry **C**lear	BCC	1E	$C = 0$
Branch if **C**arry **S**et	BCS	1F	$C = 1$
Signed Branches			
Branch if **G**rea**T**e**R**	BGTR	14	$Z \lor N = 0$
Branch if **L**ess or **EQ**ual	BLEQ	15	$Z \lor N = 1$
Branch if **G**reater or **EQ**ual	BGEQ	18	$N = 0$
Branch if **L**e**SS**	BLSS	19	$N = 1$
Branch if **N**ot **EQ**ual	BNEQ	12	$Z = 0$
Branch if **EQ**ua**L**	BEQL	13	$Z = 1$
Branch if o**V**erflow **C**lear	BVC	1C	$V = 0$
Branch if o**V**erflow **S**et	BVS	1D	$V = 1$

complemented. For example, to jump to a distant label A when an unsigned integer in R0 is greater than the unsigned integer in R1, we could code:

```
        CMPL    R0,R1
        BLEQU   SKIP
        BRW     A
SKIP:
```

6.10 | Setting the Condition Codes

In the examples presented thus far, we always placed an instruction specifically intended to set the condition codes immediately before the conditional branch. This practice leads the beginning programmer quickly to correct programs, but sometimes is unnecessary. In fact, practically all instructions will affect the condition codes, and it may well be that an instruction needed for some other reason will set the condition codes properly for the branch. For example, suppose we wish to move the contents of A into R2 and branch to L2 if the transferred number is negative. We can write:

```
MOVL  A,R2
BLSS  L2
```

without doing a specific TSTL R2. This is because MOVL will clear V and set or clear N according to whether the number moved was negative or positive, and these condition codes are the only ones needed by BLSS. A programmer who is concerned with program speed and size will examine the code with this in mind and remove unnecessary CMPLs and TSTLs. Consult Table A.1 to see exactly how every VAX-11 instruction affects, and is affected by, the condition codes.

6.11 | Shift and Rotate Instructions

An important property of positional binary representation is that a number is multiplied by two by simply shifting the bit pattern to the left, adding a zero at the right. For example, 3_{10} is written in binary as:

$$0000\ 0000\ 0000\ 0000\ 0000\ 0000\ 0000\ 0011$$

If we shift the pattern to the left by one bit we get:

$$0000\ 0000\ 0000\ 0000\ 0000\ 0000\ 0000\ 0110$$

which is 6_{10}. It should also be apparent that shifting one bit to the right will divide by two.

These facts form the basis for many arithmetic algorithms on a binary machine. For this and other reasons to be developed later, most computers have shift instructions which accomplish the above operation. In MACRO we have the arithmetic shift instruction:

```
ASHL  count, source, destination
```

where:

count   =   number of positions all bits are to be shifted. Positive count shifts left, negative shifts right.

source   =   operand to be shifted (remains unchanged).

destination =   operand where shifted result is to be placed.

This instruction can be used to multiply or divide by any power of 2. The operation performed is shown diagrammatically in Figure 6.5.

This instruction is called **arithmetic** shift because of the way that it treats the leftmost and rightmost bits. Shifting with positive count automatically zero-fills at the right, accomplishing the desired effect of multiplying by two. The right shift, with negative count, will automatically replicate the leftmost bit, thereby retaining the correct sign. For example, if we have in R0:

$$1011\ 0000\ 1111\ 0000\ 1111\ 0000\ 1111\ 0000$$

and the instruction:

```
ASHL  #-4,R0,R1
```

is executed, we get in R1:

$$1111\ 1011\ 0000\ 1111\ 0000\ 1111\ 0000\ 1111$$

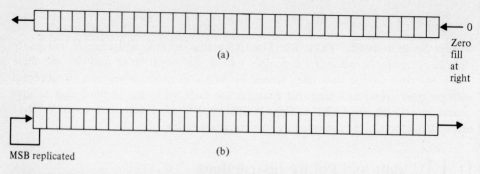

(a)

Zero
fill
at
right

MSB replicated   (b)

FIGURE 6.5/Operation of the ASHL instruction

This yields the correct result; we have divided a negative number by 2^4 and have obtained a negative result. If the leftmost bit in R0 was a zero, i.e., a positive number, the same instruction would add 0's at the left to produce a positive number one-sixteenth as large.

We call attention to the fact that shifting too far to the left produces an overflow, as expected. For example, suppose we have the positive number:

$$0100\ 0000\ 0000\ 0000\ 0000\ 0000\ 0000\ 0000$$

in R0. Then:

```
ASHL #1,R0,R1
```

would produce in R1:

$$1000\ 0000\ 0000\ 0000\ 0000\ 0000\ 0000\ 0000$$

which is negative. The erroneous result developed because twice the original number is too large to be stored as a 32-bit two's complement number.

In this event the V condition code would be set, indicating an overflow. Similarly, if we have the large negative number in R0:

$$1000\ 0000\ 0000\ 0000\ 0000\ 0000\ 0000\ 0001$$

and ASHL #1,R0,R1 is executed, we get in R1 the erroneous result:

$$0000\ 0000\ 0000\ 0000\ 0000\ 0000\ 0000\ 0010$$

Again, this operation would cause V to be set.

The ASHL instruction does not work well with 32-bit unsigned integers because it is designed to work with two's complement numbers. The C bit is *not* set when a left shift would cause an unsigned integer too large to fit in the longword. Rather, C is always cleared by ASHL. Also, a right shift on an unsigned integer that has the MSB set will give an erroneous result because of replication of this bit in the shifting.

When an odd number is divided by 2, a fractional part results. In a system that does not retain fractional parts, i.e., two's complement or positive integers, we must examine what happens. Consider first the positive 32-bit two's complement number:

$$0000\ 0000\ 0000\ 0000\ 0000\ 0000\ 0000\ 0011$$

that is 3_{10}. A right shift of one bit produces:

$$0000\ 0000\ 0000\ 0000\ 0000\ 0000\ 0000\ 0001$$

that is 1_{10}. Now consider -3_{10}, that is:

$$1111\ 1111\ 1111\ 1111\ 1111\ 1111\ 1111\ 1101$$

A right shift of one bit produces:

$$1111\ 1111\ 1111\ 1111\ 1111\ 1111\ 1111\ 1110$$

that is -2_{10}, These results can best be explained in terms of the real line. As shown below, in either case the result is truncated to the integer *at its left*.

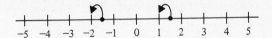

Thus we see that the arithmetic shift right one bit produces the largest integer which is less than or equal to the original number divided by 2. In mathematics this would be called the "floor function." Many readers will recognize this as similar to the INT function in BASIC or FORTRAN.

The VAX-11 has another instruction for bit shifting, namely, ROTL (**ROT**ate Longword). This differs from ASHL in that with ROTL the bits from one end are fed back into the other end during the shift, giving rise to the term **rotate.** Figure 6.6 shows the operation of ROTL. As an example, consider R0 to contain:

$$1001\ 0000\ 0000\ 0000\ 0000\ 0000\ 0000\ 1111$$

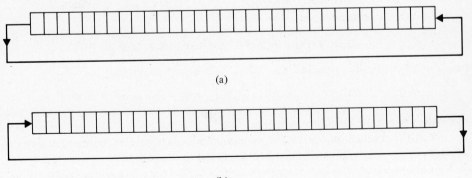

(a)

(b)

FIGURE 6.6/Operation of the ROTL instruction with (a) positive shift count and (b) negative shift count

Then the instruction:

```
ROTL   #4,R0,R1
```

produces in R1:

$$0000\ 0000\ 0000\ 0000\ 0000\ 0000\ 1111\ 1001$$

This instruction is useful for manipulation of bit patterns, but has no particular arithmetic connotation.

6.12 | Double-Precision Representation

We have repeatedly emphasized that the size of integers that can be stored is limited by the size of the storage cell. On a computer such as the VAX-11, this is usually not a problem because very large integers can be stored in a 32-bit longword. Many computers, however, only have smaller cells such as 8-bit bytes or 16-bit words. Because you may have to work on such a machine one day, and need large integers, we now develop a method for using multiple cells to get any desired number size regardless of the cell length.

Suppose we had a computer with cell size of only four bits, and all instructions worked with only 4-bit operands. If we wished to calculate unsigned integers larger than $2^4 - 1 = 15_{10}$ on this machine, we would have to use more than one cell. For example, to store $27_{10} = 1B_6$ we would use two adjacent cells.

1	0	1	1	A
0	0	0	1	A + 1

Following the convention employed in the VAX-11, we placed the low-order bits in the first cell, and continued the high-order bits into the next cell. We can see this more clearly using a horizontal display:

A + 1					A			
0	0	0	1		1	0	1	1

This is called **double precision.** Although this concept can be extended for use with more than two cells (multiple precision), we will focus on double precision in this discussion. In practice, use of still larger numbers would probably be through the use of the **floating-point** representation to be discussed in Chapter 14.

Because our hypothetical computer's instructions work on 4-bit numbers, special programming is required to perform operations on the 8-bit double-precision numbers. This is accomplished by performing the operations on the high and low cells separately, accounting for carries or borrows across the cell boundary. We will demonstrate this by showing how to add two double-precision numbers. Although we are using 4-bit cells, the concept is the same regardless of the cell length.

Consider the addition for $A = 1D$ (29_{10}) to $B = 1A$ (26_{10}) with each stored in two 4-bit words. We can represent this diagrammatically as follows:

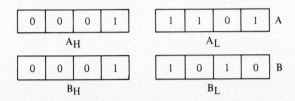

Here we use A_H and B_H to represent the cells used to store the high-order bits of each number, and A_L and B_L for the cells in which their low-order bits are stored. Now observe that the addition of A_L to B_L yields a 4-bit result and a carry:

$$
\begin{array}{rl}
B_L: & 1010 \\
A_L: & +1101 \\
B_L: & 1\leftarrow\ 0111
\end{array}
$$

Clearly the carry bit must be added to B_H:

$$
\begin{array}{rl}
B_H: & 0001 \\
\text{Carry:} & +0001 \\
B_H: & 0010
\end{array}
$$

To complete the operation, we add A_H to B_H:

$$
\begin{array}{rl}
B_H: & 0010 \\
A_H: & +0001 \\
B_H: & 0011
\end{array}
$$

The final result is:

which, when viewed as an 8-bit number, is 37_{16}.

These operations can be implemented in MACRO by use of the C condition code and the **AD**d **W**ith **C**arry (ADWC) instruction. This will yield a 64-bit result called a **quadword.** The ADWC instruction has the form:

```
ADWC    source,destination
```

which causes the *current* contents of the C condition code to be added to the destination, in addition to the source operand. Thus if there was a carry from the *previous* instruction, 1 will be added to the result.

Thus to implement double-precision addition on the VAX-11, we use the instructions:

```
ADDL    AL,BL    ; ADD LOW LONGWORDS
ADWC    AH,BH    ; ADD CARRY AND AH TO BH
```

This, of course, assumes that the high and low 32-bit segments of A and B were previously stored in locations labeled AH, AL, BH, and BL.

Normally, the low and high parts are stored in two successive longwords in main memory, and rather than assign a separate label to each part we refer to the high-order longword using an **expression operand.** For example,

```
ADDL    A,B      ; ADD LOW LONGWORDS
ADWC    A+4,B+4  ; ADD CARRY AND HIGH LONGWORDS
```

The assembler then calculates the correct PC-relative addresses for the high longwords. We will discuss expression operands more fully in Chapter 10.

Double-precision subtraction can be done similarly. To subtract B from A, we first subtract B_L from A_L. If a borrow was required from the A_H word, a 1 must be subtracted from A_H to reflect this fact. The C condition code will be set if such a borrow occurs, so this can be accomplished by use of the **SuB**tract **W**ith **C**arry instruction, SBWC. The double-precision subtraction is then accomplished by:

```
SUBL    A,B      ; SUBTRACT LOW LONGWORDS
SBWC    A+4,B+4  ; SUBTRACT BORROW AND HIGH
                 ; LONGWORDS
```

The result is then found in the two successive longwords B and B+4.

The double-precision subtraction algorithm depends on the fact that the C condition code (the carry bit) is set if there was a borrow *into* the MSB. In Section 6.6 it was explained that C was set if there was *not* a carry *out of* the MSB. These are merely two different ways of saying the same thing. That is, subtraction can be viewed either as negating the subtrahend and adding, or as actual binary subtraction. From the first point of view, subtracting a larger number from a smaller one generates a *carry out of* the MSB. From the second point of view, a *borrow into* the MSB is required. This is seen in the following example, using a 3-bit cell for convenience:

Negate and Add

101	subtrahend
011	two's complement of Subtrahend
<u>100</u>	minuend
111	difference

(No carry generated out of MSB, so C = 1.)

Binary Subtraction

1 →	100	minuend
	− <u>101</u>	subtrahend
	111	

(A borrow was required into the MSB, so C = 1.)

This observation leads some to call C the "borrow" bit in subtraction. However, we choose to call it the carry bit or the C condition code in any context. Regardless of terminology or points of view, the C bit is properly set in addition or subtraction so that the above instructions for double-precision addition and subtraction work.

Double-precision negation is sometimes required. To accomplish this, recall that negation is achieved by one's complementing the number and adding one. When doing this in double precision, we have to one's complement both parts, but the one is added only to the low part. However, when the one is added to the low part, we have to account for the possible carry into the high part. This suggests the sequence:

```
MCOML   A+4,A+4 ; ONE'S COMPLEMENT HIGH LONGWORD
MNEGL   A,A     ; NEGATE LOW LONGWORD
add 1 to A + 4 if negation caused a carry
```

However, the problem is that the C condition code is *cleared* rather than set, due to a carry that is caused by an MNEGL operation, as in subtraction. Therefore, to accomplish the desired effect, we *add* 1 to A+4 beforehand, and then *subtract* the C condition code. This suggests the following instructions:

```
MCOML   A+4,A+4
INCL    A+4
MNEGL   A,A
SBWC    #0,A+4
```

However, noting that complementing and incrementing is just negation, we finally arrive at:

```
MNEGL   A+4,A+4
MNEGL   A,A
SBWC    #0,A+4
```

for double-precision negation. Note that the *order* of these instructions is very important. Carrying out these operations by hand with a few double-precision numbers will show more clearly how they work.

When double-precision operations are done, the storage allocated for the double-precision operands must also be doubled. VAX-11 MACRO, therefore, has directives appropriate for these data types, which are called **quadwords.** To allocate storage and initialize A and B in the preceding examples we would write:

```
A:   .QUAD   39642
B:   .QUAD   ^XA1F361BC7915
```

Here we are reserving eight bytes for A and storing $9ADA_{16}$ (39642_{10}) in the lowest-order bytes. Eight bytes are also reserved for B, and we use the **radix control** symbol for hexadecimal, ^X, to allow specification of the initial value directly in hexadecimal. This large number requires six of the eight reserved bytes. If we wished to reserve storage without initialization we would write:

```
C:   .BLKQ   1
```

which would reserve one quadword.

6.13 | Multiplication and Division

Multiplication and division are significantly different from addition and subtraction. Indeed, many small computers do not have instructions for multiplication and division. If this is the case, the programmer must carry out these operations by use of the more primitive addition and subtraction instructions. This is called "software" multiply and divide. Newer or larger computers such as the VAX-11 are usually equipped with multiplication and division instructions along with instructions for addition and subtraction. These are called "hardware" multiply and divide, since these extra instructions are provided through the use of special additional circuits.

In the following paragraphs, we will discuss both software and hardware multiply and divide. The former is instructive even though hardware multiply and divide are available on your VAX-11 machine.

6.13.1 Multiplication

Software multiplication can best be explained in terms of a simple example.

EXAMPLE 6.3 Suppose we wish to multiply 3_{10} by 5_{10}. In binary, "longhand" multiplication takes the following form:

$$
\begin{array}{r}
0\,1\,1 \\
\times\,1\,0\,1 \\
\hline
0\,1\,1 \\
0\,0\,0 \\
0\,1\,1 \\
\hline
0\,1\,1\,1\,1 \\
\end{array}
$$

Observe that each nonzero partial product is just the first multiplicand shifted to the left. Also note that whenever a zero-bit occurs in the second multiplicand, the partial product is zero and need not be added. This suggests the following algorithm:

1. Clear the result register.
2. Rotate the *second* multiplicand one bit to the right.
3. If the bit shifted out at the right (and into the left) was a 1, add the first multiplicand to the result.
4. Shift the first multiplicand one bit to the left.
5. Repeat from Step 2 until all bits in the second multiplicand have been examined.

This algorithm is expressed as a MACRO program in Figure 6.7. Observe that the algorithm works only for 32-bit positive integers. Each time the WHILE loop is executed, the least significant bit (LSB) of the second multiplicand is rotated into the sign bit where it can be checked using the BEQL instruction. If it is zero, the first multiplicand is not added to the result. After addition, the second multiplicand is left-shifted arithmetically, analogous to the way we perform longhand multiplication. The loop is repeated

```
            .TITLE MULTIPLY
;
;           MULTIPLICATION BY SHIFTING
;           INPUT:
;                 R1 =FIRST MULTIPLICAND
;                 R2 =SECOND MULTIPLICAND
;           OUTPUT:
;                 R0 =PRODUCT
;
            .ENTRY  START,0
            CLRL    R0              ;CLEAR RESULT REGISTER
            MOVL    #32,R3          ;INITIALIZE LCV
WHILE:      TSTL    R3              ;DO WHILE MORE BITS IN
            BEQL    DONE            ;  2ND MULTIPLICAND,
            ROTL    #-1,R2,R2       ;MOVE LSB TO SIGN BIT
            BGEQ    L1              ;SKIP IF IT WAS A 0
            ADDL    R1,R0           ;ELSE ADD R1 TO RESULT
L1:         ASHL    #1,R1,R1        ;SHIFT R1
            DECL    R3              ;UPDATE LCV
            BRB     WHILE           ;END OF WHILE LOOP
DONE:       HALT
            .END    START
```

FIGURE 6.7/Software multiplication using shifting

32 times because there are 32 bits in the second multiplicand. A number of improvements are possible. We should add instructions to branch to an appropriate error action if overflow occurs in the multiplication process. This program could be placed in a larger program where multiplication is required. In a later chapter we will see that it could also be written as a subroutine for more convenient usage.

The VAX-11 computer has the multiply instruction MULL for hardware multiply. This instruction has two operands. For example,

```
MULL   S,R3
```

will multiply the contents of the memory location reserved for S by the contents of R3, placing the result into R3. The only complication involved in using MULL is the fact that the result may exceed 32 bits; we saw this above when we obtained a 5-bit product by multiplying two 3-bit numbers.

If there is any reason to believe that the result will not fit in a longword, the Extended **MUL**tiply can be used to produce a 64-bit result. For example,

```
EMUL   R1,R2,#0,RES
```

This is a four-operand instruction. The first two operands are the multiplicands, and the fourth is the result. The third operand is an *additive* term. Thus in the preceding example we multiplied R1 by R2, added zero, and placed the result in a quadword labeled RES.

Care must be taken when using EMUL with a register as the result operand. Because the result is 64 bits while the register is only 32 bits long, the *next* register will be overwritten. For example,

```
EMUL   R1,R2,#0,R3
```

puts a quadword result in R3 and R4.

The translation of the MULL instruction is the opcode C4, followed by two operand specifiers in the normal format. EMUL has an opcode of 7A and four operand specifiers. Both instructions always clear the C condition code. MULL sets the V condition code to indicate a product that exceeds 32-bits in length, while EMUL always clears the V bit because no overflow is possible.

6.13.2 Division

Like multiplication, division can be done with either hardware or an algorithm which uses more fundamental instructions. We will first examine software division algorithms, and then the divide instructions provided by the VAX-11.

Division algorithms vary in complexity and efficiency. The simplest algorithm, namely, repeated subtraction of the divisor from the dividend, is also the least efficient. Because of its simplicity, we will look at it first. To see how it works, consider the division of 27_{10} by 5_{10}. The quotient can be viewed as the number of times that 5_{10} can be subtracted from 27_{10} *without* a negative result. Performing the operations in binary, we have:

$$
\begin{array}{rl}
11011 & \\
-101 & (1) \\
\hline
10110 & \\
-101 & (2) \\
\hline
10001 & \\
-101 & (3) \\
\hline
01100 & \\
-101 & (4) \\
\hline
00111 & \\
-101 & (5 = \text{quotient}) \\
\hline
00010 & (\text{remainder}) \\
-101 & (6) \\
\hline
11001 & (\text{negative result})
\end{array}
$$

By this process we get the answer 5_{10} with a remainder of 2_{10}. A MACRO program employing this method is shown in Figure 6.8. We have simplified the program by assuming that the dividend and divisors are positive integers. This limitation can be removed by checking R1 and R2 prior to the division. A more fundamental shortcoming of the successive subtraction method is its inefficiency for large dividend and small divisor. In this case the number of subtractions can be quite large. Consider, for example, division of 65535_{10} by 1_{10} using this algorithm.

```
            .TITLE DIVISION ONE
;
;
;          DIVISION BY SUCCESSIVE SUBTRACTION
;
;                  DIVIDEND  = R1  (POSITIVE)
;                  DIVISOR   = R2  (POSITIVE)
;                  QUOTIENT  = R0
;                  REMAINDER = R1
;
            .ENTRY START,0
            CLRL    R0              ;INITIALIZE QUOTIENT
            BRB     WHILE           ;
LOOP:       SUBL    R2,R1           ;SUBTRACT DIVISOR
            INCL    R0              ;  AND INCREMENT QUOTIENT
WHILE:      TSTL    R1              ;LOOP WHILE REMAINDER
            BGEQ    LOOP            ;  IS POSITIVE
            ADDL    R2,R1           ;CORRECT FOR
            DECL    R0              ;  OVER-SUBTRACTION
            HALT
            .END    START
```

FIGURE 6.8/Division of positive integers using successive subtraction

A much more efficient division algorithm can be developed using the shift instructions. One frequently used algorithm is similar to "longhand" division used in decimal arithmetic. To see how this works, consider division of 27_{10} by 5_{10}, carried out in binary in a manner similar to the familiar decimal division technique:

$$
\begin{array}{r}
00101 \\
101)\overline{11011} \\
\underline{101} \\
00111 \\
\underline{00101} \\
00010 \quad \text{(Remainder)}
\end{array}
$$

Study of this technique shows that we determine if the divisor can be subtracted from the MSB. If it cannot be subtracted, we place a 0 in the quotient at the corresponding bit position, and then consider the *two* most significant bits. In the example, this continues until the divisor is compared to the three most significant bits of the dividend. Because 101 *can* be subtracted from 110, we place a 1 in the quotient and carry out the subtraction. The process then repeats until there are no further bits in the divisor. The remainder is the outcome of the last subtraction.

This process can be implemented in MACRO by using shifting operations. The strategy is to use two longwords to hold the dividend. We choose R0 and R1, with the highest-order bits stored in R1. Thus R1 contains those bits from which we try to subtract the divisor at each step. After each subtraction or attempted subtraction we execute a double-precision arithmetic shift left, bringing the next MSB into R1.

The following example will clarify this method.

EXAMPLE 6.4   We use a 6-bit cell length for convenience, and the same dividend and divisor as before. The result is developed in R5. The results of successive left shifts and subtractions are shown below:

	R1	R0	R5
Initial:	000000	011011	000000
Shift:	000000	110110	000000
Shift:	000001	101100	000000
Shift:	000011	011000	000000
Shift:	000110	110000	000000
Subtract:	000001	110000	000001
Shift:	000011	100000	000010
Shift:	000111	000000	000100
Subtract:	000010	000000	000101

In this table, "shift" means that a double-precision shift is done on (R1,R0), *and* R5 is shifted. After four shifts, we see that R1 is larger than the divisor R2, so we subtract R2 from R1 and increment R5. After two more shifts, R1 is again greater than R2, and we subtract R2 again, and again increment R5. The process stops after six shifts, since this guarantees that all bits in the dividend have gone into R1. Note that shifting R5 each time (R1,R0) is shifted ensures that each new quotient bit, either zero or one, gets put in the right position. It is evident from this example that the quotient (5_{10}) is left in R5, and the remainder resides in R1.

This procedure is implemented in MACRO in Figure 6.9. We have added a preliminary check which will determine if the divide will result in a value larger than could be represented as a 32-bit positive integer. If this occurs, the calculation is skipped.

Note that we have used the quadword version of the arithmetic shift instruction to accomplish the double-precision shift. This instruction, ASHQ, shifts a 64-bit cell. If the source operand is Rn, the register Rn + 1 is also involved in the shift.

The program in Figure 6.9 is restricted to pairs of positive integers whose quotients are less than or equal to $2^{32} - 1$. It can be modified to work on positive or negative two's complement numbers by performing a preliminary check on the signs of the inputs. One method would be to set an auxiliary register to 1 if either, but not both, of the operands is negative, and then negate those operands that are negative. The division would then be carried out as positive integers, and the result would be negated if the auxiliary register were set. The overflow check should also be modified to reflect the smaller range of two's complement numbers.

Before leaving this algorithm, let us consider an improvement that would not require use of R5. Observe from the earlier example that the low-order bits in R0 are 0 due to the shifting. In effect, the low-order positions in R0 are therefore unused as the solution progresses. This observation suggests that the quotient could be allowed to develop in R0; that is, we could increment R0 instead of R5, and delete the ASHL on R5, saving

```
        .TITLE DIVISION TWO
;
;
;       INPUT:
;           (R1,R0)= (HIGH,LOW) LONGWORDS OF DIVIDEND (POSITIVE)
;           R2      = DIVISOR (POSITIVE)
;       INTERMEDIATE USAGE:
;           R1      = REMAINDER
;           R3      = LOOP CONTROL VARIABLE
;           R5      = QUOTIENT
;       OUTPUT:
;           R0      = QUOTIENT
;           R1      = REMAINDER
;
        .ENTRY START,0
        CMPL    R2,R1           ;CHECK FOR POTENTIAL
        BLEQU   OVERFL          ;   OVERFLOW OF RESULT
        MOVL    #32,R3          ;INITIALIZE LCV
LOOP:   ASHL    #1,R5,R5        ;SHIFT RESULT
        ASHQ    #1,R0,R0        ;DOUBLE PRECISION SHIFT
                                ;   OF DIVIDEND
        CMPL    R1,R2           ;SEE IF DIVISOR CAN
        BLSSU   ENDLP           ;   BE SUBTRACTED
        SUBL    R2,R1           ;SUBTRACT DIVISOR
        INCL    R5              ;PUT 1-BIT IN QUOTIENT
ENDLP:  SOBGTR  R3,LOOP         ;LOOP IF MORE BITS
        MOVL    R5,R0           ;PLACE QUOTIENT INTO
                                ;   DESIGNATED REGISTER
OVERFL: HALT
        .END    START
```

FIGURE 6.9/Efficient software divide using shifting

one instruction and one register. In some instances, small improvements like this lead to others. Note that the final MOVL could also be eliminated.

Software division is not necessary on the VAX-11 because two hardware divide instructions are available. The normal hardware division instruction has the assembly language mnemonic of:

```
    DIVL    S,D
```

where S is the divisor and D is the dividend, which becomes the quotient. Both operands are assumed to be two's complement longword integers: The sign of the quotient is determined from the operands in the expected way.

There is also an **Extended DIV**ide instruction, **EDIV,** that is useful in conjunction with EMUL because it allows a double-precision (quadword) dividend. Also, EDIV produces a remainder that is unavailable when DIVL is used. Consider the following example:

```
        EDIV    #2,A,Q,REM
            .
            .
            .
        HALT
A:      .QUAD   4000000001
Q:      .BLKL   1
REM:    .BLKL   1
```

Here we are dividing a number too large to fit into a longword by 2. The result, 2000000000_{10}, is stored in the longword labeled Q, and the remainder, 1, will be placed in the longword labeled REM. Note that the remainder carries the sign of the quotient.

The opcodes for DIVL and EDIV are C6 and 7B, respectively. In the translation, the DIVL opcode is followed by two operand specifiers, while EDIV has four operand specifiers. Note that the second operand of EDIV must be a quadword.

Both DIVL and EDIV always clear the C condition code. The V condition code is set to 1 after either instruction if overflow occurred, or if the divisor was zero.

6.14 | Summary

This chapter dealt with numbers and operations on numbers in VAX-11 MACRO. First we discussed the impact of using the **two's complement system** as a means of representing both positive and negative numbers on the VAX-11. Although other systems are possible, the two's complement system is heavily favored by the VAX-11 instruction set.

Condition codes were introduced and related to arithmetic operations. These codes, N, Z, V, and C, are stored in the four least significant bits in the **processor status word (PSW)**. We saw that each of these has its own special uses in checking the outcome of instructions. In general, N is set when a negative result is produced, and Z is set if a zero result is produced. C and V serve several functions, but in general indicate a **carry** (unsigned overflow) or **signed overflow,** respectively. A group of branching instructions, **BVC, BVS, BCC,** and **BCS,** is available for checking the C and V bits so that appropriate action can be taken if overflow occurs. We found that the condition codes provide a means for evaluating signed and unsigned branching conditions. We saw that the difference between two 32-bit numbers will have two different interpretations, depending on whether the numbers are viewed to be unsigned integers or two's complement integers. The VAX-11, therefore, has a set of conditional branch instructions for **unsigned comparisons** (BGTRU, BLSSU, BLEQU, BGEQU, BEQLU, and BNEQU) and a different set for **signed comparisons** (BGTR, BLSS, BLEQ, BGEQ, BEQL, and BNEQ). These instructions use one or more of the condition codes to determine whether or not to branch. It was also observed that condition codes are set or cleared by many instructions. A conditional branch will react according to their *current* state, regardless of which instruction was responsible for establishing the state. In passing, we noted that the conditional branch instructions have a limited transfer range, but they can be used in conjunction with the BRW instruction to transfer to more distant addresses.

In order to expand our arithmetic capability, we introduced several other new instructions. These included **MNEGL, ASHL, ASHQ, ROTL, MULL, EMUL, DIVL,** and **EDIV. MNEGL** performs a **two's complement operation** on its operand, producing a value of equal magnitude but opposite sign, and places the result in the destination operand. The arithmetic shift instructions **ASHL** and **ASHQ** shift the bit patterns in longwords and quadwords, respectively, producing the useful arithmetic operations of multiply and divide by powers of two. The rotate instruction, **ROTL,** also shifts the bit pattern, but in this case rotates the bits out of one end of the longword and into the other.

The shift instructions provide a means for efficient **multiplication and division.** The software multiplication and division algorithms presented provide examples of these newly introduced instructions. However, most modern computers have "**hardward multiply and divide,**" represented by the MULL, EMUL, DIVL, and EDIV instructions on the VAX-11. These are more efficient and convenient.

Chapter 6 also introduced the concept of **double-precision representation.** Here, two cells are used, providing twice as many bits to represent a single integer. This allows much larger integer values in a MACRO program. We noted that special steps are necessary to perform addition, subtraction, or negation of double-precision numbers. This required dealing with the high and low cells separately, and accounting for carrys or borrows across the cell boundary with the **add with carry (ADWC)** or **subtract with carry (SBWC)** instructions.

We also introduced two new assembler directives for use with double-precision operations. The **.QUAD** directive reserves space and initializes a quadword (64 bits), while **.BLKQ** just reserves space for the quadword.

6.15 | Exercises

6.1 On a separate sheet of paper, create a table with the branch instructions BGTR, BGTRU, BLEQ, BLEQU, BGEQ, BGEQU, BLSS, BLSSU, BEQL, BEQLU, BNEQ, BNEQU, BVS, BCS, BVC, and BCC across the top, and the letters a, b, c, . . . , j down the side. In each position of this table, indicate with X if the branch will occur after a CMPL A,B instruction for each pair of A and B given below. All values are hexadecimal.

	A	B
(a)	00001F52	00001F52
(b)	FFFFFF82	0000007E
(c)	00058BA	0000020E
(d)	FFFFFFC5	FFFFFF8B
(e)	000009A0	00001E97
(f)	FFFD668C	FFFFFC29
(g)	80000000	00000001
(h)	7FFFFFFF	80000000
(i)	00000001	80000000
(j)	80000000	7FFFFFFF

6.2 Determine the N, Z, V, and C condition codes after CMPL A,B is performed for each of the pairs of A and B given in Exercise 6.1.

6.3 Repeat Exercise 6.1, indicating branches after a SUBL B,A instruction.

6.4 What is the contents of R0 after execution of the following instructions:

```
MOVL      #-1,R0
ASHL      #-4,R0
ROTL      #4,R0
```

6.5 Write a program to count the number of 1-bits (i.e., the number of bits that contain the digit 1) in a 32-bit number that is stored in R1. For example, the number 5E6B has ten 1-bits. Execute the program using the Symbolic Debugger and demonstrate that it works.

6.6 Revise the division algorithm given in Figure 6.9 to work with positive or negative two's complement numbers for dividend and divisor. Execute the program using the Symbolic Debugger, and verify that it works. Show cases that cause overflow also.

6.7 Write a program that will sort an array of positive and negative two's complement numbers into ascending order. Demonstrate its operation using the Symbolic Debugger.

6.8 Devise a program that adds two 96-bit two's complement numbers. Demonstrate your program using the Symbolic Debugger. Try it with the hexadecimal numbers:

00000001FFFFFFFE10000000

and:

0000000FFFFFFFFFFF0000000

6.9 Verify the rules for detection of two's complement overflow by showing numerical examples for each of the four cases (S^+, M^+), (S^-, M^-), (S^-, M^+), and (S^+, M^-).

6.10 Using the branch instructions, devise VAX-11 MACRO code to branch to L1 after SUBL S,M whenever M ≥ S, even if overflow occurs.

6.11 The instructions:

```
BICPSW    I^#^B1111    ; CLEARS NZVC
BISPSW    R0           ; SETS NZVC
```

set the condition codes to the values of bits <3:0> in R0. Using these instructions, devise a program that lets you test the branching conditions for the branch instructions as set forth in Table 6.3. Then test BGTR, BLEQ, and BLSSU. You may use either the Symbolic Debugger or .GETHEX and .PUTHEX for input/output.

6.12 Write a program that accepts two unsigned hexadecimal integers and computes their product using three methods: shifting software multiply, MULL, and EMUL. Use either the Symbolic Debugger or .GETHEX and .PUTHEX to input the numbers and show the results.

6.13 Write a program that accepts two unsigned hexadecimal integers and computes their quotient using three methods: shifting software divide, DIVL, and EDIV. Use either the Symbolic Debugger or .GETHEX and .PUTHEX to input the numbers and show the results. Include the remainder in the results of the software and EDIV cases.

7

Character Data and Byte Operations

7.1 | Overview

A great deal of the information processed by computers is composed of strings of alphabetic, numeric, and other character data. Examples of this include lists of mailing addresses, parts lists for inventory control, and programming language processors. Even information that is essentially numeric in nature (i.e., produced by or used in arithmetic operations) must be converted to equivalent character representations in order to be communicated to or from devices, such as printers or terminals, that are external to the computer. The importance of processing **character data** leads us to turn our attention now to the facilities of the VAX-11 and MACRO for handling information in this form.

We begin by describing how character data is represented digitally, namely, with the American Standard Code for Information Interchange, usually called **ASCII** (pronounced "ask'-ee"). Through this standard, each symbol used in representing printed information, as well as certain nonprinting **control characters,** is assigned a 7-bit code. We then introduce several new MACRO **directives used to store (or reserve space for) bytes** of character data in the main memory.

The 7-bit ASCII character codes fit conveniently into the 8-bit bytes on the VAX-11. A part of the chapter is therefore devoted to describing MACRO **instructions that operate on bytes.** We will see that most of the instructions previously introduced for operations on longwords have versions that perform the same functions on bytes. These instructions are essential for efficient programming when the data is character in nature. Moreover, there are occasions where 8-bit integers are an appropriate numeric data type, so byte instructions are also important in arithmetic contexts. After our discussion of operations on individual bytes, we will study the VAX-11 instructions for **manipulation of strings of characters.** Finally, this chapter introduces a number of instructions that enable the programmer to **examine or manipulate individual bits** in main memory cells and registers.

All of these topics will be important when we take up input and output in Chapter 8.

7.2 | Character Codes

Digital computers, as we saw earlier, are designed to store and manipulate binary information, i.e., patterns of 1's and 0's. If we wish to use such a machine to process character information, it is therefore necessary to use binary representations or "codes" for the characters to be processed. For example, the alphabet can be represented as follows:

Character	Binary Code
A	1000001
B	1000010
C	1000011
.	.
.	.
.	.

Then when we wish to store an "A" (upper-case), we can put the corresponding bit pattern into a byte storage cell, as shown here:

7	6	5	4	3	2	1	0
0	1	0	0	0	0	0	1

Conversely, when this bit pattern is *found* in a byte, we can interpret it as an upper-case "A". Note that there is nothing inherent in this bit pattern which *compels* us to interpret it in this way; it could equally well be interpreted as a representation of the positive integer 65_{10}. It is the *context,* i.e., how the data is used, that determines what it means.

7.3 | The American Standard Code for Information Interchange (ASCII)

Many possible codes can be used to represent characters. The only requirement is that there be enough bit patterns to represent each character needed. The character encodings used in the preceding examples are from a system called **ASCII,** which stands for the American Standard Code for Information Interchange. ASCII has been defined as a 7-bit code, so that there are $2^7 = 128_{10}$ unique bit patterns or codes, and 128_{10} characters can therefore be represented. These codes have been assigned to the alphabetic, numeric, and other characters as shown in Table 7.1. In this table we follow the customary practice of giving the hexadecimal and decimal representations of the binary codes. Internally, they are of course represented in binary.

In Table 7.1 there are 95 characters that appear in printed media. These are the so-called "printing characters" that include 26 upper-case letters, 26 lower-case letters, 32 punctuation characters (e.g., ".", "+", "(", etc.), 10 numeric characters, and

Table 7.1/The ASCII Codes

Hex Code	Decimal Code	Char	Hex Code	Decimal Code	Char	Hex Code	Decimal Code	Char	Hex Code	Decimal Code	Char
00	0	NUL	20	32	SP	40	64	@	60	96	`
01	1	SOH	21	33	!	41	65	A	61	97	a
02	2	STX	22	34	"	42	66	B	62	98	b
03	3	ETX	23	35	#	43	67	C	63	99	c
04	4	EOT	24	36	$	44	68	D	64	100	d
05	5	ENQ	25	37	%	45	69	E	65	101	e
06	6	ACK	26	38	&	46	70	F	66	102	f
07	7	BEL	27	39	'	47	71	G	67	103	g
08	8	BS	28	40	(	48	72	H	68	104	h
09	9	HT	29	41	)	49	73	I	69	105	i
0A	10	LF	2A	42	*	4A	74	J	6A	106	j
0B	11	VT	2B	43	+	4B	75	K	6B	107	k
0C	12	FF	2C	44	,	4C	76	L	6C	108	l
0D	13	CR	2D	45	–	4D	77	M	6D	109	m
0E	14	SO	2E	46	.	4E	78	N	6E	110	n
0F	15	SI	2F	47	/	4F	79	O	6F	111	o
10	16	DLE	30	48	0	50	80	P	70	112	p
11	17	DC1	31	49	1	51	81	Q	71	113	q
12	18	DC2	32	50	2	52	82	R	72	114	r
13	19	DC3	33	51	3	53	83	S	73	115	s
14	20	DC4	34	52	4	54	84	T	74	116	t
15	21	NAK	35	53	5	55	85	U	75	117	u
16	22	SYN	36	54	6	56	86	V	76	118	v
17	23	ETB	37	55	7	57	87	W	77	119	w
18	24	CAN	38	56	8	58	88	X	78	120	x
19	25	EM	39	57	9	59	89	Y	79	121	y
1A	26	SUB	3A	58	:	5A	90	Z	7A	122	z
1B	27	ESC	3B	59	;	5B	91	[	7B	123	{
1C	28	FS	3C	60	<	5C	92	\	7C	124		
1D	29	GS	3D	61	=	5D	93	]	7D	125	}
1E	30	RS	3E	62	>	5E	94	^	7E	126	~
1F	31	US	3F	63	?	5F	95	—	7F	127	DEL(RUB)

the blank character. The remaining 33 codes have no printed equivalent, but have special significance to the equipment that transmits, receives, prints, or generates data. Thirty-two of these are called the "control characters" and are represented in the third column of the table by their standard designations. An example of a control character is LF, which stands for linefeed and has a hexadecimal code of 0A. The very last character in the table, DEL, is also nonprinting. Its special characteristic is that the 7-bit code has all bits set. On early teletype devices that recorded characters as rows of holes punched in a paper tape, this made it ideal for deleting another character by overstriking. Although this property does not have the same importance on current devices, the DEL continues to be used as an error-correcting character in many systems. For example, on the VMS operating system, DEL moves the terminal cursor backwards and deletes the previous character. It is sometimes called the ''rub-out'' character.

The ASCII codes have several properties that make them convenient for manipulation in the computer. First, observe that the codes for the numeric characters ''0'', ''1'', ''2'', . . . , ''9'' are sequential hexadecimal (or binary) numbers: 30, 31, 32, . . . , 39. The importance of this lies in the fact that the *character code* for a digit can be obtained by using arithmetic operations on the numerical value of the digit. For example, if we have the number 4:

00000100

and we add hexadecimal 30, we get:

00110100

which is 34 in hexadecimal. From Table 7.1 we see that this is the ASCII code for the numeric character ''4''. Because of this property of the code, 30_{16} is called the ''ASCII base'' for the decimal digits 0 through 9. Similarly, 37_{16} is the ASCII base for the hexadecimial digits A through F. When we discuss output of hexadecimal and decimal numbers in Chapter 8 we will see that this is done by computing the *numeric value* of each digit and adding the ASCII base. Below we will see that the ASCII codes are then sent to the printer, which responds by printing the appropriate character.

Another useful property is that each successive alpha code is one greater than the last. This means that sorting into alphabetic order can be done using arithmetic comparisons. We see that all characters as shown in Table 7.1 are in a ''natural'' order with regard to their ASCII codes. This is called the ''collating sequence'' for the character set.

Also observe that character codes in a particular row of the table bear a simple relationship to one another. For example, the lower-case ''a'' has a code of 61_{16}, the upper-case ''A'' is 41_{16}, ''!'' is 21_{16}, and the SOH control character is 01_{16}. This implies that changing from lower- to upper-case alpha characters can be done by simply subtracting 20_{16}. Equivalently, the fifth bit of the lower-case code can just be cleared to get the upper-case code. Similarly, each control character code can be obtained by clearing the fifth and sixth bits of the printing characters in the same row. In Section 7.5 we will see that this makes it easy to generate control characters from the keyboard.

7.4 Storage of ASCII

Because ASCII is a 7-bit code, we can store one code in each byte. Note that the 7-bit code leaves an unused bit at the left in each byte. Sometimes this bit is used as a means of detecting an error (see Parity, Section 8.7). In this discussion, however, this bit is assumed to be unused and always 0.

As an example of ASCII storage, consider the storage of the character string "HI THERE!!" in main memory. If we arbitrarily choose to store this character string beginning at location 0200 we have:

Character	Hexadecimal	Binary	Address
"H"	48	01001000	0200
"I"	49	01001001	0201
" "	20	00100000	0202
"T"	54	01010100	0203
"H"	48	01001000	0204
"E"	45	01000101	0205
"R"	52	01010010	0206
"E"	45	01000101	0207
"!"	21	00100001	0208
"!"	21	00100001	0209

Observe that the leftmost characters in the string are stored first in memory. This is just the reverse of the way integers are stored, which is with the rightmost digits stored first. Although you could store strings in any order, it is customary to store character strings in this order on the VAX-11. This is because we normally view the leftmost character in a string as the "first" one, so it should logically be placed first in memory. Later we will see that special MACRO directives and VAX-11 instructions for manipulating character strings assume this order.

7.5 | ASCII, External Devices, and Control Characters

Let us now examine the use of ASCII external to the computer, i.e., in the peripheral devices. The peripheral devices, such as terminals and printers, have character codes *incorporated into their designs*. For example, an ASCII printer is designed to print the symbol "A" when it receives the bit pattern 1000001, "B" when it receives 1000010, and so on. Conversely, an ASCII keyboard will generate the bit pattern 1000001 when an upper-case "A" is typed using the shift and "A" keys.

On a "full" ASCII keyboard, each of the 128_{10} different codes, including the control characters, can be generated by some combination of one or more keys. Some of the **control characters,** such as linefeed (LF) and carriage return (CR), are generated by single keys. Any control character, however, can be generated by depressing the control key (CTRL) and the alpha key in the corresponding row in Table 7.1. For example, the backspace character BS (08_{16}) can be generated with the CLTL and h keys. The CTRL key has the effect of clearing the fifth and sixth bits of the code generated by the alpha key. For this reason control characters without assigned keys are often represented in the form CTRL-h or ^h. While the key(s) required to generate a particular code may vary from one keyboard to another, the meanings and usages of the codes are standardized to a large extent. For example, a 07_{16} code (00001111_2) will ring the bell on the device, provided one has been installed.

Here we qualify the device as "an ASCII device" because, as noted above, other code systems are possible. One other widely used code is EBCDIC, meaning Extended Binary Coded Decimal Interchange Code. Many terminals, particularly those manufactured by IBM, use these codes. When such a terminal is used in conjunction with an ASCII-oriented computer such as the VAX-11, the character codes must be translated as they go to and from the computer. Modern operating systems incorporate software that automatically detects the character codes generated by the terminal and performs needed translation without the knowledge of the user.

Some computers use special, nonstandard codes to represent character data *internally*. That is, the data may be received from an external device as ASCII or EBCDIC, and translated to a different code for internal representation. Many Control Data Corporation computers are in this category.

7.6 | Character- (Byte-) Oriented Directives

It will be recalled that we used assembler directives to reserve space for numbers, or to initialize longwords of memory with numbers. There are corresponding directives to initialize bytes of memory with character codes.

Two frequently used directives are **.ASCII** and its companion **.ASCIZ.** These are used to initialize successive bytes in memory to the ASCII codes for character strings. For example,

```
.ASCII /Computer 67/
```

will initialize eleven bytes of memory to the ASCII codes for the characters in the string "Computer 67". The first character code is stored in the *next available byte*, after the assembler has translated the preceding instruction or directive. For example, the sequence:

```
        HALT
MSG1:   .ASCII /Computer 67/
```

will generate the following memory contents. Assume that HALT is located at address 0220.

Hexadecimal	Address
00	0220
43	0221
6F	0222
6D	0223
70	0224
75	0225
74	0226
65	0227
72	0228
20	0229
36	022A
37	022B

The MACRO assembler listing shows the ASCII codes in horizontal format and right-to-left order. Thus we would see:

Memory Contents	Offset Address	Assembly Code
00	0220	HALT
37 36 20 72 65 74 75 70 6D 6F 43	0221	.ASCII/Computer 67/

The ASCII codes for the characters are as shown in Table 7.1.

To emphasize that .ASCII loads character codes beginning in the next available *byte,* let us consider the sequence:

```
HALT
.ASCII /VAX/
.ASCII /-11/
```

This generates:

Memory Contents	Offset Address	Assembly Code
00	0220	HALT
58 41 56	0221	.ASCII/VAX/
31 31 2D	0224	.ASCII/-11/

Here we see that the "−" (2D) is stored immediately after the "X" from the first string. This example also shows that long messages can be built up using successive .ASCII directives.

The **.ASCIZ** directive works exactly like .ASCII except that the *null* character 00 is added after the last character in the given string. For example,

Memory Contents	Offset Address	Assembly Code
00	0220	HALT
00 23 2A 2B	0221	.ASCIZ/+*#/

The importance of .ASCIZ is that the null character 00 can be used to mark or flag the end of a message. Indeed, it is so used by the routine for printing strings of ASCII characters described in Chapter 8.

Another character storage directive in MACRO is **.ASCIC.** This directive stores the number of characters in a string, i.e., the string length, in a byte preceding the string. For example,

Memory Contents	Offset Address	Assembly Code
43 42 41 03	0220	.ASCIC/ABC/

This is a convenience because the length of the string is frequently needed in character string manipulation.

In these examples we have arbitrarily used the slash "/" to mark the beginning and end of the string, i.e., to **delimit** the string. If the "/" character is to be *part* of the string to be stored, then it cannot be used as the delimiter. In such a case, use any character that is not otherwise used in the string as a delimiter, e.g., /, *, ., ", etc. As an example, consider:

```
.ASCII *4/3*
```

where we use "*" as the delimiter because the string "4/3" contains a "/".

It is often necessary to store the character codes for the nonprinting characters, for example, linefeed, carriage return, or bell. There are several ways of doing this. One way is by using the .ASCII or .ASCIZ directives, in which case the *decimal codes* are enclosed in $<$ . . . $>$ symbols. For example, to store linefeed, carriage return, and bell, followed by a null, we would write:

Memory Contents	Offset Address	Assembly Code
00 07 0D 0A	0220	.ASCIZ<10><13><7>

This can be combined with a string enclosed in delimiters, as follows:

```
.ASCIZ /RING BELL/<7>
```

Note that when this is done we put the $<7>$ *outside* of the string delimiters; otherwise, the $<7>$ would be considered as a string of three characters rather than the desired control character.

When we were working with numeric data, we sometimes found it necessary to set aside *n* longwords of memory using the .BLKL *n* directive. The corresponding directive to reserve one or more bytes is **.BLKB *n*.** For example, to set aside 10_{10} bytes we use:

```
.BLKB 10
```

When the assembler encounters this directive, it skips the next 10_{10} bytes before assigning an address to the succeeding instruction or directive. Note that this directive *does not* store specific values in these bytes, but merely reserves them for future use. Typically, one would use .BLKB expecting the *program* to generate results to be stored in the reserved bytes, perhaps using the byte-oriented instructions discussed later in this chapter.

In passing, observe that the directives:

```
.BLKB 40    and    .BLKL 10
```

do exactly the same thing. They are identical in effect because a block of 10_{10} sequential longwords is equivalent to 40_{10} sequential bytes. Nonetheless, it is good practice to use .BLKB to reserve space eventually to be used for byte-sized data (characters or 8-bit integers), while .BLKL should be used for allocating space for longword data types.

There is also a directive called **.BYTE** that corresponds to the .LONG directive. This can be used to initialize bytes to *numeric* values. For example,

Memory Contents	Offset Address	Assembly Code
01 01 01 01	0220	.BYTE 1,1,1,1

Observe that exactly the same contents would be obtained as a result of using the
.LONG directive:

Memory Contents	Offset Address	Assembly Code
01010101	0220	.LONG 16843009

However, it is better programming practice to use the directives that match the data
type. Obviously, the first example above is much clearer than the second if the intent
is to initialize four consecutive bytes to 1.

7.7 | Byte-Oriented Instructions

Most of the VAX-11 instructions that we have discussed in the context of
longword data also have forms that operate on byte-length data. The assembly mnemonics
for the byte-oriented instructions are like the longword instructions, but with a B suffix
instead of an L. For example,

```
MOVB   A,B
```

will move the contents of the byte whose address is A to the byte whose address is B.
Other byte-oriented instructions include CLRB, INCB, DECB, MNEGB, TSTB, and
CMPB, as well as the arithmetic ADDB, SUBB, MULB, and DIVB instructions. (Table
A.1 shows all instructions and indicates which have byte forms.)

The byte instructions perform the same operations as their word-oriented counterparts.
The major difference is that with byte instructions only eight bits are operated on instead
of 32. This requires that special care be taken when using register addressing with
byte instructions. For example, if we have $FFFFFFFF_{16}$ in R0, the instruction:

```
CLRB   R0
```

will produce FFFFFF00 in R0, not a 32-bit zero. Thus only bits (7:0) are cleared,
leaving bits (31:8) unchanged. Similarly, a MOVB instruction with register addressing
for the destination operand will affect only bits (7:0). For example,

```
MOVL   #^X12345678,R0
MOVB   #^XAB,R0
```

will leave R0 containing $123456AB_{16}$. Because of this characteristic, you must be consistent
in the use of byte instructions. For example, if we followed the preceding instruction
with:

```
CMPB   #^XAB,R0
BEQLU  OUT
```

the branch would take place because the CMPB also looks only at bits (7:0). However,
if we wrote:

```
CMPL   #^XAB,R0
BEQLU  OUT
```

the branch would *not* occur because CMPL will compare $000000AB_{16}$ with all 32 bits
of R0, which is obviously not the same.

Another consideration when using byte arithmetic instructions, e.g., ADDB or MULB, is the smaller range of values that the integers can take on. As demonstrated in Table 2.4, we can only represent integers between -128_{10} and 127_{10} in the 8-bit byte. Also the condition codes for carry and overflow are set based on the smaller cell size when byte instructions are carried out.

The autoincrement and autodecrement addressing modes are also affected by byte instructions. In Section 5.7.2 we saw that an instruction such as:

```
MOVL  (R5)+,R3
```

causes the contents of R5 to be increased by 4. However, if we write:

```
MOVB  (R5)+,R3
```

the contents of R5 is only increased by 1. The reason for this is that the autoincrement addressing mode is most often used to step through a group of sequential cells in main memory. If each cell is to be a longword, the pointer must be advanced by 4, but if the cells are only a single byte the pointer has to be advanced by 1. Similar reasoning applies to the autodecrement mode.

There are situations when it is necessary to create a 32-bit integer that has the same value as a given 8-bit integer. This is made possible by two instructions, CVTBL (ConVerT Byte to Longword) and MOVZBL (MOVe Zero-extend Byte to Longword). The CVTBL instruction is intended for converting *signed* integers. An example is:

```
CLRL   R0
MOVB   #-2,R0 ; 8-bit negative 2 in R0
CVTBL  R0,R3  ;32-bit negative 2 in R3
```

The results of these instructions are:

R0: 000000FE

R3: FFFFFFFE

Thus we see that the CVTBL performs a move with **sign extension.**

Note that if we wish to view our integers as unsigned, the CVTBL does not convert properly when the MSB is set. For example, the FE_{16} above could be viewed as an 8-bit unsigned integer (254_{10}). The proper conversion to a 32-bit unsigned integer is 000000FE, whereas we saw that CVTBL creates FFFFFFFE. For this reason the VAX-11 provides the separate instruction MOVZBL for unsigned conversions. For example,

```
MOVL    #-1,R0  ; set all bits in R0
MOVB    #254,R0 ; 8-bit integer (hex FE) to R0
MOVZBL  R0,R3   ; 32-bit integer (hex FE) to R3
```

produces:

R0: FFFFFFFE

R3: 000000FE

Let us now examine some cases of byte-oriented instructions and their effects. In Example 7.1 we show the use of several byte-oriented instructions.

EXAMPLE 7.1 For this example let us assume that the registers and memory are set as indicated below before *each* of these instructions is executed. All values are hexadecimal.

Register	Contents	Address	Contents	Address	Contents
R0	0000050A	A: 0500	41	0507	48
R1	00FFF503	B: 0501	42	0508	49
R2	00000506	C: 0502	43	0509	4A
R3	00000502	D: 0503	44	050A	4B
R4	0000050D	0504	45	050B	4C
		0505	46	050C	40
		0506	47	050D	C0

The instructions for each case are given in the first column of Table 7.2. In the next two columns we show the name and new contents of any affected registers. The last two columns show the addresses and new contents of any main memory locations affected.

TABLE 7.2/Examples of Byte Instruction Usage

	Instruction		Register Effects		Main Memory Effects	
			Register	New Value	Addr	New Value
(a)	CLRB	R0	R0	00000500	—	—
(b)	CVTBL	(R4),R1	R1	FFFFFFC0	—	—
(c)	CVTBL	-(R4),R1	R1	00000040	—	—
			R4	0000050C	—	—
(d)	MOVZBL	(R4),R1	R1	000000C0	—	—
(e)	MOVB	(R4),R1	R1	00FFF5C0	—	—
(f)	CVTBL	(R4),A	—	—	0500	C0
					0501	FF
					0502	FF
					0503	FF
(g)	CLRB	(R0)	—	—	050A	00
(h)	CLRB	(R2)+	R2	00000507	0506	00
(i)	MOVB	-(R3),(R2)+	R2	00000507	0506	42
			R3	00000501		
(j)	MNEGB	A,D	—	—	0503	BF
(k)	DECB	(R3)+	R3	00000503	0502	42
(l)	DIVB	R3,R2	R2	00000503	—	—
(m)	MULB	R3,R2	R2	0000050C	—	—
(n)	SUBB	(R3),(R2)	—	—	0506	04
(o)	ADDB	(R3),(R2)	—	—	0506	8A

In case (a) of Table 7.2, we see that the CLRB instruction operating on a register clears only the *low* byte, leaving the three high bytes unchanged. (To see this, you must remember that each byte holds two hexadecimal digits.) In general, byte operations on registers affect only the low byte. The exceptions to this are the MOVZBL and CVTBL instructions that perform zero or sign extensions as we saw previously. Cases (b), (c), and (d) further demonstrate these properties.

Cases (b) and (c) also show the usage of deferred and autodecrement addressing with byte-oriented instructions. Note that in case (b) the source operand is the contents of byte 050D which is pointed at by R4. The contents C0 (a negative number) gets put into the low byte of R1, and the *negative* sign bit gets extended into the high bytes (i.e., the 8-bit two's complement number C0 is equivalent to the 32-bit two's complement number $FFFFFFC0_{16}$). In case (c) R4 is decremented to yield 050C. Then the contents

TABLE 7.3/Byte and Character
String Instructions

Mnemonic	Opcode
ADDB	80
BICB	8A
BISB	88
BITB	93
CLRB	94
CMPB	91
CVTBL	98
DECB	97
DIVB	86
INCB	96
MCOMB	92
MNEGB	8E
MOVB	90
MOVZBL	9A
MULB	84
SUBB	82
TSTB	95
XORB	8C
MOVC3	28
CMPC3	29
LOCC	3A
SKPC	3B
BICPSW	B9
BISPSW	B8

of byte 050C is placed in the low byte of R1. In this case the sign bit is a 0, so sign extension clears the high bytes of R1. In case (d) we see that the MOVZBL clears the high bytes regardless of the sign bit of the source byte operand. The MOVB, however, copies the source byte operand into the low byte without changing the high bytes, as we can see in case (e). Case (f) demonstrates the important fact that when the destination operand is a main memory location the byte-to-longword conversion affects four bytes, even though each byte has a separate label in the assembly program.

Other examples of deferred and autoincrement addressing in byte instructions are shown in cases (g), (h), and (i). You should verify the results of these instructions.

The MNEGB instruction replaces the destination operand byte with the two's complement of the source operand byte. This is demonstrated in case (j).

Cases (k) through (o) show several arithmetic operations on bytes. These are seen to behave exactly like their longword counterparts except for the smaller allowed range of values. Observe, for example, that in case (o) we get $8A_{16}(-118_{10})$ by adding $43_{16}(67_{10})$ to 47_{16} (71_{10}). This occurs because the sum (138_{10}) is too large for an 8-bit cell. The V condition code is set by this operation.

All condition codes for the byte-oriented instructions are set or cleared according to the same rules used for the corresponding longword instructions. However, allowance is made for the shorter length of the byte. That is, the C condition code is set if the result would exceed 2^8-1, interpreted as an unsigned integer, and the V bit is set if the result would be outside of the range -128_{10} to 127_{10}.

The opcodes for byte instructions are different than those for longword instructions. Table 7.3 shows these opcodes for a number of VAX-11 byte instructions already discussed, as well as some to be introduced later in this chapter. As discussed in Section 3.4.7, the CPU is able to determine from those opcodes that the operands are bytes rather than longwords. It then adjusts the operand fetching process and the operations to be carried out by the ALU, accordingly.

7.8 | Character Constants

It is often necessary to use an ASCII character in byte-oriented instructions. For example, you may want to compare the contents of the low byte of R0 with the ASCII code for "S". One could use the hexadecimal code 53_{16}:

```
CMPB    #^X53,R0
```

However, this makes it difficult for another programmer to see what is being done. A better way is to use the facility of MACRO for representing character string constants. This is done with the notation ^A/*string*/ where ^A is called the **ASCII operator** and *string* can be any string of printable characters. The "/" at the beginning and end of the string is a convenient delimiter; actually, any character not in the string can be used. The preceding example then becomes:

```
CMPB    #^A/S/,R0
```

This causes the *assembler* to look up the ASCII code for "S" and place it in the operand specifier as a short literal operand. The translation of either of the above forms is therefore:

```
50 53 8F 91
```

7.9 | Character String Instructions

In working with character data it is frequently necessary to carry out operations on strings of characters. Examples would include moving a string of characters from one place in memory to another, searching a string for a particular character, or comparing one string with another. While these operations can always be carried out one character at a time with the byte-oriented instructions described above, many modern computers, including the VAX-11, have special instructions for this purpose. These are called **character string instructions.** We will examine four of these instructions that are frequently used, namely **MOVC3, CMPC3, LOCC,** and **SKPC.**

The MOVC3 instruction moves the contents of an entire block of bytes to a different position in main memory. Most often, the byte contents are ASCII character codes, but, in fact, the instruction works the same regardless of the contents. As an example, suppose we wish to move a string of 10_{10} characters beginning at label A to a block of bytes reserved at label B. We would write:

```
            .
            .
            .
        MOVC3 #10,A,B
            .
            .
            .
        HALT
    A:      .ASCII/0123456789/
    B:      .BLKB 10
```

The suffix 3 in MOVC3 signifies that the instruction expects three operands. The first operand is the length of the string to be moved, and the second and third are the source and destination operands, respectively. We have used short literal addressing for the length, and relative addressing for the other two operands, but any addressing mode could have been employed.

Registers R0 through R5 are used by the character string instructions. For example, after the MOVC3 is executed, R1 contains the address of the byte *following* the source string, and R3 contains the address of the byte *following* the destination string. Also R0, R2, R4, and R5 are cleared by MOVC3. The convenience of having the addresses of the next available bytes returned in R1 and R3 should be apparent. However, there is also the hazard of *losing* whatever you have stored in R0 through R5 before the MOVC3 instruction. The best policy therefore is to *avoid using R0 through R5 for other purposes* when you are using the character string instructions.

The CMPC3 instruction compares two strings, character by character, beginning at the first character of each string. The comparison stops when the two characters being compared are not equal. The condition codes are set as follows, based on the *last* compared byte in each string.

N = 1   if the byte from the first string is less than the byte from the second string, treating them as 8-bit two's complement numbers.

C = 1   if the byte from the first string is less than the byte from the second string, treating them as 8-bit unsigned numbers.

Z = 1   if all bytes from both strings are equal.

V = 0

This instruction can therefore be used to alphabetize a list of words as shown in the following example.

EXAMPLE 7.2   Write MACRO instructions to alphabetize two ASCII strings of eight characters each.

```
            .
            .
            .
            CMPC3   #8,A,B
            BLEQ    SKIP
            MOVC3   #8,A,C
            MOVC3   #8,B,A
            MOVC3   #8,C,B
    SKIP:
            HALT
    A:      .ASCII/SMITH,TJ/
    B:      .ASCII/SMITH,PB/
    C:      .BLKB 8
```

Here we compare the string in A with the one in B. Since the first six characters are the same, the condition codes are set based on comparing "T" with "P". From Table 7.1 we see that the ASCII code for "T" is greater than that for "P", so the branch does not take place, and the two strings are interchanged, using the block of eight bytes at C for temporary storage.

The LOCC and SKPC instructions are for locating and skipping characters in strings. They both have a "search character," a string length, and a string address as operands. The LOCC finds the search character in the string and places its address in R1. The SKPC finds the first character that is *not* equal to the search character and places its address in R1. Both instructions set R0 to the number of remaining characters in the string, which includes the located character. Also, both instructions set R0 to 0 and R1 to the address one byte beyond the last character in the string, if the search character is not found.

EXAMPLE 7.3   As an example of using LOCC and SKPC, suppose we need to find the first word in a line of text and place it in a block of bytes labeled WORD. The following sequence of instructions does these tasks:

```
                             •
                             •
                             •
            SKPC    #^A' ',TEXT,TEXT+1   ; SKIP LEADING SPACES
            MOVL    R1,R7                ; SAVE ADDR OF 1ST WORD
            LOCC    #^A' ',R0,(R1)       ; FIND END OF 1ST WORD
            SUBL    R7,R1                ; CALC 1ST WORD LENGTH
            MOVC3   R1,(R7),WORD         ; PUT 1ST WORD INTO WORD
                             •
                             •
                             •
            HALT
   TEXT:    .ASCIC/LINE OF TEXT/
   WORD:    .BLKB  10
```

In the SKPC instruction we make use of the fact that the length of the sentence is automatically stored in the byte preceding the string by the .ASCIC directive. Thus the TEXT label is referring to the length (using relative addressing), and TEXT+1 is the actual start of the string. The LOCC instruction then operates on the string that begins at the first nonblank character found in the SKPC. We then calculate the word length by subtracting the starting address from the end address, and use this as the length operand for the MOVC3 instruction.

All of the above character string instructions have three operands and therefore translate to an opcode followed by three operand specifiers. The opcodes are shown in Table 7.3. The operand specifiers can employ any appropriate addressing method. A more complete description of these instructions is presented in Table A.1.

The VAX-11 has several other character string instructions in addition to those discussed here. They are described in the *VAX Architecture Handbook* (Digital Equipment Corporation).

7.10 | Logical Bit Instructions

The VAX-11 has a group of instructions that perform logical operations, e.g., "and", "or", "complement", and "exclusive or", on a bit-by-bit basis. These instructions find usage in certain programming problems, and in particular in the input of characters to be discussed in Chapter 8. Although we base our discussion here on the byte form of these instructions, each has word and longword equivalents.

Let us first review the logical operators "and", "or", "complement", and "exclusive or" for single bits. Table 7.4 is the "truth table" for these operators, which defines the outcome of each possible combination of single-bit operands. This shows, for example, that "and", symbolized by $\wedge$, is true (i.e., 1) if and only if both operands are 1. The "or" operator, symbolized by $\vee$, is true if *either* operand is true. The "exclusive or", symbolized by $\forall$, is true if *one but not both* of the operands are true. "Complement", symbolized by $\sim$, is true if the single operand is false, and false if the operand is true.

The last column in Table 7.4, labeled BIC, is not as familiar as the other logical operations, but is an available VAX-11 instruction and plays an important role in programming. In effect, it says, "If a_1 is true, then the result is false, regardless of a_2. However,

TABLE 7.4/Truth Table for Logical Operators

Operands		Operators				
		BIT (AND)	BIS (OR)	XOR	COM	BIC
a_1	a_2	$a_1 \wedge a_2$	$a_1 \vee a_2$	$a_1 \veebar a_2$	$\sim a_1$	$(\sim a_1) \wedge a_2$
0	0	0	0	0	1	0
0	1	0	1	1	1	1
1	0	0	1	1	0	0
1	1	1	1	0	0	0

if a_1 is false, then the result is the same as a_2." In other words, it *clears* bits in a_2 where there is a 1-bit in the corresponding position in a_1.

The VAX-11 has an instruction for each of these logical operators. The MACRO mnemonics are as follows:

```
BITB    M,D     ; Bit test (AND)
BISB    M,D     ; Bit set  (OR)
XORB    M,D     ; Exclusive OR
MCOMB   D,D     ; Bit complement
BICB    M,D     ; Bit clear
```

These instructions examine the operands on a bit-by-bit basis and, except for BITB, establish the destination bit patterns according to the rules in Table 7.4.

In the most common usage of these instructions, the first operand is often called a "mask" because it can be viewed as a bit pattern that "masks out" the unwanted portion of the second operand. For example, if we wished to clear all bits in a byte A except the rightmost three, we could use:

```
BICB    #^B11111000,A
```

Here we are using the **binary radix control operator** ^B in order to allow representation of the mask in binary. We could also have expressed it in decimal, #248, or hexadecimal, #^XF8.

The **BICB** instruction follows the rules established in the last column in Table 7.4, i.e., the first operand (the mask) is *complemented*, then AND'ed with the second. To see this more clearly, suppose A is CD_{16}. Then we have:

$$
\begin{array}{ll}
11111000 & \text{(Mask)} \\
00000111 & \text{($\sim$Mask)} \\
11001101 & \text{(A)} \\
00000101 & \text{(Final A)}
\end{array}
$$

We see that the three LSB's have been left undisturbed while all others have been cleared or "masked out." Thus with BICB one can clear particular bits in the destination by placing one in the corresponding positions in the mask.

The **BISB** instruction will cause the destination operand bits to be *set* where there is a one in the mask. For example, using the byte instruction BISB:

```
MOVB  #^B01100011,A
BISB  #^B11110000,A
```

sets ones in the leftmost four bits of A while leaving the rightmost four bits unchanged. This is shown below:

11110000	(Mask)
01100011	(A)
11110011	(Final A)

The exclusive or, **XORB,** *complements* the destination bits selectively wherever there is a 1-bit in the mask. For example,

```
MOVL  #^X7FFFFFFF,R1
MOVL  #^XF0F0F0F0,A
XORL  R1,A
```

causes A to be set as shown here:

0111 1111 1111 1111 1111 1111 1111 1111	(Mask)
1111 0000 1111 0000 1111 0000 1111 0000	(Original A)
1000 1111 0000 1111 0000 1111 0000 1111	(Final A)

The last example employed the longword form of the exclusive or instructions, XORL. There are also word and byte forms of this instruction.

An interesting usage of the XORL is in exchanging the contents of two registers or memory locations. For example,

```
XORL  R1,R2
XORL  R2,R1
XORL  R1,R2
```

will transfer the contents of R1 to R2 and R2 to R1 without using any other registers. You can demonstrate that this works with any convenient bit patterns in R1 and R2.

The **BITB** instruction differs from the others in that it does not change either operand. It is similar in this respect to the CMPB instruction, and it is used in much the same way. That is, it is an efficient test before a branch instruction. Logically, it performs a bit-by-bit AND, as shown in table 7.4. A typical usage is when we want to execute a branch if a particular bit pattern exists in one of the operands. Consider, for example, the need to branch to OUT only if bit 4 in R1 is set, disregarding all other bits. A mask with this bit set is 00010000_2. We therefore write the instructions:

```
BITB   #^B00010000,R1
BNEQU  OUT
```

We see why this works by the following analysis. The branch takes place only if the result of the bit-by-bit ANDing is *not zero*. Observe that *only the fourth bit* of the result can be nonzero because all other mask bits are clear. Therefore, we see that only the fourth bit in R1 matters, and a nonzero result occurs only if that bit is set. Masks can be selected to cause a variety of branching conditions using BITB. Note that the 0 result occurs when the second operand *does not* equal the mask; it is for this reason that the branch instruction must reflect the *complement* of the desired branching condition.

We have already encountered the longword bit complement instruction MCOML in Section 6.11. This instruction complements each bit in the source operand and places the result in the destination operand. For example, using the byte form:

```
MOVB    #^B11110000,A
MCOMB   A,A
```

modifies A as indicated below:

$$11110000 \quad \text{(A)}$$
$$00001111 \quad (\sim\text{A})$$

As we noted in Section 2.5, this would be called the "one's complement" of A.

There are two bit manipulation instructions especially for use with the PSW. One of these, **BICPSW,** performs the bit clearing operand like BICB, but does this on the PSW. Similarly, **BISPSW** performs the bit setting operation on the PSW. These instructions can be used to set and clear bits in the PSW. An example of their usefulness was seen in Exercise 6.11.

7.11 | A Programming Example

As an example of the character manipulation capabilities of MACRO, let us consider the following problem.

EXAMPLE 7.4 Assume that a sentence is stored in a block of successive bytes beginning at the label S. Write a MACRO program that will compute the number of words in the sentence and the length of each word. The number of words is to be placed in a longword labeled N, and the lengths are to be placed in N successive bytes (as 8-bit unsigned integers) beginning at L. Assume that each word in the sentence is separated from the next by exactly one blank, and that the sentence ends with a period.

Figure 7.1(a) shows the level-1 flowchart for a solution to this problem. We use register R2 as a word counter, R1 to point at the location in L where the length of the current word is developed, and R0 to point at the current character in the sentence. The two pointers are initialized to the beginnings of their arrays prior to entering a WHILE loop. Each pass through the body of this loop counts the characters in the next word, placing the count into the next byte in the length array L. Upon completion of a pass, the sentence character pointer is left pointing at the first character of the next word, or if a period is present, at the period. The word length array pointer is incremented so that it points to the next byte in the L array for the next pass through the loop. The word counter R2 is also incremented in the body of the loop.

Because the character pointer R0 is left at the period, it can act as a loop control variable. That is, if the contents of the byte pointed at by R0 is a ".", the last word has been found. Upon exit from this loop, as a last step, we move the word count into location N as required by the problem statement.

The refinement of the major loop body is shown in Figure 7.1(b). It begins by initializing the word length (to be stored in the byte pointed at by R1) to 0, then enters a WHILE loop that is repeated as long as the character pointed at by R0 is not a

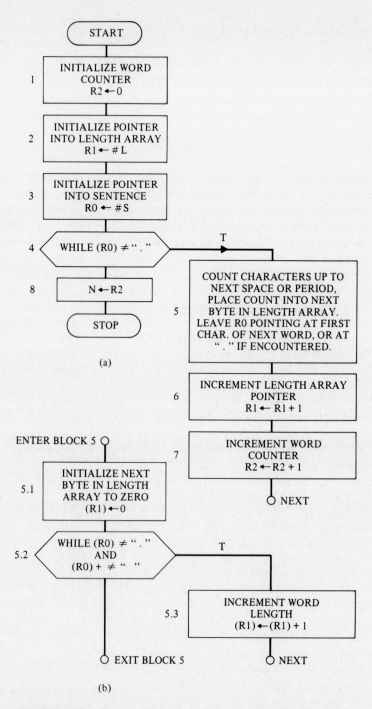

FIGURE 7.1/Flowchart for Example 7.4: (a) level-one flowchart   (b) refinement of block 5

delimiter. Note that R0 is incremented as part of the condition check, but only if a
"." is not found. The body of this loop increments the length of the current word.

The assembly program for the flowchart in Figure 7.1 is shown in Figure 7.2. For
the most part, because the instructions correspond quite closely to the flowchart blocks
described above, we shall omit a detailed description of the program operation and
focus on the usage of the byte directives and instructions. First, observe that we use
byte comparisons (CMPB) when comparing characters. This is especially important in
an instruction such as in line 11 because it is illogical to compare a longword when it
is only eight bits that need to be compared to establish equality of two single characters.

Note that the pointer R0 is incremented using autoincrement addressing in line 16.
This advances R0 to the first character of the next word if one is present. However, if
the delimiter is a period, R0 is *not* incremented. The body of the innermost loop then
has a single instruction (line 18) incrementing the word length counter. Note that we
use the byte form of the increment instruction, because the problem statement required
that the length counts be stored in bytes rather than longwords. This is efficient usage
of memory because word lengths will always be well within the range accommodated
by 8-bit, unsigned integers.

We purposely have left some inefficiencies in this program to allow discussion of
the refinement process that most programmers go through in arriving at a final program.
Note that we increment R1 in the instruction in line 20. This also could be done by
changing line 13 to autoincrement addressing. However, this would leave R1 pointing
one byte beyond where it should be when line 18 is reached. This would have to be
fixed by decrementing R1 immediately after setting it at the address of L at line 8.
Whereas this may seem to have gained nothing—trading one instruction for another—
it is in fact an improvement: we have eliminated an instruction inside the *inner* loop,
at the cost of adding one outside of both loops. This saves a number of execution
cycles equal to the number of characters in the sentence minus one. If this algorithm
were to be incorporated into a larger program, and had to be executed thousands of
times, such improvements would be quite important.

Let us make some other observations before leaving Figure 7.2. The CMPB instruction
at line 11 is seen to be translated as 2E 60 91. The 91 is the opcode for CMPB (Table
7.3). The 60 is the operand specifier for register-deferred addressing with R0. Because
the ASCII code for "." is less than 63_{10}, the assembler has selected the short literal
form rather than immediate addressing for the second operand, causing the ASCII code
2E to be stored in the second operand specifier byte. It is interesting to note that had
we chosen a character with a larger code, e.g., "@", the assembler would have used
the immediate mode, creating a slightly larger machine code program.

Note how the assembler listing displays the translation of the .ASCII directive. At
line 26, for example, we see the hexadecimal ASCII codes for the characters in the
string, printed twelve per line and in *reverse* order. Obviously, the assembler has provided
us with the *byte* contents rather than the longword contents. Also, the addresses given
relate to the first byte of each line. That is, the character codes 54, 48, and 49 are
stored in addresses 0035, 0036, and 0037. The end of the first .ASCII string is stored
in byte 0044, and the beginning of the second is stored in 0046. Line 28 shows the
allocations of 100_{10} bytes for the byte array L. Note that it begins at byte 0060 and

```
                              13-APR-1985 15:19:26   QSA1:[50,004]EX7P4.MAR;5        (1)
                                                     Assembly source code

Machine code                   Offset    Ln
                               addr
                               0000       1          .TITLE  EXAMPLE 7.4
                               0000       2  ;
                               0000       3  ; PROGRAM TO DETERMINE NUMBER OF WORDS AND LENGTHS
                               0000       4  ;       IN A SENTENCE.
                               0000       5  ;
                      0000     0000       6          .ENTRY  START,0
                   52 D4       0000       7          CLRL    R2             ;INITIALIZE WORD COUNTER
   51 00000060'8F D0           0002       8          MOVL    #L,R1          ;INITIALIZE LENGTH ARRAY POINTER
   50 00000035'8F D0           0004       9          MOVL    #S,R0          ;INITIALIZE CHARACTER POINTER
                               000B      10  WHILE1:
                   2E 60 91    0012      11          CMPB    (R0),#^A'.'    ;GET WORD IF NO PERIOD
                      16 13    0015      12          BEQLU   OUT1
                      61 94    0017      13          CLRB    (R1)           ;INITIALIZE CURRENT WORD LENGTH
                   2E 60 91    0019      14  WHILE2: CMPB    (R0),#^A'.'    ;PERIOD ENDS WORD & SENTENCE
                      09 13    001E      15          BEQLU   OUT2
                   20 80 91    0021      16          CMPB    (R0)+,#^A' '   ;SPACE ENDS WORD
                      04 13    0023      17          BEQLU   OUT2
                      61 96    0025      18          INCB    (R1)           ;INCREMENT CURRENT WORD LENGTH
                      F2 11    0027      19          BRB     WHILE2         ;CHECK NEXT CHARACTER
                      51 D6    0029      20  OUT2:   INCL    R1             ;INC. LENGTH ARRAY POINTER
                      52 D6    002B      21          INCL    R2             ;INC. WORD COUNTER
                      E5 11    002D      22          BRB     WHILE1         ;GET NEXT WORD
                               002D      23  OUT1:
     000000C4'EF 52 D0         002D      24          MOVL    R2,N           ;PLACE WORD COUNT INTO N
                      00       0034      25          HALT
                               0035      26  S:      .ASCII/THIS IS A SAMPLE/
   41 53 20 41 20 53 49 48 54
                45 4C 50 4D
                               0045      27          .ASCII/ SENTENCE WITH EIGHT WORDS./
   49 57 20 48 54 49 57 20 45 43 4E 45 54 4E 45 53 20
   52 4F 57 20 54 48 47 49 45 20
   2E 53 44
                               0060      28  L:      .BLKB   100
                               00C4      29  N:      .BLKL   1
                               00C8      30          .END    START
```

FIGURE 7.2/MACRO listing for Example 7.4

therefore ends at byte 00C3. The next available byte is then at 00C4, and we see that this value *appears* to be a longword placed in the locations reserved for L. However, in reality this is just a convenient place for the assembler to store the address of the next available byte. When the program is linked, 0's are stored in all bytes of L.

Figure 7.3 shows execution of the program under the Symbolic Debugger. We first set a breakpoint at the HALT, offset address 0034. After execution to the breakpoint, we examine the memory locations where the sentence is stored. By using the EXAMINE command with the ASCII:30 qualifier, we cause the sentence to be displayed as a line of 30 ASCII characters rather than the usual numeric codes. We then examine the bytes where the word lengths have been stored. The hexadecimal interpretation of these bytes gives the length of each word in the sentence. Location N is then examined, and we see that the program found eight words in the sentence. By examining the registers we see that R0, the sentence character pointer, is left pointing at location 025F. This is the run-time virtual address of the ".", determined as the offset plus 0200 that is added by the linker.

Similarly, R1 is left pointing at the byte where the *next* word length would have been placed had the sentence been longer. The number of words in the sentence is seen to be in register R2 and in the location assigned to N.

```
$ MACRO/LIST/DEBUG EX7P4
$ LINK/DEBUG EX7P4
$ RUN EX7P4
                        VAX-11 DEBUG Version 4.1
%DEBUG-I-INITIAL, language is MACRO, module set to 'EXP7P4'
DBG>SET BREAK START+34
DBG>GO
routine start at EXP7P4\START
break at EXP7P4\OUT1+07
DBG>EXAMINE/ASCII:30 S:L-1
EXP7P4\S:   THIS IS A SAMPLE SENTENCE WITH EIGHT WORDS.
DBG>EXAMINE/BYTE L:L+9
EXP7P4\L:    04
EXP7P4\L+01:    02
EXP7P4\L+02:    01
EXP7P4\L+03:    06
EXP7P4\L+04:    08
EXP7P4\L+05:    04
EXP7P4\L+06:    05
EXP7P4\L+07:    05
EXP7P4\L+08:    00
EXP7P4\L+09:    00
DBG>EXAMINE N
EXP7P4\N:    00000008
DBG>EXAMINE R0:R2
R0:    0000025F
R1:    00000268
R2:    00000008
DBG>EXIT
$ ▓
```

FIGURE 7.3/Execution of Example 7.4 program under the Symbolic Debugger

7.12 | Summary

Chapter 7 covered a range of topics related to the manipulation of nonnumeric data, i.e., **character data,** with the VAX-11. We began by observing that some binary code is necessary for representing character data on a binary digital computer. The **ASCII code** was presented in detail because most peripheral devices communicate with the VAX-11 using this system, and MACRO has features that make it a convenient choice. It is a 7-bit code, so that a single character fits neatly into an 8-bit byte. We saw that most often character strings are stored in successive bytes in memory.

There are several byte-oriented directives in MACRO that allow initialization of blocks of successive bytes to ASCII codes. The directive **.ASCII**/*string*/ places the codes for each character in *string* into the next available memory bytes; **.ASCIZ**/*string*/ does the same, but adds a null character at the end; and **.ASCIC**/*string*/ adds a count byte at the beginning. Other byte-oriented directives include **.BLKB** *n* which reserves *n* bytes without initialization, and **.BYTE** v_1, v_2, . . ., v_n which initializes the next *n* bytes to the values v_1, v_2, . . ., v_n.

Because character manipulation is frequently required, and the character codes reside in bytes, the VAX-11 has byte-oriented forms of most instructions. These include **CLRB, MCOMB, INCB, DECB, MNEGB, TSTB, MOVB, CMPB,** and the arithmetic instructions. These operate in essentially the same way as the previously introduced longword instructions having similar mnemonics. The byte-oriented instructions allow us to move byte-sized data to and from individual bytes in memory. We saw that certain differences therefore arise in addressing the operands. For example, the autoincrement and autodecrement modes increment the register by *one* when used in a byte-oriented instruction. This is convenient when the objective is to manipulate successive bytes, because adjacent byte addresses differ by one. For example, CLRB (R1)+ in the body of a loop will clear successive bytes beginning at the byte address in R1 upon entry to the loop.

It was observed that operations *between* bytes and longwords can also be done. In particular, **MOVB** A,R1 will move the 8-bits found in (byte) address A into the low byte of register R1. The **CVTBL** A,R1 instruction, on the other hand, moves the A byte to the low byte of R1 and extends the sign bit into the higher bytes. This is in effect a *conversion* of an 8-bit two's complement number to its 32-bit equivalent. An *unsigned* conversion is performed by **MOVZBL** A,R1, which 0-fills the high bytes of R1. On the other hand, MOVB R1,A will move the low byte of R1 into the byte reserved for A. In general, the byte-oriented instructions with register operands refer to the low byte in the register. Because the high bytes of the registers cannot be addressed, the ROTL instruction must be used to move these bytes into the low byte if needed.

Frequently it is necessary to have a "character constant" as an operand. This can be done using the **ASCII operator** ^A in MACRO. That is, CMPB A,#^A′B′ will compare the byte stored in A with the ASCII code for B, while CMPL R0,#^A′ABCD′ will compare the 32 bits in R0 with those implied by the character string "ABCD".

We also treated several VAX-11 instructions designed to operate on entire character strings at once. These include the string move instruction **MOVC3,** the string compare **CMPC3,** and the locate/skip instructions **LOCC** and **SKPC.** While you can always perform equivalent operations a character at a time with the byte instructions, the string manipulation instructions lead to more concise and efficient programs.

Chapter 7 also dealt with bit manipulation instructions, including **BITL, BICL, BISL,** and their byte-oriented equivalents **BITB, BICB,** and **BISB.** These perform logical operations on a bit-by-bit basis for two operands. Most often the first or source operand is viewed as a **mask** that "selects" or identifies the bits of concern in the second operand. For example, BITB #^B00000100,R1 tests the low byte of R1 and will produce a nonzero result if and only if bit 2 of R1 is set; all other bits in R1 are of no consequence because the corresponding bits in the mask are zero. Similarly, BISB (logical OR) will set bits in the second operand wherever a 1 occurs in the mask, and BICB clears bits in the second operand wherever a 1 occurs in the mask. Note, however, that BICB and BISB *change the second operand,* while BITB only acts to set or clear the N and Z condition codes. We also described the operation of the exclusive or, **XORB,** which will set a bit in the destination operand if there is a 1 in the corresponding position in *either* the first operand or the second, but not both. This has the effect of complementing the destination bits in the positions selected by 1's in the mask.

The chapter ended with an example that showed the use of byte directives and instructions in character manipulation.

7.13 | Exercises

7.1 Determine the ASCII characters represented by the following 8-bit hexadecimal codes:

(a) 6D   (b) 1B   (c) 53   (d) 0D
(e) 0A   (f) 07   (g) 2C   (h) 20
(i) 36   (j) 7F

7.2 Show the byte contents in hexadecimal and binary for the ASCII representation for the following characters:

(a) /   (b) r   (c) R   (d) .
(e) NUL   (f) 0   (g) 8   (h) ˆB
(i)]   (j) <

7.3 Indicate the character strings represented in each of the following longwords whose contents are given in hexadecimal. Be sure to give your answer in the correct order, remembering that the low byte holds the first character.

(a) 44 43 42 41   (b) 45 46 47 48   (c) 2322215F
(d) 34 33 32 31   (e) 0A0D4948   (f) 42624161
(g) 7D3A3D7B   (h) 2E3C3E2E   (i) 03020100

7.4 Determine the memory contents for each string as a result of the following directives:

```
.ASCII /YOU CAN LEARN ONLY/
.ASCIZ /BY PRACTICE!!/
.ASCIC /+-#( )/
```

7.5 What do the directives .ASCII /ABCD/, .BYTEˆX41ˆX42ˆX43ˆX44, and .LONGˆX44434241 have in common? Which is preferred and why?

7.6 Show the contents of each byte as a result of:

```
.ASCIZ /HI THERE!/<13><10><7>
```

7.7 Explain why you cannot use terminal keys themselves to generate the nonprinting characters in the .ASCIZ directive in Exercise 7.6, but must use the ASCII codes, e.g., 13, 10, and 7, for generating carriage return, linefeed, and bell.

7.8 The following program "decodes" a coded message stored in CODE and puts the decoded message into CLEAR. Explain how it works and what the message says.

```
1                  .TITLE  DECODE
2                  .ENTRY  START,0
3                  MOVL    #CODE,R1
4                  MOVL    #CLEAR,R2
5        LOOP:     MOVB    (R1),R3
6                  ADDB    #8,R3
7                  MOVB    R3,(R2)+
8                  CMPB    (R1)+,#248
9                  BNEQU   LOOP
10                 HALT
11       CODE:     .BYTE   69,89,91,106,103,37,41,41,248
12       CLEAR:    .BLKB   9
13                 .END    START
```

7.9 For each of the cases below show the outcome of BITB R1,R2; BICB R1,R2; BISB R1,R2; MCOMB R1,R2; and XORB R1,R2. Present your results in a table with a row for each case and a column for each instruction. (For BITB, show the N, Z, and V condition codes only. For the others, show the contents of R2 in binary.)

	R1	R2
(a)	10000000	10101010
(b)	01010100	00011001
(c)	11111000	00011111
(d)	00001111	11111111
(e)	11111111	00000000
(f)	00000000	11111111
(g)	11111111	11111111
(h)	00000000	00000000

7.10 Rework Example 7.1 using the register and memory contents shown below.

Register	Contents	Address	Contents	Address	Contents
R0	00000507	A: 0500	00	0507	07
R1	EF0FF501	B: 0501	01	0508	08
R2	0000050B	C: 0502	02	0509	09
R3	00000503	D: 0503	03	050A	0A
R4	00000508	0504	04	050B	0B
		0505	05	050C	0C
		0506	06	050D	0D

7.11 Given the register and memory contents of Exercise 7.10, in each case below show the effects on all registers and main memory locations due to the indicated instruction or instructions.

```
(a) MOVB    C,A           (b) BICL    #^XFFFFF0FF,R4
                              MOVB    (R4),(R2)

(c) MOVL    R1,C          (d) ADDL    #2,R3
(e) ROTL    #-16,D,R5         MOVZBL  (R3),R3
    MOVXBL  R5,R5             ASHL    #8(R3),R3
    ASHL    #8,R5,R5          ADDL    #8,R3
    CLRL    (R5)              CLRB    (R3)
```

7.12 Modify Example 7.3 so as to place the *second* word of TEXT into WORD. Run with the Symbolic Debugger and demonstrate that it works.

7.13 Modify Example 7.2 so that words can be delimited by any number of commas or spaces. Run your program with the Symbolic Debugger to verify its correctness.

7.14 Repeat Exercise 7.13 making use of character string instructions MOVC3, SKPC, and LOCC.

7.15 Write a program that examines a sentence and determines the number of times that each ASCII alphabetical character appears. Place the counts for each character in an array of bytes beginning at C. (*Hint:* The ASCII code minus 41_{16} plus the address of C can be used as a pointer into C.) Run your program with the Symbolic Debugger to verify its correctness.

7.16 Write a program that extracts each word from a line of text and stores it as a separate string of characters in an array of strings. Then the program must sort the array of words into alphabetical order. Assume that the words have a maximum length of ten characters.

8

Input and Output

8.1 | Overview

Most programs require certain items of data in order to begin, called the **input data,** and generate results that must be communicated to the user, called the **output data.** For example, a program that is to determine the sum of two numbers requires these numbers as input data, and the sum must be output data. In Section 4.8 we were able to sidestep these matters by using the Symbolic Debugger to load the input directly into memory locations or registers, and to examine the results in the locations or registers where they were generated. As an alternative procedure, we showed the use of preprogrammed routines for hexadecimal Input/Output (I/O) in Section 4.11. These methods allowed the complications of I/O to be temporarily set aside, but neither method is very practical for real programs. In this chapter, therefore, we take up the matter of I/O, with the objective of learning how to write programs that accept general data entry from the terminal keyboard and print or display data back to the terminal.

We will be concerned in this chapter with I/O of two kinds of data—data that have **numerical** meaning (i.e., representations of numbers), and data that do not (i.e., **character data**). We will discuss character data first, because the internal representation of the data is the same on the VAX-11 as the external representation, namely, ASCII character codes. Thus no translation or conversion is necessary prior to sending character data to the display, and character data received from the keyboard is already properly coded for use in the program. Numerical data, on the other hand, require a *translation* upon input or output because internal and external representation forms are different. However, we will find that after this translation, the I/O of numbers proceeds exactly like the I/O of character data.

Input and output from a MACRO program can be simplified through the use of what we shall call **I/O Macros.** These are in fact preprogrammed routines that deal with much of the detail of inputting or outputting one or more characters. Input/output macros are usually available as support programs of the operating system on most computers. Most of the discussion in this chapter is based on three such macros, called .TTYIN, .TTYOUT, and .PUTSTR, which are provided with this book (see Section E.1). These

184

macros are modeled after those provided with the RT-11 operating system for PDP-11 computers, and are somewhat simpler for beginners to use than those normally provided with the VAX/VMS operating system. In Chapter 17 we will discuss I/O again, using the VAX/VMS routines.

This chapter also briefly introduces I/O at a more fundamental level, namely, **programmed I/O** to the physical **device registers.** This is intended to reveal the nature of I/O programming which becomes necessary when no operating system is present, or when one must develop routines that carry out the actual communication between the computer and the peripheral device. Such routines are called **device drivers.** We will use the PDP-11 computer as a vehicle for this discussion because VAX-11 I/O at this level is more complicated and cannot be easily carried out in the normal VAX-11 environment.

8.2 | Input/Output Macros

In addition to its use as the name of the assembler used on the VAX-11, the term "macro" has a general meaning in computer science. A macro name is a single mnemonic used to invoke the assembly of a pre-defined *group* of assembly lines. In the following discussions when we say "macro," we mean a mnemonic which is not formally part of the MACRO language, but will be recognized by the assembler and cause a group of machine language instructions to be inserted into the machine language version of the program. Macros usually perform a particular task that is required at many places in the program. In Chapter 10 we will learn how to write macro definitions. Here, however, we wish simply to become familiar with the term so that it can be used in connection with input and output of character data.

The macros we will be dealing with in this chapter are for input and output of character data at your terminal. They are provided in Appendix E of this book, and must be installed on your machine as described there before you can use them.

One of these, .TTYOUT, is designed to send a single ASCII character to the terminal printer or screen. A variation of this is the macro called .PUTSTR which prints a *string* of characters. Another, called .TTYIN, is designed to accept character data from the terminal keyboard. The MACRO programmer can include and use these macros in his or her program to facilitate input and output of program data.

In the discussion in the following sections we will see that .TTYIN, .PUTSTR, and .TTYOUT use R0. It is therefore necessary to save the contents of R0 elsewhere *before each use* of any of these macros if such contents is going to be needed later. Failing to observe this rule is a frequent source of error.

In order for your program to use macros, you must make them available to the MACRO assembler and the linker. Assuming they are stored in your directory, you do this with the following assembly and linkage commands:

```
$ MACRO/LIST/DEBUG  PROG+MACLIB/LIB
$ LINK/DEBUG  PROG+SUBLIB/LIB
$ RUN PROG
```

If you do not wish to use the Symbolic Debugger, the /DEBUG can be omitted from the MACRO and LINK commands. Similarly, /LIST can be omitted if no listing file is needed.

8.3 | The .TTYOUT Macro

Of the three I/O macros discussed here, the .TTYOUT is the easiest to use. Suppose we want to print the character whose ASCII code resides in the low byte of R1. This is accomplished by the macro reference:

```
.TTYOUT R1
```

For example,

```
MOVB    #^A'X',R1
.TTYOUT R1
```

will print an "X". In this example we used register addressing for the operand of .TTYOUT. Other addressing modes may be used as well. For example, using immediate addressing:

```
.TTYOUT #^X42
```

will print a "B" (because hexadecimal 42 is the ASCII code for "B"). Finally, using relative addressing:

```
                .TTYOUT L1
                   .
                   .
                   .
    L1:         .ASCII /Q/
```

will cause a "Q" to be printed.

The .TTYOUT macro sends a *single* character to be printed on the display device, and therefore does *not* provide the familiar carriage return and linefeed after printing. This causes the *next* printable character to be placed adjacent to the last one on the same line. If this is not desired, the carriage return and linefeed codes can be sent by separate .TTYOUTs, for example:

```
.TTYOUT #^A'B'      ; Display B.
.TTYOUT #^XOD       ; Send Carriage Return.
.TTYOUT #^XOA       ; Send Linefeed.
```

Alternately, one could use the .PUTSTR macro described below which automatically sends a carriage return and linefeed after printing.

Although it is not evident in the MACRO code, the .TTYOUT macro uses R0. A frequent error is to overlook this fact, expecting R0 to be unchanged after using .TTYOUT. The following example shows this error.

```
                MOVL    #5,R0
                MOVL    #L1,R1
    LOOP:       .TTYOUT (R1)+           ;(INCORRECT)
                SOBGTR  R0,LOOP
                HALT
    L1:         .ASCII  /HELLO/
```

The programmer may hope that this prints out the word HELLO as the loop is executed in this program. However, the loop control variable R0 is being changed by .TTYOUT, so that results are unpredictable. A different register should be used for the loop control variable.

8.4 | THE .PUTSTR Macro

The .PUTSTR macro is also quite useful and easy to use. It should be used when an entire line, including a carriage return and linefeed, is to be printed. Typical usage is to print a message:

```
.PUTSTR MSG
```

where MSG is a label for the first location in a block of memory locations containing a string of characters to be printed. The character codes stored in MSG and each successive byte will be sent to the terminal display. This will continue until a null byte (00) is encountered, and then a carriage return and linefeed are sent. We have already seen this used in Chapter 1 to print a message. This is a very common usage.

The message to be printed is stored using the .ASCIZ directive, which automatically ends the message string with a null byte. The message is stored at any convenient point in the program, and the .PUTSTR is placed at the point where the printing is to be done during program execution.

In addition to fixed messages initialized by .ASCIZ, the .PUTSTR macro can be used to print strings of ASCII character codes *calculated* by the program. To demonstrate this, consider the following example.

EXAMPLE 8.1   Print the entire set of printable ASCII characters. This sequence of characters begins with the hexadecimal code 20, and ends with the hexadecimal code 7E.

Because these codes are sequential, they can be generated by initializing a register, say R1, to the space character and incrementing it in a loop. Each successive value can be stored in the next location in a byte array beginning at the label CHAR. After this array has been filled in this manner, the .PUTSTR macro can be used to print it. Remember that a null byte must be placed after the last valid character code to "turn off" the .PUTSTR process.

The listing for the MACRO program is shown in Figure 8.1. As described above, the program first fills the array CHAR with the ASCII codes, followed by the null byte. The subsequent .PUTSTR MSG causes the message created by the .ASCII directive to be printed. The <13> <10> <7> causes carriage return, linefeed, and bell character codes to be sent to the display after the message. This positions the next printing at the beginning of the next line, and rings the bell. Note that because we used .ASCII rather than .ASCIZ, the .PUTSTR macro continues after printing the MSG string rather than stopping. In this way we cause MSG *and* the results to be printed by a single use of .PUTSTR. Results of executing this program are shown in Figure 8.2. Note that as with .TTYOUT, the .PUTSTR macro disturbs R0.

```
                 .TITLE   ASCII
  ;
  ;               DISPLAY THE ASCII PRINTING CHARACTERS
  ;                    USING THE .PUTSTR MACRO
  ;
                 .ENTRY   START,0
                 MOVB     #^A' ',R0      ;INITIALIZE TO SPACE CHAR
                 MOVL     #CHAR,R1       ;INITIALIZE ARRAY POINTER
  WHILE:         CMPB     R0,#^X7F       ;CHECK FOR DEL CHAR
                 BGTRU    OUT            ;  AND STOP IF REACHED.
                 MOVB     R0,(R1)+       ;STORE CHAR & INC. POINTER
                 INCB     R0             ;CREATE NEXT CHARACTER
                 BRB      WHILE
  OUT:
                 CLRB     (R1)           ;STORE NULL BYTE
                 .PUTSTR  MSG            ;PRINT OUTPUT LABEL
                                         ;  AND OUTPUT ARRAY.
                 $EXIT_S                 ;EXIT TO VMS(SYSTEM MACRO)
  MSG:           .ASCII/ASCII PRINTING CHARACTERS:/<13><10><7>
  CHAR:          .BLKB    96             ;RESERVE BYTE ARRAY
                 .END     START
```

FIGURE 8.1/Program to print the ASCII printable characters

```
$ MACRO/LIST E8P1+MACLIB/LIB
$ LINK E8P1+SUBLIB/LIB
$ RUN E8P1
ASCII PRINTING CHARACTERS:
 !"#$%&'()*+,-./0123456789:;<=>?@ABCDEFGHIJKLMNOPQRSTUVWXYZ[\]^_`ab
cdefghijklmnopqrstuvwxyz{|}~
$ ▒
```

FIGURE 8.2/Execution of the program for Example 8.1

8.5 | The .TTYIN Macro

The role of the .TTYIN macro is to allow keyboard entry of a single ASCII character into your program. By using it repeatedly, any number of characters can be entered.

Usage of .TTYIN is slightly more complicated than the usage of .TTYOUT and .PUTSTR. In order to explain the .TTYIN, we must first introduce the concept of a "buffer."

A **buffer** is a group of memory locations that acts as temporary storage for data that is being transferred from one place to another. Data is first placed in the buffer, then withdrawn and moved to a final destination. Buffers are often required or desirable when there is a large difference in the rate of inflow and outflow of data. In the case of inputting data from a keyboard, for example, the data can be placed in the buffer by the operator at a relatively slow rate while the CPU is doing other tasks. When the buffer is full, or when the user has finished a line of input, the CPU is allowed to read the data from the buffer.

The .TTYIN macro uses the buffer concept, and the programmer must take this into account when using it. Characters are accepted into the buffer from the keyboard until the carriage return key is pressed. After the ASCII code for the carriage return is placed in the buffer, a linefeed code is *automatically placed in the buffer*. This linefeed code is supplied by the macro in much the same way as a typewriter automatically linefeeds when the carriage is returned.

In addition to filling the buffer, the .TTYIN execution causes the first character of the line to be removed from the buffer and placed into R0. On the other hand, if .TTYIN is executed, and the buffer has something in it, the next character is removed and placed into R0 without further keyboard entry. A new line is not accepted into the buffer until it has been emptied. An example will clarify the process.

Suppose we want to accept two characters from the keyboard and store them in two successive bytes beginning at label A. To accomplish this, we include these instructions at the appropriate place in our program.

```
MOVL     #A,R1        ; INITIALIZE R1 TO ADDRESS OF A
.TTYIN                ; FILLS BUFFER AND GETS
                      ;    FIRST CHARACTER INTO R0
MOVB     R0,(R1)+     ; SAVE FIRST CHAR, IN A
.TTYIN                ; GETS SECOND CHAR, INTO R0
MOVB     R0,(R1)      ; SAVE SECOND CHAR, IN A + 1
.TTYIN                ; CLEAR CR IN BUFFER
.TTYIN                ; CLEAR LF IN BUFFER
```

When this program executes, it will pause at the first .TTYIN and wait for keyboard entry. Suppose the user inputs:

```
QB<CR>
```

After completion of this input, indicated by the carriage return <CR>, the contents of R0 and the .TTYIN buffer are:

Low byte of R0:   Q

.TTYIN buffer: | B | CR | LF | | | |

Note that the second character entered is in the first position in the buffer.* The first MOVB instruction places the "Q" into the byte in memory labeled A, and advances R1 to address A + 1. After execution of the second .TTYIN, the contents of R0 and the buffer are:

Low byte of R0:   B

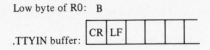

.TTYIN buffer: | CR | LF | | | | |

---

* In these diagrams we show the next available character in the first buffer cell. Actually, .TTYIN uses a pointer that advances to the right.

Note that the execution of .TTYIN caused the next character in the buffer to be moved into R0 and removed from the buffer; it *did not* cause the buffer to accept further keyboard entry because it was not empty.

After moving the second character into the location pointed at by R1, we placed two additional .TTYIN macro references. The purpose of these is to *empty the buffer* so that it is ready for reuse in case we want to get a line of characters from the keyboard later in the program. The first of these two .TTYINs leaves R0 and the buffer as follows:

Low byte of R0: < CR >

.TTYIN buffer:

LF					

After the next, we have:

Low byte of R0: < LF >

.TTYIN buffer:

It is very important to note here that our purpose was to place the first two input characters into A and A + 1. This we have done. We also emptied the buffer so that it could be used later; this was also an important step. The fact that we have left a linefeed character in R0 is not important; it will be overwritten the next time R0 is used.

To see why it is important to leave the .TTYIN buffer empty, consider the following example. Suppose a programmer wishes to accept a *single* character from each of two separate lines of keyboard entry and check to see if they are equal. To do this, the programmer writes the following (incorrect) program segment:

```
.TTYIN
MOVB    RO,A
.TTYIN
MOVL    RO,B
CMPB    A,B
BEQLU   L1
        .
        .
        .
```

One might think that two entry lines of the same character, e.g.,

```
Q<CR>
Q<CR>
```

would result in a branch to L1. However, they *do not,* because the first .TTYIN leaves the buffer and R0 to be:

Low byte of R0: Q

.TTYIN buffer:

CR	LF				

Thus the "Q" gets put into the byte at address A. The second .TTYIN gives:

Low byte of R0: < CR >

.TTYIN buffer:

LF				

Thus <CR> is put into the byte at address B, and we see that "Q" (ASCII 51_{16}) gets compared with <CR> (ASCII $0D_{16}$). Incidentally, the second line of keyboard input, Q<CR>, will not be seen by the program.

The preceding examples assumed that the entry lines from the keyboard had only the number of characters anticipated by the programmer. This permitted us to empty the buffer by inserting two .TTYINs after the last expected character was read to clear out the <CR> and <LF>. One cannot always anticipate, however, the length of the line that the user will actually put in. For example, suppose the program asks for a "yes" or "no" response and then checks only the first character to see if it is a Y or an N. Perhaps the user will actually type "YES<CR>", or even "YES, THANK YOU<CR>". What is needed to solve this problem is a set of instructions that will take the single character from the .TTYIN buffer, save it, and then clear all remaining characters. Because the end of the line will be marked with a linefeed ($0A_{16}$), the following instructions will do this:

```
G1:         .TTYIN              ; GET BUFFER & FIRST CHAR.
            MOVB    RO,S        ; SAVE FIRST CHAR.
L1:         .TTYIN              ; CLEAR
            CMPB    RO,#^XOA    ;    REST OF
            BNEQU   L1          ;      BUFFER
              .
              .
              .
            HALT
S:          .BLKB   1
```

8.6 | Examples Using .PUTSTR, .TTYIN, and .TTYOUT

Now that we have seen how the .TTYOUT, .PUTSTR, and .TTYIN macro instructions work, let's consider some examples that employ them.

EXAMPLE 8.2   Prepare a MACRO program that accepts a line of keyboard entry consisting of upper case alpha characters. After the line is entered, it should then be printed as the corresponding lower case characters.

The MACRO program for this problem is shown in Figure 8.3. The first section of the program prints a prompt message, rings the bell, and then awaits a line of keyboard input.

The entire line is accepted by the .TTYIN buffer the *first time* the .TTYIN macro is executed. On this execution, the first entered character is also placed in R0.

The ADDB instruction creates a lower case character from an upper case one. This addition is bypassed for <CR>, <LF>, and space characters. The character created

```
            .TITLE   UPPER TO LOWER
;
;         LINE OF UPPER CASE
;         ECHOED AS LOWER CASE
;
          .ENTRY   START,0
;
;   GET LINE OF INPUT & PUT INTO B ARRAY
;
            MOVL    #B,R1        ;INITIALIZE B ARRAY POINTER
            .PUTSTR PROMT        ;PROMPT FOR INPUT
LOOP:       .TTYIN               ;GET CHAR,&/OR FILL BUFFER
            CMPB    RO,#^XOD     ;SKIP IF CR
            BEQLU   L1
            CMPB    RO,#^XOA     ;    OR LF
            BEQLU   L1
            CMPB    RO,#^X20     ;    OR SPACE,
            BEQLU   L1
            ADDB    #^X20,RO     ;MAKE LOWER CASE
L1:         MOVB    RO,(R1)+     ;SAVE IN B ARRAY
            CMPB    RO,#^XOD     ;REPEAT TIL LF
            BNEQU   LOOP
            CLRB    (R1)         ;NULL BYTE TO TURN OFF .PUTSTR
;
;           PRINT   THE B ARRAY
;
            .PUTSTR B
            $EXIT_S              ;EXIT TO VMS(SYSTEM MACRO)
PROMT:      .ASCIZ/ENTER LINE OF UPPER CASE ALPHA CHARACTERS:/<7>
B:          .BLKB   80           ;80 CHARACTER ARRAY
            .END    START
```

FIGURE 8.3/Program for Example 8.2

by the addition is stored in the next byte in B, and the pointer R1 is incremented. The criterion for looping back for more characters from the buffer is whether or not a linefeed character has been encountered.

After completion of the loop, it will be noted that we have stored the carriage return and linefeed in B, as well as the lower case characters. This causes <CR> and <LF> codes to be sent to the output display, resulting in a carriage return and linefeed action. Because .PUTSTR *automatically* sends <CR> <LF>, we could have omitted these characters from the array. As is shown in Figure 8.4, the way we have programmed it gives a blank line after the output.

```
    $ MACRO/LIST E8P2+MACLIB/LIB

$ LINK E8P2+SUBLIB/LIB
$ RUN E8P2
ENTER LINE OF UPPER CASE ALPHA CHARACTERS:
ALL IS QUIET ON THE WESTERN FRONT
all is quiet on the western front

$
```

FIGURE 8.4/Execution of the program for Example 8.2

EXAMPLE 8.3 Write a MACRO program that accepts a single hexadecimal digit from the keyboard, then asks the user to enter a line with at least the number of characters indicated by the digit. Regardless of the entered line length, print out only the number of characters indicated by the digit.

The MACRO program is shown in Figure 8.5. The first .PUTSTR prompts the user for the hexadecimal digit. When read in, this digit is saved in R1 so that subsequent usages of .TTYIN will not destroy it. Assuming that the user enters only one digit and no other characters, the next two .TTYINs will clear the buffer. We then print MSG2, which acknowledges the digit and asks for a line. Note that the .TTYOUT will print the digit on a fresh line because the preceding .PUTSTR issued carriage return and linefeed characters. The next .PUTSTR, for MSG3, will appear on the same line as the digit, however, because .TTYOUT *does not* issue carriage return and linefeed.

The digit entered will actually be the ASCII code for the hexadecimal digit, so we

```
        .TITLE DEMO OF I/O MACROS
;
;       THIS PROGRAM ACCEPTS A SINGLE HEXADECIMAL
;       DIGIT,PRINTS IT OUT,THEN ACCEPTS THAT
;       NUMBER OF OTHER ASCII CHARACTERS AND
;       PRINTS THEM OUT.  ITS PURPOSE IS TO
;       DEMONSTRATE .TTYIN,.TTYOUT AND .PUTSTR.
;
        .ENTRY  START,0
        .PUTSTR MSG1            ;PROMPT USER
        .TTYIN                 ;ACCEPT HEXADECIMAL DIGIT
        MOVB    R0,R1          ;SAVE IN R1
        .TTYIN                 ;CLEAR THE CR IN .TTYIN BUFFER
        .TTYIN                 ;CLEAR THE LF IN .TTYIN BUFFER
        .PUTSTR MSG2           ;ACKNOWLEDGE THE
        .TTYOUT R1             ;   HEXADECIMAL DIGIT AND
        .PUTSTR MSG3           ;       PROMPT FOR CHARACTERS.
        MOVL    #LINE,R2       ;INITIALIZE POINTER FOR LINE
        SUBB    #^X30,R1       ;CONVERT
        CMPB    R1,#^X0A       ;   ASCII
        BLSSU   L0             ;       TO
        SUBB    #^X07,R1       ;           BINARY.
L0:
L1:     .TTYIN                 ;LOOP TO ACCEPT
        MOVB    R0,(R2)+       ;   CHARACTERS
        DECB    R1             ;       INTO
        BGTR    L1             ;           LINE.
L2:     .TTYIN                 ;CLEAR OUT
        CMPB    R0,#^X0A       ;   .TTYIN BUFFER
        BNEQU   L2             ;       TO LF.
        CLRB    (R2)           ;STORE NULL BYTE AT END OF LINE
        .PUTSTR LINE           ;PRINT IT
        $EXIT_S                ;EXIT TO VMS
MSG1:   .ASCIZ  /ENTER A HEXADECIMAL DIGIT/
MSG2:   .ASCIZ  /THANK YOU! NOW ENTER AT LEAST/
MSG3:   .ASCIZ  / CHARACTERS IN A LINE./
LINE:   .BLKB   64
        .END    START
```

FIGURE 8.5/Program for Example 8.3

```
$ MACRO E8P3+MACLIB/LIB
$ LINK E8P3+SUBLIB/LIB
$ RUN E8P3
ENTER A HEXADECIMAL DIGIT
B
THANK YOU! NOW ENTER AT LEAST
B CHARACTERS IN A LINE.
ABCDEFGHIJKLMNOP
ABCDEFGHIJK
$ ▓
```

FIGURE 8.6/Execution of the program for
Example 8.3

have to convert it to binary in order to use it as a loop control variable. This is done by subtracting the so-called ASCII base, which is 30_{16} for decimal digits, and 37_{16} for the A through F digits (see Chapter 7). The subsequent loop accepts the entered line and stores the number of characters indicated by the converted value. These are stored in a byte array beginning at LINE. The second loop clears the .TTYIN buffer.

After storing the specified number of entered characters in LINE, we clear the next byte, creating the "null character" 00. The subsequent .PUTSTR LINE will print all characters in LINE up to this null character. The operation of this program is shown in Figure 8.6.

We call attention to the fact that the program in Example 8.3 fails if the user does not follow directions precisely. We leave as an exercise the determination of what happens if more than one character is entered when the digit is asked for, or if *fewer* than the specified number of characters is entered for the line. Fixing these "bugs" is also an interesting exercise.

8.7 | Error Checking Using Parity (Optional)

Data being transmitted to or from a computer are sometimes distorted by a malfunctioning of the transmission system. The term "line noise" is often used to describe this problem. Line noise is most likely to occur when the data is being transmitted over long distances—on telephone lines, for example. However, line noise can occur even between a terminal and a nearby computer if the components are faulty or improperly adjusted. Some types of errors can actually develop within the computer itself. Because of these realities, computer programs are sometimes written to check for errors and, if any errors are found, to report their occurrence so that appropriate action can be taken. If you are working on a large, well-maintained system, this checking is probably not necessary because it is done by hardware and system programs. In some situations, however, checking for errors is the programmer's responsibility.

One frequently encountered error is the loss of a bit. For example, an ASCII "A" character code may be transmitted as:

$$1000001$$

and may arrive at its destination as:

$$0000001$$

Here it is seen that the MSB has been changed to a 0. The opposite situation can also occur, i.e., the data might be received as:

1100001

where bit 5 has been changed from a 0 to a 1. In either case the receiver has gotten a character code which is different from the one sent, and an error is said to have occurred.

Errors of this type can be discovered if the transmitter and the receiver employ what is called a **parity system.** We shall first describe the **even** parity system. In this system the transmitter sends eight bits rather than seven. The new bit, appended at the left, is set to a 1 or a 0, depending on whether the 7-bit code has an odd or even number of 1-bits. For example, instead of sending the normal ASCII "A" code, it would send:

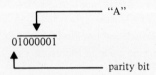

Note that the parity bit is set at 0 here, because this will give the 8-bit code an *even* number of 1-bits. On the other hand, if a "C" was to be sent, the transmitter would send:

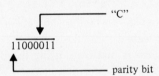

Again, note that the parity is set so as to give an even number of 1-bits in the transmitted code.

If the receiver is told that the transmitter is transmitting *even parity* as described above, the incoming character codes can easily be checked for accuracy; that is, the program can count the number of 1-bits in each character as it is received. If the count is not an even number, an error should be reported. The development of a program to do this is left as an exercise (see Exercise 8.16). It is also possible to provide this checking with the operating system software, or by hardware means. In large time-sharing systems this is most often the case, so that the MACRO programmer does not often need to be concerned with parity.

It should be apparent that an *odd* parity system will work just as well as an even parity system. In an odd parity system, the sender appends a parity bit so as to make the number of 1-bits odd, and the receiver checks for an odd number.

Both the even and odd parity systems suffer from an obvious deficiency: if *two* bits are flipped during transmission, the receiver will not be able to detect the error. However, if the equipment is well designed and maintained, this type of error is unlikely. Moreover, a serious malfunction will most likely be revealed in other ways, such as obviously incorrect results of the computations. Error-checking algorithms, which are more elaborate, are sometimes used. In fact, the VAX-11 has a special instruction for checking errors after data transmission, using what is called **cyclic redundancy checking.** This instruction is beyond the scope of this book, however.

We saw above that the parity system is dependent upon the receiver knowing whether even or odd parity is being used by the sender. External transmitting devices such as terminal keyboards usually can be set, by means of switches or special wiring, to generate either even or odd parity. The receiver must then be set accordingly either through proper programming or by settings on the hardware that provide this function.

Note that if a parity system is in use, it is necessary to remove or ignore the parity bit in the program. To see the need for this, suppose we wish to see if an incoming character is an ASCII "C". If the character is received into the low byte of R0, we might perform the following check:

```
CMPB        R0,#^A'C'
```

The assembler will translate the second operand as an ASCII "C" plus a 0 bit appended at the left. The translated machine code is therefore:

$$43 \qquad 50 \qquad 91$$

where 43_{16} is the hexadecimal code for "C."

However, if a "C" *plus even parity* is received into the low byte of R0, it will contain $C3_{16}$:

$$R0(7:0): C3$$

Obviously these are not the same, so that a subsequent BEQLU would not branch, even if the received character were a "C".

The solution to this problem is **masking,** using the BICB instruction (see Section 7.8). Recalling that BICB clears the destination operand wherever a 1-bit occurs in the mask (the first operand), we need a mask of:

Binary	Hexadecimal
10000000	80

Therefore, we change our program as follows:

```
BICB                #^X80,R0
CMPB                R0,#^A'C'
```

This will ensure that the MSBs of both operands of the CMPB instruction are zero, and that therefore only the 7-bit ASCII code has an effect on the comparison.

8.8 | I/O Without an Operating System (Optional)

The preceding sections dealt with input/output when the program is to execute on a machine with an operating system, e.g., VAX/VMS. Actually, the macros .TTYIN, .TTYOUT, and .PUTSTR provided us with access to more fundamental I/O routines within the operating system, allowing relatively straightforward input and output of character codes. However, when the computer being used *does not* have an operating system, it will be necessary to program the more detailed steps involved in I/O to the physical devices such as printers and keyboards. In this section we introduce some of the considerations when programming I/O at this fundamental level. Because the VAX-11 is somewhat complicated in this area, we focus on a simpler computer such as a rudimentary PDP-11/03.

It is also important to note that the discussion in this section applies *specifically* to situations where the user program has access to the so-called **device registers** (see below). This is usually the case on a single-user machine, such as most configurations of the PDP-11/03. Multiuser systems, such as VAX/VMS, *do not* allow programs other than the operating system itself to access these registers, and the procedures described here are not applicable. Thus if you are using a VAX/VMS or other multiuser system, you should use .TTYIN, .TTYOUT, and .PUTSTR or their equivalents for I/O as described earlier. The methods described here are known as "programmed I/O" using "polling." Other methods are discussed in Chapters 16 and 17.

8.8.1 Device Registers

External devices such as terminals communicate with the CPU through special registers collectively called **device registers.** Although these registers are not actually part of main memory, they have addresses exactly like main memory locations. There are several of these on a typical small computer configuration, allowing the computer to communicate with the operator's console, disk storage units, tape storage units, and the like. Here we are concerned only with those registers for the PDP-11 operator's console. Such a console may be a cathode ray tube (CRT) terminal or a printing terminal. Either device is composed of two parts: a keyboard and a display. Each has two associated device registers, as we will describe.

The two registers associated with the PDP-11 keyboard are called the **keyboard status register (KSR)** and the **keyboard data register (KDR).** These registers are shown in Figure 8.7. Notice that each has a specific address which is assigned when the computer is assembled. (Note that the PDP-11 has 16-bit addresses, conventionally shown in octal.)

The KSR and the KDR work together to make keyboard-generated character codes available to the CPU. The character code generated by depressing a key at the keyboard is accepted into bits 0 through 7 of the KDR. The KSR indicates by the state of bit 7

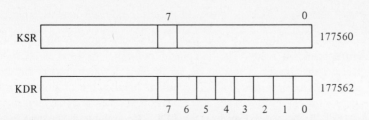

FIGURE 8.7/PDP-11 keyboard device registers

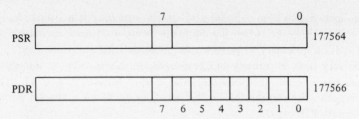

FIGURE 8.8/Printer or display device registers

whether or not the KDR is ready to be read by the CPU. That is, when a key is pressed, the corresponding ASCII code is sent to the KDR. However, because the keyboard and intermediate circuitry require some amount of time to act, this code cannot be assumed to be immediately available to the CPU. As soon as it is ready, however, bit 7 of the KSR is set to 1. The CPU can therefore check the KSR to see if the code can be read from the KDR. When the CPU *does* access the KDR, e.g., by a MOVB instruction, the KSR is *cleared*.

The KSR and KDR on the PDP-11 can be thought of as 16-bit registers. However, only bit 7 of the KSR has any significance. Similarly, the high byte of the KDR is never used.

The PDP-11 console printer or display unit also has a status and data register which we shall call the **printer data register (PDR)** and **printer status register (PSR)**. These are shown in Figure 8.8. The PDR and PSR work in conjunction with one another similarly to the KSR and KDR. In this case, however, the printer reads the character code from the PDR and begins to print it. While this printing is going on, bit 7 of the PSR is set at 0. When the printing process is complete, bit 7 of the PSR is set to 1. This indicates to the program that the PDR is empty and ready to accept another character code.

8.8.2 Printing a Character

Now that we understand the printer device registers from the preceding section, we are prepared to write a program to print a character. The strategy to be employed is as follows:

1. Test bit 7 of the PSR.
2. If bit 7 of the PSR is clear, repeat from Step 1.
3. When bit 7 of the PSR is set to 1, move the character code to be printed to the PDR.

Steps 1 and 2 constitute an "idle loop," the only purpose of which is to "kill time" until the printer is ready. This is called "polling." As soon as bit 7 of the PSR becomes 1, i.e., the printer is ready, we go to Step 3 which moves the code of the character to be printed into the PDR. The printer handles the process from this point on.

Because this discussion is based on the PDP-11 computer rather than the VAX-11, we shall express the implementation of this algorithm in MACRO-11, the assembly language for the PDP-11 family of computers. Fortunately it is quite similar to VAX MACRO. The principal difference is that registers and addresses are 16 bits in length rather than 32 bits.

MACRO-11 code to accomplish the preceding printing strategy is shown in Figure 8.9. Note that we examine bit 7 of the PSR (address 177564) by doing a TSTB followed by BPL. This works because BPL is like the VAX MACRO BGEQ instruction and examines *only* the N condition code, and N is set by TSTB only if the MSB of the *byte* is 1. We assume that the character code to be printed is stored in the low byte of R0 prior to entering this procedure.

```
LOOP:   TSTB 177564     ; TEST PRINTER STATUS
        BPL  LOOP        ; REGISTER
        MOVB RO,177566   ; PRINT RO
```

FIGURE 8.9/MACRO procedure for printing a character (PDP-11 computer)

8.8.3 Reading a Character

Reading a character code from the PDP-11 console keyboard follows a strategy similar to printing, as described above. That is, we repeatedly examine the "ready" bit in the KSR. When it is set, we know that the keyboard has completed the placing of the character code into the KDR, and it can therefore be read by the CPU. This is shown in the procedure in Figure 8.10, which places the result in register R0. Note that after the KDR is placed in R0 we clear bits (15:7). This ensures that register R0 will have only the 7-bit ASCII code in bits (7:0) of the low byte with zeros elsewhere.

```
LOOP:   TSTB    177560
        BPL     LOOP
        MOVB    177562,RO
        BIC     #177600,RO
```

FIGURE 8.10/MACRO-11 procedure for reading a character (PDP-11 computer)

8.9 | Input of Hexadecimal and Decimal Numbers

In earlier chapters we specified the starting-point data for our numerical examples by using the Symbolic Debugger, immediate addressing, e.g., MOVL #2,R0, or the initialization directives .LONG and .BYTE. These methods are not always desirable for actual programs because they require the user to be very familiar with MACRO. Moreover, if the data is established by instructions or directives, rerunning the program for new data requires reassembling and relinking on every use.

Therefore, we now take up the matter of accepting numerical data from the keyboard and converting it to the binary internal representation. Conversion is necessary because the keyboard generates a sequence of ASCII codes for the numeric *characters*, whereas internally we want the *binary* number. For example, keyboard entry of the hexadecimal number 126 sends the following three 8-bit codes (assuming no parity has been added):

$$00110001 \qquad (\text{ASCII ''1''})$$
$$00110010 \qquad (\text{ASCII ''2''})$$
$$00110110 \qquad (\text{ASCII ''6''})$$

However, the 32-bit binary representation of 126_{16} is:

$$0000 \quad 0000 \quad 0000 \quad 0000 \quad 0000 \quad 0001 \quad 0010 \quad 0110 \qquad (126_{16})$$

Thus we somehow have to convert from the sequence of input ASCII codes to the binary representation of the *value* implied by that sequence.

The conversion process will depend upon the input representation. That is, the baker's dozen could be entered in the decimal system as "13," or in the hexadecimal system as "0D"; yet the internal representation is:

$$0000 \quad 0000 \quad 0000 \quad 0000 \quad 0000 \quad 0000 \quad 0000 \quad 1101$$

in either case. We shall begin our discussion with the conversion of multidigit *hexadecimal* numbers, entered from the keyboard, to their binary internal forms. This is called hexadecimal input.

8.9.1 Hexadecimal Input

We shall develop an algorithm for this conversion based on three essential facts:

1. Keyboard entry of a number begins with the most significant digit and proceeds to the least significant digit. That is, when "176" is entered, the computer receives the "1" first.

2. The entered digits, assumed to be 0, 1, . . . , 9, A, . . . , F, are received by the computer as ASCII codes.

3. For any single hexadecimal digit, there is a unique binary value.

These observations suggest the following algorithm:

1. Clear a result register, R1.

2. Accept an ASCII character into the low byte of R0.

3. Convert the low byte of R0 to the binary equivalent of the hexadecimal digit using the algorithm:

   If the ASCII code is greater than or equal to 30_{16} and less than or equal to 39_{16}, then subtract 30_{16}.

   Else if ASCII code is greater than or equal to 41_{16} and less than or equal to 46_{16}, then subtract 37_{16}.

   Else reject as invalid digit.

4. Multiply the result register R1 by 10_{16} (hexadecimal shift left).

5. Add the binary representation of the new digit value to the result register.

6. Repeat from Step **2** until there are no more digits.

To see how this works, consider a simple example. Suppose the entered hexadecimal digits are "24". The contents of the low byte of R0 and R1 *after* each step are shown below. (Hexadecimal is used for convenience; clearly, *binary* is stored.)

Step	R0(7:0)	R1	Notes
1	?	00000000	Clear R1
2	32	00000000	Accept "2"
3	02	00000000	Convert to binary
4	02	00000000	Hex shift R1
5	02	00000002	Add new digit
2	34	00000002	Accept "4"
3	04	00000002	Convert to binary
4	04	00000020	Hex shift R1
5	04	00000024	Add new digit

The key to the success of this algorithm is that we shift the previous result in R1 to the left one hexadecimal digit, and then add the new digit. In effect, this is just like writing each new digit at the right of those received previously.

Figure 8.11 shows a MACRO program that employs the above algorithm. It has been enhanced by prompting for input by "*", and checking for invalid characters.

Let us go through Figure 8.11 to see exactly how it works. After prompting for input, the input line is read, and the first character is placed in R0 by .TTYIN. If the character is a carriage return, it loops back to get the expected linefeed, and branches out. Otherwise, the character is checked to see that it lies within the range of valid hexadecimal digits. Note that for the first check we subtract the ASCII code for a 0 from R0. If the code is less than 30_{16}, we know that it is not a valid decimal digit character, and we branch to the error handling section of the program at L3. If it passes the first test, we check to see if it is perhaps too large to be an ASCII code for a decimal digit. Now, however, we have the *binary value* in R0, because 30_{16} has already been subtracted. Thus if R0 is less than $0A_{16}$ (10_{10}), we know that a valid decimal digit was entered, and we branch to L2 for processing the digit. If it fails this test, we check to see if it is a valid hexadecimal digit in the range A through F. The CMPB R0,#^X11 followed by BLSSU to L3 has the effect of rejecting the characters that lie between "9" and "A". (See Table 7.1.) If it is not one of these characters, we subtract 07_{16}, which should give the binary value of the entered digit. However, it still might be beyond the "F" character, in which case it will be greater than $0F_{16}$. The final comparison checks for this case and branches to the error-handling instruction if it occurs. Otherwise, it falls through the branch and processes the digit.

The error-handling instructions begin at L3. These instructions clear the .TTYIN buffer, print the message stored at the MSG label, and then branch back to the beginning of the program. Note that we branch to the CLRL R0 instruction so that any portion of the previously entered number (before an invalid digit was encountered) is discarded.

The hexadecimal conversion code is composed of the two instructions MULL and ADDL. The MULL #^X10,R1 is a hexadecimal shift, as described earlier. Note that

```
            .TITLE HEXADECIMAL INPUT
    ;
    ;       ACCEPT KEYBOARD HEX   (0-FFFFFFFF) AND CONVERT TO
    ;       BINARY NUMBER IN R0.
    ;
            .ENTRY   START,0
LO:         CLRL     R1                   ;CLEAR RESULT REGISTER
            .TTYOUT  #^A'*'               ;PROMT USER FOR INPUT
L1:         .TTYIN                        ;GET CHARACTER
            CMPB     R0,#^X0D             ;IF CR
            BEQLU    L1                   ;   LOOK FOR LF.
            CMPB     R0,#^X0A             ;IF LF
            BEQLU    OUT                  ;   NUMBER IS COMPLETE.
            SUBB     #^X30,R0             ;CONVERT ASCII TO BIN.
            BLSSU    L3                   ;INVALID HEXADECIMAL DIGIT
            CMPB     R0,#^X0A             ;
            BLSSU    L2                   ;VALID ARABIC DIGIT
            CMPB     R0,#^X11             ;REJECT ":" THRU "@"
            BLSSU    L3                   ;
            SUBB     #^X07,R0             ;ASSUME A,B,C,D,E, OR F
            CMPB     R0,#^X0F             ;REJECT ABOVE F
            BGTRU    L3
L2:         MULL     #^X10,R1             ;MULTIPLY CURRENT BY HEX 10
            ADDL     R0,R1                ;ADD NEW DIGIT
            BRB      L1                   ;GET NEXT DIGIT
L3:         .TTYIN                        ;BAD CHAR. HANDLING
            CMPB     R0,#^X0A             ;CLEAR .TTYIN BUFFER
            BNEQ     L3
            .PUTSTR  MSG                  ;PRINT ERROR MSG.
            BRB      LO                   ;  AND START OVER.
OUT:        MOVL     R1,R0                ;PUT RESULT INTO R0
            $EXIT_S                       ;EXIT TO VMS
MSG:        .ASCIZ/SOME CHARACTER WAS NOT HEX. START OVER./
            .END     START
```

FIGURE 8.11/MACRO program for hexadecimal input

we could use the shift instruction ASHL #4,R1,R1 to accomplish the same result. Instead we use MULL in order to minimize the changes needed to use the program for *decimal* input. (See Section 8.9.2.)

The ADDL instruction adds the binary value of the new digit. The BRB L1 after ADDL ensures that we loop back until all digits have been read and converted. The exit from the loop occurs upon obtaining the linefeed character which follows all keyboard entry through .TTYIN. The final step in the program is to place the result into R0, because this is the customary register in which to leave the result of an input operation. Because there is no output from this program, we would have to run it with the Symbolic Debugger to prove that it works.

It should be observed that while the program in Figure 8.11 accepts hexadecimal numbers from 0 to FFFFFFFF, any subsequent interpretation of these numbers by the program is arbitrary. That is, the number FFFFFFFE could be entered and interpreted as an unsigned integer ($4,294,967,294_{10}$) or as a two's complement number (-2_{10}). Thus, in a sense, the program allows entry of negative numbers, even though a minus sign will not be accepted.

8.9.2 Decimal Input

The algorithm and program described above for hexadecimal input can, with only minor modifications, be used for *decimal* input. Indeed, the steps are the same except that the digit symbols A through F must be rejected, and the current value must be multiplied by *decimal* 10 before adding the new digit. The program in Figure 8.11 could be modified to accept decimal by the following two changes:

1. Change the invalid digit test to accept only the digits 0 through 9. This requires removal of five instructions beginning with BLSSU L2, and changing BGTRU L3 to BGEQU L3.

2. Change MULL #ˆX10,R1 to MULL #10,R1. This does a decimal shift rather than hexadecimal.

8.9.3 Output of Hexadecimal Numbers

An integer numerical value is usually represented as either a two's complement or an unsigned binary integer on the VAX-11. As such, it cannot be printed directly. For example, a common error made by beginning programmers is as follows (incorrect example):

```
        MOVL    #52,A
        .PUTSTR A
A:      .BLKL   1
```

Here the programmer may think that "52" will be printed, because that is what was put into A. The reason that this will not work is that the .PUTSTR A expects to find *ASCII codes* at address A, whereas instead there is the binary equivalent of 52_{10}, i.e.,

A: 0000 0000 0000 0000 0000 0000 0011 0100 (52_{10})

Interpreted as ASCII, this is the "4" character followed by three null characters.

Therefore, if we wish to print a number we must first *convert* it from its internal binary representation to a series of ASCII codes. This can be done by the subtractive method discussed in Section 2.4.4 in connection with decimal-to-hexadecimal conversion. This process works equally well for converting from binary to hexadecimal.

To apply the subtractive method with hexadecimal, one works with a powers-of-16 table:

n	16^n (in Hexadecimal)
0	1
1	10
2	100
3	1000
4	10000
5	100000
6	1000000
7	10000000

The *n* in this table can be viewed as the digit position index in a multidigit hexadecimal number, and the power can be viewed as the "place value." For example, in the hexadecimal number 142365, the digit 3 is in position 2; because the place value of this position is 100, this digit contributes 3×100 to the value.

The conversion strategy is to start with the highest place value and subtract it as many times as possible from the number being converted. The number of times it can be subtracted is obviously the digit value for that place. Then the next highest place value is repeatedly subtracted to find the next digit, and so on. Note that this strategy determines the digits from left to right. This is convenient because it is the order in which they must be printed.

As an example, consider determination of the hexadecimal digits for the binary number:

0000   0000   0000   0001   0110   0000   0011   0010 (00016032_{16})

By the subtraction method we determine the hexadecimal digits one at a time, as shown in the following table. (We show the work in hexadecimal, for convenience, but the computer will carry it out in binary.)

Place Value	Can Be Subtracted	Remainder	Digit
10000000	0 times	00016032	$D_7 = 0$
1000000	0 times	00016032	$D_6 = 0$
100000	0 times	00016032	$D_5 = 0$
10000	1 times	00006032	$D_4 = 1$
1000	6 times	00000032	$D_3 = 6$
100	0 times	00000032	$D_2 = 0$
10	3 times	00000002	$D_1 = 3$
1	2 times	00000000	$D_0 = 2$

Observe that because the 32-bit longword will allow a hexadecimal number of no more than eight digits, we do not need powers of sixteen greater than 16^7.

A MACRO program using this strategy is shown in Figure 8.12. The value placed in R0 by the first instruction of the program will be printed. The program uses two arrays, PV and A. The PV array holds the place values, while A is a byte array that will store the ASCII codes of the hexadecimal digits as they are determined.

The two pointers into these arrays, R1 and R3, are initialized prior to entry into the major loop of the program. The major loop, beginning at NEXT and extending to the SOBGTR instruction, is repeated eight times; each time through this loop a new digit is determined and stored in A as its ASCII code.

Inside the major loop is another loop, beginning at L2 and extending to BGEQU L2. The body of this inner loop increments the current digit value and subtracts the current place value from the number in R0. When the subtraction results in a borrow into the MSB, the C condition code is set, causing exit from the loop. This means that we have "over-subtracted." Therefore, upon exit from the loop, we correct for the over-subtraction by adding the current place value back into R0. This process *counts*

```
        .TITLE   HEXADECIMAL OUTPUT
;
;       THIS PROGRAM WILL PRINT THE NUMBER FOUND IN R0 AT
;       USERS TERMINAL AS AN 8-DIGIT HEXADECIMAL NUMBER.
;
        .ENTRY   START,0
        MOVL     #^XABCD1234,R0   ;EXAMPLE VALUE TO BE PRINTED
        MOVL     #PV,R1           ;INITIALIZE PLACE VALUE POINTER
        MOVL     #8,R2            ;INITIALIZE LCV (8 DIGITS)
        MOVL     #A,R3            ;INITIALIZE RESULT DIGIT POINTER
L1:     MOVL     #-1,R4           ;INITIALIZE DIGIT VALUE
L2:     INCL     R4               ;UPDATE DIGIT VALUE
        SUBL     (R1),R0          ;SUBTRACT PLACE VALUE
        BGEQU    L2               ;   UNTIL OVER SUBTRACTED.
        ADDL     (R1)+,R0         ;CORRECT FOR OVER SUBTRACT
        CMPB     R4,#^X0A         ;CONVERT
        BLSSU    L3               ;   DIGIT
        ADDB     #^X07,R4         ;      TO
L3:     ADDB     #^X30,R4         ;         ASCII.
        MOVB     R4,(R3)+         ;STORE CHAR. IN PRINT ARRAY
        SOBGTR   R2,L1            ;REPEAT FOR NEXT DIGIT
        .PUTSTR  A                ;PRINT RESULT
        $EXIT_S                   ;EXIT TO VMS
;       PLACE VALUES
PV:     .LONG    ^X10000000
        .LONG    ^X1000000
        .LONG    ^X100000
        .LONG    ^X10000
        .LONG    ^X1000
        .LONG    ^X100
        .LONG    ^X10
        .LONG    ^X1
A:      .BLKB    8                ;RESULT ARRAY
        .BYTE    0                ;NULL CHAR TO TURN OFF .PUTSTR
        .END     START
```

FIGURE 8.12/MACRO program to print a hexadecimal number

the number of times the place value can be subtracted. At this point we have the *binary value* of the digit in R4. The ASCII equivalent is found by adding 30_{16} if the digit value is less than $0A_{16}$, or 37_{16} if it is $0A_{16}$ or greater. This result is then saved in the next byte of A, and the A array pointer is incremented automatically.

After exit from the major loop all digits have been determined and their ASCII codes are in A. The .PUTSTR A macro then sends these ASCII codes to the printer or display, completing the program.

8.9.4 Output of Decimal Numbers

With minor modification the algorithm presented in the previous section also works for printing decimal numbers. First, observe that in decimal the place values are different, i.e., the second digit in a decimal number is worth 10 *decimal* rather than 10 *hexadecimal*. Secondly, the largest decimal number that can be represented in a 32-bit longword needs ten decimal digits (e.g., 4,294,967,295) rather than the eight required hexadecimal digits (e.g., FFFFFFFF). These observations lead us to the following modifications of the program in Figure 8.12 in order to make it convert binary numbers to decimal:

1. Initialize the LCV to 10_{10} rather than 8_{10}; that is,

```
MOVL #10,R2,
```

2. Change the place values to decimal and add place values for two more digits. For example,

```
PV:    .LONG 1000000000
       .LONG 100000000
              .
              .
              .
```

3. Change the storage array to ten digits; that is,

```
A:    .BLKB 10
```

With these minor modifications, the program will convert the 32-bit binary number in R0 to decimal for output.

It must be recognized that the program as modified treats the contents of R0 as an unsigned integer. that is, if R0 is:

$$1111 \quad 1111 \quad 1111 \quad 1111 \quad 1111 \quad 1111 \quad 1111 \quad 1110$$

it will print 4294967294, not -2. If it is desired to treat R0 as a two's complement number (which might be negative), the program would have to be modified. This modification is left as an exercise.

8.10 | Summary

The topic of this chapter has been input and output. We first examined the input and output of ASCII characters using **macros** (meaning large instructions) similar to those often supplied in operating system libraries. The macros used here included .TTYOUT which prints a single character, .TTYIN which reads a single character, and .PUTSTR which prints an array of characters. It was pointed out that these macros or their equivalents will have to be installed on your system before they can be used, if they are not already in place in the library. It was also noted that some type of system macros are *necessary* if you are working on a multiuser time-sharing computer system. This is because such a system must necessarily control access to the so-called device registers (also called I/O ports). However, small "stand-alone" computers do not require, and may not have, these macros. In such cases, the input process involves moving the input character from the keyboard data register, but only *after* looping, until the keyboard *status* register indicates that the character is ready. Similarly, output requires moving a character to the printer data register after its status register indicates that it is ready. This is called **programmed I/O.**

Section 8.7 dealt with the idea of **parity** as a means of error checking. The central concept here is setting bit 7 in the byte (otherwise unused for a 7-bit ASCII character code) so as to give an *even* number of 1-bits (even parity), or an *odd* number of 1-bits (odd parity). When the code is transmitted and one of the bits gets reversed (flipped from 1 to 0 or 0 to 1), the receiver can detect the error by counting the 1-bits. If such a system is employed, the program can check for parity transmission errors. When a parity system is in use, even if no errors are detected it will be necessary to ignore the MSB in any comparison with 7-bit ASCII codes in the program. This is facilitated with "masking" using the BICB and BICL instructions introduced in Chapter 7.

Sections 8.8 and 8.9 dealt with **input and output of numerical data.** We observed that input required the incoming ASCII codes representing hexadecimal (or decimal) digits to be converted to binary and added into the developing internal value. The algorithm which we examined for doing this took advantage of the fact that keyboard entry produces the most significant digit first. Therefore, ensuring that each digit was added in at its correct place value required only that we *shift* the previous sum one digit to the left. This shift was achieved by multiplying by 10_{16} for hexadecimal input, or 10_{10} for decimal input. Indeed, we found that the algorithm could be converted to decimal input merely by changing the multiplier from 10_{16} to 10_{10}, and changing the range of allowable digits. Numerical output required that we convert the internal binary representation to the series of ASCII codes required for hexadecimal (or decimal) representation. We found that an algorithm using repeated subtraction worked well for this purpose. In this algorithm, we determined each digit, beginning at the left, by determining how many times the place value could be subtracted. An array of place values, selected by a pointer, made this process straightforward and efficient. After determination of each digit *value* by this process, we converted it to an ASCII code and stored it for later printing. Again we found that decimal output could be achieved by very minor modifications of the hexadecimal routine.

8.11 | Exercises

8.1 Indicate that will happen upon execution of the following instructions:

```
(a) .TTYOUT  #^X2B      (b) MOVB  #7,B
                            .TTYOUT B

(c) A:  .ASCIZ /X+Y/     (d) .TTYIN
    S:  .PUTSTR A            MOVB    R0,B
                            .PUTSTR B

(e) .TTYIN
    .TTYIN
    .TTYOUT R0
```

8.2 Write a program segment that will prompt the user with a ">", then accept a single character *on the same line as the prompt*, then echo this character on the next line, and finally position the terminal display cursor at the beginning of the next line.

8.3 Modify the program in Example 7.4 to accept the sentence from the keyboard, store it, then determine and print out the number of words and the length of each word. You may use .PUTHEX (see Section 4.11) or the techniques for hexadecimal output discussed in this chapter. Label the results.

8.4 Write a program that accepts a sentence as all upper case alpha characters, and then prints it out with only the first character upper case and the rest lower case.

8.5 Modify the program of Example 8.3 so that it behaves in an acceptable manner when the user does not follow input directions precisely. Test it by responding with a 2-digit integer, and also by entering *fewer* than the requested number of characters.

8.6 Write a program that accepts two characters from the keyboard, stores them in a memory location, and then prints out the resulting bit pattern. (*Hint:* Use shift instruction to allow examination of each bit, and print out the ASCII character for either 0 or 1, as the case may be.)

8.7 Write a program that accepts four characters from the keyboard, stores them in a longword memory location (with the first entered character in the low byte), and then prints out the longword contents as four hexadecimal digits. (*Hint:* Use shifts and BICL with the appropriate mask to examine the bits in groups of four. Use these four bits to determine the appropriate ASCII code to print.)

8.8 Write a program that will accept up to 20 hexadecimal numbers in the range 0–FFFFFFFF and sort them into descending order, treating them as unsigned integers. Print out the sorted list of numbers.

8.9 Work Exercise 8.8, treating the numbers as two's complement numbers.

8.10 Write a program that behaves like a four-function, reverse-Polish calculator. That is, it should accept two hexadecimal numbers, then an operator—either ''+'', ''-'', ''*'', or ''/''. It should then print out the result. For example, 20, 2, * should produce 40.

8.11 Modify the hexadecimal input and output programs given in this chapter to work in decimal, but with the numbers restricted to unsigned integers.

8.12 Modify the hexadecimal input and output programs given in this chapter to work with positive or negative integers.

8.13 Modify the hexadecimal input and output programs given in this chapter to work in octal, but with the numbers restricted to unsigned integers.

8.14 Write a program that accepts a decimal number from the keyboard and prints its hexadecimal representation.

8.15 Write a program that accepts a hexadecimal number from the keyboard and prints its decimal representation.

8.16 Assume that a block of bytes beginning at M has somehow been filled with ASCII characters. The MSB in each of these bytes has supposedly been set to "even parity," meaning that it has been set to 0 or 1, as required, to give an even number of 1 bits in the byte. However, errors may have occurred such that a byte may no longer be in true parity. Write a program sequence that will examine each byte and move each character that doesn't have a parity error (i.e., has an even sum of bits) to a new array beginning at D. The MSB's in D should all be cleared. Errors in M should appear as DEL ($7F_{16}$) in D.

9

Subroutines and Stacks

9.1 | The Need for Subroutines

The programs that we have examined up to this point have been small and relatively simple in terms of purpose. However, it will be found that programs addressing more significant problems become large and unwieldy if one relies solely on the methods presented thus far. That is, complex programs that incorporate all of the detailed steps in a single, large set of instructions are difficult to develop, and confusing to those who wish to understand how they work. What we need then is some mechanism for dividing a large, complex programming task into a group of small, simple tasks. By far, the most important of the programming concepts that allow efficient, straightforward construction of sophisticated programs is the **subroutine.**

This chapter shows how subroutines are written and used in MACRO on the VAX-11. Most of these ideas, however, are common to many contemporary assembly languages and computers. We will first develop the essential concepts and show their application through simple examples. Full understanding of the MACRO subroutine call requires that we then introduce the concept of a data structure called a **stack.** This is an important concept in its own right, but also plays a key role in VAX-11 subroutine calls. Other related matters are also discussed in this chapter, such as how to transfer information to and from the subroutine and how to avoid disturbing the contents of the general registers during subroutine execution. Included also is a discussion of a special kind of subroutine on the VAX-11 called a **procedure.** Finally, we shall examine how subroutines can be developed and assembled separately for later use in any other program.

This chapter also introduces three new addressing modes—**displacement, displacement-deferred,** and **autoincrement-deferred**—used in connection with subroutine and procedure argument transmission.

9.2 | Characteristics of Subroutines

A subroutine is a group of instructions that has a purpose *subordinate* to the main purpose of a program. These instructions are usually physically separated from the main program. This separation is made possible by two special types of instructions, namely, **subroutine transfer instructions,** and **subroutine return instructions.** The VAX-11 has several different instructions of each type. Initially, we will use the BSBW (**B**ranch to **SuB**routine with **W**ord displacement) and RSB (**R**eturn from **SuB**routine) for subroutine return.

BSBW is placed in the "calling" program and causes control to be transferred to the first instruction in the subroutine. Unlike other branch instructions, however, a BSBW causes the machine to "remember" where it was, so that control can be transferred back to the calling program upon completion of the subroutine. The RSB instruction performs this return transfer. It is placed in the subroutine (usually at the end) and causes control to be transferred back to the calling program, specifically to the instruction following the BSBW.

Usually subroutines have a single purpose and are small. However, any number of instructions of any type can occur in the subroutine before the RSB, and the contained instructions will be executed each time control is transferred to the subroutine. It is important to note that control can be transferred to the subroutine from any number of places in the main program, and even from other subroutines. This is possible because the computer remembers where it was, so that control can be transferred back to the correct place after subroutine execution.

Subroutines contribute to programming efficiency and clarity in a number of ways. First, they allow the details of subordinate computations to be removed from the main program. This helps the programmer remain focused on the principal problem being attacked, rather than becoming distracted with details of subordinate computations. Anyone who has to read the program will also benefit from this approach. This advantage is intensified when the same calculations have to be repeated at several places in the program. Rather than being repeated, the instructions can be written once as a subroutine and used from anywhere in the program as often as needed by means of BSBW instructions. This method conserves memory space as well as programming effort.

9.3 | Elementary Subroutine Usage

A MACRO subroutine is invoked by means of the transfer instruction:

```
BSBW label
```

where *label* is the label of the first instruction in the subroutine, called its entry point. This causes PC to be set to the address of *label*, so that subroutine execution automatically begins.

The subroutine itself, occurring anywhere in the program (or even separately assembled), has the following form:

label: instruction 1

instruction 2

•

•

•

RSB

The RSB instruction causes control to be passed back to the instruction that follows the BSBW *label* instruction. That is, PC is set to the address of the instruction following the one containing the BSBW.

The translation of the BSBW instruction is:

30	opcode
dd	displacement
dd	

Here *displacement* is the number of bytes that must be added to PC to reach *label*. Because the displacement is one word (two bytes), the PC is actually set to a position *three* bytes beyond the BSBW instruction upon return.

There are two other instructions that perform essentially the same operation as BSBW. One is the BSBB (**B**ranch to **SuB**routine with **B**yte displacement), which is exactly like BSBW except that it allows only one byte for the displacement. Thus you can only use BSBB to invoke a subroutine if the subroutine entry point is within -128_{10} to $+127_{10}$ bytes of the location where BSBB is stored. BSBB is often used when the subroutine is part of the same assembly module as the routine that uses it. Most of the examples in this chapter meet this description, so we could use BSBB. We most often choose to use BSBW, however, because in practice subroutines are frequently assembled separately and linked together by the linker, so that one cannot be assured that the subroutine will be within -128_{10} to $+127_{10}$ bytes of all places where it is used.

The opcode of the BSBB is 10, and because the displacement is one byte, the translation is:

10	opcode
dd	displacement

The other form of subroutine transfer that is similar to BSBW is the JSB (**J**ump to **SuB**routine) instruction. Its usage is of the form:

```
JSB destination
```

where *destination* refers to the subroutine entry point. *Destination* can be designated *with any addressing method* other than direct register addressing. For example, we could write:

```
JSB  SUB1   (relative addressing)
JSB  (R1)   (register deferred addressing)
```

This gives the ability to transfer to subroutines located anywhere within the virtual address space, and also provides added flexibility in specifying its location. We will not have occasion to use the JSB instruction in the simple examples in this chapter, however.

Note that BSBW, BSBB, and JSB all use the same subroutine return instruction, i.e., RSB. This instruction translates to a single byte of machine code, namely, 05.

EXAMPLE 9.1 An example of a simple subroutine and its usage is shown in Fig. 9.1. Here we have written a program that will raise each of the two numbers, stored in A and B, to the power of 4, making use of a simple subroutine to perform the arithmetic. The main program is placed at the beginning, and the subroutine at the end, although this order is not important. PWR4 has been selected as a label, or name, for the subroutine.

Let us examine how this program works. The main program first moves the contents of A into R0 because PWR4 actually operates on R0. By placing A into R0, we are doing what is called "passing" or "transmitting" the argument to the subroutine; other methods of doing this are discussed later. The first BSBW PWR4 causes control to be passed to the first instruction in the subroutine, MULL R0,R0, which raises the original value to the second power. The second MULL R0,R0 then gives the fourth power, as desired, leaving the final result in R0. The RSB instruction then causes control to be passed back to the main program—specifically, to the MOVL R0,A instruction that stores the result back into A.

The next sequence of instructions in the main program raises B to the fourth power. This time the value stored in B is moved into R0, and control is again passed to

```
            .TITLE      EXAMPLE 9.1
    ;
    ;      RAISE A AND B TO FOURTH POWER USING A SUBROUTINE
    ;
            .ENTRY    START,0
            MOVL      A,R0              ;RAISE A TO 4TH POWER
            BSBW      PWR4             ;  AND PLACE BACK
            MOVL      R0,A             ;    INTO A.
            MOVL      B,R0             ;NOW B
            BSBW      PWR4             ;
            MOVL      R0,B             ;
            $EXIT_S                    ;EXIT TO VMS
A:          .LONG     4
B:          .LONG     8
    ;
    ;      END OF MAIN PROGRAM
    ;
PWR4:
    ;
    ;      FORTH POWER SUBROUTINE
    ;
            MULL      R0,R0
            MULL      R0,R0
            RSB                        ;RETURN TO CALLER
    ;
    ;      END OF SUBROUTINE
    ;
            .END      START
```

FIGURE 9.1/Example of simple subroutine usage

PWR4. Upon completion, RSB returns control to the MOVL R0,B instruction. Note that each time RSB is reached, control passes back to the instruction immediately following the most recent BSBW PWR4 instruction. As noted previously, this is because the machine can "remember" where the subroutine call came from. Next we will see exactly how the VAX-11 accomplishes this.

Subroutines are of great benefit to the programmer, but they also require consideration of factors that would not come up otherwise. These factors are:

1. *Linkage:* Linkage refers to the mechanism whereby control is transferred to the subroutine and returned to the proper place after completion. (Note that we are using a different meaning of *linkage* than that used in Section 1.3.)
2. *Argument transmission:* Subroutines usually require certain inputs and generate certain results. Therefore, there must be a mechansim for transmitting data to and from the subroutine. This is an especially important consideration when the subroutine is used with different input values from different points in the program, and when the subroutine is assembled separately.
3. *Side effects:* Ideally, a subroutine should perform only the task it was designed to perform, without disturbing other locations or registers. Any changes to memory or registers other than the intended changes are called "side effects," and are undesirable.

These considerations are taken up in the following paragraphs. We shall begin with a study of the data structure known as a **stack** because this can play a role in each of these considerations.

9.4 | Stacks

A stack is a way of organizing objects such that the most recently added object is also the next one accessible for removal. A classic example is a stack of dinner plates in a cafeteria. Clean plates are placed on top of the stack, and are also removed from the top. The stack of dishes often lies on a platform supported by a spring, so that each plate added pushes the stack down, and each one removed causes the stack to pop up.

The data structure called a stack is a way of organizing data that is completely analogous to the stack of cafeteria plates. It is an appropriate structure whenever the last item to be put into the set of data items is the next one needed for retrieval. Many problems in computer science require just such an organization. MACRO offers convenient means of using data stacks in assembly programming.

A data stack occupies a group of adjacent locations in the main memory. These locations are specifically set aside for the stack, either by the programmer or by LINK at the time the program is linked. We can picture the stack as shown in Fig. 9.2, where we assume that eight bytes have been reserved for it between virtual addresses 7FFFFFF8 and 7FFFFFFF.

First observe that the so-called bottom of the stack is one byte *higher* in memory than the first actual data position. Each added piece of data goes into the next *lower* memory location. As shown, there are four entries in the stack, with the number $1E_{16}$ occupying the "top" position. Bytes above the top will have some (probably nonzero)

Main memory

?	7FFFFFF8 last usable location
?	7FFFFFF9
?	7FFFFFFA
?	7FFFFFFB
1E	7FFFFFFC top of stack
5C	7FFFFFFD
33	7FFFFFFE
21	7FFFFFFF first usable location

80000000 bottom of stack

Registers

R4	77
R5	
SP	7FFFFFFC
PC	

FIGURE 9.2/Data stack with eight bytes

contents, but with respect to the stack, they are regarded as empty. We show this with a question mark.

It is possible to set up stacks for various purposes anywhere in main memory. However, there is one stack set up automatically by the linker called the **User Stack.** Most often, this stack will meet all programming needs. The Stack Pointer register (SP) is automatically set to point to this stack when the program begins to execute.

An item of data can be placed in the User Stack (at the top) by use of any of the move instructions, i.e., MOVL, MOVB, or MOVW, along with *autodecrement addressing* on the destination operand. For example, suppose the stack and registers are as shown in Figure 9.2. If the instruction:

```
MOVB   R4,-(SP)
```

is executed, the result will be as shown in Figure 9.3. This instruction is often called a "push" and is analogous to the action of pushing another plate onto the stack of cafeteria dishes.

In order to remove any item from the stack, we use a move instruction with autoincrement addressing on the source operand. For example, if the registers and memory are left as shown in Figure 9.3, and the instructions:

```
MOVB   (SP)+,R5
MOVB   (SP)+,R4
```

are executed, the result is as shown in Figure 9.4. A study of this will reveal that we have removed ("popped") the top two stack entries and placed them into R5 and R4, respectively. Furthermore, this action has left the stack pointer pointing at the new top of the stack. Note that we again regard the locations above the pointer as empty, even though the previous values remain undisturbed in this example.

In general, then, byte data items are added to or removed from the stack by the instructions:

```
MOVB   S,-(SP)    ; PUSH S ONTO STACK
MOVB   (SP)+,D    ; POP TOP OF STACK INTO D
```

Main memory

?	7FFFFFF8 last usable location
?	7FFFFFF9
?	7FFFFFFA
77	7FFFFFFB top of stack
1E	7FFFFFFC
57	7FFFFFFD
33	7FFFFFFE
21	7FFFFFFF first usable location

80000000 bottom of stack

Registers

R4	77
R5	
SP	7FFFFFFB
PC	

FIGURE 9.3/The stack after pushing a byte containing 77 onto it

After either push or pop instructions, the stack pointer is left properly positioned for the next push or pop operation. The other operand in each of these instructions (S or D) can use any addressing mode.

It is interesting to note that the same stack can be used for many different purposes, as long as three simple rules are followed. One rule is to always remove from the stack whatever was placed there. For example, a certain item can be placed on top of the stack at the beginning of a program. The stack can then be used for any number of pushes and pops throughout the program, and as long as every push is matched with a pop, the original item can be popped from the top of the stack at the end of the program. The second rule is to remove items in the reverse order in which they were placed in the stack. For example, if A, B, and C are pushed onto the stack, they must be popped

Main memory

?	7FFFFFF8 last usable location
?	7FFFFFF9
?	7FFFFFFA
?	7FFFFFFB
?	7FFFFFFC
57	7FFFFFFD top of stack
33	7FFFFFFE
21	7FFFFFFF first usable location

80000000 bottom of stack

Registers

R4	1E
R5	77
SP	7FFFFFFD
PC	

FIGURE 9.4/The stack after popping two bytes from it

off as C, B, and A. The third rule is not to depend on any value above the current stack pointer. The reasons for this are discussed below.

Space for the User Stack is usually allocated by VAX/VMS at the high end of User Space (see Section 3.4.3). This is why we have shown the bottom of the stack at virtual address 80000000_{16} in Figures 9.2, 9.3, and 9.4. However, if you examine the SP using the Symbolic Debugger you will find an address *lower* than this even before your program has placed anything in the stack. The reason for this is that your User Stack is also used by system software needed to run your program. For all practical purposes, however, you may consider the bottom of the User Stack to be whatever address is in SP prior to the first push in your program. It makes no difference what address this happens to be, because all of your pushes will cause the stack to "grow" to smaller addresses, and if you include a pop for every push SP will be reset to its original value at the completion of your program.

The preceding discussion is based on the idea of a stack of bytes. It is also possible to use a stack in which the items are words or longwords rather than bytes. In the case of longwords the push and pop instructions would be:

```
MOVL S,-(Rn)   ; PUSH LONGWORD
MOVL (Rn)+,D   ; POP  LONGWORD
```

Here S and D are assumed to be longword operands. We have used the longword form of the move instruction, so the stack pointer register will be incremented or decremented by four.

For example, if the stack were as we left it in Figure 9.4, and the instruction:

```
MOVL R4,-(SP)
```

were executed, the result would be as shown in Figure 9.5. Observe that the most significant bytes are pushed on the stack first, so that the longword on the stack is stored in the normal manner, i.e., with the least significant bytes at the lower addresses.

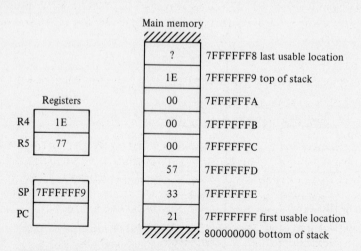

FIGURE 9.5/The stack after a longword push of 1E onto it

When data items of varying lengths are placed on the stack, you must be very careful to use the same length upon removal as used when placing them on the stack. Consider, for example, popping the $1E_{16}$ from the stack as shown in Figure 9.5 with:

```
MOVB    (SP)+,R3
```

You may think that the stack pointer would be left pointing at the 57 because you pushed $1E_{16}$ onto the stack and then popped it off. However, the MOVB instruction performs autodecrement by one, so the high-order bytes remain in the stack, and SP points to 00. Because of this possible source of error, some programmers prefer to keep the stack "longword aligned" by pushing only longwords onto it. When it is necessary to put a byte into the stack following this policy, you use **MOVZBL** instead of MOVB, and remove it with the **CVTLB** (ConVerT Longword to Byte) instruction. For example,

```
MOVZBL  SB,-(SP)    ; PUSH BYTE ONTO LONGWORD STACK
CVTLB   (SP)+,DB    ; POP BYTE FROM LONGWORD STACK
```

An added advantage of this policy is that the VAX-11 hardware can manipulate the stack faster if longword alignment is maintained. The disadvantage, of course, is that is wastes stack space.

Most often, the User Stack will meet your needs whenever a data structure of this nature appears desirable. However, it is also possible to establish different stacks at other places in main memory, using registers other than SP as pointers. This is explored when we take up stacks as general data structures in Chapter 12.

9.5 | Subroutine Linkage and the User Stack

Previously we noted that the principal difference between a normal branch and a subroutine transfer instruction is the ability to return to the location following the branch. We will now examine how the VAX-11 has provided for this transfer to and from subroutines. This is called **linkage,** and the User Stack plays a major role.

As we have seen, the transfer to a subroutine can be done with the BSBW instruction. For example,

```
BSBW    SUB1
```

transfers to a subroutine called SUB1. When BSBW executes, *two* things happen, namely:

1. The *current* PC is pushed onto the User Stack.
2. The displacement, stored after the BSBW opcode, is added to the PC.

It must be emphasized that the current PC that is saved on the User Stack in Step 1 is, in fact, the *return address*. This is because the Instruction Fetch Execute Cycle causes PC to be advanced as the BSBW operand (i.e., the displacement) is being fetched, so that PC points to the location *following* this operand before BSBW is executed. Thus we see that the User Stack provides a place to store the return address.

The second step has the effect of a normal branch instruction. Recall that the displacement, as determined by the MACRO assembler, represents the distance between the location currently pointed to by the PC and the destination. Thus when this value is added to the PC, the PC is made to point at the logically first instruction of the subroutine, called the **entry point.** The normal functioning of the Instruction Fetch Execute Cycle then causes the instructions in the subroutine to be executed.

Upon reaching the subroutine return instruction, RSB (opcode 05), the return address is simply popped off of the stack and placed into PC. In effect, this is a branch back to the instruction following the BSBW.

As an example, let us assume that the translation of the BSBW SUB1 instruction is stored at location 0220, and that the displacement to SUB1 is 20_{16}. Furthermore, let us assume that the current top of the User Stack is at location 7FFF1000. If we examine the main memory, PC, and SP before BSBW SUB1 has been executed, we see the state represented in Figure 9.6(a). After fetching and executing BSBW SUB1, the state is as shown in Figure 9.6(b). Note that the PC contains 0243, which is the sum of the displacement (20_{16}) and the address *following* the BSBW SUB1 instruction (0223_{16}). Also, the 0223 address is stored as a longword on top of the User Stack, and SP has been decremented by four bytes accordingly.

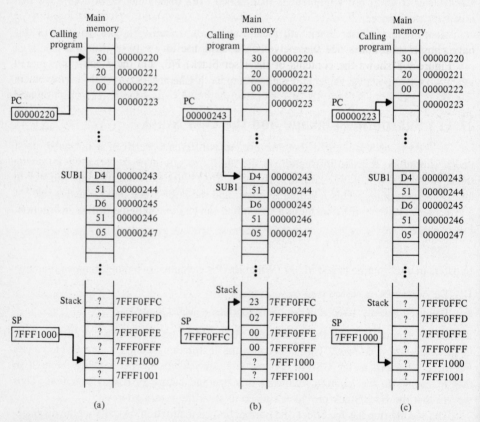

FIGURE 9.6/User Stack during subroutine transfer: (a) before transfer; (b) after transfer; (c) after return

The subroutine instructions at SUB1 can be disassembled to show that the subroutine consists of the three instructions:

```
CLRL  R1
INCL  R1
RSB
```

Thus SUB1 merely sets R1 to 1 and returns.

After the RSB has executed, the state is as shown in Figure 9.6(c). That is, the 0223 has been removed from the User Stack and placed in PC, and SP has been advanced to its original value. Execution then resumes at 0223.

We see now how the User Stack is used in subroutine linkage, i.e., to provide a mechanism for saving the return address. At first encounter, this might seem to be convenient, but not essential. Couldn't one simply use a register in which to save the return address? To see the true importance of using the stack, you must consider the linkage problem in "nested" subroutines, i.e., the case in which one subroutine calls another subroutine.

EXAMPLE 9.2   An example of subroutine nesting is shown in Figure 9.7. Here the main program calls subroutine A, subroutine A calls subroutine B, and subroutine B calls subroutine C. Because our intention is to examine only the linkage process, we have chosen subroutines that themselves do nothing useful.

Figure 9.8 shows the contents of the User Stack, PC, and the Stack Pointer (SP) as this program executes. Note that each instruction has been given a label for convenient reference. The successive states of the stack are shown *before* the instruction indicated at the bottom has been executed. Thus before the first instruction has been executed, the stack is empty and the address of the next instruction, S, is in PC. The original top of the User Stack is referred to as P. Also, for convenience we picture the User Stack as a stack of *longwords*. When the first BSBW is executed, the return address, AR, is placed on the stack. Now, the instruction at A is another BSBW, so the return address for it, BR, must be placed on the stack. Similarly, after executing the BSBW at B we see that the return points for both of the earlier subroutine calls are in the

```
            .TITLE   NESTED SUBROUTINES
      ;
      ;     TO DEMONSTRATE HOW BSBW/BSBB USE
      ;     THE USER STACK FOR LINKAGE
      ;
            .ENTRY   START,0
S:          BSBW     A              ;BRANCH TO SUB, A
AR:         $EXIT_S                 ;EXIT TO VMS
A:          BSBW     B              ;BRANCH TO SUB, B
BR:         RSB
B:          BSBW     C              ;BRANCH TO SUB, C
CR:         RSB
C:          .PUTSTR  MSG            ;PRINT MESSAGE
D:          RSB
MSG:        .ASCIZ   /HERE I AM IN SUBROUTINE C/
            .END     START
```

FIGURE 9.7/Nested subroutines (see also Figure 9.8)

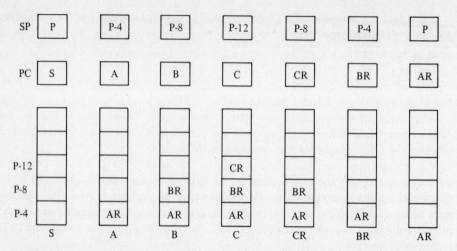

FIGURE 9.8/States of the User Stack, PC, and SP for Figure 9.7. The state is shown *immediately before* the instruction indicated with the label at the bottom has been executed. The User Stack is shown as longwords.

stack. It should be apparent that subroutines can be nested to any level with this scheme, limited only by the size of the reserved stack space. The process of always saving the return address on the stack ensures that the return address for each earlier subroutine call is saved for future use. Moreover, these addresses are available in exactly the order in which they are needed.

The rightmost three panels in Figure 9.8 show the stack, PC, and SP as control returns to the main program. Observe that the top of the stack always has the proper return point regardless of which routine we are in. At the conclusion the stack pointer is reestablished at its original value.

Actual examination of the stack at each of the states in Example 9.2 is left as an exercise (see Exercise 9.1). The User Stack can be conveniently examined using the Symbolic Debugger command:

```
EXAMINE @SP
```

which shows the contents of the top four bytes of the stack as a longword. To examine the top three longwords use:

```
EXAMINE  @SP:@SP+11
```

9.6 | Register Protection

Ideally, a subroutine should carry out a specific intended purpose and do nothing else. If nonintended changes occur as a result of calling the subroutine, it is said to have **side effects.** Side effects tend to make programming more difficult and more subject to errors, and therefore should be avoided.

One step that can be taken to prevent side effects is to "protect" the registers upon transfer to the subroutine. This is accomplished easily using the User Stack. The idea here is to push all registers used in the subroutine onto the stack immediately upon entry into the subroutine. They are then popped off the stack in reverse order, immediately before the RSB instruction. For example, a subroutine that makes use of registers R0 and R1 would be written:

```
SUB:    (Entry point)
        MOVL   R0,-(SP)
        MOVL   R1,-(SP)
        (Body of subroutine)
        MOVL   (SP)+,R1
        MOVL   (SP)+,R0
        RSB
```

It should be evident that this use of the stack does not interfere with its normal usage for linkage purposes. This is because we have followed the rule that all items pushed onto the stack must also be popped off. Thus when RSB is executed, the top of the User Stack once again contains the return address.

9.7 | An Example

Let us now consider a slightly more complex example, which demonstrates the definition and usage of a subroutine, including register protection.

EXAMPLE 9.3 Suppose we need a subroutine that performs division using the shifting method shown in Figure 6.9. This algorithm uses registers R0, R1, and R2 for transmission of input arguments, and returns the results in R0 and R1. The user would therefore expect R0 and R1 to change as a result of calling the subroutine. However, examination of the algorithm shows that R3 and R5 are also changed. When we write the subroutine we therefore must save R3 and R5 on the stack for restoration after the division is complete.

Figure 9.9 shows the subroutine implementation and use. Comparing this with Fig. 6.9 shows that the following changes have been made. First, we have given the procedure a name by putting the label DIV2 at the beginning. The first instructions upon entry push R3 and R5 onto the stack. At the end of the division process, we pop R5 and R3 off the stack, then return to the calling program. Note that the HALT has been removed and replaced by the return instruction, RSB.

Following the subroutine we have placed a sample calling program with the ENTRY label START. Because of the .END START directive, this will be the place where execution begins when the assembled version of Figure 9.9 is executed. The first three instructions set up the dividend in R0 and R1, and the divisor in R2. The BSBW DIV2 then calls the subroutine, which transfers control to the label DIV2. Upon reaching the RSB, control is returned to the $EXIT_S in the calling program.

Figure 9.10 demonstrates the program using the Symbolic Debugger. First we examine the main program using the INSTRUCTION qualifier with the EXAMINE command. This allows us to see the addresses needed to set breakpoints before and after the subroutine branch. Also, we deposit arbitrary values in R3 and R5 just to allow us to

```
            .TITLE EXAMPLE 9.3
;
;           SUBROUTINE
;
;
;           INPUT:
;               (R1,R0)= (HIGH,LOW) LONGWORDS OF DIVIDEND (POSITIVE)
;               R2      = DIVISOR (POSITIVE)
;           INTERMEDIATE USAGE:
;               R1      = REMAINDER
;               R3      = LOOP CONTROL VARIABLE
;               R5      = QUOTIENT
;           OUTPUT:
;               R0      = QUOTIENT
;               R1      = REMAINDER
;
DIV2:
            MOVL    R3,-(SP)        ;SAVE R3
            MOVL    R5,-(SP)        ;   AND R5 ON STACK.
            CMPL    R2,R1           ;CHECK FOR POTENTIAL
            BLEQU   OVERFL          ;   OVERFLOW OF RESULT.
            MOVL    #32,R3          ;INITIALIZE LCV
LOOP:       ASHL    #1,R5,R5        ;SHIFT RESULT
            ASHQ    #1,R0,R0        ;DOUBLE PRECISION SHIFT
                                    ;   OF DIVIDEND.
            CMPL    R1,R2           ;SEE IF DIVISOR CAN
            BLSSU   ENDLP           ;   BE SUBTRACTED.
            SUBL    R2,R1           ;SUBTRACT DIVISOR
            INCL    R5              ;PUT 1-BIT IN QUOTIENT
ENDLP:      SOBGTR  R3,LOOP         ;LOOP IF MORE BITS
            MOVL    R5,R0           ;PLACE QUOTIENT INTO
                                    ;   DESIGNATED REGISTER.
OVERFL:
            MOVL    (SP)+,R5        ;RESTORE R5
            MOVL    (SP)+,R3        ;   AND R3.
;
;   RETURN TO CALLER
;
            RSB
;
;   CALLING PROGRAM
;
            .ENTRY  START,0
            CLRL    R1              ;SET DIVIDEND HI WORD
            MOVL    #27,R0          ;   AND LOW WORD.
            MOVL    #2,R2           ;SET DIVISOR
            BSBW    DIV2            ;DO THE DIVIDE
            $EXIT_S                 ;EXIT TO VMS
            .END    START
```

FIGURE 9.9/Division with shifting using subroutine

confirm that they are protected through the subroutine execution. When execution stops prior to the BSBW execution, we examine (R1,R0) as a quadword and see that the desired 64-bit dividend is stored therein. After the subroutine execution, we see that R0 and R1 contain the quotient, $OD_{16} = 13_{10}$, and the remainder, 1, respectively. It is also evident that R3 and R5 were indeed protected.

```
$ MACRO/DEBUG E9P3
$ LINK/DEBUG E9P3
$ RUN E9P3
                    VAX-11 DEBUG Version 4.1
%DEBUG-I-INITIAL, language is MACRO, module set to 'EXAMPLE'
DBG>EXAMINE/INSTR START+2:START+10          {EXAMINE as instructions.}
EXAMPLE\START+02:   CLRL    R1
EXAMPLE\START+04:   MOVL    #1B,R0
EXAMPLE\START+07:   MOVL    #02,R2
EXAMPLE\START+0A:   BSBW    EXAMPLE\DIV2
EXAMPLE\START+0D:   PUSHL   #01                {This is $EXIT_S
EXAMPLE\START+0F:   CALLS   #01,@#SYS$EXIT          translation.}
DBG>DEPOSIT R3=1F1F1F1F                      {Set registers.}
DBG>DEPOSIT R5=1A1A1A1A
DBG>SET BREAK START+0A                       {Set Breaks.}
DBG>SET BREAK START+0D
DBG>GO                                            {Execute.}
routine start at EXAMPLE\START
break at EXAMPLE\START+0A
DBG>EXAMINE/QUAD R0                          {Examine as quadword.}
R0:   00000000 0000001B                      {Dividend.}
DBG>GO
start at EXAMPLE\START+0A
break at EXAMPLE\START+0D
DBG>EXAMINE R0:R1                            {Examine result.}
R0:   0000000D                               {Quotient.}
R1:   00000001                               {Remainder.}
DBG>EXAMINE R3                               {Show that R3
R3:   1F1F1F1F                                   was protected.}
DBG>EXAMINE R5                               {And  R5.}
R5:   1A1A1A1A
DBG>EXIT
$ ▓
```

FIGURE 9.10/Execution of example in Figure 9.9

9.8 | Methods of Argument Transmission

Up to this point we have used the general registers to communicate input data to a subroutine, and the results back to the calling program. This method is the most convenient and is often used if the number of arguments is small. In this section we shall discuss several other methods that can be used when there are many arguments.

Argument passing methods are often described by the terms "call by value" or "call by reference." From a programming perspective, the difference between the two is whether or not a change to the argument *within* the subroutine automatically changes the calling program variable represented by the argument. With **call by value,** only a *copy* of the argument is passed, so the calling program variable cannot be directly changed by the subroutine. For example, when we use registers to pass arguments, we are using call by value since we must explicitly place a copy of the input value into the register before the subroutine transfer, and extract the result from the register upon return.* **Call by reference,** on the other hand, means that the subroutine operates directly on the storage location of the arguments in the calling program. At the assembly programming level, this means that *addresses* of arguments are transferred to the subroutine, and indirect (deferred) addressing modes are used to operate on the arguments inside the subroutine. For this reason, call by reference is sometimes referred to as "call by address." If you are familiar with the Pascal programming language, you will recognize that the default argument passing method is call by value, and that call by reference is only used for arguments preceded by VAR. FORTRAN programmers will recognize that arguments in that language are normally passed using call by reference, although modern FORTRAN compilers often allow value arguments as well. The C language always employs call by value. In the following discussion, we will point out which of these two techniques is employed in the normal usage of the method.

9.8.1 Transferring Address of Arguments through Registers

Transferring *addresses* through registers is almost as simple as passing *values* through registers. However, there are occasions when it is advantageous to transfer addresses. One such occasion occurs when the subroutine has arrays as either input or output. In this case, by passing the address of the array, whose space is reserved by the calling program, we avoid the execution time that would be needed to transfer all of the values to arrays within the subroutine. Also, this saves memory because the subroutine makes use of the same array space reserved in the calling program. This method of argument passing is a form of call by reference.

EXAMPLE 9.4 As an example of this method, consider a subroutine to find the largest number in an array of integers. The subroutine and calling program are shown in Figure 9.11.

In Figure 9.11, observe that we use immediate addressing to place the necessary addresses into the argument registers first, then transfer to the subroutine. After return, we use the .PUTHEX routine described in Section 4.11 to print the result. Inside the subroutine, addressing is done using the register-deferred or autoincrement modes. This allows the instructions to refer to data stored in the main programs, minimizing the need for moving data.

Linkage and execution of this program are shown in Figure 9.12. The program correctly selects $1FF_{16}$ (511_{10}) as the largest of the five numbers stored in A.

9.8.2 In-Line Argument Values

Some programmers prefer to place the argument values immediately after the subroutine transfer instruction. This method, called "in-line argument values," is favored by the architecture of some computers, such as the PDP-11. It is not particularly convenient or efficient on the VAX-11, but we consider it here for completeness.

---

* However, one could argue that call by reference is being used if the register was the only storage place used for the data item.

```
              .TITLE EXAMPLE 9.4
;
;             PROGRAM TO DEMONSTRATE PASSING ADDRESSES IN REGISTERS
;                     (FINDS LARGEST IN ARRAY)
;
              .ENTRY  START,0
              MOVL    #N,R0       ;PLACE ADDR OF ARRAY LENGTH IN R0
              MOVL    #A,R1       ;PLACE ADDR OF ARRAY IN R1
              MOVL    #BIG,R2     ;PLACE ADDR OF RESULT IN R2
              BSBW    FINDIT      ;FIND LARGEST NO. IN ARRAY
              MOVL    BIG,R0      ;PRINT RESULT
              .PUTHEX             ;  IN HEXADECIMAL.
              $EXIT_S             ;EXIT TO VMS
N:            .LONG   5
A:            .LONG   67,18,4,511,-1
BIG:          .BLKL   1
;
;             END OF MAIN PROGRAM
;
FINDIT:
;     SUBROUTINE TO FIND LARGEST NO. IN ARRAY
;             (R0)=NO. OF ELEMENTS IN ARRAY
;             (R1)=FIRST ELEMENT IN ARRAY
;             (R2)=RESULT RETURNED
;
              MOVL    R1,-(SP)    ;PROTECT REGISTERS
              MOVL    R4,-(SP)    ;
              MOVL    (R1),(R2)   ;INITIALIZE BIG
              MOVL    (R0),R4     ;INITIALIZE LCV
AGAIN:        CMPL    (R1)+,(R2)  ;CMP NEXT VAL WITH BIG
              BLEQ    L1          ;REPLACE IF
              MOVL    -(R1),(R2)  ;   IT WAS BIGGER
              TSTL    (R1)+       ;RE-ADVANCE POINTER
L1:           SOBGTR  R4,AGAIN
              MOVL    (SP)+,R4    ;RESTORE REGISTERS
              MOVL    (SP)+,R1
              RSB                 ;RETURN TO CALLER
;
;     END OF FINDIT
;
              .END    START
```

FIGURE 9.11/Using addresses for argument passing

```
$ MACRO E9P4+MACLIB/LIB
$ LINK E9P4+SUBLIB/LIB
$ RUN E9P4
000001FF
$ ▓
```

FIGURE 9.12/Linking and executing program in Figure 9.11

EXAMPLE 9.5   As an example, suppose we wish to pass two input arguments, X and
Y, to a subroutine SUB1 and accept the result, say the difference between X and Y,
into a third argument Z. A subroutine and calling program using this method is shown
in Figure 9.13.

```
                .TITLE EXAMPLE 9.5
        ;
        ;       PROGRAM TO DEMONSTRATE PASSING ARGUMENTS AS
        ;       IN-LINE VALUES.
        ;
                .ENTRY  START,0
                .PUTSTR MSG
                .GETHEX                 ;GET X
                MOVL    R0,X
                .PUTSTR MSG1
                .GETHEX                 ;GET Y
                MOVL    R0,Y
                BSBW    SUB1            ;COMPUTE DIFFERENCE
        X:      .BLKL   1               ;ALLOCATE LONGWORD FOR X
        Y:      .BLKL   1               ;ALLOCATE LONGWORD FOR Y
        Z:      .BLKL   1               ;ALLOCATE LONGWORD FOR Z
                .PUTSTR MSG2
                MOVL    Z,R0            ;PRINT DIFFERENCE X-Y
                .PUTHEX
                $EXIT_S                 ;EXIT TO VMS
        MSG:    .ASCIZ/INPUT X:/
        MSG1:   .ASCIZ/INPUT Y:/
        MSG2:   .ASCIZ/DIFFERENCE IS:/
        ;
        ;       END OF MAIN PROGRAM
        ;
        SUB1:
        ;
        ;       SUBROUTINE TO COMPUTE DIFFERENCE
        ;         R5  =(SP)    NOTE: CONTENTS OF R5 LOST.
        ;         (R5)=X
        ;         (R5+4)=Y
        ;         (R5+8)=X-Y
        ;
                MOVL    (SP)+,R5        ;POP ADDR OF X
                MOVL    R1,-(SP)        ;PROTECT REGISTER R1
                MOVL    (R5)+,R1        ;GET X
                SUBL    (R5)+,R1        ;GET Y AND SUBTRACT
                MOVL    R1,(R5)+        ;PUT RESULT INTO Z,
                                        ;    ADVANCING R5 TO RETURN
                                        ;        ADDRESS.
                MOVL    (SP)+,R1        ;RESTORE R1
                MOVL    R5,-(SP)        ;PUSH RET. ADDR ONTO STACK
                RSB                     ;RETURN TO CALLER
        ;
        ;       END OF SUB1
        ;
                .END    START
```

FIGURE 9.13/Using in-line argument values

In this program we use .GETHEX to accept values for X and Y from the keyboard. We then transfer to SUB1. The arguments are stored immediately after the BSBW instruction. This would cause a problem upon return if the PC was reset in the normal way. However, in the subroutine we *adjust* the return address as we access the arguments in order to avoid this problem.

Our first action in SUB1 is to pop the top of the stack and place it into R5, which we shall call the **argument pointer.** Note that the obtained longword is the *address of the first argument* because we placed that argument immediately after the BSBW. We then use autoincrement addressing with R5 to access the arguments, and in the process R5 is advanced to become the address of the *longword following the last argument.* Just before we return, we place the contents of R5, which is now the correct return address, onto the stack. This assures proper linkage for the return because RSB resets PC to the address found on top of the stack upon return. With this method great care must be taken in matching the number of arguments in the subroutine and calling program. Otherwise, the argument pointer register will not contain the correct return address.

Let us examine in greater detail how this example works. Upon entry to the subroutine, the top of the User Stack contains the address of the longword following the BSBW instruction. The MOVL (SP)+,R5 pops the stack and places this address in R5. Because X is at this address, the MOVL (R5)+,R1 instruction gets X, advances R5 by 4, and puts X into R1. Because of the advancement, R5 now points at Y, so that SUBL (R5)+,R1 subtracts Y from R1. R5 is incremented by four in the process of getting Y, so that the MOVL R1,(R5)+ places the result into Z; the autoincrement addressing here advances R5 to one longword beyond Z, which we see to be the correct return point for the subroutine.

Because locations in the calling program are directly changed by the subroutine, this method could easily be viewed as a call by reference method. However, it can also be viewed as a call by value method. The latter would be the case if we viewed the locations following the BSBW as *temporary* storage for the arguments, rather than the permanent storage reserved for program variables. For example, we could write:

```
        MOVL    X,ARG1
        MOVL    Y,ARG2
        BSBW    SUB1
ARG1:   .BLKL   1
ARG2:   .BLKL   1
ARG3:   .BLKL   1
        MOVL    ARG3,Z
```

Because the program variables X, Y, and Z are not directly accessible in the subroutine, this is clearly a call by value technique. When the arguments are handled in this manner the space used for their transmission, i.e., ARG1, ARG2, and ARG3, is referred to as the **argument frame.** When we study VAX-11 procedures in Section 9.9, we will see that the argument frame can alternatively be placed in the User Stack. The argument frame is called the **activation record** in some languages.

9.8.3 In-Line Argument Addresses

A variation of in-line argument values is the placing of the *addresses* of the arguments in line, i.e., after the BSBW instruction. As with in-line values, it is necessary to use an argument pointer which is advanced in the subroutine in order to leave it pointing at the return address. Now, however, the argument pointer register will contain an *address of an address* of an argument. Hence, this method of argument transmission requires a new method of operand addressing, which we will take up before discussion of other aspects.

To see the need for the new addressing mode, consider the following example:

```
A:   BSBW    SUB1
     .LONG   X
```

Here X is the *label* for the location reserved for the argument X. The assembler translates this to:

A	30
A + 1	disp
A + 2	disp
A + 3	addr
A + 4	addr
A + 5	addr
A + 6	addr
A + 7	

where *disp* is the displacement of SUB1, *addr* is the address reserved for X (i.e., the value assigned by the assembler to X), and A represents the address in which the BSBW instruction is stored. When the opcode 30 is fetched for execution, PC is left pointing at A + 1, and then PC is advanced to A + 3 as the displacement is fetched. When 30 is executed, A + 3 gets placed on top of the stack and PC is set to the transfer address SUB1.

Inside the subroutine we can get the address A + 3 from the top of the stack and place it in an argument pointer, say R5:

```
MOVL   (SP)+,R5
```

When we wish to access the argument in the subroutine, we can look in R5 to get the address A + 3, then look *in* A + 3 to get *addr,* and finally extract the *contents* of *addr.* This is called **second-level indirect addressing,** as shown in Figure 9.14.

The VAX-11 has a second-level indirect addressing mode in which the register is incremented automatically. It is called **autoincrement-deferred,** and the assembly mnemonics are:

```
@(Rn)+
```

where n can be any register. To show how this works, assume that we have the following register and memory state:

Register	Contents	Address	Contents
R1:	00000200	00000200	00000400
R2:	00000000	00000400	00000111

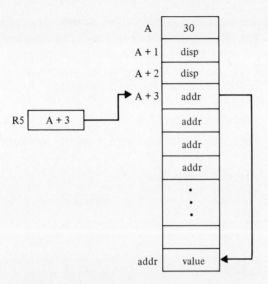

FIGURE 9.14/Second-level indirect addressing (autoincrement-deferred)

Then when the instruction:

```
MOVL @(R1)+,R2
```

is executed, we will obtain:

Register	Contents	Address	Contents
R1:	00000204	00000200	00000400
R2:	00000111	00000400	00000111

Thus we have moved the contents of 00000400 to R2. Note also that R1 has been incremented by four. This is because the contents of R1 is being used as an *address of an address,* which *must* be a longword. Presumably the next usage would want R1 to point at the next address, which would be four bytes away. Note that this is true even if a byte instruction is used. For example,

```
MOVB  @(R1)+,A
```

also increments R1 by four.

The operand specifier for autoincrement-deferred addressing is 9n, where n is the register employed. Thus the previous MOVL example translates as:

$$52 \quad 91 \quad D0$$

Note that the VAX-11 does not have second-level indirect addressing without autoincrement. However, the mnemonic @(Rn) is recognized by the MACRO assembler as implied byte displacement deferred addressing. (See Section 12.2.4.)

Now we can return to the in-line address method of argument transmission.

EXAMPLE 9.6   To demonstrate this method, Example 9.5 can be modified to use addresses instead of values. The listing in Figure 9.15 shows the program with the necessary modifications. Note that we have moved the storage allocation for X, Y, and Z after the main program $EXIT_S. In the three longwords immediately following the BSBW SUB1 we have placed the *addresses* for these arguments. (Recall that the assembler

```
                .TITLE EXAMPLE 9.6
        ;
        ;       PROGRAM TO DEMONSTRATE PASSING ARGUMENTS AS
        ;       IN-LINE ADDRESSES.
        ;                                               0
                .ENTRY  START,0
                .PUTSTR MSG
                .GETHEX                 ;GET X
                MOVL    RO,X
                .PUTSTR MSG1
                .GETHEX                 ;GET Y
                MOVL    RO,Y
                BSBW    SUB1            ;COMPUTE DIFFERENCE
                .LONG   X               ;ADDRESS OF X
                .LONG   Y               ;ADDRESS OF Y
                .LONG   Z               ;ADDRESS OF Z
                .PUTSTR MSG2
                MOVL    Z,RO            ;PRINT DIFFERENCE X-Y
                .PUTHEX
                $EXIT_S                 ;EXIT TO VMS
X:              .BLKL   1               ;ALLOCATE LONGWORD FOR X
Y:              .BLKL   1               ;ALLOCATE LONGWORD FOR Y
Z:              .BLKL   1               ;ALLOCATE LONGWORD FOR Z
MSG:            .ASCIZ/INPUT X:/
MSG1:           .ASCIZ/INPUT Y:/
MSG2:           .ASCIZ/DIFFERENCE IS:/
        ;
        ;       END OF MAIN PROGRAM
        ;
SUB1:
        ;
        ;       SUBROUTINE TO COMPUTE DIFFERENCE
        ;          R5  =(SP)      NOTE: CONTENTS OF R5 LOST
        ;          @(R5)=X
        ;          @(R5+4)=Y
        ;          @(R5+8)=X-Y
        ;
                MOVL    (SP)+,R5        ;GET ADDR OF ADDR OF X
                MOVL    R1,-(SP)        ;PROTECT REGISTER R1
                MOVL    @(R5)+,R1       ;GET X
                SUBL    @(R5)+,R1       ;GET Y AND SUBTRACT
                MOVL    R1,@(R5)+       ;PUT RESULT INTO Z,
                                        ;    ADVANCING R5 TO RETURN
                                        ;          ADDRESS.
                MOVL    (SP)+,R1        ;RESTORE R1
                MOVL    R5,-(SP)        ;PUSH RET. ADDR ONTO STACK
                RSB                     ;RETURN TO CALLER
        ;
        ;       END OF SUB1
        ;
                .END    START
```

FIGURE 9.15/Using in-line argument addresses

determines values for the labels X, Y, and Z, and it is these values, which are addresses, that get stored here as a result of the three .LONG directives.) In the subroutine itself, we have changed the addressing mode for the arguments to autoincrement-deferred. In this way we account for the fact that R5 *points to an address that contains the address* of the arguments. As each argument is referenced, the autoincrement feature advances the R5 by four, leaving it with the correct return address which is then placed on the User Stack before return. These changes make this program work exactly the same as the one in Figure 9.13.

As implemented in Figure 9.15, the in-line address method is a form of call by reference because the permanent storage location for the calling program variables are operated on directly by the subroutine. Note that this is a result of placing *addresses* in the argument frame rather than values. Nonetheless, the method can also be used to implement call by value tansmission. For example, we could write:

```
        MOVL      X,ARG1
        MOVL      Y,ARG2
        BSBW      SUB1
        .LONG     ARG1
        .LONG     ARG2
        .LONG     ARG3
        MOVL      ARG3,Z
          .
          .
          .
ARG1:   .BLKL     1
ARG2:   .BLKL     1
ARG3:   .BLKL     1
```

It should be observed that when programmed in this manner the argument space (ARG1, ARG2, and ARG3) can be reused for subroutine transfers elsewhere in the program.

9.8.4 Transmission of Address of Argument List

This method of transmitting subroutine arguments uses ideas present in several of the other methods. It is similar to the in-line address method in that it passes an address that points to a list of addresses. In this case, however, the list of argument addresses is *not* placed immediately after the BSBW instruction. Therefore, the address of the list of argument addresses is passed in a register rather than on the stack.

Argument list address transmission is of interest for two reasons. First, it conveniently allows for a large number of arguments without requiring that they be stored in adjacent memory locations. Secondly, it is often the method used in the machine code generated by compilers. In particular, a variation of this method has been formalized in the use of special VAX-11 subroutines called **procedures.** Here we study the basic ideas behind the method, which will allow us to better understand procedure calls discussed in Section 9.9

We will need yet another addressing mode for this method of argument transmission. This mode is called **displacement mode,** and has the mnemonics:

`symbol(Rn)`

Here, *symbol* can be either a numeric constant (i.e., a literal) or a symbol whose value is assigned by the assembler, e.g., a label. The operation of this mode is very simple:

the value of *symbol* is added to the contents of Rn, and the result is the address of the operand. For example, if we have:

Register	Contents	Address	Contents
R1:	00000200	00000204	0000007F
R2:	00000100		

and the instruction:

```
ADDL 4(R1),R2
```

is executed, the result is:

Register	Contents	Address	Contents
R1:	00000200	00000204	0000007F
R2:	0000017F		

Note that the contents of the location pointed at by *4 plus the contents of R1* (i.e., 00000204) has been added to R2. Used in this way, this addressing mode refers to a value in a location that is *offset or displaced* by the value of the preceding constant from the *base* address in the register employed. This is the way in which it will be used in the argument transmission mode discussed in this section. Note that the contents of the register is an *address* when used in this manner.

In other uses of displacement addressing, *symbol* is more conveniently viewed as the base address, and the value in the register as an offset. That is, we can write:

```
MOVL X(R3),R1
```

where X is a label to which the assembler assigns an address value. During execution, the contents of R3 will be added to X to find the operand. Thus Rn is like a subscript in an array in high-level languages. Indeed, many of the array examples in earlier chapters of this book could have been worked using displacement addressing rather than autoincrement. Used in this manner, *symbol* is a base address, and the register contains an integer that is an offset or displacement rather than an address. In either case, the sum of *symbol* and the register contents is used as an address. Thus displacement addressing is a form of indirect addressing.

In the machine code translation, the displacement addressing mode can have any one of three possible operand specifiers:

An   (Byte displacement)

Cn   (Word displacement)

En   (Longword displacement)

where n is the register employed. The assembler chooses the appropriate operand specifier depending on the value of the displacement. For example,

```
MOVL 6(R3),R5
```

translates as:

$$55 \quad 06 \quad A3 \quad D0$$

whereas:

```
MOVL   500(R3),R5
```

translates as:

$$55 \quad 01 \quad F4 \quad C3 \quad D0$$

Note that the *value of the symbol* is stored as part of the operand specifier.

It is also interesting to note that if R15 (PC) is used with this mode, we have what we have been calling **relative addressing.** Actually, relative addressing is a special case of displacement mode addressing when examined at the machine code level. As a convenience to assembly programmers, the special assembler mnemonics have been built into MACRO for the case when the register is PC, and this we have called relative addressing. The way this works is discussed in Chapter 12.

We now return to transmission of the address of the argument list. With this method, the arguments themselves are stored in the calling program, and not necessarily in adjacent locations. Also, the *addresses* of these arguments are stored in an array in which the first element is the number of arguments. Let us demonstrate this with the following example.

EXAMPLE 9.7   Suppose we wish to transfer the two arguments X and Y to a subroutine called SUB1, which calculates the value of Z = X + 2Y. We could write:

```
        MOVL    #ARG,R5
        BSBW    SUB1
          .
          .
          .
ARG:    .LONG   3,X,Y,Z
          .
          .
          .
X:      .LONG   10
          .
          .
          .
Y:      .LONG   20
          .
          .
          .
Z:      .BLKL   1
          .
          .
          .
```

Here we have used R5 to convey to the subroutine the *address* of a short array called ARG. The first element in ARG contains the number of arguments that follow. The symbols X, Y, and Z in the first .LONG directive are *replaced at assembly time* by the *addresses* of locations reserved for their values, so that at execution time the ARG array contains the number of arguments and their *addresses*. As we have shown, the locations reserved for the arguments themselves can be anywhere, and need not be adjacent.

Let us now consider how the arguments are accessed in the subroutine. Because the address of ARG is passed in R5, any element in ARG can be found by displacement addressing using R5. For example, the address of the first argument X is 4(R5), the address of Y is 8(R5), and so on. Here we choose the displacement number (e.g., 4 or 8) as the number of bytes between ARG and the needed argument. When the argument *values* are needed, they can be obtained by first using displacement addressing to move the address into a register, then using deferred addressing to obtain the value. For example, to compute X + 2Y, we could use the following instructions:

```
MOVL    4(R5),R1    ; ADDRESS OF X INTO R1
MOVL    8(R5),R2    ; ADDRESS OF Y INTO R2
MOVL    (R1),R3     ; X INTO R3
ADDL    (R2),R3     ; ADD Y
ADDL    (R2),R3     ; ADD Y AGAIN
```

This code can be shortened by using a new addressing mode called **displacement-deferred.** Its assembly mnemonics are:

```
@symbol(Rn)
```

which is seen to be just like displacement mode, except for the preceding @. This implies that the value found by adding the value of *symbol* to the contents of Rn is to be interpreted as the address where the *address* of the operand is to be found.

The operand specifier translation for displacement-deferred addressing is either Bn, Dn, or Fn, depending on whether the displacement is represented as byte, word, or longword, respectively.

Using this mode, the preceding code reduces to:

```
MOVL    @4(R5),R3    ; MOVES X INTO R3
ADDL    @8(R5),R3    ; ADD Y
ADDL    @8(R5),R3    ; ADD Y AGAIN
```

The complete subroutine and a demonstration calling program is shown in Figure 9.16.

Note that we have followed the convention of placing the argument count in ARG. This is done only to make this discussion compatible with out subsequent discussion of VAX-11 procedures. We do not use the count in this example, and it could be omitted.

Argument list address transmission is fundamentally a call by reference method. We leave it as an exercise to devise a call by value construction that employs the same basic idea.

9.8.5 Transmission of Arguments Using the User Stack

Sometimes the most attractive method for argument transmission is with the User Stack. This is particularly true in *recursive* subroutines, i.e., those that can "call themselves," as discussed in Chapter 13. Here we demonstrate the technique using a simple example that could be easily handled with other methods.

```
                .TITLE EXAMPLE 9.7
        ;
        ;       PROGRAM TO DEMONSTRATE PASSING ARGUMENTS WITH
        ;       ADDRESS OF ARGUMENT LIST.
        ;
                .ENTRY   START,0
                MOVL     #ARG,R5     ;ADDRESS OF ARG ARRAY TO R5
                BSBW     SUB1        ;COMPUTE Z =X + 2 Y
                .PUTSTR MSG          ; PRINT LABEL FOR OUTPUT
                MOVL     Z,R0        ;PRINT VALUE
                .PUTHEX              ;   OF Z.
                $EXIT_S              ;EXIT TO VMS
        ARG:    .LONG    3,X,Y,Z     ;ARGUMENT ADDRESS ARRAY
        X:      .LONG    8           ;INITIALIZE X
        Y:      .LONG    16          ;INITIALIZE Y
        Z:      .BLKL    1           ;RESERVE LONGWORD FOR Z
        MSG:    .ASCIZ/X + 2 Y =/
        ;
        ;       END OF MAIN PROGRAM
        ;
        SUB1:
        ;
        ;       COMPUTES Z = X + 2 Y
        ;          X=@4(R5)
        ;          Y=@8(R5)
        ;          Z=@12(R5)
        ;
                MOVL     R3,-(SP)    ;PROTECT R3
                MOVL     @4(R5),R3   ;PUT X IN R3
                ADDL     @8(R5),R3   ;ADD Y
                ADDL     @8(R5),R3   ;   TWICE.
                MOVL     R3,@12(R5)  ;PUT RESULT INTO Z
                MOVL     (SP)+,R3    ;RESTORE R3
                RSB                  ;RETURN TO CALLER
        ;
        ;       END OF SUB1
        ;
                .END     START
```

FIGURE 9.16/Using address of argument list

EXAMPLE 9.8 Suppose we need frequently to multiply by 8. Let us write a subroutine to do this, designed such that the number to be multiplied is placed on top of the stack before transfer and the result is on top of the stack upon return. The calling sequence and subroutine are then:

```
        MOVL     Y,-(SP)          ; Y TO TOP OF STACK
        BSBW     MUL8             ; MULTIPLY BY 8
A:      MOVL     (SP)+,Y8         ; STORE RESULT
        $EXIT_S
Y:      .LONG    6
Y8:     .BLKL    1
MUL8:                             ; SUBROUTINE
        ASHL     #3,4(SP),4(SP)   ; MULT Y BY 8
        RSB                       ; RETURN
          .
          .
          .
```

This demonstrates the technique of using displacement addressing in the stack to reach the argument. To see this, note that the stack contents after MUL8 is reached is:

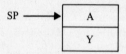

Thus the return address is pointed at by SP, and Y is in the next longword, i.e., SP+4. Recalling that with displacement addressing the operand address is the sum of the preceding value and the register contents, we see that 4(SP) refers to Y. In the example the contents of this location in the stack is multiplied by 8 as a result of the arithmetic shift. When the RSB causes the return address to be popped from the stack, the result is left at the top, as desired.

When using the stack in a subroutine it is especially important to remember that the return address *must* be at the top of the stack upon reaching RSB. In Example 9.8 we are assured of this by not disturbing it at all. Alternately, it can be removed from the stack and saved in a temporary location so that arguments in the stack can be popped. It is then necessary to place the return address back on the stack immediately before return.

The stack can be used for either call by value or call by reference transmission of arguments. In Example 9.8 we used it on a call by value basis because argument values were placed in the stack. However, by placing *addresses* in the stack and using displacement-deferred addressing in the subroutine, call by reference can also be implemented.

9.9 | VAX-11 Procedures

In addition to the subroutine transfer instructions BSBW, BSBB, and JSB described in Section 9.3, the VAX-11 supports two other instructions, **CALLG** and **CALLS,** which play similar roles. These are referred to as **procedure calls** and are used to invoke a special kind of subroutine called a **VAX-11 procedure.** Procedure calls have certain advantages over subroutine transfers, as we will explore in this section. It is also important to note that according to conventions established by Digital Equipment Corporation, procedures written in MACRO can be invoked from VAX-11 high-level languages, whereas subroutines, in general, cannot. This topic is discussed in Section 9.11.

VAX-11 procedures are the same as subroutines in many respects. Like subroutines, they provide the programmer with a means of creating a logically distinct group of instructions, physically removed from the main-line program, and that can be invoked from anywhere in the program. They differ from subroutines in the way in which they are invoked, the manner in which arguments are passed, and in the instruction used to return.

As already noted, a procedure is invoked with either the CALLG or CALLS instruction. The CALLG instruction employs an argument transmission method that is a formalization of the method of transmitting the address of the argument list (see Section 9.8.4). CALLS, on the other hand, uses the User Stack for argument transmission in a manner similar to that discussed in Section 9.8.5. In both cases, however, the transfer instruction automatically handles many of the details that have to be programmed when BSBW, BSB, or JSB is used. In particular, the argument pointer is automatically set up, and register protection is automatically performed. Regardless of whether CALLG or CALLS is used, the return instruction is **RET.** Unlike the RSB instruction used with subroutines, the procedure RET instruction automatically *restores* the protected registers and the User Stack upon return to the calling program. We shall further examine the VAX-11 procedure in the context of the following example.

EXAMPLE 9.9   Revise the program in Example 9.7 to demonstrate the use of a VAX-11 procedure. Invoke the procedure with both CALLG and CALLS.

The solution to this example is shown in Figure 9.17. Comparing this to Figure 9.16, we note the following changes necessary to make the subroutine into a procedure.

First, the entry point is designated by the:

```
.ENTRY SUB1,^M<R3>
```

directive. This establishes SUB1 as the entry point label. The ^M<R3> argument creates a 16-bit mask, called the **entry mask,** with bit 3 set, and stores this mask as the first word of the machine code version of the procedure. When the procedure is invoked, the general registers corresponding to any bits that are set in the entry mask word are automatically saved on the User Stack. Thus in this example we have requested that R3 be protected and restored after completion of SUB1. We therefore do *not* have to program separate instructions for this purpose. Further examination of the procedure shows that we have replaced R5 with the formal argument pointer register, AP. This is because CALLG and CALLS automatically place the address of the argument list into AP when the procedure is invoked. Therefore, we do not have to move the address of ARG into R5 in the calling program as we did in Section 9.8.4. Instead we call the procedure with:

```
CALLG  ARG,SUB1
```

where ARG is the argument list label as before, and SUB1 is the procedure entry point label. The final required change is to replace the RSB instruction with the RET instruction at the end of the procedure.

In the second part of the calling program we demonstrate the use of CALLS. The procedure itself is the same, regardless of whether CALLG or CALLS is used. The difference is that immediately before the CALLS we push the *addresses of the arguments* onto the stack *in reverse order*. The procedure is then invoked by:

```
CALLS  #3,SUB1
```

```
Machine code           Offset  Ln
                        addr
                       0000      1         .TITLE  EXAMPLE 9.9
                       0000      2 ; PROGRAM TO DEMONSTRATE CALLG AND CALLS PROCEDURE CALLS
                       0000      3 ;                  (FORTRAN COMPATIBLE)
                       0000      4 ;
                       0000      5 ;
                  0000 0000      6         .ENTRY  START,0
                       0002      7 ;
                       0002      8 ; USING GENERAL ARGUMENT LIST (CALLG)
                       0002      9 ;
0000005A'EF    FA      0002     10         CALLG   ARG,SUB1     ;COMPUTE Z = X + 2 Y
      00000080'EF      000D     11         .PUTSTR MSG          ;PRINT LABEL FOR OUTPUT
50  00000072'EF  D0    0017     12         MOVL    Z,R0         ;PRINT VALUE
          FFDF'  30    001E     13         .PUTHEX R0           ;  OF Z.
                       0021     14 ;
                       0021     15 ; USING STACK ARGUMENT LIST (CALLS)
                       0021     16 ;
7E  00000072'8F  D0    0021     17         MOVL    #Z,-(SP)     ;PUSH 3RD ARG ADDR ONTO STACK
7E  0000006E'8F  D0    0028     18         MOVL    #Y,-(SP)     ;PUSH 2ND ARG ADDR ONTO STACK
7E  0000006A'8F  D0    002F     19         MOVL    #X,-(SP)     ;PUSH 1ST ARG ADDR ONTO STACK
00000080'EF  03  FB    0036     20         CALLS   #3,SUB1      ;COMPUTE Z=X +2 Y
                       003D     21         .PUTSTR MSG          ;PRINT LABEL FOR OUTPUT
50  00000072'EF  D0    0047     22         MOVL    Z,R0         ;PRINT VALUE
          FFAF'  30    004E     23         .PUTHEX R0           ;  OF Z.
                       0051     24         $EXIT_S              ;EXIT TO VMS
```

238

```
00000072'0000006E'0000006A'00000003   005A   25 ARG:   .LONG    3,X,Y,Z          ;ARGUMENT ADDRESS ARRAY
                            00000008   006A   26 X:     .LONG    8                ;INITIALIZE X
                            00000010   006E   27 Y:     .LONG    16               ;INITIALIZE Y
                            00000076   0072   28 Z:     .BLKL    1                ;RESERVE LONGWORD FOR Z
      00 3D 20 59 20 32 20 2B 20 58   0076   29 MSG:   .ASCIZ/X + 2 Y =/
                                       0080   30 ;
                                       0080   31 ;
                                       0080   32 ;  END OF MAIN PROGRAM
                                       0080   33 ;
                                0008   0080   34        .ENTRY   SUB1,^M<R3>      ;MASK TO PROTECT R3
                                       0082   35 ;
                                       0082   36 ; COMPUTES Z = X + 2 Y
                                       0082   37 ;   X=@4(AP)                     ;AP POINTS
                                       0082   38 ;   Y=@8(AP)                     ;   TO ARG
                                       0082   39 ;   Z=@12(AP)                    ;   ADDR LIST.
                 53   04 BC  D0        0082   40        MOVL     @4(AP),R3        ;PUT X IN R3
                 53   08 BC  C0        0086   41        ADDL     @8(AP),R3        ;ADD Y
                 53   08 BC  C0        008A   42        ADDL     @8(AP),R3        ;   TWICE.
              0C BC   53     D0        008E   43        MOVL     R3,@12(AP)       ;PUT RESULT INTO Z
                            04        0092   44        RET                       ;RETURN TO CALLER
                                       0093   45 ;
                                       0093   46 ; END OF SUB1
                                       0093   47 ;
                                       0093   48        .END     START
```

FIGURE 9.17/Usage of VAX-11 procedures

239

where 3 is the argument count and SUB1 is the entry point label. The CALLS instruction itself pushes the argument count onto the User Stack, so that upon reaching the procedure the stack has the following contents (shown as longwords):

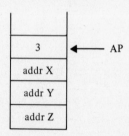

Note that the CALLS instruction has also set AP to point at the argument count. Therefore, once inside the procedure, the situation is exactly the same as when the procedure was invoked by CALLG, i.e., AP points at an argument list of the same structure as when invoked by CALLG. The only difference is that the list is on the *User Stack* instead of elsewhere in memory. Note that the stack is automatically "cleaned up" by the RET instruction, so we do not have to explicitly pop the argument list after the return.

Example 9.9 shows that many of the details of argument passing are automatically handled by the procedure calls. Another important aspect of the procedure call (either CALLG or CALLS) is the **call frame,** which helps the programmer deal with linkage, register protection, and stack usage internal to the procedure.

In a sense, the call frame is an extension of the idea of automatic saving of the PC on the User Stack for linkage back to the calling program. In addition to the return point PC, there are a number of other pieces of information that often need to be saved prior to procedure execution, and restored afterwards. Examples include the general registers that need to be protected due to usage within the procedure, special registers such as the argument pointer (AP) and the frame pointer (FP), and the processor status word (PSW). The procedure call instructions automatically save all of these and certain other information in the User Stack, and RET restores them to their pre-call contents upon return.

The structure of the call frame is shown in Figure 9.18. Note that it is above the argument frame if the procedure is called with CALLS. If called by CALLG, the argument frame is not in the stack. The call frame structure is the same in either case.

We will examine the entries in the call frame in the order in which they are pushed onto the stack, i.e., beginning with the saved registers. The registers actually saved are determined by the *mask,* defined in the program by the .ENTRY directive. For example,

```
.ENTRY  SUB2,^M<R4,R7,R8>
```

creates a mask bit pattern of:

$$0000000110010000$$

and causes the call frame to contain:

(R4)
(R7)
(R8)

when (Ri) means the contents of Ri before the call. (Registers R0 and R1 have special significance in procedures and *cannot* be placed in the mask.) Above the lowest numbered general register in the call frame are the pre-call contents of PC, FP, and AP. The presence of these in the call frame allows the RET instruction to restore these registers upon return. It should be observed that this mechanism is what allows the VAX-11 to call a procedure that calls annother procedure, that calls another procedure, and so on, and to properly return from each call with these important registers undisturbed. Of course, you could achieve the same result using subroutine branch instructions by writing explicit instructions to save these registers on the stack. However, CALLS and CALLG automatically perform these chores for you.

The longword that is immediately below the top of the call frame contains certain

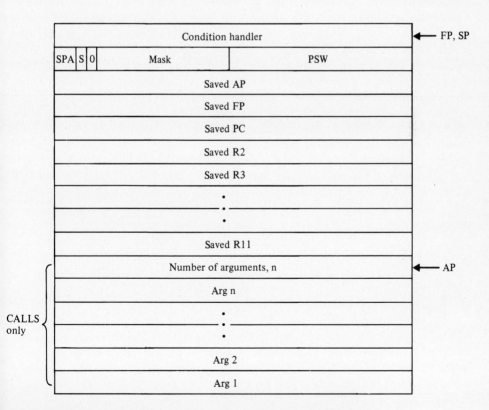

FIGURE 9.18/Procedure call frame in User Stack (shown as longwords)

other information needed to restore conditions upon return. Bits <15:0> of this longword contain the bit pattern that will be placed in the PSW upon return. Bits <15:5> are exactly as the PSW exists prior to the call, and thus these bits will be restored exactly upon return. However, bits <4:0> are zero, so that the condition codes and the trap bit (to be discussed in Chapter 16) are returned *clear*. Note, however, that any of these bits can be reset in the procedure. For example, you can capture the final condition codes at the end of the procedure and place them in bits <3:0>, causing N,Z,V, and C to be set accordingly upon return. The entry mask described previously is stored in bits <28:16>. These bits are examined in order to determine which registers are to be restored upon return. Bit 28 is always 0. Bit 29 indicates whether the procedure call was CALLS or CALLG. If it was CALLS this bit is set, indicating that the arguments are to be removed from the stack upon return. Finally, bits <31:30> contain a 2-bit unsigned integer that represents the number of bytes that SP had to be advanced in order to achieve *longword alignment* in the User Stack when the call frame was created. For example, if SP was 7FFB002 prior to the call, SP would have to be advanced by 2 to achieve longword alignment, and 10_2 would be stored in <31:30> upon entry. Upon return, this same number is subtracted from SP in order to properly restore the stack.

The top longword of the call frame is used to store the address of what is called a **condition handler.** The details of this are beyond the scope of the current discussion. The basic idea, however, is that certain error conditions can sometimes occur in a procedure, and there should be some simple and uniform means for handling these events. The VAX-11 and VMS operating system provide a centralized "condition handling facility" for this purpose. Within any procedure it is only necessary for the programmer to place the address of the appropriate handler into the first longword of the call frame. The system automatically detects the error events and invokes the routine whose address is at the top of the current call frame. If a zero is found there, it tries the top of the *calling* program call frame. This continues until a nonzero condition handler address is found, and then that condition handler address is invoked. These ideas are explored further in Chapter 16.

In addition to placing the items described above into the call frame on the User stack, the CALLG or CALLS instruction places the resulting SP into another register called the **frame pointer,** FP. On first thought, this may seem superfluous; since it means that there will then be *two* registers with which to reference the top of the stack. This is justified, however, because there are situations in which the stack is used within the procedure, changing SP in the process. In contrast, FP remains *unchanged,* providing a *fixed* reference point into the call frame, regardless of how the stack is used. Also, FP provides the call frame address needed by the RET instruction to "clean up" the stack prior to returning to the caller.

The procedure can access any of the items in the call frame using the displacement addressing mode. For example, suppose we want to have the condition codes (NZVC) upon return to the caller set to the condition codes at the conclusion of the procedure. To do this, we have to capture bits <3:0> of PSL immediately before the RET instruction in the procedure and place them into the PSW field of the call frame. The instructions to do this are:

```
MOVPSL    R8              ; CAPTURE PSL
BICL      #^XFFFFFFF0,R8  ; CLEAR HIGH BITS
BISL      R8,4(FP)        ; PUT INTO CALL FRAME
RET                       ; RETURN TO CALLER
```

The first instruction gets the entire PSL into R8. The next instruction clears bits $<31:4>$, leaving N,Z,V, and C in bits $<3:0>$. The BISL instruction then places these bits in the corresponding bits of the byte with a displacement of 4 from the frame pointer. As can be seen in Figure 9.18, this is the correct position for N,Z,V, and C in the return PSW field of the call frame.

In our discussion of the call frame we noted that R0 and R1 cannot be saved during a procedure call. If they are specified in the entry mask, an assembler error will be reported. The reason for this is that they are normally used to *return results*. For example, Pascal or FORTRAN functions return the function value this way. A 32-bit result is returned in R0, and a 64-bit result, when needed, is returned in (R1,R0).

It should be evident from the preceding discussion that the CALLG and CALLS instructions, together with the procedure return instruction, RET, offer several advantages over the BSBB, BSBW, and JSB instructions. However, it must also be noted that procedure calls are somewhat less efficient if the extra information in the call frame is not needed. For example, a simple routine that has a small number of arguments and can return a single result in a register is more efficiently implemented as a subroutine. On the other hand, if there is a need for a standardized interface between the subroutine and the calling program, a procedure should be used. The most common example of this need is when the assembly language subroutine is to be invoked by a high-level language. According to conventions established by the Digital Equipment Corporation, all high-level language processors employ the linkage and argument transmission mechanisms embodied in the CALLG/CALLS type procedures. Therefore, if you wish to be able to call a subroutine written in MACRO from a FORTRAN program, or to invoke it as a Pascal procedure, it must be written as a CALLG/CALLS type procedure. This is demonstrated in Section 9.11.

Procedures can employ either call by value or call by reference argument passing. The example shown in Figure 9.17 uses call by reference since argument *addresses* are stored in the argument frame. However, if we store argument *values* there and employ displacement instead of displacement-deferred addressing, call by value is achieved.

9.10 | Separately Assembled Subroutines

The examples up to this point have shown the subroutines and procedures integrated with the main program that uses them. In larger programming efforts, it is most often preferable to have subroutines and procedures as completely separate "modules" that are assembled separately. With this approach, both source and machine code forms of each module are saved as separate files. This has several advantages, including reduction of the size of the file that has to be continually reassembled during program development. Also, separately assembled modules can be used by many different programmers in a variety of different programs. In Examples 9.10, 9.11, and 9.12, we

```
                .TITLE EXAMPLE 9.10
        ;
        ;       DEMONSTRATES SEPARATELY ASSEMBLED MAIN PROGRAM
        ;                     AND PROCEDURE
        ;
                .EXTERNAL SUB1          ;DECLARE EXTERNALS (OPTIONAL)
                .ENTRY    START,0
        ;
        ;    USING GENERAL ARGUMENT LIST (CALLG)
        ;
                CALLG     ARG,SUB1       ;COMPUTE Z =X + 2 Y
                .PUTSTR   MSG            ;PRINT LABEL FOR OUTPUT
                MOVL      Z,R0           ;PRINT VALUE
                .PUTHEX                  ;   OF Z.
        ;
        ;    USING STACK ARGUMENT LIST (CALLS)
        ;
                MOVL      #Z,-(SP)       ;PUSH 3RD ARG ADDR ONTO STACK
                MOVL      #Y,-(SP)       ;PUSH 2ND ARG ADDR ONTO STACK
                MOVL      #X,-(SP)       ;PUSH 1ST ARG ADDR ONTO STACK
                CALLS     #3,SUB1        ;COMPUTE Z=X +2 Y
                .PUTSTR   MSG            ;PRINT LABEL FOR OUTPUT
                MOVL      Z,R0           ;PRINT VALUE
                .PUTHEX                  ;   OF Z.
                $EXIT_S                  ;EXIT TO VMS
ARG:            .LONG     3,X,Y,Z        ;ARGUMENT ADDRESS ARRAY
X:              .LONG     8              ;INITIALIZE X
Y:              .LONG     16             ;INITIALIZE Y
Z:              .BLKL     1              ;RESERVE LONGWORD FOR Z
MSG:            .ASCIZ/X + 2 Y =/
        ;
        ;       END OF MAIN PROGRAM
        ;
                .END      START
```
(a)
```
                .TITLE SUB1
                .ENTRY    SUB1,^M<R3>    ;MASK TO PROTECT R3
        ;
        ;       COMPUTES Z = X + 2 Y
        ;         X=4(AP)               ;AP POINTS
        ;         Y=8(AP)               ;   TO ARG
        ;         Z=12(AP)              ;       ADDR LIST.
        ;
                MOVL      @4(AP),R3      ;PUT X IN R3
                ADDL      @8(AP),R3      ;ADD Y
                ADDL      @8(AP),R3      ;   TWICE.
                MOVL      R3,@12(AP)     ;PUT RESULT INTO Z
                RET                      ;RETURN TO CALLER
        ;
        ;       END OF SUB1
        ;
                .END
```
(b)

FIGURE 9.19/Separately assembled routines: (a) main program; (b) procedure SUB1

will see how such object modules can be created, and consider some new situations that arise because of their separate assembly.

EXAMPLE 9.10 To demonstrate separate assembly, let us modify the procedure in Figure 9.17 appropriately. The modified form is shown in Figure 9.19. Comparison of these two figures shows that we made the following changes:

1. We moved the procedure instructions to a separate file called E9P9S.MAR.
2. We added a .TITLE directive to the subroutine.
3. We inserted an .EXTERNAL SUB1 directive to the main program.
4. We added an .END directive in the subroutine.

The .EXTERNAL directive alerts the assembler that the listed symbols, in this case just SUB1, are defined outside the module being assembled. These are then called external or global symbols. The assembler will simply mark all references to such symbols as external, rather than flag them as "undefined symbol" errors. (Actually, the MACRO assembler assumes that symbols not defined in the module are externally defined, so .EXTERNAL could be omitted. We include it here to call your attention to the concept of externally defined symbols.) Also, the .ENTRY directive in the procedure causes SUB1 to be marked as global (G) in the symbol table, meaning that other modules may refer to it. When the LINK program is used as shown in Figure 9.19, the symbol tables of all linked modules are searched for the external symbols referred to in other modules. This allows the linker to arrive at the correct addresses for subroutine transfers during execution. This process is called **resolving external references.** Because this example uses a VAX-11 *procedure* we have indicated that the label SUB1 is global by the .ENTRY directive. In the case of a separately assembled *subroutine,* this would be done by listing the name in a .GLOBAL directive or by using a double colon following the label itself at the point at which it is defined in the subroutine. For example,

```
SUB1::
```

Once the main program and procedure have been placed in separate source files, they can be separately assembled, then linked and run. These steps are shown in Figure 9.20.

```
$ MACRO E9P10M+MACLIB/LIB
$ MACRO E9P10S
$ LINK E9P10M,E9P10S+SUBLIB/LIB
$ RUN E9P10M
X + 2 Y =
00000028
X + 2 Y =
00000028
$ ▒
```

FIGURE 9.20/Separate assembly, linkage, and execution

9.11 | Procedure Calls from High-level Languages

In Section 9.9 we noted that the VAX-11 procedure linkage and argument passing conventions were compatible with high-level languages. In Examples 9.11 and 9.12, we demonstrate this by linking the MACRO procedure of Figure 9.19(b) with Pascal and FORTRAN main programs.

EXAMPLE 9.11 Figure 9.21(a) shows a short FORTRAN program that reads two integers, I and J, from the terminal keyboard. It then calls SUB1 (Figure 9.19(b)), passing I and J as the first two arguments. Thus the input values are assigned to X and Y in the MACRO subroutine, and are used to compute Z, the third argument. Because the third argument in the calling program is K, K takes on the value calculated for Z.

Figure 9.21(b) shows the compilation of the FORTRAN program, followed by linkage and execution. We observe that an input of 10 and 20 for I and J, respectively, produces a result of 50 as expected, thus demonstrating proper argument passing and linkage. Often FORTRAN programs can be made to execute much faster by coding key subroutines in assembly and linking, as shown in this example.

EXAMPLE 9.12 Figure 9.22(a) shows a short Pascal program to demonstrate linkage with the MACRO procedure SUB1 (Figure 9.19(b)). Because SUB1 is not defined within the Pascal program, it is declared EXTERNAL in the declarations section. Also, the variables X, Y, and Z are declared INTEGER because SUB1 treats them as signed integers. With the procedure declaration statement, X and Y are treated as value parameters, while Z is identified as VAR. This is because X and Y are not changed by SUB1, while Z is changed.

```
C,
C       FORTRAN PROGRAM TO DEMONSTRATE
C       MACRO SUBROUTINE USAGE
C,
        INTEGER X,Y,Z
        WRITE(*,*)'ENTER X,Y'
        READ(*,*) X,Y
        CALL SUB1(X,Y,Z)
        WRITE(*,*)'X + 2 Y ='
        WRITE(*,*) Z
        END
```

(a)

```
$ FORTRAN E9P11F
$ MACRO E9P10S
$ LINK E9P11F,E9P10S
$ RUN E9P11F
ENTER X,Y
10,20
X + 2 Y =
           50
$ ▒
```

(b)

FIGURE 9.21/MACRO procedure usage with FORTRAN: (a) FORTRAN program; (b) compilation, assembly, linkage, and execution

```
PROGRAM E9P12P(INPUT,OUTPUT);
VAR
    X,Y,Z:INTEGER;
PROCEDURE SUB1(X,Y:INTEGER; VAR Z:INTEGER);EXTERNAL;
BEGIN
    WRITELN('ENTER X Y:' );
    READLN(X,Y);
    SUB1(X,Y,Z);
    WRITELN('X + 2 Y =');
    WRITELN(Z)
END.
```
                              (a)

```
$ PASCAL E9P12P
$ MACRO E9P10S
$ LINK E9P12P,E9P10S
$ RUN E9P12P
ENTER X Y:
10 20
X + 2 Y =
            50
$ ░
```
                              (b)

FIGURE 9.22/MACRO procedure usage with Pascal: (a) Pascal program;
(b) compilation, assembly, linkage, and execution

Compilation, linkage, and execution are shown in Figure 9.22(b). We enter 10 and 20 for X and Y, and the program outputs both input values and the result, 50, as it should.

It should be observed that all VAX-11 high-level languages provided by the manufacturer expect procedures to treat arguments as we have done in SUB1. That is, the *addresses* of the arguments are in an argument list whose address is passed to the procedure. As noted previously, this is referred to as *call by reference* argument passing. Care must be taken in writing MACRO procedures that will be called by high-level languages so that the argument list itself is not changed. For example, if the procedure is to put 100 into the third argument we write:

```
MOVL   #100,@12(AP)
```
and *not:*
```
MOVL   #100,12(AP)
```

because the latter would change the *address* of the argument rather than the argument.

Because the procedure treats arguments on a call by reference basis, you might wonder how a high-level language can allow arguments to be values instead of variable names. For example, the FORTRAN call:

```
CALL SUB1 (10,20,Z)
```

and the Pascal declaration and call:

```
PROCEDURE SUB1(X,Y:INTEGER; VAR Z:INTEGER); EXTERNAL;
BEGIN
              .
              .
              .
    SUB1 (10,20,Z);
```

are valid constructs. These give the appearance of call by value argument passing. However, the compiler actually creates *temporary storage* for value arguments and places the addresses of these storage locations into the argument list.

The Pascal compiler does this for all parameters *not* preceded by VAR in the procedure declaration. The FORTRAN compiler decides based on the actual arguments in the CALL statement. Those that are not recognized as symbols, i.e., those that are literals, are treated in the above manner.

9.12 | Summary

This chapter focused on the use of **subroutines** in assembly language programming. As in high-level language programming, the use of subroutines provides a mechanism for breaking down a large programming task into a number of smaller ones. The VAX-11 provides a convenient means of implementing subroutines based upon the use of two special instructions, **BSBW** and **RSB,** and upon the so-called user stack.

The BSBW instruction transfers control to the subroutine. Its form is:

```
BSBW    label
```

where *label* is the label attached to the subroutine "entry point." Before branching to the indicated label, BSBW causes the return point PC to be saved on the User Stack.

The companion of the BSBW is the RSB instruction. This instruction is put in the subroutine at the place at which it is desired to return in the calling program. It reverses the effect of BSBW in the sense that the PC is reset to the proper address at which execution is to resume in the calling program.

Alternate subroutine transfer instructions provided by the VAX-11 include **BSBB** and **JSB.** The former is identical to BSBW except that the displacement to the subroutine entry point cannot be larger than can be placed in a byte, whereas BSBW allows a word (sixteen bits) for the displacement. JSB provides complete flexibility in that any addressing mode can be used to specify the subroutine entry point.

In this chapter we also examined the concept of a **stack** as a general means of data organization. The special property of a stack is that the most recently added item is the next available for removal. In MACRO, longword data are "pushed" onto the stack with MOVL S,−(SP), and are "popped" off by MOVL (SP)+,D.

While the stack has many other uses, it is particularly useful in subroutine transfer. We saw that VAX-11 makes use of register R14 (known as **SP**) as a **User Stack Pointer** in the sense that the BSBW instruction automatically saves the contents of the PC register in the location pointed at by SP. Operating system software, i.e., LINK, provides a number of locations at the high end of process virtual address space as a "User Stack," and sets SP to its bottom when execution begins. This usually provides enough stack space to allow general usage in the program for temporary data storage, as well as subroutine linkage. We noted that one must always retrieve information from the stack in the reverse order in which it was placed there, and must remove all items placed there. If these rules are not followed for stack usage inside the subroutine, linkage back to the main program will be lost.

The input and output data for subroutines are called **arguments,** and we examined several different ways for them to be **transmitted** back and forth. The simplest way is to pass values **through registers,** but this will not suffice if there are very many arguments. We saw that an alternative is to use a register to **pass an address** where the argument can be found. Still another alternative is to reserve the storage locations for the argument values immediately after the BSBW, i.e., **in line.** A register is used as an argument pointer to contain the address of the first argument when the subroutine is reached. The arguments can then be accessed using autoincrement addressing with the argument pointer. If all of the arguments are so referenced, the argument pointer register will contain the correct return address upon reaching the RSB instruction.

A variation of the in-line value transmission method is **in-line addresses.** Here the argument addresses are stored immediately after the BSBW, so that upon subroutine entry an argument pointer register points to an address that contains the address of the first argument. Access then requires use of the **autoincrement-deferred addressing mode,** introduced here for the first time.

Autoincrement-deferred addressing is indicated by the mnemonics $@(Rn)+$. This addressing mode causes the quantity found in the address pointed at by Rn to be interpreted as the *address* of the operand, and afterwards the register contents to be incremented. This is called **second-level indirect addressing.**

Another very flexible argument transmission method is characterized by passing a **single address through a register.** This address is that of an array containing the number of arguments, followed by the addresses of the arguments. Access to the arguments is then through the use of two newly introduced addressing modes called **displacement** and **displacement-deferred** addressing. The assembly mnemonics for displacement addressing are *symbol*(Rn), and it is understood that the operand address is the sum of *symbol* and the register contents. Displacement-deferred is indicated by @*symbol*(Rn), where the sum of *symbol* and the register contents produces the address of the location in which the operand address can be found. The principal advantage of this method of argument transmission is the flexibility allowed in the allocation of storage.

As a final method of argument transmission, we considered use of the **User Stack.** Here, arguments are simply pushed onto the stack by the calling program, and accessed internally by popping, or by using displacement addressing relative to the top of the stack. Special care must be taken because of the way the stack is used in the linkage process. This method of argument transmission plays an important role in recursive subroutines, which will be discussed in Chapter 13.

For each argument passing method, we discussed whether **call by value** or **call by reference** was employed. Call by value means that a copy of the argument is passed to the subroutine, whereas in call by reference the address is passed. Thus the latter results in the subroutine directly affecting calling program variables. We observed that most of the argument transmission methods are basically call by reference methods, but call by value can be easily implemented with minor modifications.

We also learned that the VAX-11 has a special form of subroutine called a **procedure.** The main difference between procedures and other subroutines is that certain chores related to argument passing, register protection, and linkage are automatically handled by procedure calls. Procedures are invoked by **CALLG** and **CALLS** rather than BSBW or JSB. Also, return is with the **RET** instruction. Either CALLG or CALLS can be used to invoke a procedure. The only difference is that with CALLG the arguments are stored in a list, called an **argument frame,** which is in a fixed place in memory, whereas they are pushed onto the stack immediately before the call with CALLS. Our discussion of procedures included the argument pointer AP, which helps locate items in the **call frame.** The call frame is a data structure automatically placed on the User Stack by either CALLG or CALLS. Items stored in the call frame include the return point PC, registers to be protected, and other information needed for linkage.

The chapter concluded with consideration of **separate assembly** of MACRO subroutines, and MACRO programs callable from high-level languages. The separate assembly concept allows full achievement of the advantages of subroutines in that, after it has been tested, a subroutine can be assembled once and for all and stored in object form. Programs that use it then do not need to include its source code, but simply "link" with it before execution. This is made possible with the concept of **global symbols** in the assembly process. Global symbols are those symbols that have meaning in more than one routine. Procedure names, declared with the .ENTRY directives, are global, as are symbols listed in the .GLOBAL directive and labels followed by double colons, "::". The MACRO assembler automatically assumes that any label referred to in a program module but not defined therein is a global label. The .EXTERNAL directive is sometimes used to explicitly state the labels in this category, which would include any separately assembled subroutine or procedure labels. The linker must then complete the task of assigning addresses to global labels.

The final examples in the chapter showed that VAX-11 Pascal and FORTRAN employ the argument passing and linkage conventions represented in VAX-11 procedures. Thus any properly implemented VAX-11 procedure can be invoked by Pascal or FORTRAN programs.

9.13 | Exercises

9.1 Enter and assemble the program shown in Figure 9.7, and execute it using the Symbolic Debugger. Set breakpoints at S, A, B, C, CR, BR, and AR. Examine the User Stack and PC at each break, verifying the states shown in Figure 9.5.

9.2 Write a MACRO subroutine that accepts a hexadecimal number as ASCII characters from the keyboard and returns its binary value in R0. Include a short main program to demonstrate its use. Assemble the main program and subroutine together. Link and run using the Symbolic Debugger to show that it works. (*Hint:* The program in Figure 8.11 can be converted easily to a subroutine. Be sure to protect the contents of any registers used in the subroutine, other than R0.)

9.3 Write a MACRO subroutine that prints the number found in R0 as an 8-digit hexadecimal number. Include a short main program to demonstrate its use. Assemble the main program and subroutine together. Link and run using the Symbolic Debugger to show that it works. (*Hint:* The program in Figure 8.12 can be converted easily to a subroutine. Be sure to protect the contents of all registers used in the subroutine, including R0.)

9.4 Do Exercise 9.2 for positive decimal number input.

9.5 Do Exercise 9.3 for decimal number output of a 32-bit unsigned integer placed in R0.

9.6 Assume the following initializations of registers and memory locations prior to execution of each of the sample instructions given. Indicate all changes in registers and memory locations as a result of each instruction.

Register	Contents	Label	Location	Contents
R0:	000004	W:	0500	00000001
R1:	000508		0504	00000002
R2:	00050C		0508	0000050C
R3:	000504		050C	00000500
			0510	00000500
			0514	00000508

```
(a) CLRL   4(R1)              (b) ADDL   R1,8(R2)
(c) CLRL   W(R0)              (d) SUBL   4(R1),W(R0)
(e) MOVL   R2,@4(R1)          (f) CLRL   @8(R2)
(g) CLRL   @(R1)+             (h) DECL   @(R2)+
(i) MOVL   @(R1)+,@4(R1)      (j) SUBL   -(R2),@(R2)+
```

9.7 Write a subroutine that does software multiply of 32-bit unsigned integers using the shifting algorithm (see Figure 6.7). Also write a subroutine that computes $Z = X(X + 3Y)$ where X, Y, and Z are arguments transmitted using the technique of in-line values. Write a main program that accepts values for X and Y from the keyboard and prints out Z, using the subroutine. For input/output you may use the routines developed in Exercises 9.2–9.5, or .GETHEX/.PUTHEX (Section 4.11).

9.8 Write a subroutine that searches a character string to see if it contains a given character. Pass the address of the first character of the search string in R0 and the ASCII code of the target character in R1. Return the location of the first occurrence of the target character in the search string as a value in R0. For example, if the search string is "NOW IS THE TIME!" and the target character is "S", R0 should be set to 6. If the target is not found, R0 should be set to 0. Assume that the search string is terminated with a null character. Include a main program to demonstrate its usage with several different search strings and target characters.

9.9 Write a main program that:

(a) prompts the user for "Y" or "N".

(b) if "Y", accepts an unsigned integer from the keyboard and places it on the stack.

(c) when "N" is entered, calls SUB.

(d) halts or exits upon return from SUB.

The subroutine SUB should print the entered values in the reverse order of entry and then print their sum. Assemble the main program and SUB separately. Link main, SUB, and decimal or hexadecimal input/output routines together and run.

9.10 Write a subroutine that computes the inner (dot) product of two vectors, i.e., $P = X_1 Y_1 + X_2 Y_2 + , \ldots , + X_n Y_n$. Transmit arguments using in-line addresses. Separately assembly a short main program to demonstrate it. You may use either the Symbolic Debugger or suitable decimal or hexadecimal input/output routines for this demonstration.

9.11 Write a subroutine that computes the sum of three numbers, passing the argument values in registers. Also write a calling program to demonstrate its usage. Repeat this for the following other methods of argument transmission.

(a) addresses in registers   (b) in-line values

(c) in-line addresses   (d) addresses of argument list in register

(e) values in User Stack

9.12 Devise a sequence of instructions that implements call by value using the argument list address transmission method described in Section 9.8.4.

9.13 Write a VAX-11 *procedure* that computes the sum of three numbers and returns the result in a fourth argument. Demonstrate the procedure as follows:

(a) Using a calling program written in MACRO and using CALLG.

(b) Using a calling program written in MACRO and using CALLS.

(c) Using a calling program written in Pascal.

(d) Using a calling program written in FORTRAN.

10

Macros, Conditional Assembly, and Other VAX-11 MACRO Features

10.1 | Overview

This chapter presents a collection of MACRO features that, while not essential, greatly simplify program development. We first introduce the concept of **expressions,** and the **direct assignment** directive. The central idea of expressions is that the assembler is asked to perform elementary arithmetic prior to the translation process. The assignment directive provides a means of assigning a value which is *not* an address, at assembly time, to a symbol. One advantage of this is the ability to use mnemonic symbols in place of numeric constants in the assembly code, thus improving program clarity and allowing for easy change of a parameter. Taken together, assignment and expressions allow programs that can be more easily modified.

In the second section we take up the concept of **macro instructions,** or **macros** for short. Like subroutines, macros represent a way of coding an algorithm in one place and using it as often as necessary in other parts of the program. Once defined, a macro is used simply by writing its name and operands (called arguments), much as if it were part of the MACRO language. Prior to translation, the macro body is inserted in place of the reference to its name. This results in the translation being inserted "in-line" in the object code, in contrast to subroutines that require transfer of control to remotely located machine code.

Related to macros is the concept of the **repeat block.** This feature allows the programmer to automatically replicate a block of MACRO instructions a specified number of times. MACRO allows three forms of repeat blocks, each of which is discussed in this chapter.

Another major topic taken up in this chapter is **conditional assembly.** The idea here is that certain portions of the source code can be skipped during the translation process, depending upon values assigned to certain symbols or determined from expression evaluation during assembly. This feature allows different versions of the object program to be created by making only minor changes in the source program.

The final topic of this chapter is the assembly process itself. This is presented in the form of a simplified algorithm for a two-pass assembler with some of the features found in MACRO.

10.2 Assembly Expressions and Assignment

10.2.1 Expressions as Operands

With few exceptions, up to this point we have restricted instruction operands to conform exactly to one of the given addressing modes. That is, we have primarily used operands only of forms such as Rn, (Rn), A, X(Rn), etc. On occasion, however, we have found it more convenient to have an operand of the form B + 4, such as when we dealt with double-precision operations (see Section 6.12). Operands of the latter kind are referred to as **expression** operands. We now consider more general kinds of expression operands, and how the assembler handles these forms.

MACRO allows symbolic expressions of certain limited forms, including the +, −, *, and / operators. Note that there is no hierarchy among the operators, so that evaluation proceeds from left to right, except for subexpressions in < . . . > being evaluated first. The following are examples of valid MACRO expressions.

```
A+2
A+<2*B>
EOD-DATA/4
```

If all symbols used in an expression are defined in the program module containing the expression, the assembler evaluates the expression to obtain a longword value, then uses this value in place of the expression when translating to machine code. If symbols that are *not* defined in the same module are used, the assembler assumes that they are defined in other modules, i.e., that they are external, and the linker completes the expression evaluation.

Using expressions as operands allows programming techniques not otherwise available, and if used properly tends to make programs more readable. The usage that we have already seen is that which allows reference to a memory location that is a known number of bytes away from a location that has a label. For example,

```
MOVL   A+64,R1
```

will move the contents of the longword that is 64_{10} bytes beyond A into R1. This avoids having to assign a label to the byte referenced by the operand. We saw an example of this convenience when we had to refer to the high word of a double-precision integer in Section 6.12. Note that the relative addressing mode is used here, and that the expression is evaluated during assembly. Thus, if the PC-relative address of A is, say, $0A_{16}$, the translation of the above instruction is:

$$51 \quad 0000004A \quad EF \quad D0$$

It is important to observe that the expression A + 64 does *not* mean that the *value* found in A is added to 64. To remember this, keep in mind that all symbolic expressions are evaluated at *assembly or linkage* time, whereas location contents are usually determined during execution.

10.2.2 Symbols and Direct Assignment

Up to this point we have used symbols only as labels for memory locations. Actually, MACRO allows a wider usage of symbols, and provides the **direct assignment directive** as a means of assigning values to symbols that are not labels.

Symbols have two major uses in addition to their role as labels. First, they are frequently used in place of constants in order to improve program readability. For example, the instruction:

```
CMPB   R0,#CR
```

suggests that we are checking to see if the low byte of R0 contains the carriage return control character, while:

```
CMPB   R0,#15
```

is less clear. In order for such a symbol to be used in a program, however, it must be given a value using the **direct assignment directive.**

The form of the direct assignment directive is:

$$symbol = expression$$

Customarily, the direct assignment directive begins in column one. In the most common usage, *expression* is just a constant. For example, we may write:

```
LF=12
      .
      .
      .
   CMPB   R0,#LF
```

However, the expression on the right of the equal sign could be almost any valid form, as discussed in Section 10.2.1. The only requirement is that all symbols used in expressions on the right of the equal sign *must be previously defined* in the module where employed. This is because the assembler determines values for *all* symbols on the first pass, so it cannot "look ahead" to find the value of a symbol being used in an expression defining another symbol. Thus if you wish to define a symbol such as:

```
LENGTH=A-EOA
```

where A and EOA are labels, you must place this assignment *after* these labels.

Global symbols can also be assigned values. Double equal characters indicate that the symbol is to be placed in the global symbol table for use in separately assembled modules. For example, if we write:

```
BEL==7
```

the symbol BEL will be defined as 7 in all program modules. Symbol names follow the same rules as labels do. That is, they must begin with an alpha character and be 31 or fewer characters in length.

10.2.3 Advantage of Symbols and Expressions

Use of symbols and expressions can lead to more efficient programs, as well as ones that are more easily modified. For example, let us reconsider the program in Figure 5.4. This program makes use of the quantities N and NM1, the latter meaning N − 1. Note that the way we chose to program this required two longwords of storage for N and NM1, and two instructions to compute NM1 at execution time. As an alternative, suppose we use the label EOD on the byte beyond the end of DATA, define N and NM1 as nonlabel symbols, and make other changes to the program as indicated below.

```
            ,
            ,
            ,
        MOV  #N,R1
            ,
            ,
            ,
        MOV  #NM1,R2
            ,
            ,
            ,
DATA:   .LONG 4,3,2,1
EOD:
N   =<EOD-DATA>/4
NM1=N-1
        .END START
```

The assembler will then assign addresses to DATA and EOD and compute the values of the symbols N and NM1. Note that it was necessary to change the addressing modes where N and NM1 are used because they are now values computed at assembly time rather than the contents of memory locations computed during execution. The program modified in this way is shorter by 26 bytes and runs faster than the original program. Also, observe that it is more easily modified. If it becomes necessary to sort a larger array, it is necessary only to add additional values in .LONG directives between DATA and EOD. Unlike the original program, it is not even necessary to manually count the values in the array.

10.2.4 Location Counter Usage

Of occasional value in programming is the use of the assembler **location counter** in expressions. The location counter is symbolized by a period ``.'' in the assembly code, and always has a value equal to the address of the next location available for storage of translated code or data. The location counter symbol can be used where any other symbol can be used. As an example, suppose it was necessary to branch around a block of four bytes. We could write:

```
    BRB     .+5
A:  .BYTE 10,20,30,40
    MOVL  R2,R3
```

This is equivalent to:

```
    BRB   B
A:  .BYTE 10,20,30,40
B:  MOVL  R2,R3
```

However, by using the location counter we were able to accomplish the branch without introducing a destination label. As a rule, this usage is not recommended, because it has less clarity than using a label, and greater care must be exercised if the program has to be modified later. More valuable usage of location counter addressing is demonstrated in Section 10.5.3.

When using the location counter it is important to be aware of exactly when it is advanced during the assembly cycle. The rule is that it advances *after* each part of the instruction or operand specifier has been translated. Thus the instruction:

```
A:   MOVL   #,-1,R0
```

will place the address of the instruction (i.e., the value of A) into R0. This is so because the location counter is advanced after a location for the MOVL opcode has been allocated, so that "." refers to the address of the first operand specifier, and therefore ".−1" refers to the address of MOVL. Note that the sequence:

```
LC=.
A:   MOVL   #LC,R0
```

will have the same effect, because the assignment directive does not advance the location counter.

10.2.5 Pitfalls When Using Symbolic Expressions

While use of symbolic expressions and assignments often allows savings, care must be taken to assure that the results are those intended. A common error is failing to recognize that expressions are evaluated and assignments made *at assembly or linkage time*. An example of such an error is the following (incorrect) program to clear an array beginning at A:

```
A:        .BLKL   100
START:    MOVL    #100,R0
L:        CLRL    A              (incorrect)
          A=      A+4
          SOBGTR  R0,L
```

The programmer may *believe* that the address being cleared is incremented by 4 each time through the loop, thus pointing to the next longword. Actually, though, this code has a conceptual error and, moreover, will cause assembly time error reports. Conceptually it is wrong because the expression evaluation and assignment are done only once, because they are done during assembly, while the loop is repeated only during execution. Assembler errors are generated because A is first defined as a label, and then the value is changed by direct assignment. On the second pass, the assembler will again encounter the label and report it as a multiply-defined label. As a general rule, the same symbol cannot appear on the left of both "=" and ":" in a program.

As we saw in earlier chapters, the correct way to clear the array at A is to place the address of A into a register, and then use indirect addressing and increment the register each time through the loop.

Another common error is the attempt to increment the contents of a register or memory cell using an expression. For example, the instruction:

```
MOVL   R1+1,B   (incorrect)
```

may *appear* to add 1 to the contents of R1 before moving it into B. Actually, this instruction says to add 1 to the value of the *symbol* R1, which is illegal and will result in an assembler error report. However, the instruction:

```
MOVL  A+1,B
```

will be accepted by the assembler, but the program is in error if the intention is to place 1 plus the *contents* of A into B. As before, the above code means to move the contents of the location *one byte beyond A* into B.

When expressions are used to calculate values for direct assignment to symbols, special care must be taken that all symbols within the expression are *previously* defined. That is, when you write:

```
A=B*<C+4>
```

the symbols B and C must be given values *before* this line in the program. This is because the assembler expects to be able to determine values for *all* symbols during the first pass, and it cannot find a value for A if B and C are not known until after the assignment statement. In contrast, observe that the use of the same expression *as an operand*, e.g.,

```
MOVL B*<C+4>,R1
```

does *not* require B and C to be previously defined. In this case, the operand specifier is not calculated until the second pass, and presumably B and C will receive their values somewhere within the module, so they will be known during the second pass. If an operand involves symbols defined nowhere within the module being assembled, these symbols are identified as *external*, and the linker completes the calculation of the operand specifier.

10.3 | Macro Instructions

The concept of a subroutine, introduced in the previous chapter, provides the programmer with one method for defining a group of instructions in one place and using it elsewhere in the program. This was found to be an important advantage, because it improves program clarity as well as reducing programming effort.

In this section we introduce another programming concept with similar advantages, called a **macro.** Like a subroutine, a macro is a group of instructions, defined by the programmer, that can be referred to by an assigned name. Wherever this name is referred to in the assembly source program, the entire set of defining instructions will be inserted into the source program. This results in the corresponding machine code being inserted into the object program, in much the same way as a normal assembler mnemonic causes a single machine code instruction to be translated. Indeed, the term ''macro instruction'' means literally ''large instruction.''

An assembler that allows the definition and use of macro instructions (macros for short) is called a macro assembler. VAX-11 MACRO has such capability, and in fact derives its name from this feature.

10.3.1 Definition and Use of Simple Macros

Whenever there is need to perform the same task at many different places in a program, considerable programming effort can be saved by defining a macro to do the task. This definition must *precede* the usage of the macro in the program.

The definition of a macro begins with the directive **.MACRO** and ends with the directive **.ENDM**. Everything between these directives is considered to be part of the macro definition. For example, a macro to interchange the contents of two registers or longwords in main memory can be defined as:

```
.MACRO   SWITCH,A,B,TEMP
MOVL     A,TEMP
MOVL     B,A
MOVL     TEMP,B
.ENDM    SWITCH
```

Here we have selected SWITCH as the name of the macro, and have used three **dummy arguments,** A,B, and TEMP. Obviously, A and B represent the storage locations or registers whose contents are to be switched, and TEMP represents temporary storage. Note that while the macro name in the .ENDM directive is optional, it improves clarity when there are many macros defined.

Once a macro has been defined, it can be used as if it were part of the MACRO language itself. Use of the above macro to intercahnge R1 and R2 using R0 as temporary storage would require only:

```
SWITCH   R1,R2,R0
```

This would result in the following instructions being inserted into the source program:

```
MOVL     R1,R0
MOVL     R2,R1
MOVL     R0,R2
```

Thus we see that the assembler substitutes the *actual* arguments for the dummy arguments, and then "expands" the macro. Afterwards, the normal translation process takes place. When a macro is used, it is said to be **referenced.** The action of the assembler upon encountering a macro reference is called "expansion" of the macro.

The substitution process should be viewed as the replacement of the strings of characters representing the dummy arguments by the strings representing the actual arguments. With this understanding, it is easy to see the exact meaning of a particular application of a macro. For example, if we use the above macro to write:

```
SWITCH   X,Y,T
```

it is evident that the resulting "expanded" code will be:

```
MOVL     X,T
MOVL     Y,X
MOVL     T,Y
```

Morevoer, the same macro could be used to switch the contents of the two topmost User Stack locations by writing:

```
SWITCH   4(SP),(SP),T
```

which expands to:

```
MOVL   4(SP),T
MOVL   (SP),4(SP)
MOVL   T,(SP)
```

Thus it is seen that when the macro is used, the entire string "4(SP)" is used to replace "A" in the macro definition. Similarly, "(SP)" replaces "B", and "T" replaces "TEMP".

EXAMPLE 10.1   A complete program defining and using the above macro is shown in Figures 10.1 and 10.2. Figure 10.1 shows the source file, in which it can be seen that the macro is used first with register addressing, then with relative addressing. Note that in the latter case, it is necessary to reserve memory locations for the arguments in the main program; the macro defined in this example does not provide for any data storage.

Figure 10.2 shows how the assembler expands each reference to the SWITCH macro. Observe that the first usage results in only nine bytes of machine code, because register addressing is employed. In the second usage, relative addressing makes each MOVL instruction in the expanded code translate into an eleven-byte instruction.

Figure 10.2 also shows that the assembler *does not* generate machine code at the point where the macro is defined. Rather, the code is generated only where the macro is used.

In the example in Figures 10.1 and 10.2 we have included the directive:

```
.SHOW EXPANSIONS
```

```
            .TITLE EXAMPLE 10.1
;
;      DEMONSTRATES DEFINITION AND USE OF SIMPLE MACRO
;
            .MACRO   SWITCH,A,B,TEMP
            MOVL     A,TEMP
            MOVL     B,A
            MOVL     TEMP,B
            .ENDM    SWITCH
            .SHOW    EXPANSIONS
;
;      NOW USE THE MACRO CALLED SWITCH:
;
            .ENTRY   START,0
            MOVL     #3,R1
            MOVL     #4,R2
            SWITCH   R1,R2,R0
            MOVL     #5,X
            MOVL     #6,Y
            SWITCH   X,Y,T
            $EXIT_S
X:          .BLKL    1
Y:          .BLKL    1
T:          .BLKL    1
            .END     START
```

FIGURE 10.1/Demonstration of a simple macro (source file)

```
EXAMPLE  10.1      2-JUN-1985 11:47:09   VAX-11 Macro V03-00              Page  1
                   2-JUN-1985 11:46:56  _DRA1:[SOWELLJE10P1.MAR;2        (1)
                                                     Assembly source code
Machine code
                              Offset  Ln
                              addr
                              0000    1           .TITLE EXAMPLE 10.1
                              0000    2      ;
                              0000    3      ; DEMONSTRATES DEFINITION AND USE OF SIMPLE MACRO
                              0000    4      ;
                              0000    5           .MACRO  SWITCH,A,B,TEMP
                              0000    6           MOVL    A,TEMP
                              0000    7           MOVL    B,A
                              0000    8           MOVL    TEMP,B
                              0000    9           .ENDM   SWITCH
                              0000   10           .SHOW   EXPANSIONS
                              0000   11      ;
                              0000   12      ; NOW USE THE MACRO CALLED SWITCH:
                              0000   13      ;
                        0000  0000   14           .ENTRY  START,0
                  51    03    0000   15           MOVL    #3,R1
                  52    04    0005   16           MOVL    #4,R2
                              0008   17           SWITCH  R1,R2,R0
                  50    51    0008               MOVL    R1,R0
                  51    52    000B               MOVL    R2,R1
                  52    50    000E               MOVL    R0,R2
                              0011
         00000049'EF    05    0011   18           MOVL    #5,X
         0000004D'EF    06    0018   19           MOVL    #6,Y
                              001F   20           SWITCH  X,Y,T
00000051'EF  00000049'EF      001F               MOVL    X,T
00000049'EF  0000004D'EF      002A               MOVL    Y,X
0000004D'EF  00000051'EF      0035               MOVL    T,Y
                              0040
                              0040   21      $EXIT_S
                              0040               .GLOBL  SYS$EXIT
                  01    DD    0040               PUSHL   #1
                  01    FB    0042               CALLS   #1,G^SYS$EXIT
                              0049
                00000004D    0049   22 X:        .BLKL   1
                00000051    004D   23 Y:        .BLKL   1
                00000055    0051   24 T:        .BLKL   1
         00000000'GF          0055   25           .END    START
```

FIGURE 10.2/Demonstration of a simple macro (expanded listing file).

This directive causes the listing file to show the expanded form of the macro, as we see in Figure 10.2. Had this directive been omitted, such expansion would not be shown. Instead, the listing would show only the macro references, as in the source file. After the macro has been perfected the latter is preferred, because the expanded form makes the listing lengthy and cluttered. In any case, however, the assembler generates the machine code instructions for the expanded macro and inserts them into the object program at each point of reference.

10.3.2 Macros versus Subroutines

The following important distinction can be made between macros and subroutines: reference to a macro inserts machine code "in-line" at each point of reference to it, whereas machine code for the subroutine exists at only one place and control is transferred to it and back each time it is used. The implications of this are important when either program size or speed is of concern. In general, the definition and use of a macro to perform a given task will result in a *larger* object program than if the same task were done using a subroutine. On the other hand, transfer to and from subroutines takes longer than sequential execution of in-line code. The magnitudes of these differences will depend on the size of the object code to do the task, and the number of times it is to be used in the program. As a general rule, small tasks should be defined as macros, and lengthy tasks as subroutines.

10.3.3 Internal Labels

In Section 4.5 we noted that each label in a program module must be unique because using the same label for more than one memory location would result in ambiguity. This is of concern when a macro has an internal label because every reference to the macro will generate a *repetition* of the label. For example, consider a macro to push N values stored in ARY onto the stack. This might be written as follows:

```
        .MACRO    PUSHN ,ARY ,N
        MOVL      #ARY ,R1
        MOVL      N ,R0
L1:     MOVL      (R1)+ ,-(SP)
        SOBGTR    R0 ,L1
        .ENDM     PUSHN
```

Then if we wished to use this to put two arrays A and B onto the stack, we would write:

```
        PUSHN     A ,NA
        PUSHN     B ,NB
           .
           .
           .
NA:     .LONG     5
A:      .LONG     1 ,2 ,3 ,4 ,5
           .
           .
           .
NB:     .LONG     7
B:      .LONG     11 ,12 ,13 ,14 ,15 ,16 ,17
```

When expanded, this would create two occurrences of the label L1, which is unacceptable. We will discuss two ways of dealing with this, namely, **argument labels** and **local labels.**

Argument labels require no new ideas. The labels internal to the macro are simply placed in the dummy argument list. At each use of the macro, a unique label is specified by the programmer as the actual argument. In the expansion process, the actual label is substituted for the dummy so that the fully expanded program has no repeated labels.

Labels as arguments are objectionable because they require careful selection of unique labels on each macro reference. Also, the requirement for specifying an actual argument that has no significance in the procedure where it is referenced is not good programming practice in general. In order to overcome this, MACRO provides another mechanism, which uses the concept of **local labels.** We shall first examine local labels in general, and then show how they are employed to resolve the problem of internal macro labels.

The definition of local labels depends upon the MACRO program being divided into a number of segments called **local symbol blocks.** This division is done automatically according to the rule that a new local symbol block begins with each *normal* label, i.e., those not constructed according to the rules for local labels as defined below. As an example, the code beginning with L2: and ending with the line preceding L3: in Figure 8.12 is a local symbol block, and the code beginning with L3: and ending with PV: is another. (The directive .PSECT (Section 11.4.4) and certain other directives also can be used to define local symbol blocks.)

The programmer creates a local label by making it of the form n$, where n is a decimal integer between 1 and 65535. For example, 4$, 6$, and 48$ are valid local labels. Any label so constructed will be recognized only within the local symbol block where it is defined. This has to important implications:

1. Local symbols cannot be referred to from other local symbol blocks. For example, consider:

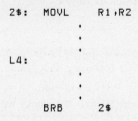

```
2$:    MOVL     R1,R2
         .
         .
         .
L4:
         .
         .
         .
       BRB      2$
```

This will not cause a branch to the MOVL instruction, because L4 begins a new local symbol block. Either the BRB will cause an "unrecognized symbol" error, or, if there is a label 2$ defined within the local symbol block beginning at L4, it will be the branch destination.

2. The same local label can be used in more than one local symbol block. When this is done, the assembler will treat each as a unique label.

It is the second characteristic that justifies the usage of local labels. If one uses local labels for branch destinations and loop labels, and uses normal labels for entry points for major blocks of code, there will be less change of duplicate labels.

MACRO uses the concept of local labels to effectively eliminate the possibility of duplicate labels during macro expansion. This is accomplished by putting the label in the dummy argument list with a prefix question mark "?", e.g.,

```
.MACRO   PUSHN,ARY,N,?L1
```

When this is done, the expansion process *generates* a local label n\$ with n between 30000_{10} and 65535_{10} to be used in place of L1. The first reference to a macro with a local label argument in any local symbol block generates 30000\$; the second generates 30001\$; and so on up to 65535\$. The count begins at 30000\$ again whenever a new local symbol block is encountered. The possibility of generating more than 35535_{10} local labels in a given local symbol block is remote, but would result in illegal duplicate labels and assembler errors if it occurred.

EXAMPLE 10.2   Figure 10.3 shows a listing for the PUSHN macro example with automatically generated local labels. The .SHOW EXPANSIONS directive is again included to show the macro expansion. We see that the label L1 is replaced by 30000\$ on the first reference, and by 30001\$ on the second.

10.3.4 Nested Macros

It is possible to have a macro reference another macro. For example, suppose we wish to create a macro to save the contents of R0 through R5 on the stack. One way of doing this is:

```
.MACRO   PUSH,X
MOVL     X,-(SP)
.ENDM    PUSH
.MACRO   SAVREG
PUSH     R0
PUSH     R1
PUSH     R2
PUSH     R3
PUSH     R4
PUSH     R5
.ENDM    SAVREG
```

Note that two separate macros are defined, namely, PUSH and SAVREG. PUSH is defined first, and then it is *referenced* in the definition of SAVREG. This technique is called **nesting** of macro references. The expansion of SAVREG will yield:

```
MOVL     R0,-(SP)
MOVL     R1,-(SP)
MOVL     R2,-(SP)
MOVL     R3,-(SP)
MOVL     R4,-(SP)
MOVL     R5,-(SP)
```

It is also possible to nest macros to more than one level, i.e., to have a macro reference a macro that references another macro, and so on.

While the preceding example is a good illustration of nested macro references, SAVREG is not a very useful macro on the VAX-11 because the CPU has a special instruction for pushing the registers onto the stack. Thus the instruction:

```
PUSHR    #^M<R0,R1,R2,R3,R4,R5>
```

```
         Machine code                    Offset  Ln      Assembly source code
                                          addr
                                         0000     1         .TITLE  EXAMPLE 10.2
                                         0000     2         .MACRO  PUSHN,ARY,N,?L1
                                         0000     3         MOVL    #ARY,R1
                                         0000     4         MOVL    N,R0
                                         0000     5   L1:   MOVL    (R1)+,-(SP)
                                         0000     6         SOBGTR  R0,L1
                                         0000     7         .ENDM   PUSHN
                                         0000     8         .SHOW   EXPANSIONS
                                         0000     9   ;
                               0000      0000    10         .ENTRY  START,0
                                         0002    11         PUSHN   A,NA
51             00000037'BF  D0           0002         MOVL    #A,R1
50             00000033'EF  D0           0009         MOVL    NA,R0
               7E   81  D0               0010  30000$:     MOVL    (R1)+,-(SP)
                    FA   50  F5          0013         SOBGTR  R0,30000$
                                         0016    12         PUSHN   B,NB
51             0000004F'BF  D0           0016         MOVL    #B,R1
50             0000004B'EF  D0           001D         MOVL    NB,R0
               7E   81  D0               0024  30001$:     MOVL    (R1)+,-(SP)
                    FA   50  F5          0027         SOBGTR  R0,30001$
                                         002A    13         $EXIT_S
                                         002A                 .GLOBL  SYS$EXIT
               00000000'GF   01  DD      002A         PUSHL   #1
                             01  FB      002C         CALLS   #1,G^SYS$EXIT
                                         0033    14   NA:   .LONG   5
00000004 00000003 00000005              0033    15   A:    .LONG   1,2,3,4,5
00000002 00000001                       0037
                  00000005              0047
                  00000007              004B    16   NB:   .LONG   7
00000000D 0000000C 0000000B             004F    17   B:    .LONG   11,12,13,14,15,16,17
00000011 00000010 0000000F              005F
                  0000000E              006B    18         .END    START
```

FIGURE 10.3/ Listing with expanded macro using local labels

accomplishes the same thing as SAVREG. The companion instruction:

```
POPR    #^M<R0,R1,R2,R3,R4,R5>
```

restores the registers from the stack.

Definitions of macros can also be nested. For example, it is possible to write:

```
.MACRO   ONE,X,Y
.MACRO   TWO,W
MULL     #2,R1
MOVL     R1,W
.ENDM    TWO
.MACRO   THREE,W
MULL     #3,R1
MOVL     R1,W
.ENDM    THREE
TWO      X
THREE    Y
.ENDM    ONE
```

Here we have defined and referenced macros named TWO and THREE internally to macro ONE. When macro ONE is referenced in a program, e.g.,

```
ONE   A,B
```

the resulting expansion is:

```
.MACRO   TWO,W
MULL     #2,R1
MOVL     R1,W
.ENDM    TWO
.MACRO   THREE,W
MULL     #3,R1
MOVL     R1,W
.ENDM    THREE
MULL     #2,R1
MOVL     R1,A
MULL     #3,R1
MOVL     R1,B
```

It should be noted that the expansion yields the assembly and machine code for the references to TWO and THREE, and also the definitions of these two macros. Thus it would now be possible to make further references to TWO and THREE later in the program. It is not possible, however, to refer to an internally defined macro until *after* the macro in which it is defined has been referenced.

Features of MACRO such as nested macro definitions have uses in advanced programming. Their importance to the beginning programmer is limited, however.

10.3.5 More on Macro Arguments

In Sections 10.3.1–10.3.4 we have seen that dummy arguments in macro definitions are treated as character strings that are replaced by the corresponding actual argument strings during expansion. We will now examine some cases in which slightly different processes are used for some kinds of arguments.

One special case is when the dummy argument is to be replaced by an actual argument string that *contains a delimiter*. Delimiters are the characters used to separate the arguments. They include the space, comma, semicolon, and tab keys.

In this case the actual argument must be enclosed in angle brackets, $< \ldots >$, causing it to be treated as a single string during expansion. As an example, suppose we wanted the capability to delay the execution of arbitrary instructions. We could define a macro instruction to do this as follows:

```
        .MACRO    DELAY,INSTR,N,?L
        MOVL      R0,-(SP)    ; SAVE R0
        MOVL      #N,R0       ; DELAY
L:      SOBGTR    R0,L        ;   N CYCLES
        MOVL      (SP)+,R0    ; RECOVER R0
        .ENDM INSTR
```

A typical reference of this could be:

```
DELAY   <BSBW SUB1>,100000
```

which would be expanded to give:

```
            MOVL    R0,-(SP)      ;SAVE R0
            MOVL    #100000,R0    ;DELAY
30000$:     SOBGTR  R0,30000$     ;   N CYCLES
            MOVL    (SP)+,R0      ;RECOVER R0
            BSBW    SUB1
```

Thus any time this macro is referenced, the machine will execute the SOBGTR instruction N times before executing the indicated instruction. Without the facility provided by the angle brackets, this macro could not have been constructed because the spaces and commas used in the instruction argument, acting as delimiters, would have caused the instruction mnemonic and each of its operands to be treated as separate macro arguments.

Another special case occurs when an argument is to be treated as a *number*. In order to force the assembler to treat an argument as a number rather than the corresponding character string, the actual argument is prefixed by a backslash "\".

EXAMPLE 10.3 As an example of this consider a macro that will store the first argument in the next available location in an array beginning at A. This might be done as follows:

```
.MACRO    NEXT,V,C
MOVL      V,A+C
.ENDM     NEXT
.MACRO    SAVE,V,C
NEXT      V,\C
C=C+4
.ENDM
```

To see how this works, let us examine Figure 10.4, which shows a listing with four expanded references to SAVE. The symbol C is first defined to be zero, and the first reference to SAVE is at source line 15. Note that the *symbol* C was substituted during the expansion of SAVE, yielding:

```
NEXT X,\C
C = C+4
```

However, when NEXT X,\C is expanded, the \C causes the *value* of C to be substituted for the dummy argument of NEXT. This yields:

```
MOVL   X,A+0
```

Subsequent references to SAVE yield:

```
MOVL   X,A+4
MOVL   Y,A+8
MOVL   Z,A+12
```

and so on, due to the C = C + 4 that is generated upon each expansion. Thus we are placing the X, Y, and Z in successive longwords beginning at A.

The final case of special argument forms to be mentioned here is called **concatenation** of arguments. The way this works and a suggestion for possible usage may be seen in the following example:

```
          .MACRO     MSG,A,B
MSG'A:    .ASCII/MESSAGE 'A:/
          .ASCIZ/A'B/
          .ENDM      MSG
```

The single quote preceding (or following) a dummy argument inside the macro means that the substituted actual argument string is to be concatenated to the existing characters at that point. If we reference the above macro with:

```
MSG  ONE,<:ENTER A VALUE>
```

the expansion is therefore:

```
MSGONE:   .ASCII/MESSAGE  ONE:/
          .ASCIZ/ONE:ENTER A VALUE/
```

This technique can be used to conveniently construct a number of messages that differ only slightly. It has many other uses also, as will be discussed in Section 10.4.1.

10.4 | Repeat Blocks

An assembly concept which has some similarity to the macro instruction is the **repeat block.** Like a macro, a repeat block causes automatic insertion of code into the assembly instructions prior to translation. However, a repeat block replicates the defining code a specified number of times at a single place in the code, rather than generating a copy at various calling points throughout the program as occurs with macro references. MACRO provides three forms of repeat blocks, indicated by the directives .REPT, .IRP, and .IRPC. These are discussed in Sections 10.4.1–10.4.3.

10.4.1 Simple Repeat Blocks (.REPT)

The simple repeat block can be used when it is necessary to insert the same sequence of instructions a definite number of times at a single place in the program. The .REPT block has the form:

```
.REPT expression
(body)
.ENDR
```

```
Machine code         Offset  Ln      Assembly source code
                     addr
                     0000     1              .TITLE  EXAMPLE 10.3
                     0000     2      ;
                     0000     3      ; NESTED MACRO DEFINITION WITH NUMERIC ARGUMENT
                     0000     4      ;
                     0000     5              .SHOW   EXPANSIONS
                     0000     6              .MACRO  NEXT,V,C        ;DEFINE
                     0000     7              MOVL    V,A+C           ;  NEXT
                     0000     8              .ENDM   NEXT            ;  MACRO.
                     0000     9              .MACRO  SAVE,V,C        ;DEFINE
                     0000    10              NEXT    V,\C            ;  SAVE MACRO
                     0000    11              C=C+4                   ;  USING
                     0000    12              .ENDM   SAVE            ;  NEXT.
                     0000    13              .ENTRY  START,0
            00000000 0002    14      C=0                             ;INIT, NUMERIC ARGUMENT.
                     0002    15              SAVE    X,C             ;SAVE X
                     0002                    NEXT    X,\C            ;  SAVE MACRO
00000043'EF D0       0002                    MOVL    X,A+0           ;  NEXT
            00000004 000D                    C=C+4                   ;  USING
                     000D    16              SAVE    X,C             ;  TWICE,
                     000D                    NEXT    X,\C            ;  SAVE MACRO
00000037'EF D0 00000047'EF 000D              MOVL    X,A+4           ;  NEXT
            00000008 0018                    C=C+4                   ;  USING
                     0018    17              SAVE    Y,C             ;SAVE Y
                     0018                    NEXT    Y,\C            ;  SAVE MACRO
```

```
0000004B'EF  0000003B'EF  D0  0018                 MOVL    Y,A+8         ;   NEXT
             0000000C          0023
                               0023                 C=C+4               ;   USING
                               0023          18     SAVE    Z,C          ;SAVE Z
                               0023                 NEXT    Z,\C         ;   SAVE MACRO
0000004F'EF  0000003F'EF  D0  0023                 MOVL    Z,A+12        ;   NEXT
             00000010          002E
                               002E                 C=C+4               ;   USING
                               002E          19     $EXIT_S
                               002E                 .GLOBL  SYS$EXIT
          01 DD               002E                 PUSHL   #1
          01 FB               0030                 CALLS   #1,G^SYS$EXIT
0000000'GF                     0037
                    0000000A   0037          20 X:  .LONG   10           ;INIT. X
                    00000014   003B          21 Y:  .LONG   20           ;INIT. Y
                    0000001E   003F          22 Z:  .LONG   30           ;INIT. Z
                    000001D3   0043          23 A:  .BLKL   100          ;ARRAY FOR STORAGE
                                                   .END    START
```

FIGURE 10.4/Nested macro call with numeric arguments

When .REPT is encountered in the assembly process, *expression* is evaluated, and all instructions and directives in the body are repeated a number of times, indicated by the value of *expression*. As a simple case to consider, suppose we want to push four copies of the contents of R0 onto the User Stack. Using a repeat block we could write:

```
.REPT   4
MOVL    R0,-(SP)
.ENDR
```

The assembler will expand this to:

```
MOVL    R0,-(SP)
MOVL    R0,-(SP)
MOVL    R0,-(SP)
MOVL    R0,-(SP)
```

The body of the repeat block can contain any instruction, macro call, or directive. This is shown in Example 10.4.

EXAMPLE 10.4   Let us again consider the need for a macro to save registers R0 through R5 on the User Stack. We will use techniques for numeric and concatenated arguments discussed in Section 10.3.5 in addition to the .REPT directive.

```
.MACRO      PUSH,N
MOVL        R'N,-(SP)
.ENDM       PUSH
.MACRO      SAVREG
N=0
.REPT   6
PUSH    \N
N=N+1
.ENDR
.ENDM       SAVREG
```

A reference to SAVREG will then generate machine code for:

```
MOVL      R0,-(SP)
MOVL      R1,-(SP)
            •
            •
            •
MOVL      R5,-(SP)
```

This expansion occurs because the sequence:

```
PUSH    \N
N=N+1
```

is repeated six times after N has been initialized to zero. Due to the "\" preceding N, the *value* of N is passed to the PUSH macro expansion and gets concatenated onto the R as discussed in Section 10.3.5.

10.4.2 Indefinite Repeat Blocks (.IRP)

The indefinite repeat block differs from the simple form in that symbol substitution is possible. Its general form is:

```
.IRP    symbol,<argument list>
(body)
.ENDM   (.ENDR also accepted)
```

This structure is placed in the program at the place where the repeated code is required. Upon expansion, the internal parameter represented by *symbol* is replaced by successive symbol strings in the *argument list*. Let us clarify this with the now-familiar objective of saving register contents on the stack. We could write:

```
.MACRO    SAVREG
.IRP    X,<R0,R1,R2,R3,R4,R5>
MOVL    X,-(SP)
.ENDM
.ENDM    SAVREG
```

Any reference of SAVREG causes the MOVL X,-(SP) instruction to be repeated, with X replaced successively by R0,R1,...,R5. Obviously, this generates the same machine code as the other macros we defined for this purpose.

This is called an *indefinite* repeat block because the repetition is done for an arbitrary number of arguments. It has several similarities to the macro. Note, for example, that it has a dummy argument (*symbol*) and actual arguments (*argument list*). Also, the rules for forming arguments are the same as for macro arguments. Finally, the end is marked by .ENDM just as for a macro. However, it is not referenced by a name like a macro.

10.4.3 Indefinite Repeat with Character Argument (.IRPC)

The repeat block directive .IRPC is almost identical to .IRP. The only difference is that the single argument is a *string* of characters, each of which becomes a substitution for the dummy argument symbol. To show this as simply as possible, the code:

```
.IRPC    X,<AB>
MOVL    X,(R1)+
.ENDM
```

is expanded to give:

```
MOVL    A,(R1)+
MOVL    B,(R1)+
```

It is left as an exercise to use this construction to define our SAVREG macro yet another way.

10.5 | Conditional Assembly

Often a program is expected to run in several different environments. This can arise due to differences in the hardware, such as various peripheral devices, or due to the absence of certain software, such as operating system library macros. The programmer can use the **conditional assembly** feature of MACRO to allow for such differences within the context of a single source program.

The basic concept of conditional assembly is that assembly language instructions are included in the source program for all anticipated program variations, but certain portions are skipped in the translation process to generate a particular version of the object program. The portions included and those skipped are controlled by decision structures constructed with special assembly directives.

Let us be clear on a very important point in this discussion. That is, we are talking about decisions that are made during the *assembly* process, not during execution. These decisions must therefore be based on symbols and expressions whose values are determinable *at assembly time*. Often this is as simple as introducing a symbol to act as a flag, with an assignment directive near the beginning of the source program to give it a value. When it is desired to assemble a different version, the value of the flag is changed and the source program is reassembled. Later in the program conditional assembly directives use this flag to determine whether or not to assemble a particular block of instructions.

MACRO provides a number of directives that can be used to construct conditional assembly decision structures. We will use these to describe single-alternative and double-alternative conditional assemblies.

10.5.1 Single-Alternative Conditional Assembly

Single-alternative conditional assembly is the case where there is a block of source code that is to be either assembled or skipped, as pictured in Figure 10.5. The implementation of Figure 10.5 in MACRO has the following general form:

```
.IF     condition  argument
        (code to be assembled if
        argument meets condition)
.ENDC
```

An alternate implementation, useful when there is only one line to be assembled or omitted, is:

```
.IIF  condition  argument, statement
```

where *statement* is any valid MACRO instruction or directive. Here *condition* can be any of the several logical operators shown in Table 10.1. The first six of these assume the argument to be an expression that can be evaluated at assembly time. The value is then compared to zero according to the condition operator, e.g., to see if it is EQ **EQ**ual to zero, or LT (**L**ess **T**han) zero. If the expression satisfies the condition, the

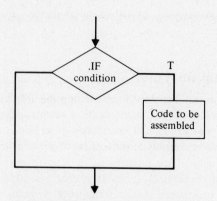

FIGURE 10.5/Single-alternative conditional assembly

TABLE 10.1/Conditional Test Operators

Condition	Arguments	Assemble Block If
EQ	Expression	Expression is equal to zero
NE	Expression	Expression is not equal to zero
GT	Expression	Expression is greater than zero
LE	Expression	Expression is less than or equal to zero
LT	Expression	Expression is less than zero
GE	Expression	Expression is greater than or equal to zero
DF	Symbol	Symbol is defined
NDF	Symbol	Symbol is not defined
B	<String>	Argument string is absent (blank)
NB	<String>	Argument string is not blank
IDN	<String 1> <String 2>	String 1 is identical to string 2
DIF	<String 1> <String 2>	String 1 is different from string 2

NOTES:

(1) Expression can be any valid symbolic expression.

(2) Symbol can be any valid symbol. It is found to be defined if it occurs to the left of :, =, ::, or ==.

(3) String can be anything that would comprise a valid macro argument enclosed in <>.

code is assembled; otherwise it is ignored. When the DF and NDF conditions are used, the argument is treated as a symbol, and a determination is made to see whether or not the symbol has been defined either as a label or by assignment. (Note that macro names, MACRO instruction mnemonics, and directive mnemonics are not recognized as defined in this sense.) The last four conditions are intended for use in macro definitions, and assume the argument to be like a macro argument. These are discussed in Section 10.5.3.

EXAMPLE 10.5   As our first example of the use of conditional assembly, suppose we wish to write a program to test the advantage of using the XOR instruction rather than the BICL and BISL instructions to accomplish the same thing. To do this, let us define a flag symbol DEFXOR that is set to zero if XOR is not to be used, or to a nonzero value otherwise. Then, in the initial version of the source program, we place the assignment directive:

```
DEFXOR =0
```

This should be near the beginning of the program so that it can be readily found and changed later. Then we insert the conditional assembly block into the source program as follows:

```
.IF      EQ        DEFXOR
.MACRO   XOR       RN,D     ; XOR MACRO
MOVL     D,-(SP)
BICL     RN,D
BICL     (SP)+,RN
BISL     RN,D
.ENDM    XOR
.ENDC
```

Because DEFXOR is zero, the macro will be expanded wherever XOR appears in the program. A study of this macro will reveal that it behaves exactly as the XOR instruction, although it is longer and considerably less efficient. If DEFXOR is set to a nonzero value and the program is reassembled, the macro will not be expanded and any XOR in the program will automatically refer to the XOR *instruction*. The two versions of the program could then be compared for length of object code and speed of execution.

Although the preceding example has only a macro definition in the conditional assembly block, any MACRO directive or instruction can be included in this block.

10.5.2 Double-Alternative Conditional Assembly

Often there is a need to assemble one block of code if a condition is true, and a different block if the condition is false. Also, there is usually code to be assembled regardless. This is what we call a double-alternative conditional assembly, as depicted in Figure 10.6.

MACRO provides for assembly control structures such as the one shown in Figure 10.6 using the conditional assembly directive described above, .IF, and three **subconditional** assembly directives, .IFF (if false), .IFT (if true), and .IFTF (if true or false). The subconditional directives can only appear inside a conditional block, but can be

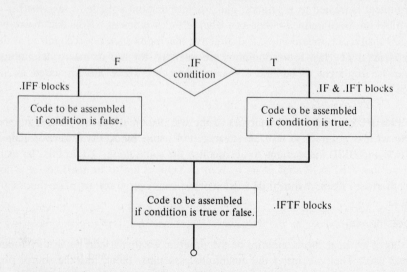

FIGURE 10.6/Double-alternative conditional assembly

used as often as necessary and in any order. They do not have a separate condition test; they are based on the test for the preceding .IF directive. The rule followed is that code is assembled or not assembled according to the most recent .IF directive. That is: (1) all code following .IF or .IFT is assembled only if the condition is true; (2) all code following an .IFF is assembled only if the condition is false; and (3) all code following an .IFTF is assembled regardless of whether the condition is true or false.

EXAMPLE 10.6 As an example of double-alternative conditional assembly, suppose we wish to demonstrate the relative efficiency of using the SOBGTR instruction rather than an equivalent loop structure using branch instructions. A program that could be used to test either approach in clearing an array is:

```
FLAG = 1 ; SET TO 0 TO TEST SOBGTR
             .IF    NE     FLAG
             .IFTF
             MOVL   #A,R2
             MOVL   #10,R1
L1:          CLRL    (R2)+
             .IFT
             DECL   R1
             BGTRU  L1
             .IFF
             SOBGTR R1,L1
             .ENDC
```

The results of assembling this with FLAG set to 1 and 0 are:

```
      FLAG=1
      ------
      MOVL   #A,R2
      MOVL   #10,R1
L1:   CLRL   (R2)+
      DECL   R1
      BGTRU  L1
```

and:

```
      FLAG=0
      -------
      MOVL   #A,R2
      MOVL   #10,R1
L1:   CLRL   (R2)+
      SOBGTR R1,L1
```

Observe that the first three instructions are assembled in any event, because they are after the .IFTF directive. Only one of the other two blocks is selected, depending upon whether FLAG is 0 or not 0.

10.5.3 Nonnumeric Conditional Tests

Table 10.1 shows several nonnumeric conditional tests. Among these are the DF and NDF conditions, which can be used to determine if a symbol has been defined as a label or through use of the assignment directive. (Note that symbols in the permanent symbol table, i.e., the MACRO instruction and directive set, and those used as macro names *cannot* be checked with these conditional tests.)

EXAMPLE 10.7 As an example of the use of NDF, consider again the need for a macro that switches the contents of two longwords or registers. We would like to use a longword of memory for the temporary location, but do not want a different location allocated each time the macro is referenced. The following definition meets this requirement:

```
        .MACRO   SWITCH,A,B
        .IF   NDF  SWTMP
        BRB      .+5
SWTMP:  .LONG    1
        .ENDC
        MOVL     A,SWTMP
        MOVL     B,A
        MOVL     SWTMP,B
        .ENDM    SWITCH
```

On the first reference to SWITCH, a memory location is reserved with the label SWTMP. The BRB .+5 instruction is also inserted to branch around this longword (see Section 10.2.4). Subsequent references to SWITCH will find SWTMP to be defined, and will simply use it rather than defining another temporary location.

The DF and NDF conditions can also be applied to logical expressions involving several symbols. The accepted logical operators are & (and), ! (or), and \ (exclusive or). For example, we would write:

```
.IF   DF   N!M
```

which would cause assembly of the subsequent conditional block if either N or M has been defined. If we write:

```
.IF   NDF   S&W
```

the conditional block is assembled only if S and W are both undefined, i.e., neither is defined.

The B and NB conditional tests allow the detection of omitted actual arguments when a macro is referenced.

EXAMPLE 10.8 As an example, suppose a macro is needed that will move M longwords from array X to array Y, but if M is not specified it should assume that ten longwords are to be transferred. This could be written as follows.

```
        .MACRO   SAVARY,X,Y,M,?L
        .IF   B     <M>
        N = 10
        .IFF
        N=M
        .ENDC
        MOVL     R0,-(SP)
        CLRL     R0
L:      MOVL     X(R0),Y(R0)
        ADDL     #4,R0
        CMPL     R0,#4*N
        BLSSU    L
        MOVL     (SP)+,R0
        .ENDM    SAVARY
```

If this is referenced as:

```
SAVARY   X1,Y1
```

then ten values are moved from X1 to Y1. On the other hand, if we write:

```
SAVARY   Z,W,44
```

the code generated will move 44_{10} values from Z to W.

The conditional tests IDN and DIF also enable examination of macro argument strings. In this case two strings are involved, and they are compared to see if they are identical (IDN) or different (DIF). As an example of a possible use of these conditions, consider the SWITCH macro developed in Section 10.3.1. Suppose we wish to alert the programmer using this macro if the TEMP location is the same as one of the locations being switched, because this would cause an error. To do so, modify the macro as follows.

```
.MACRO     SWITCH,A,B,TEMP
.IF        IDN    <A>,<TEMP>
.ERROR        ;TEMP SAME AS A
.ENDC
.IF        IDN    <B>,<TEMP>
.ERROR        ;TEMP SAME AS B
.ENDC
MOVL       A,TEMP
MOVL       B,A
MOVL       TEMP,B
.ENDM      SWITCH
```

If in any usage of SWITCH the actual argument for either A or B is identical to that for TEMP, then the **.ERROR directive** will be placed in the expanded source program.

The .ERROR directive, used in the preceding example for the first time, causes an error report in the listing. The general form of this directive is:

```
.ERROR symbol   ;   message
```

where *symbol* is any defined symbol in the program and *message* is any character string. The report in the listing will include the value of *symbol* and *message*. Also, the error will be reported to the terminal screen as are regular assembly errors.

10.5.4 Other Conditional Assemblies in Macro

We have already noted that conditional assembly in macro definitions can be a useful programming technique. We shall now examine several other directives that enlarge this capability in MACRO. These include the following.

Directive	Explanation
.MEXIT	Causes all further code in the macro to be skipped. In effect, an unconditional GO TO .ENDM in the macro expansion.
.NARG symbol	Causes the count of actual arguments to be assigned to symbol.
.NTYPE symbol,arg	Causes the addressing code of argument arg to be assigned to symbol.
.NCHR symbol, <string>	Causes the count of characters in string to be assigned to symbol.

The .MEXIT and .NARG directives are often used together.

EXAMPLE 10.9   As an example of using the preceding directions, let us devise a macro that will add up to five arguments, with the sum appearing in R0. The following macro will do this.

```
.MACRO      ADDALL ,A ,B ,C ,D ,E
.NARG       N
CLRL        R0
.IF         EQ       N
.MEXIT
.ENDC
.IRP        X ,<A ,B ,C ,D ,E>
ADDL        X ,R0
N=N-1
.IF         EQ       N
.MEXIT
.ENDC
.ENDR
.ENDM       ADDALL
```

Note that after clearing R0, the first conditional assembly will insert .MEXIT, causing no further expansion of the macro if there are no arguments. If N is greater than 0, however, the repeat block will be expanded. On each expansion there is generated successively:

```
ADDL    A ,R0
N=N-1
ADDL    B ,R0
N=N-1
    .
    .
    .
```

This continues until N is 0, whereupon the second conditional assembly generates a .MEXIT, causing the macro expansion process to stop.

The directive .NTYPE is used for detecting the addressing mode of arguments and allowing proper action to be taken. For example, the SWITCH macro of Section 10.3.1 could be modified to prohibit the use of R0 as the temporary location.

```
.MACRO      SWITCH ,A ,B ,TEMP
.NTYPE      TYPE ,TEMP
.IF         EQ       TYPE - #^X50
.ERROR      TYPE                 ;CANNOT USE R0
.MEXIT
.ENDC
MOVL        A ,TEMP
MOVL        B ,A
MOVL        TEMP ,B
.ENDM       SWITCH
```

Thus if this macro is called by an uninformed user as:

```
SWITCH      X ,Y ,R0
```

the symbol TYPE will be set to 50_{16} (i.e., the operand specifier code for R0), causing the conditional assembly block to be expanded. This expansion generates an .ERROR directive and exits from further macro expansion due to .MEXIT. Note that we have used the general form of the .ERROR directive; this will cause the value of the symbol TYPE to be printed in the listing along with the message:

```
".ERROR   TYPE;   CANNOT   USE   R0."
```

Sometimes a macro argument will be a character string whose length is needed in the macro expansion. Consider the following example of this, which uses the .NCHR directive:

```
.MACRO      SAVSTR, STRING
.NCHR       COUNT, STRING
.BYTE       COUNT
.ASCII      /STRING/
.ENDM       SAVSTR
```

When this macro is invoked, the argument string is saved, preceded by a count of its length. For example,

```
SAVSTR    <MACRO>
```

results in the expansion:

```
.BYTE     COUNT
.ASCII    /MACRO/
```

Note that the assembler *also* has placed COUNT in the symbol table and assigned it a *value*—namely, 5. This would be evident if we examined the translation (not given here).

10.6 | The Assembly Process

Throughout this book we have referred to "the assembler" constantly, but have described it only in terms of *what* it does rather than *how* it does it. A somewhat better understanding of assembly language programming can be gained by considering how the assembler works. A complete description of the MACRO assembler is beyond the scope of this book, but we can gain some understanding by considering a simplified assembler with similar features.

An assembler is nothing more than a program. It can be written in any suitable programming language, including another assembly language, or even in the same language that it is intended to assemble. For example, one could program a MACRO assembler in MACRO, FORTRAN, Pascal, or BASIC. Functionally, this program may be described as a program that reads a "source program" consisting of a list of assembly instructions and directives, and produces a list of binary numbers that represent the machine language equivalent of the source program.

Most assemblers, including MACRO, are what we call **two-pass** assemblers. This means that the source program is processed line-by-line twice in coming up with the machine language program. The reason for the second pass is the possibility of a symbol occurring in an instruction or directive *before* it is defined. This is called **forward referencing.** For example, in assembling the program:

```
CR = 15
                    CMPL      A,#CR
                      .
                      .
                      .
    A:                .BLKB    100
                      .
                      .
                      .
```

the symbol CR has a known value when the CMPL instruction is encountered, but A does not. The value to be assigned to A cannot be determined until all intervening instructions have been assigned locations. Therefore, the CMPL instruction cannot be assembled when first encountered. To resolve this problem, the first pass has as its principal purpose the building of a **symbol table.** This symbol table is a list of symbols and corresponding values, e.g.,

```
    CR      15
    A       0024
```

where 15 is the assigned value for CR and 0024 is the offset address (relative to the beginning of the program) assigned by the assembler for storage at label A. The second pass through the source program can then fully translate the instructions, referring to the symbol table as required to determine immediate values, PC relative addresses, branch destinations, and so on.

The assembly process is facilitated by the location counter, LC, first mentioned in Section 10.2.4. Just as PC always points to the next main memory address during program execution, LC always points to the next available location for assignment to an instruction or storage directive during assembly. It starts at zero and is advanced by the number of bytes required by each instruction or directive as successive lines of source code are processed. During the first pass then, LC will always provide the value to assign to a label when one is encountered.

A simplified algorithm for a two-pass assembler is described in Figure 10.7. In Figure 10.7(a) we see the major steps in building the symbol table. After initializing LC to 0, we get the first source line and break it down into "tokens," i.e., symbols and punctuation. These tokens are examined to see if one of them is an .END directive that marks the end of the module. If not, the WHILE loop is entered and the tokens are examined to see if they form a MACRO directive or instruction. If it is a direct assignment, the symbol and the value to the right of the = are placed in the symbol table. If it is a label, the symbol and the current LC are put in the symbol table. Once this has been done, the next task is to determine how much to advance LC. The "syntax" of the source line, i.e., the sequence of tokens, provides this information. For example, an instruction that translates into three bytes will cause LC to be advanced by three bytes, while the directive:

```
    .BLKB    12
```

will cause LC to be advanced by 12_{10} bytes. Some directives, e.g., direct assignment, require no storage, so LC is not advanced at all. After updating the LC, the next line is obtained and tokenized, and the WHILE loop is repeated. This continues until the .END token is found in some line, whereupon pass 1 concludes and pass 2 begins.

Begin pass 1:

1. Initialize LC = 0.

2. Get the first line of source code.

3. Break line into tokens.

4. While line is not .END directive:
    4.1 If line is assignment directive:
        Then
                Enter symbol & value into symbol table.
    4.2 If line has label:
        Then
                Enter label & LC into symbol table.
    4.3 Determine bytes required to assemble line.
    4.4 Increment LC= LC + bytes used.
    4.5 Get next line of source code.
    4.6 Break line into tokens.
    Repeat step **4.**

End pass 1.

(a)

Begin pass 2:

1. Initialize LC = 0.

2. Get first line of source code.

3. Break line into tokens.

4. While line is not .END directive:
    4.1 If line is instruction:
        Then
                Find opcode from opcode table.
                Find symbol values from symbol table.
                Form and write machine code instruction.
        Else (it must be a directive):
                Carry out directive.
    4.2 Write line and machine code to listing file.
    4.3 Determine bytes used.
    4.4 Increment LC = LC + bytes used.
    4.5 Get next line of source code.
    4.6 Break line into tokens.
    Repeat step **4.**

End pass 2.

(b)

FIGURE 10.7/Simplified algorithm for two-pass assembler: (a) pass 1; (b) pass 2

The basic structure of pass 2 is much the same as pass 1. Now, however, tokens are compared to a list of instruction mnemonics and, if found, the corresponding opcodes are taken from a built-in table. Many instructions, such as:

```
MOVL   A,B
```

also require that symbols be looked up in the symbol table. Once the opcode and symbols are known, the machine code can be formed and stored in an output file.

If a line is not an instruction it is examined to see if it is a directive. Some directives will require no action. For example, storage directives like .BLKB require no action other than the normal LC advancement. Directives like .LONG 4,5,6 will require that specific values be placed into the machine code file. The simplified algorithm shown here does not show actions required by more complex directives, such as .MACRO and .RPT.

The listing is also produced during the second pass. This is done by writing each assembled line, in both machine code and mnemonic forms, to the listing file. At the conclusion of pass 2, the entire symbol table is also written to this file.

When we compare the algorithm in Figure 10.7 with MACRO, we see that many important details have been omitted. We have already mentioned that it does not address macro expansion. Indeed, many simple assemblers do not allow macros. Other omissions include error-checking, evaluation of expressions, and the details of the several steps involved. These are proper subjects for study in the general area of language processors, which also include compilers and interpreters.

10.7 | Summary

This chapter dealt with a number of MACRO features that aid the programmer in developing clearly written and efficient assembly programs. We first saw that **expressions** involving symbols and constants can be used in the operand fields of instructions, and that **nonlabel symbols** can be given values with the **assignment** directive. These features often can be used to shorten the assembled program through elimination of unnecessary execution-time arithmetic and labels. Moreover, the use of symbols makes programs more readable and easier to maintain. The assembler **location counter,** symbolized by the period "." in the source code, can be used in expressions whenever the address of the current or next translated item is required. We also observed that all expression evaluations and assignments are carried out *at assembly time,* a factor that must be carefully observed when using these features.

The **.MACRO** directive introduced in this chapter allows the programmer, in effect, to define his or her own instructions. We saw that such instructions, called **macros,** can be referred to by name after they have been defined, and any such reference causes the entire defining code to be "expanded" into the program prior to assembly, substituting actual arguments for the dummy arguments used in the definition. Macros are like subroutines in that they provide a facility for making use of a block of source code more than once. They differ in that they result in *in-line* code in the object program, rather than jumps and returns.

Our study of macros included the problems due to internal labels. We saw that one way of dealing with this is by putting the internal label in the dummy argument list prefixed with a question mark, e.g., ?L1. This results in automatic generation of **local labels** of the form n$, where n is an integer. Such labels are "known" only within the **local symbol block** where defined. Local symbol blocks are program segments delimited by normal labels in the source code. Although generated automatically in macro expansion, local labels can also be introduced by the programmer, inside or outside of macros, using the n\$ naming convention. This is an effective means of avoiding multiply defined labels.

An important extension of macro utility is achieved through **nesting.** There are two concepts here, nesting of a macro *reference* within a macro definition, and nesting of a macro *definition* within a macro definition. The later results in the inner macro not being defined unless the outer macro is referenced.

A key feature of macros is that they are defined in terms of **dummy** arguments, for which **actual** arguments are substituted when they are expanded. The actual arguments are normally treated as strings that replace the dummy strings. However, by prefixing an actual argument with ''\'', its *value* is used instead. We also saw that actual arguments containing delimiters such as blanks or commas must be enclosed in angle brackets $<...>$.

An important rule is that the definition of a macro must precede its usage. An implication of this rule is that a macro that is defined within another macro cannot be referenced until the outer macro is referenced.

Closely related to macros are **repeat blocks.** We saw that any one of the directives **.REPT, .IRP,** and **.IRPC** will cause all code up to the .ENDR directive to be repeated a number of times, generating in-line code. The .REPT directive repeats a fixed block of code the number of times indicated by the argument expression. Both .IRP and .IRPC perform substitutions much like a macro, and generate a number of modified blocks of code equal to the number of arguments.

With **conditional assembly directives,** it is possible to include or omit blocks of assembly code during the translation process. The basic directives are **.IF** and **.ENDC,** which set off the conditional assembly block. The .IF directive has a *condition* and an *argument*. The argument, which is often a symbol or expression, is evaluated and checked according to the specified condition. If the condition is met, the block is assembled. Otherwise, it is omitted. Subconditional assembly directives **.IFT, .IFF,** and **.IFTF** can occur within the conditional block, and allow double-alternative decision structures for the conditional assembly. An important usage of conditional assembly is in making versatile macros. In this case, the conditional directives and blocks are internal to the macro definition, and the conditions are tested whenever the macros are expanded. We considered several examples of this, such as causing the macro expansion to vary depending upon the number or type of actual arguments in the macro reference.

The chapter concluded with a brief look at the **assembly process** itself. Here we saw that the assembler is a program that makes two ''passes'' through the source file. On pass 1, it determines values for all symbols found, placing both the symbols and the values in a **symbol table.** This table is then referenced as the mnemonic codes are translated to machine instructions during pass 2.

10.8 | Exercises

10.1 Using symbols, expressions, and the assignment directive, modify the program in Figure 8.12 so that it can be assembled for either hexadecimal output or decimal output, depending only on the value assigned to a *single symbol*, B. That is, if B = 16, it should be assembled for hexadecimal, and if B = 10, it should be assembled for decimal.

10.2 Modify the program in Figure 5.4 as suggested in Section 10.2.3. Assemble it and compare the listing to that shown in the figure. List all differences, and confirm how many bytes and instructions have been saved.

10.3 Translate the following instruction assuming that it will be placed in location 0500:

```
MOVL    #.+6,-(SP)
```

Explain what it does.

10.4 Write a macro that will interchange two double-precision, i.e., quadword, quantities. For each argument, assume that the high-order longword is stored in the location following the low-order longword. Demonstrate your macro in a program.

10.5 Write a macro that will add two double-precision, i.e., quadword, quantities. For each argument, assume that the high-order longword is stored in the location following the low-order longword. Demonstrate your macro in a program.

10.6 Show the expanded assembly code that results from the macro call:

```
ADDX    2,123
```

The definition of ADDX is as follows:

```
.MACRO    ADDNX, X,N
 ADDL     #N,A'X
.ENDM     ADDNX
.MACRO    ADDX,  N,STRING
C=N
.IRPC     K,<STRING>
ADDNX     K,\C
C=C+4
.ENDR
.ENDM     ADDX
```

10.7 Show the expanded assembly code that results from the macro call:

```
HEXROTL  A,-2
```

Also, describe what it does. The definition of HEXROTL is as follows:

```
.MACRO      HEXROTL,X,N
.IF     GT    N
.REPT         N
ROTL          #4,X,X
.ENDR
.IFF
.REPT         -N
ROTL          #-4,X,X
.ENDR
.ENDC
.ENDM    HEXROTL
```

10.8 Using the .IRPC directive, define a macro called SAVREG that pushes general-purpose registers R0 through R11 onto the stack.

10.9 Show how multiply defined labels can be avoided during macro expansion by using: (a) the location counter in operand expressions, and (b) the argument concatenation operator "'" in the macro definition.

10.10 Define a set of macros that simulates a Reverse Polish Notation (RPN) calculator. The following functions are required.

```
EN    X    ;   pushes contents of X onto stack
EX         ;   interchanges the upper two stack entries
PL         ;   adds the upper two stack entries and
               leaves sum on top of stack
SU         ;   subtracts top of stack from second from
               top, leaving result on top of the stack
MU         ;   multiplies upper two stack entries and
               leaves product on top of the stack
DI         ;   divides top of stack into second from
               top, leaving result on top of the stack
NE         ;   negates top of the stack
```

Demostrate these macros to evaluate the decimal expression $((2 + 4) \times 3 + 6 - 4/2)/6$.

10.11 Using conditional and subconditional assembly directives, write a macro ADDWB A1,A2,P that will generate code to add A1 to A2 regardless of whether they are byte ($P = 1$), word ($P = 2$), longword ($P = 4$), or quadword ($P = 8$) quantities.

10.12 In the following problems, assume that $Z = 2$ and $W = 4$, but no other symbols are defined. Write the resulting assembly code.

```
(a)  .IF    LE    W-3*Z        (b)  .IF    LT    W-<3*Z>
     ADDL         R1+Z,R2           MOVL         A,B
     .IFF                           .IFTF
     SUBL         R1+W,R2           MOVL         R1,R2
     .IFTF                          .IFTF
     MOVL         Z(R1),W(R2)       MOVL         C,D
     .ENDC                          .IFT
                                    ADDL         A,B
                                    .ENDC


(c)  .IF    DF    Z            (d)  .IF    NDF   Z
     .IF    NDF   W                 .IF    DF    W
     MULL         R4,R1             MULL         R4,R1
     .IFF                           .IFF
     ADDL         R4,R1             ADDL         R4,R1
     .ENDC                          .ENDC
     .ENDC                          .ENDC
```

PART II

Advanced Topics

11

Programming Considerations

11.1 | Overview

This chapter deals with a number of programming techniques and special topics that arise in the application of assembly language programming to actual problems in the commercial and industrial world. Included in the discussion are modular programming, programming style and standardization, linking and memory maps, position-independent code, and use of libraries.

The importance of these topics is difficult to see in the context of the small, textbook-type problems we have encountered thus far. However, for larger, more complex problems, their importance becomes overriding. In fact, it is widely accepted that the ability to deal with large problems through the effective use of the techniques discussed here is a far more important skill than merely translating algorithms into assembly language. Here we will describe these techniques and show their application to a problem that, while still rather small, is larger in scope than the examples of previous chapters.

11.2 | The Concept of Modular Programming

The problems addressed in examples up to this point in this book have been generally small in scope and uncomplicated, leading to a page or less of assembly language code. In practice, however, programming tasks are often more complex. Taken as a whole, real programs may require hundreds or even thousands of lines of assembly language code. A problem arises here, because the complexity of a single, large program can become so great that the programmer cannot effectively deal with it. This leads to logical errors, compounded by the natural difficulty in error tracing (debugging) in large programs. This problem was mentioned in Chapter 9 as justification for subroutines, which allow the program to be divided into a number of smaller modules. We will now demonstrate a systematic approach to programming along these lines, called **modular programming.** This topic is sometimes referred to as ''top-down'' programming, although the latter term implies a particular sequence in the design process as well as modularity.

289

In the following discussion we will attempt to distinguish between these different but closely related and equally important concepts.

The central idea behind modular programming is that even the most complicated programming tasks can be broken down into a series of smaller, more manageable tasks. Each task is then programmed as an independent program module, such as a subroutine, procedure, or macro. When this is done, several advantages are achieved. First, the smaller tasks are easier to program because they will have a more specific purpose, with more readily defined inputs and outputs and more straightforward logic. These same characteristics make the tasks of testing, debugging, and maintenance easier to perform. Finally, this breakdown allows a large programming task to be handled by a *team* of programmers, because each module can be efficiently assigned to a different individual for design, programming, and testing.

Modular design is usually done as a "top-down" process. That is, the overall problem is first defined in terms of a sequence of logical steps. Each step is described in terms of *function*, i.e., *what* is to be done, rather than *how* it is to be done. This definition can be in the form of a flowchart or "pseudocode." (We will see by example what is meant by pseudocode.) Regardless of how it is presented, this definition is referred to as the **level-one** procedure or algorithm, and is the basis for the main program module. Each step then in the level-one procedure is understood to be an independent module, to be implemented as a macro, subroutine, or VAX procedure.

Next, each of these modules is defined in more detail. This refinement shows *how* the task is to be done, and constitutes a **level-two** procedure. If the problem is a complicated one, the refinement of a level-two procedure may itself require modularization, requiring separate definition of level-three procedures. This process continues until the problem solution is completely defined in terms of a number of small, more easily understood modules. These modules have a hierarchical relationship which is often represented by a **System Program Chart** as shown in Figure 11.1. The purpose of the System Program Chart is to convey information about the program structure, i.e., how the modules are related. It does not indicate program logic, i.e., the sequence in which the modules at a given level are executed.

Once the program is designed using this technique, and complete specifications have been developed for each module, coding can begin. Normally each module will be coded and assembled separately, and the object-code versions brought together at the linkage step. This creates yet another advantage—namely, that changes that may be required in a single module will not necessitate reassembly of the entire program.

Modules can be defined as either **local** or **global.** A local (also called internal) module is available *only* to the higher-level module that it is subordinate to, while a global (also called external) module is available to *any* other module. Minor modules needed only within a single higher-level module and not subject to frequent change are often made local. In MACRO this is effected by making the module a subroutine internal to the module that needs it, and not defining its entry point as a global label. On the other hand, major modules that will require significant design, programming, and testing effort are defined to be global. Any module that is needed by more than one other module must also be made global. Global modules are subroutines with entry point labels defined to be global, using either the .GLOBAL directive or the double colon

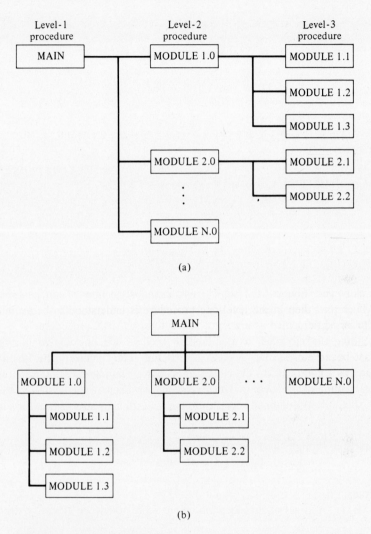

FIGURE 11.1/System program chart for modular program: (a) horizontal format; (b) vertical format

(::). As a matter of convenience each global subroutine is usually stored in a separate file. VAX-11 procedures (see Section 9.9) are always global by definition.

EXAMPLE 11.1   As an example of modular programming let us consider the need for a program to determine the statistics for a set of exam scores. This program is to accept an arbitrary number of scores, each between 0 and 100, and print out the number of scores entered, along with the high, low, and average scores. It is also to plot a histogram showing the number of scores in each decile.

The program to do these tasks would be lengthy and complex if done as a single

BEGIN:

1. Read scores from keyboard, storing values in array X and count of scores in N. (Subroutine READ)

2. Add all scores and leave sum in R0. (Subroutine SUMX)

3. Calculate average score, rounded to nearest integer, storing result in AVG. (Subroutine AVGX)

4. Find highest and lowest scores in X and store results in HIGH and LOW. (Subroutine HILO)

5. Count number of scores in each decile, storing counts in array F. (Subroutine FREQ)

6. Print N, HIGH, LOW, and AVG. (Subroutine PRNT)

7. Plot histogram of F. (Subroutine PLOT)

END;

FIGURE 11.2/Level-one procedure for test score program

module. However, Figure 11.2 shows with pseudocode how it can be broken down into seven distinct steps, each of which can be carried out with a relatively simple independent module.

In refining the modules, a specification such as the one shown in Figure 11.3 should first be developed. Its purpose is to define more precisely the function of the module and its "interface" to the calling procedure. The interface information includes input data requirements, output data expected, argument transmission methods, and how it is called. A well-defined specification gives sufficient information for a competent

Function: Prompts user for successive integer scores. Accept only those between 0 and 100. Count valid entries.

Inputs:
    R1: Address of first location where scores are to be stored (array X)

Outputs:
    R1: As input
    R2: Count of valid entries
    (R1),(R1 + 1) . . . (R1 + R2 − 1): Scores

External Calls:
    GETDEC: Gets decimal value from keyboard
    GETCHR: Gets character from keyboard

Calling sequence: MOVL #X, R1
                        BSBW READ

FIGURE 11.3/Specification for READ subroutine

programmer to develop an algorithm, program the module, and use it. The refined procedure for the READ subroutine is shown as pseudocode in Figure 11.4.

Observe that several of the tasks in Figure 11.4 are described in function only, to be defined in detail as separate modules. These include the score validation subroutine, CHKSCR, the decimal input subroutine GETDEC, and the character input subroutine GETCHR. If the detailed description of these were incorporated in the READ definition, clarity would be lost. Note also that the macro .PUTSTR is used to print user prompt messages. The subroutine includes register protection to prevent side effects.

In a complete program design, specifications and refinements for each module would be developed as exemplified above. We omit these here in the interest of brevity.

The System Program Chart for the test score program is shown in Figure 11.5. It shows each module in the entire program in relation to the others. Thus we see that the main program, SCORE, uses READ, SUMX, AVGX, HILO, FREQ, PRNT, and PLOT. Furthermore, it may be seen that READ uses GETCHR, which in turn uses the macro .TTYIN. This diagram, therefore, conveys a concise picture of the overall program structure. Note that the CHKSCR module is local to READ, because it is a single module needed only by READ. All others are defined to be global modules.

Once all modules have been designed and expressed in the form of pseudocode or flowcharts, supported by detailed specification of input, output, and linkage information, coding is straightforward. It is necessary only to convert the steps in the algorithm to

BEGIN READ:

1. Save registers R0, R1.
2. Clear count register R2.
3. Prompt "ENTER SCORE". (Macro .PUTSTR)
4. Accept decimal number from keyboard into R0. (Subroutine GETDEC)
5. Check score for 0–100 range. (Subroutine CHKSCR)
6. If not OK
       Then
       print "INVALID ENTRY, REENTER LAST VALUE"
       Goto **3**
7. Store score in location printed at by R1 and advance R1 to next longword (R1 points to location for entry).
8. Increment count register R2.
9. Prompt "MORE SCORES (Y or N)?"
10. Accept character from keyboard. (Subroutine GETCHR)
11. If "Y"
        Then goto **3**
12. Restore registers R0, R1.

END;

FIGURE 11.4/Typical level-two procedure (READ) for test score program

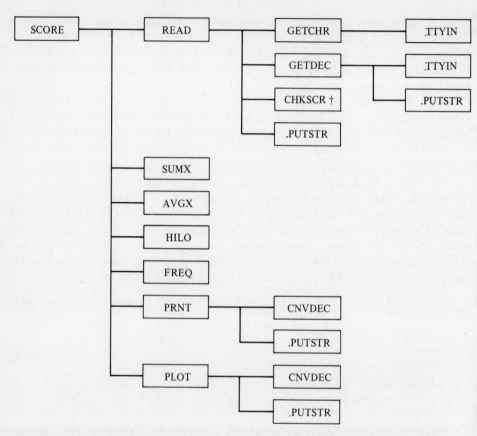

FIGURE 11.5/System program chart for test score program. †CHKSCR is local to READ.

the instructions and syntax provided by MACRO. This has been done for the preceding example, and the resulting code is presented in Appendix F. The reader is encouraged to study this code, comparing it to the design. This code also exhibits the style and standards recommended in the following section.

11.3 | Programming Style and Standardization

When one is first learning how to program, the challenge of "making it work" tends to be all-consuming, and little attention is paid to the clarity of the logic, or the general appearance of the code. While it may seem that function is more important than form, in practice it has been found that large programming projects proceed more efficiently if efforts are made to make the code easy to understand. This can be done through the use of certain programming conventions and abundant internal documentation, i.e., comments in the code. Clarity is also improved by following *uniform conventions or standards* as to the way the internal documentation is done, the placement of the instructions in a line, and other matters of appearance. Large organizations often have established "programming standards" that set forth these rules that all programmers are expected to follow. Here we shall examine some of the more important issues commonly found in such standards. These issues pertain to coding, symbols, and internal documentation.

Example 11.1, discussed in Section 11.2 and presented in Appendix F, has been coded according to these standards. Examination of that code will clarify the general statements of the standards presented next.

11.3.1 Coding Standards

MACRO is a very powerful language, allowing many programming techniques. However, clarity is enhanced if certain capabilities of the language are not used, or if absolutely necessary, used only with careful explanation in adjacent comments. The rules listed below should be followed whenever possible.

1. Line Format
   Begin labels in column 1, instruction mnemonics in column 9, operands in column 17, and comments in column 33. If operands extend beyond column 32, leave one space and begin comment.

2. Program Modularity
   Design program such that it is composed of a number of small, single-function modules (see Section 11.2).

3. Subroutine Linkage and Argument Transmission
   Use only standard argument transmission and linkage methods (see Section 9.8).

4. Subroutine Success/Failure Indication
   Use some uniform method to indicate abnormal return from subroutines. For example, the C condition code can be set, or the LSB of R0 can be set.

5. Side Effects
   Subroutines must not have any effects other than setting the designated output registers and locations. Save and restore all employed registers except result registers.

6. Structure
   Program or module control should flow down the listing except for loops. Use only standard control structures, and implement consistently (see Section 5.4).

7. Instructions vs. Data
   Do not modify instructions. Do not use instructions as data, nor data as instructions.

8. Choice of Instructions
   Use instructions for their intended purposes only, e.g., to add 8 to R1 code ADDL #8,R1 rather than CLRL (R1)+,(R1)+.

9. Location Counter Addressing
   Use location counter addressing (Section 10.2.4) only when necessary. Avoid use for branch destination.

10. Module Format
    Each program module should be organized as follows:

```
.TITLE          name
.EXTERNAL       A1,A2 ...(if required)
{prologue—see Section 11.3.3}
.PAGE
.PSECT DATA
{Allocations for local data}
{Assignment of local symbols}
{Definition of local macros}
.PAGE
.PSECT PROG
.ENTRY name, mask (if VAX procedure) or
name::          (if subroutine)
{code section, beginning with local SUBROUTINES}
.END            ; (name) or
.END            name (if main module)
```

The example in Appendix F shows this technique.

11.3.2 Symbols

Careful choice of symbols will improve clarity in a program. The following rules will help in this regard.

1. Choose meaningful mnemonic labels and symbols.

2. Use R0, . . . , R11,AP,FP,SP, and PC for the registers.

3. In a large module, use local labels, e.g., 4$,5$, etc., unless a mnemonic label would improve clarity or is needed for external reference.

4. Assign ASCII codes to standard mnemonic symbols, e.g.,

    ```
    CP=13
    BEL=7
    ```

5. Never define a symbol to be global without justification.

6. When relative addressing into tables, assign symbols to record size, field offsets in records, and table size, rather than using literals in instructions.

11.3.3 Documentation

As discussed above, all program modules must have abundant internal documentation. Some of the commonly followed documentation rules are given below, although these will vary from one organization to another.

1. Use of the Line Comment Field
    Through the use of the comment field, indicate the purpose of each instruction or group of instructions. For example,

    ```
    MOVL    R1,R0       ;INTERCHANGE
    MOVL    R2,R1       ;   REG 1   AND
    MOVL    R0,R2       ;       REG 2.
    ```

Note that successive lines of multiline comments are slant-indented to indicate that they go together. Comments must indicate the *significance* of the instruction, not just reiterate the instruction mnemonic. For example, write:

```
CLRL     R1          ;INITIALIZE SUM TO ZERO
```

rather than:

```
CLRL     R1          ;CLEAR R1
```

2. Comments in Code Body

   Comments too lengthy for the comment field should be placed "in-line" preceding the code that it describes. Such comment blocks are preceded and followed by a line containing a single semicolon in column 1. The comment itself should begin with column 3, with any desired indentation appearing in column 9. For example,

```
;
; THE FOLLOWING CODE MOVES A BLOCK
; OF DATA FROM ONE LOCATION TO
; ANOTHER.  DEFINITIONS ARE:
;      R1:  POINTS TO ORIGINAL LOCATION OF FIRST
;           ELEMENT TO BE MOVED
;      R2:  POINTS TO DESTINATION FOR FIRST ELEMENT
;      R3:  NUMBER OF BYTES TO BE MOVED.
;
```

3. Module Prologue

   Every program module must have a **prologue** section giving the following information:

   1. Version number and date of last revision.

   2. Narrative description of module function.

   3. Author.

   4. List of input arguments indicating their meaning and transmission conventions.

   5. List of output arguments indicating their meanings and transmission conventions.

   6. List of internal variables indicating their meanings.

   7. Indication of any side effects of executing the module. Normally, this should be none.

   8. List of external module calls, including brief narrative of what they do.

The prologue should begin with a line of the form:

```
;++ ***************************************************
```

and end with:

```
;-- ***************************************************
```

This allows special programs to automatically extract the prologues from a group of modules for use in external documentation of the program.

11.4 | Linkage and Memory Maps

It is sometimes necessary to know exactly where a particular instruction or data item is stored in virtual memory at execution time. We have already seen this need when we learned to use the Symbolic Debugger to examine memory contents during execution. There are other times as well when the programmer needs this information, such as when trying to determine the exact location of a program error, and when trying to make maximum use of limited memory. In order to develop these abilities, we have to examine the processes by which run-time addresses are determined. We shall begin by reviewing the address assignment process during assembly, and then examine the linkage process and the memory map.

11.4.1 Assembly-Time Addresses

Address assignment begins with the assembly process. Beginning in early chapters of this book, we saw that the assembler translates the MACRO mnemonics and assigns successive addresses to each machine code instruction or data item. This address assignment begins at 0000 for each separate module processed by the assembler. (Also see the following discussion on .PSECT.)

Thus the addresses assigned by the assembler are actually *relative* to the beginning of the module. These are the addresses shown in the column of the assembly listing to the left of the source line numbers, and are also reflected in the symbol table shown at the bottom of the listing. These are called **offset addresses** because they are the offsets from the address where the module is placed in the virtual memory address space.

If a module were assigned virtual memory addresses beginning at local 0000, the offset addresses assigned by the assembler would also be the run-time virtual addresses. To determine the location of a particular instruction or data item we would then need only examine the assembler listing. However, this is never the case for a number of reasons. First, VMS does not allow user programs to access locations 0 through 01FF, so the linker normally begins allocation with virtual address 0200_{16}. Thus the first run-time address in the executable image is 0200_{16}. Second, if there are two or more modules, they cannot all be assigned beginning at the same virtual address. Instead, each module must be allocated in successive blocks of virtual memory. Because of this, each module has a unique **loading point address** or **base address** at run-time. One of the functions of the linker is to assign these base addresses to each module as it builds an executable image of the program. Run-time virtual addresses are then the offset addresses determined by the assembler plus the base address of the module. The linker does this addition automatically in order to determine the absolute virtual addresses actually referred to in the instructions, such as those introduced through operands of the form #*label*.

Example 11.2 Let us clarify the preceding discussion with a simple example. Figure 11.6(a) shows the assembler listing for a main program that calls the subroutine defined in Figure 11.6(b). Observe that the three arrays A, B, and C are defined globally, as are the entry points START and SUB1. The last instruction of SUB1 is also given a global label ESUB1 for reasons soon to be seen. Also note that the address of A introduced by the immediate operand in line 6 of the main program is marked with an apostrophe. This means that this address must be *modified* during linkage because at run-time the absolute address of A must be used, and only the offset address relative to the module beginning is known at assembly time. The required modification is the addition of the module base address. Additionally, the address of SUB1 as used in line 9 is listed as

FEE6 (the negative of the *following* offset) and marked with an apostrophe. This means that SUB1 is global, and its address will be determined by the linker and the machine code modified accordingly. The assembler uses the negative of the offset following the branch operand specifier in order to allow later calculation by the linker of the run-time branch PC-relative destination. The need for similar modifications in the code for SUB1 can be seen by the apostrophes in Figure 11.6(b).

The assembler listing also contains a **symbol table,** as can be seen in Figure 11.6. All symbols used in the module are listed in the table, along with their values which are marked with R, X, RG, or GX. Symbols such as L1 in the main program that will be modified by addition of the base address upon linkage are marked R, meaning "relocatable." Those such as SUB1 that are listed in the .EXTERNAL directive but not defined within the module are indicated by "****** X". This means that they are externally defined, and the linker will have to provide the run-time address by using the offset address and base address of *some other module* where it is defined.

Symbols that are *defined globally within the module,* for instance by being to the left of ::, or to the left of : and appearing in the .EXTERNAL list, are marked RG. This means that the linker can determine the run-time address using the offset address

```
LINKAGE EXAMPLE 24-SEP-1985 08:49:29   VAX/VMS Macro V04-00 Page    1
                24-SEP-1985 21:24:06   _DRA1:[SOWELL]E11P2A.MAR;5 (1)
                              0000       1            .TITLE LINKAGE EXAMPLE
                              0000       2            .EXTERNAL SUB1
                    00000100  0000       3 A::        .BLKB   ^X100
                              0000  0100  4           .ENTRY  START,0
     51   00000100 8F    D0   0102       5            MOVL    #^X100,R1
     52   00000000'8F    D0   0109       6            MOVL    #A,R2
          82    FF 8F    90   0110       7 L1:        MOVB    #-1,(R2)+
          F9 51       F5      0114       8            SOBGTR  R1,L1
             FEE6'    30      0117       9            BSBW    SUB1
                              011A      10            $EXIT_S
                    00000223  0123      11 B::        .BLKB   ^X100
                              0223      12            .END    START
Symbol table
A                    00000000 RG      01
B                    00000123 RG      01
L1                   00000110 R       01
START                00000100 RG      01
SUB1                 ******** X       01
SYS$EXIT             ******** GX      01
                        +-----------------+
                        ! Psect synopsis !
                        +-----------------+
PSECT name   Allocation            PSECT No.   Attributes
. ABS .      00000000 (      0.)   00 ( 0.)    NOPIC    USR    CON    ABS
                                               LCL NOSHR NOEXE NORD
                                               NOWRT NOVEC BYTE
. BLANK .    00000223 (    547.)   01 ( 1.)    NOPIC    USR    CON    REL
                                               LCL NOSHR  EXE    RD
                                               WRT NOVEC BYTE
```

FIGURE 11.6/MACRO list file for linkage example: (a) main program

```
SUB1 EXAMPLE 25-SEP-1985 08:49:38   VAX/VMS Macro V04-00    Page 1
            24-SEP-1985 21:28:16  _DRA1:[SOWELL]E11P2B.MAR;2  (1)
                             0000    1             .TITLE  SUB1 EXAMPLE
                             0000    2             .EXTERNAL  A,B
                  00000100   0000    3 C::         .BLKB   ^X100
                             0100    4 SUB1::
    51   00000100 8F    D0   0100    5             MOVL    #^X100,R1
    52   00000000'8F    D0   0107    6             MOVL    #C,R2
    53   00000000'8F    D0   010E    7             MOVL    #A,R3
    54   00000000'8F    D0   0115    8             MOVL    #B,R4
             62   63    90   011C    9 L1:         MOVB    (R3),(R2)
             64   63    90   011F   10             MOVB    (R3),(R4)
                   52   D6   0122   11             INCL    R2
                   53   D6   0124   12             INCL    R3
                   54   D6   0126   13             INCL    R4
             F1   51    F5   0128   14             SOBGTR  R1,L1
                   05        012B   15 ESUB1::     RSB
                             012C   16             .END    ;(SUB1)
Symbol table
A                       ********  X   01
B                       ********  X   01
C                       00000000 RG   01
ESUB1                   0000012B RG   01
L1                      0000011C R    01
SUB1                    00000100 RG   01
                      +----------------+
                      ! Psect synopsis !
                      +----------------+
PSECT name  Allocation           PSECT No.   Attributes
. ABS .     00000000 (     0.)   00 (   0.)  NOPIC    USR    CON    ABS
                                             LCL NOSHR NOEXE NORD
                                             NOWRT NOVEC BYTE
. BLANK .   0000012C (   300.)   01 (   1.)  NOPIC    USR    CON    REL
                                             LCL NOSHR   EXE    RD
                                             WRT NOVEC BYTE
```

FIGURE 11.6/MACRO list file for linkage example: (b) subroutine SUB1

and base address of the current module, but the address so determined may be used in another module. Although not used in this example, symbols defined by direct assignment will also be listed in the symbol table with an equal sign between the symbol and the assigned value.

11.4.2 Linkage and the Load Maps

When the object modules for the program in Figure 11.6 are linked, the result is an executable program, sometimes called a **virtual memory image** or **image** module. The organization of the image module is shown in Figure 11.7. Part (a) of this figure shows an edited version of the file called "name.MAP" produced by the LINK program. Part (b) shows a pictorial representation. Either of these representations can be called the **load map** for the program.

The edited name.MAP file in Figure 11.7(a) is composed of three principal parts:

```
25-SEP-1985 08:50            VAX-11 Linker V04-00              Page    1
                    +------------------------+
                    ! Object Module Synopsis !
                    +------------------------+
Module Name Ident   Bytes       File                      Creation Date
LINKAGE      0         547 _DRA1:[SOWELL]E11P2A.OBJ;9 25-SEP-1985 08:49
SUB1         0         300 _DRA1:[SOWELL]E11P2B.OBJ;5 25-SEP-1985 08:49
                    +----------------------------+
                    ! Program Section Synopsis !
                    +----------------------------+
Psect   Module   Base      End        Length     Align  Attributes
.BLANK.          00000200 0000054E 0000034F (847.) BYTE 0 NOPIC,USR,
                                                          CON,REL,LCL,
                                                          NOSHR,EXE,
                                                          RD,WRT,NOVEC
        LINKAGE  00000200 00000422 00000223 (547.) BYTE 0
        SUB1     00000423 0000054E 0000012C (300.) BYTE 0
                    +------------------+
                    ! Symbols By Name !
                    +------------------+
Symbol           Value             Key for special characters:
                                   +------------------+
A                00000200-R        ! *  _ Undefined   !
B                00000323-R        ! U  _ Universal    !
C                00000423-R        ! R  _ Relocatable !
ESUB1            0000054E-R        ! X  _ External     !
START            00000300-R        +------------------+
SUB1             00000523-R
```

FIGURE 11.7/Memory map for linkage example: (a) map file from LINK

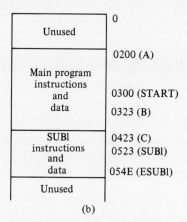

(b)

FIGURE 11.7/Memory map for linkage example: (b) diagram of virtual address space

the *Object Module Synopsis,* the *Program Section Synopsis,* and the *Symbols by Name Table.* The *Object Module Synopsis* gives information on the separately associated modules used in the LINK command. The module names are derived from the .TITLE directives. From this synopsis we also see the length of each module (decimal bytes), the names of the object files, and the date and times of creation. The *Program Section Synopsis* gives the base address and ending address for each module, as well as their lengths in hexadecimal and decimal.

The *Symbols by Name Table* gives the run-time virtual addresses of all global labels in all modules. It is instructive to compare these addresses with those in the assembler listing. We see that A is stored beginning at 00000200, and C at 00000423. Because these are the first addresses in the main program and SUB1, respectively, these addresses also indicate the load points or base addresses for the two modules. These base addresses can be confirmed in the *Program Section Synopsis* part of the report. The fact that A is stored at 00000200 indicates that the linker begins allocation of virtual addresses at this number, as stated earlier. The global label ESUB1 placed at the end of SUB1 is also listed in the load map. This label was assigned to allow us, for purposes of this example, to see the address of the last byte used by the program. This label is unnecessary and usually omitted.

In addition to the load points of each module, we are sometimes interested in other run-time virtual addresses available from the load map. For example, the **entry point** of each module is sometimes needed. Because these are always global labels, they are listed in the *Symbol by Name Table*. Thus we see that the main module entry point START is located at 00000300, and that for SUB1 is located at 00000523.

The actual map file created by the LINK/MAP command has an *Image Synopsis* section and a section giving times required for the various linkage stages. We omitted these from Figure 11.7(b) because they are not important to our discussion. Also, other options with the LINK command can be used to request additional information in the map file, such as symbol cross-references. The VAX-11 *Linker Reference Manual* can be consulted for more information on load map reports.

11.4.3 Finding Run-Time Addresses

Run-time addresses can be calculated as the sum of the offset addresses found in the assembler listing and the base addresses found in the MAP listing from the linker. For example, the run-time address of L1 in the SUB1 module is:

$$
\begin{array}{ll}
0000011C & \text{(Offset address of L1 from Figure 11.6(b))} \\
+\ 00000423 & \text{(Base address of SUB1 from Figure 11.7)} \\
\hline
0000053F & \text{(Virtual address of L1)}
\end{array}
$$

Care must be taken to be sure that the correct base address is used. A common error is to assume that the entry point is the same as the base. This is only true if there is no code or data before the module entry point.

11.4.4 Program Sections

The load map in Figure 11.7(b) shows that all of one module, including instructions and data, is stored in virtual memory first, followed by all of the next module. This creates a load module that has instructions and data intermixed, i.e.,

> data   —module 1
> instructions—module 1
> data   —module 2
> instructions—module 2

While there is nothing really wrong with this, there are situations in which it would be more desirable to have all instructions grouped together, and all data grouped together and thus separate from the instructions, i.e.,

> data   —module 1
> data   —module 2
> instructions—module 1
> instructions—module 2

One advantage of the latter organization is that it is easier to distinguish between instructions and data when we need to examine memory contents. Other advantages have to do with efficiency of memory allocation by the operating system.

MACRO allows the programmer to specify the above organization through a concept called **program sections,** implemented with the **.PSECT directive.** With this concept, the above program would be thought of as two "sections," one for data and one for program instructions. The assembler is capable of reorganizing the program in this manner, calculating offset addresses relative to the beginning of each section rather than relative to the module beginning.

When the assembler encounters the directive:

```
.PSECT   name1
```

in the source code, it begins placing all subsequent translated instructions or data into a "program section" identified by "name1". When the next directive:

```
.PSECT   name2
```

is encountered, it stops placing code in the "name1" section and starts placing it in the section called "name2". The programmer can choose any name, and there can be any number of .PSECT directives. This therefore allows the source assembly language instructions and data allocation directives to occur in a sequence convenient and logical from a programming point of view, while at the same time providing enough information so that the linker can create an efficient load module organization.

EXAMPLE 11.3 To show the usage of .PSECT to force separate data and program sections, let us modify the example in Figure 11.6. As shown in Figure 11.8, we simply place the directive:

```
.PSECT DATA
```

before all data-generating directives, and place the directive:

```
,PSECT PROG
```

before all groups of instructions. Note that in Figure 11.8(a) there are two .PSECT DATA directives because there are data both before and after the instructions.

The effects of these .PSECT directives can be seen first in the assembly listing, Figure 11.8, which should be compared with Figure 11.6. Note that in Figure 11.8(a) A is assigned the offset address 00000000, and B immediately follows the end of the 100_{16}-byte A array, in spite of the intervening instructions. Also observe that START is assigned the relocatable address 00000000, and the instructions are assigned the successive addresses up to 001A. In order to accomplish this separate address assignment into the two sections, the assembler uses a separate location counter (see Section 10.6) for each section. The location counter for a particular section begins at zero at the first

```
         LINKAGE EXAMPLE  24-SEP-1985  22:03:06   VAX/VMS Macro V04-00 Page
                          24-SEP-1985  22:01:01   _DRA1:[SOWELL]E11P3A.MAR;4 (
                                   0000    1           ,TITLE  LINKAGE EXAMPLE
                                   0000    2 ;             WITH ,PSECT USAGE
                                   0000    3           ,EXTERNAL SUB1
                           00000000    4           ,PSECT   DATA
                   00000100  0000    5 A::       ,BLKB    ^X100
                           00000000    6           ,PSECT   PROG
                                   0000    7           ,ENTRY   START,0
      51     00000100 8F    D0   0002    8           MOVL     #^X100,R1
      52     00000000'8F    D0   0009    9           MOVL     #A,R2
            82   FF 8F       90   0010   10 L1:      MOVB     #-1,(R2)+
                 F9 51       F5   0014   11           SOBGTR   R1,L1
                 FFE6'       30   0017   12           BSBW     SUB1
                                 001A   13           $EXIT_S
                           00000100   14           ,PSECT   DATA
                    00000200  0100   15 B::       ,BLKB    ^X100
                                 0200   16           ,END     START
Symbol table
     A                  00000000 RG    01
     B                  00000100 RG    01
     L1                 00000010 R     02
     START              00000000 RG    02
     SUB1               ******** X     00
     SYS$EXIT           ******** GX    02
                        +-----------------+
                        ! Psect synopsis !
                        +-----------------+
     PSECT name  Allocation          PSECT No.   Attributes
     ,  ABS  ,   00000000  (   0,)   00 (   0,)  NOPIC   USR   CON    ABS
                                                 LCL NOSHR NOEXE NORD
                                                 NOWRT NOVEC BYTE
     DATA        00000200  ( 512,)   01 (   1,)  NOPIC   USR   CON    REL
                                                 LCL NOSHR   EXE    RD
                                                 WRT NOVEC BYTE
     PROG        00000023  (  35,)   02 (   2,)  NOPIC   USR   CON    REL
                                                 LCL NOSHR   EXE    RD
                                                 WRT NOVEC BYTE
```

FIGURE 11.8/MACRO list file for .PSECT example: (a) main program

```
SUB1 EXAMPLE 24-SEP-1985 22:03:39   VAX/VMS Macro V04-00 Page    1
             24-SEP-1985 22:02:34  _DRA1:[SOWELL]E11P3B.MAR;3 (1)
                            0000    1              .TITLE  SUB1 EXAMPLE
                            0000    2 ;             WITH .PSECT USAGE
                            0000    3              .EXTERNAL  A,B
                        00000000    4              .PSECT  DATA
               00000100  0000    5 C::            .BLKB   ^X100
                        00000000    6              .PSECT  PROG
                            0000    7 SUB1::
51    00000100 8F   D0  0000    8              MOVL    #^X100,R1
52    00000000'8F   D0  0007    9              MOVL    #C,R2
53    00000000'8F   D0  000E   10              MOVL    #A,R3
54    00000000'8F   D0  0015   11              MOVL    #B,R4
          62    63   90  001C   12 L1:          MOVB    (R3),(R2)
          64    63   90  001F   13              MOVB    (R3),(R4)
                52   D6  0022   14              INCL    R2
                53   D6  0024   15              INCL    R3
                54   D6  0026   16              INCL    R4
       F1 51   F5  0028   17              SOBGTR  R1,L1
                05  002B   18 ESUB1:: RSB
                    002C   19              .END    ;(SUB1)
Symbol table
A                   ********   X    00
B                   ********   X    00
C                   00000000 RG   01
ESUB1               0000002B RG   02
L1                  0000001C R    02
SUB1                00000000 RG   02
                    +-----------------+
                    ! Psect synopsis !
                    +-----------------+
PSECT name  Allocation            PSECT No.   Attributes
. ABS .     00000000  (      0.)  00 (   0.)  NOPIC   USR   CON    ABS
                                              LCL NOSHR NOEXE NORD
                                              NOWRT NOVEC BYTE
DATA        00000100  (    256.)  01 (   1.)  NOPIC   USR   CON    REL
                                              LCL NOSHR   EXE    RD
                                              WRT NOVEC BYTE
PROG        0000002C  (     44.)  02 (   2.)  NOPIC   USR   CON    REL
                                              LCL NOSHR   EXE    RD
                                              WRT NOVEC BYTE
```

FIGURE 11.8/MACRO list file for .PSECT example: (b) subroutine SUB1

occurrence of the .PSECT directive with its name, and is incremented in the normal manner until a section of a different name is indicated by another .PSECT directive.

The assembler writes the name of each program section and the code placed in that section into the object module. The linker then puts together an image module in which sections of like name are grouped together, even though they may have come from different modules. This creates a load map such as the one shown in Figure 11.9, which should be compared with Figure 11.7. Note that in the load map in Figure 11.9 two sections are shown: DATA and PROG. Each has parts from *both* modules.

```
24-SEP-1985 22:10 VAX-11 Linker V04-00              Page   1
                  +-------------------------+
                  ! Object Module Synopsis !
                  +-------------------------+
       Module Name Ident Bytes      File                    Creation Date
       LINKAGE     0       547  _DRA1:[SOWELL]E11P3A.OBJ;2 24-SEP-1985 22:03
       SUB1        0       300  _DRA1:[SOWELL]E11P3B.OBJ;2 24-SEP-1985 22:03
                  +-------------------------+
                  ! Program Section Synopsis !
                  +-------------------------+
Psect Name Module Name    Base      End       Length       Align  Attributes
DATA                    00000200 000004FF 00000300 (768.) BYTE 0 NOPIC,USR,
                                                                  CON,REL,LCL
                                                                  NOSHR,EXE,
                                                                  RD,WRT,NOVE(
           LINKAGE      00000200 000003FF 00000200 (512.) BYTE 0
           SUB1         00000400 000004FF 00000100 (256.) BYTE 0
PROG                    00000500 0000054E 0000004F ( 79.) BYTE 0 NOPIC,USR,
                                                                  CON,REL,LCL
                                                                  NOSHR,EXE,
                                                                  RD,WRT,NOVE(
           LINKAGE      00000500 00000522 00000023 ( 35.) BYTE 0
           SUB1         00000523 0000054E 0000002C ( 44.) BYTE 0
                  +------------------+
                  ! Symbols By Name !
                  +------------------+
       Symbol        Value          Key for special characters :
       A          00000200-R        +------------------+
       B          00000300-R        ! *  _ Undefined   !
       C          00000400-R        ! U  _ Universal   !
       ESUB1      0000054E-R        ! R  _ Relocatable !
       START      00000500-R        ! X  _ External    !
       SUB1       00000523-R        +------------------+
```

FIGURE 11.9/Memory map for .PSECT example: (a) map file from LINK

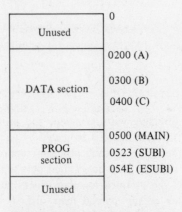

FIGURE 11.9/Memory map for .PSECT example: (b) diagram of virtual address space

11.5 | **Position-Independent Code**

In certain situations it is desirable that the machine language version of a program or subroutine be able to execute properly regardless of where it is placed in memory. An example is a library routine furnished by the operating system and needed by many different users in a multiuser environment such as VMS. In such a case, the operating system must be able to load the machine code into any available portion of the virtual memory space without having to modify it in any way. That is, it must be **Position-Independent Code,** or PIC.

Early in our study of machine and assembly language programming we learned that programs can reside anywhere in the virtual memory space. Thus it might be thought that *all* machine code is position-independent. Unfortunately, though, this is not necessarily the case, as we will see in the following examples.

EXAMPLE 11.4   Suppose there is a procedure located at virtual address 80001000_{16} (i.e., in the operating system portion of the virtual address space). Assuming that there are no arguments, transfer to this procedure could be by means of the procedure call instruction CALLS, e.g.,

```
.ENTRY   START, 0
CALLS    #0,^X80001000
```

Here we have used relative addressing for the destination operand, although 80001000_{16} is the absolute virtual address of the procedure. If this was assembled and linked using the normal 00000200_{16} virtual base address assigned by LINK, we would have the run-time instructions and virtual addresses shown here:

Machine Code	Virtual Address
0000	00000200
80000DF7 EF 00 FB	00000202
	00000209

Note here that the $80000DF7_{16}$ is the PC-relative address of the procedure. Hence at run-time:

$$00000209 + 80000DF7 = 80001000$$

is found for the destination address for the CALLS instruction. Now suppose that we were to ignore the fact that this code was linked using 00000200 as the base address, and arbitrarily enter the *same* machine code at virtual address 00000400. (This could be done, for example, by using the Symbolic Debugger.) We would then have:

Machine Code	Virtual Address
0000	00000400
80000DF7 EF 00 FB	00000402
	00000409

When the procedure destination address is computed at run-time now we get:

$$00000409 + 80000DF7 = 80001202$$

which is *not* the address of the called procedure. Therefore, the program will *not* execute correctly when loaded at this address.

The principle demonstrated in Example 11.4 is that when *relative addressing* is used to refer to *absolute virtual addresses* outside of the set of instructions in question, the resulting machine code is *not* position-independent. The code will work fine as long as the machine code has virtual addresses at run-time beginning at the location where the linker *assumed* it would be executed, but if relocated without modification elsewhere in virtual memory, it will fail. The cure for this difficulty is to use **absolute addressing** to refer to any absolute addresses outside of the routine to be relocated. Absolute addressing has the mnemonics @#addr, where addr can be either a symbol or a literal.

EXAMPLE 11.5 Modify the previous example to make the code position-independent. Use of absolute addressing accomplishes this.

```
.ENTRY   START,0
CALLS    #0,@#^X80001000
```

Regardless of its location in the virtual address space, this translates to:

Machine Code

```
             0000
8001000 9F 00 FB
```

Because the address of the instruction is not involved in the translation, this code can be located anywhere in the virtual address space without modification.

Another problem of position dependence arises when a translated instruction incorporates an *absolute virtual* address (rather than PC-relative, for example) of a location that lies *within* the body of code to be relocated. The following is perhaps the most common example of this.

EXAMPLE 11.6 Determine if the following program segment is position-independent:

```
A:             .WORD   0,2
               .ENTRY  START, 0
               MOVL    #A,R1
               MOVL    (R1),R2
                  .
                  .
                  .
```

Again assuming the standard 00000200_{16} offset provided by LINK, this translates to the run-time machine code:

Machine Code		Virtual Address	
0002	0000	00000200	A
	0000	00000204	START
51 00000200	8F D0	00000206	
52	61 D0	0000020D	

Here the underlined number is seen to be the absolute virtual address of A. However, if the machine code is relocated without modification to, say, 00000400, we would have:

Machine Code		Virtual Address	
0002	0000	00000400	A
	0000	00000404	START
51 00000200	8F D0	00000406	
52	61 D0	0000040D	

Now the address of A is 00000400, although the *code* still assumes it to be in 00000200. Once again, relocation has resulted in incorrect results. Therefore, the code is position-*dependent*.

The cure for the difficulty in Example 11.6 is to *avoid use* of absolute addresses of locations *within* the relocatable code.

EXAMPLE 11.7 Modify the code in Example 11.6 to be position-independent. The operation can be done with position-independent code by use of the move address instruction:

```
A:          .WORD    0,2
            .ENTRY   START,0
            MOVAL    A,R1
            MOV      (R1),R2
```

Regardless of where it is located in the virtual address space, these instructions translate to:

Machine Code		
0002	0000	A
	0000	START
51	F7 AF DE	
52	61 D0	

Observe that the PC-relative address of A (F7) is independent of where the code is located, making it position-*independent*. The MOVAL instruction determines the absolute virtual address of A at run-time.

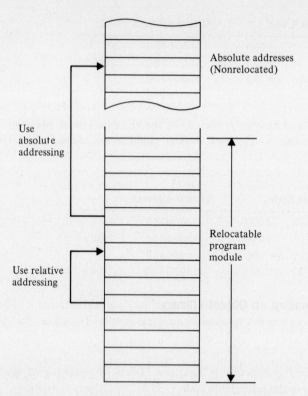

FIGURE 11.10/Requirements for position-independent code

Summarizing, we can say that position-independency has been achieved for the block of code to be relocated if:

1. It contains no *relative* addresses of locations *outside* of itself.
2. It contains no *absolute* addresses of locations *within* itself.

These rules are depicted in Figure 11.10.

11.6 | Libraries

When a new program is being developed it often happens that several of the needed modules already exist. These could be from earlier stages of a large program development effort, from an unrelated earlier project, or from the large body of programs that have been developed over many years. In any event, it is most convenient to have *access* to the needed modules without having to include them directly in the new program. That is, we would like to simply refer to the existing modules and have them immediately available to our program. We have already seen that this can be achieved through the linking process by listing each individual object module along with the new program object module. For example,

```
$ LINK   MAIN,SUBA,SUBB,SUBC
$ ▓
```

This becomes awkward, however, when the number of object modules is large. Also, the time required to link a large program can be considerable. It would be more convenient to gather all the existing modules into a single file that could be referenced whenever any of the contained object modules was required. This is indeed possible, and the composite file is called an **object library.** A related concept is a **macro library,** in which there is a collection of macro definitions in MACRO assembly language. Libraries of either kind can be "private," i.e., created by the user, or "public," i.e., provided to all users by the system. In Sections 11.6.1, 11.6.2, and 11.6.3 we shall see how libararies are created, and how they are used. Note that while the command syntax is dependent on the operating system, the concepts are generally applicable to almost any operating system. We shall show our examples assuming the VAX/VMS environment.

11.6.1 Creating an Object Library

Suppose you had developed a set of subroutines in MACRO and wanted to make them available for use in other programs. To accomplish this, you must first assemble the subroutines (with global entry point labels) as separate modules, and then merge them into a library file. The merging operation requires a special system program that not only concatenates the separate files, but also creates a "directory" so that the individual modules can be found later by the linker. In VMS this program is executed by means of the LIBRARY command, as shown in the following example.

EXAMPLE 11.8 Let us create an object library containing the subroutines in Figure 11.11. These are stored in the three separate files—SUBA.MAR, SUBB.MAR, and SUBC.MAR. First, assemble each file to create the object files.

```
$ MACRO SUBA+MACLIB/LIB
$ MACRO SUBB+MACLIB/LIB
$ MACRO SUBC+MACLIB/LIB
$ ▓
```

The object files now exist as SUBA.OBJ, SUBB.OBJ, and SUBC.OBJ. To create the library called MYLIB.OLB enter the following command:

```
$LIBRARY/CREATE/LIST=MYLIB.LIS/FULL/NAMES MYLIB.OLB SUBA,SUBB,SUBC
$ ▓
```

This creates the two files MYLIB.OLB and MYLIB.LIS. The .OLB file is to be used in a LINK operation, and the .LIS file can be printed to see the contents of the library. The listing file for the above example is shown in Figure 11.12. Note that the module name comes from the .TITLE directive in the module, while the names listed below

```
           .TITLE SUBAMOD
SUBA::     .PUTSTR MSG1
           RSB
ENTRY2::.PUTSTR MSG2
           RSB
MSG1:      .ASCIZ/SUBROUTINE SUBA/
MSG2:      .ASCIZ/SUBROUTINE SUBA,  ENTRY2/
           .END    ;(SUBA)
                    (a)


           .TITLE SUBBMOD
SUBB::     .PUTSTR MSG
           RSB
MSG:       .ASCIZ/SUBROUTINE SUBB/
           .END    ;(SUBB)
                    (b)


           .TITLE SUBCMOD
SUBC::     .PUTSTR MSG
           RSB
MSG:       .ASCIZ/SUBROUTINE SUBC/
           .END    ;(SUBC)
                    (c)
```

FIGURE 11.11/Subroutines for library example: (a)
SUBA.MAR; (b) SUBB.MAR; (c) SUBC.MAR

```
Directory of OBJ library _DRA1:[SOWELL]MYLIB.OLB;1 on 29-SEP-1985 08:13
Creation date:  29-SEP-1985 08:07:06   Creator:  VAX-11 Librarian V04-0
Revision date:  29-SEP-1985 08:07:06   Library format:   3.0
Number of modules:     3       •       Max. key length:  31
Other entries:         4               Preallocated index blocks:       4
Recoverable deleted blocks:      0     Total index blocks used:
Max. Number history records:     20    Library history records:
Module SUBAMOD     Ident 0             Inserted 29-SEP-1985 08:07:06 2 symb
ENTRY2                                 SUBA
Module SUBBMOD     Ident 0             Inserted 29-SEP-1985 08:07:06 1 symb
SUBB
Module SUBCMOD     Ident 0             Inserted 29-SEP-1985 08:07:06 1 symb
SUBC
```

FIGURE 11.12/MYLIB.LIS showing directory of object library

the modules are all labels in the module that were defined in a .GLOBAL directive or by the :: operator.

The LIST=, FULL, and NAMES command qualifiers on the LIBRARY command are optional. If omitted, the .LIS file will not be created. Also the .LIS file can be created at any time by executing the LIBRARY command without the CREATE qualifier and without the list of input object files.

The LIBRARY command has several variations that are necessary or convenient when maintaining an object library. Some of these are shown below.

To delete a module, e.g., SUBAMOD:

```
$ LIBRARY/DELETE=SUBAMOD  MYLIB.OLB
$ ▨
```

To add a module, e.g., put back SUBAMOD:

```
$ LIBRARY/INSERT  MYLIB.OLB SUBA.OBJ
$ ▓
```

To replace a module with the newest version of the .OBJ file:

```
$ LIBRARY/REPLACE  MYLIB.OLB SUBA.OBJ
$ ▓
```

11.6.2 Using an Object Library

Object libraries are used at the linkage step. The library name/LIB is simply *concatenated* with a "+" on the right-hand side of the .OBJ modules in the LINK command. For example, suppose we wish to use one or more of the three subroutines in MYLIB.OLB in a main program, as shown in Figure 11.13. Because of .PUTSTR we also need the SUBLIB.OLB module.

After assembling this program, we execute the command:

```
$ LINK  MAIN+SUBLIB/LIB+MYLIB/LIB
$ ▓
```

The LINK program will recognize SUBLIB and MYLIB as user libraries and will search them for external labels referred to in MAIN or in already-loaded library modules. When it finds a label, it extracts the module to which it belongs and links it into the image module. Modules in the library but not containing any global labels referred to in MAIN or other modules are not included in the image file created by LINK. The program can now be run in the normal manner:

```
$ RUN  MAIN
```

From the above example note that it is possible to use more than one library. LINK will search all libraries listed in the LINK command in a left-to-right order until all external labels are identified. These may all be libraries which you have created, or they can be those supplied by the system.

11.6.3 Macro Library

The LIBRARY command can also be used to create a library of macro definitions. A macro library is quite different from an object library in that it is represented in MACRO source code as opposed to object code. This is because macros are introduced at the *assembly* step rather than at the linkage step.

```
.TITLE MAIN
.EXTERNAL SUBA,SUBC,SUBC,ENTRY2
.ENTRY   START,0
BSBW     SUBA
BSBW     SUBC
BSBW     ENTRY2
$EXIT_S
.END     START
```

FIGURE 11.13/Main program using library
subroutines

EXAMPLE 11.9   As an example of defining a macro library, suppose that a file named
MYMACROS.MAR has been created containing definitions of the macros PUSH and
SAVREG (see Section 10.3.4). To create the library enter:

```
$ LIBRARY/CREATE/MACRO MYMACROS.MLB MYMACROS.MAR
$ ▨
```

This creates the file MYMACROS.MLB that will contain the macro definitions and a
directory of the contained macro names.

Then when the program that uses PUSH and/or SAVREG is to be assembled we
issue the command:

```
$ MACRO MAIN+MYMACROS/LIB
$ ▨
```

When PUSH or SAVREG is encountered during assembly, the file MYMACROS.MLB
will be searched for the macros listed. However, only those referenced in the program
will be taken from the library and included in the program.

11.7 | Summary

In the preceding sections we have dealt with several ideas that are important in the
development of large assembly language programs. One of these topics was **modular programming.**
It can be argued that a ''complicated program'' is simply one that has not been broken down
into small enough steps, and this is the idea behind modular programming. The ''top-down''
approach to modular programming suggests that the original problem be broken down into a
number of major functional steps, each of which becomes a program module. However, if any
module so defined is itself overly complicated, we describe it in terms of functional steps, and
so on until the entire problem is described in terms of simple, single-purpose modules. The
formal design procedure, applicable to large programming efforts, then suggests that each module
be described by a specification and a procedure or algorithm, expressed as a flowchart or in
pseudocode. The latter terms refer to step-by-step description using precise but informal language
that can be unambiguously interpreted by another programmer.

The modular programming idea is augmented by **standards** of style and program logic.
These standards include cosmetic things, such as formatting the line of assembly code in a uniform
way and the formatting of internal documentation. However, they also include restrictions on
usage of nonstandard control structures and on certain features of MACRO.

Both modularity and standardization address the problem of making programming easier for
people to read and follow. This is important because most often large programming projects are
handled as team efforts, and it is necessary for one programmer to be able to understand another's
work. Also, these practices make program maintenance a more manageable task.

Modular programming can be further enhanced by making each major module a separate
file so that all can be assembled and stored as separate object-code modules. This has several
advantages, including minimizing the amount of machine time for reassembly when localized
changes have to be made. When this is done, the linkage program (LINK) is used to build an
executable ''image'' which is a combined machine-code module ready for loading and executing.
In this building process, the linker assigns a **virtual base address** to each module. Whenever
necessary, the linker adds this base address to the address assigned by the assembler to arrive at
the correct run-time code for the module. Also, any global labels are given absolute virtual

addresses by the linker. Thus the linkage step is one of conversion of the code produced by the assembler to code with proper virtual addresses ready for execution. An important output of the linker is the **load map** of the program. This is a list of global symbols (labels) and their absolute virtual addresses as assigned by the linker. The programmer can use this information along with the assembler listings for each module to arrive at the run-time addresses of all data and instructions, should this be necessary.

Finally, it was shown that the **.PSECT directive** can be used to control where each portion of a module is to be located in the virtual address space. Often this feature is used to cause the image to have all data from many modules located in one section of memory, and all instructions in another. There are certain advantages to this organization.

In Section 11.6.1 we saw that a VMS command called LIBRARY can be used to create **object** or **macro libraries.** This makes code that has been thoroughly debugged available in other programs with minimal effort.

11.8 | Exercises

11.1 Based on the problem description and the level-one procedure shown in Figure 11.2, develop specifications and level-two procedures for steps 2 through 5 in Example 11.1. Use Figures 11.3 and 11.4 as guides.

11.2 Develop MACRO implementations of the procedures defined in Exercise 11.1. Follow the standards set forth in Section 11.3. Compare your work with Appendix F.

11.3 A program is required to analyze a paragraph of text entered at a keyboard. It must count the number of words, the average word length, and the average number of words per sentence and print out these values. Words are separated by spaces, commas, or periods. Develop the level-one procedure as pseudocode or flowchart.

Then write specifications and level-two procedures for each module. If necessary, modularize the level-two procedures so that each program module has a single, simple purpose. Your work must have sufficient clarity so that it can be programmed by a classmate without further communication. (Your instructor should assign Exercise 11.4 or 11.5 with this exercise.)

11.4 Using the standards set forth in Section 11.3, implement the modular program defined in Exercise 11.3. Test it using the text of Exercise 11.3 as the entered paragraph.

11.5 Using the standards set forth in Section 11.3, implement the program *defined by a classmate* for Exercise 11.3. Test it with the text of Exercise 11.3 as the entered paragraph.

11.6 Enter and assemble the program and subroutine shown in Figure 11.6. Link it with the SUB1 object module *before* the main program, i.e.,

```
$ LINK/MAP  SUB1,MAIN
```

Examine the listing and map files and determine the absolute run-time addresses of L1 in both modules. Explain the differences.

11.7 Revise the program in Figure 11.8 such that there are three sections defined as follows:

DATA: contains all data
MAIN: contains only instructions for main program
SUB1:   contains only instructions for SUB1

Assemble and link and examine the load map and listing. State why this might be more convenient than having a single instruction section.

11.8 Examine each of the following code segments and state whether or not it is position-independent. If necessary, revise to make it position-independent.

(a)
```
        ADDL  R1,R2
        MOVL  R2,R3
```

(b)
```
A:      .WORD 4
S:      MOVL  #2,R1
        ADDL  A,R1
```

(c)
```
        MOVL  #STATUS, R1
L:      TSTB  (R1)
        BGEQ  L
        MOVL  #DATA,R1
        MOVB  R0,(R1)
```

(d)
```
A:      .WORD 4
        MOVL  #A,R1
        ADDL  (R1),R3
```

(e)
```
        CLRL  ^X200
```

12

Addressing and Data Structures

12.1 | Overview

Earlier chapters introduced a number of elementary assembly programming topics and the corresponding MACRO instructions, addressing modes, and directives. This has given us the ability to develop modestly complex assembly programs, especially with the use of subroutines and macros. However, with the intent of maintaining a sharply focused discussion as we went along, we omitted a number of assembly programming techniques and features of MACRO. In particular, we introduced the various VAX-11 addressing modes on an ''as-needed'' basis, thus postponing the development of a unified view of this topic. Also, we did not develop an adequate understanding of how these addressing techniques can be used to implement various data structures in MACRO. In this chapter we intend to fill in these gaps. While this material is optional for an introductory course, the topics considered here are of substantial importance in many advanced assembly applications.

We begin this chapter by going back to the subject of **addressing modes.** We examine all of the addressing modes offered on the VAX-11 as a unified whole, supplementing earlier explanations where they were first introduced. Our purpose will be to develop an understanding of the interrelationships among these modes, which is not possible when they are considered separately.

Data structure refers to the way that the data to be processed are stored in memory. There are several more or less standard organization schemes available, such as **arrays, tables, stacks, queues,** and **linked lists.** These are briefly explained, and their implementation in MACRO is discussed.

12.2 | The VAX-11 Addressing Modes

Address specification for instruction operands can take many different forms on the VAX-11. Although we have already seen most of these forms in the context of various examples introduced in earlier chapters, we shall now see how they fit into the overall VAX-11 addressing methodology.

The VAX-11 addressing modes can be classified in many different ways. For purposes of our discussion here, we shall group them into the following categories: General Register Modes, Short Literal Mode, Indexed Modes, and Program Counter Addressing.

12.2.1 General Register Addressing Modes

The VAX-11 addressing modes that employ the general registers in determining the operand are listed in Table 12.1. This table shows the machine language hexadecimal mode specifier, as well as its name, the assembly mnemonics, and a brief explanation of how the operand is determined at run time. Most of these modes have been presented earlier, and the table indicates the section where discussion and examples can be found.

There are some unifying elements present in General Register Addressing that are important to observe. First, note that it is the hexadecimal mode specifier that allows the processor to distinguish one mode from another. Secondly, all modes employ one

TABLE 12.1/VAX-11 General Register Addressing Modes

Mode Specifier	Name	Assembly Mnemonics	Explanation
5	Register	Rn	Rn contains operand. (Section 4.3)
6	Register-Deferred	(Rn)	Rn contains address of operand. (Section 5.7)
7	Autodecrement	− (Rn)	Decrement contents of Rn by 1 if the operation is a byte operation, or by 4 if it is a longword operation, etc. After that, Rn contains address of operand. (Section 5.7)
8	Autoincrement	(Rn) +	Rn contains address of operand. After the operand is fetched or stored, Rn is incremented (by 1 if the operation is a byte operation, or by 4 if it is a longword operation, etc.). (Section 5.7)
9	Autoincrement-Deferred	@ (Rn) +	Rn contains address of address of operand. After the operand is fetched or stored, Rn is incremented by 4. (Section 9.8.3)
A,C,E	Displacement	D(Rn)	Address of operand is sign-extended D + contents of Rn. The value of D is stored in the cell following the first byte of the operand specifier. (Section 9.8.4)
B,D,F	Displacement-Deferred	@D(Rn)	Address of address of operand is sign-extended D + contents of Rn. The value of D is stored in the cell following the operand specifier. (Section 9.8.4)

NOTES:

(1) Examples of usage are shown in the indicated sections for each mode.

(2) Displacement, D, can be prefixed with B^ for byte, W^ for word, or L^ for longword. If the prefix is omitted, the assembler decides the most appropriate length. Also D can be a symbol, an expression, or a literal. Hexadecimal mode specifiers for byte, word, and longword displacements are A, C, and E, respectively, for displacement addressing, or B, D, and F for displacement-deferred.

of the general registers (R0, R1, . . . , R11, AP, FP, SP, PC). These two pieces of information, the mode specifier, and the register, are placed by the assembler into the first byte of the operand specifier in the following format:

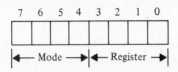

When the processor fetches and decodes this byte, it determines from the mode specifier how the register contents is to be used in locating the operand. For example, if the mode is 5, register addressing is implied, so the register contents is itself the operand. On the other hand, a mode specifier of 6 implies register-deferred addressing and will cause the register contents to be used as the *main memory address* of the operand. More complex modes use the register contents in other ways, and some cause the register contents to be modified in the process. When you choose an addressing mode, it is important that you understand exactly how it will be interpreted by the processor, and how the employed register will be altered. Most of this information is available in Table 12.1, with examples presented in the indicated sections.

Many of the data structures considered in this chapter rely heavily on displacement addressing which was introduced in Section 9.8.4. Let us review this mode briefly so that its operation will be thoroughly understood when needed later in this chapter.

First, note that the Displacement and Displacement-Deferred modes each have three distinct forms at the machine code level. The difference is the number of bytes reserved for the displacement in the operand specifier. When the displacement is small enough to fit in one byte, the byte form can be used, whereas larger displacements can use word or longword forms. The programmer can indicate which form to use by the prefixes B^ for byte, W^ for word, and L^ for longword. At run time, the displacement length is indicated by the mode specifier. For example,

```
CLRL   W^326(R1)
```

results in the word displacement being used, giving the translation:

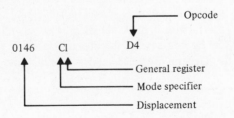

Note that the displacement size has nothing to to do with the operand size. Thus in the preceding example we are clearing a longword whose displacement ($326_{10} = 146_{16}$) is too large to fit in a byte, but small enough to fit in a word. Also, recall that if the displacement length prefix is omitted in the assembly code, the assembler chooses the correct displacement length. Most programmers therefore omit the prefix unless there is some reason for reserving a longer displacement space in the operand specifier.

Omitting the prefix, Displacement addressing is symbolized by:

```
D(Rn)
```

Here the D can be either a literal (i.e., a constant), a symbol that is a label, a symbol that is defined by direct assignment, or an expression. If it is a symbol or expression it is replaced by its numeric value at assembly time.

Regardless of whether D is a symbol or a literal, at execution time its value is added to the contents of Rn, and the value thus determined is used as the address of the operand. For example, if R1 contains 1000_{16}, and we write:

```
MOVL   4(R1),R3
```

the contents of the longword at main memory 1004 is placed in R3. The same thing is accomplished by:

```
A=4   ; DIRECT ASSIGNMENT OF 4 TO A
      MOVL   A(R1),R3
```

Furthermore, the instructions:

```
A=2
      MOVL   A+2(R1),R3
```

do the same thing. In this case we are using the *expression* A + 2 as the displacement mnemonic. At assembly time, 2 is added to the assigned value of A, so that at execution time 4 is added to the current contents of R1.

Usage of this mode is often of the form:

```
SCORE=6
         MOVL   #TABLE,R1
         MOVL   SCORE(R1),R2
```

This results in the contents of the longword at main memory location "SCORE bytes beyond TABLE" being placed in R2. We shall see that this provides a convenient means of addressing into tables.

12.2.2 Short Literal Addressing Mode

The Short Literal Addressing mode is shown in Table 12.2. This mode is different from those in Table 12.1 in that it does not employ a general register. Instead, the operand itself is stored in the first byte of the operand specifier where the register code would be stored for the General Register modes. In this case the operand specifier format is:

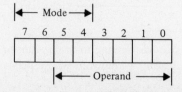

TABLE 12.2/Short Literal and Indexed Addressing

Mode Specifier	Name	Assembly Mnemonics	Explanation
0–3	Short Literal	S^#literal	The value of the literal is embedded in the operand specifier, from which it is decoded at run time. (Section 5.6.1)
4	Indexed	[Ri]	This can only appear as a suffix to certain other addressing modes. Register i acts as an index relative to a base address determined from the other part of the addressing mnemonics. (Section 12.2.3)

Note that the operand field overlaps the mode specifier field, allowing larger operands than would be possible if the operand were restricted to bits (3:0). This overlap is possible because the CPU recognizes any one of the four mode specifiers 0000, 0001, 0010, and 0011 (i.e., 0, 1, 2, and 3) as short literal addressing. Also, as we observed in Section 5.6.1, the operand must be in the range of $0–63_{10}$ in order to fit in the six bits provided.

The Short Literal addressing mode is also of interest from the computer architecture point of view. First, we can observe that this mode employs four of the possible sixteen codes that were available to the designers for mode specifiers. One might therefore ask why the machine designers chose to implement a short literal form rather than using these codes to implement additional addressing modes. For example, the VAX-11 does not give us an autodecrement-deferred mode, which presumably would have been provided if another mode specifier code were available.

We can only speculate on the designers' motives, but it is clear that the short literal form offers at least two important advantages. When compared to the alternative—namely, immediate addressing (see Section 5.6.1)—we see that the Short Literal mode saves one byte of memory at each usage. This is because it embeds the operand in the first byte of the operand specifier rather than in the succeeding byte. Considering the frequency of need for small operands, this savings could be significant in large programs. The second advantage is execution speed, because the operand fetch is avoided. Apparently, the VAX-11 designers felt that these two advantages warranted committing four mode specifier codes to this mode.

12.2.3 Indexed Addressing

Indexed addressing on the VAX-11 is a mode used in conjunction with another addressing mode, called the base mode. That is, it is not an independent mode. It has a mode specifier of 4. As indicated in Table 12.2, the indexed assembly mnemonic [Ri] is placed as a suffix to the mnemonic for the base mode. For example, we might write:

```
CLRB   (R1)[R2]
```

wherein the *base mode* is register-deferred, (R1), and R2 is the **index register.**

This mode is called *indexed* because the contents of the register in the square brackets (the index register) is used in much the same way as the index for an array in a high-level language. With this view, the array address, i.e., the address of its first element, is indicated by the base addressing mnemonics, and the index is relative to that address. That is, index 0 refers to the first element of the array, 1 refers to the second, and so on. Thus in the preceding example if R2 contained 3, the instruction would clear the byte 3 bytes beyond the first byte in an array of bytes whose starting address was in R1. Note that this works equally well with word, longword, and quadword arrays. For example, when the instructions:

```
CLRW   (R0)[R2]
```

and:

```
CLRL   (R1)[R2]
```

are executed with R2 containing 2, the second *word* beyond the one pointed at by R0 will be cleared, as well as the second *longword* beyond the one pointed at by R1.

In a more formal explanation of Indexed addressing, the operand specifier can be viewed as having two parts, referred to as the base operand specifier and the primary operand specifier. For example, the translation of:

```
CLRL   (R0)+[R3]
```

is:

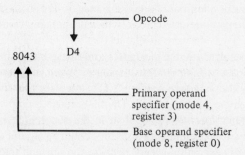

When the CPU encounters an operand specifier with the first byte containing 4 in the mode field, it obtains the contents of the register indicated in the register field and multiplies this value by the *length of the primary operand*. It is able to determine the length of the primary operand by examining the instruction opcode. For example, D4 implies a *longword* primary operand. The base operand address is then determined by evaluating the base operand specifier in the normal manner. Finally, the primary operand address is determined by adding the previous product to the base address. It is the automatic multiplication of the index by the length of the primary operand that allows the VAX-11 index mode to work with indexes that increment by 1 regardless of the length of the data elements. Note also that the CPU knows that there is a second mode specifier byte because the index mode specifier is stored first.

Not all of the VAX-11 addressing modes can be used for the base address in conjunction with the Indexed mode. Those which can are Register-Deferred, Autodecrement, Autoincrement, Autoincrement-Deferred, Displacement, and Displacement-Deferred.

The following examples demonstrate Indexed addressing using the allowed forms of the base operand.

EXAMPLE 12.1 Assume the following initializations of the registers and main memory locations prior to execution of *each* of the sample instructions given. The effects on register contents and main memory are shown.

Register	Contents	Address	Contents
R1	00000514	0514	0 0 0 0 0 0 0 0
R2	00000520	0518	F F F F F F F F
R3	0000050C	051C	A A A A A A A A
R4	00000524	0520	0 0 0 0 0 5 2 4
R5	00000002	0524	1 2 3 4 5 6 7 8
R6	FFFFFFFE	0528	B B B B B B B B
		052C	C C C C C C C C

		Register Effects		Main Memory Effects	
		Register	New Value	Address	New Values
(a)	INCW (R1)[R5]	None	—	0518	FFFF0000
(b)	INCL -(R1)[R5]	R1	00000510	0518	00000000
(c)	MOVB @(R2)[R5],R3	R3	00000534	None	—
(d)	CLRL (R4)+[R6]	R4	00000528	051C	00000000
(e)	ADDL @(R2)+[R5],R3	R2	00000524	None	—
		R3	CCCCD1D8		
(f)	CLRW 4(R4)[R6]	None	—	0524	12340000
(g)	INCB @12(R1)[R5]	None	—	0524	12355678

In Case (a), the address of the *word* to be incremented is the base address, 0514, plus 2 (bytes per word) times the index, yielding 0518. Because the word at 0518 contains FFFF (-1), incrementing produces a word-sized zero.

In Case (b), R1 is first decremented by 4 due to the longword Autodecrement base addressing. This yields a base address of 0510, to which 4 (bytes per longword) times the index (2) is added. Thus the longword at 0518 is cleared. In Case (c), the address of the base address is in R2. Thus the base address itself is 0524. Because the operand is to be a byte, the base address plus 1 times the index (2) yields an operand address of 0526. The byte in 0526 is seen to be 34, which then overwrites the low byte of the longword in R3.

Cases (d) and (e) demonstrate indexing on a base address determined in the Autoincrement and Autoincrement-Deferred modes, respectively. In Case (d), we have a negative index, so the longword that is cleared is at 0524 plus 4 (bytes per longword) times the index (− 2), or $0524 + 4 \times (- 2) = 051C$. In Case (e), the base is 0524, so the operand address is this plus (4 bytes per longword) times the index (2), or 052C. When the longword found there is added to the contents of R3 we get CCCCD1D8.

Cases (f) and (g) use Displacement and Displacement-Deferred addressing, respectively, to specify the base address. In (f), the base address is the displacement, 4, plus the contents of R4, 0528, and the index is − 2. The address of the word that will be cleared is therefore 0528 minus 4, or 0524. In Case (g), the address of the base address is in 12_{10} (C_{16}) plus 0514, which is 0520. Thus the base address is 0524, and the operand address is therefore 0526. This byte is in the longword at 0524, which after incrementing will be 35_{16}.

It should be noted that there are many situations where the programmer can employ either Autoincrement Addressing, or Register-Deferred with indexing. For example, we can clear successive elements in a longword array by placing either:

```
CLRL    (R1)+
```

or:

```
CLRL    (R1)[R2]
INCL    R2
```

in a loop, assuming appropriate initialization. In either case, R1 would be initialized to the address of the first element of the array. However, in the first case R1 is incremented (by 4), whereas in the second case R1 remains fixed while R2 is incremented (by 1). The choice between the two alternatives is made based primarily on programmer preference, although the Autoincrement mode results in a shorter program.

The indexed mode can be used to greater advantage with base modes that provide second-level indirect addressing, namely Autoincrement-Deferred and Displacement-Deferred. This is because with these modes the base mode register can be used to point at an array, while the index register points to a particular element in that array. As an example, suppose we wish to add all elements of array A to corresponding elements of array B. We could do this with the instructions:

```
            MOVL    #LIST,R1
            CLRL    R2
            MOVL    #100,R3
    LOOP:   ADDL    @(R1)[R2],@4(R1)[R2]
            INCL    R2
            SOBGTR  R3,LOOP
```

Figure 12.1 shows this addressing method diagrammatically. The addresses of A and B are stored in a main memory longword array labeled LIST. Register R1 points to the beginning of LIST, i.e., the location where the address of A is stored. Thus @(R1) points to the actual address of A, and @4(R1) points to the actual address of B. Both are indexed with R2. Techniques such as this are especially useful when arrays are arguments of subroutines. (See Exercises 12.3 and 12.5.)

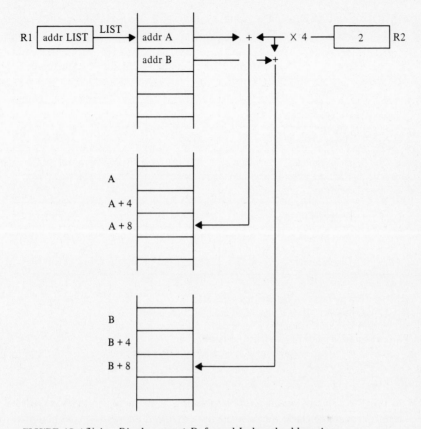

FIGURE 12.1/Using Displacement-Deferred Indexed addressing

12.2.4 Another View of VAX-11 Addressing Modes

The VAX-11 addressing modes are presented in a slightly different arrangement in Table 12.3. In the left columns of the upper portion of the table we see that there are four modes that might be called "basic," namely Register, Autodecrement, Autoincrement, and Displacement.

The upper right part of the table shows that for *each basic mode* there is a corresponding *deferred* mode (also called indirect mode). Note that the quantity determined by the basic mode is used as the operand *value,* whereas in the corresponding deferred version the same quantity is determined, but is then used as the *address* of the operand value. For example, register mode uses the register contents as the operand value, but in register-deferred mode the contents is the *address* of the operand value. Taking a more complex mode, autoincrement causes the register to be incremented, then fetches the contents of the memory location pointed at by the register, and uses it as the operand value. Autoincrement-*deferred,* on the other hand, increments the register, fetches the contents of the memory location pointed at by the register, but then goes one step

TABLE 12.3/Addressing Modes (Basic vs. Deferred)

		Basic		Deferred	
		Mode	**Mnemonic**	**Mode**	**Mnemonic**
Base	Register	5	Rn	6	(Rn)
	Autodecrement	7	– (Rn)	—	NA
	Autoincrement	8	(Rn) +	9	@(Rn) +
	Displacement	A,C,E	D(Rn)	B,D,F	@D(Rn)
Indexed	Register	—	NA	6/4	(Rn) [Ri]
	Autodecrement	7/4	– (Rn) [Ri]	—	NA
	Autoincrement	8/4	(Rn) + [Ri]	9/4	@(Rn) + [Ri]
	Displacement	A,C,E/4	D(Rn) [Ri]	B,D,F/4	@D(Rn) [Ri]

NOTES:
(1) NA = Not available or logically not applicable
(2) D = Displacement: Byte B^d;mode A(basic) or B (deferred)
  Word W^d;mode C (basic) or D (deferred)
  Longword L^d;mode E (basic) or F (deferred)
(3) Indexed addressing is always used in conjunction with a base mode.

further to use the contents as an *address* pointing at the actual operand. Observe that in this case, because the basic mode itself uses deferred addressing, the autoincrement-deferred mode is actually *second-level* deferred addressing. This is also true for the displacement modes.

The organization of Table 12.2 makes it apparent that the VAX-11 designers made a conscious decision to omit the autodecrement-deferred mode as we speculated in Section 12.2.2.

From Tables 12.1, 12.2, and 12.3 we see that the VAX-11 does not have a second-level deferred addressing mode without displacement or register incrementing/decrementing. That is, the mode that might be symbolized as:

```
@(Rn)
```

is missing from the tables. In fact, however, this syntax *will* be recognized by the assembler and translated as byte Displacement-Deferred addressing (mode specifier B) with the symbol value of zero. That is,

```
@(Rn)
```

is interpreted as:

```
@B^0(Rn)
```

Thus while the *machine code* does not have simple second-level deferred addressing, the assembly language programmer can assume that it does.

The bottom portion of Table 12.3 shows the Indexed modes that are available, paralleling the modes shown in the upper portion. There we see that most of the basic and basic deferred modes can act as base modes for indexed addressing. The only exception is register addressing. This is because with register addressing the register *contents* is the operand (and therefore *not* an address), so that indexing has no meaning.

By viewing the numerous VAX-11 addressing modes as they are presented in Table 12.3, we are able to simplify the task of remembering how they work. The basic modes in the upper left part of the table are the only ones that require memorization. The deferred modes are interpreted exactly like the basic mode, but the value found is used as an address to find the operand. However, if it is Indexed, this address is used as a base for the indexing operation, producing the final address of the actual operand.

12.2.5 Program Counter Addressing

You may have observed that in the preceding sections there was no discussion of what we earlier called Relative Addressing, Immediate Addressing, and Absolute Addressing. This is because these are not really distinct addressing modes on the VAX-11. Rather, they are special cases of the Displacement, Autoincrement, and Autoincrement-Deferred modes when the employed register is 15_{10}, i.e., the PC. Next we will see that there is one other addressing method that uses the PC, namely Relative-Deferred. These four methods are known collectively as **Program Counter Addressing.** Although they are only special cases of the actual VAX-11 modes, they appear to be different to the assembly language programmer because the assembler recognizes special syntax for them. They are perhaps the addressing methods most often used.

Table 12.4 shows the four Program Counter Addressing methods recognized by the MACRO assembler. Of these, immediate and relative have been discussed previously (Chapter 5), while Absolute and Relative-Deferred appear here for the first time. We shall see how these work from a practical, assembly programming point of view, as well as in relation to the fundamental modes.

We have already seen (in Chapter 5) that immediate addressing provides a method of introducing a value as an operand. Typical examples include:

```
MOVL    #25,R1
MOVL    #ARY,R2
```

From a programming point of view, this says to move the value following the # into the second operand. Note that what follows the #, i.e., a literal, a symbol, or an expression, is always reduced to a value at assembly time, and is therefore a constant at run time. We often use this method to introduce a constant, or to refer to an address by means of a label to which the assembler has assigned a value.

To see how immediate addressing works in terms of the fundamental modes, observe from Table 12.4 that the assembler assigns the code of 8F as the first byte of the operand specifier, and then stores the operand value in the succeeding bytes.

At run time, because of the Instruction Fetch Execute Cycle, register F (the PC) will contain the address of the immediate operand after the first byte of the operand specifier is fetched. Because the first byte is 8F (autoincrement), according to Table 12.1, the contents of this location is fetched as the operand, *and* the register (i.e., the

TABLE 12.4/Program Counter Addressing

Mode	Name	Assembly Mnemonics	Explanation
8F	Immediate	I^#symbol	Operand is the value of symbol. This value is automatically stored following the instruction. (Section 5.6.1)
9F	Absolute	@#symbol	Operand is in location whose address is the value of symbol. Symbol value is automatically stored following the instruction. (Section 12.2.5)
AF,CF,EF	Relative	symbol	Operand is in location whose address is the value of symbol. The PC-relative address of symbol (see notes) is automatically stored following the instruction. (Section 5.6.2)
BF,DF,FF	Relative-Deferred	@Symbol	Address of operand is in location whose address is indicated by value of symbol. The PC-relative address of symbol (see notes) is automatically stored following the instruction. (Section 12.2.5)
8F/4	Immediate-Indexed	I^#symbol [Ri]	Not a useful mode
9F/4	Absolute-Indexed	@#symbol [Ri]	See Note 3
AF,CF,EF/4	Relative-Indexed	symbol [Ri]	See Note 3
BF,DF,FF/4	Relative-Deferred Indexed	@symbol [Ri]	See Note 3

NOTES:

(1) Symbol can be a literal, a label, a symbol given a value by assignment, or even an expression. In all cases, a value is first determined by the assembler, then used as indicated.

(2) PC-relative address is the symbol value minus the *current* PC. (See Section 5.6.2.)

(3) In each indexed case, base address is determined as in corresponding base addressing mode (top part of table). Operand address is then determined by adding contents of Ri times operand length to the base address.

PC) is advanced by 4. This leaves the PC pointing at the next location which will contain another operand specifier, or the next instruction. Thus this mode takes advantage of the autoincrement feature to advance the PC beyond the immediate operand.

Relative addressing has also been discussed in Chapter 5. From a programming point of view, it is a convenient way of using the contents of a memory location as an operand. For example,

```
ADDL   B,R1
```

says to add the contents of the memory location whose label (i.e., address) is B to R1. Note that because the operand is the contents of a memory location, its value can change during execution; thus this mode is most naturally used when the operand is a *variable* rather than a constant.

From a machine code perspective, relative addressing is a special case of the Displacement addressing mode. When the assembler sees an unprefixed nonregister symbol as an operand, it sets the address code to AF, CF, or EF, depending on the required displacement size (i.e., mode A, C, or E, with register F) and computes the *PC-relative* address of the symbol and stores it in the next location. By PC-relative address, we mean the value assigned to the symbol (understood to be an address) *minus* the current value stored in PC. (Recall, however, that the current value means its value *after* the operand fetch. See Section 5.6.2.) Thus the PC-relative address is really the *displacement* of the operand from the current PC at run time.

Let us now see what happens during execution with relative addressing. When the first byte of the operand specifier is fetched, PC is advanced to the next location, where the PC-relative address was placed by the assembler. Now, according to Table 12.1, for displacement addressing, the address of the operand is found by adding the contents of the employed register, i.e., the *PC-contents,* to the value found at the second byte of the operand specifier. Clearly, this "undoes" the subtraction carried out by the assembler, yielding the actual address of the operand. Note that the PC is advanced by the length of the displacement whenever displacement addressing is used, so it is left pointing at the next longword containing an instruction or perhaps another operand specifier.

The **absolute** and **relative-deferred** addressing methods are simply deferred versions of the Immediate and Relative methods. That is, if we write:

```
TSTB   @#^X1000
```

we are testing the contents of the byte whose *address* is 1000. This translates to:

$$00001000\ 9F\ 95$$

When the first byte of the operand specifier (9F) is fetched PC will contain the address of the location containing 00001000. We see from Table 12.1 that because the mode is 9 and the register is F the 00001000 will be fetched and treated as the address of the operand, and PC will be incremented by 4. Note that the only difference between this and immediate addressing is the way in which the "immediate" value is used. In one case it is used as the operand, and in the other as an address of the operand.

We should also carefully compare Relative and Absolute addressing, because they have certain similarities, but also an important difference. Note that from a programming point of view the instruction:

```
MOVL   A,R1
```

has the same effect as:

```
MOVL   @#A,R1
```

That is, both access the contents of the location labeled A. The difference, however, is in how they are assembled. In the first case, relative addressing is employed and it translates as:

51 (rel addr of A) EF D0

where we see that the *PC-relative address* of A is stored as part of the operand specifier. In the second case, we have:

51 (addr of A) 9F D0

where the *absolute* address of A is seen to be stored as part of the operand specifier. In many cases this will not matter, because the computer will find the same operand by either method. We examined cases where it does make a difference when we studied *position-independent code* in Section 11.5.

The deferred counterpart of Relative addressing is exemplified by the first operand of:

```
MOVL   @ARY,R1
```

Here we are indicating that the address of the value to be moved to R1 is stored in the location labeled ARY. This is very similar to register-deferred addressing, where the address of the operand is stored in a register.

The assembler translates the above instruction as:

51 (rel addr of ARY) FF D0

where we assume that a longword is needed to store the relative address of ARY. As with Relative addressing, the actual address of ARY is found at run time by adding the current PC contents to the relative address stored immediately after the first byte of the operand specifier. However, becuase the mode is F, the value found in ARY is used as the *address* of the actual operand.

The bottom part of Table 12.4 shows that each Program Counter Addressing method can also be indexed. The mnemonics are similar to the nonindexed case except that [Ri] is added as a suffix. At run time, the base address is determined exactly as it is for the nonindexed case, and then the contents of Ri is multiplied by the operand length and added to the base address to get the operand address. Thus the instructions:

```
          CLRL    R1
LOOP:     CLRL    A[R1]
          INCL    R1
          CMPL    R1,#100
          BLSSU   LOOP
```

clear 100_{10} longwords beginning at A. This represents a common usage of Relative Indexed addressing. Absolute and Relative-Deferred Indexed addressing also have meaningful applications. However, it is difficult to conceive of a meaningful application of Immediate Indexed addressing because the addresses computed (for all but the case of index = 0) refer to locations where the machine code for successive operands and instructions is stored rather than data. Moreover, these addresses are not affected by the immediate operand itself. Nonetheless, the assembler recognizes the mnemonics for this method.

12.3 | Arrays

12.3.1 One-Dimensional Arrays

An array is a collection of similar data items, stored in a sequence of main memory locations, and identified by a single name. A simple example is an array of integers stored in successive longwords beginning at some label. Storage space for arrays is usually allocated using the .BLKL or .BLKB directives, e.g.,

```
RESULT:    .BLKL   100
```

As we saw in Chapter 5, successive items in an array, called elements, can be referenced by Register-Deferred or Autoincrement/Autodecrement addressing. For example, to increment all elements of RESULT by 1, we write:

```
        MOVL    #100,R1
        MOVL    #RESULT,R2
L:      INCL    (R2)+
        SOBGTR  R1,L
```

However, Displacement or Indexed Addressing can also be employed to address particular array elements, and one of these methods is preferred when there are two or more arrays in which corresponding elements are to be addressed. For example, the following code will add array A to array RESULT using Displacement addressing:

```
        CLRL    R1
L:      ADDL    A(R1),RESULT(R1)
        ADDL    #4,R1
        CMPL    R1,#400
        BLSSU   L
```

Note that accomplishing this with Autoincrement or Register-Deferred addressing would require two registers instead of the one used above.

Using Relative Indexed addressing to accomplish the same result gives:

```
        CLRL    R1
L:      ADDL    A[R1],RESULT[R1]
        INCL    R1
        CMPL    R1,#100
        BLSSU   L
```

Note that with Indexed mode, R1 is incremented by 1 in the assembly code, but because of the normal operation of the Indexed mode, successive *longword* addresses are referenced.

The preceding example can be programmed more compactly by using the AOBLSS (**A**dd **O**ne and **B**ranch on **LeSS** than) instruction. That is,

```
        CLRL    R1
L:      ADDL    A[R1],RESULT[R1]
        AOBLSS  #100,R1,L
```

The compact and efficient code that this allows makes the AOBLSS instruction a natural adjunct to Indexed addressing. The first operand of AOBLSS is the limit, the second is the register that is incremented automatically, and the third is the branch destination.

12.3.2 Two-Dimensional Arrays

The preceding examples use *one-dimensional* arrays. That is, an element is specifiable by a single index. For some types of data this is a natural organization. Other types of data are more naturally viewed in a two-dimensional organization.

An example is daily time records for a group of employees, where the time worked by employee I on day J might be referred to as T(I,J). As shown in Figure 12.2(a), this collection can be viewed as a two-dimensional array, with each row representing an employee and each column a day. Note that by convention, the row index is given first, so that by T(2,1) we mean the value in the second row, first column. Also, the indexes are normally assumed to begin at 1, rather than 0.

The main memory is inherently one-dimensional, so storage of two-dimensional arrays must be stored in either *row-major* or *column-major* form, as shown in parts (b)

(a)

	C1	C2	C3	C4	C5
R1	8	7	7	6	10
R2	6	5	8	8	4
R3	7	4	4	10	3

(b) column-major:

T:	8
C1	6
	7
	7
C2	5
	4
	7
C3	8
	4
	6
C4	8
	10
	10
C5	4
	3

(c) row-major:

T:	8
	7
R1	7
	6
	10
	6
	5
R2	8
	8
	4
	7
	4
R3	4
	10
	3

FIGURE 12.2/Two-dimensional array: (a) T viewed as 2-dimensional array; (b) column-major storage; (c) row-major storage

and (c) of Figure 12.2. The choice is arbitrary unless there is a need for compatibility with other program modules that use a particular arrangement. For example, FORTRAN arrays are traditionally stored by columns, whereas the C programming language stores by rows. Regardless of which order is used, an assembly language program has to *compute* the proper index in the as-stored form, given the separate row-column indexes. For example, if the array of longwords has M rows and N columns and is stored by columns, the one-dimensional index of T(I,J), relative to the first element, is

```
4[(I-1)+m(J-1)]
```

which assumes that each element occupies four bytes. However, for better efficiency the value of this one-dimensional index is often calculated by repeated addition rather than directly from this formula.

EXAMPLE 12.2 As a simple example of programming with two-dimensional arrays, consider the need to compute the weekly total hours for each employee. A program that initializes T as shown in Figure 12.2 and computes row-wise sums is shown in Figure 12.3. In this program R3 holds a one-dimensional index relative to the first element in T. The sum for each row is computed by first setting R3 to a row "base index," which is the index for the first element in each row, then incrementing R3 by the number of bytes per column each time through the innermost loop. After completing

```
        .TITLE EXAMPLE 12.2
        .ENTRY START,0
        MOVL    M,R0        ;INIT. ROW LCV
        MOVL    R0,M2       ;CALC. COL-TO-COL
        ASHL    #2,M2,M2;     INDEX INCREMENT.
        MOVL    N,R1        ;INIT. COL LCV
        CLRL    R2          ;INIT. ROW BASE INDEX
        CLRL    R3          ;INIT. 1-DIM. INDEX
        CLRL    R4          ;INIT. SUM
L1:
        ADDL    T(R3),R4    ;DEVELOP SUM
        ADDL    M2,R3       ;INC. COL INDEX
        SOBGTR  R1,L1       ;REPEAT FOR N COLS.
        MOVL    R4,W(R2)    ;STORE SUM
        CLRL    R4          ;REINIT SUM
        ADDL    #4,R2       ;INC.ROW BASE INDEX
        MOVL    R2,R3       ;SET INDEX TO NEW ROW BASE
        MOVL    N,R1        ;REINIT COL LCV
        SOBGTR  R0,L1       ;REPEAT FOR M ROWS
        $EXIT_S             ;EXIT TO VMS
T:      .LONG   8,6,7       ;HOURS BY EMPLOYEE & DAY
        .LONG   7,5,4
        .LONG   7,8,4
        .LONG   6,8,10
        .LONG   10,4,3
W:      .BLKL   3           ;HOURS BY EMPLOYEE
M:      .LONG   3           ;NO. OF EMPLOYEES
N:      .LONG   5           ;NO. OF DAYS
M2:     .BLKL   1           ;4* NO. OF DAYS
        .END    START
```

FIGURE 12.3/Two-dimensional array example

a row sum, it is saved in the one-dimensional array W. The row base index is recomputed each time through the outer loop by adding 4. This strategy should be compared to the far less efficient method of calculating R3 directly by the formula. Note that the row base index also serves as an index for the result array W.

12.3.3 Arrays of Records (Tables)

In the array of Example 12.2, each element was a longword (four bytes) containing a single entity. Sometimes it may be desirable to have each array element contain several entities, in which case we would call it a **record.** Such an array of records can be called a **table.**

EXAMPLE 12.3 Suppose we wish to store a list of names and exam scores. This might be done in an array like the one shown in Figure 12.3. We have defined a name *field* of ten bytes and a score *field* of two bytes for each record. Storage for this array could be allocated by the directive:

```
TABLE:  .BLKB 9*12   ; 9 RECORDS OF 12 BYTES
```

In order to place a name or score into this array, it is necessary to identify the record and the displacement of the appropriate field from the beginning of the record. Techniques for doing this are demonstrated in Figure 12.5. This program loads the array in Figure 12.4 from keyboard entry. R1 is used as a pointer to the first byte in each record, and R2 points to the beginning of the name field in each record. This address is moved to R0, and the macro .GETSTR accepts keyboard characters and stores them beginning at this address. The macro .GETHEX gets a hexadecimal number from the keyboard and places it in R0. (.GETHEX and .GETSTR are shown in Section E.1.) The subsequent MOVL stores this number in the score field. Observe that we use displacement addressing

Index	←——— 10 bytes ———→	←2 bytes→
0	SMITH	77
1	JOHNSON	90
2	WELLINGTON	56
3	STUMP	65
4	DAVIDSON	72
5	GARCIA	95
6	EDWARDS	82
7	JONES	77
8	ROBERTSON	52

FIGURE 12.4/An array of records: (a) logical organization

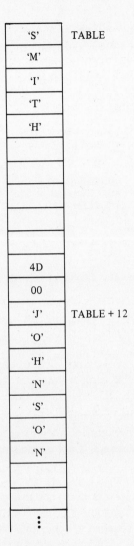

FIGURE 12.4/An array of records: (b) physical organization in main memory

here, so that the field displacement is added to the record pointer, yielding the address of the destination operand.

The two techniques for addressing into tables employed in Example 12.3 are general and should be studied carefully. When the field contains a character string, we most often need the *address* of the first byte, rather than the contents. This is because string processing procedures and the special VAX-11 string instructions discussed in Section 7.9) operate on the string using its *starting address*. Thus for strings we initialize a pointer to the NAME address in the first record. This allows autoincrement addressing

```
                    .TITLE EXAMPLE 12.3
         ;
         NAME=0      ;NAME DISPLACEMENT IN RECORD
         SCORE=10    ;SCORE DISPLACEMENT IN RECORD
         RECLEN=12   ;RECORD LENGTH
         ;
                    .ENTRY    START,0
                    MOVL      #9,R3              ;INIT LCV
                    MOVL      #TABLE,R1          ;INIT RECORD POINTER
                    MOVL      #TABLE+NAME,R2     ;INIT POINTER TO NAME
         L1:        MOVL      R2,R0              ;GET
                    .GETSTR                      ;    NAME,
                    .GETHEX                      ;GET
                    MOVW      R0,SCORE(R1)       ;    SCORE,
                    ADDL      #RECLEN,R1         ;ADVANCE TO
                    ADDL      #RECLEN,R2         ;    NEXT RECORD,
                    SOBGTR    R3,L1              ;REPEAT 9 TIMES
                    $EXIT_S                      ;EXIT TO VMS
         TABLE:     .BLKB     9*RECLEN           ;9 RECS, OF RECLEN BYTES
                    .END      START
```

FIGURE 12.5/Storing data in table of records (see Figure 12.4)

within the string by .GETSTR. Subsequently, incrementing the pointer by the record length advances it to the next record. On the other hand, when the field contains a number, e.g., a byte or longword integer, we use displacement addressing to access it. Note that when we code:

```
MOVL  R0,SCORE(R1)
```

the sum of SCORE and the contents of R1 provides the destination address. R1 is incremented by the record length in order to access the SCORE in the next record. Also note that because the record is not a standard VAX-11 data type, we cannot use the Indexed mode here.

In the preceding example, R1 and R2 are always equal because the displacement of the NAME field is 0. However, this is not always the case. The way it is programmed in Figure 12.4 ensures that the address of the NAME field is always correctly calculated even if its displacement is changed to something other than 0.

12.4 | Table Accessing Order

Tables often need to be accessed in a particular order. For example, we may want to print out the names and scores from the table in Figure 12.4 in an order determined by the scores, from highest to lowest. There are a number of ways of accomplishing this, including the following three.

1. Repeat the search for the highest remaining score, with a system of marking each record after printing it.

2. Sort the table prior to printing, using the score field of each record for comparison, and interchanging entire records when an out-of-order sequence is desired.

3. Do a sort using the score field for the comparison, but rearranging only the elements of a *parallel array* of record indexes. The array of indexes is then used to select records for printing.

Method 1 might be used if the task needed to be done only once, but would be wasteful if the table had to be accessed in the same order later. Methods 2 and 3 are both superior to 1 in this respect. However, Method 2 is not ideal for large tables because it involves moving large amounts of data. Method 3, called an **index sort,** avoids this problem, because only the indexes are moved while the table itself remains unchanged. We will therefore implement this method as an exercise in table access.

The index sort is based on an auxiliary array called the **index array,** which has an element for each record in the table. The contents of each element of the index array is used to identify a particular record in the table. For example, if we have an index array of words K, as shown in Figure 12.6(a), and R1 contains 6, the instruction sequence:

```
MOVZBW   K(R1),R3
MULL    #12,R3
```

will place the index for TABLE record number 3 into R3. Note that we had to multiply by 12, the record length, to compute the record address from the indexes stored in K. To address the SCORE for this record, we use:

```
MOVL   TABLE+SCORE(R3),R0
```

From Figure 12.4(a) we see that this places the score 65 into R0. Obviously, if we incremented R1 by 2 (the number of bytes per element in K) and repeated this sequence, we would get the score from record 4, i.e., 72. Furthermore, we see that if R1 is incremented as 0,2,4,6, . . ., this process accesses the records in whatever order is implied by the *contents* of the successive elements of K.

The aim of index sorting, then, is to rearrange the index array such that it contains

0	K	5	K
1	K + 2	1	K + 2
2	K + 4	6	K + 4
3	K + 6	0	K + 6
4		7	
5		4	
6		3	
7		2	
8		8	
(a)		(b)	

FIGURE 12.6/Index array for table sorting: (a) before sorting; (b) after sorting

the record indexes in the desired order. For example, we see from Figure 12.4(a) that the maximum score is in record 5, the next highest in record 1, and so on. In Figure 12.6(b) we see the desired sequence of indexes in K.

EXAMPLE 12.4 A program that reads a table of records and performs an index sort is shown in Figure 12.7. Reading the table is essentially the same as shown in Figure

```
            .TITLE EXAMPLE 12.4
    ;
    ;          SORT TABLE OF RECORDS
    ;
    NREC   = 9       ;NUMBER OF RECORDS
    NAME   = 0       ;NAME DISPLACEMENT IN RECORD
    SCORE  = 10      ;SCORE DISPLACEMENT IN RECORD
    RECLEN = 12      ;RECORD LENGTH
    ;
            .ENTRY   START,0
    ;
    ;    READ TABLE
    ;
            CLRL     R3                ;INIT, LCV/INDEX
            MOVL     #TABLE,R1         ;INIT RECORD POINTER
            MOVL     #TABLE+NAME,R2    ;INIT POINTER TO NAME
    L1:     MOVL     R2,R0             ;GET
            .GETSTR                    ;   NAME,
            .GETHEX                    ;GET
            MOVW     R0,SCORE(R1)      ;   SCORE,
            MOVW     R3,K(R3)          ;SET UP ARRAY OF REC INDEXES
            DIVW     #2,K(R3)          ;SO K WILL BE 0,1,2,,,
            ADDL     #RECLEN,R1        ;ADVANCE TO
            ADDL     #RECLEN,R2        ;   NEXT RECORD,
            ADDW     #2,R3             ;INC LCV/INDEX
            CMPW     R3,#2*NREC        ;REPEAT
            BLSSU    L1                ;   NREC TIMES,
    ;
    ;    SORT ACCORDING TO SCORES
    ;
    L2:     MOVL     #NREC-1,R0        ;INIT LCV
            CLRL     R1                ;INIT K INDEX
            CLRL     FLAG              ;INIT INTERCHG FLAG
    L3:     MOVZWL   K(R1),R3          ;COMPUTE
            MULL     #RECLEN,R3        ;   RECORD
            MOVZWL   K+2(R1),R5        ;      INDEXES FROM
            MULL     #RECLEN,R5        ;         K INDEX,
            CMPW     SCR(R3),SCR(R5)   ;OUT OF ORDER?
            BGEQU    E                 ;   IF YES
            MOVW     K(R1),R2          ;      THEN
            MOVW     K+2(R1),K(R1)     ;         INTERCHANGE
            MOVW     R2,K+2(R1)        ;            INDEXES,
            INCL     FLAG              ;SET INTERCHG FLAG
    E:      ADDW     #2,R1             ;ADVANCE 1 INDEX
            SOBGTR   R0,L3             ;CONTINUE THE PASS
            TSTL     FLAG              ;ANOTHER PASS
            BNEQU    L2                ;   IF THERE WAS INTERCHG,
```
(a)

FIGURE 12.7/Index sort of table of records

```
;
;              PRINT SORTED TABLE
;
              BSBW      PRT_THEM
              $EXIT_S                       ;EXIT TO VMS
;
PRT_THEM:
              CLRL      R1                  ;INIT, LCV/INDEX
L4:           MOVZWL    K(R1),R0            ;GET INDEX
              MULL      #RECLEN,R0          ;COMPUTE ADDR
              ADDL      #TABLE,R0           ;   OF RECORD,
              BSBW      PRTREC              ;PRINT A RECORD
              ADDL      #2,R1               ;INCREMENT LCV/INDEX
              CMPL      R1,#2*NREC          ;REPEAT
              BLSSU     L4                  ;   NREC TIMES,
              RSB
;
PRTREC:
              CLRL      R6                  ;INIT, LCV
              MOVL      R0,R7               ;ADDR OF RECORD TO R7
L5:           .TTYOUT   (R7)+               ;PRINT
              INCL      R6                  ;   THE
              CMPL      R6,#10              ;     NAME
              BLSSU     L5                  ;       ONLY,
              MOVZWL    (R7),R0             ;PRINT
              .PUTHEX                       ;   THE SCORE,
              RSB
;
TABLE:        .BLKB     NREC*RECLEN         ;NREC RECS, OF RECLEN BYTES
SCR = TABLE+SCORE                           ;ADDR OF FIRST SCORE
FLAG:         .BLKL     1
K:            .BLKW     NREC                ;INDEX ARRAY
;
              .END      START
```
(b)

FIGURE 12.7/Index sort of table of records (concluded)

12.5, except that instructions have been added to create the initial index array K. The sorting portion uses the bubble sort technique. However, note that it does a comparison on the SCORE field of records in TABLE, but does the interchanges on the contents of the index array K.

The outer loop, beginning at L2, is designed to continue making passes through the K array until it is in the correct order. This condition is indicated by FLAG remaining clear, signifying that no out-of-order sequence was encountered in the most recent pass. Each time through the outer loop, the inner loop LCV is set, the K index, R1, is reset to zero, and the FLAG is cleared, prior to entering the inner loop.

The inner loop indexes through the K array, using R1 as an index. For each new value of R1, we extract the corresponding element of K and the next one. These two values from K, when multiplied by the record length, point to two records in TABLE. The contents of the SCORE fields of these two records are compared, and if the first is less than the second, the values from K are interchanged and FLAG is set. (Note that the base for the R3 and R5 indexes is the sum of TABLE and SCORE defined as constant symbol SCR.) Indexing through K one time in this manner places the index of the record with smallest score in the last element of K. Eventually, there will be a pass in which no interchanges are necessary, so that FLAG remains clear, terminating the process.

Once K has been sorted it can be used to drive the printing process. This is done in the subroutine PRT_THM, which selects the record, computes the address, and then calls PRTREC to print it.

Before leaving this example, it should be noted that the techniques used here are general. For example, the program in Figure 12.7 could be modified easily to sort K alphabetically based on the name field. To do this the CMPW instruction would simply be replaced by an appropriate instruction for comparing the two character strings found in the name fields. All other parts of the program would remain unchanged.

Finally, we should note that the sort technique used in Example 12.4 is not ideal. For one thing, it could be easily improved upon simply by decrementing the upper bound on the inner loop LCV each time through the outer loop. (Why is this possible?) However, for large tables the bubble sort algorithm itself is very inefficient relative to other well-known sorting techniques (see Section 13.3). The other ideas demonstrated here, such as the use of the index array, are applicable to other sort methods.

12.5 | Character Strings

As discussed in Section 7.9, a character string is a data item composed of 0 or more ASCII character codes. For example, "HELLO", "", and "1264" are character strings of lengths 5, 0, and 4, respectively. A string of length 0 is said to be empty.

As we have seen in Chapter 7, one 7-bit ASCII character code can be stored in each byte on the VAX-11. A character string is therefore stored in successive bytes in main memory. The address of a string is defined as the address of the first character in it, or if preceded by a count, by the address of the count byte.

When more than one string is stored there must be some method of discerning where one ends and another begins. One way that this is often done is by storing an ASCII "null" character, 00, after the last character. This method, shown in Figure 12.8(a), works because most strings of practical interest do not contain the null character. An auxiliary array of pointers contains the address of the first byte of each string. As we saw in Section 7.6, the .ASCIZ directive stores a string in this manner.

An alternative scheme is shown in Figure 12.8(b). Here the number of characters in the string is stored in the first byte, followed by as many ASCII codes. With this method, lengths are limited to 256 characters. The .ASCIC directive uses this method for string storage.

In a third method, the length of strings is constant, as shown in Figure 12.8(c). This method is wasteful of space, and forces truncation of strings that are longer than anticipated. No pointer array is required, because the address of the first string and the fixed length are sufficient to locate all others.

A final method considered is shown in Figure 12.8(d). Here a separate array of

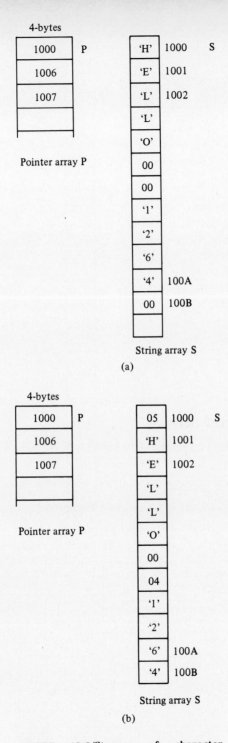

FIGURE 12.8/Storage of character strings: (a) array of null-terminated strings; (b) array of strings with preceding count byte; (c) array of fixed-length strings; (d) separately stored addresses

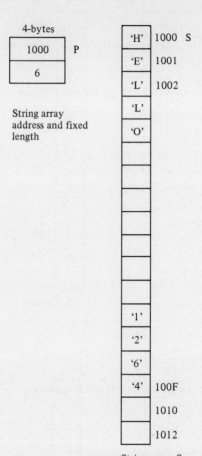

String array
address and fixed
length

(c)

Index	4-bytes	2-bytes	
6	1000	5	P
1	1005	0	
2	1005	4	
3			
	Address	Length	

Word

(d)

FIGURE 12.8/Storage of character strings (concluded)

records holds the address and length of each string. The strings themselves are then stored, without intervening nulls or counts, in a separate block of memory.

Manipulation of strings naturally depends upon how they are stored. In methods (a) and (b) if we allow one longword for pointers the address for the nth string is found in location P+4n, where P is the address of the pointer array. Thus we can use indexed addressing in P to find the address of a particular string in S, and then autoincrement to store or extract the characters in S.

EXAMPLE 12.5 Figure 12.9 demonstrates usage of method (a). This program accepts three strings from the keyboard, using the .TTYIN macro (Section 8.5), and then prints them using the .PUTSTR macro (Section 8.4). Note that the loop beginning at L2 gets a string of characters, one character at a time, storing these characters in successive bytes of S. When a <CR> <LF> sequence is found, it marks the end of the string with a null byte, and increments the pointer array index. The address of the first character of each string is stored in P prior to getting the string. Note that alternatively we could

```
        .TITLE EXAMPLE 12.5
CR=13
LF=10
NSTR=3  ;NUMBER OF STRINGS
;
        .ENTRY  START,0
;
;       FILL STRING ARRAY FROM KEYBOARD
;
        CLRL    R1              ;INIT. P INDEX
        MOVL    #S,R2           ;INIT. S INDEX
L1:     MOVL    R2,P[R1]        ;STORE STRING ADDR IN P[R1]
L2:     .TTYIN                  ;GET CHAR FROM KEYBOARD
        CMPB    R0,#CR          ;IF CR
        BEQLU   L2              ;   GET LF.
        CMPB    R0,#LF          ;IF LF
        BEQLU   EOS             ;    IT IS END OF STRING.
        MOVB    R0,(R2)+        ;STORE CHAR IN S
        BRB     L2              ;GET NEXT CHARACTER
EOS:    CLRB    (R2)+           ;MARK END OF STRING
        INCL    R1              ;INCREMENT P INDEX
        CMPL    R1,#NSTR        ;REPEAT
        BLSSU   L1              ;   NSTR TIMES.
;
;       PRINT STRING ARRAY
;
        CLRL    R1              ;INIT. LCV/INDEX
L3:     MOVL    P[R1],R0        ;PRINT
        .PUTSTR                 ;    STRING.
        INCL    R1              ;INCREMENT INDEX
        CMPL    R1,#NSTR        ;REPEAT
        BLSSU   L3              ;    NSTR TIMES.
        $EXIT_S                 ;EXIT TO VMS
P:      .BLKL   64              ;POINTER STORAGE
S:      .BLKB   512             ;STRING STORAGE
        .END    START
```

FIGURE 12.9/Implementation of string storage using method (a) of Figure 12.8

have used the .GETSTR macro (Section E.1) to get the entire string, including the trailing null character. For output, the character-by-character processing is handled by .PUTSTR, so that only one loop is required. Observe that we place the string address into R0 and reference the .PUTSTR macro without argument. We cannot use P[R1] as the argument to .PUTSTR because that would imply that the *string* was located in the P array rather than the *string address*. However, when used without argument, .PUTSTR uses the contents of R0 as the string address.

Methods of string storage (b), (c), and (d) can be implemented in much the same way as (a) is implemented. For (b) it is necessary only to place the characters beginning at the second byte, saving the first byte for a count that is developed during the input process. This count is then placed in the first byte using the address stored in P and Displacement-Deferred addressing. Method (c) does not use a pointer array at all, and increments the S index by a fixed number of bytes after getting each string. Method (d) uses the technique shown in Section 12.3.3. The input process places the string starting address in ADDR(R1); places the characters into S, developing the count at the same time; and then places the count in LEN(R1). Here ADDR is equated to 0, and LEN to 4, by direct assignment. R1 is initialized to the address of P and is incremented by 6 each time through the outer loop. The details of these implementations are left as exercises.

12.6 | Stacks and Queues

The stack, as introduced in Chapter 9, is a data structure in which data items can be conveniently removed in reverse of the order in which they were added. We have already seen an important application of a stack, namely subroutine linkage. In that application, the *User Stack* was employed, which meant that register 14, SP, was used as the pointer to the current top of the stack. However, it is possible to use another register for a pointer, and other stacks can be established at any convenient location in memory. One might set up such a stack whenever it was necessary to access data on a last-in first-out basis, and for some reason it was not desired to employ the User Stack.

When a separate stack is to be used, space must be allocated for it and the pointer must be initialized to its bottom. For example, a stack of 100_{10} longwords (400_{10} bytes) with R5 as its pointer is established and used by the instructions:

```
        MOVL    #S+400,R5    ; INITIALIZE STACK POINTER
          .
          .
          .
        MOVL    B,-(R5)      ; PUSH  B  ONTO  STACK
          .
          .
          .
        MOVL    (R5)+,R1     ; POP STACK INTO R1
          .
          .
          .
        $EXIT_S
S:      .BLKL   100          ; ALLOCATE STACK
```

Note that the pointer always contains the address of the item most recently added to the stack. An instruction with autoincrement addressing for the source operand removes this item. This is called "popping" the stack. Conversely, autodecrement addressing in a destination operand causes a push onto the stack. Care must be exercised to ensure that items are not added beyond the allocated space, leading to stack oveflow. Stack underflow is said to occur when more items are removed than were placed on the stack. If the program logic is such that either overflow or undeflow could possibly occur, the value of the pointer should be compared to the first allocated address before each push, or to the last allocated address before each pop.

The preceding example used a longword stack. It is also possible to have byte, word, or quadword stacks. It is only necessary to change the push and pop to the appropriate forms of the instructions, and to change the storage allocation directive accordingly. Recall that autoincrement and autodecrement addressing change the employed register an amount that is appropriate for the data type.

There are applications that require temporary storage of data items with removal in the same order as entry. A **queue** is a data structure with this property. An example of a need for queue is an **input buffer,** in which keyboard entry is stored prior to its being accessed by the program. Such buffering is needed whenever the rate of accessing the data may be slower than the rate of entry. A stack is inappropriate in this case, because it would provide access in the reverse order of entry.

Implementation of queues requires two pointers. One points to the next item available for removal, called the FRONT, and another points to the next place where a new item can be placed, called the REAR. This is shown in Figure 12.10. In Figure 12.10(a) the characters A,B,C,D, and E have been entered, and none have been removed. In Figure 12.10(b), A,B, and C have been removed and F and G have been inserted. Normally, insertions at REAR and removal at FRONT proceed as independent processes, except removal stops when the queue becomes empty. The empty condition is indicated by FRONT becoming equal to REAR.

Obviously, if there is continuing input the space allocated for the queue will eventually be overrun with the process described above. That is, both FRONT and REAR will advance beyond the allocated space in main memory. To avoid this, the pointers are simply reset back to the beginning of the allocated storage when the end is reached. This creates what is called a **circular queue** or **buffer.** Parts (c) and (d) of Figure 12.10 show the condition after both have "wrapped around" and started over.

Implementation of circular queues is easily done in MACRO. Sufficient space is allocated to handle the largest anticipated number of items; this will depend upon the expected relative rates of insertions and removals. Two registers are used as pointers, and are initialized to 0. The displacement addressing mode using these registers then allows insertion or removal. This is shown in Figure 12.11.

The BICL instruction in Figure 12.11 has the effect of resetting the pointer registers to 0 when they are incremented beyond the allocated 255_{10} bytes. Note that a check is made prior to removal to be sure that the queue is not empty. This assumes that the queue is large enough to ensure that overflow cannot occur. If overflow is anticipated, an additional check has to be made to distinguish between the empty and full conditions.

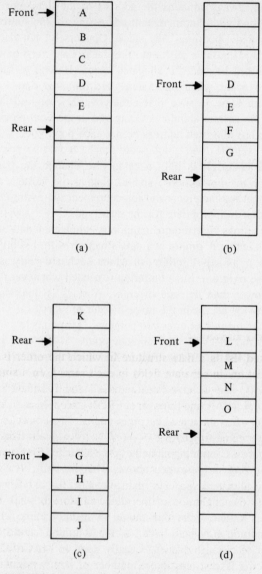

FIGURE 12.10/Circular input queue

```
        CLRL        R0                      ; REAR POINTER
        CLRL        R1                      ; FRONT POINTER
            .
            .
            .
        MOVB        B,Q(R0)                 ; ADD ITEM AT REAR
        INCL        R0                      ; ADVANCE REAR POINTER
        BICL        #^XFFFFFF00,R0          ; WRAP AROUND
            .
            .
            .
        CMPL        R0,R1                   ; CAN'T REMOVE
        BEQLU       L                       ;   IF EMPTY
        MOVB        Q(R1),C                 ; REMOVE ITEM FROM FRONT
        INCL        R1                      ; ADVANCE FRONT POINTER
        BICL        #^XFFFFFF00,R0          ; WRAP AROUND
L:          .
            .
            .
        $EXIT_S
Q:      .BLKB  255                          ; BUFFER OF 255 BYTES
```

FIGURE 12.11/Use of a circular buffer

12.7 | Linked Lists

A **linked list** is a data structure in which the order is established by one or more pointers that are in separate fields in each record. In a singly linked list, each record contains a pointer to the next record, while a doubly linked list contains a pointer to the next record and one to the previous record. "Next" and "previous" here refer to the order in which the records are to be accessed. This is called the **logical order,** as opposed to the **physical order,** of storage in main memory. The program will access a record and, after processing it, get the pointer out of it. This pointer is then used to address the next record to be processed. Linked lists are often used for tables that require efficient insertion or deletion of records, as well as for other purposes.

As an example of a singly-linked list, let us consider the table of names and scores shown in Figure 12.4. This is redrawn with an added field for the pointer in Figure 12.12. The pointer field has been added at the right, but could be anywhere in the record. It is called NEXT, because it contains the address of the next record. For convenience, we have shown the records in physically sequential memory locations beginning at 02AF, although in general the records of a linked list can be scattered throughout the memory.

Accessing a linked list requires the address of the first item to be at some known location. This is most conveniently done by creating a dummy record called BASE with the same format as the actual records. The address of the logically first list record is stored in the NEXT field of BASE. It can reside anywhere in memory.

As noted above, the access order of the records is determined by the addresses stored in the NEXT field of the records. As a concrete example of this, Figure 12.12 shows addresses in these fields that would allow access in order of the scores, from

BASE (033F)	/////////////	/////////////	02FF

|◀── 10 BYTES ──▶| 2 BYTES | 4 BYTES |

	NAME	SCORE	NEXT
TABLE (02AF)	SMITH	77	031F
02BF	JOHNSON	90	030F
02CF	WELLINGTON	56	032F
02DF	STUMP	65	02CF
02EF	DAVIDSON	72	02DF
02FF	GARCIA	95	02BF
030F	EDWARDS	82	02AF
031F	JONES	77	02EF
032F	ROBERTSON	52	033F

FIGURE 12.12/Table as a linked list

highest to lowest. As shown, it is said to be "sorted" according to the score field. In a later example we will see how these addresses can be established. Observe that BASE has 02FF in the NEXT field, which is the address of the record with the highest score. If the record at 02FF is examined, we see in its NEXT field the address of 02BF, the record which has the second highest score, 90. This continues down to the record with the lowest score, which points back to BASE.

Successive records in a linked list can be accessed using the displacement addressing mode. For example, to place the second highest score in R0 we would write:

```
NEXT  = 12
SCORE = 10
      MOVL    #BASE,R1     ; GET ADDR OF BASE
      MOVL    NEXT(R1),R1  ; GET ADDR OF 1ST REC
      MOVL    NEXT(R1),R1  ; GET ADDR OF 2ND REC
      MOVZWL  SCORE(R1),R0 ; GET SCORE OF 2ND REC
```

In the first instruction, we get the address of the BASE dummy record, 033F, into R1. The operand NEXT(R1) in the second instruction then refers to the contents of the NEXT field in BASE, namely 02FF, which gets placed into R1. Then the third instruction updates R1 to the contents of the NEXT field in the record at 02FF, namely, 02BF. Finally, the contents of the SCORE field in the record at 02BF, i.e., 90, is moved into R0 with zero-fill into the high word. This suggests the following scheme for printing all of the scores in highest-to-lowest order:

```
      MOVL    #BASE,R1
L:    MOVL    NEXT(R1),R1
      MOVZWL  SCORE(R1),R0
      .PUTHEX
      CMPL    NEXT(R1),#BASE
      BNEQU   L
```

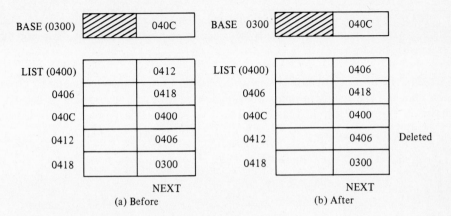

FIGURE 12.13/Deleting record from linked list

Here we use the .PUTHEX macro, which prints the contents of R0 in hexadecimal (see Section 4.11). Observe that the loop termination relies on the fact that we use the convention of linking the last record back to BASE. Other conventions are also employed.

When programming with linked list data structures, it is necessary to be able to create the linked list in the desired order, access records in it, delete records from it, and add new records to it. We have already seen how to access it. Deleting a record from it means simply breaking the record out of the chain and relinking the adjacent records. To see the process required, let us consider how to delete the record containing 'CC' in the linked list of five records in Figure 12.13. Since we access records by using the NEXT field contents, it is only necessary to change this field in the record that logically precedes the one to be deleted. Specifically, it must be changed to the address of the record that logically follows the deleted record. Thus the record containing 'BB' is given the NEXT address of the 'DD', record 0406 in this example. Note that the "deleted" record is really still there; it is simply ignored during subsequent list accesses because its address is no longer present in the chain.

The instructions for deleting must include a search for the record to be deleted. Usually this is based on the contents of some field. During the search, the address of the *previous* record is always retained in another register to facilitate its change when the target record is found. This is demonstrated by the following code, which carries out the operation suggested in Figure 12.13.

```
        F=0
        NEXT=2
        RECLEN=6
           MOVL   #BASE,R1
    L:     MOVL   R1,R0              ; SAVE PREVIOUS REC PTR
           MOVL   NEXT(R1),R1       ; UPDATE POINTER
           CMPL   R1,#BASE          ; EXIT IF
           BEQLU  OUT               ; NOT FOUND
           CMPW   F(R1),#^A'CC'     ; IS IT "CC"?
           BEQLU  DELETE            ; IF YES THEN DELETE
           BRB    L                 ; ELSE CONTINUE
    DELETE:    MOVL   NEXT(R1),NEXT(R0)
    OUT:
```

Let us now take up the matter of creating a linked list in a particular order. In the process, we will see how new records are added to such a list, completing our repertoire of linked list operations.

EXAMPLE 12.6 Let us consider how to create the list as shown in Figure 12.12, and then print out the scores in order from highest to lowest. The program to do this is shown in Figure 12.14. In Figure 12.14(a) we see that the problem is divided into

```
          .TITLE    EXAMPLE 12.6
;
;         SORTED LINKED LIST
;
;
NREC   = 9                 ;NUMBER OF RECORDS
NAME   = 0                 ;NAME DISPLACEMENT IN RECORD
SCORE  = 10                ;SCORE DISPLACEMENT IN RECORD
NEXT   = 12                ;NEXT RECORD POINTER DISPLACEMENT IN RECORD
RECLEN = 16                ;RECORD LENGTH
TABLEN = NREC*RECLEN       ;LENGTH OF TABLE
;
          .ENTRY    START,0
;
;   READ TABLE LEAVING NEXT RECORD POINTER FIELD BLANK
;
          CLRL      R3                ;INIT. LCV/INDEX
          MOVL      #TABLE,R1         ;INIT RECORD POINTER
          MOVL      #TABLE+NAME,R2    ;INIT POINTER TO NAME
L1:       MOVL      R2,R0             ;GET
          .GETSTR                     ;   NAME.
          .GETHEX                     ;GET
          MOVW      R0,SCORE(R1)      ;   SCORE.
          ADDL      #RECLEN,R1        ;ADVANCE TO
          ADDL      #RECLEN,R2        ;   NEXT RECORD.
          INCL      R3                ;INC LCV/INDEX
          CMPL      R3,#NREC          ;REPEAT
          BLSSU     L1                ;   NREC TIMES.
;
;   DO INSERT SORT TO LINK THE TABLE
;
          MOVL      #BASE,BASE+NEXT   ;INITIALIZE EMPTY LIST
          MOVL      #TABLE,R2         ;INITIALIZE LCV/REC. POINTER
L2:       BSBW      LINK              ;LINK NEXT RECORD INTO LIST
          ADDL      #RECLEN,R2        ;ADVANCE RECORD POINTER
          CMPL      R2,#EOT           ;IF NOT LAST RECORD
          BLSSU     L2                ;   THEN CONTINUE.
;
;   PRINT ORDERED SCORES
;
          MOVL      #BASE,R1          ;INIT.REC PTR TO BASE
L3:       MOVL      NEXT(R1),R1       ;GET RECORD POINTER
          MOVZWL    SCORE(R1),R0      ;GET SCORE
          .PUTHEX                     ;PRINT SCORE
          CMPL      NEXT(R1),#BASE    ;IF MORE RECORDS
          BNEQU     L3                ;   THEN CONTINUE.
          $EXIT_S                     ;EXIT TO VMS
```

FIGURE 12.14/Sorting a linked list: (a) read table and sort

```
;
LINK:
;
;    SUBROUTINE TO INSERT RECORD INTO LINKED LIST
;    SORTED BY SCORE FIELD. RECORD POINTED AT BY
;    R2 IS INSERTED BEFORE THE FIRST SMALLER SCORE
;    OR AT THE END OF THE LINKED LIST.
;
          MOVL    #BASE,R0          ;START SEARCH AT BASE
AGAIN:    MOVL    R0,R1             ;SAVE PREVIOUS SEARCH PTR.
          MOVL    NEXT(R0),R0       ;ADVANCE SEARCH POINTER
          CMPL    R0,#BASE          ;IF END OF LINKED LIST
          BEQLU   INSERT            ;   THEN ADD AT END.
          CMPW    SCORE(R0),SCORE(R2);DOES IT BELONG HERE?
          BLSSU   INSERT            ;   IF SO,INSERT IT
          BRB     AGAIN             ;   ELSE LOOK FURTHER.
INSERT:   MOVL    NEXT(R1),NEXT(R2) ;LINK NEW RECORD
          MOVL    R2,NEXT(R1)       ;RELINK PRECEDING RECORD.
          RSB                       ;RETURN TO CALLER
;
TABLE:    .BLKB   NREC*RECLEN       ;NREC RECS. OF RECLEN BYTES
EOT=TABLE+TABLEN                    ;ADDRESS OF END OF TABLE
BASE:     .BLKB   RECLEN            ;DUMMY BASE RECORD
          .END    START
```

FIGURE 12.14/Sorting a linked list: (b) inserting a record

three tasks. First, the table is entered and stored exactly as it was in Example 12.3. Observe that we have added a NEXT field simply by changing RECLEN and adding the displacement definition to the direct assignments. However, we do not read anything into this field. The second task links the records by filling the NEXT field with the correct addresses. This task begins by placing the *address* of the dummy BASE record into its own NEXT field. This, in effect, creates an empty linked list, i.e., the base is linked to itself. Then a loop is entered that steps through the table in physical order. Each time through the loop the address of the next record is placed in R2 and a branch is made to subroutine LINK. LINK, shown in Figure 12.14(b), "inserts" the record whose address is in R2 into the linked list. As we shall see below, the record itself is not moved. Rather, the correct linking address is found and placed in its NEXT field. After linking the table, the scores are printed out in the manner discussed previously. Because the linking was done according to the score, these values are accessed and printed in order from highest to lowest.

The principal new concepts of this example are embodied in Figure 12.14(b) where the LINK subroutine is shown. This is a "search and insert" process. That is, we first step through the table (in its logical order) looking for the right place to insert the new record. When we find it, we break the chain and insert the new record. We will now consider these two functions one at a time.

The search process uses a loop structure much like that used in deleting a record. At any given state of the process, there will be some number of records (initially 0) already linked into the list. We step through this list using the NEXT field contents of each record, after placing it in R0, as a "search pointer" to point to the next record to be examined. A copy of the previous search pointer is always placed in R1 so that it can be used in the insertion process at the conclusion of the search. When the search pointer is updated, we compare it to the address of BASE. If R0 ever becomes equal to BASE we know that the end of the current linked list has been encountered, and we branch to the instructions to insert the new record at the end of the list. Otherwise, we compare the SCORE field contents of the search record with that of the new record. (The latter is pointed at by R2.) If the search record score is less than the new one, we have found the correct position, i.e., it belongs immediately before the first score that it exceeds. At this point a branch is made to the insert instructions. Observe that the search process can conclude with one of two outcomes: a record with a lower score to place the new record in front of, or no such record. In *either* case, the new record is to be placed immediately after the "previous" record. Moreover, the address of this record is always in R1.

The insertion process itself is very simple, requiring only two steps:

1. The NEXT field of the new record has to be set to the address of the record that is to *follow* it in the list. Note that the needed address is available in the NEXT field of what we have called the "previous" record.

2. The NEXT field of the previous record has to be set to the address of the record that is to *precede* it in the list. Note that the address needed here is simply that of the new record.

These steps are shown diagrammatically in Figure 12.15. The MACRO instructions for the insertion are:

```
MOVL   NEXT(R1),NEXT (R2)
MOVL   R2,NEXT(R1)
```

Note that the order of these instructions is critical. If these steps are performed out of order, the address of the succeeding record is overwritten and the chain cannot be relinked.

Before leaving Example 12.6, several observations are in order. First, let us re-emphasize that the records need not be located contiguously in memory. They were

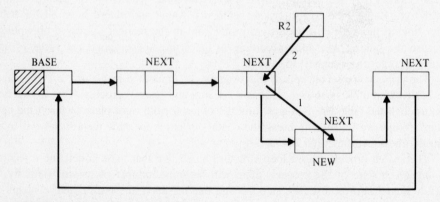

FIGURE 12.15/Insertion into linked list

contiguously located in this example simply because this was the most convenient way to create the table in the first place. In some programs it may be preferable to establish a large region of memory for miscellaneous data storage, and place each new record in any unused location in this region. In this case, a routine can be written that locates the required number of unused locations and returns the starting address. The record data is then written into it, and the NEXT field is set to the correct address to link it into the list. Indeed, one of the principal virtues provided by linked lists is the ability to do dynamic storage allocation in this way. The access, insert, delete, and add operations presented here work equally well with this scheme of storage allocation.

Finally, it should be observed that any field in the record can be used as the basis for setting the linking order. For example, instead of comparing the score fields, we could have used the CMPC3 instruction (Section 7.9) to compare the strings in the NAME field. In this manner the records could be linked alphabetically with only minor changes in the program.

12.8 | Summary

This chapter has dealt with two major topics, namely VAX-11 addressing modes and data structures in MACRO.

First, we examined the full set of VAX-11 addressing modes, both from assembly code and machine code viewpoints. Some of this was review, because most modes were introduced by way of examples in earlier chapters. However, by looking at them all together, we were better able to see certain similarities and differences. For one thing, we saw that there are only four basic general register modes (Register, Autoincrement, Autodecrement, and Displacement) and three other modes that are simply *deferred* or indirect versions of three of the basic four. (There is no deferred version of autodecrement.) Because the basic autoincrement and displacement are themselves deferred, however, their so-called deferred versions are actually *second-level* deferred modes. The advantage of thinking of the addressing modes as two groups is that the deferred modes are then seen as simple extensions of the basic modes, rather than as completely different modes.

The general register modes (both basic and deferred) are further extended by the **Indexed mode,** which is really just an argumentation of other modes. That is, it cannot be used by itself. Each of the basic modes except register addressing, as well as their deferred counterparts, can be indexed by placing [Ri] as a suffix to the normal mnemonics. The normal mnemonics then determine a base address to which the *product* of the index register contents and the operand length is added to get the actual operand address. Thus this mode allows indexing very similar to the meaning of the term in connection with arrays in high-level languages.

Another mode discussed was the **Short Literal mode,** first discussed in Chapter 5. We learned that this mode is quite different from the general register modes in that the operand value is embedded in the operand specifier. This can be used for small literal operands and provides program size and speed efficiencies.

Our re-examination of addressing modes also pointed out that the so-called immediate and relative modes are really just special cases of the true VAX-11 addressing modes. The methods called **absolute** and **relative-deferred** addressing, the latter introduced for the first time in the chapter, are similar in this respect. Together, these are referred to as **Program Counter** addressing methods, and are among the more widely used methods. The Program Counter addressing modes can also be indexed.

The data structures covered in the chapter included **arrays, tables, strings, stacks, queues, and linked lists.** Our goal was to briefly introduce the underlying concepts of each of these, and show how they are implemented in MACRO.

We saw that arrays can employ one or more indexes to identify their elements. The number of indexes is called the **dimensionality** of the array. One-dimensional arrays are straightforward, because they correspond exactly to the inherently linear organization of the main memory. Two-dimensional arrays require some scheme for storing linearly, while allowing location of elements using the two separate (row and column) indexes. Either row-major or column-major storage meets this need.

A powerful concept is found in arrays of records, which can be called **tables.** The central idea here is that each array element is a group of adjacent bytes in memory called a **record.** Each record is divided into several **fields** that can be of any length and can contain any type of data. We found that data items in a table are addressed by a *pointer* that selects the record plus a *displacement* of the desired field from the beginning of the record. The displacement addressing mode, together with direct assignment of mnemonic names to field displacements, facilitates access to the data.

The use of tables or arrays brings up the matter of accessing order. In this connection we explored different ways in which arrays and tables can be sorted according to one of the fields. The particular method called **index sort** was demonstrated in an example. Here we sorted a separate array of indexes which could then be used to control the order of access to the records in the table.

The concept of **character strings** as data entities was also discussed. We saw that there are a number of ways that a group of character strings can be stored, including null-terminated sequences, and sequences with a preceding count byte. An auxiliary array of addresses keeps track of where each string begins. It is also possible to store the byte count along with the string addresses in the auxiliary array, so that the strings themselves can be stored without intervening markers or counts.

The final topic discussed here was **linked lists.** We focused on singly linked lists, although other forms are possible. This data structure requires that the records include a field for a pointer, i.e., an address, to the next record. By *next* we refer to the *logical order,* or the order of access. Physically, the records can be located anywhere in memory, not necessarily contiguously. Once any record is accessed, the pointer to the next record can be extracted from the field that we called NEXT using indexed addressing. We developed techniques for creating such a list from a sequential table, linking it according to descending order in a particular field. This, in effect, creates a "sorted" list, although the records themselves are not moved. We also discussed how to access the linked list, how to add new records, and how to "delete" records. In the lattermost case, the record is not actually deleted, but rather it is "unlinked" from the chain. The primary advantage of linked lists over sequentially accessed structures is the ease of insertion, deletion, merging, and splitting. Also, linked lists allow for dynamic allocation of storage, a fact that was mentioned without elaboration.

12.9 | Exercises

12.1 Assume the following initializations of registers and memory locations prior to *fetching* of each of the sample instructions given. Provide the translation of each, and indicate all changes in registers and memory locations as a result of its execution.

Register	Contents	Label	Location	Contents
R0	00000004	A:	0500	00000504
R1	00000500	B:	0504	00000508
R2	00000505		0508	0000050C
PC	00001000			

(a)	MOVL A,R0	(b)	MOVL #A,R0
(c)	MOVL @#A,R0	(d)	MOVL @A,R0
(e)	MOVL 500,R0	(f)	MOVL #500,R0
(g)	MOVL @#500,R0	(h)	MOVL @500,R0
(i)	CLRL @4(R1)	(j)	CLRB @4(R1)
(k)	CLRW @(R2)+	(l)	CLRL @(R2)

12.2 Rework Example 12.1 using the following initializations of registers and main memory locations prior to execution of *each* of the instructions given there.

Register	Contents	Location	Contents
		0514	FFFFFFFF
R1	000051C	0518	11111111
R2	0000528	051C	AAAABBBB
R3	0000879	0520	88888888
R4	0000520	0524	00000528
R5	0000003	0528	0000051C
R6	FFFFFFD	052C	12345678
		0530	EEEEEEEE
		0534	ABCDEF10

12.3 Develop a subroutine that will add two one-dimensional arrays, producing their sum in a third array. Use Indexed addressing. Transmit the address of the argument list in R5 (see Section 9.8.4).

12.4 Develop a program that accepts a two-dimensional array from the keyboard in row-major order and stores it in column-major form. Allocate sufficient space for arrays containing as many as 0200_{16} total elements. The number of rows and columns should be read from the keyboard first. Use .GETHEX or a suitable alternative for keyboard input.

12.5 Write a subroutine that will compute row averages for an array with M rows and N columns. Assume that the array is stored in row-major form. Transmit the address of the argument list in R5 (see Section 9.8.4).

12.6 Write a program that accepts row and column indexes from the keyboard and prints the corresponding element of the T array shown in Figure 12.2. Assume that it is stored in column-major form. Use .GETHEX and .PUTHEX or suitable equivalents for I/O.

12.7 Repeat Exercise 12.6, but assume T to be stored in row-major form.

12.8 Assume that there are N students (100 decimal maximum) whose names, student numbers, and test scores (16-bit integers) are to be entered into memory for processing. Write a program that accepts this information from the keyboard and stores it as an array of records, i.e., a table. Use the .GETHEX and .GETSTR macros.

12.9 Develop a program that will accept a student number from the keyboard and print out the corresponding name and test score from the table referred to in Exercise 12.8.

12.10 Do Exercise 12.8 using an index array. Sort according to student number, and print the student numbers and corresponding scores.

12.11 Write a program that functions exactly like that shown in Figure 12.9, but employs the string storage method shown in Figure 12.8(b).

12.12 Write a program that functions exactly like that shown in Figure 12.9, but employs the string storage method shown in Figure 12.8(c).

12.13 Write a program that functions exactly like that shown in Figure 12.9, but employs the string storage method shown in Figure 12.8(d).

12.14 Write a program that accepts hexadecimal numbers continuously from the keyboard, placing them in a circular queue of 0200_{16} longwords. When any nonhex character is entered, the program should print the numbers currently in the queue, and then ask for more numbers. A "Q" should halt the program.

12.15 Do Exercise 12.8 using a linked list.

12.16 Develop a program that provides the user with four commands: ADD (A), DELETE (D), PRINT (P), and HALT (H). If A is entered, it should accept a name and score (16-bit integer) and store them as a linked list of records, ordered according to score. If P is entered, the current list of scores should be printed. If D is entered, a name should be accepted and, if found in the list, the record should be deleted. H should stop the program.

13

Recursive Programming

13.1 | Overview

In Chapter 9 we saw how the User Stack is used for subroutine linkage, and how it can be used for argument transmission. Furthermore, we saw that this method allowed nesting, i.e., subroutines calling other subroutines. In an extension of this same idea, Chapter 13 will show how subroutines can actually call themselves, using the stack for argument transmission and local storage. Mathematically, this concept is known as **recursion** and is characterized by a function being defined in terms of its own definition. The simplest example is the factorial function. The ease with which such functions are coded in MACRO is impressive. Due to the far-reaching importance of recursive algorithms in computer science, and the fact that this will be the first encounter for many readers, we treat this subject in some detail.

13.2 | The Concept of Recursion

In mathematics, a function is said to be *defined recursively* if it is defined in terms of itself. A simple example of this is the factorial function, $n!$, which we shall call $F(n)$. This is understood to be the result of the sequence:

$$n \times (n - 1) \times (n - 2) \times (n - 3) \times \ldots \times (1)$$

Note here that the sequence:

$$(n - 1) \times (n - 2) \times (n - 3) \times \ldots \times (1)$$

is nothing other than $(n - 1)!$. Therefore, a valid definition of $F(n)$ is:

$$F(n) = n! = n \times F(n - 1)$$

which is recursive.

Many functions can be defined in this way. Other examples include:

Power function (x^n):

$$F(0) = 1$$

$$F(n) = x \times F(n - 1)$$

Fibonacci Numbers:

$$F(0) = 0$$

$$F(1) = 1$$

$$F(n) = F(n - 1) + F(n - 2)$$

Present value of unit annual deposit at interest i:

$$F(0) = 0$$

$$F(n) = 1 + (1 + i) \times F(n - 1)$$

In each case, there are one or more **root formulas** that are nonrecursive for particular argument values, as well as the **recursive formula.** Both are essential elements of recursive calculations.

Recursive definition is also applicable to nonnumeric problems. For example, in the design of language processors such as compilers it is necessary to examine general expressions such as:

```
A+B*(C+C*E+X*(A+10)+14)
```

and to generate the machine code to carry out the indicated operations. Recursive procedures can be defined to do such translations. Applications such as this make recursion very important in computer science.

The programming of recursively defined functions or procedures requires certain capabilities of the programming language. In particular, a procedure (i.e., a subroutine or function) has to be able to *call itself.* Many widely used high-level languages (e.g., BASIC and FORTRAN) do not allow this. However, an assembly language that uses a stack for subroutine linkage, such as MACRO, is well suited to the needs of recursive programming.

Before getting into the programming details, let us try to develop a better understanding of the nature of recursion. The factorial function can be used for this purpose. Suppose we wish to compute the factorial of 4 recursively. The steps are as follows.

1.	$F(4) = 4 \times F(3)$	(Cannot complete, so Find $F(3)$.)
2.	$F(3) = 3 \times F(2)$	(Cannot complete, so Find $F(2)$.)
3.	$F(2) = 2 \times F(1)$	(Cannot complete, so Find $F(1)$.)
4.	$F(1) = 1 \times F(0)$	(Cannot complete, so Find $F(0)$.)
5.	$F(0) = 1$	(By root formula.)
6.	$F(1) = 1 \times 1 = 1$	(Complete Step 4.)
7.	$F(2) = 2 \times 1 = 2$	(Complete Step 3.)
8.	$F(3) = 3 \times 2 = 6$	(Complete Step 2.)
9.	$F(4) = 4 \times 6 = 24$	(Complete Step 1.)

We see that evaluation for a high-level argument requires that the function be evaluated for the entire sequence of lower-level arguments, down to the root formula, in this case $F(0) = 1$. This is called the "descent" process. During descent, each attempt to evaluate has to be left "pending" because the result depends on the as-yet-undetermined lower-level evaluations. Once the descent is complete, which is evident when we finally come to an argument that is the root, the "ascent" process begins. This is a matter of working backwards, completing the steps left pending during the descent.

Also, note that the intermediate results obtained during descent have to be saved for use during the ascent process. That is, in the example above, we had to retain the successive values of n (4,3,2, and 1) in order to carry out the multiplications during ascent. This is an important consideration when recursive routines are programmed. It is also important to note that these values are needed in the *reverse* of the order in which they are calculated. This suggests that a stack will be the ideal data structure for recursion.

Many problems can be programmed either recursively or otherwise. For example, other algorithms for the factorial function are easily devised. In general, a recursive algorithm will require more steps and more memory than will the alternatives. The reason recursion is used, then, is not to achieve efficiency, but because the algorithms are often (though not always) less complicated and easier to program. The first example used here, the factorial function, has been chosen for its familiarity. It is, however, a poor example because it happens to have a recursive algorithm that is both less efficient and more complicated than the alternative. As another example, therefore, we will look at a recursive implementation of a sorting method, called Quicksort, which is much simpler than its nonrecursive alternatives.

13.3 | Recursive Programming Examples

EXAMPLE 13.1   The factorial function is a convenient problem for demonstrating recursive programming. Not only is it a familiar relationship, but it has only one argument, n, and uses only one previous value of the function. A flowchart showing a recursive algorithm for this function is given in Figure 13.1. The corresponding MACRO subroutine and a calling program are shown in Figure 13.2.

The stack plays a major role in this algorithm. The number for which the factorial is to be found, n, is on top of the stack when control is passed to the subroutine. Upon return to the calling point, the result ($n!$) will be on top of the stack, having replaced the argument. Immediately upon entry, the stack contents are:

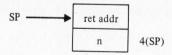

The organization of the stack during recursive calls must be kept in mind so that information can be extracted as needed. All arguments and intermediate results can be addressed from the *current* SP, regardless of the depth of recursion.

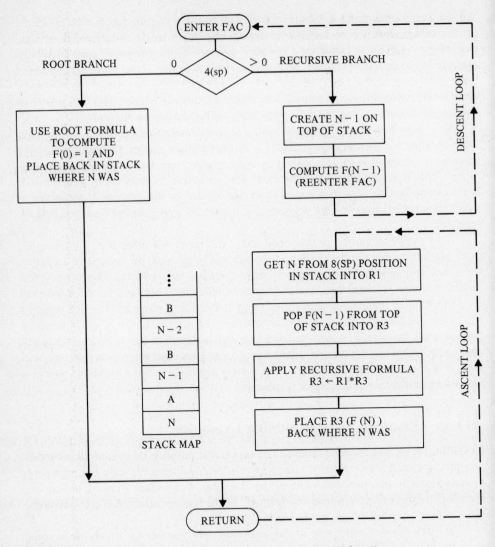

FIGURE 13.1/Flowchart for recursive calculation of the factorial function

There are two cases to be considered with this algorithm, depending upon the value of *n*. First we consider the case when *n* = 0, as would arise due to the instruction sequence:

```
MOVL    #0,-(SP)
BSBW    FAC
```

Upon return, we expect the factorial of 0, i.e., 1, to be on top of the stack.

As can be seen in Figures 13.1 and 13.2, the value of *n* is examined by testing 4(SP), because *n* is four bytes (one longword) below the current stack pointer. Since

```
            .TITLE   EXAMPLE 13.1
;
;           RECURSIVE FACTORIAL
;
            .ENTRY   START,0
            .PUTSTR  M1              ;PRINT PROMPT
            .GETHEX                  ;GET N FROM KEYBOARD
            MOVL     R0,-(SP)        ;PUT N INTO STACK
            BSBW     FAC             ;COMPUTE FACTORIAL
A:          .PUTSTR  M2              ;PRINT LABEL FOR RESULT
            MOVL     (SP)+,R0        ;POP N! FROM STACK
            .PUTHEX                  ;PRINT N!
            $EXIT_S                  ;EXIT TO VMS
M1:         .ASCIZ/ENTER N/
M2:         .ASCIZ/N! IS:/
;
;           END OF MAIN
;
FAC:
            TSTL     4(SP)           ;SEE IF ROOT CASE.
            BEQLU    FAC0            ;IF SO,BR TO FAC0
            MOVL     4(SP),-(SP)     ;IF NOT,SET UP
            DECL     (SP)            ;  (N-1) AS ARGUMENT.
            BSBW     FAC             ;     AND RECURSE.
B:          MOVL     8(SP),R1        ;GET N
            MOVL     (SP)+,R3        ;POP F(N-1)
            MULL     R1,R3           ;F(N)=N*F(N-1)
            MOVL     R3,4(SP)        ;PUT F(N) IN STACK.
            BRB      OUT
FAC0:
            INCL     4(SP)           ;F(0)=1
OUT:        RSB                      ;RETURN TO CALLING POINT
;
;           END OF FAC
;
            .END     START
```

FIGURE 13.2/MACRO implementation of recursive factorial algorithm

the contents of 4(SP) is zero, the branch takes place and the zero at 4(SP) is replaced by its factorial, namely, 1. This is followed immediately by a return to the calling point, leaving the factorial of the argument on top of the stack, as promised.

The more interesting case is when n is greater than 0. As an example, suppose the following instruction sequence is executed:

```
            MOVL     #2,-(SP)
            BSBW     FAC
A:
```

Upon reaching the TSTL 4(SP) instruction in FAC, the test fails and the recursive part of the algorithm is executed.

The recursive part of the algorithm can be explained either intuitively or precisely. The intuitive explanation requires that one simply *believe* that recursion works, without worrying about how it works. That is, when we discover that the argument is greater than zero, we set about to calculate $F(n)$ by the recursive formula:

$$F(n) = n \times F(n - 1)$$

To do this, we need $F(n - 1)$. Since we have a great deal of confidence that our subroutine FAC *will* compute the factorial of a number, we simply use it to compute $F(n - 1)$. That is, we place $n - 1$ on top of the stack and execute BSBW FAC. Upon return, $F(n - 1)$ is on top of the stack, and we can proceed with calculation of $F(n)$ by the recursive formula. This line of reasoning requires a certain boldness, but it is very effective in the design of recursive algorithms. The precise explanation, given below, should be understood, but its details tend to obscure rather than enlighten when one is designing a recursive algorithm.

The precise explanation of the recursive part of Figures 13.1 and 13.2 requires that we examine what happens when the BSBW FAC is executed from within FAC. This can best be explained by observing the evolution of the stack as shown in Figure 13.3 for calculation of 2!. For convenience of discussion, we have labeled the instructions immediately after the BSBW FAC in the main program and subroutine as A and B, respectively. Parts (a), (b), and (c) of Figure 13.3 show the states upon subroutine entry. There are three such states because FAC gets called once from the main program, and twice from itself. Parts (d), (e), and (f) show the states after the three successive returns.

On the first call from the main program, the stack has the main program return point on top, and the primary argument in the second position. Because that argument

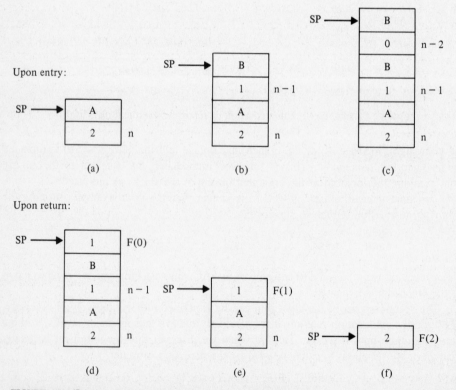

FIGURE 13.3/States of stack during recursive calculation of 2!

pointed at by 4(SP) is 2 rather than 0, the branch to FAC0 is not executed. Instead, the primary argument is duplicated on top of the stack and decremented, forming $2 - 1 = 1$. The BSBW FAC is then executed, creating the stack state shown in Figure 13.3(b) upon re-entry. The value pointed at by 4(SP) is now 1, so it is again placed on top of the stack and decremented. This is followed by BSBW FAC, so that the procedure is re-entered with the stack state shown in Figure 13.3(c). Now the value pointed at by 4(SP) is 0, so the branch to FAC0 is executed. This results in the 0 in 4(SP) being incremented to 1 (creating F(0)), and RSB is executed for the first time. This return, however, is to B, still inside FAC, because that is the address on top of the stack. The state of the stack at this point is shown in Figure 13.3(d). The instructions at B apply the recursive formula, taking the "current" $n = 1$ (really the original $n - 1$) out of position 4(SP) and $F(n - 1) = 1$ off of the top. The latter is done with a pop so that SP points to the correct return address. After the MULL instruction forms $n \times F(n - 1) = 1$, this value is placed in 4(SP), which is where SP will point after the next return. This second return is also to B, with the stack state shown in Figure 13.3(e). The actions which then take place are exactly the same as before, only this time the operands for the multiply are $n = 2$ and $F(n - 1) = 1$, so that $F(2)$ is formed and placed in 4(SP). The third return is then executed, this time causing return to the main program with $F(2) = 2$ on top of the stack.

It is helpful to think of the process just described as recursive descent, followed by ascent. This is shown by the dashed lines in the flowchart in Figure 13.1. Note that the descent loop will continue until the value pointed at by 4(SP) is 0. Every time it goes through this loop, it leaves an n and the *internal* return point (B) on the stack. When it finally takes the ROOT branch, the return will therefore be to B. This puts it in the ascent loop where it works its way back down through the stack, computing the successive factorials. It will exit the ascent loop when it works its way down to the A return point placed in the stack by the call from the main program.

EXAMPLE 13.2   Quicksort is a well-known, general-purpose sorting algorithm that has an elegant recursive implementation. It is discussed in many texts on data structures and algorithms, so we will not provide an in-depth discussion here. Instead, we will follow the algorithm as described by Sedgewick (*Algorithms*, Addison-Wesley, 1983) as we implement Quicksort in VAX MACRO.

The basic idea of Quicksort is that two small lists can usually be sorted faster than one large list. Using this idea, the original list, here called a[L], . . . , a [R], is partitioned into three parts:

left sublist : a[i] : right sublist

where a[i] is called the *partitioning* element. Now, if we can be sure that all elements in the left sublist are less than or equal to a[i], and all those in the right sublist are greater than or equal to a[i], we can sort the two sublists separately and still arrive at a properly sorted combined list. Then the basic algorithm can be described as in Figure 13.4.

This algorithm is recursive in that it is reinvoked from within itself to sort each sublist. Note that each recursive call is with a smaller sublist, and the IF R > L test will therefore eventually fail. This is the root case, requiring no action since R < = L implies an empty or single-element sublist.

```
Quicksort (L,R)
BEGIN

1. IF R > L
   THEN
      BEGIN

         1.1 Partition the list to get i.;
         1.2 Quicksort (L, i −1);
         1.3 Quicksort (i +1, R);

      END;

   ELSE
      Do nothing;
END;
```

FIGURE 13.4/Recursive Quicksort algorithm expressed as pseudocode

It is evident that the partitioning step is the key to the algorithm. The objective is to choose some element v and put it into its final position a[i] while rearranging the other elements such that the previously stated conditions on a[i] are satisfied. An efficient algorithm for doing this is given by Sedgewick and shown in Figure 13.5.

```
Partition (L,R,i)
BEGIN

1. v = a[R];
2. i = L −1;
3. j = R;
4. REPEAT
      4.1 REPEAT
             i = i + 1
          UNTIL a[i] >= v;
      4.2 REPEAT
             j = j − 1
          UNTIL a[j] <= v;
      4.3 Exchange a[i] and a[j];
      UNTIL j < = i;
5. Exchange a[i] and a[j];
6. Exchange a[i] and a[R];
END;
```

FIGURE 13.5/Partitioning algorithm for Quicksort expressed as pseudocode

The partitioning element, v, is arbitrarily taken as the rightmost element. The algorithm works by scanning the list from the left looking for an a[i] greater than v, and from the right looking for an a[j] less than v. These elements, being obviously out of place, are then exchanged. The process is repeated until the scan indexes cross. The last exchange must then be undone, and finally the partitioning element a[R] put into

```
        .TITLE QUICKSORT
A:      .ASCIC/ALLISQUIETONTHEWESTERNFRONT/
        .BYTE 0
        .ENTRY  START,0
        .PUTSTR A+1             ;PRINT ORIGINAL STRING
        MOVZBL  #1,-(SP)        ;PUSH L ONTO STACK
        MOVZBL  A,-(SP)         ;PUSH R ONTO STACK (STRING LENGTH)
        BSBW    QUICK           ;DO A QUICKSORT
        .PUTSTR A+1             ;PRINT SORTED STRING
        $EXIT_S                 ;EXIT TO VMS
;
;    QUICKSORT IMPLEMENTED AS A RECURSIVE SUBROUTINE
;
R     = 0                      ;CALL FRAME
I     = 4                      ;    OFFSETS.
SPACE = 8                      ;FRAME SPACE
RET:    .LONG 1                ;TEMP STORAGE FOR RETURN ADDRESS
QUICK:
        MOVL    (SP)+,RET       ;GET RETURN ADDRESS
        MOVL    (SP)+,R7        ;GET R
        MOVL    (SP)+,R6        ;GET L
        MOVL    RET,-(SP)       ;PUSH RETURN ADDRESS BACK ON STACK
        MOVL    FP,-(SP)        ;SAVE FRAME POINTER
        SUBL    #SPACE,SP       ;SET UP STACK SPACE
        MOVL    SP,FP           ;    FOR RECURSION PROTECTED STORAGE.
        CMPL    R7,R6           ;RETURN WHEN
        BLEQ    OUT             ;    R<=L.
;
        BSBB    PARTIT          ;PARTITION THE STRING
;
        MOVL    R9,I(FP)        ;SAVE I AND R FOR
        MOVL    R7,R(FP)        ;    USE AFTER FIRST RECURSIVE CALL.
        MOVZBL  R6,-(SP)        ;PUSH L
        MOVZBL  R9,-(SP)        ;PUSH
        DECL    (SP)            ;    I-1.
;
        BSBW    QUICK           ;SORT LEFT SUBSTRING
;
        MOVZBL  I(FP),-(SP)     ;PUSH
        INCL    (SP)            ;    I+1.
        MOVZBL  R(FP),-(SP)     ;PUSH R
;
        BSBW    QUICK           ;SORT RIGHT SUBSTRING
;
OUT:    ADDL    #SPACE,SP       ;FREE STACK FRAME
        MOVL    (SP)+,FP        ;RESTORE FRAME POINTER
        RSB
;
```

FIGURE 13.6/Recursive MACRO implementation of Quicksort: (a) Main program and Quicksort

```
PARTIT: MOVB    A[R7],R8        ;CURRENT V TO R8
        SUBL3   #1,R6,R9        ;INITIALIZE I
        MOVL    R7,R10          ;INITIALIZE J
LO:
L1:     INCL    R9              ;LOCATE V IN A
        CMPB    A[R9],R8        ;    FROM
        BLSSU   L1              ;        LEFT.
L2:     DECL    R10             ;LOCATE V IN A
        CMPB    A[R10],R8       ;    FROM
        BGTRU   L2              ;        RIGHT.
        MOVB    A[R9],T         ;INTERCHANGE
        MOVB    A[R10],A[R9]    ;    A[I]
        MOVB    T,A[R10]        ;        AND A[J].
        CMPL    R10,R9          ;REPEAT UNTIL WE GET THE
        BGTR    LO              ;    PARTITIONING ELEMENT.
        MOVB    A[R9],A[R10]    ;UNDO LAST EXCHANGE AND
        MOVB    A[R7],A[R9]     ;    PUT PARTITIONING
        MOVB    T,A[R7]         ;        ELEMENT INTO PLACE.
        RSB
T:      .BLKB   1               ;TEMP STORAGE FOR EXCHANGE
;
        .END    START
```

FIGURE 13.6/Recursive MACRO implementation of Quicksort: (b) partition

place by exchanging a[R] and a[i]. The index of the partitioning element, i, is returned. You can demonstrate that the process does partition a list in the desired manner by applying it to a short list of integers.

The preceding algorithms are implemented in MACRO in Figure 13.6. In part (a) of this figure we see Quicksort and a calling program that sorts the character string:

"ALLISQUIETONTHEWESTERNFRONT"

into the order of ascending ASCII codes. The partition algorithm is in Figure 13.6(b).

The algorithm itself is best understood in terms of the pseudocode in Figures 13.4 and 13.5. The important lesson in Figure 13.6 is the way the User Stack is employed in the assembly implementation. As in Example 13.1, argument transmission is through the stack. Now, however, we have the added problem of retaining data *other than the arguments* while the recursive call is executed. To see the need for this, note in Figure 13.4 that we need both i and R *after* the first recursive call. We cannot save these in registers or local storage because they would be changed by the first recursive call. This problem is solved in the MACRO implementation by setting up a *stack frame* upon entry to QUICK. This frame has the following structure:

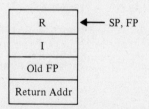

Thus R and I are at fixed offsets from the frame pointer FP, and can therefore be accessed using displacement addressing. Subsequent recursive calls will use the stack *above* this frame, leaving the data stored in the frame undisturbed and available after the call. Note that we also save the old value of FP in the stack so that it can be restored prior to return. This is necessary because the FP gets changed in the recursive call.

Finally, note that local variables such as T, RET, and those stored in registers (j, L, and v) are *not* saved in the stack frame. This is because they are *not* needed after the recursive call, and one should try to keep the stack frame as small as possible.

13.4 | Developing Recursive Subroutines

The ideas used in the previous examples can be generalized to apply to any recursive definition. The general form for recursion formulas that use one recursive evaluation is:

SUB:

1. Set up stack frame for post-recursive local data if needed
2. Conditional branch to root formula, ROOT.
3. Set up arguments for recursive call.
4. Branch to subroutine SUB.
5. Apply recursive formula.
6. Place result in proper place in stack.
7. Reset stack pointer to proper return address.
8. Go to 12.

ROOT:

9. Root formula.
10. Place result in proper place in stack.
11. Reset stack pointer to proper return address.

OUT:

12. RETURN

Arguments are always placed in the stack. In the previous examples we saw that they are accessed using displacement addressing into the stack, i.e., m(SP) where m is the number of bytes that the needed argument is from the top of the stack in a given state. A simple diagram of the stack will help in determining the proper offset in the stack. Often the result is returned on top of the stack. Care must be taken to ensure that the stack pointer points at the most recently added return point when the RSB instruction is reached.

Some recursion algorithms require more than one recursive call. The Fibonacci problem, for example, uses $F(n-1)$ and $F(n-2)$ to compute $F(n)$. Quicksort is another example of this nature. The structure for two recursive calls as in the Fibonacci problem is:

SUB:

1. Set up stack frame for post-recursive local data if needed.
2. Conditional branch to root case 1, ROOT1.
3. Conditional branch to root case 2, ROOT2.
4. Set up arguments for finding $F(n - 1)$.
5. Branch to subroutine SUB.
6. Set up arguments for finding $F(n - 2)$.
7. Branch to subroutine SUB.
8. Apply recursive formula.
9. Place result in proper place in stack.
10. Reset stack pointer to proper return address.
11. Go to **17**.

ROOT1:

12. Root formula 1.
13. Place result in proper place in stack.
14. Go to **17**.

ROOT2:

15. Root formula 2.
16. Place result in proper place in stack.

OUT:

17. RETURN

Although slightly more complicated than the single root case, the principles for the case of two root formulas are the same. It is seen that two recursive calls must be made before the recursion formula can be applied. Also, there are two conditional branches to root formulas. The stack structure is also more complex because of the need for two previous values of the function.

13.5 | Summary

The topic discussed in this chapter was **recursion** and, in particular, **recursive subroutines** in MACRO. We saw that mathematically recursion means that a function is defined in terms of itself, with separately defined "root" formula(s) to get the process started. In programming, recursion implies that a subroutine has a call to itself from within the body of its definition.

When the subroutine is called from outside (the primary call), it will usually be for some large value of argument. As soon as the subroutine determines that the root formula does not apply, it leaves the evaluation pending, decreases the argument, and calls itself (the recursive call) to evaluate for the smaller argument. This call may result in the need for another recursive call, again leaving the calculation pending. This process, called **recursive descent,** continues until the root formula applies. Then the **ascent** process begins, working its way back through the set of pending calculations.

One essential requirement for recursive programming is the retention of the intermediate results of calculations left pending during descent. Another is retention of the correct return point for each recursive call as well as the primary call. The linkage conventions used by the normal BSBW instruction, together with argument transmission through the User Stack, make recursive programming straightforward in MACRO. We saw this demonstrated with simple examples, as well as a generalized approach for more complicated problems.

13.6 | Exercises

13.1   Enter and assemble the program and recursive subroutine shown in Figure 13.2. Assemble and link with the Symbolic Debugger and execute the program with breakpoints set at FAC, A, and B. At each break, examine the stack and verify the states shown in Figure 13.3.

13.2   Create a recursive subroutine to calculate x^n, using integer values of x and n. Demonstrate using the Symbolic Debugger.

13.3   Create a program and recursive subroutine to calculate Fibonacci numbers. Link with suitable input/output routines (.GETOCT and .PUTOCT may be used). Execute the program to find the largest argument for which it can calculate the Fibonacci number.

13.4   Rewrite the program for Example 13.1 using a VAX-11 procedure instead of a subroutine.

13.5   Carry out Exercise 13.2 using a VAX-11 procedure instead of a subroutine.

13.6   Carry out Exercise 13.3 using a VAX-11 procedure instead of a subroutine.

13.7   Rewrite the program for Example 13.2 using a VAX-11 procedure instead of a subroutine.

13.8   Revise Example 13.2 to sort an array of longwords.

13.9   Develop a recursive MACRO subroutine with inputs L, R, and k that finds the kth smallest element in a list. For example, if the list is "ABLETOFLY" the character "F" should be found for k = 4. (*Hint:* Recall that the partitioning step of Quicksort produces two sublists with the properties: $\{a[L], \ldots, a[i-1]\} <= a[i] <= \{a[i+1], \ldots, a[R]\}$ Thus if i happens to equal k, we have the answer. Otherwise, if k < i the subroutine is called recursively with the right sublist seeking the kth smallest, or if k > i with the left sublist looking for the (k − i)th smallest element.)

14

Floating-Point
Representation

14.1 | Overview

In earlier chapters we restricted our numbers to those that could be represented as byte, word, or longword integers. However, in many programming problems we are required to deal with numbers that cannot be represented in these data types. For example, scientific work often requires numbers that are not integers, or that exceed the range of binary integers of reasonable lengths. Many modern computers therefore provide data types and instructions that are more appropriate for scientific programming than are binary integers.

In this chapter we will learn about **floating-point** representation of numbers, and the facilities provided by the VAX-11 for handling numbers in this format. We shall see that this representation allows us to use real numbers ranging from very small fractions to values much larger than can be represented in the longest VAX-11 integer data type. We shall see that the VAX-11 has arithmetic, comparison, and conversion instructions for dealing with floating-point data types, and that MACRO provides appropriate storage and initialization directives for them. Also, we shall see how to perform input and output of these data types.

14.2 | Floating-Point Representation and Storage

Floating-point is a way of representing a number in a digital computer that is analogous to **scientific notation.** Recall that in scientific notation the representation of magnitude is separated into two parts, one called the mantissa, and the other the exponent. For example, 359.628 can be written in scientific notation as 3.59628×10^2, wherein 3.59628 is the **mantissa** and 2 is the **exponent** on the base. Note that the same number could also be written as 0.359628×10^3. Written in this way, i.e., with the decimal point immediately preceding the most significant digit, the number is said to be **normalized,** and the mantissa can meaningfully be called the **fraction.**

These ideas can be extended to binary numbers. Thus we can represent 110100110 as $0.110100110 \times 2^{1001}$, where the fraction and exponent are both shown in base two.

Now, if we wished to store this number in the computer, we would have to store only the bit patterns:

fraction: 110100110

exponent: 1001

Note that the base is understood and therefore need not be stored. Also, the "binary point" is understood to be at the extreme left and therefore its location need not be stored. Of course, any usage of this number would have to account for the way it was stored.

The above scheme could be used directly, storing the fraction in one cell and the exponent in another. However, this would not be an efficient usage of resources because the available cell sizes, e.g., byte, word, and longword, usually do not exactly match the storage needs of the exponent and fraction. Suppose, for example, that we arbitrarily selected a word (2 bytes) for each. It is unlikely that an entire 16-bit word would be needed for the exponent, while more than one word may be needed for the fraction. This is so because with normalized floating point representation the *accuracy* to which we can work is controlled by the number of bits available for the fraction, while the allowed *size* of the number is determined by the number of bits available for the exponent. For these reasons the format for floating-point representation on the VAX-11 has been defined as shown in Figure 14.1(a). We see that 23 bits have been reserved for the fraction, eight for the exponent, and one for a sign. Figure 14.1(b) shows how this representation is actually stored in a VAX-11 main memory longword cell, or in a general register. Observe that the sign bit, exponent, and most significant bit of the fraction are stored in the *low* bytes of the longword, while the least significant bits of the fractions are stored in the high bytes. This organization was chosen by the designers in order to maintain compatibility between the VAX-11 and the PDP-11 families of computers.

We have two other points to consider regarding the way floating-point numbers are actually stored in the VAX-11. The first concerns the sign of the exponent. We

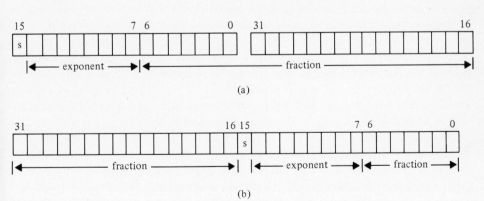

FIGURE 14.1/Floating-point representation format: (a) logical organization; (b) arrangement in VAX-11 longword

need to be able to store very small numbers as well as very large numbers, so we must allow for both positive and negative exponents. This is handled by a system known as **excess-128** representation, in which the exponent plus 128_{10} (80_{16}) is stored rather than the exponent itself. For example, the exponent in the preceding example, 1001_2, is stored as $9_{16} + 80_{16} = 89_{16}$. The full range of exponents possible with this system is then:

Actual Exponent (hexadecimal)	Excess-128 (hexadecimal)
+7F	FF
+1	81
0	80
−1	7F
−7F	01

Note that neither positive nor negative 80_{16} is listed as a valid, actual exponent. This is because either would yield 00 in the excess-128 system, and this particular value in the exponent field is used to indicate a floating-point zero as discussed below.

The other matter to be considered is called the **hidden bit,** which is a refinement of the way the fraction is stored. Observe that the normalization process places the binary point to the left of the most significant nonzero bit. This means that the first bit in what we have called the fraction is *always* a 1! Because this is so, the 1 need not be stored. This "hidden bit" is just *understood* to be there, and is restored by the computer whenever a nonzero floating-point number is processed. This means that although we have only 23 actual bits for the fraction, in effect we have 24, providing greater accuracy.

With this floating-point system, numbers can be represented to approximately seven decimal digits of accuracy, the equivalent of 24 bits. (Showing this is left as an exercise.) Positive or negative numbers as large as approximately 1.7×10^{38} (decimal) can be represented. Also, positive or negative numbers as small as approximately 0.294×10^{-38} (decimal) can be represented. However, as a consequence of the hidden bit assumption, zero cannot be represented internally in the same way as other numbers. This is because the fraction for the number $0.5_{10} = 0.1_2$ is stored as 0 after removing the hidden bit, and therefore a zero in the fraction field cannot be construed as meaning zero. To deal with this, an additional convention is adopted, whereby **floating-point zero** is represented by a zero in the *sign and exponent fields.*

A so-called "true" or "clean" zero also has the fraction bit zero. However, whenever just the sign and exponent fields are zero, a zero value will be used in all operations regardless of the contents of the fraction bits. Note that a nonzero sign bit together with a zero exponent field is *not* a legitimate floating-point number, and is called a *reserved operand.* VAX-11 floating-point instructions cause error reports if reserved operands are encountered.

The floating-point representation described above is called the F_FLOATING data type on the VAX-11. This machine also allows several other floating-point formats.

For example, the D_FLOATING data type is provided for double-precision floating-point representation. Here we shall focus on the F_FLOATING representation.

Let us now review floating-point representation by considering several examples.

EXAMPLE 14.1   Convert 384_{10} to floating-point as stored on the VAX-11.

$$384_{10} = 110000000_2 = 0.11 \times 2^{1001}$$

Fraction	$= 11$	(Store 1 because of hidden bit)
Exponent	$= 1001 = 09_{16}$	(Store 89_{16} as excess-128 value)
Sign bit	$= 0$	(Positive number)

Binary:

Sign	Exponent	Fraction
0	10001001	10000000000000000000000

Memory Longword Contents (Hexadecimal):

0000 44C0

EXAMPLE 14.2   Convert 0.5_{10} to floating point as stored on the VAX-11.

$$0.5_{10} = 0.1_2 \times 2^0$$

Fraction	$= 1$	(Store 0 because of hidden bit)
Exponent	$= 0$	(Store 80_{16} as excess-128 value)
Sign	$= 0$	(Positive number)

Binary:

Sign	Exponent	Fraction
0	10000000	00000000000000000000000

Memory Longword Contents (Hexadecimal):

0000 4000

EXAMPLE 14.3   Convert the following floating-point memory contents (shown in hexadecimal) to decimal:

0000 45E0

Binary:

Sign	Exponent	Fraction
0	10001011	11000000000000000000000

Fraction	$= 111$ (Hidden bit added)
Exponent	$= 8B$ (Excess-128)
	$= 8B - 80 = 0B_{16} = 11_{10}$
Sign	$= 0$ (Positive)
Value	$= 0.111 \times 2^{11} = 111_2 \times 2^8 = 1792_{10}$

EXAMPLE 14.4 Convert the following floating-point memory contents (shown in hexadecimal) to decimal:

$$EE00 \quad A31A$$

Binary:

Sign	Exponent	Fraction
1	01000110	00110101110111000000000

Fraction   = 100110101110111 (Hidden bit added)
Exponent = 46_{16} (Excess-128 notation)
         = $46 - 80 = -3A_{16} = -58_{10}$
Sign   = 1 (Negative)
Value   = $-0.100110101110111 \times 2^{-58}$
         = $-100110101110111 \times 2^{-73}$
         = $-19831 \times 1.058791 \times 10^{-22}$
         = $-2.099689 \times 10^{-18}$

14.3 | Floating-Point Arithmetic

Arithmetic operations on floating-point numbers are quite different from the corresponding operations on integers. Recall that with integers (unsigned or two's complement) the entire bit pattern representing the number is treated as a whole, with operations carried out uniformly on all bits. Floating-point numbers, on the other hand, are represented in two parts, namely the fraction and the exponent, and each part must be treated separately in the operations. Also, both the fraction and the exponent of the result must be calculated. In this section we show how these operations can be carried out.

When carrying out operations on the fraction part of floating-point numbers, the stored, 23-bit representation has to be augmented by two extra bits at the left and right. The bits at the left are to accommodate the hidden bit which must be accounted for in all operations, and a bit to accommodate a possible carry due to operations on the hidden bit. The two extra bits at the right, called **guard bits,** are needed to achieve the best possible accuracy when one-bits are shifted out of the fraction at the right during the operations. Thus the operational format is exemplified by:

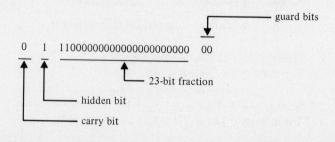

It is shown in the *VAX Architecture Handbook* (Digital Equipment Corporation) that this format allows floating-point operations to be carried out to an accuracy within 1/2 of the value of the LSB.

Examples in this section demonstrate the floating-point operations and the use of this format. Fortunately, however, most modern computers, including the VAX-11, have special floating-point instructions that perform the entire floating-point operation rather than requiring programmed operations on the separate parts. Nonetheless, it is important that the fundamental ideas of floating-point operations be understood. We will therefore examine floating-point addition, subtraction, multiplication, and division in the context of simple examples. It should be noted that we will neglect many important details concerning loss of accuracy and handling of error conditions.

14.3.1 Addition and Subtraction

Before two floating-point numbers can be added or subtracted, their exponents must be equal. The first step in either of these operations is therefore to identify the addend with the smallest exponent and shift its fraction to the right in order to achieve equality of exponents. This is called **alignment.** The number of bit positions for the shift is the positive difference between the two exponents. After thus aligning the fractions, addition or subtraction of the fractions can be carried out using normal integer operations. In the case of subtraction, or addition with one or more negative addends, the sum or difference can be negative. In this case, the results must be negated in order to get a positive fraction, and the sign bit set. The result is then **post normalized** by shifting left or right as required to place the leftmost 1-bit in the MSB position. The exponent of the result is the larger of the two original exponents, properly adjusted to reflect post-normalization of the fraction.

EXAMPLE 14.5 Add the floating-point numbers given in Examples 14.1 and 14.2 (384_{10} and 0.5_{10}).

Difference in exponents: $|89_{16} - 80_{16}| = 9_{16} = 9_{10}$
Fraction 1 : 01   10000000000000000000000   00
Fraction 2 : 00   00000000100000000000000   00   (Shifted 9 bits)
Sum   : 01   10000000100000000000000   00

Result (Binary):

Sign	Exponent	Fraction
0	10001001	10000000100000000000000

Memory (Hexadecimal):

4000 44C0

Note that we include the hidden bit. In this example, no normalization was required, so the exponent of the result is equal to the larger initial exponent.

EXAMPLE 14.6   Subtract 0.5_{10} from 384_{10} in floating-point representation. (See Examples 14.1 and 14.2.)

> Difference in exponents: $|89_{16} - 80_{16}| = 9_{16} = 9_{16}$
> Fraction 1 : 01   10000000000000000000000   00
> Fraction 2 : 00   00000000100000000000000   00   (Shifted 9 bits)
> Difference : 01   01111111100000000000000   00

Result (*Binary*):

Sign	Exponent	Fraction
0	10001001	01111111100000000000000

Memory (*Hexadecimal*):

C000 44BF

EXAMPLE 14.7   Add 0.5_{10} to itself in floating-point representation.

> Difference in exponents: $|80_{16} - 80_{16}| = 0$
> Fraction 1 : 01   00000000000000000000000   00
> Fraction 2 : 01   00000000000000000000000   00
> Sum   : 10   00000000000000000000000   00
> Normalized
> Sum   : 01   00000000000000000000000   00

Result (*Binary*):

Sign	Exponent	Fraction
0	10000001	00000000000000000000000

Memory (*Hexadecimal*):

0000 4080

Note that we normalized the fraction by shifting one position to the right and adding 1 to the exponent.

EXAMPLE 14.8   Subtract 8_{10} from 4_{10} in floating-point representation.

> $4_{10} = 100_2 = 0.1 \times 2^{11}$
> $8_{10} = 1000_2 = 0.1 \times 2^{100}$
> Difference in exponents: $|83_{16} - 84_{16}| = 1$
> Fraction 1 : 00   10000000000000000000000   00   (Shifted 1 bit)
> Fraction 2 : 01   00000000000000000000000   00
> Difference : 11   10000000000000000000000   00
> Negated
> Difference : 00   10000000000000000000000   00
> Normalized
> Difference : 01   00000000000000000000000   00

Result (*Binary*):

Sign	Exponent	Fraction
1	10000011	00000000000000000000000

Memory (*Hexadecimal*):

0000 C180

Note that subtraction of the aligned fractions required a borrow and produced a negative result, necessitating negation of the fraction and setting of the sign bit of the result. The fraction then required a shift of one bit to the left for normalization, accompanied by a decrease in the exponent by 1.

EXAMPLE 14.9   Add the numbers that have floating-point representations of FFFF 42FF and 0000 4440.

	Sign	Exponent	Fraction
Number 1:	0	10000101	11111111111111111111111
Number 2:	0	10001000	10000000000000000000000

Difference in exponents: $\mid 85_{16} - 88_{16} \mid = 3_{16} = 3_{10}$

Fraction 1:	00	00111111111111111111111	11	(Shifted 3 bits)
Fraction 2:	01	10000000000000000000000	00	
Sum:	01	10111111111111111111111	11	
Sum, rounded:	01	11000000000000000000000	00	

Result (*Binary*):

Sign	Exponent	Fraction
0	10001000	11000000000000000000000

Memory (*Hexadecimal*):

0000 4460

Note that the right shift for alignment caused three bits to be lost, but two of these were retained in the guard bits. After adding, the leftmost guard bit is set, so we round by adding 1 to the retained part of the fraction. This ensures that the result is accurate to within 1/2 of the value of the least significant bit of the fraction.

14.3.2 Multiplication and Division

Multiplication and division of floating-point numbers also involve separate manipulation of the fractions and exponents. In multiplication, the two fractions are multiplied as positive integers, yielding an integer that can be shifted to obtain the normalized fraction for the result. The exponent of the result is the sum of the multiplicand exponents, adjusted for post-normalization if required. In floating-point division the fraction of the dividend is divided by the fraction of the divisor using integer division techniques. As with multiplication, the result may require post-normalization. The exponent of the result is the difference between the dividend and divisor exponents, plus 1 if post-normalization is required.

The integer operations in the preceding steps must be performed with attention to accuracy of the result. For multiplication this means ensuring proper propagation of carries as the partial products are added (see Section 6.13). This applies even to the low-order bits to the right of the intended length of the final result. For division, care must be taken to calculate the remainder exactly at each stage. It is also possible, of course, to use extended precision integer multiply and divide instructions (e.g., EMUL and EDIV) to carry out the integer operations. In Examples 14.10 and 14.11, we demonstrate the basic techniques, leaving issues of accuracy and efficient algorithms to more advanced treatments (cf. K. Hwang, *Computer Arithmetic: Principles, Architecture, and Design,* Wiley, 1978).

EXAMPLE 14.10 Multiply 384_{10} by 0.5_{10} using floating-point arithmetic.

Calculate fraction:

$$0.1100 \times 0.1000 = 1100 \times 2^{-4} \times 1000 \times 2^{-4}$$
$$= 1100000 \times 2^{-8}$$
$$= 0.011000$$
$$= 0.1100 \times 2^{-1} \quad \text{(Normalized)}$$

Calculate exponent:

$$9 + 0 - 1 = 8_{16} = 88_{16} \quad \text{(Excess-128)}$$

Result (Binary):

Sign	Exponent	Fraction
0	10001000	1000000000000000000000000

Memory (Hexadecimal):

$$0000\ 4440$$

Observe that we factor the fraction of each multiplicand into a binary whole number and a power of 2. This allows use of integer multiplication techniques. Also, we had to subtract 1 from the sum of the multiplicand exponents to reflect post-normalization.

EXAMPLE 14.11 Divide 384_{10} by 0.5_{10} using floating-point arithmetic.

Calculate fraction:

$$0.1100 \div 0.1000 = 11000000 \times 2^{-8} \div 1000 \times 2^{-1}$$
$$= 11000 \times 2^{-4}$$
$$= 1.1000$$
$$= 0.1100 \times 2^{1} \quad \text{(Normalized)}$$

Calculate exponent:

$$9 - 0 + 1 = 0A_{16} = 8A_{16} \qquad \text{(Excess-128)}$$

Result (Binary):

Sign	Exponent	Fraction
0	10001010	10000000000000000000000

Memory (Hexadecimal):

$$0000\ 4540$$

As with multiplication, we first express the operands as integers to allow use of integer division techniques.

14.4 | Floating-Point Errors

Because all numerical calculations on digital computers are performed with a finite number of digits there is always a possibility of error. The nature of the possible errors is dependent upon the representation of the numbers as they are manipulated in the calculations, as well as on the number of digits available, both in the storage form and during intermediate steps. Here we shall examine errors that can occur with the VAX-11 F_FLOATING data type.

Errors are sometimes stated in *absolute* terms, meaning the difference between the actual value and the approximation. Alternately, we can express the *relative* error, which is the difference divided by the actual value. Thus if X is the actual value and X' is the approximation, we have the definitions:

$$\epsilon = \text{absolute error} = |X - X'|$$
$$\delta = \text{relative error} = |X - X'|/X$$

The purpose of a particular calculation will determine which of these definitions should be used as the accuracy criterion. Normally, relative error is important in scientific work, while absolute error is more important in commerce and finance.

With floating-point representation, errors can be of two basic types, which we shall call **mapping errors** and **loss of significance.** Mapping errors refer to errors that develop in the attempt to construct a machine-format number from a given real number. Loss of significance refers to a reduction in the *precision* of the results during the computation.

14.4.1 Mapping Errors

Because of the limited number of bits reserved for both the fraction and the exponent, the machine floating-point format (Fig. 14.1) can only represent a subset of the real numbers. This causes three kinds of mapping errors. As we saw in Section 14.2, a number larger in absolute value than 1.7×10^{38} (decimal) cannot be represented. Thus one kind of error that can occur is when an operation would produce a value larger than 1.7×10^{38}. This is called **floating-point overflow.** Similarly, absolute values less than 0.294×10^{-38} (decimal) cannot be represented, and an attempt to do so causes a **floating-point underflow.** Technically, both of these cases are characterized by an inability to represent the *exponent,* and are often referred to as **range errors.** The third kind of mapping error is associated with the finite length of the fractional part. One way to look at this is that the place value of the LSB of the fraction determines the width of "gaps" on the real line that cannot be represented. For example, the number:

$$0.10000000000000000000000001_2 \times 2^5 \simeq 0.160000019_{10} \times 10^2$$

whereas:

$$0.10000000000000000000000000_2 \times 2^5 = 0.160000000_{10} \times 10^2$$

and no number between these can be represented. When the need arises to represent a number in the gap, we have to select either the next higher value that can be represented, or the next lower one. Graphically this can be shown as:

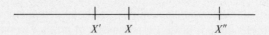

where X' and X'' are representable and X is the number we are trying to represent. Choosing X' or X'' to represent X is the final step in mapping a real number onto the set of representable floating-point numbers and can be done either by **rounding** or **chopping.** The error thereby introduced is called **roundoff error.** Many modern computers, including the VAX-11, do "optimal" rounding by choosing the *closest* representable number, so that the absolute roundoff in any single operation is at most 1/2 of the value of the gap. Thus with optimal rounding absolute and relative errors can be shown to be:

$$|\epsilon| \leq 2^{m-n-1}$$
$$|\delta| \leq 2^{-n}$$

where:

ϵ = absolute error
δ = relative error
m = exponent
n = number of fraction bits (24 for VAX-11)

As we saw in Section 14.4, rounding requires the intermediate results of the calculations to include extra bits at the right, called guard bits, in order to provide an accurate rounding bit. It can be shown that with careful selection of the algorithm for the rounding operation, at most two guard bits are required for optimal rounding. Some machines merely discard the bits beyond those needed in the final result rather than rounding. This is called "chopping." Obviously, chopping can introduce larger errors, but it is faster than rounding.

Although roundoff error is slight for single operations, when many operations are done the effects can accumulate and lead to unacceptable results. If this occurs, the solution is to change the representation of the numbers. One choice is a floating-point format with more bits in the fraction. As was mentioned previously, the VAX-11 has several floating-point data types besides the one we have studied, including one with 55 bits in the fraction (D_FLOATING) and another with 112 (H_FLOATING). Another choice is to use binary or decimal integer representation, provided that the numbers are integers, or can be scaled to allow integer representation.

14.4.2 Loss of Significance

Loss of significance develops whenever two floating-point numbers that are nearly the same size are subtracted. To understand this problem, consider the need to calculate:

$$Z = X - Y$$

where X and Y are not representable with integers. If done in floating-point, we will have in the machine *approximations* to X and Y, which we shall call X' and Y'. As we have seen, for standard VAX-11 floating-point they will have a maximum relative error of 2^{-24}, giving seven significant *decimal* digits. When the machine does the subtraction, it is obviously with X' and Y' rather than the actual values, so we get:

$$Z' = X' - Y'$$

for our approximation to Z. Now, if the *leading digits* of X' and Y' are *different*, we will get the same number of significant digits in Z' as we have in X' and Y'. However, if one or more leading digits *are the same*, cancellation occurs leaving *fewer* significant digits in Z'.

We can illustrate this using the numbers:

$$X = 0.3412345678 \times 10^0 \quad \text{and} \quad Y = 0.3412122222 \times 10^0$$

These must be converted to the machine floating-point format for storage. The techniques discussed in Section 14.2 can be used to do this conversion, yielding (in hexadecimal):

$$X' = \text{B64C 3FAE} \quad \text{and} \quad Y' = \text{B35E 3FAE}$$

If we extract the fractions from these and carry out the subtraction we get:

X' fraction:	01 01011101011011001001100 00
Y' fraction:	01 01011101011001101011110 00
Z' fraction:	00 00000000000001011101110 00
Z' normalized:	01 01110111000000000000000 00

Observe here that the normalized Z' fraction has only *nine* significant bits. Those that shifted in at the right in the normalization process will indeed be 0, but have no significance with regard to the original problem. The decimal equivalent of Z' is then:

$$Z' = 0.2235174 \times 10^{-4}$$

whereas by decimal arithmetic we can calculate (by hand):

$$Z = 0.2234560 = 10^{-4}$$

Thus we see that Z' has only three significant decimal digits, whereas X' and Y' had seven. This loss of significance may or may not be important in a particular problem, but the programmer should be aware of its occurrence.

It should be noted that loss of significant digits increases the *relative* errors, not the absolute error. For example, if X and Y are the masses of two objects measured in grams, then X', Y', *and* Z' are accurate within 1/10 of a microgram (10^{-6} grams). On the other hand, the relative error in X' and Y' is at most $2^{-24} = 5.9_{10} \times 10^{-8}$, whereas the relative error in Z' is $2^{-9} = 1.9_{10} \times 10^{-3}$:

The use of more bits in the floating-point fraction is one way to combat loss of significance. However, a better approach is to first examine the problem formulation to see if rearrangement of the calculation sequence reduces the problem. Textbooks on numerical analysis have many examples of these techniques (cf. S.D. Conte and Carl de Boor, *Elementary Numerical Analysis*, McGraw-Hill, 1972).

14.5 | **Floating-Point Directives**

MACRO has special directives which are useful when working with floating-point numbers. The directive:

```
A:   .FLOAT   f
```

or alternately:

```
A:   .F_FLOATING   f
```

will convert the decimal number f and store it in the floating-point cell (4 bytes) at address A using the format given in Figure 14.1(b). The number f can be written in a variety of ways as suggested by the following examples:

$$6$$
$$7.2$$
$$92.6E4$$
$$-4.2E-3$$

It is also possible to write:

```
ARY:   .FLOAT   a,b,c
```

where a, b, and c are decimal values to be stored in successive, floating-point cells in the array ARY.

When using this directive, you must observe the allowable range of magnitude for floating-point numbers. For example,

```
.FLOAT   1.2E43   (INCORRECT)
```

will result in an assembly error message, because 1.2E43 is outside of the allowed range for floating-point numbers. Arguments for .FLOAT smaller than 0.294E-38 are stored as floating-point zero.

A companion directive to .FLOAT is .DOUBLE. This directive will convert a decimal number to an *8-byte* floating-point representation, called D_FLOATING or double-precision. The format used is similar to that shown in Figure 14.1(b), except four additional bytes are provided for holding more low-order bits. Calculations are sometimes carried out in double-precision floating-point because this provides approximately sixteen significant decimal digits. We do not consider such problems in this book, however.

There is also a floating-point directive for allocating storage without initialization analogous to .BLKL and .BLKB. This is the .BLKF directive, exemplified by:

```
ARY:    .BLKF   10
```

where we are allocating 10_{10} floating-point cells intended for later storage of floating-point numbers. Note that we could accomplish the same thing with the .BLKL directive because longword and floating-point data types happen to be of the same length. However, the .BLKF directive more clearly indicates our intentions of using the allocated space for floating-point numbers.

14.6 | VAX-11 Floating-Point Instructions

As noted previously, the VAX-11 has many instructions designed specifically for floating-point data types. Through use of these instructions, floating-point operations such as those described in Section 14.3 can be carried out much more easily and efficiently. Additionally, there are instructions for other floating-point operations such as negation, comparison, conversion, and polynominal evaluation.

Table 14.1 shows the VAX-11 instructions for single-precision floating-point data types. It is seen there that these instructions have the same mnemonics as their integer counterparts, but with a suffix "F" rather than B, W, or L. The operands symbolized in the table by SF (source) are assumed to be floating-point numbers formatted as described in Section 14.2. Such operands come about either through floating-point directives (Section 14.5) or prior floating-point instructions.

The destination operands, DF, are automatically formatted as floating-point data types by the instructions. In general, SF and DF can be specified with any addressing mode.

The table also gives the opcodes for the floating-point instructions. It is interesting to note that the CLRF instruction has an opcode identical to CLRL. This is because single-precision floating-point data are one longword in length, and a longword with all bits cleared will be interpreted as a floating-point zero (see Section 14.2). One might think that the opcodes for MOVF and MOVL would also be the same. However, as discussed below, condition codes are set differently for floating-point operations, necessitating a different machine instruction.

The arithmetic instructions, ADDF, SUBF, MULF, and DIVF, perform the operations that we carried out manually in Section 14.4. However, the operations are implemented in the hardware so that greater efficiency is achieved. That is, ADDF automatically aligns and adds the fraction, performs needed post-normalization, and calculates the exponent of the result. Also, the algorithms used ensure accuracy to within 1/2 of the LSB in the fraction.

Several instructions in Table 14.1 deal with operations not discussed earlier. The MNEGF instruction performs floating-point negation by copying the source to the destina-

TABLE 14.1/VAX-11 Basic Floating-Point Instructions

Assembler Mnemonics		Opcode	Explanation
CLRF	DF	D4	Clear all bits in DF (floating zero)
MOVF	SF,DF	50	Copy SF to DF
ADDF	SF,DF	40	Add SF to DF
SUBF	SF,DF	42	Subtract SF from DF
MNEGF	SF,DF	52	Place negated SF into DF
CMPF	SF,DF	51	Compare SF to DF, setting condition codes
TSTF	DF	53	Compare DF to zero, setting condition codes
MULF	SF,DF	44	Multiply DF by SF
DIVF	SF,DF	46	Divide DF by SF
CVTBF	SB,DF	4C	Convert SB to DF
CVTWF	SW,DF	4D	Convert SW to DF
CVTLF	SL,DF	4E	Convert SL to DF
CVTFB	SF,DB	48	Convert SF to DB
CVTFW	SF,DW	49	Convert SF to DW
CVTFL	SF,DL	4A	Convert SF to DL (truncated)
CVTRF	SF,DL	4B	Convert SF to DL (rounded)
POLYF	X,#n,C	55	Evaluates polynominal of degree n, coefficient array C, argument X, and places result in R0.

NOTES:

SF	= floating-point source	DF	= floating-point destination
SB	= byte integer source	DB	= byte integer destination
SW	= word integer source	DW	= word integer destination
SL	= longword integer source	DL	= longword integer destination

tion and, provided that the source is not zero, negating the sign bit. The CMPF instruction performs a floating-point subtraction (SF − DF) and sets the N and Z condition codes accordingly. Like the integer comparisons, the difference is discarded and neither operand is changed. TSTF is like CMPF except that the source operand is compared to a floating-point zero.

The conversion instructions, e.g., CVTLF, perform integer-to-floating-point or floating-point-to-integer conversions. As we see in Table 14.1, instructions are available for conversion of floating-point to either byte, word, or longword integers and vice versa. The last two characters of the mnemonic indicate the data types involved. Some of these conversions are done exactly. For example, word or byte integers can be exactly represented in floating-point. On the other hand, longword integers (with low-order bits set) cannot be exactly represented in the 24-bit floating-point fraction; in this case *rounding* is performed in the conversion. The conversion from floating-point to integer is, in general, not exact because the integer data type does not allow a fractional part. The CVTFB, CVTFW, and CVTFL instructions *truncate* the floating-point to get the integer, while CVTRFL *rounds*.

The last instruction shown in Table 14.1 is POLYF. This is a special instruction for evaluation of a polynominal, e.g., $c_0 + c_1x + c_2x^2 + \ldots + c_nx^n$. The first operand is understood to be the independent variable, and the second is the order of the polynominal. The third operand gives the address of the coefficient array, where $c_0, c_1, \ldots, c_n$ are stored as floating-point data. The result is returned as a floating-point number in R0. Note that R1 and R2 are cleared and R3 points to the longword following the coefficient array after execution of POLYF.

When using floating-point instructions the appropriate branch instructions are the *signed branches*, BGTR, BLSS, BLEQ, BEQL, and BNEQ. The unsigned branches cannot be used because floating-point instructions clear the C condition code regardless of the outcome. The BVC and BVS branch instructions can be used because floating-point instructions that could produce an excessively large exponent, as a rule, set the V condition code when this occurs.

The following example illustrates programming with the VAX MACRO floating-point instructions and directives.

EXAMPLE 14.12 Develop a MACRO program to determine the present worth of an annuity (*PWA*), given by the formula:

$$PWA = \frac{(1 + i)^n - 1}{i(1 + i)^n}$$

where:

$$i = \text{interest rate as a fraction}$$
$$n = \text{number of years}$$

The program listing is shown in Figure 14.2. The values of interest and the number of years are set with directives. The result is developed in R0. The initial instructions set the result to n and skip the other calculations if the interest rate is zero. For nonzero interest, $(1 + i)$ is developed in the floating-point variable ONE_P_I. Next, $(1 + i)^n$ is developed as a floating-point number in R0, making special allowance for the case where n is zero. A copy of $(1 + i)^n$ is placed in R2 and used to calculate the denominator, followed by subtraction of 1 from R0 to get the numerator. Finally, *PWA* is calculated in R0 by floating-point division. The result is stored in *PWA* as a floating-point number, in T_PWA after truncation to an integer, and in R_PWA after rounding to an integer.

Figure 14.3 shows execution after linking with the Symbolic Debugger. We examine *PWA* both as a longword, and as a floating-point number. T_PWA and R_PWA are then examined as longword integers.

```
EXAMPLE 14.12      6-AUG-1985 22:48:59     VAX/VMS Macro V04-00      Page   1
                   6-AUG-1985 22:46:46     _DRA1:[SOWELL]E14P12.MAR;3    (1)

                                  0000              1          .TITLE   EXAMPLE 14.12
                                  0000              2  ;
                                  0000              3  ;  PRESENT VALUE OF AN ANNUITY
                                  0000              4  ;
                        0000      0000             5           .ENTRY   START,0
       50  0000071'EF  4E         0002             6           CVTLF    N,R0                ;TEST ZERO INTEREST CASE
           000006D'EF  53         0009             7           TSTF     I                   ;
                        3E 13     000F             8           BEQL     OUT
00000075'EF 08  40  50            0011             9           MOVF     I,ONE_P_I           ;CALC
           50  08  50             001C            10           ADDF     #1,ONE_P_I          ;    (1+I).
           00000071'EF D5         0023            11           MOVF     #1,R0               ;ZERO N
                        11 1B     0026            12           TSTL     N                   ;          CASE.
                                  002C            13           BLEQU    L2
       51  00000071'EF D0         002E            14           MOVL     N,R1
       50  000006D'EF  44         0035            15  L1:       MULF     ONE_P_I,R0          ;CALC
                        F6 51     003C            16           SOBGTR   R1,L1               ;    (1+I)^N.
                        52 50     003F            17  L2:       MOVF     R0,R2
       52  000006D'EF  44         0042            18           MULF     I,R2                ;    I*(1+I)^N.
                        50 08     0049            19           SUBF     #1,R0               ;CALC (1+I)^N.  1.0
                        50 52     004C            20           DIVF     R2,R0               ;CALC PWA
           00000079'EF 50         004F            21  OUT:      MOVF     R0,PWA              ;STORE PWA FLOATING
           0000007D'EF 50         0056            22           CVTFL    R0,T_PWA            ;STORE PWA TRUNCATED
           00000081'EF 50         005D            23           CVTRFL   R0,R_PWA            ;STORE PWA ROUNDED
                                  0064            24  EXIT:     $EXIT_S
           CCCD3ECC               006D            25  I:        .FLOAT   0.10                ;INTEREST RATE
           00000014               0071            26  N:        .LONG    20                  ;NO. OF YEARS
           00000079               0075            27  ONE_P_I:  .BLKF    1                   ;1+I STORAGE
           0000007D               0079            28  PWA:      .BLKF    1                   ;PWA STORAGE,FLOATING
           00000081               007D            29  T_PWA:    .BLKL    1                   ;PWA STORAGE,LONG
           00000085               0081            30  R_PWA:    .BLKL    1                   ;PWA STORAGE,LONG
                                  0085            31            .END     START
```

FIGURE 14.2/MACRO program to calculate present value of an annuity

```
$ MACRO/LIST/DEBUG E14P12
$ LINK/DEBUG E14P12
$ RUN E14P12
            VAX DEBUG Version 4.1
%DEBUG-I-INITIAL, language is MACRO, module set to 'EXAMPLE'
DBG>SET BREAK EXIT
DBG>GO
break at EXAMPLE\EXIT: PUSHL    S^#01
DBG>EXAMINE/FLOAT PWA
EXAMPLE\PWA:      8.513564
DBG>EXAMINE PWA
EXAMPLE\PWA:      378F4208
DBG>EXAMINE T_PWA:R_PWA
EXAMPLE\T_PWA:    00000008
EXAMPLE\R_PWA:    00000009
DBG>EXIT
$ ▒
```

FIGURE 14.3/Execution of program in Figure 14.2 with the Symbolic Debugger

14.7 | Floating-Point Literal Operands

Careful study of the listing in Figure 14.2 reveals an operand specifier translation that we have not seen previously, namely the **floating-point literal.** This occurs in lines 10, 11, and 19, where #1 is used as an operand in a *floating-point* instruction. We see that the assembler generates 08 for this operand in the machine code. To see how 08 can represent a floating-point 1.0, let us look at it in binary, i.e.,

7	6	5	4	3	2	1	0
0	0	0	0	0	0	0	1

Recall from Section 12.2.2 that any operand specifier with the two leftmost bits clear will be treated as literal addressing, meaning that bits $<5:0>$ represent the operand. When the opcode is of the floating-point type, these six bits are interpreted as *the three low bits of the exponent and the three high bits of the fraction* in the floating-point data type. The other parts of the floating-point number are predefined by the hardware. This is shown in the following diagram.

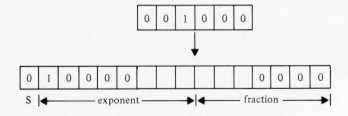

Note that the sign bit is clear, the MSB of the exponent is set, and all other bits, including the sixteen low-order bits of the fraction (not shown here) are clear. The resulting 32-bit number is 00004080, which we recognize from Example 14.7 as a

floating-point 1.0. The numbers that can be represented as floating-point literals are obviously very limited. Nonetheless, those that can be so represented are quite common numbers, and whenever this form can be used it saves four bytes of memory. For this reason the MACRO assembler always checks floating-point instructions with #n-type operands and uses the literal form if possible. We leave as an exercise the determination of all possible floating-point literals.

14.8 | **Input and Output of Floating-Point Numbers**

If floating-point operations are to be used in a program, one must consider how floating-point representation can be accepted as input from a keyboard, and how it can be output to a printer or display unit. These tasks can be done using assembly routines, or by using existing facilities provided as part of the support software for high-level languages. We shall introduce both appraoches without elaboration.

14.8.1 Using High-Level Language I/O Facilities

Let us first consider how floating I/O can be handled using existing facilities. Since a frequent use of assembly language is for critical subroutines of programs written in high-level languages, it is quite natural to handle the input and output in the high-level language. We have already seen in Chapter 9 how to call assembly routines from Pascal and FORTRAN programs. There, however, we used only integer values. In Figure 14.4 we see a FORTRAN main program that passes floating-point arguments to and from a MACRO subroutine. All I/O is then done in FORTRAN. Observe that with the FORTRAN convention for argument transmission (see Section 9.8.4), internal access to floating arguments is no different than for integer arguments. That is, the *addresses* of the real arguments are stored in locations 4,8, and 12 relative to the argument array address, which is passed in register AP. The compilation, assembly, and linkage steps are exactly as shown in Chapter 9.

```
        PROGRAM FLTIO
C
C     FORTRAN MAIN PROGRAM
C
        READ(*,*)X,Y
        CALL  SUB1(X,Y,Z)
        WRITE(*,*)Z
        END
              (a)
```

```
      .TITLE FLOATING SUBROUTINE
      .ENTRY    SUB1,^M<R2>
      MOVF      @4(AP),R2        ;GET X
      MULF      @8(AP),R2        ;MULTIPLY BY Y
      MOVF      R2,@12(AP)       ;STORE RESULT IN Z
      RET
      .END
              (b)
```

FIGURE 14.4/Floating point operations in MACRO with I/O in FORTRAN main program: (a) FORTRAN main program; (b) MACRO subroutine

```
            .TITLE   FLOATING I/O
            .EXTERNAL FINP,FOUT
            .ENTRY   START,^M<R2>
            CALLG    ARG,FINP        ;GET INPUTS
            CLRF     R2              ;INIT. SUM
            ADDF     X,R2            ;ADD X
            ADDF     Y,R2            ;ADD Y
            MOVF     R2,Z            ;STORE Z
            CALLG    ARG2,FOUT       ;OUTOUT RESULT
            RET                      ;RETURN
X:          .BLKF    1               ;STORAGE FOR X
Y:          .BLKF    1               ;STORAGE FOR Y
Z:          .BLKF    1               ;STORAGE FOR Z
ARG:        .LONG    2,X,Y           ;IN ARG LIST
ARG2:       .LONG    1,Z             ;OUT ARG LIST
            .END
                        (a)
            PROGRAM MAIN
C
            CALL START
            END
C
            SUBROUTINE FINP(A,B)
            READ(*,*)A,B
            RETURN
            END
C
            SUBROUTINE FOUT(C)
            WRITE(*,*)C
            RETURN
            END
                        (b)
```

FIGURE 14.5/Using FORTRAN I/O for MACRO assembly programs: (a) MACRO portion; (b) FORTRAN portion

Another example of using FORTRAN I/O facilities is shown in Figure 14.5. The short main program, written in FORTRAN, does nothing other than transfer control to the major routine, which is written in MACRO. The MACRO routine then calls FORTRAN subroutines that perform the I/O. This technique is probably not ideal for production programs, but it provides a convenient method for testing.

14.8.2 Floating-Point I/O from MACRO

Usage of input/output facilities of a higher-level language may not be possible or desirable in certain situations. In such cases, routines must be developed for input and output of floating-point numbers. We shall show this approach for output and briefly consider input without going into detail.

For output, the basic goal is to print two decimal integers, D and N, as ASCII character strings, "ddddddd" and "nn", where d represents fraction digits and n represents exponent digits. Conventionally, these are printed in the format:

$$\pm\ 0.dddddddE\pm nn$$

There are several methods for finding the integers D and N. One way to find N is to compare successive powers of ten with the number X, beginning with the most negative possible decimal exponent, -38. If a power is less than or equal to the number, N is incremented and the next power is tried. When this process is complete N is the exponent of 10. It can be converted to a string of ASCII digits ''nn'' using a procedure like the one shown in Figure 8.12, modified for decimal output.

To find D, first observe that we can arbitrarily choose the number of significant digits to be printed. However, this can be no more than seven decimal digits, corresponding to the maximum accuracy possible with the 24-bit binary fraction. Then note that if X is divided by $10^{(N-K)}$, the whole-number part of the result can be represented with K decimal digits. These digits will be the decimal digits to the *right* of the decimal point in a normalized decimal floating-point form.

EXAMPLE 14.13   A procedure implementing these ideas is shown in Figure 14.6(a) and (b). The macros in Figure 14.6(a) are used to generate a table of powers of ten

```
        .TITLE EXAMPLE 14.13
;
;       PROGRAMMED FLOATING-POINT OUTPUT
;
        .EXTERNAL  CNVDEC
        .MACRO GEN,K
        .FLOAT 1.E'K
        .ENDM  GEN
        .MACRO DEFPOW
POWTEN: .FLOAT 1.E-38
        K1=-37
        .REPT  75
        GEN    \K1
        K1=K1+1
        .ENDR
        .ENDM  DEFPOW
        .ENTRY START,0
        MOVL   N0,N          ;INIT. EXPONENT
        MOVL   #POWTEN,R1    ;INIT POWTEN POINTER
        CLRL   ES            ;INIT. EXP SIGN FLAG
        MOVF   X,R0          ;LOAD X INTO R0
        CLRL   IS            ;SET
        TSTF   R0            ;    INTEGER PART
        BGTR   L1            ;        SIGN
        INCL   IS            ;           FLAG.
        XORL   #^X8000,R0    ;ABS(X) INTO R0
L1:
        CMPF   (R1)+,R0      ;FIND DECIMAL EXPONENT
        BGTR   L2            ;    BY STEPPING THRU
        INCL   N             ;        POWTEN.
        BRB    L1
L2:
        SUBL   #4,R1         ;BACK UP 1 FP ENTRY IN POWTEN
        SUBL   K,R1          ;POINT TO 10**(N-K)
        DIVF   (R1),R0       ;COMPUTE INTEGER PART
        TSTL   N             ;SET SIGN FLAG
        BGEQ   L3
        INCL   ES
        MNEGL  N,N
```

FIGURE 14.6/Floating-point output: (a) conversion to decimal exponent and fraction

```
L3:
            MOVL        #ASC,R1             ;SET ASCII BUF POINTER
            TSTL        IS                  ;IF NEGATIVE
            BEQL        L4
            MOVB        #^A'-',(R1)+        ;    PUT "-" INTO BUFFER.
L4:
            MOVW        #^A'O.',(R1)+       ;PUT "O." INTO BUFFER
            CVTFL       R0,ITG              ;PUT INTEGER PART
            MOVL        ITG,R0              ;    INTO R0 & ITG.
            BSBW        CNVDEC              ;CVT TO DEC & STORE @(R1)
            MOVB        #^A'E',(R1)+        ;PUT "E" INTO BUFFER
            TSTL        ES                  ;IF EXP NEGATIVE
            BEQL        L5                  ;
            MOVB        #^A'-',(R1)+        ;    PUT "-" INTO BUFFER.
L5:
            MOVL        N,R0                ;PUT EXPONENT INTO R0
            BSBW        CNVDEC              ;PUT EXPONENT INTO BUFFER
            .PUTSTR     ASC                 ;PRINT THE BUFFER
            $EXIT_S                         ;EXIT TO VMS
ASC:        .BLKB       10                  ;ASCII BUFFER FOR FLOAT PRINT
            .BYTE       0                   ;NUL BYTE TO TURN .PUTSTR OFF
K:          .LONG       16                  ;4*NUMBER OF DIGITS (MAX 4)
X:          .FLOAT      -1.982E3            ;NUMBER TO BE PRINTED
IS:         .BLKL       1                   ;INTEGER PART SIGN FLAG
ES:         .BLKL       1                   ;EXP SIGN FLAG
N:          .BLKL       1                   ;DECIMAL EXPONENT
NO:         .LONG       -38                 ;INITIAL EXPONENT
ITG:        .BLKL       1                   ;INTEGER PART
            DEFPOW                          ;SET UP POWTEN TABLE USING MACRO
            .END        START
```

FIGURE 14.6/Floating-point output: (b) conversion to ASCII and printing

from $1.E-38$ to $1.E+38$. The first part of the executable code, beginning at .ENTRY, loads the value to be printed into the R0 register and sets a flag for its sign. The loop beginning at L1 then steps through the POWTEN table, comparing successive table values with the number. When this loop completes, N contains the decimal exponent, and R1 points to one table entry (4 bytes) beyond the actual power of ten. In the next portion of the program, beginning at L2, R1 is adjusted to point at $10^{(N-4)}$ in the table. This is divided into R0, leaving there a number that can be represented in decimal with four digits to the left of the decimal point. The sign of the exponent N is used to set a flag ES, and then N is set positive.

The conversion to ASCII and printing is shown in Figure 14.6(b). The ASCII codes are first developed in the buffer ASC, and then printed. The sign of the number, indicated by the flag IS, determines whether or not to place a "−" symbol as the first character. Next the characters "0" and "." are stored. Then the previously determined floating-point value in R0 is converted to integer and stored in ITG, then returned to R0 as an integer. The subroutine CNVDEC converts an integer found in R0 to the corresponding string of ASCII decimal characters. It stores these characters beginning at the byte pointed at by R1, advancing R1 accordingly. (CNVDEC can be seen in Appendix F.) Upon return from CNVDEC, the digits representing the fractional part are in place in the buffer. An "E", and a "−" if indicated by the ES flag, is then placed in the buffer. Finally, the exponent is loaded into the buffer, again using CNVDEC. The .PUTSTR macro is then used to print ASC. When executed, the program shown in Figure 14.6 will print:

```
-0.1982E4
```

If X is changed to −0.04314, it will print:

```
-0.4314E-1
```

Floating-point input can be accomplished in a manner somewhat parallel to that used in Example 14.13. The objective in this case is to accept a keyboard entry in floating-point notation, e.g.,

```
-643.961E-13
```

and store it in the standard internal floating-point representation. A procedure to do this would have the following major steps.

1. Read the input line as ASCII characters into a buffer. (The .TTYIN buffer will do.)

2. Set a flag if the first character is "−".

3. Store the numeric characters to the left of E in a separate buffer IBUF without the decimal point.

4. Set an exponent sign flag if "−" follows the E.

5. Store the numeric characters to the right of E in a separate buffer, EBUF.

6. Convert IBUF from ASCII to floating point.

7. Convert EBUF from ASCII to binary.

8. Use the converted EBUF as an index into a table of powers of ten, thus obtaining the floating-point value of 10 to the power of the exponent.

9. Multiply the results of Steps 6 and 8, giving the floating-point representation to be stored.

Steps 6 and 7 are very similar to the problem addressed in Figure 8.11, i.e., conversion of ASCII character codes to internal integer representation. However, that procedure must be modified to accept decimal digits. Also, Step 6 requires the result to be developed as a floating-point data type, because many floating-point numbers are too large or too small to be represented in the longword, signed integer form. The details of floating-point input are left as an exercise.

14.9 | Summary

This chapter dealt with a new way of representing numerical data, namely **floating-point** representation, which is ideal for scientific applications. The VAX-11 has several floating-point data types that are all basically similar. We focused on one of these, called F_FLOATING, which is suitable for many problems and embodies the important floating-point concepts. With this data type, 32 bits are used to store a single number. Twenty-three of the bits are used to represent the so-called mantissa or fraction, while eight bits are used to store the exponent on the (understood) binary base, and one bit is used to represent the sign. This system allows positive or negative numbers between 0.294×10^{-38} and 1.7×10^{38} to be represented. This representation allows solution of problems that cannot be handled with integers.

In our discussion of this topic we covered conversion, arithmetic operations and errors, and the available VAX-11 floating-point instructions and directives. We found that because floating-point representation stores numbers in two parts, normal integer operations cannot be used directly. However, by separate manipulation of the parts, we can perform all arithmetic operations using integer operations and recast the result into floating-point form at the conclusion. While the VAX-11 floating-point instructions perform these operations automatically, the underlying principles are important in understanding sources of floating-point errors, and in programming other computers that have only integer instructions.

Regarding errors, we learned that there are two basic categories, namely those due to **mapping** from real decimal numbers to binary, machine-format, floating-point representation, and those due to **loss of significant digits** during arithmetic operations. Mapping errors can be divided into **overflow/underflow** errors, where the number requires a binary exponent that is too large or too small to fit in the provided field, and **roundoff** errors, where the finite length of the fraction field results in loss of precision. Either of these errors can be reduced or eliminated by the use of extended floating-point data types that provide more bits for the exponent and fraction. The VAX-11 provides such data types, along with instructions for their manipulation, but we did not cover these here. Loss of significance occurs when nearly equal floating-point numbers are subtracted. The use of extended data types also helps reduce this kind of error, but in some cases rearrangement of the calculation sequence is a better solution.

The last floating-point topic covered was I/O. We learned that output can be done by separately computing the *decimal* fraction and exponent, followed by conversion to their ASCII equivalents for printing. A similar technique applies to input. Alternately, the facilities of a high-level language can be used for I/O.

14.10 | Exercises

14.1 Convert (by hand) the following *decimal* values to VAX-11 floating-point representation. Show in binary as sign, exponent, and fraction bit patterns, and as hexadecimal contents of a longword.

(a) 686   (b) -9.6×10^{12}

(c) -12 (d) 512×10^{-4}

(e) 0.35   (f) -3×10^{-8}

(g) 6.2×10^{23} (h) 0.75

14.2 Convert (by hand) the following hexadecimal floating-point longword contents to decimal.

(a) 0000 4692   (b) 0000 C692   (c) 0000 3280

(d) E400 4492   (e) 0000 0000   (f) 9249 9249

(g) 0000 8000   (h) 9249 1249   (i) 3FFF FFFF

(j) 0000 4080

14.3 Verify your answers to Exercise 14.1 by assembling a program with these numbers stored using the .FLOAT directive. Examine the .LIS file.

14.4 Use the MACRO assembler and the Symbolic Debugger to verify your answers for Exercise 14.2. Note that EXAMINE/FLOAT causes floating-point display in the symbolic Debugger.

14.5 Show that a 24-bit fraction in floating-point representation corresponds to seven decimal digits of *accuracy*.

14.6 Show that if seven-decimal-digit accuracy is to be maintained, the range of positive or negative floating-point numbers on the VAX-11 computer is approximately 0.294×10^{-38} to approximately 1.7×10^{38}.

14.7 Carry out floating-point addition of the numbers in Exercise 14.1(a) and 14.1(c).

14.8 Subtract the number in Exercise 14.1(h) from that in 14.1(a) using floating-point arithmetic.

14.9 Carry out floating-point multiplication of the numbers in Exercises 14.1(a) and 14.1(c).

14.10 Divide the number in Exercise 14.1(a) by that in Exercise 14.1(c).

14.11 Show that the maximum relative error due to optimal rounding is $1/2\ B^{1-n}$ where B is the base and n is the number of digits allowed for the fraction of a floating-point representation.

14.12 What is the number of significant *bits* of the result when the number in Exercise 14.1(c) is subtracted from that in 14.1(a)? How many significant *decimal* digits does this correspond to?

14.13 Create a recursive subroutine to calculate the future value of a unit annual deposit at interest i, using floating-point operations. Demonstrate with the Symbolic Debugger and compare the result with:

$$[(1+ i)^n-1]/i$$

14.14 Using floating-point operations, write a MACRO procedure that solves:

$$ax^2 + bx + c = 0$$

for both real roots. Create a Pascal or FORTRAN main program that accepts a, b, and c as floating-point inputs, calls your MACRO subroutine, and upon return prints the results. It should print a message if there are no real roots. Test your program with $a = 2.83$, $b = 8.12$, $c = 2.35$, and then with $a = 4.53$, $b = 6.13$, $c = 5.14$.

14.15 Develop a MACRO subroutine that will accept keyboard entry in the form $\pm 0.\text{dddddddE} \pm \text{nn}$ and return it as a floating-point value in R0.

14.16 Write a MACRO procedure callable from FORTRAN or Pascal that evaluates a polynominal of order n using the POLYF instruction. The coefficient array and argument value should be passed to the procedure in the argument list, and the result returned likewise. Test it with a Pascal or FORTRAN calling program using:

$$F(x) = 2.83x^2 + 8.12x + 2.35$$

14.17 Write subroutines to perform the floating-point arithmetic operations indicated below without using the floating-point instructions. Demonstrate with the Symbolic Debugger by comparing the results to those given by the floating-point instructions.

(a) addition   (b) subtraction   (c) negation
(d) multiplication   (e) division

15

Decimal Representation

15.1 | Overview

The floating-point data type and supporting instructions allow the VAX-11 to be conveniently and efficiently programmed for scientific applications. This data type is not well suited to business applications, however, because financial data are normally expressed in decimal. While it is possible to convert all input to floating-point or binary integers prior to doing the calculations, and then convert the results to decimal for output, this approach can result in loss of accuracy. Also, in some cases decimal processing may be more efficient. In order to better meet the needs of commercial and financial applications the VAX-11 therefore provides several data types for storing **decimal data.** Special directives and instructions are provided that allow direct manipulation of data in this form.

From the beginning of this book we have emphasized that all numbers are stored in binary, and all operations are done on strings of 1's and 0's, i.e., binary codes. Therefore, it may seem contradictory now to introduce the notions of "storing decimal" and performing "decimal arithmetic" on a digital computer. We shall see, however, that these views are indeed compatible. For decimal operations we simply store *strings* of decimal digits, using binary codes for the decimal digits 0,1, . . . , 9. These strings are readily storable in main memory cells, and can be manipulated numerically. We shall first examine how they are stored, and then we will see how the arithmetic is done.

15.2 | Advantages and Disadvantages of Decimal Representation

As noted above, the need for decimal representation and operations arises primarily in commercial and financial programming. In these fields we encounter large dollar amounts, and at the same time we expect accuracy to the nearest cent. Neither integer nor floating-point data types is well suited to these requirements.

395

To see why integer data types are not always appropriate, consider an accounting program that has accounts with balances as large as $50,000,000.00. In order to use an integer data type, we have to multiply by 100 and maintain values internally in units of cents. The maximum number to be stored is then 5,000,000,000, which exceeds the capacity of longword integers. While we could sidestep this problem by using quadword integers, doing so would require eight bytes per number and would lengthen processing time. Later we shall see that the same size number can be stored in six bytes using the decimal form. Moreover, because the data normally exist external to the machine as decimal ASCII, the complex decimal-to-binary conversion is required. On the other hand, conversion from decimal ASCII to an internal decimal representation is much easier and faster.

The preceding problem of magnitude could be solved by using floating-point representation. Indeed, floating-point numbers can be as large as 1.7×10^{38}, whereas we shall see that VAX decimal numbers are limited to approximately 1.0×10^{31}. However, floating-point representation limits our *accuracy*. For example, the normal single-precision VAX floating-point data type (F_FLOATING) provides only seven significant decimal digits of accuracy. Thus, in the example just described, the best we could hope for would be balances accurate to the nearest $10. Of course, a double-precision floating-point data type could be used, at the expense of more memory for each number. It should also be noted that floating-point mapping errors can lead to significant loss of accuracy even when it appears that you are well within the significant digits provided by the data type. For example, consider the program:

```
        .TITLE  ERRORS
A:      .FLOAT  0.7
        .ENTRY  START,0
        MOVL    #10000,R9
        CLRF    R8
AGAIN:  ADDF    A,R8
        SOBGTR  R9,AGAIN
        $EXIT_S
        .END    START
```

Here we add 0.7 ten thousand times, expecting the result in R8 to be 7000.000. Instead we get 7000.608. The reason is that the decimal fraction 0.7 cannot be exactly represented in binary. The small mapping error in representing 0.7 in floating-point builds up to become a significant error in the result. This error could be avoided by scaling the data by a factor of ten, and then using either integer or decimal representation. By choosing decimal, we achieve the needed accuracy with economical usage of memory.

The issue of efficiency is complex when decimal and other data types are compared. On one hand, significant savings can be realized by avoiding conversion of external decimal ASCII to binary integer or floating-point representation. As an illustration, it takes approximately twice as long to convert a 10-digit decimal ASCII number to longword integer or floating-point as to convert it to an internal decimal string. On the other hand, decimal arithmetic operations are much slower than either longword integer or floating-point operations. For example, decimal multiplication takes approximately 10 to 20 times longer than floating-point or integer multiplication. In general then, decimal will be preferred in programs with large amounts of decimal I/O and relatively little arithmetic. Many commercial applications are so characterized. However, if a significant amount of arithmetic is to be performed, it will probably pay to convert to floating-point or integer representation.

15.3 | Decimal Data Types

The VAX-11 has two basic data types for decimal integers, namely, **numeric strings** and **packed decimal strings.** Numeric strings are simply strings of decimal characters represented in ASCII codes, and are used primarily as a temporary form of storage for input and output. They are not used directly in arithmetic calculations. With packed decimal strings, on the other hand, the numbers are stored in a form that is more compact, and more easily used in calculations. We shall look at the form of storage for both of these types and then show how they are employed in a program.

As noted above, with the numeric string form the number is stored as the ASCII codes representing the digits (hexadecimal 31 through 39) in sequential bytes in main memory. The sign of the number is stored as a mandatory prefix "+", " ", or "−" in ASCII code, where the space " " is taken as equivalent to the "+". This is referred to as the **Leading Separate Numeric** data type. (*Note:* The VAX-11 has an alternate numeric string type called Trailing Separate Numeric in which the sign is *encoded* with the ASCII code of the last digit, but we do not consider this type here.) An example showing how the decimal number −123456 is stored as a Leading Separate Numeric (LSN) is:

2D	S
31	S + 1
32	S + 2
33	•
34	•
35	•
36	

The first byte contains $2D_{16}$ which is the ASCII code for "−". Note that the most significant digit follows the sign, and lower-order digits are stored in higher-numbered addresses. The length of an LSN string is specified *exclusive* of the sign byte. Thus the above string is of length 6. In general, the storage length is L + 1, where L is the number of digits in the string.

Packed decimal strings store the decimal digits more compactly and in a form more convenient for calculations. That is, instead of storing the entire ASCII code, only the rightmost four bits (called the low "nibble") are stored. This is possible because the high nibbles of the ASCII codes for all decimal digits are the same, and have no numerical significance. The low nibble, on the other hand, is the *numeric value of the digit* and can therefore be used directly in numerical operations. This form of representation is sometimes called **Binary Coded Decimal** (BCD). The sign of the number represented as packed decimal is also stored as a 4-bit code, but for this data type it *follows* the least significant digit. The binary codes that are not needed to represent decimal digits are used to represent the sign. Thus either 1010, 1100, 1110, or 1111 (A,C,E, or F hexadecimal) can be used to represent a positive number, while either 1011 or 1101 (B or D hexadecimal) can represent a negative number. By convention, C is preferred for positives and D for negatives. If necessary, a leading zero is stored with the most significant digit in order to have the string begin at a byte boundary in memory. The VAX-11 packed decimal string can be up to 31_{10} digits in length. As with leading numerics, the length does not include the sign. Nor does it include the leading zero if one is needed for byte alignment. The digits thus encoded are stored ''packed'' two per byte. Applying these rules, and expressing the codes in hexadecimal, the decimal integer -123456 is stored as:

01	S
23	S + 1
45	S + 2
6D	S + 3

The sign code, D in this case, shares the last byte of the string with the code for the least significant digit. Note the leading 0 added for byte alignment. The length of the string is 6, and four bytes are required for its storage. In general, the storage required is $L/2 + 1$, where L is the number of digits in the string.

Because the decimal data types can represent only integers, we cannot work directly with decimal numbers having fractional parts. However, this problem is easily solved by *scaling* the numbers. For example, a financial problem needing accuracy to one cent can be programmed entirely in terms of cents. Doing this requires only minor adjustments to input and output quantities.

15.4 | Decimal Arithmetic

The mechanics of decimal arithmetic as performed by hand need no explanation here. However, the implementation of the familiar operations, such as decimal addition, subtraction, multiplication, and division on what we have come to view as a *binary* machine does require explanation. We will show how addition and subtraction can be implemented, and from this it should be evident how other operations could be carried out. Before proceeding with this development, let us clarify that our purpose here is to briefly describe the principles of decimal arithmetic on a binary machine. Because the VAX-11, as well as many other modern computers, has decimal instructions implemented in the hardware, it is seldom necessary to program the procedures shown below to do decimal arithmetic.

Addition of packed decimal strings requires that the individual digit codes be extracted from each addend string and added, beginning at the least significant digit. Because the codes used are identical with the numerical values represented in binary, the digit codes can be added directly. If the result is less than or equal to the 9 code, it is simply placed into the result string. If it is greater than 9, a carry is indicated so that A_{16} (10_{10}) is subtracted before storing, and the left-adjacent digit code is incremented. The following example shows the technique.

EXAMPLE 15.1 Let us add 154_{10} and 265_{10} as packed decimal strings. The operations are most conveniently shown by arranging successive bytes in memory from left to right on the page, that is,

15	4C

plus:

26	5C

Skipping the sign code and starting at the lowest-order digits, the machine extracts the binary codes for the 4 and 5 and performs binary addition.

$$
\begin{array}{ll}
0100 & (4) \\
\underline{0101} & \underline{(5)} \\
1001 & (9)
\end{array}
$$

This is recognized as the code for a decimal 9, so it is stored in the lowest-order digit of the result string to the left of the sign code.

	9C

When the next digits are extracted and added, we get:

$$
\begin{array}{ll}
0101 & (5) \\
\underline{0110} & \underline{(6)} \\
1011 & (11)
\end{array}
$$

Because this is larger than the highest decimal digit value, the decimal base is subtracted.

$$
\begin{array}{ll}
1011 & (11) \\
\underline{1010} & \underline{(10)} \\
0001 & (1)
\end{array}
$$

This 1 is stored in the result string, and it is noted that a 1 must be carried to the left.

$$\boxed{1 \;\big|\; 9\text{C}}$$

Extracting the next digit from the source operand and adding, along with the carry, gives:

$$
\begin{array}{ll}
0001 & (1) \\
\underline{0010} & \underline{(2)} \\
0011 & (3) \\
\underline{0001} & \underline{(1)} \quad \text{(carry)} \\
0100 & (4)
\end{array}
$$

This is stored in the result string, completing the addition.

$$\boxed{41 \;\big|\; 9\text{C}}$$

If there had been a carry out of the last addition, the result string would have been extended accordingly.

Subtraction also proceeds from right to left, extracting digit codes from the source strings one at a time. If subtraction of the subtrahend digit from the corresponding minuend digit yields a negative number, a borrow is indicated, so the decimal base is added to get the result digit, and the left-adjacent minuend digit is decremented. If the operation on the most significant digit requires a borrow, sign adjustment is required. This is done by forming the ''tens complement'' of the result and setting the sign code negative. The following two examples clarify the procedure.

EXAMPLE 15.2 Show decimal subtraction of 136_{10} from 495_{10} when the numbers are represented as packed decimal strings.

As with addition, the digit codes are extracted one at a time from the string, working from right to left. This time, we show our work in decimal only, even though the machine must do these operations in 4-bit binary.

$$
\begin{array}{ccc}
 & \overset{8}{} & \\
4 & \cancel{9} & 5 \\
\underline{-1} & \underline{-3} & \underline{-6} \\
3 & 5 & -\cancel{1} \\
 & & 9
\end{array}
$$

Because the subtraction at the most significant digit did not require a borrow, the result does not need sign adjustment. The packed decimal result is therefore:

35	9C

EXAMPLE 15.3   Show decimal subtraction of 652_{10} from 461_{10} when the numbers are represented as packed decimal strings.

Again, we show our work in decimal, working from right to left, one digit at a time.

$$
\begin{array}{ccc}
 & 5 & \\
4 & \cancel{6} & 1 \\
-6 & -5 & -2 \\
\hline
-\cancel{2} & 0 & -\cancel{1} \\
8 & & 9
\end{array}
$$

Because a borrow was required in the most significant digit, sign adjustment is required. Form the tens complement of 809.

$$
\begin{array}{ll}
999 & \text{(maximum digit values)} \\
-809 & \text{(number to be complemented)} \\
\hline
190 & \\
\underline{\quad 1} & \text{(add 1)} \\
191 & \text{(tens complement)}
\end{array}
$$

The final result is then:

19	1D

Note that we have set the sign nibble to D (negative).

It should be apparent that the decimal multiply and divide operations could be performed using the preceding addition and subtraction procedures together with algorithms for software multiply and divide such as those given in Chapter 6.

The repeated addition and repeated subtraction methods for multiplication and division, respectively, are straightforward but inefficient. The shifting methods are more complicated than their binary counterparts because of the larger set of digits in the decimal system, which means that a larger number of single-digit products is needed in forming the partial products. That is, with binary we have only four cases, $0 \times 0 = 0$, $0 \times 1 = 0$, $1 \times 0 = 0$, and $1 \times 1 = 1$, whereas with decimal we have 100 combinations of digits for which products must be determined. These can be generated separately by binary multiplication each time a particular single-digit product is needed. As a more efficient alternative, the single-digit products could be precalculated for table look-up.

15.5 | Decimal Directives

As with other data types we have studied, the decimal data types require assembly directives for allocating space and for initializing main memory locations. Because LSN strings are really just ASCII characters, the .BLKB directive can be used for space allocation, and the .ASCII directive can be used for initializing. For example, we can write:

```
N:  .ASCIZ/-123456/
```

in order to initialize a leading separate numeric string at location N to −123456. Note that the sign is *mandatory*. If it is omitted, decimal string instructions on the number cause a "reserved operand" fault.

Initializing storage to packed decimal values can be done with the .PACKED directive. For example,

```
P:  .PACKED -123456, LEN
```

creates a packed decimal string for −123456 beginning at location P in main memory. Additionally, the symbol LEN is assigned a value equal to the length of P, i.e., 6.

15.6 | Decimal Instructions

Decimal instructions available on the VAX-11 include arithmetic, comparison, and conversion. These are shown in Table 15.1. Observe that all arithmetic and comparison instructions apply only to the packed decimal data type. The only LSN instructions are those for converting between this data type and the packed decimal type. The reason is that we normally accept input in the LSN form, convert to packed decimal for our calculations, and convert back to LSN for output.

It can also be seen in Table 15.1 that the instructions always require lengths for the decimal operands. This is because the decimal data can be of any length between 0 and 31 digits. The operand specifying these lengths can be coded as an immediate value, or a *word length* integer in memory. It is important, however, that the lengths specified in the instructions correspond to the storage lengths actually allocated.

The other operands in the decimal instructions can employ any addressing mode that leads to an address. This means that any mode except register or immediate can be used. However, in the six-operand instructions care must be taken that the destination string does not overlap either source string.

The following example demonstrates several of the decimal instructions.

EXAMPLE 15.4 Write a MACRO program that accepts an arbitrary number of costs expressed in dollars and cents and generates their sum. Use decimal arithmetic to avoid conversion errors.

The program is shown in Figure 15.1. The .GETSTR macro (Section E.1) is used to get a string character in the format ddd.cc. Because we search for the "." using the LOCC instruction, there can be any number of dollar digits up to 12. The CVTSP instruction is used to convert the input string into two packed decimal strings, representing

TABLE 15.1/VAX-11 Decimal Instructions

Assembler Mnemonics		Opcode	Explanation
Arithmetic:			
ADDP4	LS,SP,LD,DP	20	SP is added to DP
ADDP6	LS1,SP1,LS2,SP2,LD,DP	21	SP1 + SP2 placed in DP
SUBP4	LS,SP,LD,DP	22	SP is subtracted from DP
SUBP6	LS1,SP1,LS2,SP2,LD,DP	23	SP2 − SP1 is placed in DP
MULP	LS1,SP1,LS2,SP2,LD,DP	25	SP2 × SP1 is placed in DP
DIVP	LS1,SP1,LS2,SP2,LD,DP	27	SP2/SP1 is placed in DP
ASHP	C,LS,SP,R,LD,DP	F8	SP × 10^C is placed in DP (Notes 6 and 7)
MOVP	LS,SP,DP	34	SP is moved to DP
Comparison:			
CMPP3	LS,SP1,SP2	35	SP1 is compared to SP2 and condition codes are set. Both strings are of same length.
CMPP4	LS1,SP1,LS2,SP2	37	SP1 is compared to SP2 and condition codes are set. Strings are of different lengths.
Conversion:			
CVTLP	SL,LD,DP	F9	SL converted to DP
CVTPL	LS,SP,DL	36	SP converted to DL
CVTPS	LS,SP,LD,DS	08	SP converted to DS
CVTSP	LS,SS,LD,DP	09	SS converted to DP

NOTES:

(1) All operands must reside in main memory, not in registers.

(2) Registers R0–R5 are used internally by the decimal instructions.

(3) LS,LS1,LS2 = length of source; LD = length of destination. Must be represented as word-size integers.

(4) SP,SP1,SP2 = source packed string.

(5) DP,DP1,DP2 = destination packed string.

(6) C = decimal digit shift count, + left, − right.

(7) R = decimal rounding control. If C < 0, then result is rounded up if next digit beyond LD is greater than or equal to C. R = #5 for normal rounding, #0 for truncation.

(8) SL = source longword signed interger.

(9) DL = destination longword signed interger.

(10) SS = source leading separate numeric string.

(11) DS = destination leading separate numeric string.

dollars and cents, respectively. Because CVTSP operates on LSN strings, the input string must be preceded by " ", "+", or "−". Also, in order to use CVTSP on the cents portion, we overwrite the input "." with a " " to make the last three characters into a legitimate LSN string.

The arithmetic is done with packed decimal instructions. Because packed decimal does not allow fractions we work in terms of cents in the addition. Note that we allow up to 20 digits in SUM, so that the final number of dollar digits is 18. The input and addition process is repeated until the user responds "N".

Output is broken down into dollar and cents using decimal arithmetic. Note that the shift right, shift left, and subtract represent the formulas:

$$\text{DOLLARS} = \text{INT(SUM/100)}$$
$$\text{CENTS} = \text{SUM} - \text{DOLLARS*100}$$

where INT means "take the integer part." The packed decimal strings DOLLARS and CENTS are then converted to LSN strings and moved into an output buffer. The output buffer is initialized to provide the decimal point in front of the cents.

Observe the storage allocation in the program. We have allowed n + 1 bytes for

```
            .TITLE EXAMPLE 15.1
    ;
    ;   ADD $DDDDDDDDDDDD.CC USING PACKED DECIMAL STRINGS
    ;
            .ENTRY  START,0
AGAIN:  .PUTSTR MSG1            ;PROMPT FOR INPUT
        MOVL    #IBUF,R0        ;INPUT STRING
        .GETSTR                 ;    TO IBUF.
        LOCC    #^A'.',#16,IBUF ;GET CENTS
        SUBL3   #IBUF,R1,R2     ;CALC DOLLAR
        CVTLW   R2,LDOL         ;    STRING
        SUBL    #1,LDOL         ;       LENGTH.
        MOVB    #^A' ',(R1)     ;LSN FORM FOR CENTS
        CVTSP   #2,(R1),#2,CENTS;CVT TO PACKED
        CVTSP   LDOL,IBUF,LDOL,DOLLARS
    ;
    ;   SUM IN CENTS
    ;
        ASHP    #2,LDOL,DOLLARS,#5,#14,CENTS2
        ADDP4   #2,CENTS,#20,SUM;ADD CENTS
        ADDP4   #14,CENTS2,#20,SUM;ADD DOLLARS
    ;
    ;   ASK FOR MORE INPUT
    ;
        .PUTSTR MSG2
        MOVL    #IBUF,R0
        .GETSTR
        LOCC    #^A'Y',#3,IBUF  ;Z CLEARED IF FOUND
        BEQL    FINIS
        BRW     AGAIN
```

FIGURE 15.1/Adding dollar amounts in decimal: (a) input and calculations

```
FINIS:
;
;   SET UP OUTPUT
;
        ASHP    #2,#20,SUM,#0,#18,DOLLARS;TRUNCATE CENTS
        ASHP    #2,#18,DOLLARS,#5,#20,HOLD;EVEN DOLLARS
        SUBP6   #20,HOLD,#20,SUM,#2,CENTS ;  AND CENTS
        CVTPS   #18,DOLLARS,#18,OUTBUF;CVT DOLLARS TO LSN
        CVTPS   #2,CENTS,#2,CBUF      ;CVT CENTS TO LSN
        MOVC    #2,CBUF+1,OUTBUF+20
        .PUTSTR OUTBUF           ;PRINT RESULT
        $EXIT_S                  ;EXIT TO VMS
MSG1:   .ASCIZ/ENTER AMOUNT:/
MSG2:   .ASCIZ*AGAIN?(Y/N)*
IBUF:   .BLKB   80              ;INPUT BUFFER
OUTBUF:.BLKB    19              ;OUTPUT BUFFER
        .ASCII/./
        .BLKB   2
        .BYTE   0
CENTS:  .BLKB   2
LDOL:   .BLKW   1
DOLLARS:.BLKB   11
CENTS2:.BLKB    8
SUM:    .BLKB   11
HOLD:   .BLKB   11
CBUF:   .BLKB   3
        .END    START
```

FIGURE 15.1/Adding dollar amounts in decimal: (b) output and local storage

LSN strings, and (n/2 + 1) bytes for packed decimal strings. It does no harm to allocate extra space, but allocating too little will cause problems. In general, the allocation must be based on the longest length specified in any *destination* operand where the string is used.

15.7 | Summary

The topic of this chapter was **decimal programming.** We saw that decimal integers can be stored internally as strings of codes representing the individual decimal digits. These strings can be either ASCII codes with a prefixed ASCII signed code (**Leading Separate Numeric Strings**), or the 4-bit hexadecimal values packed two per byte (**Packed Decimal Strings**). The former are convenient for I/O, and the latter can be operands in special VAX-11 decimal arithmetic instructions, such as **ADDP3, SUBP3,** and so on.

The advantage of using packed decimal arithmetic is that it can give exact results for problems that can be represented in decimal integer form. Unlike floating-point, there are no mapping or round-off errors. Up to 31 decimal digits can be represented, making these data types appropriate even for large-scale commercial and financial applications. The disadvantages are that scaling is required in order to deal with fractions, and arithmetic operations are significantly slower than with other data types.

15.8 | Exercises

15.1 Show the leading separate numeric string and packed decimal string representations of the following decimal numbers. Be sure to show proper arrangement in memory.

(a) 1985 (b) +165294 (c) −49632
(d) −1207 (e) 12611 (f) −3553897

15.2 Write a MACRO subroutine that performs addition of packed decimal strings without using the packed decimal instructions. Demonstrate with the Symbolic Debugger.

15.3 Repeat Exercise 15.2 for subtraction of packed decimal strings.

15.4 Write a program that accepts a decimal numeric string from the keyboard and converts it successively to packed decimal, longword integer, and floating-point. The program should then reverse the process, converting it back to string form for terminal display with .PUTSTR. Use the CVT instructions. Then run the program with various decimal input, e.g., 1234, 1234567, and 1234567890. Explain the results.

15.5 Write a program to compare the sum of 50 seven-digit decimal numbers as computed using floating-point arithmetic with the same sum computed using decimal arithmetic. Explain any difference in the sums.

15.6 Implement the subroutine CNVDEC that is referenced in Example 14.13 using the integer-to-packed-decimal and packed-decimal-to-leading-separate-numeric conversion instructions.

15.7 Write a MACRO program that accepts two user-input decimal integers and an operation symbol (+,−,*, or #) and performs the indicated operation in decimal, printing the result. Use only *integer* instructions. Allow input integers up to 15 decimal digits, and outputs up to 31 decimal digits.

16

Exceptions and Interrupts

16.1 | Overview

This chapter deals with the important concepts of **CPU interrupts** and **exceptions.** These concepts are important when the computer hardware and software must interact with external devices or human operators. Examples include systems in which the computer is being used to control a physical device or acquire data from a laboratory experiment, and on-line database management such as airline reservation systems. These are sometimes called real-time applications because the computer must respond within the time frame established by the external events.

The term *interrupt* applies when some event outside of the program itself interrupts the normal instruction execution cycle and causes a branch to a special service routine. Interrupts are important for a number of reasons, such as the fact that they provide an efficient method for performing input/output operations. The same basic mechanism also provides a way to take appropriate action when a CPU error occurs, and this is called an *exception*. We shall see that the VAX-11 uses a method called **vectoring** for servicing exceptions and interrupts, which is an important concept in its own right.

The material discussed in this chapter is highly dependent on the hardware and software environment. In general, interrupts and exceptions cannot be programmed by a nonprivileged user in a multi-user environment. Therefore, it will not be possible to do actual hardware-level exception and interrupt programming directly from a user program operating under VMS. Nonetheless, we attempt to show the basic concepts underlying such programming. This is supplemented with discussion and examples of the software equivalents of exception and interrupt programming using special features of VMS.

Another topic discussed in this chapter is called **Direct Memory Access** (DMA). This refers to the ability of some peripheral devices to transfer data to and from main memory with minimal intervention by the CPU. DMA is important since it provides much faster data transfer than would be possible otherwise, as well as freeing the CPU for concurrent activity.

407

16.2 | Reasons for Exceptions and Interrupts

There are certain conditions under which the instruction execution sequence should be altered from that implied by the normal, programmer-controlled sequence. One example of this is when an error condition occurs, such as an illegal instruction or addressing error due to a programming error. Such events are called *exceptions*. When this happens, it is usually best to interrupt the program and take some special action, such as displaying an error report and halting. Another example is when some external device, such as the keyboard of the operator console, requires attention. An event like this is called an *interrupt*. Both of these cases can be characterized as events whose time of occurrence and location in the program cannot be anticipated by the programmer. That is, an error might occur anywhere in the code, and the need to "service" a keyboard input might occur at any moment. Rather than requiring the program to constantly check for these occurrences, modern computers are designed with *interrupt* capability. That is, the hardware itself constantly checks for exceptions and interrupt signals from various internal and external sources, and on such occurrence provides automatic branching to routines coded to deal with the event.

16.3 | Hardware Mechanism for Exceptions and Interrupts

16.3.1 Vectoring

When the CPU is interrupted, due to an exception or an interrupt, the normal sequence of instruction execution, as provided by the program, has to be altered. That is, control has to be transferred to the place where the so-called "servicing" routine is located. Because there are many different possible sources of interrupts, each of which needs it own special servicing routine, a way of transferring control to the correct routine has to be provided. On the VAX-11, this problem is solved using a technique called **vectoring.** With vectoring, each hardware element that can cause an interrupt, and each kind of possible exception, is designed to send a unique *offset address* to the CPU along with its interrupt signal. This offset address is relative to the base virtual address of a data structure called the **System Control Block** (SCB) (see Figure 16.1). The SCB base virtual address is stored in a special register called the **System Control Block Base Register** (SCBB). When the CPU receives the exception or interrupt signal, it obtains the contents of the SCBB, adds the offset sent by the interrupter, and uses the result as the virtual address of the location in the SCB where the virtual address of the service routine is stored. The CPU then automatically transfers control to the service routine address. Thus the servicing routine for a particular exception or interrupt can be stored anywhere in memory, as long as its address is stored in the location provided in the SCB. This scheme is shown diagrammatically in Figure 16.1.

Although the SCB can be placed (by the operating system) anywhere in virtual memory space, the offset addresses relative to the SCB base are uniquely determined by the exception or device causing the interrupt. Table 16.1 shows the offset addresses assigned to a number of peripheral devices and CPU exceptions. Also shown there are

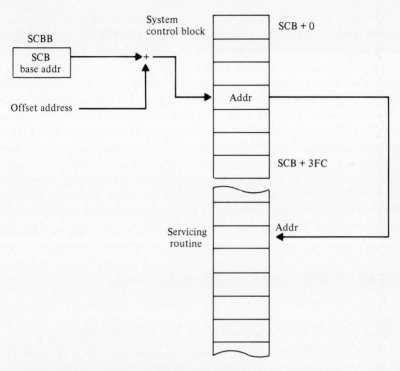

FIGURE 16.1/Exception and interrupt vectoring

TABLE 16.1/Exception and Interrupt Offsets in the System Control Block (partial list)

Source	Offset Address (hexadecimal)	Type	Priority Level (hexadecimal)
Power failure	0C	Interrupt	1E
Reserved instruction	10	Exception (fault)	*
Reserved operand	18	Exception (fault/abort)	*
Trace pending	28	Exception (fault)	*
Arithmetic errors	34	Exception (trap/fault)	*
Change mode	40 – 4C	Exception (trap)	*
Software interrupt	84 –BC	Interrupt	01– 0F
Interval timer	C0	Interrupt	18
Console terminal keyboard	F8	Interrupt	14
Console terminal display	FC	Interrupt	14
Peripheral devices	100 –3FC	Interrupt	10 –17

* Exceptions are not subject to priority; they are handled immediately.

offset addresses for the fifteen different kinds of **software interrupts.** These allow vectoring *initiated by the program* in much the same way that hardware interrupts and exceptions are handled. (Software interrupts are discussed in Section 16.8.)

On a simple, single-user computer, the programmer would write routines to service the exceptions and interrupts, and place the addresses of these routines directly into the System Control Block at the appropriate offsets. However, the typical VAX-11 with VMS normally is executing many concurrent programs, and chaos would result if every program were allowed to redefine the exception and interrupt vectors. Therefore, the operating system assumes the responsibility of maintaining the SCB, and the vectors are really addresses of operating system "dispatch" routines that direct the interrupt or exception to the actual routines that perform necessary operations. These are called **Handler Routines.** Handler routines can be those provided by the operating system, or special ones developed and specified by the programmer. We will see examples of how Handler Routines are developed in MACRO after we have examined the hardware reaction to exceptions and interrupts in greater detail.

16.3.2 Returning from Interrupts and Exceptions

The preceding discussion explained the mechanism for transferring to an exception or interrupt servicing routine, but did not explain how the machine continues after servicing the interrupt. Often the appropriate action is to resume execution of the interrupted program at the point of interruption. To do this, however, the CPU needs a return address and the processor status at the time of the interrupt. To meet this need, the CPU automatically saves the PC and PSL on a special stack at the time of interrupt. The sequence of events upon receiving an exception or interrupt signal can be described, in principle, as follows.

1.   The current contents of the PSL is pushed onto a stack.
2.   The proper address for return (after servicing the exception) is pushed onto the stack.
3.   Any information needed for servicing the exception, such as the type of an arithmetic error, is pushed onto the stack.
4.   The servicing routine address, as determined from the appropriate vector address in the SCB, is loaded into the PC.

Steps 1 and 2 make it possible to return to the place where the interrupt or exception occurred after execution of the servicing routine. Step 3 makes needed information available to the servicing routine. Step 4 transfers control to the servicing routine. By "appropriate" vector, we mean the vector address as given in Table 16.1 for whatever event caused the interrupt or exception. For example, if an arithmetic error occurred, the servicing routine address would be taken from the location offset 34 bytes from the SCB base.

As described in Section 16.3.1, the VMS servicing routine transfers control to an appropriate handler routine. The details of the handler vary depending upon whether the event was an exception or an interrupt. In either case, however, the handling software returns control to the servicing routine upon completion. Final return to the interrupted program is caused by the **REI** (**R**eturn from **E**xception or **I**nterrupt) instruction in the servicing routine. This instruction causes the first and second longwords to be popped from the stack and used to restore PC and PSL, respectively. This completely restores the machine to the state that existed before the execution or interrupt.

16.4 | Exceptions Versus Interrupts

Although the VAX-11 hardware deals with both exceptions and interrupts in essentially the same manner, there are significant differences. The most important difference is the time at which the execution of the service routine is initiated, i.e., when Step 4 takes place. Exceptions cause immediate transfer to the service routine. Interrupts, on the other hand, are serviced according to a priority system, sometimes resulting in delay. Also, there are significant differences in the way that handling routines are defined. In the following two sections we discuss exceptions and interrupts separately in order to further understand their similarities and differences, and how to use these concepts in MACRO programming.

16.5 | Unique Properties of Exceptions

16.5.1 Synchronous Events

Exceptions on the VAX-11 occur due to a variety of causes, as can be seen in Table 16.1. However, all exceptions share the characteristic of being related to the execution of a *particular instruction*. That is, given the same initial state of the machine and the same data, the exception would again occur at exactly the same instruction. For this reason exceptions are sometimes called **synchronous events,** meaning that they are synchronized with the program. Interrupts do not share this characteristic.

16.5.2 Kinds of Exceptions

Exceptions can be classified according to where in the computation cycle the error is detected. If it is detected *after the instruction is complete,* it is called a **trap.** An example would be an integer overflow, because it is only the *result* that is wrong. An exception that occurs *during execution of an instruction,* and which leaves registers and memory in a state suitable for re-execution of the instruction, is called a **fault.** An example of this would occur when an operand is not currently in physical memory so that a paging operation is required. Exceptions occurring during the instruction, but which leave the machine in a *nonrecoverable* state, are called **aborts.** Aborts are rare and are usually the result of a hardware error such as a memory parity error, or a serious system software problem.

The distinction among exception types is important in deciding what to do after detecting the exception. For example, recovery from a trap usually requires an error report and program termination because the problem is related to values of the operands. In some cases, however, resumption of execution is appropriate after a trap. If so, the place to resume is usually at the *following* instruction. This is so because, unless the servicing routine changes the operand, re-execution of the instruction would again precipitate the exception. For this reason the address of the *following* instruction is saved on the stack at the time of the trap, and is used to restore PC after servicing. Faults, on the other hand, often indicate a machine or system condition that the operating system can remove, e.g., page fault, so re-execution of the instruction that caused the fault is suggested. Appropriately, the address of this faulting instruction is the one that is saved on the stack after a fault. Aborts are by definition nonrecoverable, so exit to the operating system is appropriate action. In this case, the saved PC points to the instruction causing the exception to aid in diagnosis.

16.5.3 Enabling Arithmetic Exceptions

Although the *occurrence* of an exception is determined entirely by the instruction and its operands, whether or not the processor reacts to it depends on whether the particular exception type is *enabled* or *disabled*. Some exceptions are always enabled, while others can be enabled and disabled by specific action of the program.

The exceptions that can be enabled and disabled by the program are integer and decimal overflow, floating-point underflow, and trace traps. Each of these is represented by a bit in the PSW, shown in Figure 16.2. Setting one of these bits enables the

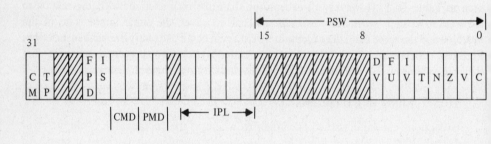

N, Z, V, C : Condition codes
T : Trace trap
IV : Interger overflow trap enable (1 = enabled)
FU : Floating-point underflow trap enable (1 = enabled)
DV : Decimal overflow trap enable (1 = enabled)
IPL : CPU interrupt priority level
CMD : Current mode field (0 = user, 1 = supervisor, 2 = executive, 3 = kernel)
PMP : Previous mode field (0 = user, 1 = supervisor, 2 = executive, 3 = kernel)
IS : Interrupt stack flag
FPD : First part done flag
TP : Trap pending flag
CM : Compatibility mode bit (0 = VAX instruction, 1 = PDP-11 instruction)

FIGURE 16.2/The Processor Status Longword (PSL)

corresponding exception. These bits can be set or cleared by means of the procedure entry mask, or by use of the BICPSW and BISPSW instructions. Placing DV, FU, or IV in the entry mask sets the corresponding bit in PSW and enables the exceptions. For example, the entry mask:

```
.ENTRY PROCA,^M<IV,R4,R5>
```

sets the integer overflow exception enable bit in the PSW, and also saves R4 and R5 on the stack. Because the IV bit is bit 5 in the PSW, it can also be set by:

```
BISPSW #^B100000
```

Similarly,

```
BICPSW #^B100000
```

will clear IV, thus enabling integer overflow exceptions.

16.5.4 Exception Programming Under VMS

Let us now consider how we might use these concepts to cause our program to take some special action upon encountering an exception, such as an integer overflow. In the absence of an operating system, we would write a routine (called the exception servicing routine) to carry out the special actions, and place the virtual address of this routine in the SCB at offset 34_{16} as described in Section 16.3. However, because VMS does not allow us to change the SCB, we cannot use this direct approach. Instead, VMS provides an alternate mechanism for accomplishing the same result as described below.

We have already seen in Section 16.3 that *all* exceptions are "intercepted" by the VMS exception servicing dispatcher routine. The dispatcher in turn invokes a routine called a **condition handler,** which takes action appropriate for the particular kind of exception. We now must consider the following two issues: how to tell VMS to invoke a condition handler routine of our choosing, and how such a routine should be constructed. Both of these issues relate to the *procedure call frame* discussed in Section 9.9.

Informing VMS about a Special Condition Handler for Exceptions

As discussed in Section 9.9 and shown in Figure 9.15, the first longword in the User Stack upon entry to a procedure contains either the address of a condition handler or a longword zero. If the longword is nonzero, the VAX-11 assumes this longword to be the *entry point address of the condition handler* that is to be used throughout the procedure. Because it is viewed as a procedure by VMS, your MACRO main program always has a call frame that was established by VMS at the time it began to execute. By default, this call frame will have a zero in its top longword. However, if you wish to use your own condition handler, you can do so by placing the address of the handler in this location. For example, if you wish a routine called MY_HANDLR to be used as a condition handler for all exceptions in the main program, you should write:

```
.ENTRY   START, ^M<IV,FU>
MOVAB    MY_HANDLR,(FP)
    .
    .
    .
$EXIT_S
.ENTRY   MY_HANDLR,^M<R4,R5>
    .
    .
    .
RET
.END START
```

Because the frame pointer FP points to the top of the call frame, the first instruction in this main program places the address of MY_HANDLR into the position where VMS will look for the condition handler. Then the enabled exceptions in the main program (i.e., IV and FU) will cause MY_HANDLR to be executed whenever either kind of exception occurs. Note that an explicit call to MY_HANDLR is *not* required.

If a procedure does not place a condition handler address at the top of its call frame, VMS finds a zero there and assumes that the condition handler of the *calling* procedure should be used. VMS can find the address of this condition handler because the FP of the *calling* procedure is stored in the third longword of the call frame of every procedure (see Figure 9.15). That is, 12(FP) will always address the previous call frame. If VMS also finds a zero at the top of the calling procedure call frame, it looks into the call frame of the *next higher level* calling procedure. This process continues until a nonzero address is found at the top of some call frame. The first nonzero found in any earlier call frame is used as the condition handler address. Figure 16.3 shows successive call frames in the User Stack due to nested procedures, and the search for a nonzero condition handler address.

In many cases, including all examples in earlier chapters of this book, neither the main program nor any of its procedures defined condition handlers. In such cases the search continues until the call frame of the VMS procedure that called the user program is found. This call frame, set up by VMS, will contain the address of the *system default condition handler*. Thus when you take no specific action to create condition handlers you get the default VMS responses to exceptions. If you have been working the exercises in earlier chapters, you no doubt have seen many of these responses due to programming errors, e.g., "reserved operand fault," followed by the contents of PC and PSL.

Writing Special Condition Handlers for Exceptions

Let us now consider how to write an exception handler. First, the condition handler must be a VAX-11 *procedure*. It must contain instructions to carry out whatever actions are desired for one or more types of exceptions. Other rules that must be followed are:

1. Place any registers used by the procedure, other than R0 and R1, in the entry mask.

2. Any argument needed should be referenced indirectly using the FP of the procedure that *established* the handler.

3. Conditions not dealt with by the handler should be "resignaled" so that VMS can find an appropriate handler for all exceptions.

The meanings of these rules will become clear when we look at Examples 16.1.

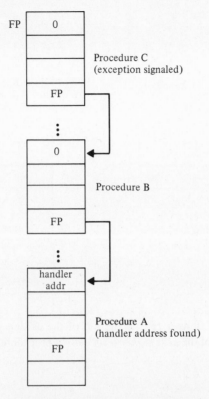

FIGURE 16.3/Searching user stack for nonzero condition handler address

Earlier we noted that VMS employs an exception service dispatcher. One of the functions of this dispatcher is to set up two data tables that become available within the condition handler procedure. These are called the **Signal Array** and the **Mechanism Array.** The addresses of these tables are in the procedure argument list shown in Figure 16.4.

The Signal Array contains the name of the condition that occurred, and in some cases special arguments needed to deal with it. It also contains the PC and PSL at the time of the exception. The names are symbols that are predefined by the MACRO assembler to allow identification of the exception that actually occurred.

Table 16.2 shows names of several of the exceptions sometimes dealt with in user-provided condition handlers. A more complete list can be found in the *VAX/VMS System Service Reference Manual* (Digital Equipment Corporation).

The Mechanism Array provides other information that may be needed in the handler. For example, the FP in this array is that of the procedure that *established* the handler. That is, FP points to the longword where we stored the address of the handler. Thus FP can be used to access local variables stored in the stack immediately above the call frame *of the establisher* (e.g., the main program). This provides a convenient way to

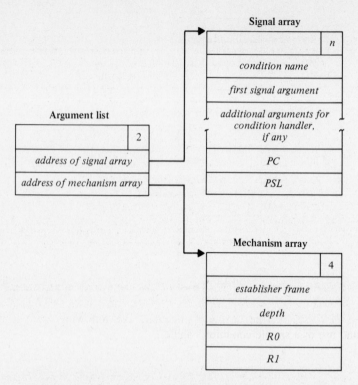

You can define symboblic names to refer to these arguments using the
$CHFDEF macro instruction. The symbolic names are:

Symbolic Offset	Value
CHF$L_SIGARGLST	Address of signal array
CHF$L_MCHARGLST	Address of mechanism array
CHF$L_SIG_ARGS	Number of signal arguments
CHF$L_SIG_NAME	Condition name
CHF$L_SIG_ARG1	First signal-specific argument
CHF$L_MCH_ARGS	Number of mechanism arguments
CHF$L_MCH_FRAME	Establisher frame address
CHF$L_MCH_DEPTH	Frame depth of establisher
CHF$L_MCH_SAVR0	Saved register 0
CHF$L_MCH_SAVR1	Saved register 1

FIGURE 16.4/Argument list and data structures for condition handlers. Copyright © 1982, Digital Equipment Corporation. All rights
reserved. Reprinted with permission.

pass arguments between the handler and the establisher. The *depth* entry in the Mechanism
Array is the frame number of the establisher relative to the procedure where the exception
occurred. For example, *depth* would be 2 for the case shown in Figure 16.3. The R0
and R1 stored in the Mechanism Array are the contents of these registers when the
exception occurred.

TABLE 16.2/Exception Condition Names

Condition Name (Type)	Explanation
SS$_BREAK (fault)	Breakpoint instruction encountered
SS$_DECOVE (trap)	Decimal overflow
SS$_FLTDIV (trap)	Floating/decimal divide by zero
SS$_FLTDIV_F (fault)	Floating divide by zero fault
SS$_FLTOVF (trap)	Floating overflow
SS$_FLTOVF_F (fault)	Floating overflow fault
SS$_FLTUND (trap)	Floating underflow
SS$_FLTUND_F (fault)	Floating underflow fault
SS$_INTDIV (trap)	Integer divide by zero
SS$_INTOVF (trap)	Integer overflow
SS$_TBIT (fault)	Trace bit is pending following an instruction

The information contained in the data structures in Figure 16.4 allows the condition handler to deal with any of the VAX-11 exceptions. The action taken by the condition handler will of course depend on the application. The following example shows the definition and use of a simple condition handler.

EXAMPLE 16.1   Create a condition handler to count the number of integer overflows that occur during program execution.

The program is shown in Figure 16.5. The handler is established in the main program by placing its entry point label EXCPT into the call frame. Local storage is allocated on the stack by decrementing SP by 4. The symbol COUNT_IV is used as an offset from FP for referencing this location, which is where we will keep the count of integer overflows. A hexadecimal integer is accepted from the keyboard using .GETHEX. Because integer overflow exceptions are normally disabled, we enable them by setting bit 5 of PSW. The loop at L1 increments the low byte of R10, beginning at -128_{10}, as a means of generating integer overflows.

Note that no explicit call is made to the condition handler. Yet, at the conclusion of the loop, we print out the count and expect to get the number of integer overflows. Thus we depend on the VAX/VMS exception service routine to invoke EXCPT upon each interger overflow.

The handler EXCPT is defined as a procedure following the main program. We use the entry mask to protect R4, R5, and R6 because they are used within the handler. The first task of the handler is to ascertain the exception type. To do this, we get the Signal Array address out of EXCPT's argument list using the predefined symbolic offset from AP, CHF$L_SIGARGLST. The condition name is then addressed in the Signal Array using the symbolic offset CHF$L_SIG_NAME. This is compared to SS$_INTOVF, which is the symbolic name for the integer overflow condition shown in Table 16.2. If these are not equal, it is a different kind of exception, so we branch to 10$ where the predefined SS$_RESIGNAL value is placed in R0 prior to return. This is called **resignaling** and has the effect of causing the VMS exception service dispatcher to continue searching the call frame sequence for another handler for any exceptions not handled by EXCPT.

```
                .TITLE EXAMPLE 16.1
        COUNT_IV==-4                      ;COUNT OFFSET FROM FP
                .ENTRY  START,^M<>
                MOVAB   EXCPT,(FP)         ;DEFINE EXCEPTION HANDLER
                SUBL    #4,SP              ;SPACE FOR COUNT OF IV'S
                CLRL    COUNT_IV(FP)       ;CLEAR COUNT
                .GETHEX                    ;GET NUM OF TIMES TO LOOP
                MOVL    R10,NUM            ;  AND PLACE IN MEMORY.
                BISPSW  #^B100000          ;SET INTEGER OVERFLOW TRAP
                MOVB    #-128,R10          ;DUMMY
                MOVL    NUM,R1             ;   PROGRAM
        L1:     INCB    R10                ;      TO GENERATE
                SOBGTR  R1,L1              ;          INTEGER OVERFLOWS.
                MOVL    COUNT_IV(FP),R0    ;PRINT COUNT
                .PUTHEX                    ;  OF INTEGER OVERFLOWS.
        EXIT:   $EXIT_S                    ;EXIT TO VMS
        NUM:    .BLKL   1                  ;STORAGE FOR LOOP LIMIT
        ;
        ;   EXCEPTION HANDLER
        ;
                .ENTRY  EXCPT,^M<R4,R5,R6>
                MOVL    CHF$L_SIGARGLST(AP),R4;GET SIG ARG LIST TO R4
                CMPL    #SS$_INTOVF,CHF$L_SIG_NAME(R4);CHECK FOR
                BNEQ    10$                ;            INT OVERFLOWS.
                MOVL    CHF$L_MCHARGLST(AP),R5;GET MCH ARG LIST TO R5
                MOVL    CHF$L_MCH_FRAME(R5),R6;GET FP OF MAIN PROG
                INCL    COUNT_IV(R6)           ;INCREMENT COUNT OF IVS
                MOVZWL  #SS$_CONTINUE,R0       ;RET WITH CONTINUE SIGNAL
                BRB     OUT
        10$:
                MOVZWL  #SS$_RESIGNAL,R0   ;LET ANOTHER HANDLER DO IT
                                           ;  IF NOT INT OVERFLOW.
        OUT:    RET                        ;RETURN TO VMS DISPATCHER
                .END    START
```

FIGURE 16.5/Counting integer overflow exceptions with exception handler

In our case, this will cause all exceptions other than integer overflow to be handled by the system default exception handler.

When the exception is an integer overflow, the establisher FP is extracted from the Mechanism Array and placed in R6. The COUNT_IV offset symbol is then used with displacement addressing from R6 to increment the count variable in the main program. Note that because we made COUNT_IV a global symbol, the EXCPT procedure could even be separately assembled and linked. After incrementing the count, we place SS$_CONTINUE into R0 as a signal. This causes the VMS exception servicing dispatcher to return to the interrupted routine and continue processing.

16.5.5 The Trace Trap Bit

Suppose we wanted to display the contents of the registers or certain memory locations after execution of each instruction. This is called **tracing** and is a useful aid in debugging a program. The VAX-11 provides the capability to do this without making major changes to the program being debugged. As shown in Figure 16.2, bit 4 of the PSW is called the T or **trace trap bit.** When this bit is set, the CPU will be interrupted after the next instruction and trapped through the vector at offset 28_{16} in the SCB. To use this feature, the program must place the servicing routine address at this offset in SCB and set the T bit in the PSW. Once this is done, the next instruction will cause a trap to the servicing routine, which can contain any desired instructions.

When operating under VMS we cannot perform the above programming steps directly. However, a trace can still be performed by using a VMS facility called the **System Services.** To enable tracing, the T-bit in the PSW must be set using either the entry mask or the BISPSW instruction. For example,

```
.ENTRY  START,^M<T>
```

will enable tracing throughout the program. Then an exception handler is defined in the same manner as in Example 16.1. In fact, the same handler could be used with few modifications. With reference to Figure 16.5, it would be necessary to add the following instructions after the 10$ label:

```
        CMPL  #SS$_TBIT,CHF$L_SIG_NAME(R4)
        BNEQ  20$
        {instructions to print desired registers etc}
        BRB  OUT
20$:
```

The tracing can be turned on and off with the BISPSW and BICPSW instructions.

16.6 | Interrupts

As noted previously, the term *interrupt* in the VAX-11 context refers specifically to those CPU interrupts that are caused by randomly occurring, external events, such as the need for attention by peripheral devices. These are sometimes referred to as *asynchronous* events because, in contrast to exceptions, they are not "synchronized" with the program. That is, if the program was re-executed, chances are that the interrupt would *not* occur again at the same instruction.

While interrupts work in much the same way as exceptions, they have a different purpose and are different in the way that they are used. Their purpose is to allow the CPU to do other tasks while awaiting the need to service a peripheral device. This way of handling I/O is in contrast to the programmed I/O method considered in Section 8.8.1, in which the program constantly tested the device status register while waiting. Interrupt-driven I/O can greatly improve the speed in certain applications, and in some cases represents the only viable approach.

16.6.1 Interrupt Enabling

Before developing these ideas further, we need to discuss the role of the **device status registers** and the **processor status longword** (PSL) in interrupt programming. These registers allow interrupts to be enabled or disabled, and to be dealt with in order of priority.

Interrupt-generating devices have status registers that include bits called INTR ENBL (interrupt enable) and READY. This register is the same as that discussed in Section 8.8.1, and is shown in Figure 16.6 with the INTR ENBL and READY bits identified.

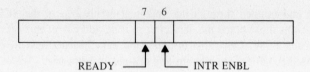

FIGURE 16.6/Device status register

If the INTR ENBL bit is cleared, as it is normally unless set by the program, the associated device cannot interrupt the CPU. If it is set, then an interrupt signal is sent to the CPU whenever the READY bit in the same register changes from 0 to 1. This means that one of the tasks necessary in programming for interrupts is setting the INTR ENBL in the status register for the device being used.

It was stated above that interrupt occurs whenever INTR ENBL is set and READY changes from 0 to 1. It is also true that if the READY bit is set and the INTR ENBL changes from 0 to 1, an interrupt will occur. Because of this, an interrupt will occur immediately upon execution of an instruction that sets INTR ENBL for a device that is normally in the ready state, such as a display or printer.

Having the INTR ENBL bit set is actually just one of two requirements for a device being allowed to interrupt the processor. The other requirement is that the *CPU interrupt priority level* (IPL) must be lower than that of the device. Device priority levels are fixed, as shown in Table 16.1. On the other hand, CPU priority (IPL) can be set in the program and is indicated by bits $<20:16>$ in the PSL. If IPL is *lower* than the priority level of the interrupt request, the service routine is executed immediately. Otherwise, it is deferred until the IPL is reduced. The IPL changes frequently because interrupt servicing routines usually raise it to a higher level so as to keep less important tasks from interrupting. When the executing process completes, IPL is automatically reduced to the previous level due to the action of the REI (return from interrupt) instruction.

Suppose, for example, that a program is executing at IPL of 0 (the normal condition) and an interrupt from the console keyboard is detected. Because this interrupt request has a priority of 14_{16} (see Table 16.1), control is transferred to its service routine, and IPL is raised to 14_{16}. If a peripheral with a priority of 17_{16} requests an interrupt before the keyboard routine completes, the service routine of this second device is initiated, raising the IPL to 17_{16}. The second routine could then be interrupted by the interval timer (priority 18_{16}) or a power failure (priority $1E_{16}$). Eventually, however, each service routine completes with an REI instruction, lowering IPL and allowing the interrupted, lower-priority tasks to complete.

16.6.2 Device Drivers

Because of the multi-user operating system, direct interaction with peripheral devices as just described is never done within the context of a VAX/VMS user program. Instead, VAX/VMS provides access to these devices with the System Services routines. These routines in turn invoke **device driver** routines that are specific to each peripheral device. It is within the context of a device driver that interrupt programming is normally done, using the concepts just described. Many device drivers are provided with VMS, including those for terminals, line printers, and mass storage devices. By following VMS protocols, user-developed drivers for other devices can be invoked through the VMS facilities. Details on device drivers can be found in the *VAX/VMS Guide to Writing a Device Driver,* and other information on interrupt I/O programming can be found in the *VAX/VMS Real-Time User's Guide* (Digital Equipment Corporation).

16.6.3 The Asynchronous System Trap and System Service

Previously we noted that VMS does not allow interrupt programming in a direct sense. However, through a group of routines called the VMS System Services we are provided with a similar concept, called an **Asynchronous System Trap** (AST). This concept allows user programs to respond to asynchronous events and execute special servicing routines in a manner that parallels interrupt programming at the hardware level. The System Services provide a variety of functions, including I/O to terminals, line printers, and other peripheral devices. In Section 16.6.3 we focus on terminal I/O to exemplify use of the System Services and AST programming. The *VAX/VMS System Services Reference Manual* (Digital Equipment Corporation) may be consulted for a complete description of the capabilities and usage of these routines.

Establishing a Channel

The System Service I/O routines communicate with peripheral devices through a software data path called a **channel.** Before a program can do any I/O with a device, it is necessary to "connect" a channel to the device. Normally the programmer knows the device by a physical name, e.g., _TXB3 (terminal 3), or by a logical name, e.g., SYS$INPUT (a generic reference to the user's terminal). The **$ASSIGN_S** System Service macro performs the task of connecting a named device to a channel. Specifically, this macro takes the known physical or logical name as an input argument and returns a channel number. The channel number is then referenced in subsequent I/O operations with the device.

As an example, suppose we wish to establish a channel for terminal I/O. The appropriate device logical name is either SYS$INPUT or SYS$OUTPUT, and we would therefore write:

```
TERM_NAME:  .ASCID/SYS$INPUT/   ; DEFINE DEVICE NAME
TERM_CHAN:  .BLKW 1             ; STORAGE FOR CHAN. INDENTIFIER
            $ASSIGN_S DEVNAM=TERM_NAME,CHAN=TERM_CHAN
            BLBC  RO,ERROR       ; ERROR HANDLING
```

Here the .ASCID directive is used to store the SYS$INPUT device name as a character string descriptor* at the location labeled TERM_NAME.

Following the device name, a word is reserved for storage of the channel number at the location labeled TERM_CHAN. The $ASSIGN_S macro then determines a channel number for the device and stores the channel number at TERM_CHAN.

---

* A character string descriptor consists of two longwords, the first of which contains the string length in bits <15:0> and the second of which contains a pointer to the actual string location. Many system routines require string arguments of this form.

All System Services return R0 with the low bit clear if for any reason the requested operation cannot be carried out. The BLBC (**B**ranch on **L**ow **B**it **C**lear) instruction in the preceding example will therefore branch to the location labeled ERROR if VMS cannot establish a channel number for the named device. If the assignment is successful, the branch is not taken and terminal I/O can subsequently be carried out with channel TERM_CHAN. When I/O to the device is completed, the channel can be deassigned with the $DASSGN_S macro. For example,

```
$DASSGN_S  CHAN=TERM_CHAN
BLBC    R0,ERROR
```

will deassign the terminal channel created previously. However, the channel will be automatically deassigned upon completion of your program, so explicit deassigning is not often required.

Device Input or Output

Input or output to an assigned channel is done with the **$QIO_S** System Service macro. This service derives its name from the function it actually performs. That is, it places an input or output request in a *queue,* which is a collection of all pending VMS I/O requests. This is called "queuing" the input or output. After doing so, or attempting to do so, $QIO_S returns control to the user program at the instruction following the $QIO_S. Note that the I/O process itself now proceeds independently of the program that queued it, and its completion must be viewed as an asynchronous event. Meanwhile, the user program continues, and VMS sends a signal to the user program when the requested I/O is actually completed. The user program must somehow detect the signal and react accordingly. Here we shall describe two methods for this detection. One is analogous to the hardware-level programmed I/O described in Section 8.8 using the software equivalent of the device status register. The other uses an Asynchronous System Trap, which is the software equivalent of an interrupt.

The $QIO_S System Service macro can perform either input or output, and allows several variations in the way these are done. The arguments determine the exact operation being requested. In general, the form for terminal I/O using $QIO_S is:

```
$QIO_S -
   CHAN   = address where channel number is stored,-
   FUNC   = #function code for read or write,-
   IOSB   = address of quadword I_O status block,-
   ASTADR = entry point address for AST handler routine,-
   P1     = address of input or output buffer,-
   P2     = #buffer length
```

Because of the number and length of the arguments, we use the MACRO assembler *continuation character* "-" and place each argument on a separate line. The channel parameter (CHAN) is usually equated to the label of the channel number as determined in the associated $ASSIGN_S. The function code (FUNC) indicates whether a read or a write is requested. That is,

```
FUNC = #IO$_READVBLK
```

requests a read operation, or:

```
FUNC = #IO$_WRITEVBLK
```

requests a write operation. These symbols are predefined by the System Services and will be available if you place the macro reference **$IODEF** in the definitions section of your program. IOSB and ASTADR are optional arguments, and normally one or the other is used. If IOSB (**I/O** Status **B**lock) is given, $QIO_S will store the completion status in a *quadword* at the indicated address. You should include this argument if you intend to check for completion in a manner similar to programmed I/O. On the other hand, ASTADR should be equated to the entry point label of an Asynchronous System Trap handling procedure if you intend to handle I/O completion asynchronously (i.e., like an interrupt). The parameters P1 and P2 give $QIO_S the address and length of a buffer for the input or output characters.

The techniques just described are demonstrated in the following example.

EXAMPLE 16.2 Consider the need for a program that continuously accepts numerical inputs from the terminal keyboard and enters them into a sorted list. This program is to be run under VMS so that we cannot access the terminal keyboard and display device registers directly.

One approach is to use the .GETHEX routine described in Section 4.11. The disadvantage of this approach is that when the list gets long, the time required to sort the new number into the list becomes lengthy. Therefore, there might be a significant delay before the next number can be entered. Instead, we would like the program to accept input as fast or slowly as the keyboard operator types, while allowing the processor to work on sorting whenever there is a pause in the input. That is, we seek to *overlap* the entry process and the sorting process in order to maintain good keyboard response and high processor utilization.

An interrupt method for accepting keyboard entry would meet this need. However, because we cannot do interrupt programming directly under VMS, we choose to use the equivalent software concept of Asynchronous System Traps in conjunction with the $QIO_S System Service macro. Also, in order to demonstrate the equivalent of programmed I/O using System Services, we will echo the keyboard to the terminal display using the completion status returned by $QIO_S.

With this approach, the main program logic is shown in Figure 16.7. After setting up the data structures and other needed initializations, the program enters a loop that constantly merges new entries into the list. The variable NSORT represents the number of items currently in the list, and STP is a stopping flag. Both of these variables have their values updated by the keyboard AST handling routine. Also, new numbers are placed into the list by the AST handling routine. If STP is not set, a check is made to see whether the list has increased since last sorted. If it has, the list is sorted. In either case, the program continuously loops back until the STP flag is set.

Note that the main program algorithm has no branch to an input routine. Rather, we are depending on the AST mechanism to handle this branching. This cannot be shown in a flowchart because the asynchronous event could occur *anywhere* in the loop. The loop will be interrupted any time a key is pressed at the keyboard. In a sense, the keyboard process may be thought of as going on in parallel with the loop and sorting process.

The MACRO program for this example is shown in Figure 16.8. Let us first examine

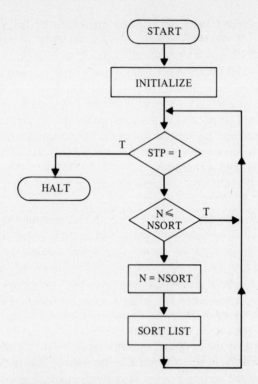

FIGURE 16.7/Main program for AST-driven data entry

the initializations in the main program, as shown in Figure 16.8(a). Note that we include the $IODEF System Service macro to define standard symbols that we will use in the program. Next, the data structures that the $ASSIGN_S and $QIO_S macro will use are defined. The input and output buffers are defined to be one byte in length so that we can handle input one character at a time. This is followed by local storage for program variables.

The main program is shown in Figure 16.8(b). It begins by assigning a channel for terminal I/O and performing initializations of program variables. Immediately before entering the loop, we perform "read enable" using the subroutine READ_ENABLE. As described below, READ_ENABLE queues the first request for keyboard input. After this, the main program loop is begun, with logic as shown in Figure 16.7.

The sort routine is shown in Figure 16.8(c). A bubble sort technique is used, in which passes are made through the list until no further interchanges take place. Note that the length of the sorted list is NSORT, rather than N. This is because the length of the list N might get changed while a sort is in progress due to AST servicing. One must always be careful when programming with ASTs that the concurrent processes do not interfere with one another.

The routines that actually queue the I/O requests are shown in Figure 16.8(d). The

FIGURE 16.8/(Pages 425–427) Interrupt-driven data entry: (a) symbol definitions and initializations; (b) main program

```
        .TITLE EXAMPLE 16.2
;
;       INTERRUPT DRIVEN INPUT UNDER VAX/VMS
;
;   SYMBOL DEFINITIONS AND INITIALIZATIONS
;
IBL = 1                         ;INPUT BUFFER LENGTH
OBL = 1                         ;OUTPUT BUFFER LENGTH
LF  = 10                        ;LINEFEED
CR  = 13                        ;CARRIAGE RETURN
        $IODEF                  ;SYS MACRO TO DEFINE IO SYMBOLS
TERM_NAME:-
        .ASCID /SYS$INPUT/      ;DEFINE TERMINAL LOGICAL NAME
TERM_CHAN:-
        .BLKW 1                 ;STORAGE FOR CHANNEL NUMBER
OUT_IOSB:-
        .BLKQ 1                 ;STORAGE FOR OUTPUT STATUS BUFFER
IN_BUF: .BLKB IBL               ;STORAGE FOR INPUT BUFFER
OUT_BUF:.BLKB OBL               ;STORAGE FOR OUTPUT BUFFER
;
;   STORAGE
;
STP:    .BLKL  1                ;RESERVE
V:      .BLKL  1                ;
N:      .BLKL  1                ;     STORAGE
NSORT:  .BLKL  1                ;
LLAST:  .BLKL  1                ;       SPACE.
LIST:   .BLKL  1000             ;1000. DECIMAL LIST SPACE
```

(a)

```
;
;   PROGRAM
;
        .ENTRY  START,0
;
;   INITIALIZATIONS
;
        $ASSIGN_S -             ;GET THE CHANNEL
          DEVNAM=TERM_NAME,-    ;    NUMBER FOR
          CHAN  =TERM_CHAN      ;      TERMINAL.
        BLBS    R0,LO           ;EXIT TO VMS
        BRW     ERROR           ;    IF ASSIGN_S FAILS.
LO:     MOVW    #SS$_NORMAL,OUT_IOSB ;INIT. OUTPUT STATUS BUFFER
        CLRL    STP             ;INIT. STOP FLAG
        CLRL    V               ;INIT. VALUE LOCATION
        CLRL    N               ;INIT. LEN. OF ENTERED LIST
        CLRL    NSORT           ;INIT. LEN. OF SORTED LIST
        MOVL    #LIST,LLAST     ;INIT. ADDR. OF NEXT LIST ENTRY
        BSBW    READ_ENABLE     ;BEGIN WAIT FOR FIRST KEYBOARD ENTRY
;
;   CONTINUOUSLY ACCEPT NEW ENTRIES AND SORT LIST REAL-TIME.
;
LOOP:
        TSTL    STP             ;QUIT IF KBIH
        BNEQ    QUIT            ;    SETS STOP FLAG.
        CMPL    N,NSORT         ;IDLE LOOP IF
        BLEQU   LOOP            ;    N HAS NOT CHANGED.
        MOVL    N,NSORT         ;SORT LEN.=ENTERED LEN.
        BSBW    SORT            ;SORT THE LIST
        BRB     LOOP            ;KEEP RUNNING TIL STP=0
QUIT:
EXIT:   $EXIT_S                 ;NORMAL EXIT TO VMS
;
;   ERROR EXIT
;
ERROR:
        .PUTSTR ERR_MSG
        $EXIT_S R0              ;EXIT AND SIGNAL
ERR_MSG:.ASCIZ/IO ERROR/
```

(b)

```
;
;      SORTING ROUTINE
;
SORT:
          MOVL      NSORT,R2          ;SET SORT PASS
          DECL      R2                ;   LCV.
          BLEQU     OUTSORT           ;NOTHING TO SORT
          MOVL      #1,MORE           ;SET FLAG FOR INIT.SORT PASS
WHILE:    TSTL      MORE              ;MAKE MORE PASSES UNTIL
          BEQL      OUTSORT           ;   NO MORE SWITCHES.
          CLRL      MORE              ;PREPARE SWITCH FLAG
          MOVL      #LIST,R11         ;SET LIST PTR. TO TOP OF LIST
          MOVL      R2,R3             ;INIT. PASS LCV , R3
PASS:     CMPL      (R11),4(R11)      ;SKIP SWITCH
          BLEQU     L2                ;   IF ADJ. ENTRIES IN ORDER.
          MOVL      (R11),TEMP        ;OTHERWISE
          MOVL      4(R11),(R11)      ;   DO THE
          MOVL      TEMP,4(R11)       ;      SWITCH AND
          INCL      MORE              ;         SET THE FLAG.
L2:       ADDL      #4,R11            ;INCREMENT LIST PTR.
          SOBGTR    R3,PASS           ;COMPLETE THE PASS
          BRB       WHILE             ;CONTINUE MAKING PASSES
OUTSORT:
          RSB                         ;RETURN TO MAIN PROGRAM
TEMP:     .BLKL     1                 ;TEMP. STORAGE FOR SWITCH
MORE:     .BLKL     1                 ;PASS FLAG
```

(c)

```
;
;      READ AND WRITE ROUTINES
;
READ_ENABLE:
          $QIO_S    CHAN=TERM_CHAN,-;SET CHANNEL TO TERMINAL
                FUNC      =#IO$_READVBLK,-;THIS IS FOR A READ OPERATION
                ASTADR    =KB_AST_H,- ;SET ADDR OF KEYBD. INTERRUPT HDLR.
                P1        =IN_BUF,-   ;SET ADDR OF INPUT BUFFER
                P2        =#IBL       ;SET INPUT BUFFER LENGTH
          BLBS      R0,10$            ;ERROR EXIT
          BRW       ERROR             ;   IF ENABLE FAILS.
10$:      RSB                         ;RETURN TO CALLER
WRITE:
          TSTW      OUT_IOSB          ;WAIT IF
          BEQL      WRITE             ;   DISPLAY NOT READY.
          CMPW      OUT_IOSB,#SS$_NORMAL;ERROR EXIT
          BEQL      20$               ;   IF
          BRW       ERROR             ;      STATUS ERROR.
20$:      $QIO_S    CHAN=TERM_CHAN,-;SET CHANNEL TO TERMINAL
                FUNC      =#IO$_WRITEVBLK,-;THIS IS FOR A WRITE OPERATION
                IOSB      =OUT_IOSB,- ;WE WILL USE THE IO STATUS
                P1        =OUT_BUF,-  ;SET THE OUTPUT BUFFER
                P2        =#OBL       ;SET OUTPUT BUFFER LENGTH
          BLBS      R0,30$            ;ERROR EXIT
          BRW       ERROR             ;   IF WRITE DOESN'T GET QUEUED.
30$:      RSB                         ;RETURN TO CALLER
```

(d)

FIGURE 16.8/Interrupt-driven data entry: (c) sorting routine; (d) read and write routines

```
;
;     KEYBOARD AST SERVICING PROCEDURE
;
          .ENTRY  KB_AST_H,^M<R10>
          MOVB    IN_BUF,R10          ;READ DATA FROM KEYBOARD INPUT BUFFER
          BICL    #^XFFFFFF80,R10     ;MASK UNUSED HIGH BITS
          BSBW    PRTIT               ;ECHO INPUT
          CMPB    R10,#^A'S'          ;"S" WILL SET STOP FLAG
          BEQL    STPSET
          CMPB    R10,#CR             ;CR WILL INDICATE
          BEQL    COMP                ;    ENTRY IS COMPLETE.
          SUBB    #^X30,R10           ;REMOVE ASCII BASE
          BLSSU   L3                  ;IGNOR
          CMPB    R10,#10             ;    NON-DECIMAL
          BGEQU   L3                  ;      CHARACTERS.
          MULL    #10,V               ;DECIMAL SHIFT PREVIOUS VALUE
          ADDL    R10,V               ;ADD ENTERED DIGIT TO VALUE
L3:       BRB     OUTKBIH             ;
STPSET:   INCL    STP                 ;SET STOP FLAG
          BRB     OUTKBIH             ;
COMP:     INCL    N                   ;INC. ENTERED LIST LENGTH
          MOVL    V,@LLAST            ;PUT ENTERED VALUE AT BOT. OF LIST
          ADDL    #4,LLAST            ;ADVANCE "LAST ENTRY" POINTER
          CLRL    V                   ;RESET ENTERY VALUE LOCATION
OUTKBIH:
          BSBW    READ_ENABLE         ;RE-ENABLE KEYBOARD READ
          RET                         ;RETURN FROM KB INTERRUPT
;
;    INPUT ECHO TO SCREEN
;
PRTIT:
          MOVB    R10,OUT_BUF         ;PRINT THE
          BSBW    WRITE               ;   CHARACTER.
          CMPB    R10,#CR             ;SEND A LF
          BNEQ    L4                  ;    IF IT
          MOVB    #LF,OUT_BUF         ;      WAS
          BSBW    WRITE               ;          CR.
L4:       RSB                         ;RETURN TO CALLER
;
;    END OF PROGRAM
;
          .END    START
```

(e)

FIGURE 16.8/Interrupt-driven data entry: (e) interrupt servicing procedure

first of these is READ_ENABLE, which is basically a $QIO_S to queue a keyboard input request. Note that we set the ASTADR argument to KB_AST_H, which is the entry point address of the keyboard AST handler. This means that the next time a keyboard entry for this process is detected by VMS, control will be transferred to KB_AST_H.

Following the READ_ENABLE routine in Figure 16.8(d) is a routine called WRITE. The function of WRITE is to queue a write to the terminal display. Observe that this routine begins by testing the first word of the terminal I/O status buffer, OUT_IOSB. Because OUT_IOSB is initialized to the System Service "normal exit" value (i.e.,

SS$_NORMAL, which is not zero), the looping branch to WRITE does not take place the first time the routine is entered. Instead, a terminal display write is immediately queued by the $QIO_S call. Because the IOSB argument is given and is equated to OUT_IOSB, $QIO_S will maintain the status of the write request in OUT_IOSB. This status buffer is *cleared upon queuing the request,* then set to $SS_NORMAL when the write completes successfully. Note that control is returned immediately to the calling routine after the $QIO_S, rather than waiting for completion. However, if WRITE should be called *again* before the first write has completed, the entry point loop will cause the routine to be delayed until the previous request is complete. Obviously, we could place the wait loop after the $QIO_S. However, the approach used here has the advantage of allowing useful processing elsewhere in the program while waiting for the write request to complete.

The AST handling routine, KB_AST_H, is shown in Figure 16.8(e). We immediately read the input buffer, IN_BUF. It is not necessay to check the status buffer because control cannot get to this routine unless a keyboard entry has completed. After getting a character, we jump to subroutine PRTIT to echo it to the terminal display. After echoing, we check to see if an "S" was entered, and set the "stop flag" STP to 1 and return if it was. Otherwise, the character is converted to binary and added to the "entry value" which is built up in V. Note that control is returned to the point of interrupt after each entered *digit* is converted. When the entered character is a carriage return, the servicing routine branches to COMP where the completed entry value is placed at the bottom of the list, the list length N is incremented, and the value V is reset to 0.

16.7 | Software Interrupts

The concept of vectoring to a servicing routine through an address at a fixed place in memory has applications other than exceptions and interrupts. Many computers provide a mechanism that allows this vector process to be initiated *by the program.* This is called a **software interrupt** or **software trap,** and results in transfer to a service routine identified by the vector. In a sense, this is much like a subroutine transfer, but it has a number of advantages. For one thing, by using the vectoring mechanism, the service routine need not be involved in the linking process. For example, a service routine implemented in this way can be stored as part of the operating system rather than as part of the user program, and yet can be accessed by the user program. Also, the hardware interrupt priority system can be used for scheduling service routine execution. Many operating systems provide services to user programs with the software interrupt mechanism.

As with other kinds of interrupts, VAX-11 software interrupts can only be executed by privileged programs, preventing most users from employing this programming technique directly. Nonetheless, we shall explore the mechanism in order to better understand the concepts involved. Then we will learn how to use the VMS System Services to do a very similar kind of programming using Asynchronous System Traps.

16.7.1 Software Interrupts on the VAX-11

The VAX-11 supports fifteen priority levels for software interrupts. That is, with this mechanism one can request execution of a service routine at a high priority level if it needs to be done immediately, or at a lower priority if it is not time-critical. As with other interrupts, the processor will not execute the service routine until the processor priority drops below the priority level specified for the software interrupt. From Table 16.1 we see that interrupt priority levels 1 through F_{16} are assigned to software interrupts. Because all hardware priority levels are higher than software priority levels, hardware interrupts always take precedence over software interrupts.

The software interrupt vectors are stored in the System Control Block (SCB) like those for hardware interrupts and exceptions. Table 16.1 shows that the vectors for the software interrupt priority levels 1 through F_{16} are stored in the SCB at offsets 84_{16} through BC_{16}. Because there is a one-to-one correspondence between these vectors and the priority levels, there can only be one service routine for each software priority level. Conversely, the processor needs only the priority level to determine the location of the service vector.

Given the above information it is evident that software interrupt programming on the VAX-11 requires the following steps. First, the service routine must be stored at a known location in memory. Secondly, the address of this routine must be placed in the SCB at an offset location between 84_{16} and BC_{16}. The offset will determine the priority level for the interrupt, as noted above. Once these steps have been carried out, a software interrupt is "requested" by placing the interrupt priority level into a special, privileged register called the **Software Interrupt Request Register** (SIRR). This precipitates the normal interrupt sequence, as described in Section 16.3. The processor determines the service vector offset from the priority level placed in SIRR. However, only privileged programs can alter SIRR, preventing most users from using this programming technique.*

16.7.2 Using Asynchronous System Traps to Simulate Software Interrupts

The Asynchronous System Trap (AST), described in Section 16.6.3, provides a mechanism for simulation of software interrupts for user programs running under VMS. Although this mechanism does not afford the full advantages of an actual VAX-11 software interrupt, it does allow us to exemplify very similar programming techniques.

In Section 16.6.3 we saw that the AST concept involved definition of a service routine, and then identification of this routine with an asynchronous event, such as completion of an I/O operation. These same steps must be followed in preparing for software interrupt simulation. Then, in order to simulate a software interrupt, all we need is a method for "requesting" an AST interrupt by an explicit program instruction, rather than waiting for an asynchronous event. The needed method is provided through the **$DCLAST_S (Declare AST)** macro that is part of the System Services. The parameters

---

* The VAX-11 has an alternate software interrupt mechanism through the change mode instructions CHMK, CHME, CHMS, and CHMU, as described in the *VAX Architecture Handbook*.

for this macro include the address of the servicing routine, and an optional argument. For example, we could write:

```
$DCLAST_S ASTADR = MY_SERVICE_ROUTINE,-
          ASTPRM = #2
```

This causes transfer to MY_SERVICE_ROUTINE, and the argument value, in this case 2, becomes available at 4(AP) within this procedure (see Figure 16.4). Often the argument is used as a "request number" identifying the desired service, so that a single service routine can perform several different functions.

EXAMPLE 16.3   As an example of $DCLAST_S usage consider the need for terminal I/O. We would like three services, namely, open the terminal (SYS$INPUT) for I/O, read a single character from the keyboard into the low byte of R10, and display the single character stored in the low byte of R10 at the terminal.

The program is shown in Figure 16.9. In Figure 16.9(a) we see a main program that exercises the specified functions. The service routine address label is IO. Within the main program, the terminal is first opened by a $DCLAST_S with the parameter

```
        .TITLE EXAMPLE 16.3
;
;    SOFTWARE INTERRUPTS
;

        .ENTRY  START,0
        $DCLAST_S   ASTADR=IO,ASTPRM=#0;OPEN TERMINAL CHANNEL
        $DCLAST_S   ASTADR=IO,ASTPRM=#4;READ INTO R10
        $DCLAST_S   ASTADR=IO,ASTPRM=#8;WRITE FROM R10
        MOVB        #^A'X',R10
        $DCLAST_S   ASTADR=IO,ASTPRM=#8;WRITE FROM R10
        $EXIT_S
                        (a)
;
;    SERVICE ROUTINE
;
;
;    SYMBOL DEFINITIONS AND INITIALIZATIONS
;
IBL=1                           ;INPUT BUFFER LENGTH
OBL=1                           ;OUTPUT BUFFER LENGTH
        $IODEF                  ;SYS MACRO TO DEFINE IO SYMBOLS
TERM_NAME:-
        .ASCID /SYS$INPUT/      ;DEFINE TERMINAL LOGICAL NAME
TERM_CHAN:-
        .BLKW 1                 ;STORAGE FOR CHANNEL NUMBER
OUT_IOSB:-
        .BLKQ 1                 ;STORAGE FOR OUTPUT STATUS BUFFER
IN_IOSB:-
        .BLKQ 1                 ;STORAGE FOR INPUT STATUS BUFFER
IN_BUF: .BLKB IBL               ;STORAGE FOR INPUT BUFFER
OUT_BUF:.BLKB OBL               ;STORAGE FOR OUTPUT BUFFER
                        (b)
```

FIGURE 16.9/Software traps for vectoring to service routines using System Services: (a) main program; (b) service routine symbols and definitions

```
        .ENTRY  IO,^M<R11>
        MOVL    4(AP),R11           ;GET PARAMETER N
        JMP     @FUN(R11)           ;GO TO FUNCTION N
FUN:    .LONG   OPEN,IN_CHAR,OUT_CHAR;FUNCTION TABLE
;
;   FUNCTIONS
;
OPEN:   $ASSIGN_S -                 ;GET THE CHANNEL
          DEVNAM=TERM_NAME,-        ;   NUMBER FOR
          CHAN  =TERM_CHAN          ;      TERMINAL.
        BLBS    R0,10$              ;EXIT TO VMS
        BRW     ERROR               ;   IF ASSIGN_S FAILS.
10$:    MOVW    #SS$_NORMAL,OUT_IOSB;INIT. OUTPUT STATUS BUFFER
        BRB     IO_END              ;RETURN
OUT_CHAR:MOVB   R10,OUT_BUF         ;LOAD OUTPUT BUFFER
10$:    TSTW    OUT_IOSB            ;WAIT IF
        BEQL    10$                 ;   DISPLAY NOT READY.
        CMPW    OUT_IOSB,#SS$_NORMAL;ERROR EXIT
        BEQL    20$                 ;   IF
        BRW     ERROR               ;         STATUS ERROR.
20$:    $QIO_S  CHAN=TERM_CHAN,-    ;QUEUE THE IO REQUEST
          FUNC    =#IO$_WRITEVBLK,-,;THIS IS FOR A WRITE OPERATION
          IOSB    =OUT_IOSB,-       ;WE WILL USE THE IO STATUS
          P1      =OUT_BUF,-        ;SET THE OUTPUT BUFFER
          P2      =#OBL             ;SET OUTPUT BUFFER LENGTH
        BLBS    R0,30$              ;ERROR EXIT
        BRW     ERROR               ;   IF WRITE DOESN'T GET QUEUED.
30$:    BRB     IO_END              ;RETURN
IN_CHAR:$QIO_S  CHAN=TERM_CHAN,-    ;QUEUE THE IO REQUEST
          FUNC    =#IO$_READVBLK,-  ;THIS IS FOR A READ OPERATION
          IOSB    =IN_IOSB,-        ;WE WILL USE THE IO STATUS
          P1      =IN_BUF,-         ;SET ADDR OF INPUT BUFFER
          P2      =#IBL             ;SET INPUT BUFFER LENGTH
        BLBS    R0,10$              ;ERROR EXIT
        BRW     ERROR               ;   IF ENABLE FAILS.
10$:    TSTW    IN_IOSB             ;WAIT IF
        BEQL    10$                 ;   KEYBOARD NOT DONE.
        CMPW    IN_IOSB,#SS$_NORMAL ;ERROR EXIT
        BEQL    20$                 ;   IF
        BRW     ERROR               ;        STATUS ERROR.
20$:    MOVB    IN_BUF,R10          ;GET CHARACTER TO R10
        BRB     IO_END              ;RETURN
IO_END: RET                         ;RETURN TO CALLER
;   ERROR EXIT
ERROR:  .PUTSTR ERR_MSG
        $EXIT_S R0                  ;EXIT AND SIGNAL
ERR_MSG:.ASCIZ/IO ERROR/
        .END    START
```

(c)

FIGURE 16.9/Software traps for vectoring to service routines using System Services: (c) service routine

set to 0. This is followed by a read from the keyboard, function 4, with immediate write back to the display, function 8. Then an ASCII 'X' is placed in R10, followed by another write, thus demonstrating all functions.

Figure 16.9(b) contains needed declarations for the $QIO_S service to be used in the I/O service routine. These are explained in Section 16.6.3.

The I/O service routine is defined in Figure 16.9(c). The argument is obtained from the call frame and used to index a function table for a JMP destination. At each function label we find the necessary System Service calls to perform the function. Both the input and output functions are performed using programmed I/O.

Note that any procedure that is properly designed as an AST service routine can be invoked with $DCLAST_S. Thus this macro provides a mechanism for testing such procedures without dependence on an asynchronous event.

16.8 | Interval Timer Interrupts and Timer Services

The VAX-11 CPU includes an **interval timer** that provides a basis for timing the execution of instruction sequences, as well as other uses. The diagram shown in Figure 16.10 shows how this timer operates. The device has three registers, called the **Interval Count Control/Status Register** (ICCS), the **Interval Count Register** (ICR), and the **Next Interval Count Register** (NICR). The hardware automatically increments ICR every microsecond whenever the R (Run) bit in ICCS is set. When this incrementation results in a carry out of bit 31 of ICR, two events occur: the I (Interrupt) bit in ICCS is set, and the contents of NICR is loaded into ICR. Thus if the program places -*n* in NICR and sets the R bit in ICCS, the I bit in ICCS will be set after *n* microseconds. If the program has also *enabled* timer interrupts by setting the E bit in ICCS, a processor interrupt will result. One of the actions of the interrupt servicing routine can be to clear the I bit so that the cycle will be repeated continuously, generating interrupts every *n* microseconds. Often the servicing routine will also increment a program location, providing a measure of elapsed time since the timer was started. This location can then be interrogated before and after the instruction sequence or other process to be timed.

As with interrupts in general, a user program under VMS cannot directly deal with the interval timer interrupts for two reasons. First, the interval timer registers are privileged and therefore are not addressable with normal instructions. Secondly, the vector offset address in the SCB is fixed by VMS to point at the system interrupt dispatcher. However, the System Services routines allow us to devise a timer using similar principles.

In order to provide the software equivalent of the hardware interval timer, System Services provide us with four basic tools for timing. Two of these, $BINTIM_S and $ASCTIM_S, are conversion routines for converting between internal and external time representation. The other two, $SETIMR_S and $CANTIM_S, allow setting and cancelling of timers.

Before we see how the timer services work, we must consider the internal and external representation of time intervals on the VAX-11.* The internal representation

---

* There are also conventions for representing absolute time. See Exercises 16.12 and 16.13.

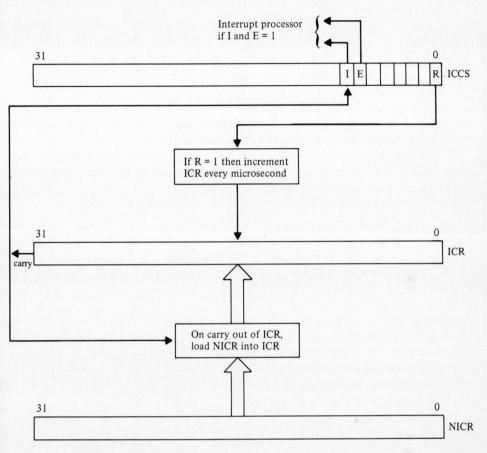

FIGURE 16.10/VAX-11 interval timer

of time is a quadword integer that is the *negative* of the desired time interval expressed in 100-nanosecond (i.e., 10^{-7} second) units. For example, the representation for 5 seconds is found as follows:

$$5 \text{ seconds}/10^{-7} = 5 \times 10^7 \text{ 100-nanosecond units}$$

$$(-5 \times 10^7)_{10} = \text{FFFFFFFF FD050F80}_{16}$$

The external representation of time intervals is an ASCII string of the form:

$$\text{dddd hh:mm:ss.cc}$$

where:

dddd = days

hh = hours

mm = minutes

ss = seconds

cc = hundredths of a second

Furthermore, the System Service routines require that the ASCII string be stored in descriptor form, i.e., the string length followed by its address.

The $BINTIM_S macro allows conversion of the external time interval representation to the internal representation. For example, a 5-second interval is stored as the internal representation at address T_I by the following sequence:

```
T_I:     .BLKQ  1
T_E_D:   .ASCID/0000 00:00:05.00/
             .
             .
             .
         .ENTRY     START, 0
         $BINTIM_S     TIMBUF = T_E_D,-
                       TIMADR = T_I
```

Conversely, $ASCTIM_S converts the internal form to the external ASCII string. In this conversion, however, we must indicate whether we want days, hours, minutes, and seconds, or just hours, minutes, and seconds. For example, in order to convert the internally formated 5-second interval determined previously back into external representation including days, we would write:

```
CT_I:    .QUAD  ^XFFFFFFFFFD050F80
CT_E_D:  .LONG  16
         .LONG  CT_E
CT_E:    .BLKB  16
             .
             .
             .
         .ENTRY START,0
             .
             .
             .
         $ASCTIM_S     TIMBUF = CT_E_D,-
                       TIMADR = CT_I,-
                       TIMLEN = CT_E_D,-
                       CVTFLG = #0
```

Here the $ASCTIM_S converts the internal form stored at CT_I to the external form pointed to by the descriptor at CT_E_D. We have allowed sixteen bytes at CT_E where the ASCII string itself will be stored by $ASCTIM_S. Because we have set the conversion flag CVTFLG to 0, the external form will include the days, and the converted string length will be 16. The converted string length is stored in the low word of the longword at CT_E_D because TIMLEN is set to that address.

The timer is set by the $SETIMR_S macro. The parameters needed by this macro are the address of an internally represented time interval, and the address of an AST service routine. This will cause the service routine to be executed after expiration of the given time interval. For example, if we wish to display the value in R0 after 5 seconds of execution time, we could write:

```
.ENTRY     START 0
           .
           .
           .
$SETTIMR   DAYTIM = CT_I,-;SET
           ASTADR = PRT   ;  TIMER
           .
           .
           .
$EXIT_S
.ENTRY     PRT,0           ;SERVICE ROUTINE
.PUTHEX                    ;PRINT R0
RET
```

When the AST is serviced it is automatically cleared and the timer is no longer operative. This means that if you want the service routine to be executed repeatedly, the service routine should reset the timer. For example, we could program as follows in order to increment TIME by DT every DT seconds:

```
$SETIMR_S DAYTIM = DT,-       ;SET
          ASTADR = INC_TIME   ;  TIMER
          .
          .
          .
.ENTRY      INC_TIME, 0       ;SERVICE ROUTINE
ADDL        DT,TIME           ;DOUBLE PRECISION
ADWC        DT+4,TIME+4       ;  ADD DT TO TIME
$SETTIMR_S  DAYTIM = DT,-     ;RESET
            ASTADR = INC_TIME ;  TIMER
RET
```

In this program it is assumed that DT is initialized to the internal representation of the negative of a small time increment, perhaps 0.01 seconds. Also, TIME must be initialized to a quadword 0. When it is desired to display the time, TIME must be converted to external form.

As noted above, timers are automatically cancelled when they expire. However, in some cases it is desirable to explicitly cancel a timer. This can be done by:

```
$CANTIM_S
```

This will terminate the execution of the INC_TIME routine in the previous example.

Note that the above timer is somewhat inaccurate for two reasons. First, there may be a delay before servicing the AST due to other concurrent processes. Secondly, time is required to execute the servicing routine. To minimize these effects, DT should be made as large as possible, considering the approximate length of the task being timed.

16.9 | Direct Memory Access (DMA)

We have previously considered two different types of I/O, namely, programmed I/O and interrupts (or their software equivalents using System Services). With programmed I/O, the CPU continually tests the device status register until it is ready, and then executes an instruction that transfers the data. This is called polling and, as previously mentioned, it is wasteful in that it ties up the CPU while waiting for a relatively slow I/O process. In other cases, the I/O device may be faster than the CPU can carry out the polling, resulting in loss of data. With interrupts, we avoid the loss of CPU availability during the waiting period, since the device itself will notify the CPU when it is ready. However, the CPU is still required to execute one or more instructions for each item of data transferred, and again may not be able to keep up with rapid I/O processes. There are other I/O methods that reduce the I/O burden on the CPU and greatly speed up the process. One of these is called Direct Memory Access (DMA). This method is possible with certain high-speed devices such as magnetic disks or tape storage units.

The basic idea of DMA is implied by its name, i.e., the I/O device accesses the main memory *directly* rather than having the data pass through the CPU. For example, a group of data items can be transferred directly from a magnetic disk storage unit to main memory without ever being acted upon by the CPU. This is in contrast to programmed or interrupt I/O in which each data item is brought into the CPU, then transferred to main memory. It should be obvious that DMA is potentially much faster than the other methods. In some situations this is merely a welcome improvement in performance. However, in cases such as automatic data acquisition from high-speed events in a laboratory, it may be the only viable method.

With DMA, the CPU is involved only at the beginning and the end of the transfer. The exact details vary depending on the device, but usually the following steps are involved. First, the program places needed information into the device registers. This will include as a minimum the number of data items to be transferred, the type of data (words or bytes), and the main memory address that the data is coming from on output or going to on input. Then a program instruction places a code into the device command register which initiates the transfer. From this point on, the device itself carries out the transfer. For example, on input it automatically sends an address to main memory, followed by a value to be stored there. It also increments the address for the next item, and decrements the count. All of this takes place in the DMA device. This process continues until the specified number of items has been transferred. While this is going on, the CPU is completely free to do other tasks. When the transfer is complete, a CPU interrupt is generated by the device, causing a transfer of control using the appropriate vector stored in the SCB. The interrupt servicing routine can then take appropriate action, such as processing the data or beginning another transfer.

This description of the DMA process is somewhat oversimplified. One thing not mentioned is the possibility of both the I/O device and the CPU needing the data transfer bus at the same time. This is solved by the I/O device requesting the bus from the CPU whenever it is ready to transmit a data item. If the CPU is not using the bus, it grants this request. Otherwise, the CPU completes its current operation, and then grants the bus request from the I/O device. This is called "cycle stealing" because the DMA process is depriving the CPU of the ability to proceed, resulting in loss of the equivalent of a few instruction fetch execute cycles.

The *PDP-11 Peripherals Handbook* (Digital Equipment Corporation) contains full descriptions of capabilities and programming details for most I/O devices. It should be consulted for DMA programming of specific devices.

16.10 | Summary

This chapter introduced the concepts of **exceptions** and **interrupts.** These concepts are similar in that they both refer to an automatic change in the sequence of instruction execution due to an *event,* rather than due to the normal branch or procedure call instructions. If the event is **synchronized** with the program, i.e., is attributable to a particular instruction, it is called an **exception** and usually reflects a program or system error. Interrupts, on the other hand, refer to **asynchronous** events, such as power failures or completion of a concurrent I/O process. Exceptions are further categorized as **traps, faults,** or **aborts,** depending on where in the instruction the exception occurred, and whether or not recovery is possible.

Exceptions and interrupts are also similar in the way that they are directed to the appropriate **servicing** or **handling** routine. In either case a process called **vectoring** is employed, whereby the address of a servicing routine is found in a data structure called the **System Control Block** (SCB). The exception or interrupt causes the current state of the machine, i.e., PC and PSL, to be saved on the stack, and control to be transferred to the address found in the SCB. The type of exception or interrupt determines which vector in the SCB is used.

In spite of these similiarities, exceptions and interrupts differ in certain ways. One key difference is that, as a rule, exceptions are due to computational or hardware errors, whereas interrupts are signals from hardware peripheral devices. Also, exceptions are handled when they occur, whereas interrupts are subject to a *priority level* system. That is, the processor always operates at some interrupt priority level called **IPL,** and each interrupting device or event has associated with it a prescribed priority level. A pending interrupt is not serviced until the CPU IPL drops below the prescribed priority level of the pending interrupt.

Exceptions and interrupts play an important role in the operating system itself. That is, these hardware-level mechanisms allow system resources to be shared, and help ensure efficient overall system operation. However, the security and stability of a multi-user system such as VMS on the VAX-11 require that normal user programs *not* be allowed direct access to the SCB. Furthermore, access to registers that are involved in exception and interrupt programming is restricted. Thus, instead of direct use of the hardware-provided interrupt features, the VAX-11 MACRO programmer writing programs to run under VAX/VMS must use operating system facilities to accomplish the same goals. Nonetheless, the chapter attempted to explain the hardware exception and interrupt mechanisms because of their fundamental importance.

The software mechanism provided by VMS for handling exceptions is the **VAX procedure call frame.** Specifically, the programmer places the address of the exception handler in the procedure call frame, and VMS automatically transfers to that address upon occurrence of any enabled exception. We saw that most arithmetic exceptions are normally disabled, but can be enabled by the **entry mask,** or by the **BISPSW instruction.** These tools give the MACRO programmer complete control over exception programming.

The equivalent of interrupt programming is handled with the VAX/VMS **System Service** routines using **Asynchronous System Traps** (ASTs). The basic idea here is that VMS detects interrupts that are related to your program (as opposed to those due to other concurrent programs) and issues a *signal* indicating the event. The System Service routines allow you to specify the handler routine to be executed upon detection of the signal. We saw that the most common use of ASTs is in asynchronous I/O programming. The System Service routine called **$QIO_S** was seen to be the primary mechanism for I/O programming with this technique. Basically, $QIO_S *queues* an I/O request and immediately returns to the point where it was invoked. This allows I/O to proceed concurrently with execution of other parts of the program. Also, $QIO_S can be used for programmed I/O, as described in Chapter 8.

While studying the VAX/VMS System Service routines we encountered two other useful services, namely, **software interrupts** and **timer services.** The $DCLAST_S service is a way to *force* execution of an AST servicing routine rather than waiting for an asynchronous event. This service is intended as a VMS equivalent of the similar hardware level service often called a **software interrupt** or **trap.** Software interrupts are important in that they are widely used to implement operating system services using the interrupt vector structure. We demonstrated the equivalent of this programming technique as an example of $DCLAST_S usage.

The last System Services considered were those related to *timing*. We saw that the **$SETIMR_S** service sets a timer with a specific expiration interval, and specifies a service routine to be executed upon expiration. Companion services allowed timer cancellation, and conversion between internal and external time interval representations. Together these services allow timing of instruction execution sequences, as well as other programming techniques.

Finally, we touched briefly on the **Direct Memory Access** (DMA) method of I/O. The key idea here was that the CPU initiates a transfer of data to or from memory and then proceeds with other activities while the transfer completes. This greatly enhances overall system performance, especially for programs requiring large amounts of I/O.

16.11 | Exercises

16.1 Assume that you are to develop a program for a VAX-11 in the absence of an operating system. Your program will be the only one executing on the machine. Express in pseudocode the steps necessary to implement an arithmetic exception handling system. It should report all arithmetic exceptions, indicating the type, as well as current PC contents. Execution should continue after integer overflow traps, floating underflow traps, and floating underflow faults, but all other exceptions should halt the processor. Assume that your program will operate with all necessary privileges.

16.2 Assuming the same environment described in Exercise 16.1, express in pseudocode the steps necessary to detect console keyboard interrupts, and display the typed characters on the console display device.

16.3 Develop an exception handler for a program to run under VMS. It should handle all exceptions listed in Table 16.2, reporting type and current PC, and then *resignal* for normal default VMS exception handling. That is, both your messages and the normal VMS messages should appear. Devise a suitable test program and prepare hard copy of terminal activity during your tests.

16.4 Create the program shown in Figure 16.5. Assemble and link it with the Symbolic Debugger. Execute to a breakpoint set at EXCPT. Locate the FP stored in EXCPTs call frame, then use this to locate the call frame of the main program. Verify the contents of the latter call frame according to the discussion in Sections 9.9 and 16.5.4. Then revise the program by converting the four lines constituting the "dummy program" to a procedure call. Repeat your examination of the call frame sequence. Describe all differences.

16.5 Develop a tracing facility using techniques described in Section 16.5.5. It should display registers R0 through R11 after each instruction is executed. Test your solution in the context of a simple program.

16.6 Using the facilities of the VAX/VMS System Services, develop a macro that behaves exactly like .TTYOUT. Test your macro in the context of a simple program.

16.7 Using the facilities of the VAX/VMS System Services, develop a macro that behaves exactly like .PUTSTR. Test your macro in the context of a simple program.

16.8 Using the facilities of the VAX/VMS System Services, develop a macro that behaves exactly like .TTYIN. Be sure that it uses a buffer and reacts to successive references exactly like .TTYIN. Test your macro in the context of a simple program.

16.9 Create the program shown in Figure 16.8. Assemble and link with the Symbolic Debugger. Set the breakpoint at OUTKBIH. Execute the program and enter several numbers. Verify that the current list of numbers is always sorted when it stops at OUTKBIH each time.

16.10 Implement the I/O service routine of Figure 16.9. Rewrite the program in Figure 8.5 using these routines instead of .PUTSTR, .TTYIN, or .TTYOUT.

16.11 Use the INC_TIME routine described in Section 16.8 to determine the time required to perform $100,000_{10}$ floating-point multiplications on the VAX-11 that you use. Try DT values of 0.01, 0.10, and 1.00 and note the effect on the result. Explain these effects.

16.12 Repeat Exercise 16.11 using the macro $GETTIM_S which returns the absolute time in system internal format. For example, $GETTIM_S TIMADR=TIME places the current time in a quadword labeled TIME. Compare results with those of Exercises 16.11 and explain any differences.

16.13 The $SETTIMR_S System Service accepts time-of-year as well as the time intervals used in examples in this chapter. To set time-of-year, the TIMBUF parameter of the $BINTIM_S System Service is specified in the following form:

```
T_E_D: ASCID/30_SEP_1985 14:45:15,28/
```

When this is input to $BINTIM_S as the TIMBUF parameter, the internal form created is a *positive* quadword integer. A positive input to $SETIMR_S indicates that the timer is to expire at the indicated *time-of-year* rather than after an interval. Demonstrate this to yourself by writing a program that loops until a specified clock time. Execute the VMS command SHOW TIME to determine the current time, and encode this time plus 5 minutes to test your program.

16.14 Many terminals have a "no-scroll" mode and allow characters to be displayed at specified locations on the screen. This normally requires sending an "escape sequence" indicating the row and column, followed by the character to be displayed. Determine the details of this in the user's manual for your terminal. Then write a timer servicing routine similar to INC_TIM that displays the elapsed time at the upper left corner of the screen during execution of a sample program.

17

Input/Output Using the Record Management Services (RMS)

17.1 | Overview

In earlier chapters we dealt with input and output at several different levels. First, we learned to use preprogrammed macros (.TTYIN, .TTYOUT, .PUTSTR, .GETHEX, and .PUTHEX) for elementary terminal I/O. In Chapter 8 we briefly described programmed I/O that is applicable when it is necessary (and permissible) to directly access the hardware device registers. In Chapter 16 we learned how to do I/O to devices such as terminals using the VMS facility called the System Service routines, in particular the $QIO_S routine.

We now wish to introduce another class of I/O service routines provided by VMS, called the **Record Management Services** or **RMS.** This group of routines differs from the System Services in that it allows the programmer to assume a higher-level view of the I/O process. With the System Services we were required to view the process in terms of I/O of individual data elements going to or from particular devices. With RMS we are instead allowed to view the process as transferring *collections* of data, called **records,** to and from **files.** Low-level details such as the physical devices involved in the transfer are automatically handled by the operating system.

A study of the RMS is important both for practical and fundamental reasons. The practical reason is that RMS allows us to read from, create, and write to files from our MACRO programs. The fundamental reason is that it affords us the opportunity to glimpse one important aspect of a modern operating system. That is, practically all modern operating systems are similar to VMS in that they provide file- and record-oriented I/O software that is employed by nearly all high-level software running on the computer. This not only circumvents the need for direct user access to the physical devices, but also makes I/O programming more convenient and leads to efficient overall system operation.

The presentation of RMS in this chapter is intended to be introductory rather than comprehensive. The coverage is sufficient to allow input from and output to sequential files with fixed length records. RMS has many more capabilities, as described in the

VAX-11 Record Management Services Reference Manual (Digital Equipment Corporation).

17.2 | Record and File Input and Output

In Section 12.3.3 we dealt with collections of records in main memory, referring to these collections as *tables*. If the information must be stored after program execution the records must be written to an auxiliary storage device, such as a disk or tape storage unit. A collection of records stored on auxiliary storage is referred to as a *file*. A very important programming capability is the reading and writing of records from and to files. While these tasks can be done using the $QIO_S System Service routines described in Chapter 16, VAX/VMS provides more convenient means through the Record Management Services (RMS) routines.

Several steps must be carried out in order to perform file I/O from a MACRO program using RMS. These steps are:

1. Define the attributes of the records and the file.
2. Create the file if it does not exist, or open it if it does exist.
3. Establish a "connection" between the program and the file.
4. Perform the actual input or output a record at a time.
5. Close the file.

Sections 17.3–17.5 describe each of these steps for elementary I/O operations on files of the simplest type, namely, *sequential files* with *fixed length* records.

17.3 | Establishing File and Record Attributes

In order to carry out its tasks, RMS needs certain information about the file and records contained therein. For example, it needs to know the name of the file as it is known to VMS, the size of the records, and how the records are organized in the file. This information is specified in two data structures, called **control blocks,** which must be included in any program accessing the file. The **Record Access Block** (RAB) describes the record attributes, while the **File Access Block** (FAB) describes the file attributes. RMS provides macros that serve to define and initialize these data structures within the MACRO program as described below.

17.3.1 Initializing the File Access Block (FAB)

The **$FAB macro** is used to define the FAB for all files to be accessed by the program. Because $FAB allocates space as well as performing initialization of FAB parameters, rather than generating executable instructions, it should be placed *before* the executable part of the program. The exact form of the $FAB reference will depend on whether the file already exists or is to be created, and on whether input, output, or both are to be performed.

For example, if you intend to do input operations from an *existing* file called SCORES.DAT, the appropriate $FAB reference is:

```
IN_FAB:   $FAB   FNM = <SCORES.DAT>,-; FILE NAME
                 FAC = GET            ; TO BE INPUT FROM
```

Here FNM means *file name* and FAC means *file access* type. This $FAB therefore establishes a FAB at address IN_FAB for the VMS file called SCORES.DAT and authorizes GET (input) operations. On the other hand, to allow creation of a *new* file called PAY.DAT, we would use:

```
PAY_FAB:   $FAB  FNM = <PAY.DAT>,-  ; FILE NAME
                 FAC = PUT,-        ; TO BE OUTPUT TO
                 ORG = SEQ,-        ; SEQUENTIAL ORGANIZATION
                 RFM = FIX,-        ; FIXED RECORD LENGTH
                 MRS = 80           ; 80 CHARACTER RECORDS
```

Observe that we set the file access parameter FAC to PUT because we intend to output to PAY.DAT. The file organization (ORG) is specified to be sequential (SEQ). Also supported by RMS (but not described here) are relative and indexed file organizations. As specified by the *record format* (RFM) and maximum record size (MRS) parameters, the file is to consist of fixed length records, each containing 80 characters. RMS also allows variable length records, although we do not discuss this format here.

As a final $FAB example, consider the need for a file called SCRATCH.DAT that is to be created if it does not already exist, and that will be used for input and output (appending records) in the same program. Then we must write:

```
SCR_FAB: $FAB FNM = <SCRATCH.DAT>,-;FILE NAME
              FAC = <GET,PUT>,-   ; EITHER READ OR WRITE
              ORG = SEQ,-         ; SEQUENTIAL ORGANIZATION
              RFM = FIX,-         ; FIXED RECORD LENGTH
              MRS = 130,-         ; 130 CHARACTER RECORDS
              FOP = CIF           ; CREATE IF NOT EXISTING
```

Note that the file access parameters are enclosed in angle brackets because we are specifying more than one method of access. The *file options* parameter (FOP) is set to CIF, which means that when the file creation is requested (see $CREATE below), your directory will first be checked to see if SCRATCH.DAT exists. If it does exist, that file will be used; otherwise, a new file will be created.

In each of the above examples, a label precedes the $FAB. This allows the FAB to be referred to in subsequent RMS macros (such as $RAB and $OPEN) as discussed below.

17.3.2 Initializing the Record Access Block (RAB)

The **Record Allocation Block** (RAB) is a data structure used by RMS to store information about the records in a file. Although the RAB has many parameters that are useful in more advanced file operations, here we shall be concerned only with those that define the buffers used by RMS during the I/O operations, and the one that associates a record with its file.

The Record Management Services also provide a macro for allocating and initializing the RAB. This macro is called **$RAB,** and takes on several possible forms, depending on the particular operations to be done in the program. An appropriate RAB for preparing to input from the SCORES.DAT file (for which we created the FAB earlier) is established by:

```
IN_RAB:$RAB  FAB = IN_FAB,-   ;IDENTIFY WITH FAB
         UBF     = IN_BUF,-   ;IDENTIFY INPUT BUFFER
         USZ     = 80         ;SPECIFY INPUT BUFFER SIZE
```

Note that every RAB must be associated with a FAB. This association is established by equating the FAB parameter in the $RAB macro to the label of a previous $FAB macro. The UBF and USZ parameters identify, respectively, the address and length of a *user buffer* (allocated in your program) for RMS to use during input. Thus the program containing the above $RAB must also have a buffer allocation directive such as:

```
IN_BUF:  .BLKB  80   ;INPUT BUFFER
```

The RAB for output operations must give the address and length of the record to be stored, as well as the associated FAB. The $RAB to do this for the PAY.DAT file mentioned previously is:

```
PAY_RAB:  $RAB FAB = PAY_FAB,-  ;IDENTIFY WITH FAB
          RBF      = OUT_BUF,-  ;IDENTIFY OUTPUT BUFFER
          RSZ      = 80         ;RECORD SIZE
```

Here RBF stands for Record Buffer and is set equal to an address of this buffer which must be allocated somewhere in the program. RSZ represents the length of this buffer. The purpose of this buffer is to temporarily hold an "image" of a record before it is output to the file.

We just saw that the RABs for input and output specify buffers. Input employs a *user buffer,* UBF, while output employs a *record buffer,* RBF. If both input and output are to be done on the file, both buffers should be specified, as well as their lengths. Also, note that an input operation *changes* the value of RBF and RSZ. This is explained further in the following discussion of input and output.

17.4 | Creating, Opening, and Closing Files

Before file I/O operations can be carried out the file must exist in the VMS directory, and it must be "opened," i.e., made available in the context of the program. After I/O operations have been completed, the file should be "closed." RMS provides macros for each of these tasks.

An existing file is opened for I/O with the $OPEN macro. For example, the SCORES.DAT file referred to in Section 17.3.1 is opened with:

```
$OPEN FAB = IN_FAB
```

where IN_FAB is the label of the FAB for the SCOES.DAT file. Because $OPEN is a macro that generates executable code (as opposed to space allocation and initialization) it should be placed in the executable part of the program rather than in the data section. Also, because errors can occur, such as if the specified file cannot be found, a check should be made after the macro reference. All RMS macros that generate executable code return with the low bit of R0 cleared as an error indication. Therefore, we can use the BLBS (**B**ranch on **L**ow **B**it **S**et) instruction to branch around error-handling instructions following the macro reference. For example, we can write:

```
        $OPEN   FAB = IN_FAB
        BLBS    R0,L1
        .PUTSTR/FILE OPENING ERROR/
        $EXIT_S
L1:
```

This prints a message and exits the program if the $OPEN failed. Otherwise, the low bit of R0 will be set and the execution will continue at L1.

Sometimes the output file does not exist and must be created by the program. In this case we use the $CREATE macro instead of $OPEN. For example, the PAY.DAT file described previously can be created with:

```
$CREATE  FAB = PAY_FAB
```

where PAY_FAB is the FAB label. Because $CREATE leaves the file open for I/O after creation, it is not necessary to use $OPEN. Like $OPEN, the $CREATE macro belongs in the executable code section of your program. It also should be followed with an error check similar to that shown above for the $OPEN.

After all I/O operations have been completed, the file should be closed. This can be done explicitly with the $CLOSE macro, e.g.,

```
$CLOSE  FAB = PAY_FAB
```

Because all files are automatically closed by the $EXIT_S System Service macro, $CLOSE can often be omitted. However, every open file places certain resource demands on the operating system, so it is considered good practice to close a file when operations on it are complete.

17.5 | Transferring Records to and from the File

The actual transfer of records to and from a file can be done with the RMS **$PUT** and **$GET macros.** The transfer is through the buffers specified in the RAB, and the file that the record is transferred to is indicated by the FAB parameter in the RAB. Although the association between the record and its file is indicated by the $RAB macro, the actual data path must be activated at run-time with the **$CONNECT macro.**

Typically, an output operation to an open file requires the following form:

```
        $CONNECT    RAB = {address of RAB}
        BLBS        R0,L1
        {error handling}
L1:     {instructions to construct record image of RBF buffer}
        $PUT        RAB = {address of RAB}
        BLBS        R0,L2
        {error handling}
L2:
```

The record image constructed in the RBF buffer can contain any kind of data, e.g., integer, floating-point, or character string. The record length is specified by the RSZ parameter in the RAB, which must agree with the MRS parameter in the FAB. The

$PUT then transfers this record image to the file specified by the FAB parameter. Assuming that the specified FAB defines a fixed-record-length, sequential file, the record image is place into the next available record in the file.

A typical record input from a file requires the following sequence:

```
        $CONNECT    RAB = {address of RAB}
        BLBS        R0,L1
        {error handling}
L1:     $GET        RAB = {address of RAB}
        BLBS        R0,L2
        {error handling}
L2:     {instructions to transfer record from UBF to desired location}
```

Here the $GET causes a record to be transferred from the file specified by the FAB to the UBF buffer. Assuming a fixed-record-length, sequential file, this record will be the next sequential record, and will be USZ bytes in length. Note that the file record length was established by the MRS parameter when the file was created. If a $GET is attempted with a USZ different from the file record size, $GET will return an error condition in R0. Note that because the next $GET will place the next record into the UBF buffer, program instructions must be provided to either process each record before the next

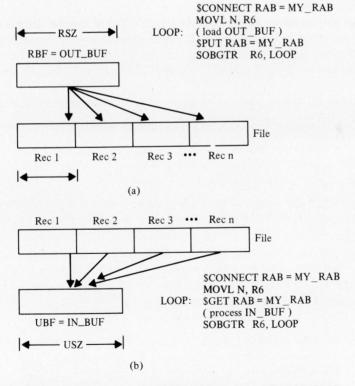

FIGURE 17.1/Input and output operations on a sequential, fixed-record-length file: (a) output; (b) input

$GET, or to transfer it to a table for later processing. (Alternately, the buffer address can be changed in the RAB. See Section 17.6.)

Because files are collections of records, and usually many or all of these records are processed by the program, the preceding input and output sequences are most often done within loop structures. Figure 17.1 shows input and output of successive records in a sequential, fixed-record-length file. Note that the $CONNECT macro reference is outside the loop because it needs to be done only once. As indicated in Figure 17.1(a), each output record resides temporarily in the RBF buffer prior to transfer to the file. Similarly, Figure 17.1(b) shows that each input record is placed into UBF for processing or transfer by the program.

17.6 | Input and Output Operations on Same File

We observed in previous sections that input and output operations, i.e., $GET and $PUT, use information stored in the FAB and RAB data structures. As long as only input or only output is performed on a given file, the needed information in these data structures does not change and the initializations done by $FAB and $RAB at assembly time are sufficient. However, when both input and output (appending records) are done it is important to note that some of the RAB data *needed* by the $PUT macro are *changed* by the $GET macro. This means that when a $PUT is to be done after a $GET from the same file, the changed RAB data must be restored. Because the $RAB macro is analogous to assembler initialization directives, it cannot be used for this purpose. Instead, the equivalent run-time macro **$RAB_STORE** can be used, or the RAB fields can be changed directly with MOVL and MOVW instructions are shown below.

For example, if we intended to perform both input and output from the file SCRATCH.DAT we would establish the RAB as:

```
MY_RAB:  FAB = MY_FAB ,-
         UBF = IN_BUF ,-
         USZ = REC_SIZE ,-
         RBF = OUT_BUF ,-
         RSZ = REC_SIZE
```

At assembly time, this initializes the FAB address, and the address and lengths of both buffers. However, the first $GET changes the RBF field *to the address where the record was placed by the $GET*. That is, upon return from the $GET, the RBF parameter will be set to the address of the UBF. Also, the RSZ parameter is changed to the length of the record just read from the file. Therefore, if a $PUT is subsequently done, the output record will *not* be taken from the address specified by the original RBF parameter. Before any $PUT we must therefore write:

```
$RAB_STORE  RBF = OUT_BUF , RSZ = REC_SIZE
```

which is the run-time equivalent of $RAB. Alternately, the RAB fields can be addressed directly using predefined symbols. For example, the instructions:

```
MOVL  #OUT_BUF ,MY_RAB+RAB$L_RBF
MOVW  #REC_SIZE ,MY_RAB+RAB$W_RSZ
```

are equivalent to the preceding $RAB_STORE. In general, every RAB field can be addressed in this manner because the MACRO assembler recognizes predefined symbolic offsets of the form RAB$W_symbol for word-sized fields and RAB$L_symbol for long-word-sized fields in the RAB data structure. FAB fields can be addressed similarly. The *VAX-11 Record Management Services Manual* provides a full list of symbolic offsets.

17.7 | RMS Examples

The following examples show elementary usage of the RMS I/O facilities. In both cases we work with fixed-record-length sequential files stored on the system default mass storage device.

EXAMPLE 17.1   Write a MACRO program that creates a file called TSTFILE.DAT and writes ten records into it. The file should be organized sequentially and have 80-byte, fixed-length records. The program should display each record as it is written to the file.

The program is shown in Figure 17.2. The .PSECT directive ensures that the FAB and RAB are longword-aligned, *as required.* Note that output access is established by setting the FAC parameter to PUT in the $FAB macro. Also, because the file is to be created, we establish its record size, and organization. Because we will be writing to it, the $RAB gives the RBF and RSZ parameters. The output buffer OUT_BUF for the RBF parameter is allocated immediately after the RAB, although other locations are also permissible. The null byte after OUT_BUF marks its end for displaying the record with the .PUTSTR macro. A table is initialized with ASCII strings in order to provide sample records for output.

The executable program begins by creating the file identified by MY_FAB. The $CREATE macro is followed by error-handling instructions, as are all other RMS run-time macros used in the program. If successfully created, a data path between the program and the file is created with the $CONNECT macro. Afterwards, a loop is entered to output the ten records set up in TABLE. Register R7 is used to index into TABLE, and the MOVC5 instruction is used to move each record into the output buffer. Note that because the records in TABLE are only 20 characters in length, we specify a "+" character to fill the 80-character file record.

The .PUTSTR macro then prints OUT_BUF, followed by output to the file with $PUT. Adding T_SIZE to R7 causes the next record in TABLE to be referenced the next time through the loop. After the last record has been written, the file is closed with the $CLOSE macro. However, because we return immediately to VMS with $EXIT_S, this explicit closing is not required.

EXAMPLE 17.2   Devise a MACRO program to read the records from TSTFILE.DAT as created in Example 17.1 The program should display the records as they are read from the file, and store them in a table allocated in the program. Figure 17.3 shows the program for this example. The overall structure closely parallels the program that creates the file, Figure 17.2. Note that in this case the $FAB does not give the file organization or record characteristics because the file already exists. RMS will determine these attributes from the file itself. Also, the FAC parameter is set to GET because we intend to read the file. In the RAB, we identify a suitable user buffer, UBF, and its size, USZ. The same record size is used as was used in file creation. Because the file contains ten 80-byte records, we allocate TABLE accordingly.

```
                .TITLE EXAMPLE_17.2
                .PSECT PROGRAM,LONG
       T_SIZE   = 20                        ;TABLE RECORD SIZE
       REC_SIZE = 80
       MY_FAB: $FAB  FNM = <TSTFILE.DAT>,-;FILE NAME
                     FAC = PUT,-            ;TO BE OUTPUT TO
                     ORG = SEQ,-
                     RFM = FIX,-
                     MRS = REC_SIZE
       MY_RAB: $RAB  FAB = MY_FAB,-
                     RBF = OUT_BUF,-
                     RSZ = REC_SIZE
       OUT_BUF:.BLKB REC_SIZE
               .BYTE  0                     ;NULL BYTE FOR .PUTSTR
       TABLE:  .ASCII/THIS IS RECORD 0   /
               .ASCII/THIS IS RECORD 1   /
               .ASCII/THIS IS RECORD 2   /
               .ASCII/THIS IS RECORD 3   /
               .ASCII/THIS IS RECORD 4   /
               .ASCII/THIS IS RECORD 5   /
               .ASCII/THIS IS RECORD 6   /
               .ASCII/THIS IS RECORD 7   /
               .ASCII/THIS IS RECORD 8   /
               .ASCII/THIS IS RECORD 9   /
               .ASCII/THIS IS RECORD 10  /
               .ENTRY START,0
               $CREATE FAB = MY_FAB
               BLBS    R0,L1
               .PUTSTR MSG1
               $EXIT_S
       MSG1:   .ASCIZ /FILE CREATE ERROR/
       L1:     $CONNECT RAB = MY_RAB
               BLBS    R0,L2
               .PUTSTR MSG2
               $EXIT_S
       MSG2:   .ASCIZ /RECORD CONNECT ERROR/
       L2:     CLRL    R7
               MOVL    #10,R6               ;WRITE 10 RECORDS
       ;            MOVE A RECORD TO OUT_BUF
       L3:     MOVC5   #T_SIZE,TABLE[R7],#^A'+',#REC_SIZE,OUT_BUF
               .PUTSTR OUT_BUF              ;ECHO TO SCREEN
               $PUT    RAB = MY_RAB         ;WRITE OUT_BUF TO FILE
               BLBS    R0,L4
               .PUTSTR MSG3
               $EXIT_S
       MSG3:   .ASCIZ/FILE PUT ERROR/
       L4:     ADDL    #T_SIZE,R7           ;ADVANCE TO NEXT RECORD
               SOBGTR  R6,L3
               $CLOSE  FAB = MY_FAB
               $EXIT_S
               .END    START
```

FIGURE 17.2/MACRO program to create sequential file of fixed-length records

In the executable program we see the same structure as used in file creation. That is, the file is opened, the record is connected, and then a loop reads successive records. Each incoming record is taken from IN_BUF and moved to the appropriate record in TABLE.

```
          .TITLE EXAMPLE_17.2
          .PSECT PROGRAM,LONG
T_SIZE    = 80                          ;TABLE RECORD SIZE
REC_SIZE = 80
MY_FAB: $FAB     FNM = <TSTFILE.DAT>,-;FILE NAME
                 FAC = GET              ;TO BE INPUT FROM
MY_RAB: $RAB     FAB = MY_FAB,-
                 UBF = IN_BUF,-
                 USZ = REC_SIZE
IN_BUF: .BLKB REC_SIZE
        .BYTE    0                      ;NULL BYTE FOR .PUTSTR
TABLE:  .BLKB    T_SIZE
        .BLKB    T_SIZE
        .BLKB    T_SIZE
        .BLKB    T_SIZE
        .BLKB    T_SIZE
        .BLKB    T_SIZE
        .BLKB    T_SIZE
        .BLKB    T_SIZE
        .BLKB    T_SIZE
        .BLKB    T_SIZE
        .ENTRY   START,0
        $OPEN FAB = MY_FAB
        BLBS     R0,L1
        .PUTSTR  MSG1
        $EXIT_S
MSG1:   .ASCIZ /FILE OPEN ERROR/
L1:     $CONNECT RAB = MY_RAB
        BLBS     R0,L2
        .PUTSTR  MSG2
        $EXIT_S
MSG2:   .ASCIZ /RECORD CONNECT ERROR/
L2:     CLRL     R7
        MOVL     #10,R6                 ;GET 10 RECORDS
L3:     $GET     RAB = MY_RAB           ;GET RECORD FROM FILE TO IN_BUF
        BLBS     R0,L4
        .PUTSTR  MSG3
        $EXIT_S
MSG3:   .ASCIZ/FILE GET ERROR/
L4:     .PUTSTR  IN_BUF
;            PUT INTO TABLE
        MOVC5    #REC_SIZE,IN_BUF,#^A/+/,#T_SIZE,TABLE[R7]
        ADDL     #T_SIZE,R7             ;ADVANCE TO NEXT RECORD
        SOBGTR   R6,L3
        $CLOSE   FAB = MY_FAB
EXIT:
        $EXIT_S
        .END     START
```

FIGURE 17.3/MACRO program to read sequential file of fixed-length records

17.8 | Summary

This chapter introduced the VAX **Record Management Services** (RMS). We saw that RMS provides the MACRO programmer with routines for input and output operations on **VMS files.** RMS is also important in a fundamental sense because it is representative of similar I/O service systems provided by most modern operating systems. Such services allow convenient

I/O programming in a multi-user environment where individual users cannot directly access peripheral devices, as well as assuring efficient usage of system resources.

The RMS services were seen to be provided through various macro instructions. Two of these, namely **$FAB** and **$RAB,** are *declarative*, in that they define and initialize data structures at assembly time. Similar to MACRO storage allocation directives, $FAB and $RAB must be in the data section of the program. Other RMS macros generate run-time code and therefore belong in the executable part of the program. This group includes **$OPEN, $CLOSE, $CREATE, $CONNECT, $GET, $PUT, $RAB_STORE,** and **$FAB_STORE.**

The use of any file requires a **File Access Block** (FAB) and **Record Access Block** (RAB) within the program. The FAB defines file attributes, while the RAB defines records within the file. These data structures are created and initialized at assembly time with $FAB and $RAB, but can also be changed at run-time through $RAB_STORE, $FAB_STORE, or direct addressing of the fields.

Prior to using a file, it must be opened with the $OPEN macro. Also, the $CONNECT macro must be executed in order to activate a connection between the record and the file. Once the file is opened and the record is connected, $GET brings a record from the file, and $PUT writes a record to the file. In both cases, transfer is through buffers that must be allocated in the program. Upon completion of all I/O from and/or to a particular file, it should be closed with the $CLOSE macro.

17.9 | Exercises

17.1 Create the program of Example 17.1 and execute it. Verify that it executes properly by displaying the TSTFILE.DAT file using the TYPE command.

17.2 Create the program of Example 17.2. Demonstrate that it works using a file created with the program in Figure 17.2, or with the editor. Use the Symbolic Debugger to break at the EXIT label and examine TABLE.

17.3 Improve the efficiency of the program in Example 17.1 by modifying the RBF address after each pass through the loop rather than moving the record to a buffer at a fixed location.

17.4 Repeat Exercise 17.3 but make the change to the program of Example 17.2.

17.5 Write a program to create a file containing records with the NAME and SCORE fields as shown in Figure 12.12. Note that the SCORE field contains word-length integers, not ASCII strings.

17.6 Modify the program of Example 12.6 to read the records from a file, and write the sorted table to a second file. Test the program with the data created in Exercise 17.5.

17.7 Modify the program of Example 17.2 to allow input and output. Set breakpoints at L1 and L4. Examine UBF and RBF fields at L1, and then again after proceeding to L4. Why are they different?

17.8 Terminal I/O can be done with RMS. The keyboard and display screen are viewed as "files" with the names SYS$INPUT and SYS$OUTPUT, respectively. Write a program that reads a line from the keyboard and echoes it to the screen. (*Note:* Because VMS also echoes the keyboard to the screen, your input will be shown twice. You can turn off the VMS echo with SET TERM/NOECHO.)

Appendixes

Programming Reference

The following notes apply to Table A.1:

1. Normal settings of N,Z,V, and C condition codes are:

    $N = 1$ if result is less than 0
    $Z = 1$ if result is 0
    $V = 1$ if operation caused a signed overflow
    $C = 1$ if operation caused an unsigned overflow

2. Set means set to 1. Cleared means cleared to 0.

3. The suffix "x" means that the instruction has forms for different data types. Possible substitutions for x are shown below the mnemonic with associated opcodes: B = byte, W = word, L = longword, Q = quadword, O = octaword, F = F_floating, D = D_floating, G = G_floating, H = H_floating.

4. The suffix "n" means that the instruction has forms for different numbers of operands. For instructions with 2 or 3 operands, 2-operand form and opcodes are shown in the table. For the 3-operand form, the third operand is the destination while the first two are unchanged source operands. Opcodes for 3-operand instructions are equal to 2-operand opcode plus 1 for 1-byte opcodes, or plus 100_{16} for 2-byte opcodes.

5. S and D mean source and destination operand, respectively. Any addressing mode is allowed unless stated otherwise in explanation. Data type is inferred from the instruction, e.g., MOVL moves a longword. In general, source operands are not changed. Except for conversion instructions, destination bits beyond the length of the data type are unaffected.

6. For character string instructions R1 and R3 return address of the byte following last character in source and destination strings, respectively, or address of a located character. R0 returns number of remaining bytes, including located byte, or zero. R2 and R4 are cleared.

7. Several VAX-11 instructions are omitted from this table because their explanations would be beyond the scope of this text. Also, explanations given are simplified. See the *VAX Architecture Handbook* (Digital Equipment Corporation) for more information.

TABLE A.1/MACRO Instructions

Assembly Mnemonics and Opcodes		Explanation	Effects on Condition Codes
Integer and Floating-Point Arithmetic			
MOVx	S,D	Copy of data type x found in S placed into D. Bits of D beyond length of data type x are not affected. Section 4.2.1.	N,Z: Note 1
B	90		V: Cleared
W	B0		C: Unaffected
L	D0		
Q	7D		
O	7DFD		
F	50		
D	70		
G	50FD		
H	70FD		
MOVZxx	S,D	Converts S to wider unsigned integer in D by zero-filling to left. Section 7.7.	N: Cleared
BW	9B		Z: Note 1
BL	9A		V: Cleared
WL	3C		C: Unaffected
MNEGx	S,D	Two's complement of S is placed into D, i.e., D becomes the negation of S. Section 6.2.	N,Z: Note 1
B	8E		V (integer): Note 1
W	AE		C (integer): Cleared if D = 0
L	CE		V,C (floating): Cleared
F	52		
D	72		
G	52FD		
H	72FD		
CLRx	D	All bits of D are cleared to 0. Section 4.2.3.	N,V: Cleared
B	94		Z: Set
W	B4		C: Unaffected
L,F	D4		
Q,D,G	7C		
O	7CFD		
H	7CFD		

Assembly Mnemonics and Opcodes		Explanation	Effects on Condition Codes
ADDxn	S,D	S is added to D. Section 4.2.2. Three-operand form available (Note 4).	N,Z,V: Note 1 C (floating): Cleared C (integer): Set if carry from MSB
B2	80		
W2	A0		
L2	C0		
F2	40		
D2	60		
G2	40FD		
H2	60FD		
SUBxn	S,D	S is subtracted from D. Section 5.2. Three-operand form available (Note 4).	N,Z,V: Note 1 C (floating): Cleared C (integer): Set if borrow into MSB
B2	82		
W2	A2		
L2	C2		
F2	42		
D2	62		
G2	42FD		
H2	62FD		
INCx	D	D is incremented by 1. Section 4.2.4. Incrementing largest positive signed integer yields largest negative integer and sets V.	N,Z,V: Note 1 C: Set if carry from MSB
B	96		
W	B6		
L	D6		
DECx	D	D is decremented by 1. Section 5.4.3. Decrementing largest negative integer yields largest positive signed integer and sets V.	N,Z,V: Note 1 C: Set if borrow into MSB
B	97		
W	B7		
L	D7		
MULxn	S,D	Product $S \times D$ is placed into D. Section 6.13.1. Three-operand form available (Note 4).	N,Z,V: Note 1 C: Cleared
B2	84		
W2	A4		
L2	C4		
F2	44		
D2	64		
G2	44FD		
H2	64FD		

453

Assembly Mnemonics and Opcodes		Explanation	Effects on Condition Codes

Integer and Floating-Point Arithmetic (continued)

EMUL	S1,S2, S3,D 7A	Extended integer multiply and add. (S1 × S2) + S3 is placed into D. S1, S2, and S3 must be longword and D is quadword. S3 is sign extended before addition. Section 6.13.1.	N,Z: Note 1 V,C: Cleared
DIVxn B2 W2 L2 F2 D2 G2 H2	S,D 86 A6 C6 46 66 46FD 66FD	Quotient D/S is placed into D. Three-operand form available (Note 4). For integers, overflow occurs if and only if largest negative integer is divided by −1. Section 6.13.2.	N,Z: Note 1 V: Set on overflow or zero divide C: Cleared
EDIV	S1,S2 Q, R 7B	Extended precision integer divide. S2/S1 is placed in Q with remainder in R. Remainder has same sign as S2. S1, Q, and R must be longwords and S2 must be quadword. If S1 = 0, then Q becomes (31:0) of S2 and R becomes 0. Section 6.13.2.	N,Z: Note 1 V: Set on overflow or zero divide C: Cleared
ADWC	S,D D8	Add with carry. The current C condition code and S are added to D. Section 6.12.	N,Z,V,C: Note 1
SBWC	S,D D9	Subtract with carry. The current C condition code and S are subtracted from D. Section 6.12.	N,Z,V,C: Note 1
POLYx F D G H	S,N,C 55 75 55FD 75FD	Polynominal of degree N (word) and coefficient array C (address) is evaluated for argument S. Result is returned in R0 for POLYF, (R0,R1) for POLYD or POLYG, or (R0,R1,R2,R3) for POLYH. Note that R0–R5 are changed by all POLYx instructions. Section 14.6.	N: Set if R0 < 0 Z: Set if R0 = 0 V: Set on floating overflow C: Cleared

454

Assembly Mnemonics and Opcodes		Explanation	Effects on Condition Codes
Logical and Bit Manipulation			
BICxn	S,D	Clears each bit in D that is set in S. Used to clear unwanted portions of D. Section 7.9. (See Note 4.)	N,Z: Note 1
B2	8A		V: Cleared
W2	AA		C: Unaffected
L2	CA		
BISxn	S,D	Sets each bit in D that is set in S. Used to set particular bits in D. Logical OR. Section 7.9. (See Note 4.)	N,Z: Note 1
B2	88		V: Cleared
W2	A8		C: Unaffected
L2	C8		
MCOMx	S,D	Ones complement of S is placed into D. Logical complement operation. Section 7.9. (See Note 4.)	N,Z: Note 1
B	92		V: Cleared
W	B2		C: Unaffected
L	D2		
BITx	S,D	See *Test and Compare* in this table. Section 7.9.	See *Test and Compare*
B	93		
W	B3		
L	D3		
XORxn	S,D	Exclusive OR. A particular bit in D is set only if it is originally set in either S or D, but not in both. Section 7.9. (See Note 4.)	N,Z: Note 1
B2	8C		V: Cleared
W2	AC		C: Unaffected
L2	CC		
EXTV	N,L,B,D	Extract the bit field of size L beginning N bits beyond base addresses B and place into longword D. Sign extended if L < 32.	N,Z: Note 1
	EE		V,C: Cleared
EXTZV	N,L,B,D	Like EXTV except zero extend to left to fill D.	N,Z: Note 1
	EF		V,C: Cleared

Assembly Mnemonics and Opcodes		Explanation	Effects on Condition Codes
Test and Compare			
CMPx	S1,S2	S1 is compared to S2 using suffi-	N: Set if S1 < S2 in signed sense
B	91	cient precision to avoid overflow.	Z: Set if S1 = S2
W	B1	Condition codes are set or cleared	V: Cleared
L	D1	accordingly, but S1 and S2 are	C (integer): Set if S1 < S2 in un-
F	51	not changed. Section 5.2.	signed sense
D	71		C (floating): Cleared
G	51FD		
H	71FD		
TSTx	S	S is compared to 0 using sufficient	N: Set if S < 0 in signed sense
B	95	precision to avoid overflow. Con-	Z: Set if S = 0
W	B5	dition codes are set or cleared	V: Cleared
L	D5	accordingly, but S is not	C: Cleared
F	53	changed. Section 5.2.	
D	73		
G	53FD		
H	73FD		
BITx	S,D	S is ANDed with D bit by bit inter-	N: Set if MSB of S AND D is 1
B	93	nally. S and D are unchanged.	Z: Set if all bits of S AND D
W	B3	Affects only condition codes.	are 0
L	D3	Yields nonzero if and only if ev-	V: Cleared
		ery set bit in S is matched with	C: Unaffected
		a set bit in D. Section 7.9.	
Rotate/Shift			
ROTL	N,S,D	S is rotated N bits left if N is posi-	N,Z: Note 1
	9C	tive, or right if N is negative.	V: Cleared
		MSB rotates into LSB if left, and	C: Unaffected
		LSB rotates into MSB if right.	
		Result is placed into D leaving	
		S unchanged. N is byte, and S	
		and D are longwords. Section	
		6.11.	

Assembly Mnemonics and Opcodes		Explanation	Effects on Condition Codes
ASHx L Q	N,S,D 78 79	S is arithmetically shifted N bits left if N is positive, or right if N is negative. Right shift preserves sign and left shift loads 0's at the right. Result is placed into D leaving S unchanged. N is byte, and S and D are longwords or quadwords. Section 6.11.	N,Z: Note 1 V: Set on left shift if any bit shifted into MSB is different from original MSB C: Cleared
Address and Stack Manipulation			
MOVAx B W L,F Q,D,G O,H	S,D 9E 3E DE 7E 7EFD	Address of S is placed into longword D. Sections 5.7.1, 11.5.	N,Z: Note 1 V: Cleared C: Unaffected
PUSHAx B W L,F Q,D,G O,H	S 9F 3F DF 7F 7FFD	Address of S is placed onto User Stack.	N,Z: Note 1 V: Cleared C: Unaffected
PUSHL	S DD	The longword S is pushed onto the User Stack. Same as MOVL S, –(SP) but is one byte shorter.	N,Z: Note 1 V: Cleared C: Unaffected
PUSHR	M BB	Pushes registers identified by set bits in mask M onto User Stack. Higher-numbered registers are pushed first. Section 10.3.4.	N,Z,V,C: Unaffected
POPR	M BA	Removes registers identified by set bits in mask M from User Stack. Lower-numbered registers are popped first. Section 10.3.4.	N,Z,V,C: Unaffected
PSW/PSL Manipulation			
BICPSW	M B9	Like BICW, but PSW is the destination. Bits <15:8> of M (word) must be clear. Used to clear bits in PSW. Exercise 6.15, Section 16.5.3.	N,Z,V,C: Set or cleared according to current N,Z,V,C and <3:0> of M

457

Assembly Mnemonics and Opcodes		Explanation	Effects on Condition Codes

PSW/PSL Manipulation (*continued*)

BISPSW	M B8	Like BISW, but PSW is the destination. Bits <15:8> of M (word) must be clear. Used to set bits in PSW. Exercise 6.15, Section 16.5.3.	N,Z,V,C: Set or cleared according to current N,Z,V,C and <3:0> of M
MOVPSL	D DC	D longword is replaced by PSL. Section 9.9.	N,Z,V,C: Unaffected

Character String Manipulations

MOVC3	L,S,D 28	Character string of L bytes located at S is moved to D. S and D can overlap. L is word operand. Section 7.9.	N,V,C: Cleared Z: Set
MOVC5	LS,S, F,LD,D 2C	Character string of LS bytes located at S is moved to string of LD bytes at D using F as fill if LD>LS. If LD<LS, first LD bytes of S are moved. R0 returns number of unmoved bytes. Note 6.	N: Set if LS<LS in signed sense Z: Set if LS = LD V: Cleared C: Set if LS<LD in unsigned sense
CMPC3	L,S1,S2 29	Bytes of string at S1 are compared to those at S2. Comparison continues until inequality is detected, or until L bytes have been compared. Condition codes are set by result of last comparison. Section 7.9. Note 6.	N: Set if last compared byte of S1 is less than that of S2 using signed comparison Z: Set if last compared byte of S1 is equal to that of S2 V: Cleared C: Set if last compared byte of S1 is less than that of S2 using unsigned comparison

Assembly Mnemonics and Opcodes		Explanation	Effects on Condition Codes
CMPC5	LS,S, F,LD,D 2D	Like CMPC3 except source is of length LS and destination is of length LD. If LS ≠ LD, shorter is extended with fill character F.	See CMPC3.
LOCC	C,L,S 3A	Bytes of string at S are compared with byte C. Comparison continues until *equality* is detected or L bytes have been compared. Section 7.9. Note 6.	N,V,C: Cleared Z: Cleared if character C is found in S
SKPC	C,L,S 3B	Bytes of string at S are compared with C. Comparison continues until *inequality* is detected or L bytes have been compared. Section 7.9. Note 6.	N,V,C: Cleared Z: Cleared if inequality is detected.

Control and Branches (See also Table A.4)

JMP	A 17	Jump to address A. Any addressing mode that evaluates to an address can be used. Unlimited range.	N,Z,V,C: Unaffected
BRx B W	A 11 31	Branches unconditionally to A. Range limited to byte (B) or word (W) displacement. Section 5.2.	N,Z,V,C: Unaffected
BBS	P,B,A E0	Branches to A if bit that is in position P relative to base address B is set. Range is limited to byte displacement.	N,Z,V,C: Unaffected
BBC	P,B,A E1	Like BBS but branches on bit clear.	N,Z,V,C: Unaffected
BLBS	S,A E8	Branches to A if low bit of longword S is set. Section 16.6.3.	N,Z,V,C: Unaffected
BLBC	S,A E9	Branches to A if low bit of longword S is clear. Section 16.6.3.	N,Z,V,C: Unaffected

Assembly Mnemonics and Opcodes		Explanation	Effects on Condition Codes

Control and Branches (continued)

Assembly Mnemonics and Opcodes		Explanation	Effects on Condition Codes
ACBx B W L F D G H	L,K,I,A 9D 3D F1 4F 6F 4FFD 6FFD	Add, compare, and branch. K is added to index I and new index is compared to limit L. For positive K, branch to A occurs if new index is less than or equal to the limit. For negative K, branch to A occurs if new index is greater than or equal to the limit. Used to implement DO, WHILE, and FOR loops. Range is limited to word displacement.	N: Set if index <0 Z: Set if index =0 V: Note 1 C: Unaffected
AOBLSS	L,I,A F2	Add 1 to index I and branch to A if new index is less than limit L. L and I are longword integers. Range is limited to byte displacement.	N: Set if index <0 Z: Set if index =0 V: Set on index overflow C: Unaffected
AOBLEQ	L,I,A F3	Same as AOBLSS except branches on index less than or equal to limit.	N: Set if index <0 Z: Set if index =0 V: Set on index overflow C: Unaffected
SOBGTR	I,A F5	Subtract 1 from index I and branch to A if new index is greater than zero. Range limited to byte displacement. Section 5.5	N: Set if index <0 Z: Set if index =0 V: Set on index overflow C: Unaffected
SOBGEQ	I,A F4	Same as SOBGTR except branches on index greater than or equal to zero.	N: Set if index <0 Z: Set if index =0 V: Set on index overflow C: Unaffected

460

Assembly Mnemonics and Opcodes		Explanation	Effects on Condition Codes
CASEx	S,B,L	Branches to case address Cn if selector S minus base B equals n. Table T of displacements to cases follows the CASEx instruction. If S-B is not in range 0 to L, control falls through to code following table.	N: Set if signed (S-B)<L
T: .WORD	C0-T		Z: Set if (S-B)=L
.WORD	C1-T		V: Cleared
.			C: Set if unsigned (S-B)<L
.			
.			
.WORD	CL-T		
B	8F		
W	AF		
L	CF		
BSBx	A	Branch to subroutine at address A. Range is limited to byte (B) or word (W) displacement. Address of location following displacement operand is pushed onto the User Stack. Return with RSB. Section 9.3.	N,Z,V,C: Unaffected
B	10		
W	30		
JSB	A	Jump to subroutine at address A. Any addressing mode that evaluates to an address can be used. Unlimited range. Address of location following operand specifier is pushed onto User Stack. Return with RSB. Section 9.3.	N,Z,V,C: Unaffected
	16		
RSB		Return from subroutine by popping longword from top of User Stack into PC. Section 9.3.	N,Z,V,C: Unaffected
	05		
CALLG	ARG,A	Procedure call with argument list. ARG is address of argument list and A is address of procedure. Return with RET. Section 9.9.	N,Z,V,C: Cleared
	FA		
CALLS	#N,A	Procedure call with stack argument list. N is number of arguments previously pushed onto User Stack, and A is address of procedure. Return with RET. Section 9.9.	N,Z,V,C: Cleared
	FB		

461

Assembly Mnemonics and Opcodes		Explanation	Effects on Condition Codes
Control and Branches (*continued*)			
RET	04	Return from procedure. Restores SP, registers in entry mask, and PSW to state that existed when called. Section 9.9.	N,Z,V,C: Restored to calling settings
Privileged Instructions			
CHMm	#n	Changes mode to Kernal (K), Exec-	N,Z,V,C: Cleared
K	BC	utive (E), Supervisor (S), or User	
E	BD	(U), and vectors to operating sys-	
S	BE	tem routine specified by n.	
U	BF		
PROBEn	M,L,B	Verifies that bytes between base B	N,V,C: Cleared
R	OC	and base plus length L addresses	Z: Cleared if accessible
W	OD	have read (R) or write (W) accessibility for mode M.	
REI	02	Return from exception or interrupt. Pops PC and PSL from stack, causing a return from servicing routine.	N,Z,V,C: Taken from PSL found in stack
LDPCTX	06	Loads process context	N,Z,V,C: Unaffected
SVPCTX	07	Saves process context	N,Z,V,C: Unaffected
MFPR	R,A DB	Contents of privileged register R is moved to A.	N: Set if R<0 Z: Set if R=0 V: Cleared C: Unaffected

TABLE A.1/MACRO Instructions (*concluded*)

Assembly Mnemonics and Opcodes		Explanation	Effects on Condition Codes
MTPR	A,R DA	Contents of A is moved to privileged register R.	N: Set if A<0 Z: Set if A=0 V: Cleared C: Unaffected
BPT	03	Generates breakpoint fault, causing vectoring to servicing routine specified in offset $2C_{16}$ in System Control Block.	N,Z,V,C: Cleared
HALT	00	Stops processor operation. Section 4.4.1.	N,Z,V,C: Unaffected

TABLE A.2/Signed Integer/Floating-Point Conversion

Opcode (Conversion Rule)

(a) CVTxy S,D

x \ y	B	W	L	F	D	G	H
B		99 (s)	98 (s)	4C (e)	6C (e)	4CFD (e)	6CFD (e)
W	33 (t)		32 (s)	4D (e)	6D (e)	4DFD (e)	6DFD (e)
L	F6 (t)	F7 (t)		4E (r)	6E (e)	4EFD (e)	6EFD (e)
F	48 (t)	49 (t)	4A (t)		56 (e)	99FD (e)	98FD (e)
D	68 (t)	69 (t)	6A (t)	76 (r)			32FD (e)
G	48FD (t)	49FD (t)	4AFD (t)	33FD (r)			56FD (e)
H	68FD (t)	69FD (t)	6AFD (t)	F6FD (r)	F7FD (r)	76FD (r)	

(b) CVTRxy S,D

x \ y	L
F	4B (r)
D	6B (r)
G	48FD (r)
H	68FD (r)

NOTES:

(1) S is converted from data type x to data type y and placed into D.

(2) B = byte; W = word; L = longword; F = F_floating; D = D_floating; G = G_floating; H = H_floating.

(3) Conversion rules:

Sign-extension (s) is used in going from short to long integers.

High bits are truncated (t) when an integer result does not fit into y data type.

Conversion to floating-point is either exact (e) or rounded (r).

(4) N and Z set if result is negative or zero, respectively, cleared otherwise. V set if converted number will not fit in y data type. C always cleared.

(5) See Sections 7.7 and 15.6 for examples.

TABLE A.3/VAX-11 Decimal Instructions (Partial List)

Assembler Mnemonics and Opcode	Explanation	Effects on Condition Codes
Arithmetic		
ADDP4 LS,SP,LD,DP 20	SP is added to DP.	N,Z,V,C: Note 1
ADDP6 LS1,SP1,LS2,SP2,LD,DP 21	SP1+SP2 is placed in DP.	N,Z,V,C: Note 1
SUBP4 LS,SP,LD,DP 22	SP is subtracted from DP.	N,Z,V,C: Note 1
SUBP6 LS1,SP1,LS2,SP2,LD,DP 23	SP2-SP1 is placed in DP.	N,Z,V,C: Note 1
MULP LS1,SP1,LS2,SP2,LD,DP 25	SP2×SP1 is placed in DP.	N,Z,V,C: Note 1
DIVP LS1,SP1,LS2,SP2,LD,DP 27	SP/SP1 is placed in DP.	N,Z,V,C: Note 1
ASHP C,LS,SP,R,LD,DP F8	$SP \times 10^C$ is placed in DP. Decimal arithmetic shift (Notes 7 and 8).	N,Z,V,C: Note 1
MOVP LS,SP,DP 34	SP is moved to DP.	N,Z,V: Note 1 C: Unaffected
Comparison		
CMPP3 LS,SP1,SP2 35	SP1 is compared to SP2 and condition codes are set. Both strings are of same length.	N: Set if SP1<SP2; cleared otherwise Z: Set if SP1=SP2 V,C: Cleared
CMPP4 LS1,SP1,LS2,SP2 37	SP1 is compared to SP2 and condition codes are set. Strings are of different lengths.	N: Set if SP1<SP2; cleared otherwise Z: Set if SP1=SP2 V,C: Cleared
Conversion		
CVTLP SL,LD,DP F9	SL converted to DP	N,Z,V,C: Note 1
CVTPL LS,SP,DL 36	SP converted to DL	N,Z,V,C: Note 1
CVTPS LS,SP,LD,DS 08	SP converted to DS	N,Z,V,C: Note 1
CVTSP LS,SS,LD,DP 09	SS converted to DP	N,Z,V,C: Note 1

NOTES:

(1) Normal settings of N,Z,V, and C condition codes for decimal operations are:

N = 1 if result is negative

Z = 1 if result is zero

V = 1 if destination string is too short for result (decimal overflow)

C = 0

(*Notes continued next page*)

(Notes continued)

(2) R1, R3, and R5 normally return the address of the most significant digit of the first, second, and third packed decimal operands, respectively. R0, R2, and R4 are normally cleared.

(3) All string operands must reside in main memory, not in registers, and must not overlap.

(4) LS,LS1,LS2 = length of source; LD = length of destination. Must be represented as word-size integers.

(5) SP, SP1, SP2 = source packed decimal string.

(6) DP, DP1, DP2 = destination packed decimal string.

(7) C = decimal digit shift count, + left, − right.

(8) R = decimal rounding control. If C < 0, then result is rounded up if next digit beyond LD is greater than or equal to C. R=#5 for normal rounding, #0 for truncation.

(9) SL = source longword signed integer.

(10) DL = destination longword signed integer.

(11) SS = source leading separate numeric string.

(12) DS = destination leading separate numeric string.

(13) See Section 15.6 for examples.

TABLE A.4/Condition Codes for Branch Instructions

Construction and Usage	Assembly Mnemonic	Opcode	Branch Conditions
Unsigned Branches			
Branch if GreaTeR, Unsigned	BGTRU	1A	$C \lor Z = 0$
Branch if Less or EQual, Unsigned	BLEQU	1B	$C \lor Z = 1$
Branch if Greater or EQual, Unsigned	BGEQU	1E	$C = 0$
Branch if LeSS, Unsigned	BLSSU	1F	$C = 1$
Branch if Not EQual, Unsigned	BNEQU	12	$Z = 0$
Branch if EQuaL, Unsigned	BEQLU	13	$Z = 1$
Branch if Carry Clear	BCC	1E	$C = 0$
Branch if Carry Set	BCS	1F	$C = 1$
Signed Branches			
Branch if GreaTeR	BGTR	14	$Z \lor N = 0$
Branch if Less or EQual	BLEQ	15	$Z \lor N = 1$
Branch if Greater or EQual	BGEQ	18	$N = 0$
Branch if LeSS	BLSS	19	$N = 1$
Branch if Not EQual	BNEQ	12	$Z = 0$
Branch if EQuaL	BEQL	13	$Z = 1$
Branch if oVerflow Clear	BVC	1C	$V = 0$
Branch if oVerflow Set	BVS	1D	$V = 1$

NOTES:

(1) N, Z, V, and C are condition codes at the time of branch execution.

(2) N, Z, V, and C are all unchanged by the branch instruction.

(3) See also *Control and Branch* instructions, Table A.1

(4) See Sections 5.2 and 6.7 for examples.

TABLE A.5/VAX-11General Register Addressing Modes

Mode Specifier (Hexadecimal)	Name	Assembly Mnemonics	Explanation
5	Register	Rn	Rn contains operand. Section 4.3.
6	Register-Deferred	−(Rn)	Rn contains address of operand. Section 5.7.
7	Autodecrement	−(Rn)	Decrement contents of Rn by 1 if the operation is a byte operation, or by 4 if it is a longword operation, etc. After that, Rn contains address of operand. Section 5.7.
8	Autoincrement	(Rn)+	Rn contains address of operand. After the operand is fetched or stored, Rn is incremented (by 1 if the operation is a byte operation, or by 4 if it is a longword operation, etc.). Section 5.7.2.
9	Autoincrement-Deferred	@(Rn)+	Rn contains address of address of operand. After the operand is fetched or stored, Rn is incremented by 4. Section 9.8.3.
A,C,E	Displacement	D(Rn)	Address of operand is sign-extended D plus contents of Rn. The value of D is stored in the cell following the first byte of the operand specifier. Section 9.8.4.
B,D,F	Displacement-Deferred	@D(Rn)	Address of address of operand is sign-extended D plus contents of Rn. The value of D is stored in the cell following the operand specifier. Section 9.8.4.

NOTES:

(1) Examples of usage are shown in the indicated sections for each mode.

(2) Displacement, D, can be prefixed with B^ for byte, W^ for word, or L^ for longword. If prefix is omitted, assembler decides most appropriate length. Also D can be a symbol, an expression, or a literal. Mode specifiers for byte, word, and long displacements are A, C, and E, respectively, for displacement addressing, or B, D, and F for displacement-deferred addressing.

TABLE A.6/Short Literal and Indexed Addressing

Mode Specifier	Name	Assembly Mnemonics	Explanation
0–3	Short Literal	S^#literal	The value of the literal is embedded in the operand specifier, from which it is decoded at run time. Sections 5.6.1, 12.2.2, 14.7.
4	Indexed	[Ri]	This can only appear as a suffix to certain other addressing modes. Register i acts as an index relative to a base address determined from the other part of the addressing mnemonics. Section 12.2.3. See also Table A.7.

TABLE A.7/Addressing Modes (Basic vs. Deferred)

		Basic		Deferred	
		Mode	Mnemonics	Mode	Mnemonic
Base	Register	5	Rn	6	(Rn)
	Autodecrement	7	−(Rn)	−	NA
	Autoincrement	8	(Rn)+	9	@(Rn)+
	Displacement	A,C,E	D(Rn)	B,D,F	@D(Rn)
Indexed	Register	−	NA	6/4	(Rn) [Ri]
	Autodecrement	7/4	−(Rn) [Ri]	−	NA
	Autoincrement	8/4	(Rn) + [Ri]	9/4	@(Rn) + [Ri]
	Displacement	A,C,E/4	D(Rn) [Ri]	B,D,F/4	@(Rn)[Ri]

NOTES:

(1) NA = Not available or logically not applicable

(2) D = Displacement: Byte B^d;mode A (basic) or B (deferred)
      Word W^d;mode C (basic) or D (deferred)
      Longword L^d;mode E (basic) or F (deferred)

(3) Indexed addressing is always used in conjunction with a base mode.

TABLE A.8/Program Counter Addressing

Mode	Name	Assembly Mnemonics	Explanation
8F	Immediate	I^#symbol	Operand is the value of symbol. This value is automatically stored following the instruction. Section 5.6.1.
9F	Absolute	@#symbol	Operand is in location whose address is the value of symbol. Symbol value is automatically stored following the instruction. Section 12.2.5.
AF,CF,EF	Relative	symbol	Operand is in location whose address is the value of symbol. The PC-relative address of symbol (see notes) is automatically stored following the instruction. Section 5.6.2.
BF,DF,FF	Relative Deferred	@symbol	Address of operand is in location whose address is indicated by value of symbol. The PC-relative address of symbol (see notes) is automatically stored following the instruction. Section 12.2.5.
8F/4	Immediate Indexed	I^ # symbol [Ri]	Not a useful mode.
9F/4	Absolute Indexed	@#symbol [Ri]	See Note 3.
AF,CF,EF/4	Relative Indexed	symbol [Ri]	See Note 3.
BF,DF,FF/4	Relative Deferred Indexed	@symbol [Ri]	See Note 3.

NOTES:

(1) *Symbol* can be a literal, a label, a symbol given a value by assignment, or an expression. In all cases, a value is first determined by the assembler, then used as indicated.

(2) PC-relative address is the symbol value minus the *current* PC. (See Section 5.6.2.)

(3) In each indexed case, a *base address* is determined as described in the corresponding base addressing mode (top part of table). The operand address is then determined by adding the contents of Ri times the operand length to the base address.

TABLE A.9/VAX MACRO Directives

Assembly Mnemonics	Explanation
General	
.TITLE *string*	Assigns *string* as title of the module. Section 4.7.
.END *label*	Marks end of module and sets the starting address for execution to *label*. Section 4.7.
.END	Marks end of module. Use this form for subroutines. Section 9.12.
.ENTRY *label*,^M<>	Defines *label* as symbolic name for procedure entry point and establishes an entry mask at that location. The mask indicates registers to be protected during procedure execution. Sections 4.7, 9.9.
.GLOBAL *list*	Places symbols in *list* in the global symbol table. This is necessary when symbols are referenced in separately assembled modules. Alternately, symbol can be placed to left of :: or = = to cause them to be global. Section 9.10.
.EXTERNAL *list*	Identifies symbols in *list* as being defined in separate module. This is optional because MACRO assembler assumes external for all undefined symbols. Section 9.10.
Symbol:	Any *symbol* to left of : is taken as internal label. Section 4.5.
Symbol::	Any *symbol* to left of :: is taken as a global label. Section 9.10.
Symbol = *Expression*	Assigns the value determined by *expression* to local *symbol*. Section 10.2.2.
Symbol = = *Expression*	Like =, but also makes *symbol* global. Section 10.2.2.
Storage and Location Counter Control	

.BLKx n
    B
    W
    L
    Q
    O
    F
    D
    G
    H
    A
	Advances the location counter by n times the length (bytes) of the data type. Used to reserve n data type cells without initialization. The n can be a previously defined symbol or an expression involving such symbols. Sections 5.6.2, 7.6.

.BYTE n1,n2... .WORD .LONG .QUAD .OCTA .F__FLOATING (.FLOAT) .D__FLOATING (.DOUBLE) .G__FLOATING .H__FLOATING .SIGNED__BYTE .SIGNED__WORD .ADDRESS	Reserves space and initializes one data type cell for each listed value. Expressions or symbols can be included in list provided that all symbols are defined prior to usage. Sections 5.6.2, 7.6.

TABLE A.9/VAX MACRO Directives (*continued*)

Assembly Mnemonics	Explanation
Storage and Location Counter Control (continued)	
.ASCII/string/<n>	Reserves space and initializes bytes to the ASCII codes corresponding to characters between delimiters or decimal numbers enclosed in < >. Delimiters can be any character not included in string. Delimited strings and <n> can occur in any order. Section 7.6.
.ASCIZ/string/<n>	Like .ASCII except string is followed by NUL character (00). Section 7.6.
.ASCIC/string/<n>	Like .ASCII except string is preceded by a count byte. Section 7.6.
.ASCIC/string/<n>	Like .ASCII except string is stored in descriptor format. Section 16.6.3.
.PACKED *dec-string, symbol*	Reserves and initializes a packed decimal string to value given by *dec-string*. If given, *symbol* is equated to number of digits. Section 15.5.
.ALIGN *data-type*	The location counter is advanced so as to place the next item assembled at an address divisible by the *data type* length. *Data-type* can be BYTE, WORD, LONG, QUAD, or PAGE, but cannot exceed alignment length of the program section. See .PSECT.
Macro and Conditional Assembly	
.MACRO *name*, a1, a2, . . .	Defines macro called *name* with arguments a1, a2. . . . Section 10.3.1.
.ENDM *name*	Ends definition of macro called *name* (*name* is optional). Also used to end .IRP and .IRPC blocks. Sections 10.3, 10.4.
.REPT *expression*	Repeats instructions up to .ENDR a number of times determined by *expression*. Section 10.4.
.ENDR	Ends .REPT blocks. Section 10.4.
.IF *cond arg*	Instructions up to next .ENDC or .IFF will be assembled if *arg* meets *condition*. Section 10.5.
.ENDC	Ends conditional assembly block. Section 10.5.
.IFF (.IF_FALSE)	Can only be between .IF and .ENDC. Instructions up to next .IFT or .ENDC will be assembled only if *arg* does *not* meet condition in previous .IF. Section 10.5.
.IFT (.IF_TRUE)	Can only be used between .IF and .ENDC. Instructions up to next .IFF or .ENDC will be assembled only if *arg* meets condition in previous .IF. Section 10.5.
.IFTF (.IF_TRUE_FALSE)	Can only be used between .IF and .ENDC. Instructions up to next .IFF, .IFT, or .ENDC will be assembled regardless of *arg* in previous .IF. Section 10.5.
.IIF *cond arg, statement*	*Statement* can be any instruction or directive and is assembled only if *arg* meets condition *cond*. Section 10.5.
.MEXIT	Can only be used between .MACRO and .ENDM. Causes all subsequent instructions and directives in the macro to be skipped. Section 10.5.

TABLE A.9/VAX MACRO Directives (*concluded*)

Assembly Mnemonics	Explanation
Macro and Conditional Assembly (continued)	
.NARG *symbol*	Can only be used between .MACRO and .ENDM. Causes the count of actual arguments to be assigned to *symbol*. Section 10.5.4.
.NTYPE *symbol, arg*	Can only be used between .MACRO and .ENDM. Causes the addressing code of *arg* to be assigned to *symbol*. Section 10.5.4.
.NCHR *symbol, <string>*	Causes the count of characters in *string* to be assigned to *symbol*. Section 10.5.4.
.ERROR *symbol, message*	Causes *message* and *symbol* to be printed in .LIS file. Used to generate macro error reports. Section 10.5.3.
Miscellaneous	
.SHOW EXPANSIONS	Causes all subsequent macro expansions and repeat blocks to be listed. Useful for seeing how macro expansion works. Section 10.3.1.
.NOSHOW DEFINITIONS	Causes all subsequent macro and repeat block definitions to be suppressed in the .LIS file.
.NOSHOW (.NLIST)	Listing suppressed up to the next .SHOW directive.
.SHOW (.LIST)	Causes listing to resume after a prior .NOSHOW.
.PSECT *name, data-type*	Causes subsequent code to be assembled into section called *name*, aligned so as to begin at an address divisible by length of *data-type*. *Data-type* can be BYTE, WORD, LONG, QUAD, or PAGE. Sections 17.7, 11.4.4.
.PAGE	Causes a form-feed character to be placed in the .LIS file. Will cause a page eject on a line printer.

B

The EDT Text Editor

B.1 | Overview

A text editor is a system-supplied program that allows you to create or modify text files. These files can be viewed as a collection of lines of text of any kind, e.g., MACRO programs, Pascal programs, and data. On a typical VAX-11 installation there will be several different text editors from which to choose. While each of these has the same essential capabilities, they differ slightly in the details of their usage. Appendix B discusses one text editor, namely EDT (V2.0), which is the standard editor provided by Digital Equipment Corporation and available on any VMS system. Although lacking in certain advanced features found in other editors, it has the advantages of almost universal availability and support.

An important characteristic of a text editor is the manner in which the user is allowed to interact with the text. In one mode of interaction, called **line-editing mode,** the file is treated as a collection of lines of text that can be modified, deleted, or added to on a one-at-a-time basis. A quite different interaction mode is called **full-screen editing.** This mode allows editing of an entire screenful of lines at one time, with the portion to be modified selected by a cursor that is controlled by terminal keys. Full-screen editing is usually viewed as a more convenient editing mode, but requires a visual display terminal (VDT) with special features, such as the VT100 terminal by Digital Equipment Corporation. Line editing, on the other hand, can be performed on any kind of terminal. EDT provides both line and full-screen editing modes, so that you can select the mode that best suits you and your equipment.

Only a minimum set of commands necessary for convenient creation and alteration of MACRO programs with EDT will be presented here. Readers wishing to use the more extensive capabilities of this editor should consult the *EDT Editor Manual* (Digital Equipment Corporation).

B.2 | File Handling with EDT

When EDT is to be executed, the name of the file to be edited is given. If this file does not exist, it is created so that new text can be inserted. If it does exist, it is read into a portion of memory called the EDT "buffer." Only the contents of this buffer is changed by EDT commands, until EDT is left with the EX command. EX causes the buffer to be written into a new version of the file, thus making your changes permanent. However, the original file is saved under the old version number so that if you wish to go back to the original version you can simply delete the edited version. This is explained further in Section D.6.1.

B.3 | EDT Commands

This section presents the EDT entry and exit commands common to both line and full-screen editing modes. Commands that apply only to the line editing mode are presented in Section B.4, while those for full-screen editing are presented in Section B.5. A short summary of frequently used EDT commands is presented in Table B.1.

TABLE B.1/Summary of EDT Commands

Action	Line Editing Mode	Full-Screen Editing Mode
Enter Editor: New or existing file.	EDIT/EDT *fnl* <CR>	EDIT/EDT *fnl* <CR> * C <CR>

Insert Text:	* I <CR>
	   text
	 * ^Z
	   (Inserts before line pointer)
		No command required. Typed *text* is inserted at the cursor. <CR> ends line and inserts new empty line.

Leave Editor: Saving changes.	* EX <CR>	^Z * EX <CR>
Discarding changes.	* QUIT <CR>	^Z * QUIT <CR>
Pointer or Cursor Movement:		
Beginning of buffer.	* % BE <CR>	GOLD TOP
End of buffer.	* % E <CR>	GOLD BOTTOM
Down 1 line.	* <CR>	↓ or LINE
Down *n* lines.	* +*n* <CR>	[ADVANCE] GOLD *n* LINE
Up 1 line.	* −1 <CR>	↑ or [BACKUP] LINE
Up *n* lines.	* −*n* <CR>	[BACKUP] GOLD *n* LINE
Forward 16 lines.	Not available	[ADVANCE] SECT
Backward 16 lines.	Not available	[BACKUP] SECT
Forward 1 character.	Not available	→ or [ADVANCE] CHAR
Forward *n* characters.	Not available	[ADVANCE] GOLD *n* CHAR
Backward 1 character.	Not available	← or [BACKUP] CHAR
Backward *n* characters.	Not available	[BACKUP] GOLD *n* CHAR
Forward 1 word.	Not available	[ADVANCE] WORD

Action	Line Editing Mode	Full-Screen Editing Mode
Pointer or Cursor Movement (*continued*)		
Forward *n* words.	Not available	[ADVANCE] GOLD *n* WORD
Backward 1 word.	Not available	[BACKUP] WORD
Backward *n* words.	Not available	[BACKUP] GOLD *n* WORD
Beginning of line.	Not applicable	BACKSPACE
End of line.	Not applicable	EOL
Position at entry:	At first line	Beginning of line where line pointer is set upon entry to full-screen mode.
Display: Buffer. *n* lines.	 * % WH <CR> * T. #*n* <CR>	 Not applicable Not applicable
Delete: Current line. Forward *n* lines. To end of line. To beginning of line. Current character. Previous character. Current word. Marked text. Undelete character. Undelete word. Undelete line. Move text: Move lines. Move character.	 * D <CR> * D.#*n* <CR> Not available Not available Not available Not available Not available Not available Not available Not available Not available * MOVE l₁:l₂ TO l₃ Not available	 [BACKSPACE] DEL__L GOLD *n* DEL__L GOLD DEL__EOL LINEFEED DEL__C DELETE DEL__W SELECT (*move cursor*) CUT GOLD UND__C GOLD UND__W GOLD UND__L SELECT (*move cursor*) CUT (*move cursor*) GOLD PASTE SELECT (*move cursor*) CUT (*move cursor*) GOLD PASTE
Find string	* ''*string*'' <CR> or '*string*' <CR>	GOLD FIND (*string*) ENTER or FNDNXT
Substitute string:	*S/*old*/*new*/ <CR>	SELECT (*new string*) CUT (*move cursor*) SELECT (*old string*) GOLD REPLACE
Read/write second file: Read into buffer. Write buffer to file.	 * INC *fn2* <CR> * WR *fn2* <CR>	 GOLD COMMAND INC *fn2* ENTER GOLD COMMAND WR *fn2* ENTER
On-line help:	* HELP <CR> or * HELP *command* <CR>	HELP

NOTES:

(1) <CR> means the RETURN key.

(2) See Figure B.3 for full-screen commands.

(3) *n* means integer typed from keyboard (*not* numeric keypad).

(4) *fn1, fn2, fn3* means file specifications including type extension.

475

B.3.1 Entering EDT (Line or Full-Screen Editing)

EDT is entered with the VMS EDIT command. This command is the same regardless of whether you wish to do line or full-screen editing. The command line necessary for entering EDT is:

```
$EDIT/EDT  filename.extension <CR>
*▨
```

Here *filename.extension* is the file that you wish to create or modify. If it does not exist in your current directory, it will be created and you will be informed that it is a new file. The symbol <CR> means to press the RETURN key. The asterisk * is the EDT line editing "command prompt," signifying that EDT is in the line editing mode and is waiting for your command. Available line editing commands are discussed below. The computer response is indicated by an underline.

To change to the full-screen mode, enter CHANGE or C in response to the command prompt. Screen editing commands are explained in Section B.5.

Because EDT is the default editor under VMS, the /EDT qualifier on the EDIT command is optional.

B.3.2 Leaving EDT (Line or Full-Screen Editing)

After the file has been created or modified and you wish to leave EDT, one of two commands can be entered: EXIT or QUIT. If you use EXIT (EX is an acceptable abbreviation), the edited file will be saved under a new version number, and control will be returned to the operating system. Using QUIT (cannot be abbreviated) results in a return to the operating system *without saving the edited file*. This is used when for some reason you wish to abandon the changes which you have made in the file.

Normally, then, an EDT line editing session looks like this:

```
$ EDIT/EDT  MYFILE.MAR <CR>
*▨
```

    (various editing operations)

```
* EX <CR>
$ ▨
```

Note that if you have been editing in the full-screen mode you must enter ^Z to obtain the * command prompt before QUIT or EX can be executed.

B.4 | Line Editing

B.4.1 The HELP Command

The first EDT command to become familiar with is called HELP. This command invokes an on-line help facility that allows you to inquire about the details of using any EDT command. When typed by itself, i.e.,

```
*HELP <CR>
```

you are presented with instructions and a list of subtopics to choose from. Typing it with a command word gives specific information about that command. For example,

```
*HELP INSERT <CR>
```

will tell you how to use the INSERT command.

B.4.2 Creating a New File

To create a new file, enter the EDIT/EDT command line with a new file name, including its extension. Then, to the first command prompt (*) enter the INSERT command (abbreviated I). This sequence is shown below, along with the computer response (underlined).

```
$EDIT/EDT  MYPROG.MAR <CR>
input file does not exist
[EOB]
*I [CR]
```

The entire file creation sequence for the line editing mode is shown below. A <CR> is required after each user-input.

```
$ EDIT/EDT  MYPROG.MAC
input file does not exist
[EOB]
*I
                .TITLE MYPROG
                .ENTRY START,0
                CLRL    R0
                INCL    R0
                HALT
                .END    START
    ^Z
*EX
$ ▨
```

It must be observed that while in the insert mode *everything* that is typed is accepted as text without regard to its meaning. This means that EDT will not respond to its commands. A very common and frustrating error when working with an editor is to be in Insert mode without realizing it, and expect EDT to respond to its normal commands. In addition to the frustration of "nothing working right," when you finally do realize what has happened and leave the Insert mode, you find that all of your attempts have been entered as text into your file! To avoid such difficulties, be sure to issue ^Z when you have finished inserting new lines.

File creation in the full-screen mode is discussed in Section B.5.2.

B.4.3 Modifying a File

EDT provides a number of commands that can be used to modify a file. However, before we discuss these, we need to discuss some general aspects of EDT. First, note that the file is viewed as a collection of lines of text. When EDT is entered, each of these lines is given a number, beginning with 1 for the first line. These line numbers are temporary and are removed upon completion of the editing session. While editing, however, they provide a convenient means for referring to particular lines in the file. EDT also uses what is called the "current line pointer." At any instant this pointer has the value of the "current" line number. It is represented by the period (.) in some commands. The line numbers and current line pointer play an important role in the use of many of the EDT line editing commands discussed below.

Most EDT line editing commands have the form:

```
*Command range
```

where *command* is the name or abbreviation for the command, and *range* indicates the lines to which the command is to be applied. In general, *range* is of the form:

start:finish

or:

start#number

If the :, #, and *finish* are missing, only the line numbered *start* is affected. As a simple example of this, consider the DELETE command, abbreviated D. To delete line 3 of the file being edited, enter:

```
*D 3
 1     line deleted
         4              (next line is displayed here)
*▨
```

As the response indicates, one line was deleted and the current line pointer was advanced to line 4. The following examples show forms of the range specification:

*	D	3:10	Deletes lines 3 through 10
*	D	.	Deletes current line (. is optional)
*	D	3#4	Deletes 4 lines beginning with line 3
*	D	.#4	Deletes 4 lines beginning with current line
*	D	BEFORE	Deletes *all* lines in file before current line
*	D	REST	Deletes current line and all following lines in the file
*	D	WHOLE	Deletes entire file

Although these examples of the various range specifications are shown using the DELETE command, they work equally well for all other commands that require a range specification. Note in particular that the period (.) range specification means the current line. Thus to display the current line and the next 24, enter the TYPE command as follows:

```
*T .#24    types 24 lines beginning with the current line
```

With the understanding gained from the examples above, we can now look at the EDT line editing commands. These are grouped below into major categories according to their general purpose. Abbreviations are used instead of the full command word. Also, several common range specifications are shown for each command.

Commands to Move Current-Line Pointer

<u>*%BE</u>	Move to Beginning of file (first line).
<u>*%E</u>	Move to End of file (EOB mark).
<u>*F"KZW"</u>	Find the next line containing KZW searching down. Does not print the line.
<u>*"KZW"</u>	Find next line containing KZW searching down. Prints the line.*
<u>*+5</u>	Move 5 lines down.*
<u>*-5</u>	Move 5 lines up.*
<u>*10</u>	Move to line 10.*

Commands to Display the File

<u>*T .#3</u> (. #3)	Display three lines beginning with the current line.
<u>*T WHOLE</u> (%WH)	Display entire file.
<u>*T "KZW"</u> ("KZW")	Display next line containing "KZW".

Note that the TYPE command can be abbreviated with T, or with nothing at all, i.e., just a carriage return, called the "null" abbreviation. This leads to the shorter form of the above instructions (shown in parentheses). When this is done, however, words like WHOLE and BEGIN or their abbreviations must be preceded by %.

Commands to Alter Lines in the File

<u>*D</u>	Delete current line.
<u>*D .#5</u>	Delete five lines beginning with current line.
<u>*S/CAT/DOG/.:"CAT"</u>	Substitute DOG for next occurrence of CAT. This is a combined search and replace.
<u>*S/MOVL/ADDL/</u>	Substitute ADDL for MOVL only in current line.
<u>*S/MOVL/MOVB/.#4</u>	Substitute MOVB for all occurrences of MOVL in four lines beginning with the current line.
<u>*S/HALT/$EXIT_S/%WH</u>	Substitute $EXIT_S for all occurrences of HALT in the whole file.
<u>*I</u>	Switch to Insert mode. All subsequent text is entered into the file *before* the current line. Return to command mode with ^Z.
<u>*R</u>	Delete current line *and* enter Insert mode. All subsequent text entry replaces current line. Return to command mode with ^Z.

Note that other characters, e.g., " or $ can be used instead of / in the SUBSTITUTE command. This is necessary when one of the strings contains a /. For example, S "A/B"B/A".

---

* Note that these are actually forms of the TYPE command with the null abbreviation.

Commands to Read or Write Files

`*INC file.ext`   Read contents of file.ext into file being edited; lines read will be inserted before current line. (INC is an abbreviation for INCLUDE.)

`*WR file.ext 2:4`   Write lines 2 through 4 of file being edited into file.ext. Edited file is not changed. (WR is an abbreviation for WRITE.)

Commands to Reorder Lines

`*M 7:20 TO 5`   Move lines 7 through 20 to immediately before line 5; delete them from original position. (M is an abbreviation for MOVE.)

`*M 7#5`   Move five lines beginning with line 7 to immediately before current line; delete them from original position.

`*CO 7:20 TO 5`   Copy lines 7 through 20 to immediately before line 5 without deleting them from their current position. (CO is an abbreviation for COPY.)

Commands to Leave EDT

`*EX`   Create a new version of the file using the edited buffer and leave EDT. (EX is an abbreviation for EXIT.)

`*QUIT`   Leave EDT *without* saving modified file (all changes are lost).

Note that because the EX command causes a *new* version of the permanent file to be created, the previous version continues to exist. This is important if it is necessary to go back to the previous version after leaving EDT with the EX command. That is, simply delete the new version.

B.5 | Full-Screen Editing with EDT

If you use a video display terminal (VDT) rather than a printing-type terminal you may find it more convenient (although not necessary) to use the full-screen editing mode provided by EDT.* By full-screen we mean that a 22-line segment of the file (called a *window*) is displayed on the screen. This is shown in Figure B.1. The window

---

* Digital Equipment Corporation refers to this mode as ''keypad editing'' because most commands are implemented as single keystrokes on the keypad.

```
;
;    SYMBOL DEFINITIONS AND INITIALIZATIONS
;
IBL=1                                   ;INPUT BUFFER LENGTH
OBL=1                                   ;OUTPUT BUFFER LENGTH
        $IODEF                          ;SYS MACRO TO DEFINE IO SYMBOLS
TERM_NAME:-
        .ASCID /SYS$INPUT/              ;DEFINE TERMINAL LOGICAL NAME
TERM_CHAN:-
        .BLKW 1                         ;STORAGE FOR CHANNEL NUMBER
OUT_IOSB:-
        .BLKQ 1                         ;STORAGE FOR OUTPUT STATUS BUFFER
IN_IOSB:-
        .BLKQ 1                         ;STORAGE FOR INPUT STATUS BUFFER
IN_BUF: .BLKB IBL                       ;STORAGE FOR INPUT BUFFER
OUT_BUF:.BLKB OBL                       ;STORAGE FOR OUTPUT BUFFER
        .ENTRY  IO,^M<R11>
        MOVL    4(AP),R11               ;GET PARAMETER N
        JMP     @FUN(R11)               ;GO TO FUNCTION N
FUN:    .LONG   OPEN,IN_CHAR,OUT_CHAR   ;FUNCTION TABLE
;
;    FUNCTIONS
;
OPEN:
        $ASSIGN_S _                     ;GET THE CHANNEL
          DEVNAM=TERM_NAME,-            ;   NUMBER FOR
          CHAN  =TERM_CHAN      ;         TERMINAL
        BLBS    R0,10$                  ;EXIT TO VMS
        BRW     ERROR           ;    IF ASSIGN_S FAILS
10$:    MOVW    #SS$_NORMAL,OUT_IOSB    ;INIT. OUTPUT STATUS BUFFER
        BRB     IO_END                  ;RETURN
OUT_CHAR:
        MOVB    R10,OUT_BUF             ;LOAD OUTPUT BUFFER
10$:    TSTW    OUT_IOSB                ;WAIT IF
        BEQL    10$             ;    DISPLAY NOT READY
        CMPW    OUT_IOSB,#SS$_NORMAL    ;ERROR EXIT
        BEQL    20$             ;    IF
        BRW     ERROR           ;         STATUS ERROR
20$:    $QIO_S  CHAN=TERM_CHAN,-        ;QUEUE THE IO REQUEST
          FUNC  =#IO$_WRITEVBLK,-       ;THIS IS FOR A WRITE OPERATION
          IOSB  =OUT_IOSB,-             ;WE WILL USE THE IO STATUS
          P1    =OUT_BUF,-              ;SET THE OUTPUT BUFFER
          P2    =#OBL                   ;SET OUTPUT BUFFER LENGTH
        BLBS    R0,30$                  ;ERROR EXIT
        BRW     ERROR           ;    IF WRITE DOESN'T GET QUEUED
30$:    BRB     IO_END                  ;RETURN
IN_CHAR:
        $QIO_S  CHAN=TERM_CHAN,-        ;QUEUE THE IO REQUEST
          FUNC  =#IO$_READVBLK,-        ;THIS IS FOR A READ OPERATION
          IOSB  =IN_IOSB,-              ;WE WILL USE THE IO STATUS
```

RE B.1/Window in full-screen editing mode

can be moved forward or backward in the file to select the displayed portion. Within the window is a marker called the *cursor*, which you can move to any character in the display using simple commands. You use the cursor to select the position where you wish to make the changes.

Once you have positioned the cursor, there are commands that allow you to make the desired changes. For example, the character, word, or line where the cursor rests can be deleted, changed from upper to lower case, or moved to another location. Inserting new text requires no special commands because any newly typed characters are simply inserted at the cursor location. All changes are displayed as they are completed so that you can immediately verify the result. This is one important reason why most users find full-screen editing to be more efficient than line editing.

B.5.1 The VT100 Keyboard

In this section we assume that you are using a DEC VT100 video display terminal, or another brand that emulates this unit. The importance of this is that the full-screen editing mode makes use of special terminal features that may not be available with other terminal types, or may be available but implemented differently.

The VT100 keyboard is shown in Figure B.2. Note that the keyboard is divided into two parts, namely the *typing keys,* Figure B.2(a), and the *keypad keys,* Figure B.2(b). The typing keys include the normal typewriter keys, plus special ones such as the arrow keys ↑, ↓, ←, and →, and the control key (CTRL). The keypad has a row of *function keys* (PF1, PF2, PF3, and PF4) at the top, and a set of numeric keys arranged somewhat like the keys on a calculator. Full-screen editing makes extensive use of the keypad keys, as well as the arrow, backspace, and control keys on the typing keyboard.

Terminals of other brands that emulate the VT100 terminal often have keyboards that are arranged differently. Also, the markings on the keys are often different from the VT100 keys. Therefore, when you use such a terminal, it will be necessary to determine the keys that are equivalent to the VT100 keypad, arrow, and control keys. You can do this by inquiring locally, or by reading the user's manual for your terminal. Also, the EDT full-screen HELP command, described below, can be used to determine how EDT interprets each key on your keyboard.

As we shall see in later sections, nearly all of the full-screen editing mode commands are invoked with one or two keystrokes on either the typing keyboard or the keypad. The key that invokes a particular command will, of course, depend upon the keyboard layout of your terminal.

Figure B.3 shows the commands assigned to each key for the VT100 keypad. We see that there is either one or two command words on each key in this diagram. When there are two, the upper command word applies if the key is pressed by itself. The lower command word is selected by pressing the GOLD key, followed by the command key. Here GOLD key means the upper left key in the keypad diagram in Figure B.3; it is *not* gold in color on the actual keyboard.

Note that this means two separate keystrokes, not pressing both keys at once. In

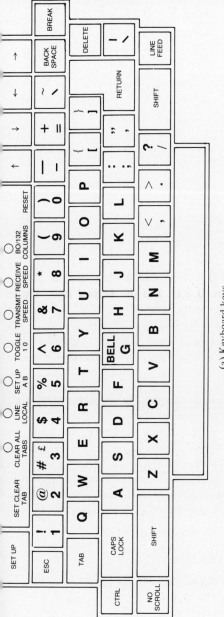

(a) Keyboard keys

PF1	PF2	PF3	PF4
7	8	9	—
4	5	6	,
1	2	3	ENTER
0		.	

(b) Keypad keys

FIGURE B.2/VT 100 keyboard and keypad. Copyright © 1982. Digital Equipment Corporation. All rights reserved. Reprinted with permission.

PF1	PF2	PF3	PF4
GOLD	HELP	FNDNXT FIND	DEL L UND L
7 PAGE COMMAND	8 SECT FILL	9 APPEND REPLACE	– DEL W UND W
4 ADVANCE BOTTOM	5 BACKUP TOP	6 CUT PASTE	' DEL C UND C
1 WORD CHNGCASE	2 EOL DEL EOL	3 CHAR SPECINS	ENTER ENTER SUBS
0 LINE OPEN LINE		SELECT RESET	

FIGURE B.3/EDT keyboard commands. Copyright © 1980, Digital Equipment Corporation. All rights reserved. Reprinted with permission. This material has been adapted in part from copyrighted publications of Digital Equipment Corporation. This material is the sole responsibility of the author.

the following discussion, we will usually refer to a command by its name only, e.g., BOTTOM, even though the command may require this two-keystroke sequence.

Because programs other than EDT make different uses of the keypad keys, the command words shown in Figure B.3 do *not* appear on the physical keys. When you begin using EDT you may therefore wish to place a copy of Figure B.3 near the keyboard for quick reference. Note that the actual key markings (for the VT100) are shown in the upper right corners of the keys in this figure in order to help you locate the corresponding keyboard keys. After a short period of use you will be able to remember the keys at least for the frequently used commands.

B.5.2 Creating a New File in Full-Screen Mode

To create a new file in full-screen mode begin by entering EDT in the normal manner, and then issue the CHANGE command (abbreviated C). For example,

```
$ EDIT/EDT MYPROG.MAR <CR>
Input file does not exist
[EOB]
*C <CR>
```

This will cause your screen to be cleared and the cursor to appear at the top left screen position, above the end-of-buffer [EOB] mark. At this point you can begin typing, and the entered text will appear on the screen. When you reach the end of a line, press the RETURN key to end the line and advance to the first column of the next line. The [EOB] mark moves down automatically.

When you have finished typing your file, you leave the full-screen mode with a CTRL-Z command. This returns you to line editing mode and produces the line editing command prompt (*). You then return to VMS with the EXIT command in the normal manner. For example,

```
^Z
*EX <CR>
$ ▓
```

B.5.3 Modifying a File in the Full-Screen Mode

To modify an existing file in the full-screen mode, enter EDT in the usual manner, and then issue the CHANGE command. For example,

```
$ EDIT/EDT MYPROG.MAR <CR>
1          .TITLE MY FIRST TRY
*C <CR>
```

This causes your screen to be cleared and the first 22 lines of your file to be displayed. The cursor will be in the first column of the first line of the file, which corresponds to the upper left screen position.

In order to modify the file, you normally move the cursor to the place where it is to be changed, and then delete unwanted characters and/or type in new ones. The commands to move the cursor and delete text are discussed below. Most commands are implemented on the keypad. Each keypad command uses either a single keypad key to execute the *upper command* for the key (see Figure B.3), or the *GOLD key* followed by the command key to execute the *lower command* for the key. For example, to delete the character at the cursor location, you execute the DEL C (**DEL**ete Character) command by pressing the single key:

To restore the character just deleted you need the UND C command (**UND**elete Character), so you press the *two-key sequence:*

The available full-screen commands are summarized in Table B.1 and discussed in the following sections.

B.5.4 The HELP Command

The EDT full-screen mode has a built-in facility that provides you with immediate help in using any command. This facility is invoked by use of the HELP keypad command (Figure B.3). When you enter:

```
┌─────────────────┐
│                 │
│      HELP       │
│                 │
└─────────────────┘
```

EDT responds by clearing the screen and displaying a diagram of the keypad similar to Figure B.3. At this point you can press any key in order to get a screen display of instructions for use of the command associated with that key. For example, depressing:

```
┌─────────────────┐
│                 │
│      SECT       │
│                 │
└─────────────────┘
```

will display a description of the SECT command. Then you can either see the description for another command by pressing another key, return to the keypad diagram display by pressing RETURN, or return to your editing session by pressing the space bar.

The HELP facility allows an experimental method for determining the key assignments for non-VT100 terminals. Such terminals usually have some form of keypad. The key for a particular command will often be physically located similar to the key for that command on the VT100. Using this assumption as a starting point, enter the HELP facility and begin pressing the keypad keys and noting the descriptions that are displayed.

B.5.5 Cursor Movement in Full-Screen Mode

There are many ways to move the cursor in full-screen mode. The easiest way is to use the arrow keys, which move the cursor in the expected direction a character at a time. In addition, there are command keys for moving in larger steps, e.g., by words, lines, or sections. Before we take up specific commands, however, it is helpful to consider the general rules that EDT follows in cursor movement.

A basic rule followed by EDT is that the cursor control commands cannot be used to move the cursor to positions where you have not previously typed visible characters or spaces. This means that you cannot use a cursor control command to move to the left of the beginning, or to the right of the end, of a line. The end of a line is the position of the cursor at the time the RETURN key was pressed. This may extend beyond the visible text due to typed spaces.

An additional rule is that when you reach the end or the beginning of a line and continue executing the same command, the cursor will continue to move in the *same direction in the file*. Thus the right arrow key causes the cursor to advance to the beginning of the *next* line when you attempt to move past the right end of a line. Similarly, the left arrow causes the cursor to go to the end of the previous line when the beginning of a line is reached. Other cursor movement commands cause similar reactions at the line boundaries.

Another consequence of not allowing the cursor to go beyond the end of a line is observed when attempting vertical movement from a long line to a short one. That is, if an upward movement command would cause the cursor to be placed beyond the end of the preceding line, it will be placed *at the end of that line* instead.

As the cursor moves forward or backward in the display window, EDT automatically moves the window in the file so as to keep the portion of interest in the middle eight lines of the screen display. That is, if downward movement attempts to place the cursor below line 14 of the display, the window moves downward in the file. Similarly, upward movement causes the window to be moved up so as to keep the cursor no closer than seven lines from the top of the display. The exception to this is upon entry, when the cursor is at the top left side of the display, and the window is not relocated until you move down past line 14 of the file.

The behavior of EDT in response to cursor control commands is more understandable if the preceding general rules are kept in mind.

UP, DOWN, LEFT, RIGHT

The UP, DOWN, LEFT, and RIGHT commands (the arrow keys on most keyboards) are for moving the cursor in the indicated direction a character at a time. They are the preferred commands when you have to move only a few characters from the current cursor location. Continuous cursor motion results if you hold one of these keys down rather than pressing and releasing it.

As discussed previously, the cursor reaction to the UP, DOWN, LEFT, and RIGHT commands is affected by the line boundaries. For example, you cannot use the RIGHT command to move to column 17 in order to place a comment on a short MACRO instruction line. Instead, you must use the space bar (or the TAB key) to actually extend the line to the desired column, and then type the new material.

ADVANCE/BACKUP Commands

The ADVANCE and BACKUP commands do not themselves move the cursor. Instead, they establish the direction of cursor motion for certain cursor controls and other commands. The commands affected are:

CHAR	FIND
LINE	FINDNXT
WORD	SECTION
EOL	CHGCASE
PAGE	SUBSTITUTE
	TAB ADJUST

After pressing the ADVANCE key, all subsequent commands in the above list function by moving forward in the file, i.e., to the right and down. Pressing BACKUP causes these commands to operate in the reverse direction, i.e., to the left and up. The UP, DOWN, LEFT, and RIGHT commands are unaffected by ADVANCE and BACKUP.

Note that in Table B.1 we show the ADVANCE and BACKUP commands in square brackets preceding certain control commands. This means that you only have to use ADVANCE or BACKUP if the direction is not already properly set. Once issued, ADVANCE or BACKUP remain in effect until the opposite command is issued.

Movement by Entities

EDT recognizes a number of different textual entities, such as characters, words, lines, sections, and pages. The command abbreviations and definitions of these entities are:

CHAR or C: One character

WORD or W: A string of characters delimited by space or punctuation mark at each end

LINE or L: Column 1 to the RETURN character

SECT: Sixteen lines

PAGE: A group of lines delimited by the form-feed character <FF>

As can be seen in Figure B.3, there are keypad commands for CHAR, WORD, LINE, SECT, and PAGE. These commands cause the cursor to move by the suggested entity. The direction of movement will depend upon whether ADVANCE or BACKUP is in effect. For example, the three keystrokes:

ADVANCE BOTTOM	LINE OPEN LINE	LINE OPEN LINE

will move the cursor down two lines.

These commands are useful for moving the cursor larger distances through the file. In particular, SECT is a convenient way of scanning the file by moving the displayed window forward and backward.

Movement to Text Boundaries

The movement-by-entity commands are supplemented by four commands that move the cursor to the text "boundaries." These boundaries are the top and bottom of the file, and the beginning and end of lines. TOP and BOTTOM are keypad commands that require the GOLD key. For example,

GOLD	BACKUP TOP

moves the cursor to the top of the file, while:

GOLD	ADVANCE BOTTOM

takes you to the bottom. These commands are unaffected by the ADVANCE/BACKUP setting.

The command to locate to the end of a line, called EOL, is also on the keypad (Figure B.3). This command *is* affected by ADVANCE/BACKUP. That is,

ADVANCE	EOL DEL EOL

places the cursor at the end of the *current* line, whereas:

```
┌─────────────┐    ┌─────────────┐
│             │    │    EOL      │
│   BACKUP    │    │   DEL EOL   │
│             │    │             │
└─────────────┘    └─────────────┘
```

takes you to the end of the *preceding* line.

To get to the beginning of the current line, use the BACKSPACE command. This command is *not* on the keypad, but is normally associated with the physical key labeled "backspace" on the typewriter keyboard (Figure B.2). Successive BACKSPACEs move the cursor upward in the file, always positioning it at a line beginning.

Searching for Character Strings

Often it is desired to locate the cursor to a place in the file that is marked by a particular character string. The FIND and FINDNXT commands are ideal for this purpose. These are keypad commands, as can be seen in Figure B.3. For example, to locate to the string "START", enter:

```
┌─────────────┐    ┌─────────────┐
│             │    │  FINDNXT    │
│    GOLD     │    │   FIND      │
│             │    │             │
└─────────────┘    └─────────────┘
```

This causes EDT to display *Search for:* at the bottom of the screen. You respond with the desired string, followed by the ENTER keypad command (*not* the keyboard RETURN key). That is:

```
                          ┌─────────────┐
Search for:   START       │    ENTER    │
                          └─────────────┘
```

The window will then be moved appropriately and the cursor located at the first character of the string. Note that no distinction is made between upper and lower cases in searching, so that the above command will also find "start" or "Start".

To locate to another occurrence of the same string, use the FINDNXT (find next) command. That is,

```
      ┌─────────────┐
      │  FINDNXT    │
      │   FIND      │
      └─────────────┘
```

locates to the next occurrence of START.

Both FIND and FINDNXT are affected by the ADVANCE/BACKUP setting. If ADVANCE is set, the search is conducted from the current location forward, while BACKUP causes a backward search.

B.5.6 Commands to Alter the Text

Text alteration in the EDT full-screen mode can be done in several ways, including:

- Deletion of entities (characters, words, or lines)
- Insertion of new text

- Moving text from one place to another
- Substitution of a new string for an existing string

All of these are accomplished by various keypad commands as described below.

Deletion of Entities

Text can be deleted by character, word, or line. The deletion of a character can be done with either the DELETE key on the typewriter keyboard, or the DEL C keypad command. The difference is that DELETE deletes the character to the *left* of the current cursor and moves the cursor left one position, while the DEL C deletes the character that the cursor is located on and leaves the cursor stationary. Note that in either case if the end-of-line character (i.e., as caused by RETURN) is deleted, the result is the joining together of two lines. For example, if DELETE is pressed when the cursor is in column 1 of some line, that line will be joined with the preceding line. (If this happens accidentally, you can restore the original arrangement by pressing RETURN or UND C.)

Word deletion is done with the DEL W command. Because this command actually deletes from the cursor through the next occurring space, you should position the cursor at the first character of the word to be deleted. In a like manner, the LINEFEED key deletes the word to the *left* of the cursor.

Lines or portions of lines can be deleted in several ways. The DEL L command deletes from the cursor through the next end-of-line, and moves the succeeding line up to the cursor. Therefore, to delete an entire line, you should first move the cursor to the beginning of that line (with BACKSPACE), and then execute DEL L. If you wish to delete a line or a portion of a line *without* moving the next line up, use DEL EOL (**DEL**ete to the **E**nd of **L**ine) instead. This command deletes the character selected by the cursor and all visible characters and spaces to the right, but *leaves* the end-of-line character. On the other hand, if you need to delete the left portion of the line, use CTRL U. This deletes all characters from the first in the line to (but not including) the one selected by the cursor.

All of the above deletion commands can be reversed or undone if necessary. That is, if you have just deleted a line and then realize that it should not have been deleted, you can use the UND L (**UND**elete **L**ine) command to restore it. This works regardless of whether you used DEL L, DEL EOL, or CTRL U to delete the line. Similarly, UND C restores a deleted character, and UND W restores a deleted word. Note, however, that this works only on the most recently deleted entity of the type being restored.

Insertion of New Text

New text is inserted at the cursor as you type noncommand keys on the typewriter keyboard. Therefore, no special insert command is needed. The cursor and any existing text are advanced to the right as each character is typed. A RETURN terminates the current line, moves any existing, succeeding lines down, and positions the cursor at column 1 of the next line. The cursor-selected character and any characters to the right are moved to this new line with the cursor.

The OPENLINE command is like RETURN except that an invisible end-of-line character is inserted *after* the cursor. This has the effect of splitting the line, moving the right portion to a new line, and leaving the cursor positioned for inserting new text on the original line.

Moving Text

While in the EDT full-screen mode, moving text from one position in the file to another is done with the aid of *auxiliary buffers*. These buffers include the entity delete buffers for character, word, and line, and the CUT buffer. The basic idea is that text is stored in one of these auxiliary buffers as it is removed from the main text buffer (i.e., the one you are editing), and then reinserted at a new position after you move the cursor. For example, suppose you have the lines:

```
    MOVL   A,B
※MOVL   B,T
    MOVL   T,A
```

with the cursor position indicated by ※, and you execute the delete line command:

```
┌─────────┐
│ DEL L   │
│ UND L   │
└─────────┘
```

The line containing MOVL B,T is thereby deleted and moved into the *deleted-line* buffer (that can contain *only one line*). Now if you move the cursor to the beginning of the first line, i.e.,

```
※   MOVL   A,B
    MOVL   T,A
```

and execute the UND L command:

```
┌─────────┐      ┌─────────┐
│         │      │ DEL L   │
│ GOLD    │      │ UND L   │
│         │      │         │
└─────────┘      └─────────┘
```

the deleted line is reinserted before the first line. This gives:

```
※   MOVL   B,T
    MOVL   A,B
    MOVL   T,A
```

A similar sequence can be used to move single characters or single words. Remember that each entity buffer can hold only one entity and the reinsertion occurs in front of the cursor.

When you want to move text that consists of an arbitrary string of characters rather than single entities, you use the SELECT, CUT, and PASTE commands. The SELECT command identifies the text to be moved, CUT removes it and places it in the CUT buffer, and PASTE reinserts it in front of wherever you position the cursor.

To use the SELECT command, move the cursor to the first character of the text to be moved. Then press the SELECT key on the keypad. This marks the beginning of the selected text. To complete the selection process, move the cursor to the last character to be selected. Any of the cursor movement commands can be used to do this. (On the VT100 terminal, the selected characters are shown in reverse video.) Then press the CUT key. This removes the text between the initial selected character and the cursor, placing it in the CUT buffer.

If you make a mistake in using the SELECT command, you can recover with the RESET command. This cancels the effect of the SELECT operation.

The PASTE command inserts the contents of the CUT buffer in front of the cursor. This can be repeated as often as desired if you wish to replicate the text in the CUT buffer.

The utility of the SELECT, CUT, and PASTE commands is extended with the APPEND command. After using SELECT and CUT the first time, you can SELECT another text string. Like the CUT command, APPEND deletes the selected text and places it in the CUT buffer. However, it *adds it* to the CUT buffer rather than deleting the current CUT buffer contents. With this facility you can move through your file "picking up" scattered fragments of text and moving them to a common location.

Replacing and Subtracting Text

The REPLACE and SUBS (**SUBS**titute) commands allow you to change an existing string or strings in the file text to another string. The only difference between these two commands is that SUBS also does an automatic "find" operation as we shall see below.

To use REPLACE, you first load the new string into the CUT buffer. This can be done by the sequence:

$$\boxed{\begin{array}{c}\text{SELECT}\\\text{RESET}\end{array}} \qquad \textit{new string} \qquad \boxed{\text{CUT}}$$

where *new string* is typed as if you were inserting it. Note that typing after SELECT adds to the selected region. This can be done anywhere on the screen because the CUT command deletes it. Then move the cursor to the first character of the string to be replaced, and SELECT that string in the usual manner. The sequence:

$$\boxed{\text{GOLD}} \qquad \boxed{\begin{array}{c}\text{APPEND}\\\text{REPLACE}\end{array}}$$

then deletes the selected text and replaces it with the contents of the CUT buffer.

As an alternative to identifying the text to be replaced with the SELECT process, you can instead use the FIND command. With this method you load the CUT buffer as described previously. Then the FIND command sequence is executed, using the string to be replaced as the search string. When the search string is found, the REPLACE command is executed as described above. If desired, the next occurrence of the search string can be replaced by using the FINDNXT command followed by REPLACE.

The SUBS command is like the REPLACE/FINDNXT sequence combined. That is, you load the CUT buffer in the usual way, and execute FIND with the string to be replaced as the search string. After these steps, the sequence:

```
┌───────────┐        ┌───────────┐
│           │        │   ENTER   │
│   GOLD    │        │   SUBS    │
│           │        │           │
└───────────┘        └───────────┘
```

both replaces the search string with the CUT buffer *and* advances to the next occurrence of the search string. Naturally, executing SUBS again repeats the process, so you can easily do the substitution throughout the file. Any occurrence of the search string that you don't want to replace can be skipped by use of the FINDNXT command.

B.5.7 Miscellaneous Full-Screen Commands

The commands just discussed to move the cursor and alter the text provide the essential full-screen editing capabilities. In this section we describe some commands that you may find useful, but that are not essential.

Repeated Commands

The GOLD n command allows you to specify that a subsequent command is to be repeated n times. For example, the sequence:

```
┌───────────┐   ┌───────────┐   ┌───────────┐
│           │   │           │   │   SECT    │
│   GOLD    │   │     3     │   │   FILL    │
│           │   │           │   │           │
└───────────┘   └───────────┘   └───────────┘
```

causes the cursor to move by three sections in the direction set by the most recent ADVANCE/BACKUP command. Note that the 3 is typed from the typewriter keyboard, not the keypad. If the command to be repeated itself requires the GOLD key, the GOLD key must be pressed again after the repeat number is typed. For example, to insert the contents of the CUT buffer twice enter the sequence:

```
┌───────────┐ ┌───────────┐ ┌───────────┐ ┌───────────┐
│           │ │           │ │           │ │   CUT     │
│   GOLD    │ │     2     │ │   GOLD    │ │   PASTE   │
│           │ │           │ │           │ │           │
└───────────┘ └───────────┘ └───────────┘ └───────────┘
```

To cancel a repeat sequence before you execute it, use the RESET command.

Changing Case

Alphabetic characters in the text can be changed from lower to upper case or vice versa with the CHGCASE command. To change the case of the cursor-selected character only, enter the sequence:

```
┌───────────┐        ┌───────────┐
│           │        │   WORD    │
│   GOLD    │        │  CHGCASE  │
│           │        │           │
└───────────┘        └───────────┘
```

Other entities, e.g., words or lines, also can be changed like this. To change the case of strings of arbitrary length, mark them with the SELECT command sequence, and then execute the CHGCASE sequence.

Inserting Special Characters

Some characters that you may want to enter into your file may have special meaning to EDT, and therefore cannot be entered in the normal manner. For example, the linefeed character, if entered with the LINEFEED key, will be interpreted by EDT as "delete to the beginning of the line." To insert this character into the file and avoid having it interpreted by EDT, you can specify its ASCII decimal code using the SPECINS (**SPEC**ial **INS**ert) command. The sequence for this example is:

where 10 is the ASCII decimal code for linefeed.

Using Line Editing Commands in Full-Screen Mode

Sometimes you may wish to use the EDT line editing commands while in the full-screen mode. This can be done with the COMMAND keypad command. The sequence:

causes a prompt "COMMAND:" to appear at the bottom of the screen. You respond with the desired command (see Section B.4), followed by the ENTER keypad command. For example, to change all occurrences of "MOVL" to "MOVB", you would enter the sequence:

COMMAND: S/MOVL/MOVB/%WH | ENTER |

Provided that the command executed is not QUIT or EXIT, you are returned to full-screen mode with the text buffer altered by the command.

C

The Symbolic Debugger

C.1 | Purpose of Debugging Tools

Assembly language programs that are not working properly are difficult to debug because errors are often caused by a misunderstanding of the action of instructions, directives, and/or addressing modes. A powerful method of debugging such a program is a system-supplied program that allows you to execute your program one instruction at a time, or up to some pre-selected "breakpoint," and then stop to allow examination of the contents of each register and memory location. The **Symbolic Debugger** is such a system program available under VAX/VMS.

Many commands are provided by the Symbolic Debugger, including those for setting breakpoints, running the program, examining locations, modifying locations and registers, and single-step execution. Because this program allows memory locations and registers to be examined and set, it can also be used as a primitive means of input/output while learning to program in assembly.

C.2 | Features of the VAX-11 Symbolic Debugger

The VAX-11 Symbolic Debugger is an exceptionally powerful and flexible debugging tool. It is called "symbolic" because it allows you to refer to symbols, e.g., labels, defined in your program. While nearly every computer and operating system has some type of debugging tool, not all have this characteristic. Furthermore, it allows you to specify the data type when examining or changing memory locations or registers. For example, you can ask for a location to be displayed represented as a byte or longword integer, as a floating-point number, or as an instruction. An interactive **HELP** facility is also provided, so that you can request help in executing a particular command without leaving the Symbolic Debugger. Although we use it in this book only for debugging MACRO programs, the Symbolic Debugger also works with other VAX languages such as Pascal and FORTRAN.

The Symbolic Debugger has numerous commands for efficient control of your debugging session. In Appendix C we discuss the most important of these commands, focusing

495

on those particularly useful in debugging MACRO programs. These commands are summarized in Table C.1, and are discussed below. Detailed information on all features can be found in the *VAX-11 Symbolic Debugger Reference Manual* (Digital Equipment Corporation).

TABLE C.1/Symbolic Debugger Command Summary

Command	Qualifier	Action
EXAMINE *addr*	/BYTE,/WORD,/LONG, /QUADWORD,/**OCTA**WORD, /FLOAT,/ASCII:n,/INSTRUCTION, /OCTAL,/DECIMAL,/HEXIDECIMAL, /SYMBOL,/NOSYMBOL,/SOURCE	Displays contents of register or location indicated by *addr*.
DEPOSIT *addr=val*	/BYTE,/WORD,/LONG, /QUADWORD,/**OCTA**WORD, /FLOAT,/ASCII:n,/INSTRUCTION	Deposits *val* into register or location indicated by *addr*.
EVALUATE *expres*	/OCTAL,/DECIMAL,/HEXADECIMAL	Displays the value of *expres*.
GO *addr*	none	Starts execution at *addr*. If *addr* omitted, starts at entry point or current breakpoint.
SET BREAK *addr*	none	Sets breakpoint at *addr*.
SET WATCH *addr*	none	Sets watchpoint at *addr*.
CANCEL BREAK *addr*	/ALL	Removes breakpoint at *addr*, or all breakpoints.
CANCEL WATCH *addr*	/ALL	Removes watchpoint at *addr*, or all watchpoints.
SHOW BREAK	none	Displays all current breakpoints.
SHOW WATCH	none	Displays all current watchpoints.
STEP *n*	/INSTRUCTION,/INTO,/OVER, /LINE,/SYSTEM,/NOSYSTEM, /SOURCE,/NOSOURCE	Executes *n* instructions from current breakpoint or entry point. If *n* omitted, 1 is assumed.
SET MODE *base*	none	Sets the assumed number system to *base* (HEX, DEC, OCT).

TABLE C.1/Symbolic Debugger Command Summary (*continued*)

Command	Qualifier	Action
SET MODULE *name*	/ALL	Sets debugger to recognize symbols defined in module *name* or in all linked modules.
SET TYPE *type*	/OVERRIDE	Sets the assumed data type to *type*, e.g., BYTE, WORD.
SHOW MODE	none	Displays current assumed number base.
SHOW MODULE	none	Displays current assumed module for symbol definitions.
SHOW TYPE	none	Displays current assumed data type.
HELP	none	Provides interactive help in using the debugger.
EXIT	none	Leave the debugger.

C.3 | Preparing to Use the Symbolic Debugger

In order to use the Symbolic Debugger you must first assemble and link your program using the DEBUG command qualifier at each step. This causes the MACRO assembler and the LINK program to set up the tables necessary for symbolic debugging.

Then when you issue a RUN command for your program, the Symbolic Debugger "takes over." From that point on, you issue Symbolic Debugger commands, such as to set breakpoints, run the program, examine contents, etc. To use the Symbolic Debugger effectively, you may need to look at the MACRO listing of your program in order to determine addresses and label locations.

For example, to debug PROG1.MAR, issue the following commands:

```
$ MACRO/DEBUG/LIST PROG1 <CR>
$ LINK/DEBUG PROG1 <CR>
$ ▒
```

At this point you have an executable file named PROG1.EXE that consists of your program linked with the Symbolic Debugger. Naturally, PROG1 could be replaced by any MACRO file name.

C.4 | Running Under the Symbolic Debugger

To execute under the Symbolic Debugger, enter:

```
$ RUN PROG1 <CR>
```

where PROG1 is the .EXE file produced by linking with the Symbolic Debugger. The file extension is assumed and need not be given. The response will be:

```
VAX-11 DEBUG Version 4.0
%DEBUG-I-INITIAL, language is MACRO, Module set to PROG1
DBG> ▓
```

The response message indicates that the Symbolic Debugger options are set appropriately for debugging a MACRO program. Also, it says that the *module* is set to PROG1, which means that all symbols defined in the assembly module with PROG1 in the .TITLE directive will be recognized by the debugger. (If you are debugging a program with several separately assembled modules, you may want to use the SET MODULE command to include symbols from all the modules. See Section C.7.8.) The prompt DBG> means that the Symbolic Debugger is in control and awaits your command.

C.5 | Leaving the Symbolic Debugger

Return to the operating system can be accomplished in two ways. The first way is to issue the EXIT command in response to the command prompt, e.g.,

```
DBG> EXIT <CR>
```

The second way is to enter ^C. If your program gets into an infinite loop while executing under the Symbolic Debugger, the ^C returns you the Symbolic Debugger command prompt. Entering EXIT or another ^C will then cause exit to the operating system.

C.6 | Command Format

In general, Symbolic Debugger command lines are of the form:

```
command/qualifier parameter <CR>
```

In this command line, *command* is the command name or abbreviation, */qualifier* is an optional part of the command line that modifies the action of the command, and *parameter* indicates the object of the action. For example, in the command line:

```
DBG> EXAMINE/DECIMAL X <CR>
```

EXAMINE is the command, DECIMAL is a qualifier indicating that we wish the output to be in decimal representation, and X is the parameter, which in this case is a symbol representing the location to be examined.

As indicated in Table C.1, there is a wide range of possible commands. Many, but not all, allow qualifiers. In some cases, more than one qualifier can be given. For example, we could use the command line:

```
DBG> EXAMINE/DECIMAL/BYTE R3 <CR>
```

to see the contents of the first byte of R3 represented in decimal.

In cases where one or more qualifiers are allowed, default settings will be used if you do not give the qualifier. These defaults are automatically set according to the language of the program being debugged. For example, when the language is MACRO, *hexadecimal* is the default **mode** for number representation, and *longword* is the default data **type** for EXAMINE and DEPOSIT operations. If desired, however, you can reset these defaults using the SET MODE and SET TYPE commands (see Section C.7.8).

The *parameter* of a command is often an address or a range of addresses where the command action is to be taken. These addresses can be run-time virtual addresses expressed literally, or symbols representing run-time virtual addresses. For example, we can examine the contents of location 0212_{16} with the command:

```
DBG> EXAMINE 212 <CR>
```

Note that we use hexadecimal representation. Similarly, the location with the label FLAG (in the MACRO source) is examined with the command:

```
DBG> EXAMINE FLAG <CR>
```

When you want to examine a range of locations, give the first and last address separated with a colon. That is,

```
DBG> EXAMINE A:C <CR>
```

displays the contents of the locations at labels A through C inclusively. On the other hand, if you wish to see the contents of A and C, but *not* the contents of locations between, use a comma, i.e.,

```
DBG> EXAMINE A,C <CR>
```

The addresses can also be expressions. For example, an array of 17_{10} bytes beginning at label TABLE can be examined with the command:

```
DBG> EXAMINE/BYTE TABLE:TABLE+10 <CR>
```

Note that any literal numbers used in expressions are interpreted as the default mode, i.e., hexadecimal for MACRO debugging.

Because symbols are allowed for address specifications, the Symbolic Debugger interprets any address parameter beginning with a nonnumerical character as a symbol. Therefore, when you specify a hexadecimal literal in an addressing expression, the leftmost digit cannot be A,B,C,D,E, or F. A leading zero can be used to avoid such literals. Also, the Symbolic Debugger appends leading zeros to output hexadecimal numbers as needed to avoid nonnumeric leading digits.

All Symbolic Debugger commands and qualifiers can be abbreviated with one or more leading characters of the command or qualifier keyword. Frequently used commands can be abbreviated with the first character alone. For example,

```
DBG> E/B TABLE:TABLE+10 <CR>
```

is the same as the preceding example. When there is more than one keyword usable in the same context and having the same leading character, the less frequently used command is abbreviated with a sufficient number of leading characters to be unambiguous. For example, EXIT is abbreviated EXI to distinguish it from the EXAMINE. Table C.1 shows acceptable abbreviations in boldface. Experimentation is the best way to become familiar with acceptable abbreviations.

C.7 | **Frequently Used Commands**

C.7.1 Examining and Changing Memory Location Contents

A frequent use of the Symbolic Debugger is to examine the contents of memory locations. To do this, enter EXAMINE or E after the command prompt, followed by the address. For example,

```
DBG> E A   <CR>
PROG1\A:    0000013A
DBG> ▒
```

Here we examine the contents of the location with the label A. The response tells us that the name of the module in which A is defined is PROG1, and the longword contents of A is $13A_{16}$. As explained in Section C.6, we could have asked for the contents of A to be expressed in decimal or other representation instead.

Indirect addressing can also be used with the EXAMINE command. For example, to see the contents of the location whose address is in C, we can issue the command:

```
DBG> E @C   <CR>
PROG1\A:    000001BA
```

Thus we see that the address in C is that of A, and the contents of A is $1BA_{16}$.

The EXAMINE command can also be used to display memory contents interpreted as MACRO instructions. To do this, use the INSTRUCTION qualifier, i.e.,

```
DBG> E/I   START+2 <CR>
PROG1\START+2:  CLRL  R0
```

This is sometimes called *disassembly* because the machine code is converted to assembly language code, the reverse of the assembly process. Note that in order for the Symbolic Debugger to do this properly, the address given must be the first byte of an instruction. Otherwise it will be out of step, and the disassembled code will bear no resemblance to the original program. Thus we specified START+2 above because the first instruction is normally two bytes beyond the procedure entry address.

Table C.1 shows all of the type qualifiers that can be specified with EXAMINE. Among these we see all of the integer data types, the floating-point types, and ASCII:n. The ASCII qualifier causes successive bytes to be interpeted as an ASCII string of length n. For example, if "ABC" is stored at label A, we get:

```
DBG> E/A:3 A  <CR>
PROG1/A:  "ABC"
```

Note that while most of the EXAMINE qualifiers specify data type, the OCTAL, DECIMAL, and HEXADECIMAL qualifiers specify the numeric mode. These can be specified in addition to a type qualifier. For example, to see the contents of a word at A represented in hexadecimal we would use:

```
DBG> E/W/H  A  <CR>
PROG1\A:  2A29
```

The SYMBOL and NOSYMBOL qualifiers affect the way addresses are displayed in response to the EXAMINE command. The SYMBOL qualifier means to display addresses symbolically. Because this is the default setting for MACRO debugging, we do not have to give this qualifier explicitly. However, if you wish to see virtual addresses expressed literally, use the NOSYMBOL qualifier (abbreviated N). For example,

```
DBG> E/W/H/N  20C  <CR>
0000020C\A:  2A29
```

The SOURCE qualifier is used to examine source code lines in high-level languages. In MACRO debugging we use the INSTRUCTION qualifier for this purpose and do not need the SOURCE qualifier.

Once you have issued an EXAMINE command you can examine successive locations by entering the EXAMINE with qualifiers but without an address. For example,

```
DBG> E/B  A <CR>
PROG1\A: 41
DBG> E/B <CR>
PROG1\A + 1: 42
DBG> E/B <CR>
PROG1\A +2: 43
DBG> ▨
```

Similarly, you can go backwards by using the "`^`" key, i.e.,

```
DBG> E/B  ^  <CR>
PROG1\A + 1: 42
```

This technique works equally well for any type of qualifier, and the advancement or decrement is properly adjusted to reflect the type length. In particular, you can examine successive instructions with E/I <CR>. Of course, if you wish to see a sequence of instructions, you can also use an address range, i.e.,

```
DBG> E/I START+2:START+6
PROG1/START+2:  CLRL  R0
PROG1/START+4:  INCL  R0
PROG1/START+6:  INCL  R0
DBG> ▨
```

Sometimes it is desired to change the contents of a location. To do this, use the DEPOSIT command. From Table C.1 we see that all type qualifiers available for the EXAMINE command can also be used with DEPOSIT. For example, to deposit 856_{16} in the word at location B, enter:

```
DBG> D/W  B=856  <CR>
DBG> ▨
```

If you wish to represent the value to be deposited in a base other than the current default, use the %DEC, %HEX, %OCT, or %BIN *lexical operators*. That is, to enter 64_{10} into the word at B, use:

```
DBG> D/W  B=%DEC 64  <CR>
DBG> ▨
```

As with EXAMINE, the DEPOSIT command can employ indirect addressing using the @ character as a prefix to the parameter.

The DEPOSIT command is also useful for making minor, temporary changes to the program. This is accomplished by using the INSTRUCTION qualifier with the new instruction enclosed in quote marks. For example,

```
DBG> D/I  START+2="CLRL R5"  <CR>
DBG> *
```

This will change the first instruction to CLRL R5. This provides a convenient means of making program or data changes directly to the machine code without going through source file editing and reassembling. Of course, permanent changes *must* eventually be done in the source program, because changes made with the Symbolic Debugger are only temporary and in no way change the MACRO source file. Also, the new instruction must be the same length as the one replaced.

C.7.2 Examining and Changing the General Purpose Registers

The general purpose registers, R0 through R11, AP, FP, SP, and PC, can also be examined or (except for PC) changed with the Symbolic Debugger. The procedure is much the same as for memory locations, except that instead of the address we use the normal register symbols. For example, to examine R0, R1, and SP, enter the following sequence:

```
DBG> E  R0,R1,SP <CR>
0\%R0:   00000000
0\%R1:   00000000
0\%SP:   7FFF7A38
DBG> *
```

If it is desired to examine several sequential registers, e.g., R0, R1, and R2, just use the range notation. For example,

```
DBG> E R0:R2  <CR>
0\%R0:   00000000
0\%R1:   00000000
0\%R2:   00000000
DBG> *
```

To change the contents of a register, use the DEPOSIT command exactly as it is done for memory locations. That is,

```
DBG> D R1=%DEC 64  <CR>
```

places 64_{10} into R1, whereas

```
DBG> D/W R5=0FFFF <CR>
```

places $FFFF_{16}$ into the low word of R5.

C.7.3 Evaluating Symbols and Expressions

The Symbolic Debugger has a command called EVALUATE that evaluates the symbol or expression given as the parameter. The most frequent use of this is in determining the current value of a symbol. For example, suppose you want to know the virtual address corresponding to the label A. This is found by the command:

```
DBG> EV A  <CR>
0000020C
```

telling us that A is 0000020C.

This command can also be used to perform calculations in the default number base. For example, the following command evaluates a hexadecimal expression:

```
DBG> EV 1A15 + 0BBC/0A  <CR>
00001341
```

Note that the rules for expression evaluation are not necessarily the same as the default language. In particular, the precedence rules for arithmetic operators are like those found in high-level languages, whereas MACRO expressions do not follow precedence rules.

C.7.4 Examining the Processor Status Longword (PSL)

As discussed in Sections 6.3 and 16.5.2, the Processor Status Longword (PSL) contains important information such as the condition codes and trap enable flags. Sometimes it is helpful to examine these codes and flags during a debugging session. The EXAMINE command can be used to do this. The symbol PSL is used as the address parameter. That is,

```
DBG> E PSL  <CR>
0\%PSL:
        CMP TP FPD IS CURMOD PRVMOD IPL DV FU IV T N Z V C
         0   0   0   0 USER   USER    0   0  0  0 0 1 0 0 1
DBG> ▒
```

We see that the fields that are normally of most interest are displayed and labeled. The meanings of these are defined in Figure 16.2. In particular, note that the condition codes are displayed.

The PSL can also be set while debugging. To do this, use the DEPOSIT command. The %BIN lexical operator is convenient for this purpose. For example, to clear N and C and set Z and V, we would enter:

```
DBG> D PSL=%BIN 0110  <CR>
DBG> ▒
```

C.7.5 Execution

The Symbolic Debugger can also be used to execute your program. To do this, you need to issue the GO command. For example, if the starting address is START, the GO command is:

```
DBG> G START  <CR>
```

This will initiate the instruction execution sequence, causing instructions in your program to be executed one after the other until some stopping condition is encountered. Possible stopping conditions are: reaching the end of your program (i.e., $EXIT_S or HALT), encountering a breakpoint or watchpoint (see Section C.7.6), or occurrence of an exception. Normally, you will want to set breakpoints and/or watchpoints prior to issuing the GO command.

As shown above, we are using the GO command with the entry point address. Because programs are actually VAX procedures (see Section 9.9), the first instruction is two bytes beyond the entry point. This causes the Symbolic Debugger to do a "routine start," which means that it automatically skips the first two bytes.

The GO command can also be used to start execution anywhere in your program. The general form is:

```
DBG> G address  <CR>
```

where *address* can be any literal virtual address or label *of an instruction.* (You would not want to begin execution in a data area, or in the middle of an instruction!) The response will be the terminal output produced by your program, followed by a message saying what caused the termination.

The GO command can also be issued without a parameter. When this is done for the first time in a debugging session, a routine start is performed at the program entry point. If the program has halted due to a breakpoint or watchpoint, the GO command without a parameter continues execution with the breakpoint or watchpoint address.

If you issue a GO command and the program appears to be in an endless loop, or for any reason you wish to stop execution, CTRL-Y or CTRL-C can be used. Either will return you to the Symbolic Debugger command prompt.

C.7.6 Setting Breakpoints and Watchpoints

Breakpoints are addresses where you wish execution to stop when your program is being executed under control of the Symbolic Debugger. A common situation where this is needed is when you wish to examine memory locations, registers, etc., after your program has executed up to a particular instruction. You can set breakpoints at any instruction address.

Sometimes you are interested in stopping execution whenever a particular memory location will be changed, rather than at a predetermined instruction. You can accomplish this by setting a *watchpoint,* naming the location being watched. The Symbolic Debugger then stops after execution of any instruction that changed that location.

Breakpoints are set by giving the command:

```
DBG> SET BREAK address  <CR>
```

where *address* is a literal virtual address, a label, or an expression giving the virtual address. You can set as many breakpoints as you wish. When a breakpoint is encountered, execution stops and a message is printed, e.g.,

```
break at PROG\T: MOVL R1,R0
```

where T is the breakpoint address, and the instruction at the right is the one that will be executed next if execution is continued.

Watchpoints are set by the command:

```
DBG> SET WATCH address  <CR>
```

where *address* is a virtual address, label, or expression that gives the address of the location to be watched. When a watched location is *changed* the program execution stops and the instruction that changed it is displayed along with the old and new values. The following example shows the effect of watching location B:

```
DBG> SET  WATCH B  <CR>
DBG> GO  START  <CR>
watch of PROG1\B at PROG\START+0B: ADDL2 R1,L^PROG1\B
      old value: 02130000
      new value: 02130222
break at PROG1\START + 2E
```

This shows that the contents of B increased by 222_{16} as a result of an ADDL instruction at START + 0B.

Normally, you would use the EXAMINE command to determine contents of locations and registers after the breakpoint or watchpoint stops the program. If desired, you can use the GO command to contine to the next breakpoint, watchpoint, or program termination. No parameter is required for the GO command in this case. Alternatively, you can use the single-step command to proceed to the next instruction.

Breakpoints and watchpoints can be cancelled using the CANCEL BREAK and CANCEL WATCH commands, respectively. For example, to cancel all breakpoints and the watchpoint at B, we give the commands:

```
DBG> CANCEL BREAK/ALL  <CR>
DBG> CANCEL WATCH B  <CR>
```

At any time you can see the breakpoint and watchpoint settings with the SHOW BREAK and SHOW WATCH commands.

C.7.7 Step-by-Step Execution

Occasionally it may be necessary to examine the progress of the computations after execution of each instruction. This can be done by setting breakpoints at each instruction. A more convenient way, however, is to use the STEP command. We will see that any number of instructions can be executed before interruption when using this feature.

The simplest form of the STEP command uses no parameters and causes execution of a single program instruction. If a MACRO program is being debugged, this means that a single VAX-11 instruction is performed. For example, to execute the next program instruction we enter:

```
DBG> S <CR>
stepped to PROG1\START+4: INCL R0
```

The response shows us the *next* instruction to be executed. Obviously, this can be repeated as often as desired.

If you wish to execute the next *n* instructions, use the STEP command with parameter *n*. For example, to execute the next five instructions, enter:

```
DBG> S 5  <CR>
stepped to PROG1\START + 14: MOVL R1,R5
```

As can be seen in Table C.1, the STEP command also has several possible qualifiers. These are set by default to values that are nearly always appropriate. The exception to this is the INTO qualifier, which allows the STEP command to step "into" a called VAX procedure. Thus you must use STEP/INTO when you see that the next instruction to be executed is a CALL and you wish to step through instructions within the procedure. If you did not use the INTO qualifier, the entire procedure would be executed as a single "step," and the next stopping point would be the instruction following the CALL.

C.7.8 The SET and SHOW Commands

In the discussion of commands in preceding sections we encountered qualifiers and parameters that affect the actions of commands. As we pointed out along the way, these have default settings that are usually appropriate. However, with the SET commands we can change these default values if desired. Also, the SHOW commands allow display of current settings. Table C.1 lists the available SET and SHOW commands. Here we will discuss only those that pertain to MACRO debugging and that have not been introduced in earlier sections.

The SET MODE command can be used to change the default number base. For example, to use decimal instead of hexadecimal, enter:

```
DBG> SET MODE DECIMAL  <CR>
```

This may be convenient if you are examining or depositing a lot of decimal data. This could then be overridden on particular commands with the HEX qualifier and the %HEX lexical operator.

The SET MODULE command is necessary when your program comprises several, separately assembled modules. By the command:

```
DBG> SET MODULE/ALL  <CR>
```

you tell the Symbolic Debugger to include symbols from all of the linked modules. Without this command you could only reference those labels in the main program module. When there are conflicting symbols among modules you will then have to give a complete description in your symbol references. For example, if B is a label in both PROG1 *and* SUB1,

```
DBG> E SUB1\A  <CR>
```

examines A in SUB1. Alternatively, you could temporarily set the module to SUB1, i.e.,

```
DBG> CANCEL MODULE\ALL  <CR>
DBG/ SET MODULE SUB1    <CR>
```

The SET STEP command allows you to reset the default parameters for the STEP command. For example,

```
DBG> SET STEP INTO  <CR>
```

will cause all subsequent STEP commands to step into called VAX procedures unless the OVER qualifier is used.

The SET TYPE command allows you to reset the default data type to be used in depositing and examining locations and registers. For example, if you wish to normally examine and deposit data as bytes rather than longwords, enter:

```
DBG> SET TYPE BYTE  <CR>
```

Then when you wish to see a longword you would use the LONG qualifier on the EXAMINE command.

The SHOW commands, for the most part, parallel the SET commands, allowing you to see the current settings of the parameters that can be set. The exception is the SHOW CALLS instruction that has no SET counterpart. This command displays the currently active procedures, as evidenced by the call frames on the User Stack. This is useful when you have stepped into several levels of procedure calls.

D

VMS Operating System

D.1 | Overview

In order to show specific examples of machine interaction in the body of this text it was necessary to assume a particular operating system. The widely used Digital Equipment Corporation (DEC) operating system called VAX/VMS was used for this purpose. Appendix D summarizes the more important VMS commands for reference purposes.

The operating system provides a framework of programs that allow the programmer to use the computer more effectively. Among the essential services provided by the operating system are:

1. Interpretation of keyboard commands, e.g., RUN, DIR, etc. This is done by the "command language interpreter" program of the operating system.
2. Systematic storage and retrieval of files.
3. A collection of supporting "utility" programs that allow manipulation of files, e.g., copy, create, modify, merge, and delete.
4. Libraries of macros and object programs to support application programs.
5. A collection of language processors such as assemblers, compilers, and interpreters.
6. The allocation of resources such as main memory, CPU time, and use of peripheral devices to multiple, simultaneous users.

VAX computers are nearly always run under control of either the VAX/VMS operating system provided by Digital Equipment Corporation, or the UNIX operating system developed by Bell Laboratories. In this appendix we consider only VMS because the VAX MACRO assembler is not available under the UNIX system. It should be noted, however, that the UNIX system is delivered with an assembler called *as* that is very similar to MACRO, but not identical to it. For one thing, it does not support macro definition and usage. Also, it employs different symbols at certain places in the assembler mnemonics. Therefore, if UNIX and the *as* assembler are used in conjunction with this book, adjustments must be made for these differences. Additionally, the student will require

508

supplemental materials providing guidance in the use of editors and debugging tools appropriate for the UNIX environment.

In the following sections the essential features of the VAX/VMS system are presented. These features are summarized in Tables D.1 and D.2. While the information given here should be adequate for using MACRO, the description of this operating system is by no means complete. A complete description of all VAX/VMS commands can be found in the *DCL Command Language Summary* (Digital Equipment Corporation).

TABLE D.1/VMS Commands (partial list)

Operation	Command
MACRO Programming	
Create or Edit MACRO file	EDIT/EDT *fn*.MAR
Assemble	MACRO *fn*+MACLIB/LIB (MACLIB is Fig. E.1)
Link	LINK *fn*+SUBLIB/LIB (SUBLIB is Fig. E.2)
Execute	RUN *fn*
Debug	Use /DEBUG qualifier on MACRO and LINK commands
Logging Off	LOG
File Manipulation	
Create a file	CREAT *fn.type* {enter text} ^Z (see also EDIT/EDT, Sec. B.4.1)
Delete a file	DELETE *fn.type;version*
Delete all but *n* most recent versions	PURGE/K=*n fn.type*
Append file *fn1* to end of *fn2*	APPEND *fn1.type fn2.type*
Create a library	LIBRARY/CREATE/type *libname fn*
Edit a file	EDIT/EDT *fn.type* (see Appendix B)
Copy file *fn1* to *fn2*	COPY *fn1.type fn2.type*
Rename file *fn1* to *fn2*	RENAME *fn1.type fn2.type*
Display a file at terminal	TYPE *fn.type*
Queue a file for printing at *site*	PRINT/QUEUE=*site fn.type*
Change file protection	SET PROTECTION *fn.type/PROT=* (OWNER=RWED,SYSTEM=RWED, GROUP=RE,WORLD=RE)
Directory Commands	
Establish default directory to *name*	SET DEFAULT [*name*]
Create subdirectory *sub* in directory *name*	CREATE/DIRECTORY [*name.sub*]
Display default directory name	SHOW DEFAULT
Display files in directory *name*	DIRECTORY [*name*]
Delete subdirectory *.sub* from directory *name*	DELETE [*name*]*sub*.DIR (*name.sub* must be empty)

TABLE D.1/VMS Commands (*continued*)

Operation	Command
Information Commands	
Display default protection for file creation	SHOW PROTECTION
Display protection for a file	DIRECTORY/PROTECTION *fn.type*
Display terminal characteristics currently assumed by VMS	SHOW TERMINAL
Display current users	SHOW USERS
Display current time	SHOW TIME
Display files queued for printing at *site*	SHOW QUEUE=*site*
Commands for Setting Environment	
Changing password	SET PASSWORD
Changing default protection for new files	SET PROTECTION=(OWNER=RWED, SYSTEM=RWED GROUP=RE,WORLD= RE)/DEFAULT
Tell VMS you are using a VT100 terminal	SET TERMINAL/DEVICE=VT100
Tell VMS you have an unknown terminal	SET TERMINAL/DEVICE=UNKNOWN

TABLE D.2/Terminal Key Commands

Key	Function
Process Control	
CTRL-C	During command entry, cancels command processing. CTRL-C is displayed as Cancel.
	Certain applications enable CTRL-C as the cancel key. For these applications, CTRL-C cancels the operation in progress. If CTRL-C is not enabled, then the action is changed to an interrupt (CTRL-Y).
CTRL-Y	During Command entry, interrupts command processing. CTRL-Y echoes as Interrupt.
	Under most conditions, CTRL-Y will return the user to the $ prompt. The program running will still be active.
CTRL-Z	Signals the end of the file for data entered from the terminal. CTRL-Z is displayed as Exit.
CTRL-S	Suspends terminal output until CTRL-Q is pressed
CTRL-Q	Restarts terminal output that was suspended by CTRL-S.
CTRL-U	Discards the current input line (provided NO_ LINE_EDIT is in effect).

TABLE D.2/Terminal Key Commands (*continued*)

Key	Function
Process Control (continued)	
CTRL-X	Discards the current line and deletes data in the type-ahead buffer.
RETURN (<CR>)	Transmits the current line to the system for processing. (On some terminals, the RETURN key is labeled CR).
	Before the terminal session, initiates login sequence.
Command Line Editing (when LINE EDIT is set)	
CTRL-B and ↑	Displays the last command line issued. If pressed again, displays the previous command in the recall buffer. The recall buffer stores the 20 most recently issued commands.
↓	Displays the next line in the recall buffer.
CTRL-D and ←	Moves the cursor one character to the left.
CTRL-F and →	Moves the cursor one character to the right.
CTRL-H and BACKSPACE	Moves the cursor to the beginning of the line.
CTRL-E	Moves the cursor to the end of the line.
CTRL-R	Retypes the current input line and leaves the cursor positioned at the end of the line
CTRL-J and LINEFEED	Deletes the word to the left of the cursor.
CTRL-U	Deletes characters from the beginning of the line to the cursor. (This overrides the standard CTRL-U function, which discards the current input line.)
CTRL-A	Switches between overstrike mode and insert mode. The default mode (as set with SET TERMINAL/ LINE_EDIT) is reset at the beginning of each line.
DELETE	Deletes the last character entered at the terminal. (On some terminals, the DELETE key is labeled RUBOUT.)
TAB	Moves the printing element or cursor on the terminal. The system provides tab stops at every eighth character position on a line. Tab settings are hardware terminal characteristics that can generally be modified by the user.

NOTES:

(1) CTRL form works regardless of terminal. Arrow keys only work if VMS recognizes your terminal key definitions.

(2) Before Command Line Editing will work you may have to execute the SET TERMINAL/ LINE_EDIT command.

D.2 | Log-on and Log-off Procedures

Sign-on to the VMS system begins by establishing a physical connection between the terminal and the computer. This will depend on local factors, and may require using a telephone and modem (e.g., an acoustical coupler). You must obtain directions for this from local support people.

After establishing the connection, you must initiate the interaction by depressing the carriage return key once or twice, causing a prompt for your "username." After entering your assigned username, it asks for a "password." The sequence is therefore:

```
<CR>
<CR>
Username: myusername<CR>   (You must use your assigned
                             username.)
Password: mypassword<CR>   (You must use your assigned
                             password. It will not be
                             echoed to the screen as you
                             type.)
Welcome to VAX/VMS Version 4.1
$
```

Here the response of the system is indicated by underlining. Some systems will give additional messages when you sign on.

The phrase "myusername" means a specific username issued for each user. You must obtain your own username from the system manager or your instructor. Similarly, the password is specially assigned.

The $ is the system prompt provided by VAX/VMS. It signifies that VMS is waiting for your command, e.g., to use the editor (EDIT), or to assemble a program (MACRO). VMS always returns with this prompt whenever it completes an operation. (Some VMS systems may use a slightly different prompt. This will be apparent the first time you sign on.)

In order to sign off of VMS, issue the command:

```
$ LOG <CR>
```

The exact response to the LOG command varies depending on the installation.

D.3 | Special Keys

In addition to the command words that must be typed out or abbreviated, VMS recognizes certain keys or key combinations as commands. For example, CTRL-Y or CTRL-C will interrupt a process. Table D.2 shows these keys and their meanings to VMS.

Of special interest are the commands for redisplay and editing of prior command lines. For example, if a command failed because of a typing error, you can redisplay the line with CTRL-B (or the up arrow key), edit it as necessary, and reissue the command with the RETURN key. The second portion of Table D.2 shows the command line editing commands. Depending upon defaults established by your system, it may be necessary for you to issue the SET TERMINAL/LINE_EDIT command before you use these commands.

D.4 | The VMS HELP Facility

VMS has extensive on-line documentation available through the HELP command. To use this facility, enter:

```
$ HELP item   <CR>
```

where *item* is the command word or topic for which you need help. If you do not know the correct topic or command word for what you are interested in, HELP HINTS will give you a short table of topic headings that are available. Once you begin executing HELP, you will be given information on the topic you entered with, and options for getting information on command qualifiers and other, more detailed, information.

In this manner the HELP facility provides you with nearly all the information about VMS commands that could be found in the manuals.

D.5 | VMS Command Formats

Whenever VMS displays the command prompt "$" you are allowed to enter any VMS command. These commands are interpreted by the Digital Command Language (DCL) interpreter, which is a component of VMS. Thus DCL is the "user interface" to VMS.

A typical command has a command name suggestive of the action to be performed, possibly followed by qualifiers and an object of the action. For example, in:

```
$ MACRO/LIST  MYPROG <CR>
```

the command name is MACRO, indicating that the VAX MACRO assembler is to be executed; /LIST is a qualifier saying that a listing file is to be generated; and MYPROG is the file to be acted upon, i.e., the file containing the MACRO program to be assembled. After completion of the command, the $ prompt is again displayed.

The above form of the VMS command line has several convenient variations. For example, the object of the command can be left off, which will cause VMS to prompt you for the omitted information. Thus the preceding command could be issued as:

```
$ MACRO/LIST <CR>
  File:MYPROG <CR>
```

Also, command names and qualifiers can be abbreviated to any unambiguous shorter form. Thus we could enter:

```
$ MAC/LIS  MYPROG <CR>
```

to accomplish the same result.

Sometimes commands with all desired qualifiers and objects are too long to fit on one line. By entering the hyphen character "-" at the end of a line, you can continue the command on the next line. Thus we could enter:

```
$ MACRO/LIST - <CR>
_$ MYPROG <CR>
```

and again cause MYPROG to be assembled. Note that the prompt for a continuation line is "_$" instead of "$" alone.

If for any reason a command cannot be carried out successfully, a system error message will be displayed. For example, if we attempt to assemble a nonexistent file, we get:

```
$ MACRO/LIST  MYPROG <CR>
%MACRO-E-OPENING, error opening QSA1:[050,004]MYPROG.MAR; as input
-RMS-E-FNF, file not found
```

The message always begins with "%", which is followed by a mnemonic for the VMS facility that issued the message, in this case, the MACRO assembler. The following symbol, E in this case, indicates the severity of the error, where F = fatal, I = informational, W = warning, E = error, and S = success. The phrase following the severity code is a mnemonic for the error, which is spelled out in more detail at the right. If some other VMS facility was also involved in the failure, its name and error report appears on a continuation line. In the preceding example we see that the Record Management System (RMS) was also involved, generating the "file not found," message. If the messages do not clearly identify the cause of the error, you can refer to the *VAX/VMS System Messages and Recovery Procedures Manual* for more help. A short summary of error messages is given in Appendix G.

D.6 | VMS Files and Directories

D.6.1 File Specifications

When you refer to a file in a command, VMS must be able to quickly locate the one you intended from among the many files catalogued at that moment. To perform this task VMS employs a general file specification of the form:

device:[directory] filename.type;version

Here *device* is the storage device where it resides, *directory* is the name of the catalog of file names, *filename* is a string of one to nine characters that identifies your file, *type* is an extension to the name that suggests its contents, and *version* indicates the number of times it has been modified. Taken together, these five items uniquely identify your file.

An example of the general file specification form is:

```
QSA1:[050,004]MYPROG.MAR;3
```

This refers to the third version of the file named MYPROG, which is of type MAR and is catalogued in the [050,004] directory (see Section D.6.3). It resides on the QSA1 device, which is probably the default system disk storage unit.

Fortunately, we seldom need to use the entire specification for a file because of a set of *default assumptions* made by VMS when certain times are omitted. For example, omission of the ";version" part of the specification causes VMS to assume the most recent version, i.e., the highest version number that it can find. Similarly, omitting "device:" causes the default system mass storage device to be used, and omitting "[directory]" results in the current *default directory* being used. Thus in most instances we could use just:

```
MYPROG.MAR
```

to refer to the above file. Even the type extension can be omitted if the command that the file name is being used in can reasonably be expected to assume the correct type. Thus we can write:

```
$ MACRO  MYPROG <CR>
```

because the MACRO command assumes a .MAR type extension.

The version number of a file is incremented automatically each time a file is modified. Moreover, the older version is *retained*. For example, when MYPROG.MAR is first created with the editor, it will appear in the directory as:

```
MYPROG.MAR;1
```

After modifying it one time with the editor the directory will show:

```
MYPROG.MAR;1  MYPROG.MAR;2
```

This makes it possible to go back to an older version by simply deleting the files with the higher version numbers. However, once you are sure you will not need older versions they should be deleted to prevent your available file space from being filled with useless files. The PURGE command is useful for this purpose. For example,

```
$ PURGE/KEEP=2 <CR>
$
```

will delete older versions of all files in the directory, keeping only the two most recent versions. Omitting the /KEEP=n qualifier causes only the most recent file versions to be kept. As a housekeeping policy, you should execute PURGE at the end of each terminal session.

Unless you specify otherwise when creating a file, your files will be on the system default storage device, and will be catalogued in your default directory. In elementary programming there is seldom need to override the system default device. However, it is not uncommon to need to access a file in someone else's directory, or to work with a subdirectory. In these cases you will have to specify the directory name. Directories are discussed in Section D.6.3.

Certain system commands can refer to several files at once. With these commands, the * can be used in place of either the file name or extension, thereby referring to all files that match the given part. For example, *.MAR refers to all files in your directory with the .MAR type extension. The "%" character can also be used in a file name reference, meaning "Accept any character" in that position. For example,

```
PROG%%.MAR
```

refers to PROG01.MAR, PROGAB.MAR, and all other file names in your directory which are six characters long, begin with PROG, and have the type extension .MAR. Certain commands such as COPY and DIR are greatly enhanced by these conventions.

The * and % used in this way are sometimes called "wild cards," in analogy to the usage of this term in certain card games.

D.6.2 Protection of Files

VMS files are secured against unauthorized access by a protection system that employs a User Identification Code (UIC) (see Section D.6.3) and a set of access privileges assigned by the file owner. Because of this protection system, a file can only be accessed for a particular purpose by persons authorized by the user. For example, properly setting the protection of a file can allow another user to read it, but not to delete it or write into it. All files have some protection established when they are created. This will either be the protection explicitly specified by the creator, or the default protection established by the system.

For purposes of file protection, VMS recognizes four classes of users and four access privilege levels. The user classifications are as follows:

1. The File Owner. This will normally be the user who created the file, as identified by a User Identification Code (UIC).

2. The Group to which the Owner belongs. For example, if the Owner's UIC is (050,004) all users in group number 050 are members of the Owner's group.

3. The System Users. These are users with special privileges, such as system programmers and the system manager.

4. The World, which encompasses all of the above classifications and all other users of the system.

The four access privilege levels are Read (R), Write (W), Execute (E), and Delete (D). The system allows each user class to be granted either no access privileges at all, or one or more of these levels. For example, the protection specification:

$$
\begin{aligned}
\text{System} &= \text{RD} \\
\text{Owner} &= \text{RWED} \\
\text{Group} &= \text{RE} \\
\text{World} &=
\end{aligned}
$$

means that the owner can read, write, execute, and delete the file, other group members can read and execute it, system programmers can read and delete it, and the world user (i.e., those other than system, owner, or group) has no access to the file at all.

You can determine what access privileges you and other users have to a particular file with the DIRECTORY command using the PROTECTION qualifier. For example, to see the protection for the file MYFILE.MAR, enter:

```
$ DIR/PROTECTON MYFILE.MAR <CR>
MYFILE.MAR;1   (RWED,RWED,RE,RE)
$
```

The access privileges are given in the order: System, Owner, Group, World. Thus we see that the System and Owner have full privileges, but all others can only read and execute it. (Of course, the Execution privilege is meaningless for a file of this type.)

If you wish to modify the protection of a file, use the SET PROTECTION command.

For example, to give all members of your group Read and Write privileges for MYFILE-.MAR, enter:

```
$ SET PROTECTION MYFILE.MAR/PROTECTION=(GROUP=RW) <CR>
$ ▒
```

Also, if you want *all new files you can create* to have a particular protection other than the system default, you can change your default protection with the same command. For example,

```
$ SET -
-$ PROTECTION=(SYSTEM=RE,OWNER=RWED,GROUP=RE,WORLD)/DEFAULT
$ ▒
```

will cause all *new* files to have these protection settings. Note that we have given no WORLD access privileges. A particular user, therefore, has only those access privileges granted by the other categories to which he/she belongs. It is a good idea to check your default protection settings when you get a new account. This can be done with the SHOW PROTECTION command.

D.6.3 Directories

The term *directory* used in connection with file specifications refers to a special file that contains the names of other files. When an account is established for a new VMS user, a "root" or "home" directory is created for this user. Unless otherwise specified by the system manager, the name selected for this directory will be the same as the User Identification Code (UIC), which is of the form $[g,m]$, where g is the *group* number and m is the *member* number. For example, if your assigned group is 050 and you are member 004, your directory will be:

```
[050,004]
```

which alternatively can be written as:

```
[050004]
```

This becomes your *default* directory when you log into VMS. Unless you change your default directory or specify otherwise when you create a file, all of your files will be catalogued in this directory. You see the contents of this directory when you enter the DIR command by itself. Many beginning programmers work entirely within this directory and thereby avoid ever having to specify a directory in a file specification. However, it is sometimes more convenient to use the VMS facilities for working with other directories.

Many VAX system managers define your root directory to be the same as your *username*. In this case your main directory would be like [SMITH] rather than [050,004].

When you wish to use a file created by someone else you will need to use a directory other than your root directory. For example, suppose your instructor has placed the I/O macro library (see Section E.2) in directory [100,001]. To access it in a MACRO command, enter:

```
$ MACRO/LIST  MYPROG+[100,001]MACLIB/LIB <CR>
```

This makes the MACLIB.MLB file available for the MACRO command without being present in your directory. Alternatively, you could copy it over into your directory by:

```
$ COPY [100,001]MACLIB.MLB MACLIB.MLB <CR>
```

Another important VMS feature is the ability to create a **subdirectory.** As the name implies, a subdirectory is a directory within a directory. A subdirectory is sometimes created to catalog all files of a similar nature, or all files pertaining to a particular project. For example, you may find it convenient to create a subdirectory to contain all of your MACRO program files, and another to hold your Pascal files. Both subdirectories would appear as files with type extension ''.DIR'' when you examined your default directory.

The CREATE/DIRECTORY command is used to create a subdirectory. Assume, for example, that your root directory is [050,004] and you wish to create a subdirectory called MACRO. This is accomplished by:

```
$ CREATE/DIRECTORY [050004.MACRO] <CR>
```

Note that the format for specifying a subdirectory name in a command or file specification is:

```
[main.sub]
```

where *main* is the main directory name and *sub* is the selected subdirectory name. Also note that the UCI format is not acceptable in this context. Therefore, if your root directory name is in the UIC format, it must be written as a string of six digits *without the comma.*

It is also possible to create subdirectories within subdirectories. For example, you could create a subdirectory for your I/O routines within your MACRO subdirectory:

```
$ CREATE/DIRECTORY [050004.MACRO.IO] <CR>
$ ▒
```

VMS allows you to have up to eight subdirectory levels under your root directory. When you do this you are creating a directory/subdirectory *hierarchy.*

Once a subdirectory has been created you can place files into it, or use files that are already there, in two ways. One way is to use the subdirectory name as part of the file specification. For example,

```
$ COPY MYFILE.MAR [050004.MACRO]MYFILE.MAR <CR>
$ ▒
```

places a copy of MYFILE.MAR (found in the default directory) into the subdirectory named MACRO. This file can then be deleted from your default directory and subsequently used from its new home in the subdirectory.

Alternatively, you can change your *default* directory to be the subdirectory. The SET DEFAULT command performs this function. For example,

```
$ SET DEFAULT [050004.MACRO] <CR>
$ ▒
```

changes your default directory to the new subdirectory. As long as you remain in this subdirectory all file specifications *without a directory specification* refer to files in the subdirectory. For this reason it is more convenient to switch over to your MACRO subdirectory whenever you do MACRO programming, and to remain there until you finish.

If you wish to go back to your root directory, use the SET DEFAULT command with your root directory, i.e.,

```
$ SET DEFAULT [050004] <CR>
$ ▓
```

Alternatively, you can "backup" in the hierarchy by using the hyphen inside the file specification brackets. That is, if you are in [050004.MACRO] and enter:

```
$ SET DEFAULT [-] <CR>
$ ▓
```

you are transferring to the [050004] directory. Thus the syntax [-] can be thought of as referring to the next higher level in the hierarchy.

Subdirectories can be referenced with the shortened syntax [.*name*]. When this syntax is used VMS assumes that *name* is a subdirectory of the current default directory or subdirectory. For example, if we have [050004] for the current default directory:

```
$ TYPE [.MACRO]MYPROG.MAR <CR>
```

displays the file MYPROG.MAR that is catalogued in [050004.MACRO]. Note, however, that this syntax will not work if your root directory is in the UIC format. That is, if your system manager has set [050,004] as your main default directory, you have to first execute the command:

```
$ SET DEFAULT [050004] <CR>
$ ▓
```

before the [.*name*] syntax will be accepted.

Also, you can determine which directory you are in at any time with the SHOW DEFAULT command, i.e.,

```
$ SHOW DEFAULT <CR>
QSA1:[050004]
$ ▓
```

The DIRECTORY command can be used to display files in any directory or subdirectory. For example, to see the files in [050004.MACRO] enter:

```
$ DIR [050004.MACRO] <CR>
MYPROG.MAR;1
$ ▓
```

Omission of the directory name, of course, gives the files in the current default directory.

Deletion of a subdirectory is a matter of deleting its name.DIR file. However, before this can be done you must first delete all files that are catalogued in it. Also, you may have to change the protection level of the name.DIR file, granting deletion privileges to its owner. The latter step is often necessary because the CREATE/DIREC-TORY command sets protection of the new name.DIR file to that of the *predecessor* directory, and your root directory, as established for you by the system manager, normally *does not* grant Deletion privileges to the Owner. The command sequence to delete [050004.MACRO.IO] is therefore:

```
$ DELETE [050004.MACRO.IO]*.*;* <CR>
$ SET PROTECTION [050004.MACRO]IO.DIR/PROT=(OWNER=RWD) <CR>
$ DELETE [050004.MACRO]IO.DIR <CR>
$ ▓
```

D.7 | Command Procedures

When your work with VMS requires repeated usage of the same set of commands you can often improve your efficiency by creation and use of a **command procedure.** As the name implies, a command procedure is a file that contains one or more VMS commands. Such files have the type extension .COM and can be executed by typing a file name with the prefix "@". An example will clarify this technique.

Suppose you frequently assemble, link, and run a MACRO program stored in a file named MYPROG.MAR. Using the editor, we create a suitable command file as follows:

```
$EDIT MLR.COM
*I
        $MACRO/LIST  MYPROG+MACLIB/LIB
        $LINK        MYPROG+SUBLIB/LIB
        $RUN         MYPROG
^Z
*EX
$ ▒
```

Note that the "$" is placed at the beginning of each command line.

When you wish to assemble, link, and run MYPROG, just type:

```
$ @MLR <CR>
```

This causes all three steps to be carried out sequentially.

The preceding example gives the general idea of a command procedure, but it has two major flaws. First, you will have to rewrite it when you begin working on a different program. Secondly, it continues on to the next command even if the previous command failed. We would prefer to have the command procedure interrupted before linking if the assembly step detected errors, or to skip the RUN command if the linkage step failed. Both of these faults are corrected below:

```
$ EDIT MLR.COM
*I
        $ON ERROR THEN EXIT
        $MACRO/LIST  'P1'+MACLIB/LIB
        $LINK        'P1'+SUBLIB/LIB
^Z      $RUN         'P1'
*EX
$ ▒
```

The ON ERROR THEN EXIT command causes VMS to check the *completion status* after each subsequent command. Then, when any subsequent command causes an error, the command procedure automatically exits to VMS. Thus we skip the remainder of the procedure upon detection of an error at either the assembly or linkage steps.

In the improved command procedure, 'P1' is a **dummy parameter.** Dummy parameters are replaced by actual values that are given when the command procedure is executed. For example, to execute this command procedure with MYPROG, enter:

```
$ @MLR MYPROG <CR>
```

Here ''MYPROG'' will be substituted for 'P1' in the command procedure. Thus any MACRO file could be assembled, linked, and executed with the same command procedure.

Command procedures can be much more elaborate than shown in these examples. For one thing, you can use up to eight dummy parameters, P1, P2, . . . , P8. Full details are presented in the *VAX/VMS Guide to Using Command Procedures* (Digital Equipment Corporation).

E

Simplified I/O Macros and Subroutines

E.1 | Description

In this book we have relied on preprogrammed macros to permit simplified input and output from MACRO programs. For example, .GETHEX and .PUTHEX were used for input and output of hexadecimal numbers in Chapter 4. Also, in Chapter 8 and thereafter, we made use of the character input and output macros, .TTYIN, .TTYOUT, .GETSTR, and .PUTSTR. This appendix defines these macros and the subroutines necessary for their operation. In addition, a set of macros and supporting subroutines for file input and output are presented here. The installation and usage of all of these macros and subroutines are described in Sections E.2 and E.3. Tables E.1 and E.2 provide a summary of the available macros.

TABLE E.1/Terminal Input/Output Macros

Macro	Usage	Purpose
.TTYIN	.TTYIN A	Accepts single character from terminal keyboard, placing it in byte argument A or R0. (Section 8.5)
.TTYOUT	.TTYOUT A	Sends a single character from byte argument A or R0 to terminal. (Section 8.3)
.GETSTR	.GETSTR A	Accepts a line from terminal keyboard and stores it as a null-terminated string at A, or at byte address found in R0.
.PUTSTR	.PUTSTR A	Sends a null-terminated string located at A to the terminal. If A is omitted, the byte address found in R0 is used as string starting address. <CR> and <LF> are also sent. (Section 8.)
.GETHEX	.GETHEX A	Accepts a hexadecimal number in the range 0–FFFFFFFF from the terminal keyboard, placing it in A or in R0. (Section 4.11)
.PUTHEX	.PUTHEX A	Sends the contents of A or R0 to the terminal as a hexadecimal number. <CR> and <LF> are also sent. (Section 4.11)

NOTES:
(1) Usage requires assembling with MACLIB.MLB macro library and linking with SUBLIB.OLB.

(2) If argument A is omitted, R0 is assumed.

TABLE E.2/File Input/Output Macros

Macro	Usage	Purpose
.FILE_SETUP	.FILE_SETUP *name,n* (must be placed before .ENTRY)	Sets up buffers and argument lists necessary for use of VMS file *name* as file *n* in subsequent file I/O macros.
.FILE_IN	.FILE_IN *n,*A	Reads single character from file *n*, placing it into byte argument A or R0.
.FILE_OUT	.FILE_OUT *n,*A,EOF	Sends a single character from byte argument A or R0 to file *n*.
.FILE_GETSTR	.FILE_GETSTR *n,*A	Reads a <CR> <LF> terminated record from file *n* and stores it as a null-terminated string at A.
.FILE_PUTSTR	.FILE_PUTSTR *n,*A,EOF	Writes a null-terminated string located at A to file *n* as a <CR> <LF> terminated record.
.FILE_RESET	.FILE_RESET *n,*EOF	Repositions file *n* to beginning if EOF omitted, or to end if EOF present.
.FILE_CLOSE	.FILE_CLOSE *n*	Closes file *n*.

NOTES:
(1) Usage requires assembling with MACLIB.MLB macro library and linking with SUBLIB.OLB.

(2) If file already exists it will be opened by first input or output operation. If it does not exist, it is created on first input or output operation.

(3) If argument A is omitted, R0 is assumed.

(4) End of file argument EOF has significance only on *first* output operation, and on all reset operations. Include EOF if you want subsequent output to be appended to end of existing file. For a new file, or overwriting existing file, omit the EOF on first output operation.

E.2 | Installation

Before any of the I/O macros can be used they must be installed on your VAX computer following the procedures given here. The steps required include entry of the source code and creation of the libraries. It is best to create the libraries in a special directory, such as that of the instructor, with WORLD=READ access protection (see Section D.6.2). Then all users can either copy the libraries to their private directories, or simply access them by giving the special directory each time they are used.

E.2.1 Source Code Entry

The first step is entry of the source code for both macros and subroutines. The source code for the macros is given in Figure E.1, and that for the subroutines is given in Figure E.2. These should be entered as two separate files. The EDT editor (Section B.1) can be used for this purpose, as shown below.

```
$ EDIT MACLIB.MAR
* I
        (type in Figure E.1)
^ Z
* EX
$ EDIT SUBLIB.MAR
* I
        (type in Figure E.2)
^ Z
* EX
$ ※
```

As an alternate procedure, the source code for Figures E.1 and E.2 can be obtained on magnetic tape or diskette. If you wish to use this alternative, contact your Addison-Wesley representative, or the author at the Department of Computer Science, California State University, Fullerton, Fullerton, CA 92634. Note that it may take four to six weeks to obtain the necessary materials for this approach.

```
        .NOSHOW
;   TERMINAL INPUT/OUTPUT MACROS
        .MACRO          .TTYIN,A
        BSBW            T$TYIN
        .IF NB          <A>
        MOVB            R0,A
        .ENDC
        .ENDM           .TTYIN
        .MACRO          .TTYOUT,A
        .IF NB          <A>
        MOVZBL          A,R0
        .ENDC
        BSBW            T$TYOUT
        .ENDM           .TTYOUT
        .MACRO          .GETSTR,A
        .IF NB          <A>
        MOVAB           A,R0
        .ENDC
        BSBW            G$ETSTR
        .ENDM           .GETSTR
        .MACRO          .PUTSTR,A
        .IF NB          <A>
        MOVAB           A,R0
        .ENDC
        BSBW            P$UTSTR
        .ENDM           .PUTSTR
;   HEXADECIMAL I/O MACROS
        .MACRO          .GETHEX,A
        BSBW            G$ETHEX
        .IF NB          <A>
        MOVL            R0,A
        .ENDC
        .ENDM           .GETHEX
        .MACRO          .PUTHEX,A
        .IF NB          <A>
        MOVL            A,R0
        .ENDC
        BSBW            P$UTHEX
        .ENDM           .PUTHEX
```

(a)

FIGURE E.1/Input/output macro source file

```
;     File I/O   MACROS
          .MACRO        .FILE_SETUP,NAME,N
          .PSECT        PROGRAM,LONG
          .ALIGN        LONG
          .IF   NDF     REC_LEN
REC_LEN = 132
          .ENDC
FAB_'N: $FAB            FNM=<NAME>,FAC=<GET,PUT,TRN>,MRS=REC_LEN,RFM=VAR,ORG=SEQ
                        ,FOP=CIF
RAB_'N: $RAB            FAB=FAB_'N,UBF=BUF_IN_'N,RBF=BUF_OUT_'N,USZ=REC_LEN -
                        ,RSZ=REC_LEN,ROP=<TPT>,CTX=0
OPEN_FLAG_'N:           .BYTE 0
BUF_IN_'N:              .BLKB REC_LEN
BUF_OUT_'N:             .BLKB REC_LEN
INDEX_'N:               .WORD -1
RSZ_'N = RAB_'N + RAB$W_RSZ
USZ_'N = RAB_'N + RAB$W_USZ
ROP_'N = RAB_'N + RAB$L_ROP
CTX_'N = RAB_'N + RAB$L_CTX
UBF_'N = RAB_'N + RAB$L_UBF
          .ALIGN  LONG
;                                    4(AP)   8(AP)    12(AP)     16(AP)     20(AP)
ARG_'N:                 .LONG 11,FAB_'N,RAB_'N,OPEN_FLAG_'N,BUF_IN_'N,BUF_OUT_'N
;                          24(AP)   28(AP) 32(AP) 36(AP) 40(AP) 44(AP)
                        ,INDEX_'N,RSZ_'N,ROP_'N,CTX_'N,UBF_'N,USZ_'N
          .ENDM         .FILE_SETUP
          .MACRO        .FILE_IN,N,A
          MOVL          AP,-(SP)
          MOVL          #ARG_'N,AP
          BSBW          F$ILE_IN
          .IF NB        <A>
          MOVB          R0,A
          .ENDC
          MOVL          (SP)+,AP
          .ENDM         .FILE_IN
          .MACRO        .FILE_OUT,N,A,POS
          .IF NB        <A>
          MOVZBL        A,R0
          .ENDC
          .IF   IDN     <EOF>,<POS>
          MOVL          #^X100,CTX_'N
          .IFF
          MOVL          #2,CTX_'N
          .ENDC
          MOVL          AP,-(SP)
          MOVL          #ARG_'N,AP
          BSBW          F$ILE_OUT
          MOVL          (SP)+,AP
          .ENDM         .FILE_OUT
```

(b)

FIGURE E.1/Input/output macro source file (*continued*)

```
.MACRO          .FILE_GETSTR,N,A
MOVL            AP,-(SP)
MOVL            #ARG_'N,AP
.IF NB          <A>
MOVAB           A,R0
.ENDC
BSBW            F$ILE_GETSTR
MOVL            (SP)+,AP
.ENDM           .FILE_GETSTR
.MACRO          .FILE_PUTSTR,N,A,POS
.IF NB          <A>
MOVAB            A,R0
.ENDC
.IF  IDN        <EOF>,<POS>
MOVL            #^X100,CTX_'N
.IFF
MOVL            #2,CTX_'N
.ENDC
MOVL            AP,-(SP)
MOVL            #ARG_'N,AP
BSBW            F$ILE_PUTSTR
MOVL            (SP)+,AP
.ENDM           .FILE_PUTSTR
.MACRO          .FILE_RESET,N,POS
$CLOSE          FAB=<FAB_'N>
CLRB            OPEN_FLAG_'N
MOVW            #-1,INDEX_'N
.IF  IDN        <EOF>,<POS>
MOVL            #^X100,CTX_'N
.IFF
MOVL            #2,CTX_'N
.ENDC
.ENDM           .FILE_RESET
.MACRO          .FILE_CLOSE,N
$CLOSE          FAB=<FAB_'N>
.ENDM           .FILE_CLOSE
.SHOW
```

(c)

FIGURE E.1/Input/output macro source file (*concluded*)

```
          .TITLE   INPUT_OUTPUT SUBROUTINES
;
;   TO SUPPORT FILE AND TERMINAL I/O MACROS
;
          .PSECT   PROGRAM,LONG
CR       = 13
LF       = 10
PROMPT   = ^A'*'
REC_LEN  = 132
;
          .ALIGN  LONG
O_FAB:   $FAB     FNM=<SYS$OUTPUT>,FAC=PUT          ;TERMINAL OUTPUT FAB
O_RAB:   $RAB     FAB=O_FAB,RBF=OUTBUF,USZ=REC_LEN ;TERMINAL OUTPUT RAB
I_FAB:   $FAB     FNM=<SYS$INPUT>,FAC=GET           ;TERMINAL INPUT FAB
I_RAB:   $RAB     FAB=I_FAB,UBF=INBUF,USZ=REC_LEN  ;TERMINAL INPUT RAB
;
MSG0:    .ASCIZ/ERROR---.TTYOUT FAILED ON OPEN/
MSG1:    .ASCIZ/ERROR---.TTYOUT FAILED ON CONNECT/
MSG2:    .ASCIZ/ERROR---.TTYOUT FAILED ON PUT/
MSG3:    .ASCIZ/ERROR---.TTYIN FAILED ON OPEN/
MSG4:    .ASCIZ/ERROR---.TTYIN FAILED ON CONNECT/
MSG5:    .ASCIZ/ERROR---.TTYIN FAILED ON GET/
MSGF1:   .ASCIZ/ERROR---.FILE_ OPERATION FAILED ON OPEN/
MSGF2:   .ASCIZ/ERROR---.FILE_ OPERATION FAILED ON CONNECT/
MSGF3:   .ASCIZ/ERROR---.FILE_ OPERATION FAILED ON PUT/
MSGF4:   .ASCIZ/ERROR---.FILE_ OPERATION FAILED ON GET/
MSGH:    .ASCIZ/ERROR--- SOME CHARACTER WAS NOT HEX.   START OVER./
;
;   LOCAL STORAGE FOR TERMINAL I/O
;
O_OPEN:  .BYTE    0                  ;SYS$OUTPUT OPEN FLAG(1=OPEN,0=NOT OPEN)
OUTBUF:  .BLKB    REC_LEN            ;BUFFER FOR TERMINAL OUTPUT.
D:       .LONG    0                  ;INPUT BUFFER POINTER.
E:       .BYTE    1                  ;INPUT BUF NON-EMPTY FLAG (1=EMPTY,0=NOT)
I_OPEN:  .BYTE    0                  ;INPUT OPEN FLAG(1=OPEN,0=CLOSED)
INBUF:   .BLKB    82                 ;BUFFER FOR INPUT LINE.
                        (a)
```

FIGURE E.2/Input/output subroutine source file

CODE SECTION

```
$TYIN::
        MOVL      R1,-(SP)              ;SAVE R1
        TSTB      I_OPEN                ;SKIP OPEN
        BNEQ      2$                    ;  IF ALREADY OPENED.
        INCB      I_OPEN                ;SET THE INPUT OPEN FLAG
        $OPEN     FAB=I_FAB             ;OPEN TERMINAL FOR INPUT
        BLBS      RO,1$                 ;ERROR
        MOVAB     MSG3,RO               ;   TRAP
        BSBW      P$UTSTR               ;        AND
        $EXIT_S                         ;              REPORT.
1$:     $CONNECT  RAB=I_RAB             ;ESTABLISH CHANNEL FOR TERMINAL INPUT
        BLBS      RO,2$                 ;ERROR
        MOVAB     MSG4,RO               ;   TRAP
        BSBW      P$UTSTR               ;        AND
        $EXIT_S                         ;              REPORT.
2$:     TSTB      E                     ;SKIP FILLING BUFFER
        BEQL      3$                    ;  IF IT IS NOT EMPTY.
        CLRB      E                     ;CLEAR THE EMPTY FLAG.
;
;  LOAD THE BUFFER
;
        $GET      RAB=I_RAB             ;FILL THE BUFFER.
        MOVAB     I_RAB+RAB$W_RSZ,RO    ;ADDR OF LENGTH OF INPUT.
        MOVZWL    (RO),RO               ;LENGTH TO RO
        ADDL      #INBUF,RO             ;1 PAST END OF INPUT.
        MOVB      #CR,(RO)+             ;PLACE CR AND
        MOVB      #LF,(RO)              ;  LF AT END OF ENTERED LINE.
        MOVAB     INBUF,RO              ;SET BUFFER POINTER
        MOVL      RO,D                  ;   AND LOAD FIRST CHARACTER
        MOVZBL    (RO),RO               ;         INTO RO.
        INCL      D                     ;SET BUFFER TO NEXT CHAR.
        BRB       4$                    ;RETURN TO CALLER.
;
;  NON-EMPTY BUFFER ENTRY POINT
;
3$:     MOVL      D,RO                  ;SET UP RO AS BUFFER POINTER.
        MOVZBL    (RO),RO               ;PUT NEXT CHAR INTO RO.
        INCL      D                     ;ADVANCE BUFFER POINTER.
        CMPB      #LF,RO                ;IF END OF LINE
        BNEQ      4$                    ;  THEN
        INCB      E                     ;      SET THE NON-EMPTY FLAG.
4$:     MOVL      (SP)+,R1              ;RESTORE R1
        RSB                             ;   AND RETURN TO CALLER.
```

(b)

FIGURE E.2/Input/output subroutine source file (*continued*)

```
;
T$TYOUT::
        MOVL    R1,-(SP)        ;SAVE R1
        MOVL    R0,-(SP)        ;SAVE CHAR TO BE PRINTED.
        TSTB    O_OPEN          ;SKIP OPEN
        BNEQ    2$              ;   IF ALREADY OPENED.
        INCB    O_OPEN          ;SET OPEN FLAG
        $OPEN   FAB=O_FAB       ;OPEN TERMINAL FOR OUTPUT
        BLBS    R0,1$           ;ERROR
        MOVAB   MSG0,R0         ;   TRAP
        BSBW    P$UTSTR         ;      AND
        $EXIT_S                 ;         REPORT.
1$:     $CONNECT RAB=O_RAB      ;ESTABLISH CHANNEL.
        BLBS    R0,2$           ;ERROR
        MOVAB   MSG1,R0         ;   TRAP
        BSBW    P$UTSTR         ;      AND
        $EXIT_S                 ;         REPORT.
2$:     MOVW    #1,O_RAB+RAB$W_RSZ;SET BUFFER LENGTH TO 1 CHAR.
        MOVB    (SP),OUTBUF     ;CHAR TO BE PRINTED TO BUFFER.
        $PUT    RAB=O_RAB       ;PRINT THE BUFFER.
        BLBS    R0,3$           ;ERROR
        MOVAB   MSG2,R0         ;   TRAP
        BSBW    P$UTSTR         ;      AND
        $EXIT_S                 ;         REPORT.
3$:     MOVL    (SP)+,R0        ;RESTORE R0
        MOVL    (SP)+,R1        ;   AND  R1.
        RSB                     ;RETURN TO CALLER.
;
G$ETSTR::
;
;     ACCEPTS A STRING AND STORES IT WITH A TERMINATING
;     NULL BEGINNING AT ADDRESS IN R0.
;
        MOVL    R0,-(SP)        ;SAVE
        MOVL    R2,-(SP)        ;  REGISTERS
        MOVL    R0,R2
        .TTYOUT #PROMPT         ;PROMPT USER FOR INPUT
1$:     .TTYIN                  ;GET CHAR FROM KEYBOARD
        CMPB    R0,#CR          ;IF CR
        BEQL    1$              ;   GET LF.
        CMPB    R0,#LF          ;IF LF
        BEQL    2$              ;   ITS END OF STRING.
        MOVB    R0,(R2)+        ;STORE CHARACTER
        BRB     1$              ;NEXT CHARACTER
2$:     CLRB    (R2)+           ;MARK END OF STRING
        MOVL    (SP)+,R2        ;RESTORE
        MOVL    (SP)+,R0        ;   REGISTERS.
        RSB                     ;RETURN TO CALLER
```
(c)

FIGURE E.2/Input/output subroutine source file (*continued*)

```
$UTSTR::
        MOVL      R1,-(SP)              ;SAVE R1
        MOVL      R2,-(SP)              ;   AND R2.
        MOVL      R0,-(SP)              ;SAVE ADDRESS OF STRING TO BE PRINTED.
        TSTB      O_OPEN                ;SKIP OPEN
        BNEQ      2$                    ;   IF ALREADY OPENED .
        INCB      O_OPEN                ;SET OPEN FLAG.
        $OPEN     FAB=O_FAB             ;OPEN TERMINAL FOR OUTPUT
        BLBS      R0,1$                 ;ERROR
        $EXIT_S                         ;   TRAP.
1$:     $CONNECT  RAB=O_RAB             ;ESTABLISH CHANNEL FOR TERMINAL
        BLBS      R0,2$                 ;ERROR
        $EXIT_S                         ;   TRAP.
2$:     MOVL      (SP)+,R0              ;INIT STRING POINTER
        MOVAB     OUTBUF,R1             ;INIT OUTBUF POINTER.
        CLRW      R2                    ;INIT CHAR COUNTER.
3$:     TSTB      (R0)                  ;STOP ON
        BEQL      4$                    ;   FINDING NUL
        INCW      R2                    ;COUNT THE CHARACTERS.
        MOVB      (R0)+,(R1)+           ;PUT CHAR FROM STRING TO OUTBUF
        BRB       3$                    ;NEXT CHARACTER
4$:     MOVB      #CR,(R1)+             ;APPEND CR
        MOVB      #LF,(R1)+             ;   & LF TO BUFFER.
        ADDW      #2,R2                 ;ADJUST COUNT FOR CR & LF.
        MOVW      R2,O_RAB+RAB$W_RSZ    ;SET BUFFER PRINT LENGTH.
        $PUT      RAB=O_RAB             ;PRINT THE BUFFER.
        MOVL      (SP)+,R2              ;RESTORE THE
        MOVL      (SP)+,R1              ;   REGISTERS.
        RSB                             ;RETURN TO CALLER.
```

(d)

FIGURE E.2/Input/output subroutine source file (*continued*)

```
;
G$ETHEX::
;
;       G$ETHEX CONVERTS KEYBOARD HEX   (0-FFFFFFFF) TO
;       BINARY NUMBER IN R0.
;
        MOVL    R1,-(SP)            ;SAVE R1 IN STACK
1$:     CLRL    R1                  ;CLEAR RESULT REGISTER
        .TTYOUT #PROMPT             ;PROMT USER FOR INPUT
2$:     .TTYIN                      ;GET CHARACTER
        CMPB    R0,#CR              ;IF CR
        BEQL    2$                  ;   LOOK FOR LF.
        CMPB    R0,#LF              ;IF LF
        BEQL    5$                  ;   NUMBER IS COMPLETE.
        SUBL    #48,R0              ;CONVERT ASCII TO BIN.
        BLSSU   4$                  ;INVALID OCTAL DIGIT
        CMPB    R0,#LF              ;
        BLSSU   3$                  ;VALID ARABIC DIGIT
        CMPB    R0,#17              ;REJECT ":" THRU "@"
        BLSSU   4$                  ;
        SUBB    #7,R0               ;ASSUME A,B,C,D,E, OR F
        CMPB    R0,#15              ;REJECT ABOVE F
        BGTRU   4$
3$:     ASHL    #4,R1,R1            ;MULTIPLY CURRENT BY 16.
        ADDL    R0,R1               ;ADD NEW DIGIT
        BRW     2$                  ;GET NEXT DIGIT
4$:     .TTYIN                      ;BAD CHAR. HANDLING
        CMPB    R0,#LF              ;CLEAR .TTYIN BUFFER
        BNEQ    4$
        .PUTSTR MSGH               ;PRINT ERROR MSG.
        BRW     1$                  ;  AND START OVER.
5$:     MOVL    R1,R0               ;PUT RESULT INTO R0
        MOVL    (SP)+,R1            ;RESTORE R1
        RSB                         ;RETURN TO CALLING POINT.
```
(e)

FIGURE E.2/Input/output subroutine source file (*continued*)

```
;
P$UTHEX::
;
;        P$UTHEX DISPLAYS CONTENTS OF RO AS HEX
;        NUMBER AT USERS TERMINAL.
;
         MOVL     RO,-(SP)           ;SAVE
         MOVL     R1,-(SP)           ;  REGISTERS
         MOVL     R2,-(SP)           ;    IN
         MOVL     R3,-(SP)           ;       STACK.
         MOVL     R4,-(SP)           ;
         MOVAL    3$,R1              ;INITIALIZE PLACE VALUE POINTER
         MOVL     #8,R2              ;INITIALIZE LCV (8 DIGITS)
         MOVAL    4$,R3              ;INITIALIZE RESULT DIGIT POINTER
1$:      MOVL     #-1,R4             ;INITIALIZE DIGIT VALUE
2$:      INCL     R4                 ;UPDATE DIGIT VALUE
         SUBL     (R1),RO            ;SUBTRACT PLACE VALUE
         BCC      2$                 ;    UNTIL OVER SUBTRACTED.
         ADDL     (R1)+,RO           ;CORRECT FOR OVER SUBTRACT
         CMPB     R4,#10             ;CONVERT
         BLSSU    6$                 ;    DIGIT
         ADDB     #7,R4              ;        TO
6$:      ADDB     #48,R4             ;          ASCII.
         MOVB     R4,(R3)+           ;STORE CHAR. IN PRINT ARRAY
         SOBGTR   R2,1$              ;REPEAT FOR NEXT DIGIT
         .PUTSTR  4$                 ;PRINT RESULT
         MOVL     (SP)+,R4           ;RESTORE REGISTERS
         MOVL     (SP)+,R3
         MOVL     (SP)+,R2
         MOVL     (SP)+,R1
         MOVL     (SP)+,RO
         RSB                         ;RETURN TO CALLING POINT
                            (f)
```

FIGURE E.2/Input/output subroutine source file (*continued*)

```
;           PLACE VALUES
3$:         .LONG       ^X10000000
            .LONG       ^X1000000
            .LONG       ^X100000
            .LONG       ^X10000
            .LONG       ^X1000
            .LONG       ^X100
            .LONG       ^X10
            .LONG       ^X1
4$:         .BLKB       8                   ;RESULT ARRAY
            .BYTE       0                   ;NULL CHAR TO TURN OFF .PUTSTR
            .ALIGN      LONG
;
;   SUBROUTINES TO SUPPORT SIMPLE FILE I/O MACROS
;
O$PEN::
            TSTB        @12(AP)             ;SKIP OPEN
            BNEQ        2$                  ;   IF ALREADY OPENED.
            INCB        @12(AP)             ;SET OPEN FLAG
            $CREATE FAB=@4(AP)              ;OPEN OR CREATE IF NOT PRESENT
            BLBS        R0,1$               ;ERROR
            .PUTHEX                         ;
            MOVAB       MSGF1,R0            ;   TRAP
            BSBW        P$UTSTR             ;      AND
            $EXIT_S                         ;         REPORT.
1$:         MOVL        @36(AP),@32(AP)     ;SET ROP FOR APPEND OR TRUNCATE.
            $CONNECT RAB=@8(AP)             ;ESTABLISH FILE CHANNEL
            BLBS        R0,2$               ;ERROR
            .PUTHEX                         ;
            MOVAB       MSGF2,R0            ;   TRAP
            BSBW        P$UTSTR             ;      AND
            $EXIT_S                         ;         REPORT.
2$:         RSB                             ;RETURN TO CALLER
```

(g)

FIGURE E.2/Input/output subroutine source file (*continued*)

```
;
F$ILE_IN::
        MOVL    R1,-(SP)                ;SAVE R1
        BSBW    O$PEN                   ;OPEN THE FILE IF NOT OPEN
        CMPW    @24(AP),#-1             ;SKIP FILLING BUFFER
        BNEQ    4$                      ; IF IT IS NOT EMPTY.
;
;   LOAD THE BUFFER
;
        $GET    RAB=@8(AP)              ;FILL THE BUFFER.
        BLBS    R0,1$                   ;ERROR
        .PUTHEX                         ;
        MOVAB   MSGF4,R0                ;    TRAP
        BSBW    P$UTSTR                 ;       AND
        $EXIT_S                         ;          REPORT.
1$:     DECW    @28(AP)                 ;WE KEEP REC. SIZE-1 IN RSZ
        MOVZWL  @28(AP),R0              ;SET R0 TO 2ND FROM
        MOVL    R0,R1                   ;   LAST & R1 TO LAST
        DECL    R0                      ;           INDEXES.
        CMPB    @16(AP)[R0],#CR         ;IF CR
        BNEQ    2$                      ;    AND LF
        CMPB    @16(AP)[R1],#LF         ;       PRESENT,
        BEQL    4$                      ;          ACCEPT AS IS.
2$:     INCL    R1                      ;ELSE
        CMPL    R1,#<REC_LEN-2>         ;   CHECK
        BLEQ    3$                      ;       LENGTH
        MOVZWL  #<REC_LEN-2>,R1         ;          AND
3$:     MOVB    #CR,@16(AP)[R1]         ;             APPEND CR
        INCL    R1                      ;               AND
        MOVB    #LF,@16(AP)[R1]         ;                  LF.
        INCL    R1                      ;RESET RSZ TO
        MOVW    R1,@28(AP)              ;   NEW REC.SIZE-1.
;
;   NON-EMPTY BUFFER ENTRY POINT
;
4$:     INCW    @24(AP)                 ;INCREMENT INDEX
        MOVZWL  @24(AP),R1              ;USE R1 AS INDEX
        CMPW    @24(AP),@28(AP)         ;RESET INDEX
        BLSSU   5$                      ;   WHEN END
        MOVW    #-1,@24(AP)             ;      OF BUFFER.
5$:     MOVZBL  @16(AP)[R1],R0          ;PUT NEXT CHAR INTO R0
        MOVL    (SP)+,R1                ;RESTORE R1
        RSB                             ;      AND RETURN TO CALLER.
                        (h)
```

FIGURE E.2/Input/output subroutine source file (*continued*)

```
;
F$ILE_OUT::
        MOVL    R1,-(SP)              ;SAVE R1
        MOVL    R0,-(SP)              ;SAVE CHAR TO BE PRINTED
        BSBW    O$PEN                 ;OPEN THE FILE
        MOVL    (SP)+,R0              ;GET CHAR TO BE PRINTED
        INCW    @24(AP)               ;INC THE COUNT
        MOVZWL  @24(AP),R1            ;GET CURRENT INDEX OF CHAR IN BUFFER
        CMPW    R1,#<REC_LEN-1>       ;ON BUF OVERFLOW
        BNEQU   1$                    ;   FORCE
        MOVZBL  #CR,R0                ;       END OF
1$:     CMPW    R1,#REC_LEN           ;           RECORD
        BNEQU   2$                    ;               BY OVER-WRITING
        MOVZBL  #LF,R0                ;                   CR & LF.
2$:     MOVB    R0,@20(AP)[R1]        ;PUT CHAR INTO THE BUFFER
        CMPB    @20(AP)[R1],#LF       ;SKIP PUT
        BNEQU   4$                    ;   IF NOT
        DECW    R1                    ;       END
        CMPB    @20(AP)[R1],#CR       ;           OF
        BNEQU   4$                    ;               RECORD.
        MOVW    @24(AP),@28(AP)       ;SET BUF SIZE TO INDEX
        INCW    @28(AP)               ;       PLUS 1.
        $PUT    RAB = @8(AP)          ;PUT BUFFER INTO THE FILE
        BLBS    R0,3$                 ;ERROR
        .PUTHEX                       ;
        MOVAB   MSGF3,R0              ;       TRAP
        BSBW    P$UTSTR               ;           AND
        $EXIT_S                       ;               REPORT.
3$:     MOVW    #-1, @24(AP)          ;RESET THE INDEX
4$:     MOVL    (SP)+,R1              ;RESTORE R1
        RSB                           ;RETURN TO CALLER.
```

(i)

FIGURE E.2/Input/output subroutine source file (*continued*)

```
;
F$ILE_GETSTR::
;
;     READS A RECORD FROM A FILE AND STORES IT AS A NUL-TERMINATED
;     STRING BEGINNING AT ADDRESS IN RO.
;
            MOVL      RO,-(SP)        ;SAVE REGISTERS
            MOVL      R2,-(SP)        ;SAVE REGISTERS
            MOVL      RO,R2           ;INIT STRING POINTER
1$:         BSBW      F$ILE_IN        ;GET CHAR FROM FILE
            CMPB      RO,#CR          ;IF CR
            BEQL      1$              ;   GET LF.
            CMPB      RO,#LF          ;IF LF
            BEQL      2$              ;   ITS END OF RECORD.
            MOVB      RO,(R2)+        ;STORE CHARACTER
            BRB       1$              ;NEXT CHARACTER
2$:         CLRB      (R2)+           ;MARK END OF STRING
            MOVL      (SP)+,R2        ;RESTORE
            MOVL      (SP)+,RO        ;   REGISTERS.
            RSB                       ;RETURN TO CALLER
;
F$ILE_PUTSTR::
            MOVL      R1,-(SP)        ;SAVE R1
            MOVL      R2,-(SP)        ;   AND R2.
            MOVL      RO,-(SP)        ;SAVE ADDRESS OF STRING TO BE FILED
            BSBW      O$PEN           ;OPEN THE FILE IF NOT OPEN
            MOVL      (SP)+,RO        ;INIT STRING POINTER
            MOVAB     @20(AP),R1      ;INIT BUF_OUT_N POINTER
            CLRW      R2              ;INIT CHAR COUNTER
1$:         TSTB      (RO)            ;STOP ON
            BEQL      2$              ;   FINDING NUL
            INCW      R2              ;COUNT THE CHARACTERS.
            MOVB      (RO)+,(R1)+     ;PUT CHAR FROM STRING TO BUF_OUT_N
            BRB       1$              ;NEXT CHARACTER
2$:         MOVB      #CR,(R1)+       ;APPEND CR
            MOVB      #LF,(R1)+       ;   & LF TO BUFFER.
            ADDW      #2,R2           ;ADJUST COUNT FOR CR & LF.
            MOVW      R2,@28(AP)      ;SET BUFFER RSZ TO PRINT LENGTH
            $PUT      RAB=@8(AP)      ;PRINT THE BUFFER.
            MOVL      (SP)+,R2        ;RESTORE THE
            MOVL      (SP)+,R1        ;   REGISTERS.
            RSB                       ;RETURN TO CALLER
            .END
```

(j)

FIGURE E.2/Input/output subroutine source file (*concluded*)

E.2.2 Library Creation

To create the macro library enter:

$ LIBRARY/CREATE/MACRO MACLIB.MLB MACLIB.MAR <CR>

The subroutines can then be assembled by the command:

```
$ MACRO SUBLIB+MACLIB/LIB <CR>
```

Finally, the subroutines are placed in an object library by:

```
$ LIBRARY/CREATE/OBJECT SUBLIB.OLB SUBLIB.OBJ <CR>
```

If desired, the object file SUBLIB.OBJ can then be deleted.

In order to make these libraries available to other users, enter the commands:

```
$ SET PROTECTION MACLIB.MLB/PROT=(WORLD=RE) <CR>
$ SET PROTECTION SUBLIB.OLB/PROT=(WORLD=RE) <CR>
```

E.3 | Usage

E.3.1 Terminal I/O

The terminal I/O macros are shown in Table E.1. In general, usage in the MACRO program requires only insertion of the macro name, optionally followed by an argument. If the argument name is omitted, R0 is assumed. The character I/O macros, .TTYIN and .TTYOUT, use byte operands, whereas the string macros, .GETSTR and .PUTSTR, use byte address operands. The operands for the hexadecimal macros, .GETHEX and .PUTHEX, are longwords. Detailed examples of usage are shown in the sections indicated under the column headed "Purpose" in the table. Also, Figure E.3 demonstrates usage of each macro.

E.3.2 File I/O

Table E.2 presents a set of macros that allows usage of VMS files in the context of a MACRO program. These macros are designed to function in much the same way as the terminal I/O macros shown in Table E.1. For example, .FILE_IN works like .TTYIN, but gets the data from a file instead of the terminal. There is a file counterpart for each of the character and string terminal I/O macros. In addition, there are macros to set up the file before usage, to reset it to the beginning or to the end, and to close it.

Examples of usage of these macros can be seen in Figure E.3. Observe that a .FILE_SETUP macro for each file to be used must be placed in the nonexecutable portion of the program. This macro accepts a VMS file name as an argument and establishes necessary buffers and argument lists for it in your program. It also assigns an arbitrarily selected internal identifier n to the file. This identifier is used to specify the file in subsequent I/O macros. All other macros create instructions and therefore must occur in the executable portion of the program.

The file macros treat a file as a collection of variable length RMS records, each of which is terminated by a <CR> <LF> sequence. For example, successive output characters are automatically stored in a buffer until the <CR> <LF> sequence is encountered, whereupon the buffer is written as a record into the file. On input, a record is read into a buffer, from which characters are extracted one at a time. When <CR> <LF> is encountered, the buffer is marked as empty so that the *next* record is read when the next character is requested. The records are limited to 132_{10} characters,

```
        .TITLE I_O_DEMO
R    = 13
F    = 10
KSLSH = ^A'\'
        .FILE_SETUP <TEST.FIL>, 1
        .FILE_SETUP <TEST2.FIL>,2
SG1:    .ASCIZ/ENTER SEVERAL LINES TO BE PUT INTO TEST.FIL,TERMINATED WITH \:/
SG2:    .ASCIZ/HOW MANY TIMES DO YOU WANT IT COPIED INTO TEST2.FIL?/
SG3:    .ASCIZ/YOU ENTERED:/
SG4:    .ASCIZ/PLEASE ENTER LAST LINE TO BE PUT INTO TEST2.FIL:/
TOR:    .BLKB       2500        ;LOCAL STORAGE FOR TEST.FIL
IRST:   .BLKB       132         ;LOCAL STORAGE FOR FIRST LINE OF TEST.FIL
AST:    .BLKB       132         ;LOCAL STORAGE FOR LAST LINE OF TEST2.FIL
        .ALIGN      LONG
        .ENTRY      START,0

   ACCEPT LINES FROM KEYBOARD AND PLACE IN TEST.FIL

        .PUTSTR     MSG1        ;DEMONSTRATE .PUTSTR
1:      .TTYIN                  ;DEMONSTRATE .TTYIN
        CMPB        RO,#BKSLSH  ;IF "\"
        BEQL        L2          ;   LAST LINE WAS INPUT.
        .FILE_OUT 1             ;DEMONSTRATE .FILE_OUT
        BRB         L1          ;GET NEXT CHARACTER
2:      .FILE_OUT 1,#BKSLSH     ;APPEND
        .FILE_OUT 1,#CR         ;   TRAILER
        .FILE_OUT 1,#LF         ;       RECORD.
3:      .TTYIN                  ;CLEAR
        CMPB        RO,#LF      ;   .TTYIN
        BNEQ        L3          ;       BUFFER.

   RESET TEST.FIL,  READ IT,  AND WRITE TO TEST2.FIL

        .PUTSTR     MSG2        ;ASK FOR REPEAT COUNT
        .GETHEX     R10         ;DEMONSTRATE .GETHEX
        .PUTSTR     MSG3        ;DEMONSTRATE
        .PUTHEX     R10         ;   .PUTHEX.
4:      .FILE_RESET 1           ;RESET TEST.FIL
5:      .FILE_IN  1             ;GET FROM TEST.FIL
        .FILE_OUT 2             ;PUT INTO TEST2.FIL
        CMPB        RO,#BKSLSH  ;IF "\"
        BNEQ        L5          ;   LAST LINE WAS INPUT.
        .FILE_IN  1             ;GET THE
        .FILE_OUT 2             ;   CR
        .FILE_IN  1             ;       AND
        .FILE_OUT 2             ;           LF.
        DECL        R10         ;REPEAT
        BLEQU       L6          ;   THE
        BRW         L4          ;       PROCESS.
                (a)
```

FIGURE E.3/Program demonstrating usage of terminal and file I/O macros

```
L6:         .FILE_RESET 2            ;
            .PUTSTR  MSG4            ;PROMPT FOR LAST LINE
            .GETSTR  LAST            ;DEMONSTRATE .GETSTR
            .FILE_PUTSTR 2,LAST,EOF ;DEMONSTRATE .FILE_PUTSTR
;
;    READ TEST.FIL,STORE LOCALLY IN STOR,AND ECHO TO TERMINAL
;
            .FILE_RESET 1            ;RESET TEST.FIL TO BEGINNING.
            MOVL      #STOR,R2       ;INITIALIZE STOR POINTER
L7:         .FILE_IN  1,(R2)         ;INPUT TO STOR
            .TTYOUT   (R2)           ;DEMONSTRATE .TTYOUT
            CMPB      (R2)+,#BKSLSH ;IF "\"
            BNEQ      L7             ;   THEN LAST LINE FOUND.
            .FILE_IN  1,(R2)         ;GET TR  CR & LF,
            .TTYOUT   (R2)+          ;   DEMONSTRATING .TTYOUT
            .FILE_IN  1,(R2)         ;       AND .FILE_IN
            .TTYOUT   (R2)+          ;          AND .TTYOUT.
;
;    GET FIRST LINE FROM TEST.FIL AND DISPLAY AT TERMINAL
;
            .FILE_RESET 1            ;RESET TEST.FIL
            .FILE_GETSTR 1,FIRST     ;DEMONSTRATE .FILE_GETSTR
            .PUTSTR FIRST            ;DISPLAY IT AT TERMINAL
;
;    CLOSE ALL FILES AND RETURN TO VMS
;
            .FILE_CLOSE 1            ;CLOSE
            .FILE_CLOSE 2            ;   BOTH FILES.
L8:         $EXIT_S                  ;EXIT TO VMS
            .END      START
```

(b)

FIGURE E.3/Program demonstrating usage of terminal and file I/O macros (concluded)

including the <CR> <LF>. If this limit is exceeded on output, the <CR> <LF> sequence is automatically inserted. On input, if the end of the VMS record is encountered before the <CR> <LF> sequence is found, this sequence is also automatically inserted. This allows .FILE_IN and .FILE_GETSTR to work on files that may not have <CR> <LF> terminated records.

File opening and positioning depend upon whether the first I/O activity is for input or for output. On the first output operation, the file is opened if it exists, or created and opened if it does not exist. If the EOF argument is *omitted,* any existing records in the file are *discarded* and the output records are placed at the beginning of the file. That is, the existing file is overwritten. Alternatively, if the EOF argument is *included* an existing file will be positioned to its *end.* Thus EOF is used to appended new output records at the end of an existing file. Note that the EOF argument has no effect on output operations after the first.

Input can be either from a file that exists at the time the program begins, or from a file created by prior output operations in the program. In the former case, the first input operation automatically begins on the first record in the file. In the latter case, the .FILE_RESET macro must be used (without the EOF argument) to position the file back to the beginning before input can be done.

Several errors can occur in using the file I/O macros. One common error is attempting to perform an I/O operation on a file for which you have not included a .FILE__SETUP macro. This causes an Undefined Symbol error report at the linkage step, listing the symbols ARG_n, CTX_n, FAB_n, INDEX_n, and OPEN_FLAG_n where n is the file identifier. A common run-time error is reading beyond the end of your file. This may come about by trying to read from a nonexistent file, or by trying to read more records than are actually in the file. In either case, the message is:

```
0001827A
ERROR---,FILE_OPERATION FAILED ON GET
```

The number 0001827A is an RMS *condition code*, meaning an end-of-file error. Different condition codes can also appear with other kinds of run-time file errors. The *VAX Record Management Service Reference Manual* (Digital Equipment Corporation) can be consulted for a complete list of condition codes.

Another frequently occurring run-time error in using the file macros is:

```
% System_F_ACCVIO, access violation
```

This is usually caused by an addressing error. For example, you might erroneously code:

```
.FILE_OUT 3,13
```

in an attempt to write a carriage return character (ASCII 13_{10}) to file 3. However, without a prefix # symbol, this will be a reference to virtual address 00000013. Because user programs cannot access virtual address below 00000200, this results in an access violation error.

E.3.3 Assembly and Linkage with I/O Macros

In order to make the I/O macros available in your program you must include the macro library in the assembly step. This is accomplished by the command:

```
$ MACRO fn+[directory]MACLIB/LIB
```

where *fn* is the name of your MACRO program line and *directory* is the directory where MACLIB.MLB is stored (see Section E.2).

It is also necessary to link with the subroutine library, i.e.,

```
$ LINK fn+[directory]SUBLIB/LIB
```

Alternatively, you can copy MACLIB.MLB and SUBLIB.OLB to your directory and then omit [*directory*] in the above commands.

F

An Example of Modular Programming

This program is the implementation of the design developed in Section 11.2.

```
.TITLE TEST SCORE ANALYSIS
.EXTERNAL READ, SUMX, AVGX, HILO, FREQ, PRNT, PLOT
*************************************************************************/*

VERSION: 2.0                               LAST REVISED:  22 SEPT 1985

FUNCTION: COMPUTES HIGH, LOW, AVERAGE SCORES AND
          PLOTS FREQUENCY IN EACH DECILE FOR
          TEST SCORES IN RANGE 0-100.

AUTHOR: E. F. SOWELL

-----------------------------------------------------------------------
```

```
-----------------------------------------------------------------------

INPUTS:
          AN ARRAY OF SCORES FROM THE KEYBOARD FOR
          SUBROUTINE READ.

OUTPUT:
      N: NUMBER OF SCORES
   HIGH: HIGHEST SCORE
    LOW: LOWEST SCORE
    AVG: AVERAGE SCORE (ROUNDED)
      F: ARRAY OF COUNTS IN EACH DECILE

INTERNALS:
          R0, R1, R2, R3: USED VARIOUSLY AND RESTORED.

EXTERNAL CALLS:
          READ: READS SCORES INTO (R1) AND COUNT INTO R2.
          SUMX: SUMS SCORES INTO R0.
          AVGX: COMPUTES AVERAGE INTO R0.
          HILO: FINDS ADDRESS OF LOW (R2) AND HIGH (R3).
          FREQ: COUNTS SCORES INTO EACH DECILE (R2).
          PRNT: PRINTS N, HIGH, AVG, AND LOW.
          PLOT: PLOTS FREQUENCY HISTOGRAM.

 ***********************************************************************
      .PAGE
```

```
;---------------------------------------------------------------
;
;                       L O C A L     D A T A
;
;---------------------------------------------------------------
        .PSECT  DATA
X:      .BLKL   1000            ;SCORES
N:      .BLKL   1               ;COUNT
AVG:    .BLKL   1               ;AVERAGE SCORE
HIGH:   .BLKL   1               ;HIGH SCORE
LOW:    .BLKL   1               ;LOW SCORE
F:      .BLKL   100             ;FREQ. ARRAY
ARG:    .LONG   N,HIGH,AVG,LOW  ;ARG LIST FOR PRNT
;
;---------------------------------------------------------------
;
        .PAGE
;
;---------------------------------------------------------------
;
;                       C O D E     S E C T I O N
;
;---------------------------------------------------------------
        .PSECT  PROG
        .ENTRY  START,0
        MOVL    #X,R1           ;READ DATA FROM KEYBOARD
        BSBW    READ            ;  INTO X ARRAY, AND
        MOVL    R2,N            ;    READ COUNT INTO R2.
        BSBW    SUMX            ;SUM ALL SCORES INTO R0
        BSBW    AVGX            ;AVERAGE SCORE INTO R0
        MOVL    R0,AVG          ;  AND SAVE.
        MOVL    R2,R0           ;FIND HIGH
        BSBW    HILO            ;  AND
        MOVL    (R2),LOW        ;    LOW
        MOVL    (R3),HIGH       ;      SCORES.
        MOVL    #F,R2           ;COUNT SCORE FREQUENCIES
        BSBW    FREQ            ;  IN DECILES, STORED IN F.
        MOVL    #ARG,R1         ;PRINT N, HIGH,
        BSBW    PRNT            ;  AVG, AND LOW.
        BSBW    PLOT            ;PLOT HISTOGRAM OF F
        $EXIT_S                 ;EXIT TO VMS
        .END    START
;
;---------------------------------------------------------------
;
```

```
      .TITLE READ
      .EXTERNAL  GETDEC, GETCHR
***************************************************************************

VERSION: 2.0                              LAST REVISED: 22 SEPT 1985

FUNCTION:  PROMPTS USER FOR SUCCESSIVE INTEGER SCORES
           BETWEEN 0 AND 100, SAVING THEM IN AN ARRAY.
           ALSO COUNTS ENTRIES.

AUTHOR: E. F. SOWELL

-------------------------------------------------------------------------

INPUTS:
         R1: ADDRESS OF THE FIRST LOC. WHERE DATA IS TO BE STORED

OUTPUTS:
         R1: AS INPUT
(R1)-(R1+R2): ARRAY OF SCORES

INTERNALS:
         R0: USED BY GETDEC, GETCHR, .PUTSTR, BUT IS RESTORED
             TO INPUT VALUE

SIDE EFFECTS:
             NONE

EXTERNAL CALLS:
      GETDEC: GETS DECIMAL VALUE FROM KEYBOARD
      GETCHR: GETS CHARACTER FROM KEYBOARD

***************************************************************************
      .PAGE
-------------------------------------------------------------------------

               L O C A L   D A T A

-------------------------------------------------------------------------

      .PSECT   DATA
T1:  .ASCIZ /ENTER SCORE (0 TO 100):/
T2:  .ASCIZ /MORE SCORES (Y OR N)?/
MSG: .ASCIZ /INVALID.  REENTER LAST VALUE./

-------------------------------------------------------------------------

               L O C A L   S Y M B O L S

-------------------------------------------------------------------------
```

```
YES    = ^A'Y'
MINSCR = 0
MAXSCR = 100
       .PAGE
;
;-----------------------------------------------------------------------------
;
;                     C O D E    S E C T I O N
;
;-----------------------------------------------------------------------------
;
;                     L O C A L    S U B R O U T I N E
;
;-----------------------------------------------------------------------------
;
       .PSECT  PROG
CHKSCR:          ;(CHECKS SCORES)
       CMPL    R0,#MINSCR        ;SET CARRY BIT
       BLSSU   OUT               ;IF SCORE
       CMPL    #MAXSCR,R0        ;   OUT OF RANGE.
OUT:   RSB                       ;RETURN TO READ
;
;-----------------------------------------------------------------------------
;
;      ENTRY POINT
;
READ::
       MOVL    R0,-(SP)          ;SAVE
       MOVL    R1,-(SP)          ;REGISTERS
       CLRL    R2                ;INIT COUNTER
REPEAT: .PUTSTR PRMT1            ;ASK FOR INPUT
       BSBW    GETDEC            ;GET SCORE (RETURN IN R0)
       BSBW    CHKSCR            ;CHECK
       BCC     OK                ;  SCORE.
       .PUTSTR ERRMSG            ;PROMPT
       BRB     REPEAT            ;   IF BAD SCORE.
OK:    MOVL    R0,(R1)+          ;STORE SCORE
       INCL    R2                ;INCREMENT COUNT
       .PUTSTR PRMT2             ;PROMPT
       BSBW    GETCHR            ;   FOR MORE.
       CMPB    R0,#YES           ;GET NEXT
       BEQL    REPEAT            ;   SCORE.
       MOVL    (SP)+,R1          ;RESTORE
       MOVL    (SP)+,R0          ;   REGISTERS.
       RSB                       ;RETURN TO CALLER
       .END    ;(READ)
;
;-----------------------------------------------------------------------------
;
```

```
      .TITLE    GET CHARACTER
*****************************************************************************

VERSION: 2.0                              LAST REVISED:  22 SEPT 1985

FUNCTION:  INPUTS A SINGLE CHARACTER INTO R0
           BUT CONTINUES TO READ JUST TO EMPTY
           THE BUFFER.

AUTHOR:  E. F. SOWELL

----------------------------------------------------------------------------

 INPUTS:
      NONE

 OUTPUT:

      R0: INPUT CHARACTER IS IN LOW BYTE.

 INTERNALS:
      R5: TEMP STORAGE (RESTORED)

*****************************************************************************
                   L O C A L    S Y M B O L S
----------------------------------------------------------------------------

= 10

----------------------------------------------------------------------------

                   C O D E     S E C T I O N
----------------------------------------------------------------------------


      .PSECT    PROG
TCHR::
      MOVL      R5,-(SP)          ;SAVE REGISTER 5 ON STACK
      .TTYIN                      ;GET LINE FROM KEYBOARD
      MOVL      R0,R5             ;SAVE FIRST CHAR
ST:   .TTYIN                      ;GET RID OF REST OF LINE
      CMPB      R0,#LF
      BNEQ      REST
      MOVL      R5,R0             ;PUT FIRST CHAR BACK INTO R0
      MOVL      (SP)+,R5          ;RESTORE R5
      RSB                         ;RETURN TO CALLER
      .END      ;(GETCHR)

----------------------------------------------------------------------------
```

```
        .TITLE  GETDEC
;++ ********************************************************************
;
;   VERSION: 2.0                        LAST REVISED: 22 SEPT 1985
;
;   FUNCTION:    GETS DECIMAL ASCII CHARACTERS FROM THE KEYBOARD
;                AND CONVERTS THEM TO BINARY.
;
;   AUTHOR:   E. F. SOWELL
;
;-------------------------------------------------------------------------
;   INPUTS:
;       NONE
;
;   OUTPUT:
;      R0: VALUE ENTERED FROM KEYBOARD
;
;   INTERNALS:
;      R3: TEMP STORAGE (RESTORED)
;
;
;-- ********************************************************************
;
;                  L O C A L    D A T A
;
;-------------------------------------------------------------------------
      .PSECT    DATA
BAD:    .ASCIZ   /BAD INPUT.....TRY AGAIN/
;
;-------------------------------------------------------------- --
;
;                  L O C A L    S Y M B O L S
;
;-------------------------------------------------------------------------
;
CR = 13
LF = 10
;
      .PAGE
;-------------------------------------------------------------------------
;
;                   C O D E    S E C T I O N
;
;-------------------------------------------------------------------------
;
        .PSECT   PROG
GETDEC::
        MOVL     R3,-(SP)          ;SAVE R3 ON STACK
GO:     CLRL     R3                ;CLEAR RESULT REGISTER
G1:     .TTYIN                     ;GET LINE FROM KEYBOARD
        CMPB     R0,#CR            ;IF CR
        BEQL     G1                ;  GET LF.
        CMPB     R0,#LF            ;IF LF
        BEQL     GEND              ;NUMBER IS FINISHED
        SUBL     #^A'0',R0         ;REMOVE ASCII BASE
        BCS      G2                ;BAD CHARACTER
        CMPB     R0,#10
        BCC      G2                ;BAD CHARACTER
        MULL     #10,R3            ;DECIMAL SHIFT OF PREVIOUS RESULT
        ADDL     R0,R3             ;COMBINE NEW DIGIT
        BRB      G1                ;GET NEXT CHARACTER
```

```
:         .TTYIN                        ;GET RID OF
          CMPB      R0,#LF              ;  REST
          BNEQ      G2                  ;    OF LINE
          PUTSTR    BAD                 ;        PRINT MESSAGE.
          BRB       GO                  ;THROW AWAY BAD NO. & GET ANOTHER
ND:
          MOVL      R3,R0               ;PUT NUMBER INTO OUTPUT REGISTER
          MOVL      (SP)+,R3            ;RESTORE R3
          RSB                           ;RETURN TO CALLER
          .END      ;(GETDEC)
          .TITLE    SUMX
+ ***********************************************************************

VERSION: 2.0                            LAST REVISED:   22 SEPT 1985

FUNCTION: ADDS INTEGERS FROM ARRAY.

AUTHOR: E. F. SOWELL

------------------------------------------------------------------------

INPUTS:
          R1: ADDRESS OF FIRST LOC. WHERE DATA IS STORED
          R2: NUMBER OF VALUES TO BE ADDED

OUTPUTS:
          R0: SUM
          R1: AS INPUT
          R2: AS INPUT

INTERNALS:
          NONE

SIDE EFFECTS:
          NONE

EXTERNAL CALLS:
          NONE

- ***********************************************************************
          .PAGE
------------------------------------------------------------------------

                CODE    SECTION

------------------------------------------------------------------------

          .PSECT    PROG
MX::
          MOVL      R1,-(SP)            ;SAVE
          MOVL      R2,-(SP)            ;  REGISTERS.
          CLRL      R0                  ;INIT. SUM
OP:       ADDL      (R1)+,R0            ;ADD R2 VALUES
          SOBGTR    R2,LOOP             ;  INTO R0.
          MOVL      (SP)+,R2            ;RESTORE
          MOVL      (SP)+,R1            ;  REGISTERS.
          RSB                           ;RETURN TO CALLER
          .END      ;(SUMX)

------------------------------------------------------------------------
```

```
        .TITLE   AVGX
;++ ****************************************************************
;
;   VERSION: 2.0                              LAST REVISED:  22 SEPT 198█
;
;   FUNCTION:  FINDS AVERAGE BY DIVIDING SUM BY COUNT.
;
;   AUTHOR: E. F. SOWELL
;
;-----------------------------------------------------------------
;
;   INPUTS:
;             R0: SUM OF SCORES
;             R2: NUMBER OF SCORES
;
;   OUTPUT:
;             R0: AVERAGE (ROUNDED TO THE NEAREST INTEGER)
;             R2: AS INPUT
;
;   INTERNALS:
;             R1: USED IN DIVIDE OPERATION, BUT RESTORED
;
;   SIDE EFFECTS:
;             NONE
;
;   EXTERNAL CALLS:
;             NONE
;
;-- ****************************************************************
        .PAGE
;-----------------------------------------------------------------
;
;                   C O D E    S E C T I O N
;
;-----------------------------------------------------------------
;
        .PSECT   PROG
AVGX::
        MOVL     R1,-(SP)          ;SAVE REGISTERS
        MOVL     R3,-(SP)
        MOVL     R4,-(SP)
        CLRL     R1                ;CLEAR DIVIDEND HIGH LONGWORD.
        EDIV     R2,R0,R3,R4       ;QUOTIENT TO R3, REMAINDER TO R4
        MOVL     R3,R0             ;QUOTIENT TO R0
        MOVL     R4,R1             ;REMAINDER TO R1
        ASHL     #1,R1,R1          ;ROUND RESULT
        CMPL     R1,R2             ;   RATHER
        BLSSU    OUT               ;      THAN
        INCL     R0                ;         TRUNCATE.
OUT:    MOVL     (SP)+,R4          ;RESTORE
        MOVL     (SP)+,R3          ;   REGISTERS
        MOVL     (SP)+,R1          ;      FROM STACK.
        RSB                        ;RETURN TO CALLER
        .END     ;(AVGX)
;
;-----------------------------------------------------------------
;
```

```
    .TITLE HILO
****************************************************************************

VERSION: 2.0                              LAST REVISED:  22 SEPT 1985

FUNCTION:  FINDS ADDRESS OF THE LOWEST
           AND THE HIGHEST VALUES IN THE ARRAY OF SCORES.

AUTHOR:  E. F. SOWELL

----------------------------------------------------------------------------

INPUTS:
        R0: COUNT OF SCORES
        R1: ADDRESS OF FIRST LOCATION WHERE DATA IS STORED

OUTPUTS:
        R0: AS INPUT
        R1: AS INPUT
        R2: ADDRESS OF LOWEST VALUE
        R3: ADDRESS OF HIGHEST VALUE

INTERNALS:
        NONE

SIDE EFFECTS:
        NONE

EXTERNAL CALLS:
        NONE

----------------------------------------------------------------------------
    .PAGE
----------------------------------------------------------------------------

                  C O D E    S E C T I O N

----------------------------------------------------------------------------


    .PSECT  PROG
LO::
    MOVL    R0,-(SP)          ;SAVE
    MOVL    R1,-(SP)          ;  REGISTERS.
    MOVL    R1,R2             ;INITALIZE RESULT
    MOVL    R1,R3             ;  POINTERS.
OP:
    CMPL    (R1),(R2)         ;CHECK VALUE AGAINST
    BGEQU   1$                ;  CURRENT LOW VALUE.
    MOVL    R1,R2             ;ESTABLISH NEW LOW POINTER
:   CMPL    (R1),(R3)         ;CHECK VALUE AGAINST
    BLEQU   2$                ;  CURRENT HIGH VALUE.
    MOVL    R1,R3             ;ESTABLISH NEW HIGH POINTER
:   ADDL    #4,R1             ;INC. BY FOUR
    SOBGTR  R0,LOOP           ;NEXT VALUE
    MOVL    (SP)+,R1          ;RESTORE
    MOVL    (SP)+,R0          ;  REGISTERS.
    RSB                       ;RETURN TO CALLER
    .END    ;(HILO)
```

```
        .TITLE   FREQUENCY COUNTER
;++ **********************************************************************
;
;   VERSION: 2.0                              LAST REVISED: 22 SEPT 1985
;
;   FUNCTION:    CREATES AN ARRAY OF COUNTS OF
;                SCORES IN N INTERVALS BETWEEN
;                MINSCR AND MAXSCR.
;
;   AUTHOR: E. F. SOWELL
;
;----------------------------------------------------------------------
;
;   INPUTS:
;            R0:  COUNTS
;            R1:  ADDRESS OF FIRST LOCATION WHERE DATA IS STORED
;            R2:  ADDRESS OF FIRST LOCATION OF RESULTS
;
;   OUTPUTS:
;            R0:  AS INPUT
;            R1:  AS INPUT
;            R2:  AS INPUT
;            (R2) TO (R2+2 N):   ARRAY OF FREQUENCIES
;
;   INTERNALS:
;            R4:      USED AS LCV AND DIVISION REGISTERS
;                     BUT RESTORED.
;
;   SIDE EFFECTS:
;            NONE
;
;   EXTERNAL CALLS:
;            NONE
;
;-- **********************************************************************
        .PAGE
;
;
;                    L O C A L    S Y M B O L S
;
;----------------------------------------------------------------------
;
MAXSCR=100                      ;MAX SCORE
MINSCR=0                        ;MIN SCORE
N     =10                       ;NUMBER OF INTERVALS
W     =<MAXSCR-MINSCR>/N        ;INTERVAL WIDTH
;
;----------------------------------------------------------------------
        .PAGE
;----------------------------------------------------------------------
;
;                    C O D E    S E C T I O N
;
;----------------------------------------------------------------------
;
        .PSECT   PROG
FREQ::
        MOVL     R0,-(SP)       ;SAVE
        MOVL     R1,-(SP)       ;  REGISTERS
        MOVL     R2,-(SP)       ;    ON THE
        MOVL     R4,-(SP)       ;      STACK.
        MOVL     #N+1,R4        ;CLEAR
```

```
P1:   CLRL      (R2)+              ;  RESULTS
      SOBGTR    R4,LOOP1           ;    ARRAY,
      MOVL      4(SP),R2           ;RESTORE FREQUENCY POINTER
P2:                                ;OFFSET IN
      MOVL      (R1)+,R4           ;  FREQ ARRAY
      DIVL      #W,R4              ;    IS
      ASHL      #2,R4,R4           ;        (SCORE/W)*4,
      ADDL      R2,R4              ;COMPUTE ADDRESS IN FREQ ARRAY
      INCL      (R4)               ;COUNT AT SCORE
      SOBGTR    R0,LOOP2           ;NEXT SCORE
      MOVL      (SP)+,R4           ;RESTORE
      MOVL      (SP)+,R2           ;  REGISTERS ,
      MOVL      (SP)+,R1           ;    FROM THE
      MOVL      (SP)+,R0           ;        STACK,
      RSB                          ;RETURN TO CALLER
      .END      ;(FREQ,)
```

```
      .TITLE    PRINT
      .EXTERNAL CNVDEC
************************************************************************

VERSION: 2,0                       LAST REVISED:   22 SEPT 1985

FUNCTION   PRINTS TESTS STATISTICS,

AUTHOR:    E, F, SOWELL
```

```
INPUTS:
        R1: ADDRESS OF ARRAY OF RESULT ADDRESS
      (R1): ADDRESS OF NO, OF SCORES
     4(R1): ADDRESS OF HIGHEST SCORE
     8(R1): ADDRESS OF AVBERAGE SCORE
    12(R1): ADDRESS OF LOWEST SCORE

OUTPUTS:
    R1: AS INPUT

INTERNALS:
    R0: ARGUMENT TRANSMISSION (RESTORED)
    R2: TEMP, FOR R1 (RESTORED)

SIDE EFFECTS:
    NONE

EXTERNAL CALLS:
    CNVDEC: CONVERTS R0 TO A STRING OF ASCII DECIMAL CHARACTERS

************************************************************************
      .PAGE
```

```
;-------------------------------------------------------------------------
;
;                        L O C A L     D A T A
;
;-------------------------------------------------------------------------
;
        .PSECT    DATA
MSG1:   .ASCII  <13><10><13><10>/                                        /
        .ASCII  /TEST STATISTICS/
        .ASCIZ  <13><10><13><10>/RESULTS:/
NUM:    .ASCIZ  <13>/   NUMBER TAKING TEST=   /
HIGH:   .ASCIZ  <13>/   HIGHEST SCORE     =   /
AVG:    .ASCIZ  <13>/   AVERAGE SCORE     =   /
LOW:    .ASCIZ  <13>/   LOWEST SCORE      =   /
;
;-------------------------------------------------------------------------
        .PAGE
;-------------------------------------------------------------------------
;
;             C O D E      S E C T I O N
;
;-------------------------------------------------------------------------
;
        .PSECT    PROG
PRNT::
        MOVL    R0,-(SP)          ;SAVE
        MOVL    R1,-(SP)          ;  REGISTERS
        MOVL    R2,-(SP)          ;    ON STACK,
        MOVL    R1,R2             ;R1 WILL BE USED BY CNVDEC
        .PUTSTR MSG1              ;PRINT HEADER
        MOVL    @(R2)+,R0         ;CONVERT
        MOVL    #NUM+23,R1        ;  AND
        BSBW    CNVDEC            ;    PRINT
        CLRB    (R1)              ;      NUMBER
        .PUTSTR NUM               ;        OF TESTS,
        MOVL    @(R2)+,R0         ;CONVERT
        MOVL    #HIGH+23,R1       ;  AND
        BSBW    CNVDEC            ;    PRINT
        CLRB    (R1)              ;      HIGHEST
        .PUTSTR HIGH              ;        SCORE,
        MOVL    @(R2)+,R0         ;CONVERT
        MOVL    #AVG+23,R1        ;  AND
        BSBW    CNVDEC            ;    PRINT
        CLRB    (R1)              ;      AVERAGE
        .PUTSTR AVG               ;        SCORE,
        MOVL    @(R2)+,R0         ;CONVERT
        MOVL    #LOW+23,R1        ;  AND
        BSBW    CNVDEC            ;    PRINT
        CLRB    (R1)              ;      LOWEST
        .PUTSTR LOW               ;        SCORE,
        MOVL    (SP)+,R2          ;RESTORE
        MOVL    (SP)+,R1          ;  REGISTERS
        MOVL    (SP)+,R0          ;    FROM STACK,
        RSB                       ;RETURN TO CALLER
        .END    ;(PRINT)
;
;-------------------------------------------------------------------------
;
```

```
    .TITLE   CNVDEC
**************************************************************************
VERSION: 2.0                              LAST REVISED:   23 SEPT 1985

FUNCTION: CONVERTS R0 INTO 3-DIGIT DECIMAL ASCII IN
          BUFFER POINTED TO BY R1.

AUTHOR:  E. F. SOWELL

------------------------------------------------------------------------

INPUTS:
        R0: CONTAINS NUMBER TO BE CONVERTED.
        R1: POINTER TO THE BUFFER FOR OUTPUT STRING.

OUTPUT:
        R0: AS INPUT.
        R1: POINTS TO NEXT AVAILABLE BUFFER BYTE.

INTERNALS:
        R2: USED AS LOOP CONTROL (RESTORED)
        R3: PLACE VALUE ARRAY POINTER (RESTORED)
        R4: DIGIT VALUE (RESTORED)

SIDE EFFECTS:
        NONE

EXTERNAL CALLS:
        NONE

**************************************************************************
------------------------------------------------------------------------

            L O C A L    D A T A

------------------------------------------------------------------------

    .PSECT     DATA
    .LONG 100,10,1            ;PLACE VALUES

------------------------------------------------------------------------

            C O D E      S E C T I O N

------------------------------------------------------------------------

    .PSECT    PROG
DEC::
    MOVL      R0,-(SP)         ;SAVE
    MOVL      R2,-(SP)         ;   REGISTERS
    MOVL      R3,-(SP)         ;      IN
    MOVL      R4,-(SP)         ;        STACK.
    MOVL      #PV,R3           ;INITIALIZE PLACE VALUE POINTER
    MOVL      #3,R2            ;INITIALIZE LCV (3 DIGITS)
    MOVL      #-1,R4           ;INITIALIZE DIGIT VALUE
    INCL      R4               ;UPDATE DIGIT VALUE
    SUBL      (R3),R0          ;SUBTRACT PLACE VALUE
    BCC       2$               ;    UNTIL OVER SUBTRACTED.
    ADDL      (R3)+,R0         ;CORRECT FOR OVER SUBTRACT
```

```
        ADDL    #^X30,R4        ;CONVERT DIGIT TO ASCII CHAR.
        MOVB    R4,(R1)+        ;STORE CHAR. IN PRINT ARRAY
21$:    SOBGTR  R2,1$           ;REPEAT FOR NEXT DIGIT
        CLRB    (R1)            ;STORE NULL BYTE
        MOVL    (SP)+,R4        ;RESTORE
        MOVL    (SP)+,R3        ;   REGISTERS
        MOVL    (SP)+,R2        ;      FROM
        MOVL    (SP)+,R0        ;         THE STACK.
        RSB                     ;RETURN TO CALLER
        .END    ;(CNVDEC)
;
;-----------------------------------------------------------------------
;

        .TITLE  PLOT
        .EXTERNAL CNVDEC
;++ ********************************************************************
;
;   VERSION: 2.0                                LAST REVISED:  22 SEPT
;
;   FUNCTION  PLOTS HISTOGRAM OF SCORE FREQUENCIES.
;
;   AUTHOR: E. F. SOWELL
;
;-----------------------------------------------------------------------
;
;   INPUTS:
;           R2: ADDRESS OF FREQUENCY ARRAY
;
;   OUTPUT:
;           R2: AS INPUT
;
;   INTERNALS:
;           R0: USED AS LOOP CONTROL (RESTORED)
;           R1: USED AS POINTER (RESTORED)
;
;   SIDE EFFECTS:
;           NONE
;
;   EXTERNAL CALLS:
;           CNVDEC:  CONVERTS  R0  TO A STRING OF  ASCII  DECIMAL
;                    CHARACTERS.
;
;-- ********************************************************************
        .PAGE
;-----------------------------------------------------------------------
;
;               L O C A L    D A T A
;
;-----------------------------------------------------------------------
;
        .PSECT  DATA
BUF:    .BLKB   80              ;PLOT LINE BUFFER
MSG1:   .ASCII  <13><13>/                        /
        .ASCIZ  /FREQUENCY PLOT/
```

```
------------------------------------------------------------------------

              L O C A L     S Y M B O L S

------------------------------------------------------------------------

H    = ^A'-'
     = ^A' '
     = ^A'!'
R    = ^A'*'
SCR  = 100                    ;MAX SCORE
SCR  = 0                      ;MIN SCORE
     = 10                     ;NUMBER OF INTERVALS
     = <MAXSCR-MINSCR>/N      ;INTERVAL WIDTH

       .PAGE
  ----------------------------------------------------------------------

              C O D E     S E C T I O N

------------------------------------------------------------------------
       .EVEN
       .PSECT  PROG
T::
       MOVL    R0,-(SP)            ;SAVE
       MOVL    R1,-(SP)            ;  REGISTERS.
       .PUTSTR MSG1               ;PRINT HEADER
       CLRL    R0                 ;INIT LCV
       MOVL    #BUF,R1            ;SET
       BSBW    CNVDEC             ;
       CMPL    #MAXSCR,R0         ;   UP
       BEQL    L1                 ;
       MOVB    #DASH,(R1)+        ;     LABEL
       ADDL    #W-1,R0            ;
       BSBW    CNVDEC             ;        FOR
       CMPL    R1,#BUF+9          ;
       BGEQU   L2                 ;          EACH
       MOVB    #SPA,(R1)+         ;
       BRB     L1                 ;            LINE
       MOVB    #BAR,(R1)+         ;              OF PLOT.
       MOVL    (R2)+,R3           ;SET UP
       BEQL    L4                 ;   CORRECT NUMBER
       MOVB    #STAR,(R1)+        ;     OF *'S
       DECL    R3                 ;       IN EACH LINE
       BRB     L3                 ;         OF PLOT.
       CLRB    (R1)+              ;STORE NULL CHAR.
       MOVL    R0,-(SP)           ;PROTECT R0 FROM .PUTSTR
       .PUTSTR BUF                ;PRINT LINE
       MOVL    (SP)+,R0           ;RESTORE R0
       CMPL    #MAXSCR,R0         ;QUIT IF
       BEQL    OUT                ;   LAST LINE.
       INCL    R0                 ;OTHERWISE DO
       BRW     L0                 ;   NEXT LINE OF PLOT.
T:
       MOVL    (SP)+,R1           ;RESTORE
       MOVL    (SP)+,R0           ;  REGISTERS.
       RSB                        ;RETURN TO CALLER
       .END    ;(PLOT)
```

Command file for assembly and linkage of SCORE program. Change "[SOWELL.IO]" to the directory where I/O macros and subroutines are available on your computer. (See Appendix E.)

```
$MACRO/DEBUG    SCORE+[SOWELL.IO]MACLIB/LIB
$MACRO/DEBUG    READ+[SOWELL.IO]MACLIB/LIB
$RENAME READ.OBJ READX.OBJ
$MACRO/DEBUG    GETCHR+[SOWELL.IO]MACLIB/LIB
$MACRO/DEBUG    GETDEC+[SOWELL.IO]MACLIB/LIB
$MACRO/DEBUG    SUMX+[SOWELL.IO]MACLIB/LIB
$MACRO/DEBUG    AVGX+[SOWELL.IO]MACLIB/LIB
$MACRO/DEBUG    HILO+[SOWELL.IO]MACLIB/LIB
$MACRO/DEBUG    FREQ+[SOWELL.IO]MACLIB/LIB
$MACRO/DEBUG    PRNT+[SOWELL.IO]MACLIB/LIB
$MACRO/DEBUG    CNVDEC+[SOWELL.IO]MACLIB/LIB
$MACRO/DEBUG    PLOT+[SOWELL.IO]MACLIB/LIB
$LINK/MAP/FULL/CROSS_REFERENCE -
        SCORE,-
        READX,-
        GETCHR,-
        GETDEC,-
        SUMX,-
        AVGX,-
        HILO,-
        FREQ,-
        PRNT,-
        CNVDEC,-
        PLOT+-
        [SOWELL.IO]SUBLIB/LIB
```

G

Dealing with Errors

G.1 | The Purpose of This Appendix

One of the frustrations encountered in learning to program is the cryptic error message. This is particularly acute in assembly language because messages are extremely brief, and errors are all too common. This appendix is intended to help you understand these error messages, and to give you some suggestions for correcting the problem. Unfortunately, we are not always able to give a definite cause of the error because often a single error identification code can be caused by several different programming errors. Once the problem is localized, however, it is usually not too difficult to identify the fault from among the listed possible causes of the error code.

The VMS system can produce over 3,000 different messages. These are all listed in the *VAX/VMX System Message and Recovery Procedures Reference Manual* (Digital Equipment Corporation). That manual provides a full description of the possible causes and corrective actions, if required, for all system messages. This appendix provides a small subset of these entries, selected to be most helpful to the beginning MACRO programmer. Therefore, only those messages that can be generated by the MACRO, LINK, RUN, and Symbolic Debugger commands are considered. In order to arrive at a concise but helpful list, messages that do not often occur in elementary programming are omitted. Also omitted are those for which the explanation and corrective action are evident from the interactive error report alone. It is anticipated that the messages given here will meet most of your needs in a one-semester course. However, you may occasionally need to consult the above manual for less common errors, especially if you are working in the later chapters of this book.

G.2 | Format of VMS Error Messages

The VMS operating system employs a uniform format for reporting errors, regardless of which system facility experienced the problem. This format is:

```
%FACILITY-L-IDENT, text
```

where FACILITY is the name of the *system facility* that failed, e.g., MACRO or LINK, L is a *severity level code,* and IDENT is an *abbreviation for the error.* The *text* that follows IDENT is a brief description of the error. If other system facilities also failed due to the same problem, their error messages are given in the same format, except the prefix "-" will be used instead of "%".

The severity level indicator, L, can be one of five values, namely:

S—Success

I—Informational

W—Warning

E—Error

F—Fatal, or severe error

The first two, S and I, are not errors, but are sometimes issued by system programs to indicate a successful outcome of an operation. Warnings, W, mean that something unexpected occurred which may need your attention. Errors, E, mean that the result of the operation is technically in error, but an attempt is made to continue execution. Fatal errors, F, are an indication that the system could not continue execution. You should carefully examine W and E messages, but sometimes no corrective action is required. However, fatal errors will always require some correction to your program, or to the command that produced the message.

In the following sections, discussion and tables of Assembly, Linkage, Execution, and Symbolic Debugger errors are presented.*

G.3 | Assembly Errors

Certain programming errors can be detected during the assembly process. These errors are printed at the terminal after the MACRO command line. For example,

```
$ MACRO/LIST MYPROG
                E7 AF DE 001A 4 MOVAL A/R0,R2
%MACRO-E-OPRNDSYNX, operand syntax error!
There were 1 error, 0 warnings, and 0 information
messages, on lines:
   4(1)
MACRO/LIST MYPROG
$ ▓
```

Note that the offending line from the listing file is displayed above the error report line, and a symbol "!" points to the syntax error. If desired, the listing file can be examined to see all error reports in the context of the rest of the program.

Often the cause of the problem and the needed corrections can be seen from the error report displayed at the terminal. For example, the above error report leaves little doubt that one of the operands of the MOVAL instruction has a syntax error. Careful inspection reveals that "/" should be deleted.

If you cannot see the problem from the terminal report, try looking it up in Table G.1. This table lists many of the assembler errors commonly encountered by beginning

---

* The material in Appendix G has been adapted in part from copyrighted publications of Digital Equipment Corporation. This material is the sole responsibility of the author.

MACRO programmers. It is organized alphabetically by the error identifier, e.g., OPRNDSYNX. The explanations given there provide a more complete description of the problem, and a suggested corrective action. Note that Table G.1 omits many of the possible MACRO error messages, such as those that are so simple that elaboration is unnecessary, and those that deal with more advanced programming. The *VAX/VMS System Message and Recovery Procedures Reference Manual* (Digital Equipment Corporation) can be consulted for error identifiers not found in Table G.1.

TABLE G.1/MACRO Assembler Errors

ADRLSTSYNX,   address list syntax error

Explanation: The address list in the .ADDRESS directive contains a syntax error.

User Action: Correct the syntax.

ALIGNXCEED,   alignment exceeds PSECT alignment

Explanation: The .ALIGN directive specified an alignment larger than the program section alignment. For example, the .PSECT directive specified byte alignment (the default) and the .ALIGN directive specified a longword alignment, or a .PSECT directive specified an invalid alignment.

User Action: Correct the conflicting alignments. The .PSECT directive should specify the largest alignment required by the program section.

ASCTOOLONG,   ASCII string too long

Explanation: Either the string in an .ASCIC directive was more than 255 characters or the string in an .ASCID directive was more than 65535 characters.

User Action: Reduce the length of the string.

ASGNMNTSYN,   assignment syntax error

Explanation: A direct assignment statement contains a syntax error.

User Action: Check the syntax of the assignment. Attempt to reduce the complexity of any expressions used.

BADENTRY,   bad format for .ENTRY statement

Explanation: The .ENTRY directive did not specify an entry point name and a correct entry mask.

User Action: Correct the .ENTRY directive syntax.

BADLEXARG,   illegal lexical function argument

Explanation: The argument to a macro string operator is invalid. String arguments can be macro arguments or strings delimited by angle brackets or the circumflex delimiters. Symbol arguments can be absolute symbols or decimal integers.

User Action: Correct the argument syntax.

BADLEXFORM,   illegal format for lexical function

Explanation: The macro string operator contained a syntax error.

User Action: Correct the macro string operator syntax.

BLKDIRSYNX,   block directive syntax error

Explanation: A conditional block or a repeat block directive contained a syntax error.

TABLE G.1/MACRO Assembler Errors (*continued*)

User Action: Correct the directive syntax.

BLKEXPNABS,   block expression not absolute

Explanation: The expression specifying the amount of storage to be allocated in a .BLKA, .BLKB, .BLKD, .BLKF, .BLKG, .BLKH, .BLKO, or .BLKW directive contained an undefined symbol or was a relative expression.

User Action: Replace the expression with an absolute expression that does not contain any undefined symbols. Sometimes the problem can be fixed by reordering statements so as to place symbol assignments before the block directive.

BRDESTRANG,   branch destination out of range

Explanation: The address specified in the branch instruction was too far from the current PC. Branch instructions with byte displacements have a range of -128 bytes to $+127$ bytes from the current PC. Branch instructions with word displacements have a range of -32768 bytes to $+32767$ bytes from the current PC.

User Action: Use a branch instruction with a word displacement instead of one with a byte displacement; use a jump (JMP) instruction instead of a branch instruction. Alternatively, change the program logic so that the branch destination is closer to the branch instruction.

DATALSTSYN,   data list syntax error

Explanation: The data list in the directive contained a syntax error. For example, the directive .LONG 3,,5 contains a data list syntax error because there is no data item between the two commas. Otherwise, a repeat count may not be terminated.

User Action: Correct the syntax of the data list.

DATATRUNC,   data truncation error

Explanation: The specified value did not fit in the given data type. The assembler truncated the value to make it fit.

User Action: Reduce the value or the number of characters in an ASCII string, or change the data type.

ENDWRNGMAC,   statement ends wrong MACRO

Explanation: The .ENDM directive specified a different name from its corresponding .MACRO directive. Macros may be improperly nested.

User Action: Correct the name in the .ENDM directive to ensure that the .ENDM directive and .MACRO directive correspond as required. Be sure that a nested macro is ended before the outer macro is ended.

EXPOVR32,   expression overflowed 32 bits

Explanation: The value of the expression could not be stored in a longword (32 bits). The assembler truncated the value to 32 bits.

User Action: Check the expression for errors. If more than 32 bits are actually needed, devise separate expressions for high and low longwords.

ILLASCARG,   illegal ASCII argument

Explanation: Either the argument to an .ASCIx directive did not have enclosing delimiters, or an expression was not enclosed in angle brackets.

User Action: Correct the syntax of the argument.

TABLE G.1/MACRO Assembler Errors (*continued*)

ILLBRDEST, illegal branch destination

Explanation: The destination of a branch instruction was not an address, for example, BRB 10(R9).

User Action: Change the destination of the branch instruction or use a jump (JMP) instruction.

ILLEXPR, illegal expression

Explanation: A radix operator, e.g., ^X, was not followed by a number, or left and right angle brackets did not match in an expression.

User Action: Correct the syntax of the expression.

ILLMASKBIT, reserved bits set in ENTRY mask

Explanation: The register save mask in an .ENTRY or .MASK directive specified R0, R1, AP, or FP registers (corresponding to bits 0, 1, 12, and 13).

User Action: Remove these registers from the register save mask.

ILLMODE, illegal mode

Explanation: An invalid addressing mode for the instruction was specified.

User Action: Specify a legal addressing mode.

ILLINDXREG, invalid index register

Explanation: The base mode may change the value of the register, and the index register is the same as the register in the base mode. Otherwise, the base mode is literal or immediate mode, or PC was used as the index register.

User Action: Use a different register for indexing. Do not attempt to index with literal or immediate base addressing. Do not use PC as an index register.

ILLREGHERE, this register may not be used here

Explanation: The PC register cannot be used in the following addressing modes: register, register-deferred, autodecrement, autoincrement, and autoincrement-deferred.

User Action: Use another register.

ILLREGNUM, illegal register number

Explanation: A register name was not the AP, FP, SP, or PC register name, or register was not in the range R0 through R12.

User Action: Correct the illegal register name.

INVALIGN, invalid alignment

Explanation: An unrecognized keyword, or no integer, or no keyword followed the .ALIGN directive.

User Action: Correct the syntax of the .ALIGN directive.

MAYNOTINDX, this mode may not be indexed

Explanation: The base mode was immediate or literal mode.

User Action: Change the base addressing mode, or remove the index.

MULDEFLBL, multiple definition of label

Explanation: The same label was defined twice in the module.

TABLE G.1/MACRO Assembler Errors (*continued*)

User Action: Delete the second label definition or change one of the labels to a different symbol name.

MCHINSTSYN,   machine instruction syntax error

Explanation: A syntax error occurred in an instruction, for example, MOVL, A.

User Action: Correct the instruction syntax.

NOTINMACRO,   statement not in MACRO body

Explanation: A .NARG, .ENDM, or .ENDR directive was used outside the context of a macro.

User Action: Check your macro definitions for correct placement of .ENDM directive. Note that .NARG can be used only inside macros.

NOTPSECOPT,   not a valid PSECT option

Explanation: The attribute specified in the .PSECT directive was invalid.

User Action: Check the options for the .PSECT directive. Delete the invalid attribute or replace it with a valid one.

NOTINANIF,   statement outside condition body

Explanation: A .IF_FALSE, .IF_TRUE, .IF_TRUE_FALSE, .IFF, .IFT, or .IFTF subconditional directive was not in a conditional assembly block.

User Action: Note that these directives can only be placed in a conditional block. Replace the subconditional directive with a conditional directive, or delete the subconditional directive.

OPENIN,   error opening 'file-spec' as input

Explanation: The assembler encountered an I/O error when opening an input source or macro library file; file-spec is the file specification of the file being opened. This message is produced when the file cannot be found.

User Action: First check the file-spec for typing errors. Then retry the assembly, or make a new copy of the input file and retry the assembly.

OPRNDSYNX,   operand syntax error

Explanation: An instruction operand contained a syntax error, e.g., (R4)A.

User Action: Correct the operand syntax, e.g., A(R4).

PSECOPCNFL,   conflicting PSECT options

Explanation: The values specified in a .PSECT directive conflicted with each other or were not the same as the values specified in the preceding .PSECT directive that specified the same program section name.

User Action: Correct the conflicting values in the .PSECT directive(s).

SYMDCLEXTR,   symbol declared external

Explanation: A label definition or direct assignment statement specified a symbol that was previously declared external in an .EXTERNAL directive.

User Action: Delete the external declaration or change the name of the internal symbol.

SYMDEFINMO,   symbol is defined in module

Explanation: An .EXTERNAL directive specified a label that was previously defined in the module.

User Action: Delete the external declaration or rename the internal symbol.

TABLE G.1/MACRO Assembler Errors (*concluded*)

SYMOUTPHAS, symbol out of phase

Explanation: A label definition specified a label that was redefined later in the module. Otherwise, a local label definition specified a local label that was redefined later in the same local label block.

User Action: Ensure that the label is defined only once in the module, or that the local label is defined only once in the local label block.

SYMNOTABS, symbol is not absolute

Explanation: The argument in a macro string operator was a relative symbol or was undefined.

User Action: Ensure that the symbol is defined as an absolute symbol.

TOOMNYARGS, too many arguments in MACRO call

Explanation: The macro call contained more actual arguments than there were dummy arguments in the .MACRO directive in the macro definition.

User Action: Ensure that the macro call corresponds to the macro definition. Also, check for a misplaced comma between macro name and first actual argument.

UNDEFXFRAD, undefined transfer address

Explanation: The .END directive specified a transfer address that was not defined in the module or specified in an .EXTERNAL directive.

User Action: Be sure that the label in the .END directive is the same as used in the .ENTRY directive.

UNDEFSYM, undefined symbol

Explanation: A local label was referred to but not defined in a local label block. Otherwise, if GLOBAL was disabled, the symbol was referred to but not defined in the module or specified in an .EXTERNAL directive.

User Action: Define the local label or symbol or specify the symbol in an .EXTERNAL directive.

UNTERMARG, unterminated argument

Explanation: The string argument was missing a delimiter, or the macro argument was missing an angle bracket.

User Action: Add a delimiter or an angle bracket to the string argument.

UNTERMCOND, unterminated conditional

Explanation: A conditional assembly block was not terminated by the .ENDC directive. The assembler inserted the .ENDC directive before the .END directive.

User Action: Add the .ENDC directive to the conditional assembly block.

G.4 | Linkage Errors

Certain programming errors cannot be detected by the assembler, but result in error reports when linkage is attempted. These are printed immediately after the LINK command line. The errors most commonly encountered in elementary programming are shown in Table G.2, along with corrective actions.

A frequent source of problems at linkage is failure to define a symbol in a module,

TABLE G.2/Linkage Errors

MULDEF, symbol 'symbol-name' multiply defined in module 'module-name' file 'file-name'

Explanation: A global symbol is defined with different values. This happens when you link separately assembled modules that have identical global labels defined more than once.

User Action: Check listings of all of your modules for occurrence of 'symbol-name'. Note that symbols *not defined* in a module are assumed to be global. Either define 'symbol-name' locally, or choose unique names for all global symbols.

NUDFSYMS, 'number' undefined symbol(s)

Explanation: There were 'number' undefined symbols encountered by the linker. This message is issued at the end of Pass 1 of the link. The undefined symbols are listed in subsequent UNFSYM messages.

User Action: Ensure that all symbols referenced are defined. Note that because assembler assumes undefined symbols to be global, it cannot detect errors of this type.

UDFSYM, 'symbol-name'

Explanation: This message is output for each undefined symbol. 'Symbol-name' is the offending symbol.

User Action: Determine why the symbols are undefined and correct the condition. (See NUDFSYMS.)

USRTFR, image 'image-name' has no user transfer address

Explanation: Your program does not contain a transfer address.

User Action: Check to be sure there is an .ENTRY directive with an entry point label, and an .END directive with the same label.

USEUNDEF, undefined symbol 'symbol-name' referenced in psect 'psect-name' offset 'address' in module 'module-name' file 'file-name'

Explanation: This indicates the exact location where a symbol reported in a prior UDFSYM message was used in your program.

User Action: This message goes away when you correct the undefined symbol problem. (See NUDFSYMS and UDFSYM.)

---

whereupon the asssembler assumes it to be global. Recall that a symbol is defined by appearing to the left of ''='' or '':''. When the linker finds no module in which the symbol is defined, it generates error messages. For example, if we used symbols A and B in a program but did not define them, we would get at link time:

```
$ LINK SHO_ERR
% LINK-W-NUDFSYMS, 2 undefined symbols:
% LINK-I-UNFSYM,          A
% LINK-I-UNFSYM,          B
% LINK-W-USEUNDEF, undefined symbol A referenced
          in psect . BLANK . offset % X00000007
          in module TYRIT file  DRA1:[SOWELL]SHO ERR.OBJ;1
% LINK-W-USEUNDEF, undefined symbol B referenced
          in psect .BLANK . offset % X0000000C
          in module TYRIT file  DRA1:[SOWELL]SHO ERR.OBJ;1
$ ▧
```

Note that the NUDFSYMS gives the total number of undefined symbols, and there is one UNFSYM and one USEUNDEF for each such symbol.

On the other hand, symbols that are intended to be global can be defined *only once* in the group of modules being linked. Symbols are made global by appearing in the .GLOBAL directive, or by appearing to the left of "::" or "==".

Another common linkage error is the lack of a "transfer address." This usually means that none of the modules being linked have .ENTRY and .END directives with corresponding labels.

G.5 | Execution Errors

There are many kinds of programming errors that cannot be detected until an attempt is made to actually execute the program. These are called "execution-time" or "run-time" errors. An example is the program:

```
        .TITLE TYRIT
        .WORD   0,2
A:      .BLKB 10
B:      .BLKB 10
        .ENTRY S,0
        MOVL    #^XA0000000,R3
        MOVL    A(R3),B
        $EXIT_S
        .END S
```

The second move instruction is correct insofar as the assembler and linker can determine. However, at execution time the large negative value in R3 causes a reference to an invalid address. This causes an *access violation* error as shown below:

```
$ RUN SHO_ERR
% SYSTEM-F-ACCVIO,  access violation,  reason  mask=01,
virtual address=A0000204, PC=00000221, PSL=03C00008
% TRACE-F-TRACEBACK, symbolic stack dump follows
module name    routine name    line  rel PC      abs PC
TYRIT          S                     00000009    00000221
$ ▓
```

This error, identified by ACCVIO, is perhaps the most frequently encountered execution-time error. It is nearly always caused by improper indirect addressing, which results in an effective address outside your program. To fix the problem you have to re-examine your operands and be sure that registers used in indirect addressing contain valid addresses.

Other frequent execution-time errors include reserved operand (ROPRAND and RADRMODE) and reserved opcode (OPCDEC and OPCCUS) errors. These can be caused by errors in program logic that result in branches to noninstruction areas in the virtual address space. Also, note that the HALT instruction is not a valid instruction for a user program. Thus, whenever its opcode (00) is encountered, an OPCDEC error occurs. This can be due to either the occurrence of the HALT instruction in your source code, or a program logic error that transfers control to a noninstruction area.

Table G.3 summarizes the more common execution-time errors. Many of these are arithmetic faults such as overflow and division by zero. Such errors require that you re-examine the arithmetic operations and logic of your program.

TABLE G.3/Execution Errors

ACCVIO, access violation, reason mask=xx, virtual address=location, PC=location, PSL=xxxxxxxx

Explanation: Your program attempted to read from, or write to, an unauthorized memory location that is protected from the current mode. This message indicates an exception condition and is followed by a register and stack dump to help locate the error. The reason mask is a longword whose lowest three bits, if set, indicate that the instruction caused a length violation (bit 0), referenced the process page table (bit 1), and attempted to read/modify operation (bit 2). Most likely, you have an addressing error, such as indirect addressing without initializing the register. This message is also displayed when an attempt has been made to make the user stack larger than the user's virtual address space permits.

User Action: Examine the instruction at the given PC and check the addressing used in that instruction. Be sure any registers used for deferred or indexed modes have the correct contents before the instruction is executed. If not an addressing error, check for excessive stack pushes, such as in an infinite loop or improper recursion.

BADSTACK,   bad stack encountered during exception dispatch

Explanation: An exception condition occurred during the execution of the program. Otherwise, the exception dispatcher noted an inconsistency in the call stack while searching for condition handlers.

User Action: Check for a programming error in the user-defined condition handler. Also, check to be sure you have left the stack in the proper state before RSB instructions.

BREAK,   breakpoint fault at PC location, PSL='xxxxxxxx'

Explanation: A breakpoint instruction was encountered. This message indicates an exception condition that was not handled by the condition handler, and is usually followed by a display of the condition arguments, registers, and stack at the time of the exception.

User Action: Examine the PC and virtual address displayed in the message to correct the instruction that caused the error.

DECOVF,   arithmetic trap, decimal overflow at PC='xxxxxxxx', PSL='xxxxxxxx'

Explanation: A decimal overflow caused an arithmetic overflow condition.

User Action: Examine the PC location displayed in the message and check the program listing to verify that the operands are specified correctly.

FLTDIV,   arithmetic trap, floating/decimal divide by zero at PC='xxxxxxxx', PSL='xxxxxxxx'

Explanation: An arithmetic exception condition occurred as a result of an attempt to divide a floating point/decimal number by zero.

User Action: Examine the PC location displayed in the message. Check the program listing to verify that operands are specified correctly.

FLTDIV_F,   arithmetic fault, floating divide by zero at PC='xxxxxxxx', PSL='xxxxxxxx'

Explanation: During a floating-point operation, an attempt was made to divide by zero.

User Action: Examine the PC location displayed in the message. Check the program listing to verify that operands are specified correctly.

FLTOVF,   arithmetic trap, floating overflow at PC='xxxxxxxx', PSL='xxxxxxxx'

Explanation: An arithmetic exception condition occurred as a result of floating-point overflow.

TABLE G.3/Execution Errors (*continued*)

User Action: Examine the PC location displayed in the message. Check the program listing to verify that operands are specified correctly.

FLTOVF_F,   arithmetic fault, floating overflow at PC='xxxxxxxx', PSL='xxxxxxxx'

Explanation: During an arithmetic operation, a floating-point value exceeded the largest representable value for that data type.

User Action: Examine the PC location displayed in the message. Check the program listing to verify that operands are specified correctly.

FLTUND,   arithmetic trap, floating underflow at PC='xxxxxxxx', PSL='xxxxxxxx'

Explanation: An arithmetic exception condition occurred as a result of floating-point underflow.

User Action: Examine the PC location displayed in the message. Check the program listing to verify that operands are specified correctly.

FLTUND_F,   arithmetic fault, floating underflow at PC='xxxxxxxx', PSL='xxxxxxxx'

Explanation: During an arithmetic operation, a floating-point value became less than the smallest representable value for that data type.

User Action: Examine the PC location displayed in the message. Check the program listing to verify that operands are specified correctly.

INTDIV,   arithmetic trap, integer divide by zero at PC='xxxxxxxx', PSL='xxxxxxxx'

Explanation: An arithmetic exception condition occurred as a result of an attempt to divide by zero.

User Action: Examine the PC location displayed in the message. Check the program listing to verify that operands are specified correctly.

INTOVF,   arithmetic trap, integer overflow at PC='xxxxxxxx', PSL='xxxxxxxx'

Explanation: The integer overflow trap was enabled, and an exception condition occurred as a result of an integer overflow.

User Action: Examine the PC location displayed in the message. Check the program listing to verify that operands are specified correctly.

OPCCUS,   opcode reserved to customer fault at PC='location', PSL='xxxxxxxx'

Explanation: An illegal operation code beginning with FC was encountered during execution of the program. This message indicates an exception condition and is usually followed by a display of the condition arguments, registers, and stack at the time of the exception.

User Action: Examine the PC displayed in the message. Also examine the entire source code carefully, and if necessary, single-step through the program. Most likely, your program logic caused a branch to a location that does not contain an instruction.

OPCDEC,   opcode reserved to DIGITAL fault at PC='location', PSL='xxxxxxxx'

Explanation: The operation code at the indicated address is not known. This message indicates an exception condition and is usually followed by a display of the condition arguments, registers, and stack at the time of the exception.

User Action: Examine the PC displayed in the message. Also examine the entire source code carefully, and if necessary, single-step through the program. Most likely, your program logic caused a branch to a location that does not contain an instruction.

TABLE G.3/Execution Errors (*concluded*)

ROPRAND,   reserved operand fault at PC 'location', PSL='xxxxxxxx'

Explanation: An instruction contains an operand in a format that is not acceptable. This message indicates an exception condition and is usually followed by a display of the condition arguments, registers, and stack at the time of exception.

User Action: Examine the PC displayed in the message to determine the instruction that caused the error. Then check source code near that instruction for a programming error. If the instruction is not really part of your program, check program logic for branch errors.

RADRMOD,   reserved addressing fault at PC 'location', PSL='xxxxxxxx'

Explanation: An instruction specifies an addressing mode that is illegal within the context of its use. This message indicates an exception condition and is usually followed by a display of the condition arguments, registers, and stack at the time of the exception.

User Action: Examine the PC displayed in the message to determine the instruction that caused the error. Then check source code near that instruction for a programming error. If the instruction is not really part of your program, check program logic for branch errors.

For some types of execution-time errors, the reported message may be meaningless. For example, a bad branch instruction may transfer control to a data area or unused portion of memory where a completely unrelated error message is generated. These errors are very hard to locate, but are best approached by studying the listing file for logical errors. Stepping through the program a single instruction at a time (Section C.7.7) is also effective.

G.6 | Symbolic Debugger Errors

When you execute your program under control of the Symbolic Debugger you can get DEBUG errors as well as any of the execution-time errors discussed in Section G.5. The DEBUG errors are listed in Table G.4. The DEBUG errors fall mostly into three categories, namely, syntax errors, addressing errors, and symbol errors. Syntax errors have to do with improper entry of debugger commands. Appendix C or the interactive HELP facility can be used to resolve these problems. Addressing errors,

TABLE G.4/Symbolic Debugger Errors

ACCADDCOM,   access violation in address computation for xxx

Explanation: The address computation for xxx resulted in reference to invalid address. This normally means that a register value or a descriptor needed in the address computation is uninitialized or corrupted.

User Action: Examine the contents of registers and locations used in the address calculation. Be sure any registers used are initialized.

TABLE G.4/Symbolic Debugger Errors (*concluded*)

BADSTARTPC,   cannot access start PC = xxx

Explanation: Location xxx is not an accessible address and therefore cannot be executed. This is often caused when a GO command with no address specification is entered after the program has terminated. The debugger tries to execute an instruction at location 0, which is not accessible.

User Action: Give a different address specification in the GO command or, if the program has terminated, exit from the debugger and reinitiate the program with the RUN command.

BADTARGET,   target location protected, cannot perform deposit

Explanation: The target address of the DEPOSIT command cannot be made writable. The DEPOSIT command cannot be performed.

User Action: Check the way in which you expressed the address for the command. Note that you cannot deposit at locations outside your own program.

BADWATCH,   cannot watch protected address xxx

Explanation: A SET WATCH command specified an invalid address. Note that you cannot place a watchpoint on a dynamically allocated variable because these variables are stored on the stack.

User Action: Do not use watchpoint on this address.

NOACCESSW,   no write access to virtual address nnn

Explanation: A DEPOSIT, SET BREAK, or SET TRACE command specified the address nnn. The debugger does not have write access to that location. The debugger requires write access in order to be able to set up breakpoints and tracepoints.

User Action: Check the way in which you expressed the address for the command. Note that you cannot deposit, break, or trace at locations outside your own program.

NOSYMBOL,   symbol xxx is not in the symbol table

Explanation: The symbol xxx cannot be located in the debugger's symbol table. This can be caused when the module that defines the symbol has not been added to the symbole table, or when a symbol name that is not in the program has been entered.

User Action: First, be sure you assembled and linked with the /DEBUG option. Then check the spelling of the symbol. Otherwise, you may have to add the required module to the symbol table with the SET MODULE command.

NOUNIQUE,   symbol xxx is not unique

Explanation: The symbol specified is used in more than one module that you included in the SET MODULE command.

User Action: Specify the scope of the symbol in the path name. For example, SUB1\A indicates the symbol A as used in module SUB1.

---

such as NOACCESSW and BADTARGET, are usually the result of improper specification of the address in a command. You may benefit from rereading portions of Appendix C. Symbol errors, such as NOSYMBOL are sometimes encountered when debugging a program that was linked from several separately assembled modules. You will have to use the SET MODULE command to resolve these difficulties (Section C.7.8).

Glossary

Abort: An exception that may have left the machine in state such that the instruction cannot be restarted.

Absolute address: An address in the machine code program that represents a virtual main memory address, rather than the distance between two addresses.

Accumulator: A special register that acts as a destination for most or all operations on certain computers.

Address: The unique number that refers to a particular location in main memory. *See* Physical address and Virtual address.

Address space: The set of all possible addresses. *See also* Physical address space and Virtual address space.

Address translation buffer: A storage unit within the CPU that holds recently accessed virtual addresses and their physical address translations.

Addressing: The way in which an operand is identified.

Alignment: Regarding stacks and program sections, the advancement of the location counter at assembly-time, or program counter at run-time, in order to ensure that the next item will be placed at an address evenly divisible by a particular data type length. For example, longword alignment ensures placement at an address divisible by four. In floating-point operations, the shifting of the mantissa to achieve alignment of the binary points before addition or subtraction.

ALU: *See* Arithmetic logic unit.

AP: *See* Argument pointer.

Arabic digits: The symbols used to represent numbers in decimal, i.e., 0,1,2, . . . , 9.

Architecture: Those aspects of the computer that define its operation as seen by an assembly or machine code programmer. For example, the instruction set, registers, addressing modes, and instruction format.

Argument frame: A group of contiguous memory cells containing arguments or argument addresses for access within a subroutine or procedure. Can be at a fixed address in the calling procedure or on the stack.

Argument pointer (AP): The register R12 that is used to pass the address of the argument frame to a subroutine or procedure.

Argument transmission: The mechanism whereby arguments are made available to a subroutine or procedure by the calling procedure and vice versa.

Arguments: The quantities that are provided to or returned from a subroutine or macro.

Arguments, actual/dummy: Actual arguments are those used when a macro is invoked. Dummy arguments are those used in its definition. Actual arguments replace the dummy arguments during expansion.

Arithmetic logic unit (ALU): The electronic assembly that actually carries out instructions. On a microprogrammed computer such as the VAX-11, there is not a distinct ALU. Instead, this function is performed by the internal data path.

Arithmetic shift: Moving the bit pattern in a cell to the right or left in a manner that preserves the algebraic sign and other arithmetic properties.

Array: A data structure in which all elements are identical, and each can be identified by one or more indexes.

ASCII: A system of binary codes for printable and control characters. American Standard Code for Information Interchange. *See* Table 7.1.

ASCII base: The value that must be added to the value of a digit to get the ASCII code for the digit symbol. In hexadecimal, the ASCII base is 30 for 0,1, . . . , 9 and 37 for A,B, . . . , F.

Assembler: The program that translates an assembly language program to machine code.

Assignment: *See* Direct assignment.

AST: *See* Asynchronous system trap.

Asynchronous: Not synchronized with the program. That is, an asynchronous event can happen at any time. *Contrast with* Synchronous.

Asynchronous system trap (AST): A signaling system provided through the VMS System Services that allows user programs to simulate interrupt programing. Both hardware and software interrupts can be simulated.

Autoincrement/autodecrement: Addressing modes indicated by (Rn)+ or −(Rn), respectively. *See* Section 5.7.2.

Base: The number that, when raised to successive powers, produces the position values in a positional notation number system. With index addressing, base means base address, such as the first address of an array or table. *See also* Offset.

Binary: A system in which numbers are represented by a sequence of 1's and 0's called bits. In the positional binary system, each bit represents the coefficient of a power of 2.

Bit: Short for binary digit. A bit can be a 0 or a 1.

Bit pattern (bit string): A group of 0's and 1's, e.g., 10111010. This term is a way of referring to the contents of a byte, word, or register without imparting a particular meaning to it.

Bootstrap: To enter a minimal machine code program that gives the computer the capability to read a larger program from a peripheral device. In early computers, this was done manually, but modern machines boostrap from built-in, read-only memory.

Borrow: In subtraction, the process of adding the place value of the next higher digit to a digit of the minuend in order to allow subtraction of a larger digit in the subtrahend. The higher digit is decremented by 1.

Breakpoint: An address where program execution is to be stopped during the use of the Symbolic Debugger. See Appendix C.7.6.

Buffer: A block of storage locations in which data is placed temporarily. Used when rates of entry and removal are different. Usually organized as a queue.

Bus: A group of electrical conductors for transmission of digital information. Often used to connect elements of digital computer systems.

Byte: A unit of information composed of 8 bits. Also viewed as a unit of memory. The VAX-11 assigns unique addresses to each byte in virtual main memory.

Cache memory: A high-speed memory within the CPU used to hold recently fetched data or instructions for possible re-use. Used to accelerate the instruction fetch-execute cycle.

Call by reference: A method of argument transmission whereby the address of the argument is passed rather than its value. This allows the subroutine to change the value of the argument in the calling procedure. *See also* Call by value.

Call by value: A method of argument transmission whereby the value of the argument is passed rather than its address. This prevents the called procedure from changing the argument in the calling procedure.

Call frame: The group of longwords pushed on the user stack when a procedure is called. Contains saved registers and other information needed to restore the state of the process upon return. Same as Stack frame.

Carry: An addition to the left adjacent digit necessitated by a sum larger than the maximum allowed digit value. If this occurs while adding the MSB's, a carry error condition occurs, setting the C condition code.

Cell: A unit of storage for digital information, e.g., byte, word, or longword.

Central processor unit (CPU):   The unit within the computer consisting of the arithmetic logic unit, general registers, program status register, and control unit.

Character code: A numeric code, usually expressed in binary, for representing a character. For example, 1000001 represents "A" in the ASCII system.

Character string: A group of characters in a specified sequence, e.g., "ABC", "123", and "A+B*C".

Circular buffer/queue: A queue in which the pointers are reset to the beginning when they reach the end.

Code: Often used to refer to a program or program segment, either in machine language, assembly, or any computer language.

Collating sequence: The sequence into which characters are sorted, usually based on numerical values of their codes. When ASCII is used, this sequence is as shown in Table 7.1.

Column-major: A one-dimensional arrangement of a two-dimensional array in which all elements of the first column are followed by those of the second column, and so on.

Compiler: A program that translates an entire program module from a high-level language, e.g., FORTRAN, into a machine language program. *Contrast with* Interpreter.

Complement: *See* One's complement and Two's complement.

Concatenation: Joining together. Thus "ABC" concatenated with "123" is "ABC123".

Condition codes: The four rightmost bits in the processor status word (PSW). These bits are set or cleared depending on whether the previous result yielded a negative (N), zero (Z), overflow (V), or carry out of the MSB (C). *See* Table A.1.

Condition handler: A procedure that performs error handling for conditions such as overflow. *See* Section 16.5.4.

Conditional assembly: A group of assembly program lines that are assembled or skipped depending on a condition check of some symbol or expression at assembly time.

Console: The terminal, composed of a keyboard and display device, that the operator uses to control the computer. *See* Section 3.4.5.

Contents: Refers to the bit pattern currently held in a register or main memory location.

Contiguous: A group of locations with sequential addresses in main memory or mass storage are said to be contiguous.

Control character: A character code that does not correspond to a printing character but has some other significance, e.g., 13_{10} is the carriage return control character.

Control (transfer of): Resetting PC, the pointer to the program instruction to be executed next.

Control unit: That part of the CPU which issues the control signals that cause instructions to be fetched and sent to the ALU. On microprogrammed computers like the VAX-11, the control unit is represented by the control store and the microsequencer units.

CPU: *See* Central processor unit.

CPU priority: *See* Interrupt priority level.

CU: *See* Control unit.

Data path: In general, the interconnections for transmission of parallel, binary signals among computer components. *See also* Internal data path.

Data type: This term is used to refer to a class of data with common attributes, e.g., an 8-bit signed integer is a data type, as is a particular 32-bit floating-point representation.

DEC: Digital Equipment Corporation.

Decimal: A system in which numbers are represented by a sequence of digits selected from 0,1,2, . . . , 9. Each digit acts as a coefficient on successive powers of 10.

Deferred addressing: Addressing mode whereby the referenced register or location contains the address of the operand rather than the operand itself. Also called indirect addressing.

Delimiter: Any character that marks the beginning and/or end of a string of characters. Thus in /ABCD/ the "/" is the delimiter. In normal text, spaces and punctuation marks "delimit" words.

Descriptor: A data structure which contains the address of and other information about a data item, but not the data item itself. Sometimes used for passing arguments to procedures.

Destination: The main memory location or register where the result of an operation is to be placed.

Device driver: A procedure that interacts directly with a peripheral device and provides a high-level interface to the device. Normally, the operating system provides most device drivers.

Device register: A register that is associated with a peripheral device such as a printer, keyboard, or line clock. Such devices usually have a status register, a data register, and others if required.

Direct assignment: The use of the direct assignment directive to give a symbol a value, e.g., A = 4. The equal sign (= or ==) signifies direct assignment.

Direct memory access (DMA): The capability to transfer data directly between a peripheral device and the main memory with minimal CPU intervention.

Directives: An instruction recognized by the assembler that does not generate a machine code instruction. Rather, it causes the assembler to take some action, e.g., reserve a block of cells.

Directory: A special file that contains the names of other files. See Appendix D.6.3.

Disassembly: Translation of machine code into assembly language.

Displacement: The number of bytes that must be added to the current PC to arrive at the destination PC in a branch or to obtain the operand address in relative addressing. Also called the PC-relative address.

Displacement addressing: The addressing mode indicated by X(Rn) where X is any symbol, expression, or value. The contents of Rn is added to the value of X to determine the operand address.

Displacement deferred addressing: The addressing mode indicated by @X(Rn) where X is any symbol, expression, or value. The contents of Rn is added to the value of X to determine the address of the operand address.

Destination operand: The operand that is affected by the instruction. The second operand in two operand instructions, or the third in three operand instructions.

DMA: *See* Direct memory access.

Double precision: The representation of numbers using twice the normal cell length. Thus a double-precision two's complement number on the VAX-11 occupies two longwords or 64 bits.

EBCDIC: Extended Binary Coded Decimal Interchange Code. A character code system like ASCII but employing eight bits rather than seven.

Editor (text): A program that allows creation and modification to text files.

EDT: A text editor program often used under VAX/VMS to create and modify MACRO programs and other text files. *See* Appendix B.

Effective address: The actual address of the operand, as determined by the addressing mode at run-time.

Entry mask: The one-word mask at the beginning of every VAX procedure that indicates registers to be protected through the call, and any needed trap enabling. Created by the .ENTRY directive.

Entry point: The starting address for a subroutine or procedure. For a subroutine, the address of the first instruction. For a procedure, the address of the entry mask.

Event: The occurrence of some change in conditions or the detection of some activity that concerns the program, e.g., a keyboard entry, a page fault, or an attempt to execute an illegal instruction. Events are classified as either *exceptions* or *interrupts* on the VAX.

Exception: An event that is caused by the instruction being executed. Examples include illegal operand or instruction, a page fault, or arithmetic overflow. Results in transfer of control to a condition handler. *Contrast with* Interrupt.

Expansion: The process whereby the assembler replaces a macro reference by its defining instructions.

Expressions: An algebraic expression such as A + 2 or <X+2>/4. Such expressions are evaluated by the MACRO assembler and reduced to a value.

External reference: The use of a symbol that is not defined in the module being assembled.

Fault: An exception occurring in the middle of an instruction, but such that the instruction can be restarted after removal of the exception condition. The most common example is a page fault.

Fetch: Fetch refers to the CPU getting an instruction, operand, address, or any other data item out of the main memory. The CPU must send the address of the desired item to the main memory.

Field: A subunit of a record. For example, a record holding name, identification number, and score has three fields, one for each of these items.

File: A collection of data stored on a mass storage device. Often this data is a program in source, object, or load module form.

Flag: Any symbol, location, or register whose value or contents control some program action.

Floating-point: A system in which a number is represented as a fraction (mantissa) and an exponent, each stored separately.

Forward reference: The use of a symbol in a program before the place where it is defined.

FP: *See* Frame pointer.

Frame pointer (FP): The register (R13) that is set by CALLS or CALLG to point at the procedure call frame.

General register: One of the 16 registers defined by the VAX architecture for general programming and certain processor uses: R0, R1, . . . , R11, AP, FP, SP, and PC.

Giga: In computer usage, 2^{30}. In normal metric usage, 10^9.

Global: A symbol that can be referred to outside of the module in which it is defined is said to be global or external. *Contrast with* Local.

Hexadecimal (Hex): A positional system for number representation in which the base is 16. Used as a shorthand for binary, because hex to binary (and reverse) conversion is very easy. Bit strings of length 4 convert directly to hex digits.

High-level language: A computer programming language that allows a problem to be conveniently defined by the programmer, rather than in the machine language or assembly. FORTRAN, Pascal, and BASIC are examples of high-level languages.

I/O: *See* Input/output.

I/O system: The hardware elements that allow the computer to communicate with the outside world. Typically a bus and bus interface module.

Image: *See* Load module.

Immediate addressing: The addressing method indicated by #A or I^#A. The assembler places the value of A immediately after the instruction code.

In-line: Instructions or data that are placed directly following the previous item in memory, as opposed to being placed remotely.

Index addressing: The addressing method whereby the effective address of the operand is determined by adding an index value to a base address. On the VAX, index addressing is indicated by the [Ri] suffix on certain other addressing modes.

Indirect addressing: *See* Deferred addressing.

Input/output (I/O): The processes whereby data is transferred to (input) and from (output) the computer. This transfer can be to/from external storage devices, or keyboards, card readers, display devices, and so on.

Instruction: A bit pattern that has a particular meaning to the computer. Can also refer to the assembly mnemonics for a machine code instruction.

Instruction buffer: A temporary storage place within the CPU that holds the most recently fetched instruction.

Instruction fetch execution cycle: The process whereby an instruction is fetched, decoded, its operands fetched, and executed. The design of the machine is such that this process continues automatically once started and until HALT is encountered.

Instruction format: The machine language organization of the various parts of an instruction, e.g., opcode and operand specifiers.

Instruction set: A collective term meaning all of the machine code instructions that a particular computer recognizes.

Internal data path: The assembly of electronic components within the VAX-11 CPU that performs the arithmetic and logic operations and implements the various registers used by the CPU.

Internal label: A label that is defined within the module being assembled.

Interpreter: A program that translates a programming language, e.g., BASIC, into machine code one statement at a time for immediate execution. *Contrast with* Compiler.

Interrupt: In general, an asynchronous event that triggers an automatic transfer of control to a special "servicing" routine.

Interrupt priority level (IPL):   The value represented by bits $<20{:}16>$ in the PSL. An interrupt-enabled device with a higher priority (*See* Table 16.1) can interrupt the CPU.

Interrupt vector: The contents of a longword in the system control block, interpreted as the address of an interrupt servicing routine. Each interrupting device or event has a unique location in the SCB, and therefore a unique interrupt vector.

Invoke: To use a previously defined subroutine or procedure.

Label: An identifier for a memory location. In MACRO, a symbol appearing to the left of : or ::, or in the .ENTRY directive.

LC: *See* Location counter.

LCV: *See* Loop control variable.

Leading decisions: The technique whereby the decision whether to execute a repeated task is made before the task is encountered, e.g., the WHILE loop.

Leading separate numeric (LSN):   A decimal string storage method whereby ASCII decimal characters are stored with a preceding sign character.

Least significant bit (LSB):   The rightmost bit in a bit string.

Library: A collection of existing programs, subroutines, or macros.

Link (LINK):   Linking refers to the process of converting one or more object programs into a load module. LINK is the system-supplied program that does this.

Linkage: The method used to ensure proper return to the calling program after execution of a subroutine or procedure. On the VAX, the return point PC is stored on the stack for linkage.

Linked list: A data structure in which a pointer to the logically next item is stored along with each item is called a singly linked list. Doubly linked lists also store pointers to previous items.

Listing: The contents of the .LIS file created by the assembler. Contains the machine code and source code side by side, along with the address of each instruction and data item relative to the beginning of the module.

Load: Place a machine language program into the computer memory in preparation for its execution.

Load module: The machine code program properly linked for execution. Also called "memory image" or "image" module. The output of the LINK program with file name extension .EXE.

Local: A symbol that cannot be referred to outside of a limited area, e.g., a module, is said to be local. Sometimes called internal. *Contrast with* Global.

Local label: A label of the form n$. Recognized only within its local symbol block.

Local symbol block: A group of MACRO instructions delimited by nonlocal labels.

Location: Refers to a particular cell in main memory. Each location has a 32-bit address.

Location counter (LC): A pointer to the next available location for storage of translated code during the assembly process.

Logical order: The order of items in a list that reflects some logical scheme, e.g., alphabetical or numerical order, or order implied by a linked list. May be different from physical order in memory.

Longword: A unit of information that is 32 bits in length. Also a memory cell of this length.

Loop control variable (LCV): A register or memory location that is used to determine exit conditions from a loop.

LSB: *See* Least significant bit.

LSN: *See* Leading separate numeric.

Machine language (Code): Instructions or a program expressed as binary (or equivalent octal or hex) codes recognized directly by the computer hardware. Also called native code.

MACRO: The assembly language for VAX computers.

Macro instruction: A group of instructions that can be introduced into the assembly code by giving a single instruction in the assembly source program. Some macros, e.g., $EXIT__S, are supplied by the system. Others are written by the programmer to meet special needs. *See* Chapter 10.

Main memory unit (MMU): The collection of cells where data and program instructions are stored. Also called central memory.

Mask: A bit pattern that is used as the source operand in certain instructions, such as BISL. The pattern is selected to have a 0 or a 1 in each position that produces the desired effect, e.g., test, set, or clear, in the corresponding bit of the destination.

Mass storage device: A device for permanent storage of data or programs accessible by the computer. Disk storage units are the most common. Also called secondary storage.

Memory: *See* Main memory unit (MMU).

Memory management system: The hardware and software that controls placement of programs and data in physical memory and converts virtual addresses to physical addresses.

Microprogrammed: A term applied to the type of computer in which the instructions are implemented as a low-level program called microcode. Microcode is stored in the control store and is executed by the microsequencer.

Microsequencer: The hardware element that interprets the microcode to carry out an instruction.

Minuend: The number from which another number (the subtrahend) is to be subtracted in a subtraction problem, e.g., in A − B, A is the minuend and B is the subtrahend.

MMU: *See* Main memory unit.

Mnemonic: As used in assembly programming, a short string of alphabetical characters that represent an opcode e.g., MOVL, and ADDB.

Mode: The description of an addressing method in machine and assembly language programming. Also, on the VAX-11, the privilege level that a program operates under. The least privileged is User mode, followed by Executive, Supervisor, and Kernel mode. Operating system programs run at the higher privilege modes.

Module: An independent group of instructions such as a subroutine or program.

Most significant bit (MSB): The leftmost bit in a bit string.

MSB: *See* Most significant bit.

Negation: The mathematical operation of changing the sign of a number, e.g., negating 2 yields -2, and negating -3 yields 3. In the two's complement number system, negation is accomplished by finding the two's complement.

Nibble: A unit of information four bits in length. Half of a byte.

Normalize: A process that adjusts the exponent in floating-point number such that the point is immediately to the left of the most significant nonzero digit.

Null byte: A byte containing all zeros, i.e., the ASCII NUL character.

Null-terminated string: A character string stored in sequential bytes of memory and followed by a null byte.

Numeric string: The method of storing numbers where the digit codes are stored in separate, contiguous bytes. Leading separate numeric is an example.

Object program (module): A program expressed as machine code but not linked for execution. The output of the assembler with file name extension .OBJ.

Octal: A positional system for number representation in which the base is 8. Used as a shorthand for binary, because octal to binary (and reverse) conversion is very easy. Bit strings of length 3 convert directly to octal digits.

Offset: In index addressing, offset is the distance in bytes between the base address and the desired address. Offset is also used to mean an address given relative to a load point of a module.

One's complement: The bit pattern formed by changing all 1's to 0's and all 0's to 1's in a binary number. Also the number system that uses the one's complement of positives to represent the negatives.

Opcode: The numerical code, often expressed in hexadecimal, that represents a particular machine language instruction.

Operand: The data item referred to in an instruction.

Operand specifier: The numerical code, often expressed in hexadecimal, that indicates how the operand is to be found.

Operating system: The program that provides overall control of the computer. It processes user commands such as RUN, MACRO, and DIR. It also keeps track of user files, and performs many other tasks necessary for convenient use of the computer. *See* Appendix D.1.

Operation code: *See* Opcode.

Overflow (signed overflow): An error condition caused by an arithmetic operation that invalidates the sign bit. Causes the V condition code to be set. *See also* Unsigned overflow.

Packed decimal: A method of storing decimal numbers whereby the digit values, represented in binary, are used as four-bit codes and are stored two per byte, followed by a sign code.

Page fault: The exception caused by referencing a virtual address that is not currently in physical main memory. The memory management system automatically reads in the needed page (512 bytes) and removes the exception.

Paging: The process of bringing in one page (512 bytes) of program or data from secondary memory into main memory. This is done automatically by the memory management system whenever a page fault is detected.

Parity: The setting or clearing of the MSB in a byte containing a character code so that the number of 1-bits is even (even parity) or odd (odd parity). This allows error checking after transmission.

PC: *See* Program counter.

PC relative addressing: *See* Relative addressing.

PDP-11: A computer manufactured by Digital Equipment Corporation that is the predecessor of the VAX-11.

Peripheral devices: Components of a computer system other than the CPU and main memory unit. Printers, mass storage devices, and keyboards are peripheral devices.

Physical address: The address used by the hardware to identify a location in physical memory. Comprises a page number and a byte address within the page.

Physical address space: The set of all possible addresses for physical main memory and I/O device registers. On the VAX, all 30-bit numbers.

Physical memory: The actual hardware main memory unit. *Contrast with* Virtual memory.

Place value: In a positional number system, the weight associated with a digit in a particular position. The base raised to a power equal to the digital position index.

Pointer: The register or location containing the address of the operand in deferred addressing.

Polling: Repeated checking of a peripheral device such as a printer or keyboard to see if it is ready to receive data from or send data to the CPU.

Pop: Remove an item from the top of a stack.

Position independent code: A segment of machine code that could be moved to a different position in virtual memory, without modification, and work properly.

Positional notation: A means for representing a number in which each digit position implies a definite position or place value. Decimal, binary, octal, and hexadecimal are examples.

Privileged: A status mode assigned to a process on the VAX computer that allows certain restricted instructions to be executed. *See also* Mode.

Procedure (VAX procedure): A special type of subroutine on the VAX that is invoked by the CALLG and CALLS instructions.

Process space: The lower half of virtual address space on the VAX. All user programs operate in process space. *Contrast with* System space.

Processor status word/longword (PSW/PSL): The PSL is a special register within the CPU that contains the status of the CPU. This includes the condition codes, trap bit, processor priority bits, and certain other information. The two low bytes of PSL are referred to as the processor status word (PSW).

Program counter (PC): Register 15, used to hold the address of the next instruction to be executed.

Program counter addressing: Addressing modes 8 through F used with R15 (PC) as the register. See Table 12.4.

Programmed I/O: I/O that is achieved by direct polling of device status registers and interaction with device data registers.

Prologue: The comment section at the beginning of a program module defining its purpose, data, and other information.

Pseudocode: A method of expressing an algorithm that uses normal language with IF, THEN, ELSE, and WHILE clauses. Indentation is used to "set off" the clauses. An alternative to flowcharting.

Pseudo-ops: Another term for an assembler directive. *See* Directive.

PSL: *See* Processor status longword.

PSW: *See* Processor status word.

Push: Place an item on top of a stack.

Quadword: A unit of information 64-bits in length. Also eight contiguous bytes in main memory.

Queue: A data structure in which the last item entered is the last to be removed.

Radix control: A prefix notation in assembly mnemonics that explicitly gives the base (radix) of the following number. For example, each of the following represent the same number: ^D14 (decimal); ^XE (hexadecimal); ^O16 (octal); and ^B1110 (binary).

Real line: A line extending from minus to plus infinity on which every real number can be placed.

Recursive: When a mathematical function, a subroutine, or a procedure is defined in terms of itself.

Reference: The use of a symbol, macro, or subroutine.

Register: Most often this refers to one of the sixteen general registers in the CPU: R0, R1, . . . , R11, AP, FP, SP, and PC. Also used in a general sense to mean high-speed electronic elements within the computer or peripheral devices that can hold a bit pattern. These are often used for special purposes and are distinct from the main memory unit.

Register addressing: The addressing mode in which the operand is in a general register.

Register deferred addressing: The addressing mode in which the operand address is in a general register.

Register protection: The act of placing the contents of registers on the user stack so the registers can be used in a procedure of subroutine and restored to their pre-call values upon return.

Relative addressing: The addressing method indicated by a symbol, e.g., A. The assembler places the PC-relative address of the operand immediately after the addressing mode code.

Relative deferred addressing: The addressing method indicated by @*symbol*. Like relative addressing, but the immediate value gives the PC-relative address of the operand's address.

Relocation: The process whereby the addresses in the object program are adjusted to reflect the locations in virtual address space where the program is to be placed for execution. Performed by LINK.

Repeat block: An assembler construct in which a group of assembler instructions are to be repeated, e.g., .IRP, and .IRPC.

Representation: The manner in which a number is represented, e.g., binary, decimal, hexadecimal, or Roman numerals.

Rotate left/right: Shifting a bit pattern in a memory cell or register such that the bits shifting out of one end are shifted into the opposite end in a circular manner.

Routine start: When the VAX processor starts execution of a procedure two bytes beyond the entry point in order to bypass the entry mask.

Row-major: A one-dimensional arrangement of a two-dimensional array in which all elements of the first row are followed by those of the second row, and so on.

Run-time address: The address of an instruction or data item when the program is executed. The .EXE file has run-time addresses.

Second-level indirect addressing: Any addressing method which begins with the address of the address of the operand, e.g., autoincrement deferred.

Secondary memory: Storage devices used to store portions of programs and data not currently needed in physical main memory. Usually a disk storage unit.

Servicing routine: A group of instructions that carries out certain actions when an interrupt or exception occurs.

Shift left/right: Moving a bit pattern left or right in a memory cell or register. *See also* Arithmetic shift and Rotate left/right.

Short literal addressing: When the operand is embedded in the mode code and register fields of the operand specifier. Only a limited range of values can be accommodated with this mode.

Side effect: When a subroutine, procedure, or macro has an effect on memory or registers other than the intended effect.

Sign bit: The MSB in a signed integer data type. Note that while the MSB is always referred to as the sign bit, it is not always restricted to that role. When the cell is not viewed as a signed integer, it has no special significance. Also the 15th bit in floating-point representation.

Sign extension: The process of replicating the MSB of two's complement integer when it is moved into a larger cell. This ensures an arithmetically correct conversion. For example, CVTBL does sign extension.

Sign magnitude: A numerical representation scheme wherein the negative values are formed by setting the sign bit, and magnitudes are represented identically regardless of sign.

Signed branches: Those branch instructions intended for use with signed integers: BGTR, BLSS, BGEQ, and BLEQ.

Signed number: The representation of a number in a system that allows both positive and negative values, such as the two's complement system. On the VAX, a two's complement number.

Signed overflow: *See* Overflow.

Software interrupt: A programmed transfer of control that is implemented using the vectoring process of interrupts. Requires use of privileged instructions on the VAX. *See also* Asynchronous system trap.

Source program: A program in the form originally expressed by the programmer, e.g., a MACRO program. Usually saved with file name extension .MAR.

SP (stack pointer): *See* Stack pointer.

Stack: A data structure in which the last item entered is the next available for removal. A register usually acts as a pointer to the most recently entered item, which is said to be on "top" of the stack. *See* User stack.

Stack frame: *See* Call frame.

Stack pointer (SP): Register 14, used as a pointer for the user stack.

Storage cell: A group of contiguous bytes in memory used to store a particular data type, e.g., byte, word, or longword.

Store: This term refers to the CPU sending a data item to the main memory. The CPU also has to send the address where it is to be stored.

String: Usually just a shorter way of saying character string. However, other kinds of strings are possible, e.g., bit strings.

Subroutine: A separate program module to which control is transferred for performance of a particular task. After completion, control is returned to the calling point. *See also* Procedure.

Subtrahend: The number to be subtracted in a subtraction problem, i.e., in A − B, B is the subtrahend and A is the minuend.

Summand: One of the numbers to be added to an addition problem.

Symbolic debugger: The system program used to debug programs under VMS. Symbolic means that program-defined symbols can be referenced during debugging.

Symbol table: The list of all symbols used or defined in an assembly program, along with the values assigned to each. Included in the .LIS file.

Synchronous: Synchronized with the program. For example, an event that is caused by a particular instruction is a synchronous event.

System program: A program that is provided to all users of a computer as part of the operating system, e.g., the MACRO assembler and EDT.

System program chart: A chart that shows the hierarchy among various program modules.

System space: The upper half of the VAX virtual address space. Used by the operating system.

Table: In programming, this refers to a one-dimensional array in which each element is a record composed of several fields. Similar to a two-dimensional array except that items in a record can be of different types whereas elements in an array are all of the same type.

Trailing decisions: A loop programming technique wherein the first decision whether to repeat the loop is made after completing the loop one time. The REPEAT-UNTIL control structure.

Translate: To convert a program from its source form to machine code. If the source is assembly language, the translation is called *assembly*.

Trap: An exception that occurs after the instruction execution is complete, e.g., integer overflow. *See also* Exception.

Two's complement: The number system used on the VAX-11 and other computers to represent signed integers. Also used as a synonym for the verb "to negate" in the two's complement system.

UNIBUS: A particular implementation of the bus concept. A Digital Equipment Corporation trademark.

UNIX: An operating system for VAX-11 (and other) computers developed by Bell Laboratories.

Unprivileged: Not having sufficient privilege to execute certain instructions. On the VAX-11, a user-mode process is unprivileged. *See* Mode.

Unsigned branch: Those branch instructions intended for use with unsigned integers only: BGTRU, BLSSU, BLEQU, and BGEQU.

Unsigned number: The representation of a number in a system that does not allow for a sign. The positional binary system for positive integers is an example.

Unsigned overflow: Error condition caused by a carry out of, or a borrow into, the MSB, setting the C condition code.

User stack: The stack used by programs operating in user mode on the VAX. SP is the pointer, and many VAX instructions employ this stack. *See also* Mode.

Utilities: Programs that perform frequently needed operations such as copying files. Usually provided by the operating system.

VAX procedure: *See* Procedure.

VAX/VMS: An operating system supplied by Digital Equipment Corporation for VAX-11 computers.

Vectoring: Transferring to a servicing routine through the use of special memory locations containing the routine address. On the VAX, these special memory locations are in the system control block (SCB).

Virtual address: The address referred to by the assembly and machine code. These are translated to physical main memory addresses by the memory management system.

Virtual address space: The collection of all legal virtual addresses. On the VAX-11 0 to $2^{32}-1$.

Virtual memory: The architectural concept that allows for use of virtual addresses in programs. Without the virtual memory concept, programs would have to use physical addresses.

VMS: *See* VAX/VMS.

Word: On the VAX-11, a unit of memory two bytes in length, or a unit of information this length. Otherwise, used to refer to the fundamental unit of digital information processed by a particular computer. By this definition, the VAX-11 has 32-bit words, while the PDP-11 has 16-bit words, and the CDC Cyber computers have 60-bit words.

Word length: The number of bits in the fundamental unit of a computer's memory: 16 on the PDP-11, and 32 on the VAX-11.

Zero extend: The process of filling the higher order bits with zeros when a smaller data type is placed into a larger cell. For example, MOVZBL does zero extend. Unsigned conversion to a larger integer data.

Answers to Selected Exercises

Chapter 1

4. (d) COPY firstfile.ext,secondfile.ext newfile.ext

Chapter 2

1. (a) $11110111_2 = 1*2^7 + 1*2^6 + 1*2^5 + 1*2^4 + 0*2^3 + 1*2^2 + 1*2^1 + 1*2^0$
$$= 128 + 64 + 32 + 16 + 0 + 4 + 2 + 1$$
$$= 247_{10}$$
—using the double dabble technique.

(b) $1010_2 = 1 \quad 0 \quad 1 \quad 0$

$1 \quad 2 \quad 5 \quad 10 = 10_{10}$

2. (c)
```
  1111
+ 111
10110₂
```
(f)
```
 1100100
-101111
0110101₂
```

3. (b) 1111101000_2

Hexadecimal: $11 \mid 1110 \mid 1000$
$\qquad\qquad\quad 3 \mid \ E \ \mid \ 8 = 3E8_{16}$

Decimal: $3*16^2 + 14*16^1 + 8*16^0 = 1000_{10}$

4. (c) 384_{10}

	Subtraction Method		Division Method
Hexadecimal:	$384 - 256 = 128$	$d2 = 1$	$384/16 = 24$ remainder $= 0$
	$128 - 16 \ = 112$		$24/16 \ = 1$ remainder $= 8$
	$112 - 16 \ = \ 96$		$1/16 \ \ = 0$ remainder $= 1$
	$96 - 16 \ = \ 80$		
	$80 - 16 \ = \ 64$		$384_{10} \ = 180_{16}$
	$64 - 16 \ = \ 48$		
	$48 - 16 \ = \ 32$		
	$32 - 16 \ = \ 16$		
	$16 - 16 \ = \ \ 0$	$d1 = 8$	
	0	$d0 = 0$	
	$384_{10} = 180_{16}$		

	Subtraction Method		Division Method	
Binary:	$384 - 256 = 128$	$d8 = 1$	$384/2 = 192$	remainder $= 0$
	$128 - 128 = 0$	$d7 = 1$	$192/2 = 96$	remainder $= 0$
	64	$d6 = 0$	$96/2 = 48$	remainder $= 0$
	32	$d5 = 0$	$48/2 = 24$	remainder $= 0$
	16	$d4 = 0$	$24/2 = 12$	remainder $= 0$
	8	$d3 = 0$	$12/2 = 6$	remainder $= 0$
	4	$d2 = 0$	$6/2 = 3$	remainder $= 0$
	2	$d1 = 0$	$3/2 = 1$	remainder $= 1$
	0	$d0 = 0$	$1/2 = 0$	remainder $= 1$
	$384_{10} = 110000000_2$		$384_{10} = 110000000_{22}$	

5. (a) CC_{16}
Decimal: $12*16^1 + 12*16^0 = 204_{10}$
Binary: C $\mid$ C $\mid$
1100 $\mid$ 1100 $\mid$ $= 11001100_2$

6. (b) 147_8
Decimal: $1*8^2 + 4*8^1 + 7*8^0 =$
64 + 32 + 7 $=$ 103_{10}
Binary: 1 $\mid$ 4 $\mid$ 7 $\mid$
1 $\mid$ 100 $\mid$ 111 $\mid$ $= 1100111_2$

7. (e)   1234
+9876
$AAAA_{16}$

8. (d)   375
-177
176_8

11. (g) -195_{16}
195_{10} in Hexadecimal = $0000\ 00C3_{16}$
Binary = $0000\ 0000\ 0000\ 0000\ 0000\ 0000\ 1100\ 0011_2$
Two's Complement = $1111\ 1111\ 1111\ 1111\ 1111\ 1111\ 0011\ 1101_2$
Two's Complement Hex = $FFFFFF3D_{16}$

12. (b) $80006DB6_{16}$ (NOTE: MSB indicates a negative value, therefore negate before conversion)
Binary = $1000\ 0000\ 0000\ 0000\ 0110\ 1101\ 1011\ 0110_2$
Two's Complement = $0111\ 1111\ 1111\ 1111\ 1001\ 0010\ 0100\ 1010_2$
Hexadecimal = $7FFF924A_{16}$
Decimal = 2147455562_{10}
Signed = -2147455562_{10}

13. (e)   8000000F
$-1000000F$
7000000F   Overflow is indicated by the positive result. (Subtracting a positive value from a negative value should always yield a negative result.)

  (f)   7000000F
$-1000000F$
60000000   No Overflow, result is positive.

Chapter 3

1. (a) 29652_{10}

Hexidecimal: 000073D4   Binary: 0000 0000 0000 0000 0111 0011 1101 0100

Address	Contents	Contents
00	D4	1101 0100
01	73	0111 0011
02	00	0000 0000
03	00	0000 0000

2. (e) $00A1_{16}$

8. (b) $PC = 0103_{16}$

Chapter 4

1.

Instruction		Machine Code		
(a) MOVL	R5,R3	53	55	D0
(g) ADDL	SP,AP	5C	5E	C0

2.

Machine Code			Instruction	
(f) 57	53	D0	MOVL	R3,R7

6. (e) $R0 = 8$

8. (c) $2(X + Y)$

```
                .TITLE   EX. 4.8C
                .ENTRY   START, 0
        ;
        ; WITH X=25, Y=10
        ; PROGRAM WILL COMPUTE 2(X+Y)
        ;
        ; ASSUME: R1 = 25
        ;         R2 = 10
        ;
        ; COMPUTE X+Y
        ;
                ADDL     R1,R2
        ;
        ; COMPUTE 2(X+Y)
        ;
                ADDL     R2,R2
        ;
                $EXIT_S
                .END     START
```

Chapter 5

1.

	BGTRU	BLSSU	BLEQU	BGEQU	BEQLU	BNEQU	BRB
(c)	X			X		X	X

2. (e) 119E − (11A2 + 2) = FA = Displacement
Therefore, the instruction is FA13

4. *Hint:* Using the ideas from the bubble sort algorithm, set up a loop that executes 9 times. In the body of the loop, compare R1 to R2, R2 to R3, etc., exchanging if necessary.

8. α = address of branch instruction.
β = address of destination.
displacement = β − (α + 3)

9. (d) R2 = 9

10. (g) BLSSU displacement = −5
Branch 3 bytes backward from the location where the opcode is stored.

11. (h) R3 = 220
address 220 = 701

16. After execution of instruction at A, the INCL instruction becomes a BRB instruction back to the first instruction, resulting in an endless loop.

Chapter 6

1.

	BGTR	BGTRU	BLEQ	BLEQU	BGEQ	BGEQU	BLSS	BLSSU
(e)			X	X			X	X
	BEQL	BEQLU	BNEQ	BNEQU	BVS	BCS	BVC	BCC
			X	X		X	X	
	BGTR	BGTRU	BLEQ	BLEQU	BGEQ	BGEQU	BLSS	BLSSU
(j)		X	X			X	X	
	BEQL	BEQLU	BNEQ	BNEQU	BVS	BCS	BVC	BCC
			X	X			X	X

2. (e) NZVC = 1001
(j) NZVC = 1000

3.

	BGTR	BGTRU	BLEQ	BLEQU	BGEQ	BGEQU	BLSS	BLSSU
(e)			X	X			X	X
	BEQL	BEQLU	BNEQ	BNEQU	BVS	BCS	BVC	BCC
			X	X		X	X	
	BGTR	BGTRU	BLEQ	BLEQU	BGEQ	BGEQU	BLSS	BLSSU
(j)	X	X			X	X		
	BEQL	BEQLU	BNEQ	BNEQU	BVS	BCS	BVC	BCC
			X	X	X			X

8. *Hint:* Add the words 32 bits at a time, adding the carry to the next higher longword. Thus, six instructions are needed including three ADWC's.

10.

```
        BVS    OVFL
        BGEQ   L1
        BRB    OUT
OVFL:   BLSS   L1
OUT:
```

Chapter 7

1. (f) BEL or ^G (control key and G)

2. (h) $02_{16} = 00000010_2$
(j) $3C_{16} = 00111100_2$

3. (e) "01"<CR><LF>

9.

	BITB	BICB	BISB	MCOMB	XORB
(e)	NZVC = 01??	00000000	11111111	00000000	11111111

10.

	Register	New Value	Addr	New Value
(f)	—	—	0500	08
			0501	00
			0502	00
			0503	00
(i)	R3	502	050B	02
	R2	50C		

11. (b)

	R4	500	050B	00

Chapter 8

1. (d) An input line is accepted in the .TTYIN buffer, and the first character is placed in R0, then into B. The .PUTSTR will initiate printing of memory contents beginning at address B, stopping at the first byte containing a null character (00). The input character is therefore printed, along with others found until the null character is reached.

13. Octal Input:

```
        :
        SUBB    #^X30,R0        ;CONVERT ASCII TO BINARY.
        BLSSU   L3              ;CODE TOO LOW FOR OCTAL DIGIT.
        CMPB    R0,#^X08        ;CHECK UPPER BOUND.
        BLSSU   L2              ;VALID OCTAL CHARACTER.
        BRW     L3              ;INVALID OCTAL CHARACTER.
L2:     MULL    #^X8,R1         ;MULTIPLY CURRENT BY OCTAL 10.
        :
```

Octal Output:

```
        :
        MOVL    #11,R2          ;INITIALIZE LCV (11 DIGITS)
        :
L1:     MOVL    #-1,R4          ;INITIALIZE DIGIT VALUE.
L2:     INCL    R4              ;UPDATE DIGIT VALUE.
        SUBL    (R1),R0         ;SUBTRACT PLACE VALUE
        BGEQU   L2              ;   UNTIL OVER SUBTRACTED.
        ADDL    (R1)+,R0        ;CORRECT FOR OVER SUBTRACT.
        ADDB    #^X30,R4        ;CONVERT TO ASCII.
        MOVB    R4,(R3)+        ;STORE CHAR IN PRINT ARRAY.
        SOBGTR  R2,L1           ;REPEAT FOR NEXT DIGIT.
        :
```

(continued next page)

```
PV: .LONG    ^010000000000
    .LONG    ^01000000000
    .LONG    ^0100000000
    .LONG    ^010000000
    .LONG    ^01000000
    .LONG    ^0100000
    .LONG    ^010000
    .LONG    ^01000
    .LONG    ^0100
    .LONG    ^010
    .LONG    ^01
A:  .BLKB    11                ;RESULT ARRAY.
    .BYTE    0                 ;NULL CHAR TO TURN OFF .PUTSTR
```

Chapter 9

6. (c) 0504 = 00000000 (registers unaffected)

(i) R1 = 50C   0500 = 00000500

11. (d)

```
ADD:
;
; R1 CONTAINS THE ADDRESS OF THE FOLLOWING LIST OF ARGUMENTS
;
;   R1 =>  ARG1    0  OFFSET
;          ARG2    4
;          ARG3    8
;
    ADDL    (R1)+,(R1)       ; ARG2 = ARG1 + ARG2
    ADDL    (R1)+,(R1)       ; ARG3 = ARG2 + ARG3
    RSB
    .ENTRY   START,0
    MOVL     #ARG,R1         ;LOAD PTR TO ARGUMENT.
    BSBW     ADD            ;CALL ADD ROUTINE.
    $EXIT_S
ARG: .LONG    10,20
     .BLKL    1
     .END START
```

Chapter 10

1.

```
B = 16                    ; CHANGE TO 10 FOR DECIMAL.

D = 10-<<B-10>/3>   ; D IS NUMBER OF DIGITS-10 OR 8.
S = 7 * <<B-10>/3>  ; SETS PV TO PV10 IF B = 10
PV = PV10 + S       ;  OR PV16 IF B = 16
```

(continued next page)

```
PV10:  .LONG  1000000000
       .LONG  100000000
       .LONG  10000000
       .LONG  1000000
       .LONG  100000
       .LONG  10000
       .LONG  1000
       .LONG  100
       .LONG  10
       .LONG  1
PV16:  .LONG  ^X10000000
       .LONG  ^X1000000
       .LONG  ^X100000
       .LONG  ^X10000
       .LONG  ^X1000
       .LONG  ^X100
       .LONG  ^X10
       .LONG  ^X1
```

```
4.     .MACRO  XCHG   QUAD1, QUAD2      ;START OF MACRO DEF.
               MOVL   QUAD1, R0         ; STORE QUAD 1 IN
               MOVL   QUAD1+4,R1        ;   TEMP REG STORAGE.
               MOVL   QUAD2, QUAD1      ; MOVE QUAD 2 INTO
               MOVL   QUAD2+4, QUAD1+4  ;   QUAD 1.
               MOVL   R0, QUAD2         ; MOVE SAVED QUAD 1
               MOVL   R1, QUAD2+4       ;   INTO QUAD 2.
       .ENDM   XCHG                     ;END OF MACRO DEF.
```

```
9. (a)  .MACRO  PUSHN, ARY, N
                MOVL   #ARY, R1
                MOVL   N, R0
                MOVL   (R1)+,-(SP)
                SOBGTR R0, .-6
        .ENDM   PUSHN
```

12. (d) Since Z is defined, the condition for the outer IF structure is false. Therefore, nothing assembles.

Chapter 11

8. (b) No Modifications required.

   (d)
```
A:     .WORD  4

       MOVAL  A, R1
       ADDL   (R1), R3
```

Chapter 12

1. (c) R0 = 00000504
   (e) R0 = 00000504

2. (c) R3 = 000008AA
   (e) R2 = 0000052C
       R3 = EEEE1AAD

```
11.  L1:    CLRW    COUNT                ;RESET CHAR COUNT.
             MOVL    R2, P(R1)            ;STORE STRING ADDRESS.
             TSTB    (R2)+                ;LEAVE FIRST BYTE FOR COUNT.
                :
             MOVB    RO, (R2)+            ;STORE CHARACTER.
             INCW    COUNT                ;UPDATE CHAR COUNT.
                :
        EOS: MOVB    COUNT, @P(R1)        ;STORE COUNT IN FIRST BYTE.
             TSTL    (R1)+                ;INCREMENT P INDEX.
        ; TO PRINT.
        L3:  MOVL    P(R1), R2            ;GET ADDRESS OF STRING.
             MOVB    (R2)+, R3            ;PUT NO. OF CHARS IN R3.
        PR:  MOVB    (R2)+, RO            ;GET CHAR.
                :
             SOBGTR R3, PR                ;DO COUNT TIMES.
        COUNT: .BLKW   1
```

Chapter 13

```
2.          .TITLE   EXPONENTIAL RECURSION.

            .ENTRY   START, 0
            MOVL     X,-(SP)
            MOVL     N,-(SP)
            BSBW     PWR
            MOVL     (SP),RO
            $EXIT_S
      X:    .LONG    16
      N:    .LONG    3
      PWR:  TSTL     4(SP)
            BNEQ     ELSE
      THEN: MOVL     #1,4(SP)
            BRB      DONE
      ;SET UP STACK FOR A CALL
      ;OF PWR (N-1)
      ELSE: MOVL     4(SP),RO
            DECL     RO
            MOVL     8(SP),-(SP)
            MOVL     RO,-(SP)
            BSBW     PWR
      ;(SP) NOW HAS X TO SOME PWR LESS
      ;THAN N, SO MULTIPLY (SP) BY 4(SP)
      ;TO GET X TO THE NEXT HIGHER POWER.
            MOVL     (SP)+, R1
            MOVL     (SP)+, RO
            MULL     RO,R1
            MOVL     R1,4(SP)
      DONE: RSB
            .END     START
```

Chapter 14

1. (a) 686_{10} $= 1010101110_2 = 0.101010111 \times 2^{1010}$
   SIGN $= 0$
   FRACTION $= 0101011100000000000000000$ (as stored)
   EXPONENT $= 10000111$ (as stored)
   LONGWORD $= 8000\ 452B$

   (f) *Hint:* Use subtraction with negative powers of 2 to convert to binary, then normalize.
   -3×10^{-8} $= 0.100000001101100101011001 \times 2^{-11000}$
   SIGN $= 1$
   FRACTION $= 00000001101100101011001$ (as stored)
   EXPONENT $= 01101000$ (as stored)
   LONGWORD $= D959\ B400$

   (h) 0.75 $= 0.11 \times 2^{-0}$
   SIGN $= 0$
   FRACTION $= 10000000000000000000000$ (as stored)
   EXPONENT $= 10000000$ (as stored)
   LONGWORD $= 0000\ 4040$

2. (d) $E400\ 4492$
   SIGN $= 0$
   EXPONENT $= 10001001$ (as stored)
   FRACTION $= 00100101110010000000000$ (as stored)
                  $= 0.29378125 \times 10^3$

   (i) $3FFF\ FFFF$
   SIGN $= 1$
   EXPONENT $= 11111111$
   FRACTION $= 11111111001111111111111111$
                  $= -1.6964271 \times 10^{38}$

Chapter 15

	Leading Numeric String	Packed Decimal String
1. (a) $1985 =$	2B	01
	31	98
	39	5C
	38	
	35	
(d) $-1207 =$	2D	01
	31	20
	32	7D
	30	
	37	

4. The differences in results are caused by the lack of precision in the floating-point representation. 1234567890 requires 10 decimal digits. Since floating-point only allows 24 bits of fractional storage, resulting in 7 decimal digits accuracy, a mapping error occurs.

Chapter 16

6.

```
            .TITLE EXERCISE .16.6
            .MACRO TTYOUT.A
            .IF   NB   <A>
            MOVL   A.RO
            .ENDC
            BSBW   WRITE
            .ENDM TTYOUT
L1:         .ASCII/Q/
            .ENTRY   START.0
            TTYOUT  #^A'B'
            TTYOUT  L1
            MOVB    #^A'W'.RO
            TTYOUT
            $EXIT_S
            $IODEF
WRITE:
            MOVB   RO.OUT_BUF
            TSTB   IS_ASSIGNED
            BNEQ   20$
            INCB   IS_ASSIGNED
            $ASSIGN_S DEVNAM=TERM_NAME.CHAN=TERM_CHAN
            BLBS   RO.10$
            BRW    ERROR
10$:        MOVW   #SS$_NORMAL.OUT_IOSB
20$:        TSTW   OUT_IOSB
            BEQL   20$
            CMPW   OUT_IOSB.#SS$_NORMAL
            BEQL   30$
            BRW    ERROR
30$:        $QIO_S CHAN=TERM_CHAN.-
                   FUNC = #IO$_WRITEVBLK.-
                   IOSB = OUT_IOSB.-
                   P1   = OUT_BUF.-
                   P2   = #1
            BLBS    RO.40$
            BRW     ERROR
40$:        RSB
ERROR:      .PUTSTR ERR_MSG
            RSB
IS_ASSIGNED:.BYTE  0
ERR_MSG:.ASCIZ/IO ERROR/
TERM_NAME:.ASCID/SYS$INPUT/
TERM_CHAN:.BLKW 1
OUT_IOSB: .BLKQ  1
OUT_BUF:  .BLKB  1
            .END START
```

11. For the VAX 11/730, we get 19.00 seconds, 19.50 seconds, and 26.86 seconds for DT = 1.0 second, 0.10 second, and 0.01 second, respectively. The differences are due to time required for more interrupts when DT is too small. An alternate timing method is to invoke $GETTIM_S before and after, and subtract. This gives 18.31 seconds.

Chapter 17

3. Replace the instruction at L3 with:

```
L3:   MOVAB   TABLE[R2],MY_RAB+RAB$L_RBF
```

Also, remove the terminal echo and make REC_SIZE and T_SIZE equal.

Index

N = negative

Z = zero

V = Overflow

C = carry

Left table

OP	Mnemonic	Description	Arguments	N Z V C
9D	ACBB	Add compare and branch byte	limit.rb, add.rb, index.mb, displ.bw	0 0 0 0
6F	ACBD	Add compare and branch D_floating	limit.rd, add.rd, index.md, displ.bw	
4F	ACBF	Add compare and branch F_floating	limit.rf, add.rf, index.mf, displ.bw	
4FFD	ACBG	Add compare and branch G_floating	limit.rg, add.rg, index.mg, displ.bw	
6FFD	ACBH	Add compare and branch H_floating	limit.rh, add.rh, index.mh, displ.bw	
F1	ACBL	Add compare and branch long	limit.rl, add.rl, index.ml, displ.bw	
3D	ACBW	Add compare and branch word	limit.rw, add.rw, index.mw, displ.bw	
58	ADAWI	Add aligned word interlocked	add.rw, sum.mw	
80	ADDB2	Add byte 2-operand	add.rb, sum.mb	
81	ADDB3	Add byte 3-operand	add1.rb, add2.rb, sum.wb	
60	ADDD2	Add D_floating 2-operand	add.rd, sum.md	
61	ADDD3	Add D_floating 3-operand	add1.rd, add2.rd, sum.wd	
40	ADDF2	Add F_floating 2-operand	add.rf, sum.mf	
41	ADDF3	Add F_floating 3-operand	add1.rf, add2.rf, sum.wf	
40FD	ADDG2	Add G_floating 2-operand	add.rg, sum.mg	
41FD	ADDG3	Add G_floating 3-operand	add1.rg, add2.rg, sum.wg	
60FD	ADDH2	Add H_floating 2-operand	add.rh, sum.mh	
61FD	ADDH3	Add H_floating 3-operand	add1.rh, add2.rh, sum.wh	
C0	ADDL2	Add long 2-operand	add.rl, sum.ml	
C1	ADDL3	Add long 3-operand	add1.rl, add2.rl, sum.wl	
20	ADDP4	Add packed 4-operand	addlen1.rw, addaddr1.ab, sumlen.rw, sumaddr.ab, [R0-3.wl]	
21	ADDP6	Add packed 6-operand	addlen1.rw, addaddr1.ab, addlen2.rw, addaddr2.ab, sumlen.rw, sumaddr.ab, [R0-5.wl]	
A0	ADDW2	Add word 2-operand	add.rw, sum.mw	
A1	ADDW3	Add word 3-operand	add1.rw, add2.rw, sum.ww	
D8	ADWC	Add with carry	add.rl, sum.ml	
F3	AOBLEQ	Add one and branch on less or equal	limit.rl, index.ml, displ.bb	
F2	AOBLSS	Add one and branch on less	limit.rl, index.ml, displ.bb	
78	ASHL	Arithmetic shift long	cnt.rb, src.rl, dst.wl	
79	ASHQ	Arithmetic shift quad	cnt.rb, src.rq, dst.wq	
F8	ASHP	Arithmetic shift and round packed	cnt.rb, srclen.rw, srcaddr.ab, round.rb, dstlen.rw, dstaddr.ab, [R0-3.wl]	
E5	BBC	Branch on bit clear	pos.rl, base.vb, displ.bb, [field.rv]	
E0	BBS	Branch on bit set	pos.rl, base.vb, displ.bb, [field.rv]	
E7	BBCC	Branch on bit clear and clear	pos.rl, base.vb, displ.bb, [field.mv]	
E3	BBCS	Branch on bit clear and set	pos.rl, base.vb, displ.bb, [field.mv]	
E4	BBSC	Branch on bit set and clear	pos.rl, base.vb, displ.bb, [field.mv]	
E6	BBSS	Branch on bit set and set	pos.rl, base.vb, displ.bb, [field.mv]	
E1	BBCCI	Branch on bit clear and clear interlocked	pos.rl, base.vb, displ.bb, [field.mv]	
E2	BBSSI	Branch on bit set and set interlocked	pos.rl, base.vb, displ.bb, [field.mv]	
1E	BCC	Branch on carry clear	displ.bb	
1F	BCS	Branch on carry set	displ.bb	
13	BEQL	Branch on equal	displ.bb	
13	BEQLU	Branch on equal unsigned	displ.bb	
18	BGEQ	Branch on greater or equal	displ.bb	
1E	BGEQU	Branch on greater or equal unsigned	displ.bb	
14	BGTR	Branch on greater	displ.bb	
1A	BGTRU	Branch on greater unsigned	displ.bb	
8A	BICB2	Bit clear byte 2-operand	mask.rb, dst.mb	
8B	BICB3	Bit clear byte 3-operand	mask.rb, src.rb, dst.wb	
CA	BICL2	Bit clear long 2-operand	mask.rl, dst.ml	
CB	BICL3	Bit clear long 3-operand	mask.rl, src.rl, dst.wl	
B9	BICPSW	Bit clear processor status word	mask.rw	
AA	BICW2	Bit clear word 2-operand	mask.rw, dst.mw	
AB	BICW3	Bit clear word 3-operand	mask.rw, src.rw, dst.ww	
88	BISB2	Bit set byte 2-operand	mask.rb, dst.mb	
89	BISB3	Bit set byte 3-operand	mask.rb, src.rb, dst.wb	
C8	BISL2	Bit set long 2-operand	mask.rl, dst.ml	
C9	BISL3	Bit set long 3-operand	mask.rl, src.rl, dst.wl	
BB	BISPSW	Bit set processor status word	mask.rw	
A8	BISW2	Bit set word 2-operand	mask.rw, dst.mw	
A9	BISW3	Bit set word 3-operand	mask.rw, src.rw, dst.ww	

Middle table

OP	Mnemonic	Description	Arguments	N Z V C
93	BITB	Bit test byte	mask.rb, src.rb	
D3	BITL	Bit test long	mask.rl, src.rl	
B3	BITW	Bit test word	mask.rw, src.rw	
E9	BLBC	Branch on low bit clear	src.rl, displ.bb	
E8	BLBS	Branch on low bit set	src.rl, displ.bb	
15	BLEQ	Branch on less or equal	displ.bb	
1B	BLEQU	Branch on less or equal unsigned	displ.bb	
19	BLSS	Branch on less	displ.bb	
1F	BLSSU	Branch on less unsigned	displ.bb	
12	BNEQ	Branch on not equal	displ.bb	
12	BNEQU	Branch on not equal unsigned	displ.bb	
03	BPT	Break point fault	[-(KSP).w*]	
11	BRB	Branch with byte displacement	displ.bb	
31	BRW	Branch with word displacement	displ.bw	
10	BSBB	Branch to subroutine with byte displacement	displ.bb, [-(SP).wl]	
30	BSBW	Branch to subroutine with word displacement	displ.bw, [-(SP).wl]	
FDFF	BUGL	VMS bugcheck		
FEFF	BUGW	VMS bugcheck		
1D	BVC	Branch on overflow clear	displ.bb	
1C	BVS	Branch on overflow set	displ.bb	
FA	CALLG	Call with general argument list	arglist.ab, dst.ab, [-(SP).w*]	
FB	CALLS	Call with argument list on stack	numarg.rl, dst.ab, [-(SP).w*]	
8F	CASEB	Case byte	selector.rb, base.rb, limit.rb, displ.bw-list	
CF	CASEL	Case long	selector.rl, base.rl, limit.rl, displ.bw-list	
AF	CASEW	Case word	selector.rw, base.rw, limit.rw, displ.bw-list	
BD	CHME	Change mode to executive	param.rw, [-(ySP).w*]	
BC	CHMK	Change mode to kernel	param.rw, [-(KSP).w*] y = MINU(E, PSL<current-mode>)	
BE	CHMS	Change mode to supervisor	param.rw, [-(ySP).w*] y = MINU(S, PSL<current-mode>)	
BF	CHMU	Change mode to user	param.rw, [-(SP).w*]	
94	CLRB	Clear byte	dst.wb	
7C	CLRD	Clear D_floating	dst.wd	
D4	CLRF	Clear F_floating	dst.wf	
7C	CLRG	Clear G_floating	dst.wg	
7CFD	CLRH	Clear H_floating	dst.wh	
D4	CLRL	Clear long	dst.wl	
7CFD	CLRO	Clear octaword	dst.wo	
7C	CLRQ	Clear quad	dst.wq	
B4	CLRW	Clear word	dst.ww	
91	CMPB	Compare byte	src1.rb, src2.rb	
29	CMPC3	Compare character 3-operand	len.rw, src1addr.ab, src2addr.ab, [R0-3.wl]	
2D	CMPC5	Compare character 5-operand	src1len.rw, src1addr.ab, fill.rb, src2len.rw, src2addr.ab, [R0-3.wl]	
71	CMPD	Compare D_floating	src1.rd, src2.rd	
51	CMPF	Compare F_floating	src1.rf, src2.rf	
51FD	CMPG	Compare G_floating	src1.rg, src2.rg	
71FD	CMPH	Compare H_floating	src1.rh, src2.rh	
D1	CMPL	Compare long	src1.rl, src2.rl	
35	CMPP3	Compare packed 3-operand	len.rw, src1addr.ab, src2addr.ab, [R0-3.wl]	
37	CMPP4	Compare packed 4-operand	src1len.rw, src1addr.ab, src2len.rw, src2addr.ab, [R0-3.wl]	
EC	CMPV	Compare field	pos.rl, size.rb, base.vb, [field.rv], src.rl	
B1	CMPW	Compare word	src1.rw, src2.rw	
ED	CMPZV	Compare zero-extended field	pos.rl, size.rb, base.vb, [field.rv], src.rl	
0B	CRC	Calculate cyclic redundancy check	tbl.ab, initialcrc.rl, strlen.rw, stream.ab, [R0-3.wl]	
6C	CVTBD	Convert byte to D_floating	src.rb, dst.wd	
4C	CVTBF	Convert byte to F_floating	src.rb, dst.wf	
4CFD	CVTBG	Convert byte to G_floating	src.rb, dst.wg	
6CFD	CVTBH	Convert byte to H_floating	src.rb, dst.wh	
98	CVTBL	Convert byte to long	src.rb, dst.wl	
99	CVTBW	Convert byte to word	src.rb, dst.ww	

Opcode index

OP	Mnemonic	OP	Mnemonic
00	HALT	3D	ACBW
01	NOP	3E	MOVAW
02	REI	3F	PUSHAW
03	BPT	40	ADDF2
04	RET	40FD	ADDG2
05	RSB	41	ADDF3
06	LDPCTX	41FD	ADDG3
07	SVPCTX	42	SUBF2
08	CVTPS	42FD	SUBG2
09	CVTSP	43	SUBF3
0A	INDEX	43FD	SUBG3
0B	CRC	44	MULF2
0C	PROBER	44FD	MULG2
0D	PROBEW	45	MULF3
0E	INSQUE	45FD	MULG3
0F	REMQUE	46	DIVF2
10	BSBB	46FD	DIVG2
11	BRB	47	DIVF3
12	BNEQ	47FD	DIVG3
12	BNEQU	48	CVTFB
13	BEQL	48FD	CVTGB
13	BEQLU	49	CVTFW
14	BGTR	49FD	CVTGW
15	BLEQ	4A	CVTFL
16	JSB	4AFD	CVTGL
17	JMP	4B	CVTRFL
18	BGEQ	4BFD	CVTRGL
19	BLSS	4C	CVTBF
1A	BGTRU	4CFD	CVTBG
1B	BLEQU	4D	CVTWF
1C	BVS	4DFD	CVTWG
1D	BVC	4E	CVTLF
1E	BGEQU	4EFD	CVTLG
1F	BLSSU	4F	ACBF
20	ADDP4	4FFD	ACBG
21	ADDP6	50	MOVF
22	SUBP4	50FD	MOVG
23	SUBP6	51	CMPF
24	CVTPT	51FD	CMPG
25	MULP	52	MNEGF
26	CVTTP	52FD	MNEGG
27	DIVP	53	TSTF
28	MOVC3	53FD	TSTG
29	CMPC3	54	EMODF
2A	SCANC	54FD	EMODG
2B	SPANC	55	POLYF
2C	MOVC5	55FD	POLYG
2D	CMPC5	56	CVTFD
2E	MOVTC	56FD	CVTGH
2F	MOVTUC	57	Reserved
30	BSBW	58	ADAWI
31	BRW	59	Reserved
32	CVTWL	5A	Reserved
32FD	CVTDH	5B	INSQHI
33	CVTWB	5C	INSQTI
33FD	CVTGF	5D	REMQHI
34	MOVP	5E	REMQTI
35	CMPP3	5F	MATCHC
36	CVTPL	60	ADDD2
37	CMPP4	60FD	ADDH2
38	EDITPC	61	ADDD3
39	MATCHC	61FD	ADDH3
3A	LOCC	62	SUBD2
3B	SKPC	62FD	SUBH2
3C	MOVZWL	63	SUBD3
		63FD	SUBH3
		64	MULD2
		64FD	MULH2

INSTRUCTION SET (continued)

OP	Mnemonic	Description	Arguments	N	Z	V	C
68	CVTDB	Convert D_floating to byte	src. rd, dst. wb				
76	CVTDF	Convert D_floating to F_floating	src. rd, dst. wf				
32FD	CVTDH	Convert D_floating to H_floating	src. rd, dst. wh				
6A	CVTDL	Convert D_floating to long	src. rd, dst. wl				
69	CVTDW	Convert D_floating to word	src. rd, dst. ww				
48	CVTFB	Convert F_floating to byte	src. rf, dst. wb				
99FD	CVTFD	Convert F_floating to D_floating	src. rf, dst. wd				
98FD	CVTFG	Convert F_floating to G_floating	src. rf, dst. wg				
56	CVTFH	Convert F_floating to H_floating	src. rf, dst. wh				
4A	CVTFL	Convert F_floating to long	src. rf, dst. wl				
49	CVTFW	Convert F_floating to word	src. rf, dst. ww				
48FD	CVTGB	Convert G_floating to byte	src. rg, dst. wb				
33FD	CVTGF	Convert G_floating to F_floating	src. rg, dst. wf				
56FD	CVTGH	Convert G_floating to H_floating	src. rg, dst. wh				
4AFD	CVTGL	Convert G_floating to long	src. rg, dst. wl				
49FD	CVTGW	Convert G_floating to word	src. rg, dst. ww				
68FD	CVTHB	Convert H_floating to byte	srd. rh, dst. wb				
F7FD	CVTHD	Convert H_floating to D_floating	srd. rh, dst. wd				
F6FD	CVTHF	Convert H_floating to F_floating	srd. rh, dst. wf				
76FD	CVTHG	Convert H_floating to G_floating	srd. rh, dst. wg				
6AFD	CVTHL	Convert H_floating to long	srd. rh, dst. wl				
69FD	CVTHW	Convert H_floating to word	srd. rh, dst. ww				
F6	CVTLB	Convert long to byte	src. rl, dst. wb				
6E	CVTLD	Convert long to D_floating	src. rl, dst. wd				
4E	CVTLF	Convert long to F_floating	src. rl, dst. wf				
4EFD	CVTLG	Convert longword to G_floating	src. rl, dst. wg				
6EFD	CVTLH	Convert longword to H_floating	src. rl, dst. wh				
F9	CVTLP	Convert long to packed	src. rl, dstlen. nw, dstaddr. ab, [R-03.wl], dst. wl				
F7	CVTLW	Convert long to word	src. rl, dst. ww				
36	CVTPL	Convert packed to long	srclen. nw, srcaddr. ab, dstlen. nw, dstaddr. ab, [R0-3.wl]				
08	CVTPS	Convert packed to leading separate	srclen. nw, srcaddr. ab, dstaddr. ab, [R0-3.wl]				
24	CVTPT	Convert packed to trailing	srclen. nw, srcaddr. ab, tbladdr. ab, dstlen. nw, dstaddr. ab, [R0-3.wl]				
6B	CVTRDL	Convert rounded D_floating to long	src. rd, dst. wl				
4B	CVTRFL	Convert rounded F_floating to long	src. rf, dst. wl				
4BFD	CVTRGL	Convert rounded G_floating to long	src. rg, dst. wl				
6BFD	CVTRHL	Convert rounded H_floating to long	src. rh, dst. wl				
09	CVTSP	Convert leading separate to packed	srclen. nw, srcaddr. ab, dstlen. nw, dstaddr. ab, [R0-3.wl]				
26	CVTTP	Convert trailing to packed	srclen. nw, srcaddr. ab, tbladdr. ab, dstlen. nw, dstaddr. ab, [R0-3.wl]				
33	CVTWB	Convert word to byte	src. rw, dst. wb				
6D	CVTWD	Convert word to D_floating	src. rw, dst. wd				
4D	CVTWF	Convert word to F_floating	src. rw, dst. wf				
4DFD	CVTWG	Convert word to G_floating	src. rw, dst. wg				
6DFD	CVTWH	Convert word to H_floating	src. rw, dst. wh				
32	CVTWL	Convert word to long	src. rw, dst. wl				
97	DECB	Decrement byte	dif. mb				
D7	DECL	Decrement long	dif. ml				
B7	DECW	Decrement word	dif. mw				
86	DIVB2	Divide byte 2-operand	divr. rb, quo. mb				
87	DIVB3	Divide byte 3-operand	divr. rb, divd. rb, quo. wb				
66	DIVD2	Divide D_floating 2-operand	divr. rd, quo. md				
67	DIVD3	Divide D_floating 3-operand	divr. rd, divd. rd, quo. wd				
46	DIVF2	Divide F_floating 2-operand	divr. rf, quo. mf				
47	DIVF3	Divide F_floating 3-operand	divr. rf, divd. rf, quo. wf				
46FD	DIVG2	Divide G_floating 2-operand	divr. rg, quo. mg				
47FD	DIVG3	Divide G_floating 3-operand	divr. rg, divd. rg, quo. wg				
66FD	DIVH2	Divide H_floating 2-operand	divr. rh, quo. mh				
67FD	DIVH3	Divide H_floating 3-operand	divr. rh, divd. rh, quo. wh				
C6	DIVL2	Divide long 2-operand	divr. rl, quo. ml				
C7	DIVL3	Divide long 3-operand	divr. rl, divd. rl, quo. wl				
27	DIVP	Divide packed	divrlen. nw, divraddr. ab, divdlen. nw, divdaddr. ab, quolen. nw, quoaddr. ab				

Next column

OP	Mnemonic	Description	Arguments	N	Z	V	C
A6	DIVW2	Divide word 2-operand	divr. rw, quo. mw				
A7	DIVW3	Divide word 3-operand	divr. rw, divd. rw, quo. ww				
38	EDITPC	Edit packed to character string	srclen. rw, srcaddr. ab, pattern. ab, dstaddr. ab, [R0-5.wl]				
7B	EDIV	Extended divide	divr. rl,divd. rq, quo. wl, rem. wl				
74	EMODD	Extended modulus D_floating	mulr. rd, mulrx. rb, muld. rd, int. wl, fract. wd	0			
54	EMODF	Extended modulus F_floating	mulr. rf, mulrx. rb, muld. rf, int. wl, fract. wf	0			
54FD	EMODG	Extended modulus G_floating	mulr. rg, mulrx. rw, muld. rg, int. wl, fract. wg	0			
74FD	EMODH	Extended modulus H_floating	mulr. rh, mulrx. rw, muld. rh, int. wl, fract. wh	0			
7A	EMUL	Extended multiply	mulr. rl, muld. rl, add. rl, prod. wq				
FD	ESCD	Escape D					
FE	ESCE	Escape E					
FF	ESCF	Escape F					
EE	EXTV	Extract field	pos. rl, size. rb, base. vb, [field.rv], dst. wl	0			
EF	EXTZV	Extract zero-extended field	pos. rl, size. rb, base. vb, [field.rv], dst. wl	0			
EB	FFC	Find first clear bit	startpos. rl, size. rb, base. vb, [field. rv], findpos. wl				
EA	FFS	Find first set bit	startpos. rl, size. rl, base. vb, [field. wv], findpos. wl				
00	HALT	Halt (kernel mode only)					
96	INCB	Increment byte	sum. mb				
D6	INCL	Increment long	sum. ml				
B6	INCW	Increment word	sum. mw				
0A	INDEX	Index calculation	subscript. rl, low. rl, high. rl, size. rl, indexin. rl, indexout. wl	0			
5C	INSQHI	Insert at head of queue, interlocked	entry. ab, header. aq	0			
5D	INSQTI	Insert at tail of queue, interlocked	entry. ab, header. aq	0			
0E	INSQUE	Insert into queue	entry. ab, addr. wl				
F0	INSV	Insert field	src. rl, pos. rl, size. rb, base. vb, [field. wv]				
17	JMP	Jump	dst. ab				
16	JSB	Jump to subroutine	dst. ab, [-(SP)+. wl]				
06	LDPCTX	Load process context (kernel mode only)	[PCB. r*, -(KSP). w*]				
3A	LOCC	Locate character	char. rb, len. rw, addr. ab, [R0-1. rw]				
39	MATCHC	Match characters	len1. rw, addr1. ab, len2. rw, addr2. ab, [R0-3. wl]				
92	MCOMB	Move complemented byte	src. rb, dst. wb				
D2	MCOML	Move complemented long	src. rl, dst. wl				
B2	MCOMW	Move complemented word	src. rw, dst. ww				
DB	MFPR	Move from processor register (kernel mode only)	procreg. rl, dst. wl				
8E	MNEGB	Move negated byte	src. rb, dst. wb				
72	MNEGD	Move negated D_floating	src. rd, dst. wd				
52	MNEGF	Move negated F_floating	src. rf, dst. wf				
52FD	MNEGG	Move negated G_floating	src. rg, dst. wg				
72FD	MNEGH	Move negated H_floating	src. rh, dst. wh				
CE	MNEGL	Move negated long	src. rl, dst. wl				
AE	MNEGW	Move negated word	src. rw, dst. ww				
9E	MOVAB	Move address of byte	src. ab, dst. wl				
7E	MOVAD	Move address of D_floating	src. aq, dst. wl				
DE	MOVAF	Move address of F_floating	src. al, dst. wl				
7E	MOVAG	Move address of G_floating	src. aq, dst. wl				
7EFD	MOVAH	Move address of H_floating	src. ao, dst. wl				
DE	MOVAL	Move address of long	src. al, dst. wl				
7EFD	MOVAO	Move address of octaword	src. ao, dst. wl				
3E	MOVAW	move address of word	src. aw, dst. wl				
90	MOVB	Move byte	src. rb, dst. wb				
28	MOVC3	Move character 3-operand	srclen. rw, srcaddr. ab, dstaddr. ab, fill. rb, [R0-5.wl]				
2C	MOVC5	Move character 5-operand	srclen. rw, srcaddr. ab, fill. rb, dstlen. rw, dstaddr. ab, [R0-5.wl]				
70	MOVD	Move D_floating	src. rd, dst. wd				
50	MOVF	Move F_floating	src. rf, dst. wf				
50FD	MOVG	Move G_floating	src. rg, dst. wg				
70FD	MOVH	Move H_floating	src. rh, dst. wh				

Numeric Order (continued)

		N	Z	V	C
65	MULD3				
65FD	MULH3				
66	DIVD2				
66FD	DIVH2				
67	DIVD3				
67FD	DIVH3				
68	CVTDB				
68FD	CVTHB				
69	CVTDW				
69FD	CVTHW				
6A	CVTDL				
6AFD	CVTHL				
6B	CVTRDL				
6BFD	CVTRHL				
6C	CVTBD				
6CFD	CVTBH				
6D	CVTWD				
6DFD	CVTWH				
6E	CVTLD				
6EFD	CVTLH				
6F	ACBD				
6FFD	ACBH				
70	MOVD				
70FD	MOVH				
71	CMPD				
71FD	CMPH				
72	MNEGD				
72FD	MNEGH				
73	TSTD				
73FD	TSTH				
74	EMODD				
74FD	EMODH				
75	POLYD				
75FD	POLYH				
76	CVTDF				
76FD	CVTHG				
77	Reserved				
78	ASHL				
79	ASHQ				
7A	EMUL				
7B	EDIV				
7C	CLRD				
7C	CLRQ				
7C	CLRO				
7CFD	CLRH				
7CFD	CLRO				
7D	MOVQ				
7DFD	MOVO				
7E	MOVAD				
7E	MOVAQ				
7E	MOVAH				
7EFD	MOVAO				
7F	PUSHAD				
7F	PUSHAQ				
7FFD	PUSHAH				
7FFD	PUSHAO				
80	ADDB2				
81	ADDB3				
82	SUBB2				
83	SUBB3				
84	MULB2				
85	MULB3				
86	DIVB2				
87	DIVB3				
88	BISB2				
89	BISB3				
8A	BICB2				
8B	BICB3				
8C	XORB2				
8D	XORB3				
8E	MNEGB				
8F	CASEB				
90	MOVB				
91	CMPB				
92	MCOMB				
93	BITB				
94	CLRB				
95	TSTB				
96	INCB				
97	DECB				
98	CVTBL				
98FD	CVTBW				
99	CVTFG				
99FD	CVTFH				
9A	MOVZBL				
9B	MOVZBW				
9C	ROTL				
9D	ACBB				
9E	MOVAB				
9F	PUSHAB				
A0	ADDW2				
A1	ADDW3				
A2	SUBW2				
A3	SUBW3				
A4	MULW2				
A5	MULW3				
A6	DIVW2				
A7	DIVW3				
A8	BISW2				
A9	BISW3				
AA	BICW2				
AB	BICW3				
AC	XORW2				
AD	XORW3				
AE	MNEGW				
AF	CASEW				
B0	MOVW				
B1	CMPW				
B2	MCOMW				
B3	BITW				
B4	CLRW				
B5	TSTW				
B6	INCW				
B7	DECW				
B8	BISPSW				
B9	BICPSW				
BA	POPR				
BB	PUSHR				
BC	CHMK				
BD	CHME				
BE	CHMS				
BF	CHMU				
C0	ADDL2				
C1	ADDL3				
C2	SUBL2				
C3	SUBL3				
C4	MULL2				
C5	MULL3				
C6	DIVL2				
C7	DIVL3				